Library of America, a nonprofit organization,
champions our nation's cultural heritage
by publishing America's greatest writing in
authoritative new editions and providing resources
for readers to explore this rich, living legacy.

MARGARET FULLER

Margaret Fuller

COLLECTED WRITINGS

Brigitte Bailey, Noelle A. Baker,
and Megan Marshall, *editors*

THE LIBRARY OF AMERICA

MARGARET FULLER: COLLECTED WRITINGS
Volume compilation and backmatter copyright © 2025 by
Literary Classics of the United States, Inc., New York, N.Y.
All rights reserved.
No part of this book may be reproduced in any manner whatsoever without
the permission of the publisher, except in the case of brief
quotations embodied in critical articles and reviews.

Published in the United States by Library of America.
Visit our website at www.loa.org.

"Tasso's Oak, Rome," engraving by J. G. Strutt belonging to Margaret
Fuller, inscribed "From the Wreck of the Elizabeth." Courtesy of
Lucilla Fuller Marvel.

This paper exceeds the requirements of
ANSI/NISO Z39.48–1992 (Permanence of Paper).

Distributed to the trade in the United States
by Penguin Random House Inc.
and in Canada by Penguin Random House Canada Ltd.

Library of Congress Control Number: 2024943677
ISBN 978–1–59853–803–8

First Printing
The Library of America—388

Manufactured in the United States of America

Contents

SUMMER ON THE LAKES, IN 1843 3

WOMAN IN THE NINETEENTH CENTURY 189

SHORT PUBLISHED WORKS

New England, 1839–1844
Translator's Preface: *Conversations with Goethe in the Last Years of His Life* 341
A Short Essay on Critics 352
A Record of Impressions: Produced by the Exhibition of Mr. Allston's Pictures in the Summer of 1839 359
The Magnolia of Lake Pontchartrain 371
Leila 378
Yuca Filamentosa 384
from Bettine Brentano and Her Friend Günderode 387

New York, 1844–1846
Emerson's Essays 397
French Novelists of the Day: Balzac, George Sand, Eugene Sue 404
Review of *Etherology; or The Philosophy of Mesmerism and Phrenology* by J. Stanley Grimes 415
Our City Charities 420
Prevalent Idea That Politeness Is Too Great a Luxury to Be Given to the Poor 427
Review of *Narrative of the Life of Frederick Douglass, An American Slave* by Frederick Douglass 429
The Irish Character 434
Review of *Tales* by Edgar Allan Poe 437
The Wrongs of American Women. The Duty of American Women 438
Review of *Poems* by Henry Wadsworth Longfellow 445
Review of *The Poetical Works of Percy Bysshe Shelley* 454
1st January, 1846 465
Review of *Mosses from an Old Manse* by Nathaniel Hawthorne 475

ix

CONTENTS

Review of *Memoirs, Official and Personal* by
Thomas L. M'Kenney 478
Review of *Ormond; Or, the Secret Witness* and *Wieland;
Or, the Transformation* by Charles Brockden Brown. . 485
Farewell 489
American Literature: Its Position in the Present Time,
and Prospects for the Future 491

Europe, 1846–1850

Letters from England 509
Liverpool and Manchester
Things and Thoughts in Europe No. V 518
Scotland, Mary Queen of Scots, and Ben Lomond
Things and Thoughts in Europe No. X.............. 528
London and Paris, French Theater and Literature
Things and Thoughts in Europe No. XIII 537
Paris, Lyons, Naples
To a Daughter of Italy........................... 544
Poem in The People's Journal
Things and Thoughts in Europe No. XVIII.......... 549
*American Tourists and European and
American Politics*
Things and Thoughts in Europe No. XIX............ 555
Living in "the real Rome"
Things and Thoughts in Europe No. XXV 565
The Revolutions of 1848 in Italy
Things and Thoughts in Europe No. XXVI 572
Revolutionary Rome
Things and Thoughts in Europe No. XXVIII 582
Proclamation of the Roman Republic
Undaunted Rome 589
"I write you from barricaded Rome"
Things and Thoughts in Europe No. XXXIII......... 592
The French Army Bombs and Occupies Rome
Italy 602
"The next revolution, here and elsewhere, will be radical"

UNPUBLISHED WRITINGS

"Possent quia posse videntur" (c. pre-fall 1819) 609
Autobiographical Romance (1840) 612

CONTENTS

Fictional Autobiographical Fragment (c. 1841–42) 634
A Credo (1842) 637
To Beethoven (1843) 644
Chamois (c. 1844) 646

JOURNALS
Poems and Selections from Journal Fragments
   (1833–1844) 653
from S. M. Fuller's bouquet.—Journal (c. 1836–1837) . . . 657
from Reflections Journal (c. 1839) 660
from Bound Journal (c. 1839–40) 666
from 1842 Journal (August 18–September 25, 1842) 670
from October 1842 Journal 686
from Journal Fragments (c. 1840, 1844) 690
from Manuscript Tracing Journal (1844) 698
from Italy 1849 Journal 709

LETTERS
To Timothy Fuller, April 24, 1817? 717
   First Letter
To Timothy Fuller, January 16, 1820 717
   "I do not like Sarah, call me Margaret alone"
To the Marquis de Lafayette, June 16, 1825? 719
   "The avenues of glory are seldom accessible"
To Susan Prescott, July 11, 1825 719
   "I am determined on distinction"
To James Freeman Clarke, August 7, 1832 721
   "I wish to talk with you now about the Germans"
To James Freeman Clarke, April 19, 1836 723
   Writing a Biography of Goethe
To Caroline Sturgis, November 16, 1837 725
   Defending Transcendentalism
To Ralph Waldo Emerson, March 1, 1838 727
   "I want to see you and still more to hear you"
To Lidian Jackson Emerson, August 19, 1838 729
   "Fret not that kindest heart"
To Sophia Ripley?, August 27, 1839 730
   "My plan for the proposed conversations"
To Unknown Correspondent, November 25, 1839 733
   "My class is singularly prosperous"

xii CONTENTS

To William Henry Channing, March 22, 1840 734
"When I write, it is into another world"

To Ralph Waldo Emerson, September 29, 1840 736
"Did you not ask for a 'foe' in your friend?"

To Henry David Thoreau, December 1, 1840 738
Rejecting a Dial *Submission*

To William Henry Channing, April 5, 1841 739
Beethoven's Fifth Symphony

To Ralph Waldo Emerson, April 9, 1842 740
Handing Over Editorship of The Dial

To Sophia Peabody, June 4, 1842 741
Peabody's Wedding to Nathaniel Hawthorne

To George T. Davis, December 17, 1842 743
"I have not lived my own life"

To Richard F. Fuller, July 29, 1843 745
Visiting the Territory of Wisconsin

To Caroline Sturgis, May 3, 1844 747
"The Carbuncle"

To Ralph Waldo Emerson, July 13, 1844 748
"You are intellect, I am life"

To Elizabeth Hoar, October [28?], 1844 749
Visiting Sing Sing Prison

To William Henry Channing, November 17, 1844 750
Woman in the Nineteenth Century

To Eugene Fuller, March 9, 1845 751
Horace Greeley and the New-York Tribune

To James Nathan, May 4?, 1845 753
"I feel chosen among women"

To James Nathan, May 23, 1845 755
"An approaching separation, presses on my mind"

To Evert A. Duyckinck, June 28, 1846 758
"I shall not alter a line or a word"

To Caroline Sturgis, November 16?, 1846 760
England and Paris

To Ralph Waldo Emerson, November 16, 1846 762
Meeting Thomas Carlyle

To Elizabeth Hoar, January 18, 1847 766
"You wished to hear of George Sand"

CONTENTS xiii

To Marcus and Rebecca Spring, April 10, 1847 767
  "I wish to be free and absolutely true to my nature"
To Richard F. Fuller, October 29, 1847. 769
  "I find myself so happy here alone and free"
To William Henry Channing, March 29, 1848 769
  Revolution
To Jane Tuckerman King, April 1848 770
  "I have done . . . things that may invoke censure"
To Costanza Arconati Visconti, May 27, 1848. 771
  "Everything confirms me in my radicalism"
To Charles King Newcomb, June 22, 1848 772
  "Poor one, alone, all alone!"
To Giovanni Angelo Ossoli, August 22, 1848 774
  Waiting to Deliver Her Child
To Giovanni Angelo Ossoli, September 7, 1848 775
  "This dear Baby in my arms"
To Giuseppe Mazzini, March 3, 1849 776
  "The best friends, . . . must be women."
To William Henry Channing, March 10, 1849 777
  "I am not what I should be on this earth"
To Caroline Sturgis Tappan, March 16, 1849 778
  "No secret can be kept"
To Giovanni Angelo Ossoli, June 1849 782
  "In the event we both die"
To Ralph Waldo Emerson, June 10, 1849 784
  "Rome is being destroyed"
To Costanza Arconati Visconti, August 1849 786
  *"I have united my destiny with that of an obscure
    young man"*
To Caroline Sturgis Tappan, August 28, 1849. 787
  "On the brink of losing my little boy"
To Margarett Crane Fuller, August 31, 1849 787
  "It was only great love for you that kept me silent"
To Costanza Arconati Visconti, October 16, 1849. 791
  "He is to me a source of ineffable joys"
To Emelyn Story, c. November 1849. 792
  "Ossoli is forming some taste for books"

CONTENTS

To Elizabeth Barrett Browning, December 6, 1849..... 793
    Remembering Edgar Allan Poe

To William Henry Channing, December 17, 1849...... 795
    "This false state of society"

To Arthur Hugh Clough, February 16, 1850.......... 797
    "I like also much living with my husband"

To Costanza Arconati Visconti, April 6, 1850 799
    "I am absurdly fearful about this voyage"

To Lewis Cass Jr., May 2, 1850 800
    "I leave Italy with profound regret"

Chronology 805
Note on the Texts. 825
Notes 841
General Index. 894
Index of Fuller's Poetry Titles and First Lines. 914

MARGARET FULLER

SUMMER ON THE LAKES,
IN 1843

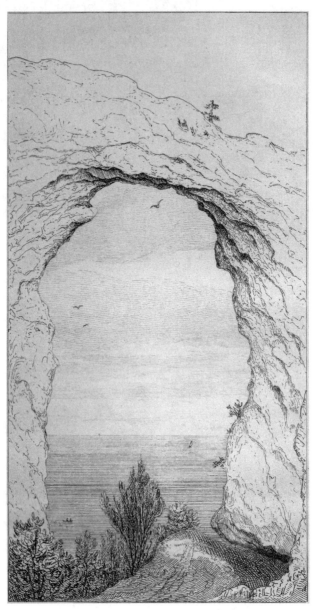

ARCHED ROCK AT MACKINAW

Summer days of busy leisure,
Long summer days of dear-bought pleasure,
You have done your teaching well;
Had the scholar means to tell
How grew the vine of bitter-sweet,
What made the path for truant feet,
Winter nights would quickly pass,
Gazing on the magic glass
O'er which the new-world shadows pass;
But, in fault of wizard spell,
Moderns their tale can only tell
In dull words, with a poor reed
Breaking at each time of need.
But those to whom a hint suffices
Mottoes find for all devices,
See the knights behind their shields,
Through dried grasses, blooming fields.

To a Friend

Some dried grass-tufts from the wide flowery plain,
A muscle shell from the lone fairy shore,
Some antlers from tall woods which never more
To the wild deer a safe retreat can yield,
An eagle's feather which adorned a Brave,
Well-nigh the last of his despairing band,
For such slight gifts wilt thou extend thy hand
When weary hours a brief refreshment crave?
I give you what I can, not what I would,
If my small drinking-cup would hold a flood,
As Scandinavia sung those must contain
With which the giants gods may entertain;
In our dwarf day we drain few drops, and soon must
    thirst again.

Chapter I

Niagara, June 10, 1843.

SINCE YOU ARE TO SHARE with me such foot-notes as may be made on the pages of my life during this summer's wanderings, I should not be quite silent as to this magnificent prologue to the, as yet, unknown drama. Yet I, like others, have little to say where the spectacle is, for once, great enough to fill the whole life, and supersede thought, giving us only its own presence. "It is good to be here," is the best as the simplest expression that occurs to the mind.

We have been here eight days, and I am quite willing to go away. So great a sight soon satisfies, making us content with itself, and with what is less than itself. Our desires, once realized, haunt us again less readily. Having "lived one day" we would depart, and become worthy to live another.

We have not been fortunate in weather, for there cannot be too much, or too warm sunlight for this scene, and the skies have been lowering, with cold, unkind winds. My nerves, too much braced up by such an atmosphere, do not well bear the continual stress of sight and sound. For here there is no escape from the weight of a perpetual creation; all other forms and motions come and go, the tide rises and recedes, the wind, at its mightiest, moves in gales and gusts, but here is really an incessant, an indefatigable motion. Awake or asleep, there is no escape, still this rushing round you and through you. It is in this way I have most felt the grandeur—somewhat eternal, if not infinite.

At times a secondary music rises; the cataract seems to seize its own rhythm and sing it over again, so that the ear and soul are roused by a double vibration. This is some effect of the wind, causing echoes to the thundering anthem. It is very sublime, giving the effect of a spiritual repetition through all the spheres.

When I first came I felt nothing but a quiet satisfaction. I found that drawings, the panorama, &c. had given me a clear notion of the position and proportions of all objects here;

I knew where to look for everything, and everything looked as I thought it would.

Long ago, I was looking from a hill-side with a friend at one of the finest sunsets that ever enriched this world. A little cow-boy, trudging along, wondered what we could be gazing at. After spying about some time, he found it could only be the sunset, and looking, too, a moment, he said approvingly "that sun looks well enough;" a speech worthy of Shakspeare's Cloten, or the infant Mercury, up to everything from the cradle, as you please to take it.

Even such a familiarity, worthy of Jonathan, our national hero, in a prince's palace, or "stumping" as he boasts to have done, "up the Vatican stairs, into the Pope's presence, in my old boots," I felt here; it looks really *well enough*, I felt, and was inclined, as you suggested, to give my approbation as to the one object in the world that would not disappoint.

But all great expression, which, on a superficial survey, seems so easy as well as so simple, furnishes, after a while, to the faithful observer its own standard by which to appreciate it. Daily these proportions widened and towered more and more upon my sight, and I got, at last, a proper foreground for these sublime distances. Before coming away, I think I really saw the full wonder of the scene. After awhile it so drew me into itself as to inspire an undefined dread, such as I never knew before, such as may be felt when death is about to usher us into a new existence. The perpetual trampling of the waters seized my senses. I felt that no other sound, however near, could be heard, and would start and look behind me for a foe. I realized the identity of that mood of nature in which these waters were poured down with such absorbing force, with that in which the Indian was shaped on the same soil. For continually upon my mind came, unsought and unwelcome, images, such as never haunted it before, of naked savages stealing behind me with uplifted tomahawks; again and again this illusion recurred, and even after I had thought it over, and tried to shake it off, I could not help starting and looking behind me.

As picture, the Falls can only be seen from the British side. There they are seen in their veils, and at sufficient distance to appreciate the magical effects of these, and the light and shade. From the boat, as you cross, the effects and contrasts are more melodramatic. On the road back from the whirlpool, we saw them as a reduced picture with delight. But what I liked best was to sit on Table Rock, close to the great fall. There all power of observing details, all separate consciousness, was quite lost.

Once, just as I had seated myself there, a man came to take his first look. He walked close up to the fall, and, after looking at it a moment, with an air as if thinking how he could best appropriate it to his own use, he spat into it.

This trait seemed wholly worthy of an age whose love of *utility* is such that the Prince Puckler Muskau suggests the probability of men coming to put the bodies of their dead parents in the fields to fertilize them, and of a country such as Dickens has described; but these will not, I hope, be seen on the historic page to be truly the age or truly the America. A little leaven is leavening the whole mass for other bread.

The whirlpool I like very much. It is seen to advantage after the great falls; it is so sternly solemn. The river cannot look more imperturbable, almost sullen in its marble green, than it does just below the great fall; but the slight circles that mark the hidden vortex, seem to whisper mysteries the thundering voice above could not proclaim,—a meaning as untold as ever.

It is fearful, too, to know, as you look, that whatever has been swallowed by the cataract, is like to rise suddenly to light here, whether up-rooted tree, or body of man or bird.

The rapids enchanted me far beyond what I expected; they are so swift that they cease to seem so; you can think only of their beauty. The fountain beyond the Moss Islands, I discovered for myself, and thought it for some time an accidental beauty which it would not do to leave, lest I might never see it again. After I found it permanent, I returned many times to watch the play of its crest. In the little waterfall beyond, nature seems, as she often does, to have made a study for some larger design. She delights in this,—a sketch within a sketch, a dream within a dream. Wherever we see it, the lines of the great buttress in the fragment of stone, the hues of the waterfall, copied in the flowers that star its bordering mosses, we are delighted; for all the lineaments become fluent, and we mould the scene in congenial thought with its genius.

People complain of the buildings at Niagara, and fear to see it further deformed. I cannot sympathize with such an apprehension: the spectacle is capable to swallow up all such objects; they are not seen in the great whole, more than an earthworm in a wide field.

The beautiful wood on Goat Island is full of flowers; many of the fairest love to do homage here. The Wake Robin and May Apple are in bloom now; the former, white, pink, green, purple, copying the rainbow of the fall, and fit to make a garland for its presiding deity when he walks the land, for they are of imperial size, and shaped like stones for a diadem. Of the May Apple, I did not raise one green tent without finding a flower beneath.

And now farewell, Niagara. I have seen thee, and I think all who come here must in some sort see thee; thou art not to be got rid of as easily as the stars. I will be here again beneath some flooding July moon and sun. Owing to the absence of light, I have seen the rainbow only two or three times by day; the lunar bow not at all. However, the imperial presence needs not its crown, though illustrated by it.

General Porter and Jack Downing were not unsuitable figures here. The former heroically planted the bridges by which we cross to Goat Island, and the Wake-Robin-crowned genius has punished his temerity with deafness, which must, I think, have come upon him when he sank the first stone in the rapids. Jack seemed an acute and entertaining representative of Jonathan, come to look at his great water-privilege. He told us all about the Americanisms of the spectacle; that is to say, the battles that have been fought here. It seems strange that men could fight in such a place; but no temple can still the personal griefs and strifes in the breasts of its visiters.

No less strange is the fact that, in this neighborhood, an eagle should be chained for a plaything. When a child, I used often to stand at a window from which I could see an eagle chained in the balcony of a museum. The people used to poke at it with sticks, and my childish heart would swell with indignation as I saw their insults, and the mien with which they were borne by the monarch-bird. Its eye was dull, and its plumage soiled and shabby, yet, in its form and attitude, all the king was visible, though sorrowful and dethroned. I never saw another of the family till, when passing through the Notch of the White Mountains, at that moment striding before us in all the panoply of sunset, the driver shouted, "Look there!" and following with our eyes his upward-pointing finger, we saw, soaring slow in majestic poise above the highest summit, the bird of Jove. It was a glorious sight, yet I know not that I felt more on seeing the bird in all its natural freedom and royalty, than when, imprisoned and insulted, he had filled my early thoughts with the Byronic "silent rages" of misanthropy.

Now, again, I saw him a captive, and addressed by the vulgar with the language they seem to find most appropriate to such occasions—that of thrusts and blows. Silently, his head averted, he ignored their existence, as Plotinus or Sophocles might that of a modern reviewer. Probably, he listened to the voice of the cataract, and felt that congenial powers flowed free, and was consoled, though his own wing was broken.

The story of the Recluse of Niagara interested me a little. It is wonderful that men do not oftener attach their lives to localities of great beauty—that, when once deeply penetrated, they will let themselves so easily be borne away by the general stream of things, to live any where and any how. But there is something ludicrous in being the hermit of a showplace, unlike St. Francis in his mountain-bed, where none but the stars and rising sun ever saw him.

There is also a "guide to the falls," who wears his title labeled on his hat; otherwise, indeed, one might as soon think of asking for a gentleman usher to point out the moon. Yet why should we wonder at such, either, when we have Commentaries on Shakspeare, and Harmonies of the Gospels?

And now you have the little all I have to write. Can it interest you? To one who has enjoyed the full life of any scene, of any hour, what thoughts can be recorded about it, seem like the commas and semicolons in the paragraph, mere stops. Yet I suppose it is not so to the absent. At least, I have read things written about Niagara, music, and the like, that interested *me*. Once I was moved by Mr. Greenwood's remark, that he could not realize this marvel till, opening his eyes the next morning after he had seen it, his doubt as to the possibility of its being still there, taught him what he had experienced. I remember this now with pleasure, though, or because, it is exactly the opposite to what I myself felt. For all greatness affects different minds, each in "its own particular kind," and the variations of testimony mark the truth of feeling.

I will add a brief narrative of the experience of another here, as being much better than anything I could write, because more simple and individual.

"Now that I have left this 'Earth-wonder,' and the emotions it excited are past, it seems not so much like profanation to analyze my feelings, to recall minutely and accurately the effect of this manifestation of the Eternal. But one should go to such a scene prepared to yield entirely to its influences, to forget one's little self and one's little mind. To see a miserable worm creep to the brink of this falling world of waters, and watch the trembling of its own petty bosom, and fancy that this is made alone to act upon him excites—derision?—No,—pity."

As I rode up to the neighborhood of the falls, a solemn awe imperceptibly stole over me, and the deep sound of the ever-hurrying rapids prepared my mind for the lofty emotions to be experienced. When I reached the hotel, I felt a strange indifference about seeing the aspiration of my life's hopes. I lounged about the rooms, read the stage bills upon the walls, looked over the register, and, finding the name of an acquaintance, sent to see if he was still there. What this hesitation arose from, I know not; perhaps it was a feeling of my unworthiness to enter this temple which nature has erected to its God.

At last, slowly and thoughtfully I walked down to the bridge leading to Goat Island, and when I stood upon this frail support, and saw a quarter of a mile of tumbling, rushing rapids, and heard their everlasting roar, my emotions overpowered me, a choaking sensation rose to my throat, a thrill rushed through my veins, "my blood ran rippling to my finger's ends." This was the climax of the effect which the falls produced upon me—neither the American nor the British fall moved me as did these rapids. For the magnificence, the sublimity of the latter I was prepared by descriptions and by paintings. When I arrived in sight of them I merely felt, "ah, yes, here is the fall, just as I have seen it in picture." When I arrived at the terrapin bridge, I expected to be overwhelmed, to retire trembling from this giddy eminence, and gaze with unlimited wonder and awe upon the immense mass rolling on and on, but, somehow or other, I thought only of comparing the effect on my mind with what I had read and heard. I looked for a short time, and then with almost a feeling of disappointment, turned to go to the other points of view to see if I was not mistaken in not feeling any surpassing emotion at this sight. But from the foot of Biddle's stairs, and the middle of the river, and from below the table rock, it was still "barren, barren all." And, provoked with my stupidity in feeling most moved in the wrong place, I turned away to the hotel, determined to set off for Buffalo that afternoon. But the stage did not go, and, after nightfall, as there was a splendid moon, I went down to the bridge, and leaned over the parapet, where the boiling rapids came down in their might. It was grand, and it was also gorgeous; the yellow rays of the moon made the broken waves appear like auburn tresses twining around the black rocks. But they did not inspire me as before. I felt a foreboding of a mightier emotion to rise up and swallow all others, and I passed on to the terrapin bridge. Everything was changed, the misty apparition had taken off its many-colored crown which it had worn by day, and a bow of silvery white spanned its summit. The moonlight gave a poetical indefiniteness to the distant parts of the waters, and while the rapids were glancing in her beams, the river below the falls was black as night, save where the reflection of the sky gave it the appearance of a shield of blued steel. No gaping tourists loitered, eyeing with their glasses, or sketching on cards the hoary locks of the ancient river god. All tended to harmonize with the natural grandeur of the scene. I gazed long. I saw how here mutability and unchangeableness were united. I surveyed the conspiring waters rushing against the rocky ledge to overthrow it at one mad plunge, till, like toppling ambition, o'erleaping themselves, they fall on t'other side, expanding into foam ere they reach the deep channel where they creep submissively away.

Then arose in my breast a genuine admiration, and a humble adoration of the Being who was the architect of this and of all. Happy were the first discoverers of Niagara, those who could come unawares upon this view and upon that, whose feelings were entirely their own. With what gusto does Father Hennepin describe "this great downfall of water," "this vast and prodigious cadence of water, which falls down after a surprising and astonishing manner, insomuch that the universe does not afford its parallel. 'Tis true Italy and Swedeland boast of some such things, but we may well say that they be sorry patterns when compared with this of which we do now speak."

Chapter II

THE LAKES

Scene, Steamboat—*About to leave Buffalo—Baggage coming on board—Passengers bustling for their berths—Little boys persecuting everybody with their newspapers and pamphlets—J., S. and M. huddled up in a forlorn corner, behind a large trunk—A heavy rain falling.*

M. Water, water everywhere. After Niagara one would like a dry strip of existence. And at any rate it is quite enough for me to have it under foot without having it over head in this way.

J. Ah, do not abuse the gentle element. It is hardly possible to have too much of it, and indeed, if I were obliged to choose amid the four, it would be the one in which I could bear confinement best.

S. You would make a pretty Undine, to be sure!

J. Nay, I only offered myself as a Triton, a boisterous Triton of the sounding shell. You, M. I suppose, would be a salamander, rather.

M. No! that is too equivocal a position, whether in modern mythology, or Hoffman's tales. I should choose to be a gnome.

J. That choice savors of the pride that apes humility.

M. By no means; the gnomes are the most important of all the elemental tribes. Is it not they who make the money?

J. And are accordingly a dark, mean, scoffing,——

M. You talk as if you had always lived in that wild unprofitable element you are so fond of, where all things glitter, and nothing is gold; all show and no substance. My people work in the secret, and their works praise them in the open light; they remain in the dark because only there such marvels could be bred. You call them mean. They do not spend their energies on their own growth, or their own play, but to feed the veins of mother earth with permanent splendors, very different from what she shows on the surface.

Think of passing a life, not merely in heaping together, but making gold. Of all dreams, that of the alchymist is the most poetical, for he looked at the finest symbol. Gold, says one of our friends, is the hidden light of the earth, it crowns the mineral, as wine the vegetable order, being the last expression of vital energy.

J. Have you paid for your passage?

M. Yes! and in gold, not in shells or pebbles.

J. No really wise gnome would scoff at the water, the beautiful water. "The spirit of man is like the water."

S. Yes, and like the air and fire, no less.

J. Yes, but not like the earth, this low-minded creature's chosen dwelling.

M. The earth is spirit made fruitful,—life. And its heart-beats are told in gold and wine.

J. Oh! it is shocking to hear such sentiments in these times. I thought that Bacchic energy of yours was long since repressed.

M. No! I have only learned to mix water with my wine, and stamp upon my gold the heads of kings, or the hieroglyphics of worship. But since I have learnt to mix with water, let's hear what you have to say in praise of your favorite.

J. From water Venus was born, what more would you have? It is the mother of Beauty, the girdle of earth, and the marriage of nations.

S. Without any of that high-flown poetry, it is enough, I think, that it is the great artist, turning all objects that approach it to picture.

J. True, no object that touches it, whether it be the cart that ploughs the wave for sea-weed, or the boat or plank that rides upon it, but is brought at once from the demesne of coarse utilities into that of picture. All trades, all callings, become picturesque by the water's side, or on the water. The soil, the slovenliness is washed out of every calling by its touch. All river-crafts, sea-crafts, are picturesque, are poetical. Their very slang is poetry.

M. The reasons for that are complex.

J. The reason is, that there can be no plodding, groping words and motions, on my water as there are on your earth. There is no time, no chance for them where all moves so rapidly, though so smoothly, everything connected with water must be like itself, forcible, but clear. That is why sea-slang is so poetical; there is a word for everything and every act, and a thing and

THE LAKES

an act for every word. Seamen must speak quick and bold, but also with utmost precision. They cannot reef and brace other than in a Homeric dialect—therefore,—(Steamboat bell rings.) But I must say a quick good-by.

M. What, going, going back to earth after all this talk upon the other side. Well, that is nowise Homeric, but truly modern.

J. is borne off without time for any reply, but a laugh—at himself, of course.

S. and M. retire to their state-rooms to forget the wet, the chill and steamboat smell in their just-bought new world of novels.

Next day, when we stopped at Cleveland, the storm was just clearing up; ascending the bluff, we had one of the finest views of the lake that could have been wished. The varying depths of these lakes give to their surface a great variety of coloring, and beneath this wild sky and changeful lights, the waters presented kaleidoscopic varieties of hues, rich, but mournful. I admire these bluffs of red, crumbling earth. Here land and water meet under very different auspices from those of the rock-bound coast to which I have been accustomed. There they meet tenderly to challenge, and proudly to refuse, though not in fact repel. But here they meet to mingle, are always rushing together, and changing places; a new creation takes place beneath the eye.

The weather grew gradually clearer, but not bright; yet we could see the shore and appreciate the extent of these noble waters.

Coming up the river St. Clair, we saw Indians for the first time. They were camped out on the bank. It was twilight, and their blanketed forms, in listless groups or stealing along the bank, with a lounge and a stride so different in its wildness from the rudeness of the white settler, gave me the first feeling that I really approached the West.

The people on the boat were almost all New Englanders, seeking their fortunes. They had brought with them their habits of calculation, their cautious manners, their love of polemics. It grieved me to hear these immigrants who were to be the fathers of a new race, all, from the old man down to the little girl, talking not of what they should do, but of what they should get in the new scene. It was to them a prospect, not of the unfolding nobler energies, but of more ease, and larger accumulation. It wearied me, too, to hear Trinity and Unity discussed in the poor, narrow doctrinal way on these free waters; but that will soon cease, there is not time for this clash of opinions in the West, where the clash of material interests is so noisy. They will need the spirit of religion more than ever to guide them, but will find less time than before for its doctrine. This change was to me, who am tired of the war of words on these subjects, and believe it only sows the wind to reap the whirlwind, refreshing, but I argue nothing from it; there is nothing real in the freedom of thought at the West, it is from the position of men's lives, not the state of their minds. So soon as they have time, unless they grow better meanwhile, they will cavil and criticise, and judge other men by their own standard, and outrage the law of love every way, just as they do with us.

We reached Mackinaw the evening of the third day, but, to my great disappointment, it was too late and too rainy to go ashore. The beauty of the island, though seen under the most unfavorable circumstances, did not disappoint my expectations. But I shall see it to more purpose on my return.

As the day has passed dully, a cold rain preventing us from keeping out in the air, my thoughts have been dwelling on a story told when we were off Detroit, this morning, by a fellow passenger, and whose moral beauty touched me profoundly.

Some years ago, said Mrs. L., my father and mother stopped to dine at Detroit. A short time before dinner my father met in the hall Captain P., a friend of his youthful days. He had loved P. extremely, as did many who knew him, and had not been surprised to hear of the distinction and popular esteem which his wide knowledge, talents, and noble temper commanded, as he went onward in the world. P. was every way fitted to succeed; his aims were high, but not too high for his powers, suggested by an instinct of his own capacities, not by an ideal standard drawn from culture. Though steadfast in his course, it was not to overrun others, his wise self-possession was no less for them than himself. He was thoroughly the gentleman, gentle because manly, and was a striking instance that where there is strength for sincere courtesy, there is no need of other adaptation to the character of others, to make one's way freely and gracefully through the crowd.

My father was delighted to see him, and after a short parley in the hall—"We will dine together," he cried, "then we shall have time to tell all our stories."

P. hesitated a moment, then said, "My wife is with me."

"And mine with me," said my father, "that's well; they, too, will have an opportunity of getting acquainted and can entertain one another, if they get tired of our college stories."

P. acquiesced, with a grave bow, and shortly after they all met in the dining-room. My father was much surprised at the appearance of Mrs. P. He had heard that his friend married abroad, but nothing further, and he was not prepared to see the calm, dignified P. with a woman on his arm, still handsome, indeed, but whose coarse and imperious expression showed as low habits of mind as her exaggerated dress and gesture did of education. Nor could there be a greater contrast to my mother, who, though understanding her claims and place with the certainty of a lady, was soft and retiring in an uncommon degree.

However, there was no time to wonder or fancy; they sat down, and P. engaged in conversation, without much vivacity, but with his usual ease. The first quarter of an hour passed well enough. But soon it was observable that Mrs. P. was drinking glass after glass of wine, to an extent few gentlemen did, even then, and soon that she was actually excited by it. Before this, her manner had been brusque, if not contemptuous towards her new acquaintance; now it became, towards my mother especially, quite rude. Presently she took up some slight remark made by my mother, which, though it did not naturally mean anything of the sort, could be twisted into some reflection upon England, and made it a handle, first of vulgar sarcasm, and then, upon my mother's defending herself with some surprise and gentle dignity, hurled upon her a volley of abuse, beyond Billingsgate.

My mother, confounded, feeling scenes and ideas presented to her mind equally new and painful, sat trembling; she knew not what to do, tears rushed into her eyes. My father, no less distressed, yet unwilling to outrage the feelings of his friend by doing or saying what his indignation prompted, turned an appealing look on P.

Never, as he often said, was the painful expression of that sight effaced from his mind. It haunted his dreams and disturbed his waking thoughts. P. sat with his head bent forward, and his eyes cast down, pale, but calm, with a fixed expression, not merely of patient wo, but of patient shame, which it would not have been thought possible for that noble countenance to wear, "yet," said my father, "it became him. At other times he was handsome, but then beautiful, though of a beauty saddened and abashed. For a spiritual light borrowed from the worldly perfection of his mien that illustration by contrast, which the penitence of the Magdalen does from the glowing earthliness of her charms."

Seeing that he preserved silence, while Mrs. P. grew still more exasperated, my father rose and led his wife to her own room. Half an hour had passed, in painful and wondering surmises, when a gentle knock was heard at the door, and P. entered equipped for a journey. "We are just going," he said, and holding out his hand, but without looking at them, "Forgive."

They each took his hand, and silently pressed it, then he went without a word more.

Some time passed and they heard now and then of P., as he passed from one army station to another, with his uncongenial companion, who became, it was said, constantly more degraded. Whoever mentioned having seen them, wondered at the chance which had yoked him to such a woman, but yet more at the silent fortitude with which he bore it. Many blamed him for enduring it, apparently without efforts to check her; others answered that he had probably made such at an earlier period, and finding them unavailing, had resigned himself to despair, and was too delicate to meet the scandal that, with such a resistance as such a woman could offer, must attend a formal separation.

But my father, who was not in such haste to come to conclusions, and substitute some plausible explanation for the truth, found something in the look of P. at that trying moment to which none of these explanations offered a key. There was in it, he felt, a fortitude, but not the fortitude of the hero, a religious submission, above the penitent, if not enkindled with the enthusiasm of the martyr.

That, he replied, I cannot tell you. He was a moment silent, then continued with an impassive look of cold self-possession, that affected me with strange sadness.

"The name of the person you will hear, of course, at the time, but more I cannot tell you. I need, however, the presence, not only of legal, but of respectable and friendly witnesses. I have hoped you and your husband would do me this kindness. Will you?"

Something in his manner made it impossible to refuse. I answered before I knew I was going to speak, "We will," and he left me.

I will not weary you with telling how I harassed myself and my husband, who was, however, scarce less interested, with doubts and conjectures. Suffice it that, next morning, P. came and took us in a carriage to a distant church. We had just entered the porch when a cart, such as fruit and vegetables are brought to market in, drove up, containing an elderly woman and a young girl. P. assisted them to alight, and advanced with the girl to the altar.

The girl was neatly dressed and quite handsome, yet something in her expression displeased me the moment I looked upon her. Meanwhile the ceremony was going on, and, at its close, P. introduced us to the bride, and we all went to the door.

Good-by, Fanny, said the elderly woman. The new-made Mrs. P. replied without any token of affection or emotion. The woman got into the cart and drove away.

From that time I saw but little of P. or his wife. I took our mutual friends to see her, and they were civil to her for his sake. Curiosity was very much excited, but entirely baffled; no one, of course, dared speak to P. on the subject, and no other means could be found of solving the riddle.

He treated his wife with grave and kind politeness, but it was always obvious that they had nothing in common between them. Her manners and tastes were not at that time gross, but her character showed itself hard and material. She was fond of riding, and spent much time so. Her style in this, and in dress, seemed the opposite of P.'s; but he indulged all her wishes, while, for himself, he plunged into his own pursuits.

For a time he seemed, if not happy, not positively unhappy; but, after a few years, Mrs. P. fell into the habit of drinking, and

I have said that my father was not one of those who are ready to substitute specious explanations for truth, and those who are thus abstinent rarely lay their hand on a thread without making it a clue. Such an one, like the dexterous weaver, lets not one color go, till he finds that which matches it in the pattern; he keeps on weaving, but chooses his shades, and my father found at last what he wanted to make out the pattern for himself. He met a lady who had been intimate with both himself and P. in early days, and finding she had seen the latter abroad, asked if she knew the circumstances of the marriage. "The circumstances of the act I know," she said, "which sealed the misery of our friend, though as much in the dark as any one about the motives that led to it."

We were quite intimate with P. in London, and he was our most delightful companion. He was then in the full flower of the varied accomplishments, which set off his fine manners and dignified character, joined, towards those he loved, with a certain soft willingness which gives the desirable chivalry to a man. None was more clear of choice where his personal affections were not touched, but where they were, it cost him pain to say no, on the slightest occasion. I have thought this must have had some connexion with the mystery of his misfortunes.

One day he called on me, and, without any preface, asked if I would be present next day at his marriage. I was so surprised, and so unpleasantly surprised, that I did not at first answer a word. We had been on terms so familiar, that I thought I knew all about him, yet had never dreamed of his having an attachment, and, though I had never inquired on the subject, yet this reserve, where perfect openness had been supposed, and really, on my side, existed, seemed to me a kind of treachery. Then it is never pleasant to know that a heart, on which we have some claim, is to be given to another. We cannot tell how it will affect our own relations with a person; it may strengthen or it may swallow up other affections; the crisis is hazardous, and our first thought, on such an occasion, is too often for ourselves, at least, mine was. Seeing me silent, he repeated his question.

To whom, said I, are you to be married?

then such scenes as you witnessed grew frequent. I have often heard of them, and always that P. sat, as you describe him, his head bowed down and perfectly silent all through, whatever might be done or whoever be present, and always his aspect has inspired such sympathy that no person has questioned him or resented her insults, but merely got out of the way, so soon as possible.

Hard and long penance, said my father, after some minutes musing, for an hour of passion, probably for his only error.

Is that your explanation? said the lady. O, improbable. P. might err, but not be led beyond himself.

I know his cool gray eye and calm complexion seemed to say so, but a different story is told by the lip that could tremble, and showed what flashes might pierce those deep blue heavens; and when these over intellectual beings do swerve aside, it is to fall down a precipice, for their narrow path lies over such. But he was not one to sin without making a brave atonement, and that it had become a holy one, was written on that downcast brow.

The fourth day on these waters, the weather was milder and brighter, so that we could now see them to some purpose. At night was clear moon, and, for the first time, from the upper deck, I saw one of the great steamboats come majestically up. It was glowing with lights, looking many-eyed and sagacious; in its heavy motion it seemed a dowager queen, and this motion, with its solemn pulse, and determined sweep, becomes these smooth waters, especially at night, as much as the dip of the sail-ship the long billows of the ocean.

But it was not so soon that I learned to appreciate the lake scenery; it was only after a daily and careless familiarity that I entered into its beauty, for nature always refuses to be seen by being stared at. Like Bonaparte, she discharges her face of all expression when she catches the eye of impertinent curiosity fixed on her. But he who has gone to sleep in childish ease on her lap, or leaned an aching brow upon her breast, seeking there comfort with full trust as from a mother, will see all a mother's beauty in the look she bends upon him. Later, I felt that I had really seen these regions, and shall speak of them again.

In the afternoon we went on shore at the Manitou islands, where the boat stops to wood. No one lives here except woodcutters for the steamboats. I had thought of such a position, from its mixture of profound solitude with service to the great world, as possessing an ideal beauty. I think so still, after seeing the woodcutters and their slovenly huts.

In times of slower growth, man did not enter a situation without a certain preparation or adaptedness to it. He drew from it, if not to the poetical extent, at least, in some proportion, its moral and its meaning. The woodcutter did not cut down so many trees a day, that the hamadryads had not time to make their plaints heard; the shepherd tended his sheep, and did no jobs or chores the while; the idyl had a chance to grow up, and modulate his oaten pipe. But now the poet must be at the whole expense of the poetry in describing one of these positions; the worker is a true Midas to the gold he makes. The poet must describe, as the painter sketches Irish peasant girls and Danish fishwives, adding the beauty, and leaving out the dirt.

I come to the west prepared for the distaste I must experience at its mushroom growth. I know that where "go ahead" is the only motto, the village cannot grow into the gentle proportions that successive lives, and the gradations of experience involuntarily give. In older countries the house of the son grew from that of the father, as naturally as new joints on a bough. And the cathedral crowned the whole as naturally as the leafy summit the tree. This cannot be here. The march of peaceful is scarce less wanton than that of warlike invasion. The old landmarks are broken down, and the land, for a season, bears none, except of the rudeness of conquest and the needs of the day, whose bivouac fires blacken the sweetest forest glades. I have come prepared to see all this, to dislike it, but not with stupid narrowness to distrust or defame. On the contrary, while I will not be so obliging as to confound ugliness with beauty, discord with harmony, and laud and be contented with all I meet, when it conflicts with my best desires and tastes, I trust by reverent faith to woo the mighty meaning of the scene, perhaps to foresee the law by which a new order, a new poetry is to be evoked from this chaos, and with a curiosity as ardent, but not so selfish as that of Macbeth, to call up the apparitions of future kings from the strange ingredients of the witch's caldron. Thus, I will not grieve that all the noble trees are gone already from this island to feed this caldron, but believe it will have Medea's virtue, and reproduce them in the form of new intellectual growths, since centuries cannot again adorn the land with such.

On this most beautiful beach of smooth white pebbles, interspersed with agates and cornelians, for those who know how to find them, we stepped, not like the Indian, with some humble offering, which, if no better than an arrow-head or a little parched corn, would, he judged, please the Manitou, who looks only at the spirit in which it is offered. Our visit was so far for a religious purpose that one of our party went to inquire the fate of some Unitarian tracts left among the woodcutters a year or two before. But the old Manitou, though, daunted like his children by the approach of the fire-ships which he probably considered demons of a new dynasty, he had suffered his woods to be felled to feed their pride, had been less patient of an encroachment, which did not to him seem so authorized by the law of the strongest, and had scattered those leaves as carelessly as the others of that year.

But S. and I, like other emigrants, went not to give, but to get, to rifle the wood of flowers for the service of the fire-ship. We returned with a rich booty, among which was the uva ursi, whose leaves the Indians smoke, with the kinnick-kinnick, and which had then just put forth its highly-finished little blossoms, as pretty as those of the blueberry.

Passing along still further, I thought it would be well if the crowds assembled to stare from the various landings were still confined to the kinnick-kinnick, for almost all had tobacco written on their faces, their cheeks rounded with plugs, their eyes dull with its fumes. We reached Chicago on the evening of the sixth day, having been out five days and a half, a rather longer passage than usual at a favorable season of the year.

Chicago, June 20.

There can be no two places in the world more completely thoroughfares than this place and Buffalo. They are the two correspondent valves that open and shut all the time, as the life-blood rushes from east to west, and back again from west to east.

Since it is their office thus to be the doors, and let in and out, it would be unfair to expect from them much character of their own. To make the best provisions for the transmission of produce is their office, and the people who live there are such as are suited for this; active, complaisant, inventive, business people. There are no provisions for the student or idler; to know what the place can give, you should be at work with the rest, the mere traveller will not find it profitable to loiter there as I did.

Since circumstances made it necessary for me so to do, I read all the books I could find about the new region, which now began to become real to me. All the books about the Indians, a paltry collection, truly, yet which furnished material for many thoughts. The most narrow-minded and awkward recital still bears some lineaments of the great features of this nature, and the races of men that illustrated them.

Catlin's book is far the best. I was afterwards assured by those acquainted with the regions he describes, that he is not to be depended on for the accuracy of his facts, and, indeed, it is obvious, without the aid of such assertions, that he sometimes yields to the temptation of making out a story. They admitted, however, what from my feelings I was sure of, that he is true to the spirit of the scene, and that a far better view can be got from him than from any source at present existing, of the Indian tribes of the far west, and of the country where their inheritance lay.

Murray's travels I read, and was charmed by their accuracy and clear broad tone. He is the only Englishman that seems to have traversed these regions, as man, simply, not as John Bull. He deserves to belong to an aristocracy, for he showed his title to it more when left without a guide in the wilderness, than he can at the court of Victoria. He has, himself, no poetic force at description, but it is easy to make images from his hints. Yet we believe the Indian cannot be looked at truly except by a poetic eye. The Pawnees, no doubt, are such as he describes them, filthy in their habits, and treacherous in their character, but some would have seen, and seen truly, more beauty and dignity than he does with all his manliness and fairness of mind. However, his one fine old man is enough to redeem the rest, and is perhaps the relic of a better day, a Phocion among the Pawnees.

Schoolcraft's Algic Researches is a valuable book, though a worse use could hardly have been made of such fine material.

Had the mythological or hunting stories of the Indians been written down exactly as they were received from the lips of the narrators, the collection could not have been surpassed in interest, both for the wild charm they carry with them, and the light they throw on a peculiar modification of life and mind. As it is, though the incidents have an air of originality and pertinence to the occasion, that gives us confidence that they have not been altered, the phraseology in which they were expressed has been entirely set aside, and the flimsy graces, common to the style of annuals and souvenirs, substituted for the Spartan brevity and sinewy grasp of Indian speech. We can just guess what might have been there, as we can detect the fine proportions of the Brave whom the bad taste of some white patron has arranged in frock-coat, hat, and pantaloons.

The few stories Mrs. Jameson wrote out, though to these also a sentimental air has been given, offend much less in that way than is common in this book. What would we give for a completely faithful version of some among them. Yet with all these drawbacks we cannot doubt from internal evidence that they truly ascribe to the Indian a delicacy of sentiment and of fancy that justifies Cooper in such inventions as his Uncas. It is a white man's view of a savage hero, who would be far finer in his natural proportions; still, through a masquerade figure, it implies the truth.

Irving's books I also read, some for the first, some for the second time, with increased interest, now that I was to meet such people as he received his materials from. Though the books are pleasing from their grace and luminous arrangement, yet, with the exception of the Tour to the Prairies, they have a stereotype, second-hand air. They lack the breath, the glow, the charming minute traits of living presence. His scenery is only fit to be glanced at from dioramic distance; his Indians are academic figures only. He would have made the best of pictures, if he could have used his own eyes for studies and sketches; as it is, his success is wonderful, but inadequate.

McKenney's Tour to the Lakes is the dullest of books, yet faithful and quiet, and gives some facts not to be met with elsewhere.

I also read a collection of Indian anecdotes and speeches, the worst compiled and arranged book possible, yet not without clues of some value. All these books I read in anticipation of a canoe-voyage on Lake Superior as far as the Pictured Rocks, and, though I was afterwards compelled to give up this project, they aided me in judging of what I afterwards saw and heard of the Indians.

In Chicago I first saw the beautiful prairie flowers. They were in their glory the first ten days we were there—

"The golden and the flame-like flowers."

The flame-like flower I was taught afterwards, by an Indian girl, to call "Wickapee;" and she told me, too, that its splendors had a useful side, for it was used by the Indians as a remedy for an illness to which they were subject.

Beside these brilliant flowers, which gemmed and gilt the grass in a sunny afternoon's drive near the blue lake, between the low oakwood and the narrow beach, stimulated, whether sensuously by the optic nerve, unused to so much gold and crimson with such tender green, or symbolically through some meaning dimly seen in the flowers, I enjoyed a sort of fairyland exultation never felt before, and the first drive amid the flowers gave me anticipation of the beauty of the prairies.

At first, the prairie seemed to speak of the very desolation of dullness. After sweeping over the vast monotony of the lakes to come to this monotony of land, with all around a limitless horizon,—to walk, and walk, and run, but never climb, oh! it was too dreary for any but a Hollander to bear. How the eye greeted the approach of a sail, or the smoke of a steamboat; it seemed that any thing so animated must come from a better land, where mountains gave religion to the scene.

The only thing I liked at first to do, was to trace with slow and unexpecting step the narrow margin of the lake. Sometimes a heavy swell gave it expression; at others, only its varied coloring, which I found more admirable every day, and which gave it an air of mirage instead of the vastness of ocean. Then there was a grandeur in the feeling that I might continue that walk, if I had any seven-leagued mode of conveyance to save fatigue, for hundreds of miles without an obstacle and without a change.

But after I had rode out, and seen the flowers and seen the sun set with that calmness seen only in the prairies, and

CHICAGO 29

the cattle winding slowly home to their homes in the "island groves"—peacefullest of sights—I began to love because I began to know the scene, and shrank no longer from "the encircling vastness."

It is always thus with the new form of life; we must learn to look at it by its own standard. At first, no doubt my accustomed eye kept saying, if the mind did not, What! no distant mountains? what, no valleys? But after a while I would ascend the roof of the house where we lived, and pass many hours, needing no sight but the moon reigning in the heavens, or starlight falling upon the lake, till all the lights were out in the island grove of men beneath my feet, and felt nearer heaven that there was nothing but this lovely, still reception on the earth; no towering mountains, no deep tree-shadows, nothing but plain earth and water bathed in light.

Sunset, as seen from that place, presented most generally, low-lying, flaky clouds, of the softest serenity, "like," said S., "the Buddhist tracts."

One night a star shot madly from its sphere, and it had a fair chance to be seen, but that serenity could not be astonished.

Yes! it was a peculiar beauty of those sunsets and moonlights on the levels of Chicago which Chamouny or the Trosachs could not make me forget.

Notwithstanding all the attractions I thus found out by degrees on the flat shores of the lake, I was delighted when I found myself really on my way into the country for an excursion of two or three weeks. We set forth in a strong wagon, almost as large, and with the look of those used elsewhere for transporting caravans of wild beastesses, loaded with every thing we might want, in case nobody would give it to us—for buying and selling were no longer to be counted on—with a pair of strong horses, able and willing to force their way through mud holes and amid stumps, and a guide, equally admirable as marshal and companion, who knew by heart the country and its history, both natural and artificial, and whose clear hunter's eye needed neither road nor goal to guide it to all the spots where beauty best loves to dwell.

Add to this the finest weather, and such country as I had never seen, even in my dreams, although these dreams had been haunted by wishes for just such an one, and you may judge

SUMMER ON THE LAKES

whether years of dullness might not, by these bright days, be redeemed, and a sweetness be shed over all thoughts of the West.

The first day brought us through woods rich in the moccasin flower and lupine, and plains whose soft expanse was continually touched with expression by the slow moving clouds which

> "Sweep over with their shadows, and beneath
> The surface rolls and fluctuates to the eye;
> Dark hollows seem to glide along and chase
>   The sunny ridges,"

to the banks of the Fox river, a sweet and graceful stream. We reached Geneva just in time to escape being drenched by a violent thunder shower, whose rise and disappearance threw expression into all the features of the scene.

Geneva reminds me of a New England village, as indeed there, and in the neighborhood, are many New Englanders of an excellent stamp, generous, intelligent, discreet, and seeking to win from life its true values. Such are much wanted, and seem like points of light among the swarms of settlers, whose aims are sordid, whose habits thoughtless and slovenly.

With great pleasure we heard, with his attentive and affectionate congregation, the Unitarian clergyman, Mr. Conant, and afterward visited him in his house, where almost everything bore traces of his own handywork or that of his father. He is just such a teacher as is wanted in this region, familiar enough with the habits of those he addresses to come home to their experience and their wants; earnest and enlightened enough to draw the important inferences from the life of every day.

A day or two we remained here, and passed some happy hours in the woods that fringe the stream, where the gentlemen found a rich booty of fish.

Next day, travelling along the river's banks, was an uninterrupted pleasure. We closed our drive in the afternoon at the house of an English gentleman, who has gratified, as few men do, the common wish to pass the evening of an active day amid the quiet influences of country life. He showed us a book-case filled with books about this country; these he had collected for years, and become so familiar with the localities that, on coming here at last, he sought and found, at once, the very spot he wanted, and where he is as content as he hoped to be, thus realizing Wordsworth's description of the wise man, who "sees what he foresaw."

A wood surrounds the house, through which paths are cut in every direction. It is, for this new country, a large and handsome dwelling; but round it are its barns and farm yard, with cattle and poultry. These, however, in the framework of wood, have a very picturesque and pleasing effect. There is that mixture of culture and rudeness in the aspect of things as gives a feeling of freedom, not of confusion.

I wish it were possible to give some idea of this scene as viewed by the earliest freshness of dewy dawn. This habitation of man seemed like a nest in the grass, so thoroughly were the buildings and all the objects of human care harmonized with what was natural. The tall trees bent and whispered all around, as if to hail with sheltering love the men who had come to dwell among them.

The young ladies were musicians, and spoke French fluently, having been educated in a convent. Here in the prairie, they had learned to take care of the milk-room, and kill the rattlesnakes that assailed their poultry yard. Beneath the shade of heavy curtains you looked out from the high and large windows to see Norwegian peasants at work in their national dress. In the wood grew, not only the flowers I had before seen, and wealth of tall, wild roses, but the splendid blue spiderwort, that ornament of our gardens. Beautiful children strayed there, who were soon to leave these civilized regions for some really wild and western place, a post in the buffalo country. Their no less beautiful mother was of Welsh descent, and the eldest child bore the name of Gwynthleon. Perhaps there she will meet with some young descendants of Madoc, to be her friends; at any rate, her looks may retain that sweet, wild beauty, that is soon made to vanish from eyes which look too much on shops and streets, and the vulgarities of city "parties."

Next day we crossed the river. We ladies crossed on a little foot-bridge, from which we could look down the stream, and see the wagon pass over at the ford. A black thunder cloud was coming up. The sky and waters heavy with expectation. The motion of the wagon, with its white cover, and the laboring horses, gave just the due interest to the picture, because it seemed as if they would not have time to cross before the storm came on. However, they did get across, and we were a mile or two on our way before the violent shower obliged us to take refuge in a solitary house upon the prairie. In this country it is as pleasant to stop as to go on, to lose your way as to find it, for the variety in the population gives you a chance for fresh entertainment in every hut, and the luxuriant beauty makes every path attractive. In this house we found a family "quite above the common," but, I grieve to say, not above false pride, for the father, ashamed of being caught barefoot, told us a story of a man, one of the richest men, he said, in one of the eastern cities, who went barefoot, from choice and taste.

Near the door grew a Provence rose, then in blossom. Other families we saw had brought with them and planted the locust. It was pleasant to see their old home loves, brought into connection with their new splendors. Wherever there were traces of this tenderness of feeling, only too rare among Americans, other things bore signs also of prosperity and intelligence, as if the ordering mind of man had some idea of home beyond a mere shelter, beneath which to eat and sleep.

No heaven need wear a lovelier aspect than earth did this afternoon, after the clearing up of the shower. We traversed the blooming plain, unmarked by any road, only the friendly track of wheels which tracked, not broke the grass. Our stations were not from town to town, but from grove to grove. These groves first floated like blue islands in the distance. As we drew nearer, they seemed fair parks, and the little log houses on the edge, with their curling smokes, harmonized beautifully with them.

One of these groves, Ross's grove, we reached just at sunset. It was of the noblest trees I saw during this journey, for the trees generally were not large or lofty, but only of fair proportions. Here they were large enough to form with their clear stems pillars for grand cathedral aisles. There was space enough for crimson light to stream through upon the floor of water which the shower had left. As we slowly plashed through, I thought I was never in a better place for vespers.

That night we rested, or rather tarried at a grove some miles beyond, and there partook of the miseries so often jocosely portrayed, of bedchambers for twelve, a milk dish for universal handbasin, and expectations that you would use and lend your "hankercher" for a towel. But this was the only night, thanks to the hospitality of private families, that we passed thus, and it was well that we had this bit of experience, else might we have pronounced all Trollopian records of the kind to be inventions of pure malice.

With us was a young lady who showed herself to have been bathed in the Britannic fluid, wittily described by a late French writer, by the impossibility she experienced of accommodating herself to the indecorums of the scene. We ladies were to sleep in the bar-room, from which its drinking visiters could be ejected only at a late hour. The outer door had no fastening to prevent their return. However, our host kindly requested we would call him, if they did, as he had "conquered them for us," and would do so again. We had also rather hard couches; (mine was the supper table,) but we yankees, born to rove, were altogether too much fatigued to stand upon trifles, and slept as sweetly as we would in the "bigly bower" of any baroness. But I think England sat up all night, wrapped in her blanket shawl, and with a neat lace cap upon her head; so that she would have looked perfectly the lady, if any one had come in; shuddering and listening. I know that she was very ill next day, in requital. She watched, as her parent country watches the seas, that nobody may do wrong in any case, and deserved to have met some interruption, she was so well prepared. However, there was none, other than from the nearness of some twenty sets of powerful lungs, which would not leave the night to a deadly stillness. In this house we had, if not good beds, yet good tea, good bread, and wild strawberries, and were entertained with most free communications of opinion and history from our hosts. Neither shall any of us have a right to say again that we cannot find any who may be willing to hear all we may have to say. "A's fish that comes to the net," should be painted on the sign at Papaw grove.

Chapter III

In the afternoon of this day we reached the Rock river, in whose neighborhood we proposed to make some stay, and crossed at Dixon's ferry.

This beautiful stream flows full and wide over a bed of rocks, traversing a distance of near two hundred miles, to reach the Mississippi. Great part of the country along its banks is the finest region of Illinois, and the scene of some of the latest romance of Indian warfare. To these beautiful regions Black Hawk returned with his band "to pass the summer," when he drew upon himself the warfare in which he was finally vanquished. No wonder he could not resist the longing, unwise though its indulgence might be, to return in summer to this home of beauty.

Of Illinois, in general, it has often been remarked that it bears the character of country which has been inhabited by a nation skilled like the English in all the ornamental arts of life, especially in landscape gardening. That the villas and castles seem to have been burnt, the enclosures taken down, but the velvet lawns, the flower gardens, the stately parks, scattered at graceful intervals by the decorous hand of art, the frequent deer, and the peaceful herd of cattle that make picture of the plain, all suggest more of the masterly mind of man, than the prodigal, but careless, motherly love of nature. Especially is this true of the Rock river country. The river flows sometimes through these parks and lawns, then betwixt high bluffs, whose grassy ridges are covered with fine trees, or broken with crumbling stone, that easily assumes the forms of buttress, arch and clustered columns. Along the face of such crumbling rocks, swallows' nests are clustered, thick as cities, and eagles and deer do not disdain their summits. One morning, out in the boat along the base of these rocks, it was amusing, and affecting too, to see these swallows put their heads out to look at us. There was something very hospitable about it, as if man had never shown himself a tyrant near them. What a morning that was! Every sight is worth twice

ROCK RIVER

as much by the early morning light. We borrow something of the spirit of the hour to look upon them.

The first place where we stopped was one of singular beauty, a beauty of soft, luxuriant wildness. It was on the bend of the river, a place chosen by an Irish gentleman, whose absenteeship seems of the wisest kind, since for a sum which would have been but a drop of water to the thirsty fever of his native land, he commands a residence which has all that is desirable, in its independence, its beautiful retirement, and means of benefit to others.

His park, his deer-chase, he found already prepared; he had only to make an avenue through it. This brought us by a drive, which in the heat of noon seemed long, though afterwards, in the cool of morning and evening, delightful, to the house. This is, for that part of the world, a large and commodious dwelling. Near it stands the log-cabin where its master lived while it was building, a very ornamental accessory.

In front of the house was a lawn, adorned by the most graceful trees. A few of these had been taken out to give a full view of the river, gliding through banks such as I have described. On this bend the bank is high and bold, so from the house or the lawn the view was very rich and commanding. But if you descended a ravine at the side to the water's edge, you found there a long walk on the narrow shore, with a wall above of the richest hanging wood, in which they said the deer lay hid. I never saw one, but often fancied that I heard them rustling, at daybreak, by these bright clear waters, stretching out in such smiling promise, where no sound broke the deep and blissful seclusion, unless now and then this rustling, or the plash of some fish a little gayer than the others; it seemed not necessary to have any better heaven, or fuller expression of love and freedom than in the mood of nature here.

Then, leaving the bank, you would walk far and far through long grassy paths, full of the most brilliant, also the most delicate flowers. The brilliant are more common on the prairie, but both kinds loved this place.

Amid the grass of the lawn, with a profusion of wild strawberries, we greeted also a familiar love, the Scottish harebell, the gentlest, and most touching form of the flower-world.

The master of the house was absent, but with a kindness beyond thanks had offered us a resting place there. Here we were taken care of by a deputy, who would, for his youth, have been assigned the place of a page in former times, but in the young west, it seems he was old enough for a steward. Whatever be called his function, he did the honors of the place so much in harmony with it, as to leave the guests free to imagine themselves in Elysium. And the three days passed here were days of unalloyed, spotless happiness.

There was a peculiar charm in coming here, where the choice of location, and the unobtrusive good taste of all the arrangements, showed such intelligent appreciation of the spirit of the scene, after seeing so many dwellings of the new settlers, which showed plainly that they had no thought beyond satisfying the grossest material wants. Sometimes they looked attractive, the little brown houses, the natural architecture of the country, in the edge of the timber. But almost always when you came near, the slovenliness of the dwelling and the rude way in which objects around it were treated, when so little care would have presented a charming whole, were very repulsive. Seeing the traces of the Indians, who chose the most beautiful sites for their dwellings, and whose habits do not break in on that aspect of nature under which they were born, we feel as if they were the rightful lords of a beauty they forbore to deform. But most of these settlers do not see it at all; it breathes, it speaks in vain to those who are rushing into its sphere. Their progress is Gothic, not Roman, and their mode of cultivation will, in the course of twenty, perhaps ten, years, obliterate the natural expression of the country.

This is inevitable, fatal; we must not complain, but look forward to a good result. Still, in travelling through this country, I could not but be struck with the force of a symbol. Wherever the hog comes, the rattlesnake disappears; the omnivorous traveller, safe in its stupidity, willingly and easily makes a meal of the most dangerous of reptiles, and one whom the Indian looks on with a mystic awe. Even so the white settler pursues the Indian, and is victor in the chase. But I shall say more upon the subject by-and-by.

While we were here we had one grand thunder storm, which added new glory to the scene.

ROCK RIVER

One beautiful feature was the return of the pigeons every afternoon to their home. Every afternoon they came sweeping across the lawn, positively in clouds, and with a swiftness and softness of winged motion, more beautiful than anything of the kind I ever knew. Had I been a musician, such as Mendelsohn, I felt that I could have improvised a music quite peculiar, from the sound they made, which should have indicated all the beauty over which their wings bore them. I will here insert a few lines left at this house, on parting, which feebly indicate some of the features.

Familiar to the childish mind were tales
 Of rock-girt isles amid a desert sea,
Where unexpected stretch the flowery vales
 To soothe the shipwrecked sailor's misery.
Fainting, he lay upon a sandy shore,
And fancied that all hope of life was o'er;
But let him patient climb the frowning wall,
Within, the orange glows beneath the palm tree tall,
And all that Eden boasted waits his call.

Almost these tales seem realized to-day,
When the long dullness of the sultry way,
Where "independent" settlers' careless cheer
Made us indeed feel we were "strangers" here,
Is cheered by sudden sight of this fair spot,
On which "improvement" yet has made no blot,
But Nature all-astonished stands, to find
Her plan protected by the human mind.

Blest be the kindly genius of the scene;
 The river, bending in unbroken grace,
The stately thickets, with their pathways green,
 Fair lonely trees, each in its fittest place.
Those thickets haunted by the deer and fawn;
Those cloudlike flights of birds across the lawn;
The gentlest breezes here delight to blow,
And sun and shower and star are emulous to deck the show.

Wondering, as Crusoe, we survey the land;
Happier than Crusoe we, a friendly band;
Blest be the hand that reared this friendly home,
The heart and mind of him to whom we owe

Hours of pure peace such as few mortals know;
May he find such, should he be led to roam;
Be tended by such ministering sprites—
Enjoy such gaily childish days, such hopeful nights!
And yet, amid the goods to mortals given,
To give those goods again is most like heaven.

Hazelwood, Rock River, June 30th, 1843.

The only really rustic feature was of the many coops of poultry near the house, which I understood it to be one of the chief pleasures of the master to feed.

Leaving this place, we proceeded a day's journey along the beautiful stream, to a little town named Oregon. We called at a cabin, from whose door looked out one of those faces which, once seen, are never forgotten; young, yet touched with many traces of feeling, not only possible, but endured; spirited, too, like the gleam of a finely tempered blade. It was a face that suggested a history, and many histories, but whose scene would have been in courts and camps. At this moment their circles are dull for want of that life which is waning unexcited in this solitary recess.

The master of the house proposed to show us a "short cut," by which we might, to especial advantage, pursue our journey. This proved to be almost perpendicular down a hill, studded with young trees and stumps. From these he proposed, with a hospitality of service worthy an Oriental, to free our wheels whenever they should get entangled, also, to be himself the drag, to prevent our too rapid descent. Such generosity deserved trust; however, we women could not be persuaded to render it. We got out and admired, from afar, the process. Left by our guide—and prop! we found ourselves in a wide field, where, by playful quips and turns, an endless "creek," seemed to divert itself with our attempts to cross it. Failing in this, the next best was to whirl down a steep bank, which feat our charioteer performed with an air not unlike that of Rhesus, had he but been as suitably furnished with chariot and steeds!

At last, after wasting some two or three hours on the "short cut," we got out by following an Indian trail,—Black Hawk's! How fair the scene through which it led! How could they let themselves be conquered, with such a country to fight for!

OREGON 39

Afterwards, in the wide prairie, we saw a lively picture of nonchalance, (to speak in the fashion of dear Ireland.) There, in the wide sunny field, with neither tree nor umbrella above his head, sat a pedler, with his pack, waiting apparently for customers. He was not disappointed. We bought, what hold in regard to the human world, as unmarked, as mysterious, and as important an existence, as the infusoria to the natural, to wit, pins. This incident would have delighted those modern sages, who, in imitation of the sitting philosophers of ancient Ind, prefer silence to speech, waiting to going, and scornfully smile in answer to the motions of earnest life,

> "Of itself will nothing come,
> That ye must still be seeking?"

However, it seemed to me to-day, as formerly on these sublime occasions, obvious that nothing would come, unless something would go; now, if we had been as sublimely still as the pedler, his pins would have tarried in the pack, and his pockets sustained an aching void of pence!

Passing through one of the fine, park-like woods, almost clear from underbrush and carpeted with thick grasses and flowers, we met, (for it was Sunday,) a little congregation just returning from their service, which had been performed in a rude house in its midst. It had a sweet and peaceful air, as if such words and thoughts were very dear to them. The parents had with them all their little children; but we saw no old people; that charm was wanting, which exists in such scenes in older settlements, of seeing the silver bent in reverence beside the flaxen head.

At Oregon, the beauty of the scene was of even a more sumptuous character than at our former "stopping place." Here swelled the river in its boldest course, interspersed by halcyon isles on which nature had lavished all her prodigality in tree, vine, and flower, banked by noble bluffs, three hundred feet high, their sharp ridges as exquisitely definite as the edge of a shell; their summits adorned with those same beautiful trees, and with buttresses of rich rock, crested with old hemlocks, which wore a touching and antique grace amid the softer and more luxuriant vegetation. Lofty natural mounds rose amidst the rest, with the same lovely and sweeping outline, showing everywhere the plastic power of water,—water, mother of beauty, which, by its sweet and eager flow, had left such lineaments as human genius never dreamt of.

Not far from the river was a high crag, called the Pine Rock, which looks out, as our guide observed, like a helmet above the brow of the country. It seems as if the water left here and there a vestige of forms and materials that preceded its course, just to set off its new and richer designs.

The aspect of this country was to me enchanting, beyond any I have ever seen, from its fullness of expression, its bold and impassioned sweetness. Here the flood of emotion has passed over and marked everywhere its course by a smile. The fragments of rock touch it with a wildness and liberality which give just the needed relief. I should never be tired here, though I have elsewhere seen country of more secret and alluring charms, better calculated to stimulate and suggest. Here the eye and heart are filled.

How happy the Indians must have been here! It is not long since they were driven away, and the ground, above and below, is full of their traces.

"The earth is full of men."

You have only to turn up the sod to find arrowheads and Indian pottery. On an island, belonging to our host, and nearly opposite his house, they loved to stay, and, no doubt, enjoyed its lavish beauty as much as the myriad wild pigeons that now haunt its flower-filled shades. Here are still the marks of their tomahawks, the troughs in which they prepared their corn, their caches.

A little way down the river is the site of an ancient Indian village, with its regularly arranged mounds. As usual, they had chosen with the finest taste. It was one of those soft shadowy afternoons when we went there, when nature seems ready to weep, not from grief, but from an overfull heart. Two prattling, lovely little girls, and an African boy, with glittering eye and ready grin, made our party gay; but all were still as we entered their little inlet and trod those flowery paths. They may blacken Indian life as they will, talk of its dirt, its brutality, I will ever believe that the men who chose that dwelling-place were able to

ANCIENT INDIAN VILLAGE

feel emotions of noble happiness as they returned to it, and so were the women that received them. Neither were the children sad or dull, who lived so familiarly with the deer and the birds, and swam that clear wave in the shadow of the Seven Sisters. The whole scene suggested to me a Greek splendor, a Greek sweetness, and I can believe that an Indian brave, accustomed to ramble in such paths, and be bathed by such sunbeams, might be mistaken for Apollo, as Apollo was for him by West. Two of the boldest bluffs are called the Deer's Walk, (not because deer do *not* walk there,) and the Eagle's Nest. The latter I visited one glorious morning; it was that of the fourth of July, and certainly I think I had never felt so happy that I was born in America. Wo to all country folks that never saw this spot, never swept an enraptured gaze over the prospect that stretched beneath. I do believe Rome and Florence are suburbs compared to this capital of nature's art.

The bluff was decked with great bunches of a scarlet variety of the milkweed, like cut coral, and all starred with a mysterious-looking dark flower, whose cup rose lonely on a tall stem. This had, for two or three days, disputed the ground with the lupine and phlox. My companions disliked, I liked it.

Here I thought of, or rather saw, what the Greek expresses under the form of Jove's darling, Ganymede, and the following stanzas took form.

Ganymede to His Eagle,

SUGGESTED BY A WORK OF THORWALDSEN'S
Composed on the height called the Eagle's Nest, Oregon, Rock River, July 4th, 1843.

Upon the rocky mountain stood the boy,
    A goblet of pure water in his hand,
His face and form spoke him one made for joy,
    A willing servant to sweet love's command,
But a strange pain was written on his brow,
And thrilled throughout his silver accents now—

"My bird," he cries, "my destined brother friend,
    O whither fleets to-day thy wayward flight?
Hast thou forgotten that I here attend,

From the full noon until this sad twilight?
A hundred times, at least, from the clear spring,
   Since the full noon o'er hill and valley glowed,
I've filled the vase which our Olympian king
   Upon my care for thy sole use bestowed;
That at the moment when thou should'st descend,
A pure refreshment might thy thirst attend.

Hast thou forgotten earth, forgotten me,
   Thy fellow bondsman in a royal cause,
Who, from the sadness of infinity,
   Only with thee can know that peaceful pause
In which we catch the flowing strain of love,
Which binds our dim fates to the throne of Jove?

Before I saw thee, I was like the May,
   Longing for summer that must mar its bloom,
Or like the morning star that calls the day,
   Whose glories to its promise are the tomb;
And as the eager fountain rises higher
   To throw itself more strongly back to earth,
Still, as more sweet and full rose my desire,
   More fondly it reverted to its birth,
For, what the rosebud seeks tells not the rose,
The meaning foretold by the boy the man cannot disclose.

I was all Spring, for in my being dwelt
   Eternal youth, where flowers are the fruit,
Full feeling was the thought of what was felt,
   Its music was the meaning of the lute;
But heaven and earth such life will still deny,
For earth, divorced from heaven, still asks the question *Why?*

Upon the highest mountains my young feet
   Ached, that no pinions from their lightness grew,
My starlike eyes the stars would fondly greet,
   Yet win no greeting from the circling blue;
Fair, self-subsistent each in its own sphere,
   They had no care that there was none for me;
Alike to them that I was far or near,
   Alike to them, time and eternity.

But, from the violet of lower air,
   Sometimes an answer to my wishing came,

GANYMEDE

Those lightning births my nature seemed to share,
   They told the secrets of its fiery frame,
The sudden messengers of hate and love,
The thunderbolts that arm the hand of Jove,
And strike sometimes the sacred spire, and strike the sacred grove.

Come in a moment, in a moment gone,
They answered me, then left me still more lone,
They told me that the thought which ruled the world,
As yet no sail upon its course had furled,
That the creation was but just begun,
New leaves still leaving from the primal one,
But spoke not of the goal to which *my* rapid wheels would run.

Still, still my eyes, though tearfully, I strained
To the far future which my heart contained,
And no dull doubt my proper hope profaned.

At last, O bliss, thy living form I spied,
   Then a mere speck upon a distant sky,
Yet my keen glance discerned its noble pride,
   And the full answer of that sun-filled eye;
I knew it was the wing that must upbear
My earthlier form into the realms of air.

Thou knowest how we gained that beauteous height,
Where dwells the monarch of the sons of light,
Thou knowest he declared us two to be
The chosen servants of his ministry,
Thou as his messenger, a sacred sign
Of conquest, or with omen more benign,
To give its due weight to the righteous cause,
To express the verdict of Olympian laws.

And I to wait upon the lonely spring,
   Which slakes the thirst of bards to whom 'tis given
The destined dues of hopes divine to sing,
   And weave the needed chain to bind to heaven.
Only from such could be obtained a draught
For him who in his early home from Jove's own cup has quaffed.

To wait, to wait, but not to wait too long,
Till heavy grows the burthen of a song;

O bird! too long hast thou been gone to-day,
My feet are weary of their frequent way,
The spell that opes the spring my tongue no more can say.

If soon thou com'st not, night will fall around,
My head with a sad slumber will be bound,
And the pure draught be spilt upon the ground.

Remember that I am not yet divine,
Long years of service to the fatal Nine
Are yet to make a Delphian vigor mine.

O, make them not too hard, thou bird of Jove,
Answer the stripling's hope, confirm his love,
Receive the service in which he delights,
And bear him often to the serene heights,
Where hands that were so prompt in serving thee,
Shall be allowed the highest ministry,
And Rapture live with bright Fidelity.

The afternoon was spent in a very different manner. The family, whose guests we were, possessed a gay and graceful hospitality that gave zest to each moment. They possessed that rare politeness which, while fertile in pleasant expedients to vary the enjoyment of a friend, leaves him perfectly free the moment he wishes to be so. With such hosts, pleasure may be combined with repose. They lived on the bank opposite the town, and, as their house was full, we slept in the town, and passed three days with them, passing to and fro morning and evening in their boats. (To one of these, called the Fairy, in which a sweet little daughter of the house moved about lighter than any Scotch Ellen ever sung, I should indite a poem, if I had not been guilty of rhyme on the very last page.) At morning this was very pleasant; at evening, I confess I was generally too tired with the excitements of the day to think it so.

Their house—a double log cabin—was, to my eye, the model of a Western villa. Nature had laid out before it grounds which could not be improved. Within, female taste had veiled every rudeness—availed itself of every sylvan grace.

In this charming abode what laughter, what sweet thoughts, what pleasing fancies, did we not enjoy! May such never desert those who reared it and made us so kindly welcome to all its pleasures!

Fragments of city life were dexterously crumbled into the dish prepared for general entertainment. Ice creams followed the dinner drawn by the gentlemen from the river, and music and fireworks wound up the evening of days spent on the Eagle's Nest. Now they had prepared a little fleet to pass over to the Fourth of July celebration, which some queer drumming and fifing, from the opposite bank, had announced to be "on hand."

We found the free and independent citizens there collected beneath the trees, among whom many a round Irish visage dimpled at the usual puffs of Ameriky.

The orator was a New Englander, and the speech smacked loudly of Boston, but was received with much applause, and followed by a plentiful dinner, provided by and for the Sovereign People, to which Hail Columbia served as grace.

Returning, the gay flotilla hailed the little flag which the children had raised from a log-cabin, prettier than any president ever saw, and drank the health of their country and all mankind, with a clear conscience.

Dance and song wound up the day. I know not when the mere local habitation has seemed to me to afford so fair a chance of happiness as this. To a person of unspoiled tastes, the beauty alone would afford stimulus enough. But with it would be naturally associated all kinds of wild sports, experiments, and the studies of natural history. In these regards, the poet, the sportsman, the naturalist, would alike rejoice in this wide range of untouched loveliness.

Then, with a very little money, a ducal estate may be purchased, and by a very little more, and moderate labor, a family be maintained upon it with raiment, food and shelter. The luxurious and minute comforts of a city life are not yet to be had without effort disproportionate to their value. But, where there is so great a counterpoise, cannot these be given up once for all? If the houses are imperfectly built, they can afford immense fires and plenty of covering; if they are small, who cares?—with such fields to roam in. In winter, it may be borne; in summer, is of no consequence. With plenty of fish, and game, and wheat, can they not dispense with a baker to bring "muffins hot" every morning to the door for their breakfast?

LOG CABIN AT ROCK RIVER

WOMEN IN THE WEST

Here a man need not take a small slice from the landscape, and fence it in from the obtrusions of an uncongenial neighbor, and there cut down his fancies to miniature improvements which a chicken could run over in ten minutes. He may have water and wood and land enough, to dread no incursions on his prospect from some chance Vandal that may enter his neighborhood. He need not painfully economise and manage how he may use it all; he can afford to leave some of it wild, and to carry out his own plans without obliterating those of nature.

Here, whole families might live together, if they would. The sons might return from their pilgrimages to settle near the parent hearth; the daughters might find room near their mother. Those painful separations, which already desecrate and desolate the Atlantic coast, are not enforced here by the stern need of seeking bread; and where they are voluntary, it is no matter. To me, too, used to the feelings which haunt a society of struggling men, it was delightful to look upon a scene where nature still wore her motherly smile and seemed to promise room not only for those favored or cursed with the qualities best adapting for the strifes of competition, but for the delicate, the thoughtful, even the indolent or eccentric. She did not say, Fight or starve; nor even, Work or cease to exist; but, merely showing that the apple was a finer fruit than the wild crab, gave both room to grow in the garden.

A pleasant society is formed of the families who live along the banks of this stream upon farms. They are from various parts of the world, and have much to communicate to one another. Many have cultivated minds and refined manners, all a varied experience, while they have in common the interests of a new country and a new life. They must traverse some space to get at one another, but the journey is through scenes that make it a separate pleasure. They must bear inconveniences to stay in one another's houses; but these, to the well-disposed, are only a source of amusement and adventure.

The great drawback upon the lives of these settlers, at present, is the unfitness of the women for their new lot. It has generally been the choice of the men, and the women follow, as women will, doing their best for affection's sake, but too often in heartsickness and weariness. Beside it frequently not being a choice or conviction of their own minds that it is best to be here, their part is the hardest, and they are least fitted for it. The men can find assistance in field labor, and recreation with the gun and fishing-rod. Their bodily strength is greater, and enables them to bear and enjoy both these forms of life.

The women can rarely find any aid in domestic labor. All its various and careful tasks must often be performed, sick or well, by the mother and daughters, to whom a city education has imparted neither the strength nor skill now demanded.

The wives of the poorer settlers, having more hard work to do than before, very frequently become slatterns; but the ladies, accustomed to a refined neatness, feel that they cannot degrade themselves by its absence, and struggle under every disadvantage to keep up the necessary routine of small arrangements.

With all these disadvantages for work, their resources for pleasure are fewer. When they can leave the housework, they have not learnt to ride, to drive, to row, alone. Their culture has too generally been that given to women to make them "the ornaments of society." They can dance, but not draw; talk French, but know nothing of the language of flowers; neither in childhood were allowed to cultivate them, lest they should tan their complexions. Accustomed to the pavement of Broadway, they dare not tread the wild-wood paths for fear of rattlesnakes!

Seeing much of this joylessness, and inaptitude, both of body and mind, for a lot which would be full of blessings for those prepared for it, we could not but look with deep interest on the little girls, and hope they would grow up with the strength of body, dexterity, simple tastes, and resources that would fit them to enjoy and refine the western farmer's life.

But they have a great deal to war with in the habits of thought acquired by their mothers from their own early life. Everywhere the fatal spirit of imitation, of reference to European standards, penetrates, and threatens to blight whatever of original growth might adorn the soil.

If the little girls grow up strong, resolute, able to exert their faculties, their mothers mourn over their want of fashionable delicacy. Are they gay, enterprising, ready to fly about in the various ways that teach them so much, these ladies lament that "they cannot go to school, where they might learn to be quiet." They lament the want of "education" for their daughters, as if

EDUCATION 49

the thousand needs which call out their young energies, and the language of nature around, yielded no education.

Their grand ambition for their children, is to send them to school in some eastern city, the measure most likely to make them useless and unhappy at home. I earnestly hope that, ere long, the existence of good schools near themselves, planned by persons of sufficient thought to meet the wants of the place and time, instead of copying New York or Boston, will correct this mania. Instruction the children want to enable them to profit by the great natural advantages of their position; but methods copied from the education of some English Lady Augusta, are as ill suited to the daughter of an Illinois farmer, as satin shoes to climb the Indian mounds. An elegance she would diffuse around her, if her mind were opened to appreciate elegance; it might be of a kind new, original, enchanting, as different from that of the city belle as that of the prairie torch-flower from the shopworn article that touches the cheek of that lady within her bonnet.

To a girl really skilled to make home beautiful and comfortable, with bodily strength to enjoy plenty of exercise, the woods, the streams, a few studies, music, and the sincere and familiar intercourse, far more easily to be met here than elsewhere, would afford happiness enough. Her eyes would not grow dim, nor her cheeks sunken, in the absence of parties, morning visits, and milliner's shops.

As to music, I wish I could see in such places the guitar rather than the piano, and good vocal more than instrumental music.

The piano many carry with them, because it is the fashionable instrument in the eastern cities. Even there, it is so merely from the habit of imitating Europe, for not one in a thousand is willing to give the labor requisite to ensure any valuable use of the instrument.

But, out here, where the ladies have so much less leisure, it is still less desirable. Add to this, they never know how to tune their own instruments, and as persons seldom visit them who can do so, these pianos are constantly out of tune, and would spoil the ear of one who began by having any.

The guitar, or some portable instrument which requires less practice, and could be kept in tune by themselves, would be far more desirable for most of these ladies. It would give all they want as a household companion to fill up the gaps of life with a pleasant stimulus or solace, and be sufficient accompaniment to the voice in social meetings.

Singing in parts is the most delightful family amusement, and those who are constantly together can learn to sing in perfect accord. All the practice it needs, after some good elementary instruction, is such as meetings by summer twilight, and evening firelight naturally suggest. And, as music is an universal language, we cannot but think a fine Italian duet would be as much at home in the log cabin as one of Mrs. Gore's novels.

The sixth July we left this beautiful place. It was one of those rich days of bright sunlight, varied by the purple shadows of large sweeping clouds. Many a backward look we cast, and left the heart behind.

Our journey to-day was no less delightful than before, still all new, boundless, limitless. Kinmont says, that limits are sacred; that the Greeks were in the right to worship a god of limits. I say, that what is limitless is alone divine, that there was neither wall nor road in Eden, that those who walked there lost and found their way just as we did, and that all the gain from the Fall was that we had a wagon to ride in. I do not think, either, that even the horses doubted whether this last was any advantage.

Everywhere the rattlesnake-weed grows in profusion. The antidote survives the bane. Soon the coarser plantain, the "white man's footstep," shall take its place.

We saw also the compass plant, and the western tea plant. Of some of the brightest flowers an Indian girl afterwards told me the medicinal virtues. I doubt not those students of the soil knew a use to every fair emblem, on which we could only look to admire its hues and shape.

After noon we were ferried by a girl, (unfortunately not of the most picturesque appearance) across the Kishwaukie, the most graceful stream, and on whose bosom rested many full-blown water-lilies, twice as large as any of ours. I was told that, *en revanche*, they were scentless, but I still regret that I could not get at one of them to try.

Query, did the lilied fragrance which, in the miraculous times, accompanied visions of saints and angels, proceed from water or garden lilies?

KISHWAUKIE

Kishwaukie is, according to tradition, the scene of a famous battle, and its many grassy mounds contain the bones of the valiant. On these waved thickly the mysterious purple flower, of which I have spoken before. I think it springs from the blood of the Indians, as the hyacinth did from that of Apollo's darling.

The ladies of our host's family at Oregon, when they first went there, after all the pains and plagues of building and settling, found their first pastime in opening one of these mounds, in which they found, I think, three of the departed, seated in the Indian fashion.

One of these same ladies, as she was making bread one winter morning, saw from the window a deer directly before the house. She ran out, with her hands covered with dough, calling the others, and they caught him bodily before he had time to escape.

Here (at Kishwaukie) we received a visit from a ragged and barefoot, but bright-eyed gentleman, who seemed to be the intellectual loafer, the walking Will's coffeehouse of the place. He told us many charming snake stories; among others, of himself having seen seventeen young ones reënter the mother snake, on the intrusion of a visiter.

This night we reached Belvidere, a flourishing town in Boon county, where was the tomb, now despoiled, of Big Thunder. In this later day we felt happy to find a really good hotel.

From this place, by two days of very leisurely and devious journeying, we reached Chicago, and thus ended a journey, which one at least of the party might have wished unending.

I have not been particularly anxious to give the geography of the scene, inasmuch as it seemed to me no route, nor series of stations, but a garden interspersed with cottages, groves and flowery lawns, through which a stately river ran. I had no guidebook, kept no diary, do not know how many miles we travelled each day, nor how many in all. What I got from the journey was the poetic impression of the country at large; it is all I have aimed to communicate.

The narrative might have been made much more interesting, as life was at the time, by many piquant anecdotes and tales drawn from private life. But here courtesy restrains the pen, for I know those who received the stranger with such frank kindness would feel ill requited by its becoming the means of fixing many spy-glasses, even though the scrutiny might be one of admiring interest, upon their private homes.

For many of these, too, I was indebted to a friend, whose property they more lawfully are. This friend was one of those rare beings who are equally at home in nature and with man. He knew a tale of all that ran and swam, and flew, or only grew, possessing that extensive familiarity with things which shows equal sweetness of sympathy and playful penetration. Most refreshing to me was his unstudied lore, the unwritten poetry which common life presents to a strong and gentle mind. It was a great contrast to the subtleties of analysis, the philosophic strainings of which I had seen too much. But I will not attempt to transplant it. May it profit others as it did me in the region where it was born, where it belongs. The evening of our return to Chicago the sunset was of a splendor and calmness beyond any we saw at the West. The twilight that succeeded was equally beautiful; soft, pathetic, but just so calm. When afterwards I learned this was the evening of Allston's death, it seemed to me as if this glorious pageant was not without connection with that event; at least, it inspired similar emotions,—a heavenly gate closing a path adorned with shows well worthy Paradise.

Farewell, ye soft and sumptuous solitudes!
Ye fairy distances, ye lordly woods,
Haunted by paths like those that Poussin knew,
When after his all gazers eyes he drew;
I go,—and if I never more may steep
An eager heart in your enchantments deep,
Yet ever to itself that heart may say,
Be not exacting; thou hast lived one day;
Hast looked on that which matches with thy mood,
Impassioned sweetness of full being's flood,
Where nothing checked the bold yet gentle wave,
Where nought repelled the lavish love that gave.
A tender blessing lingers o'er the scene,
Like some young mother's thought, fond, yet serene,
And through its life new-born our lives have been.
Once more farewell,—a sad, a sweet farewell;
And, if I never must behold you more,

FAREWELL

In other worlds I will not cease to tell
The rosary I here have numbered o'er;
And bright-haired Hope will lend a gladdened ear,
And Love will free him from the grasp of Fear,
And Gorgon critics, while the tale they hear,
Shall dew their stony glances with a tear,
If I but catch one echo from your spell;—
And so farewell,—a grateful, sad farewell!

Chapter IV

CHICAGO AGAIN

CHICAGO HAD BECOME INTERESTING to me now, that I knew it as the portal to so fair a scene. I had become interested in the land, in the people, and looked sorrowfully on the lake on which I must soon embark, to leave behind what I had just begun to enjoy.

Now was the time to see the lake. The July moon was near its full, and night after night it rose in a cloudless sky above this majestic sea. The heat was excessive, so that there was no enjoyment of life, except in the night, but then the air was of that delicious temperature, worthy of orange groves. However, they were not wanted;—nothing was, as that full light fell on the faintly rippling waters which then seemed boundless.

A poem received shortly after, from a friend in Massachusetts, seemed to say that the July moon shone there not less splendid, and may claim insertion here.

Triformis

So pure her forehead's dazzling white,
    So swift and clear her radiant eyes,
Within the treasure of whose light
    Lay undeveloped destinies,—
Of thoughts repressed such hidden store
    Was hinted by each flitting smile,
I could but wonder and adore,
    Far off, in awe, I gazed the while.

I gazed at her, as at the moon,
    Hanging in lustrous twilight skies,
Whose virgin crescent, sinking soon,
    Peeps through the leaves before it flies.
Untouched Diana, flitting dim,
    While sings the wood its evening hymn.

TRIFORMIS

II

Again we met. O joyful meeting!
  Her radiance now was all for me,
Like kindly airs her kindly greeting,
  So full, so musical, so free.
Within romantic forest aisles,
  Within romantic paths we walked,
I bathed me in her sister smiles,
  I breathed her beauty as we talked.

So full-orbed Cynthia walks the skies,
  Filling the earth with melodies,
Even so she condescends to kiss
  Drowsy Endymions, coarse and dull,
Or fills our waking souls with bliss,
  Making long nights too beautiful.

III

O fair, but fickle lady-moon,
  Why must thy full form ever wane?
O love! O friendship! why so soon
  Must your sweet light recede again?
I wake me in the dead of night,
  And start,—for through the misty gloom
Red Hecate stares—a boding sight!—
  Looks in, but never fills my room.

Thou music of my boyhood's hour!
  Thou shining light on manhood's way!
No more dost thou fair influence shower
  To move my soul by night or day.
O strange! that while in hall and street
  Thy hand I touch, thy grace I meet,
Such miles of polar ice should part
  The slightest touch of mind and heart!
But all thy love has waned, and so
  I gladly let thy beauty go.

Now that I am borrowing, I will also give a letter received
at this time, and extracts from others from an earlier traveller,

and in a different region of the country from that I saw, which, I think, in different ways, admirably descriptive of the country.

"And you, too, love the Prairies, flying voyager of a summer hour; but *I* have only there owned the wild forest, the wide-spread meadows; there only built my house, and seen the livelong day the thoughtful shadows of the great clouds color, with all-transient browns, the untrampled floor of grass; there has Spring pranked the long smooth reaches with those golden flowers, whereby became the fields a sea too golden to o'erlast the heats. Yes! and with many a yellow bell she gilded our unbounded path, that sank in the light swells of the varied surface, skirted the untilled barrens, nor shunned the steep banks of rivers darting merrily on. There has the white snow frolicsomely strown itself, till all that vast, outstretched distance glittered like a mirror in which only the heavens were reflected, and among these drifts our steps have been curbed. Ah! many days of precious weather are on the Prairies!

"You have then found, after many a weary hour, when Time has locked your temples as in a circle of heated metal, some cool, sweet, swift-gliding moments, the iron ring of necessity ungirt, and the fevered pulses at rest. You have also found this where fresh nature suffers no ravage; amid those bowers of wild-wood, those dream-like, bee-sung, murmuring and musical plains, swimming under their hazy distances, as if there, in that warm and deep back ground, stood the fairy castle of our hopes, with its fountains, its pictures, its many mystical figures in repose. Ever could we rove over those sunny distances, breathing that modulated wind, eyeing those so well-blended, imaginative, yet thoughtful surfaces, and above us wide—wide a horizon effortless and superb as a young divinity.

"I was a prisoner where you glide, the summer's pensioned guest, and my chains were the past and the future, darkness and blowing sand. There, very weary, I received from the distance a sweet emblem of an incorruptible, lofty and pervasive nature, but was I less weary? I was a prisoner, and you, plains, were my prison bars.

"Yet never, O never, beautiful plains, had I any feeling for you but profoundest gratitude, for indeed ye are only fair, grand

PRAIRIE & LONG GROVE IN THE DISTANCE

and majestic, while I had scarcely a right there. Now, ye stand in that past day, grateful images of unshattered repose, simple in your tranquillity, strong in your self-possession, yet ever musical and springing as the footsteps of a child.

"Ah! that to some poet, whose lyre had never lost a string, to whom mortality, kinder than is her custom, had vouchsafed a day whose down had been untouched,—that to him these plains might enter, and flow forth in airy song. And you, forests, under whose symmetrical shields of dark green the colors of the fawns move, like the waters of the river under its spears,—its cimeters of flag, where, in gleaming circles of steel, the breasts of the wood-pigeons flash in the playful sunbeam, and many sounds, many notes of no earthly music, come over the well-relieved glades,—should not your depth pass into that poet's heart,—in your depths should he not fuse his own?"

The other letters show the painter's eye, as this the poet's heart.

"Springfield, Illinois, May 20, 1840.

"Yesterday morning I left Griggsville, my knapsack at my back, pursued my journey all day on foot, and found so new and great delight in this charming country, that I must needs tell you about it. Do you remember our saying once, that we never found the trees tall enough, the fields green enough. Well, the trees are for once tall, and fair to look upon, and one unvarying carpet of the tenderest green covers these marvellous fields, that spread out their smooth sod for miles and miles, till they even reach the horizon. But, to begin my day's journey. Griggsville is situated on the west side of the Illinois river, on a high prairie; between it and the river is a long range of bluffs which reaches a hundred miles north and south, then a wide river bottom, and then the river. It was a mild, showery morning, and I directed my steps toward the bluffs. They are covered with forest, not like our forests, tangled and impassable, but where the trees stand fair and apart from one another, so that you might ride every where about on horseback, and the tops of the hills are generally bald, and covered with green turf, like our pastures. Indeed, the whole country reminds me perpetually of one that has been carefully cultivated by a civilized people, who had been suddenly removed from the earth, with all the works of their hands, and the land given again into nature's keeping. The solitudes are not savage; they have not that dreary, stony loneliness that used to affect me in our own country; they never repel; there are no lonely heights, no isolated spots, but all is gentle, mild, inviting,—all is accessible. In following this winding, hilly road for four or five miles, I think I counted at least a dozen new kinds of wild flowers, not timid, retiring little plants like ours, but bold flowers of rich colors, covering the ground in abundance. One very common flower resembles our cardinal flower, though not of so deep a color, another is very like rocket or phlox, but smaller and of various colors, white, blue and purple. Beautiful white lupines I find too, violets white and purple. The vines and parasites are magnificent. I followed on this road till I came to the prairie which skirts the river, and this, of all the beauties of this region, is the most peculiar and wonderful. Imagine a vast and gently-swelling pasture of the brightest green grass, stretching away from you on every side, behind, toward these hills I have described, in all other directions, to a belt of tall trees, all growing up with noble proportions, from the generous soil. It is an unimagined picture of abundance and peace. Somewhere about, you are sure to see a huge herd of cattle, often white, and generally brightly marked, grazing. All looks like the work of man's hand, but you see no vestige of man, save perhaps an almost imperceptible hut on the edge of the prairie. Reaching the river, I ferried myself across, and then crossed over to take the Jacksonville railroad, but, finding there was no train, passed the night at a farm house. And here may find its place this converse between the solitary old man and the young traveller.

Solitary

My son, with weariness thou seemest spent,
And toiling on the dusty road all day,
Weary and pale, yet with inconstant step,
Hither and thither turning,—seekest thou
To find aught lost, or what dark care pursues thee?
If thou art weary, rest, if hungry, eat.

Traveller

Oh rather, father, let me ask of thee
What is it I do seek, what thing I lack?
These many days I've left my father's hall,
Forth driven by insatiable desire,
That, like the wind, now gently murmuring,
Enticed me forward with its own sweet voice
Through many-leaved woods, and valleys deep,
Yet ever fled before me. Then with sound
Stronger than hurrying tempest, seizing me,
Forced me to fly its power. Forward still,
Bound by enchanted ties, I seek its source.
Sometimes it is a something I have lost,
Known long since, before I bent my steps
Toward this beautiful broad plane of earth.
Sometimes it is a spirit yet unknown,
In whose dim-imaged features seem to smile
The dear delight of these high-mansioned thoughts,
That sometimes visit me. Like unto mine
Her lineaments appear, but beautiful,
As of a sister in a far-off world,
Waiting to welcome me. And when I think
To reach and clasp the figure, it is gone,
And some ill-omened ghastly vision comes
To bid beware, and not too curiously
Demand the secrets of that distant world,
Whose shadow haunts me.—On the waves below
But now I gazed, warmed with the setting sun,
Who sent his golden streamers to my feet,
It seemed a pathway to a world beyond,
And I looked round, if that my spirit beckoned
That I might follow it.

Solitary

Dreams all, my son. Yes, even so I dreamed,
And even so was thwarted. You must learn
To dream another long and troublous dream,
The dream of life. And you shall think you wake,
And think the shadows substance, love and hate,
Exchange and barter, joy, and weep, and dance,
And this too shall be dream.

EVENING THOUGHTS

Traveller

Oh who can say
Where lies the boundary? What solid things
That daily mock our senses, shall dissolve
Before the might within, while shadowy forms
Freeze into stark reality, defying
The force and will of man. These forms I see,
They may go with me through eternity,
And bless or curse with ceaseless company,
While yonder man, that I met yesternight,
Where is he now? He passed before my eyes,
He is gone, but these stay with me ever.

That night the young man rested with the old,
And, grave or gay, in laughter or in tears,
They wore the night in converse. Morning came,
The dreamer took his solitary way;
And, as he pressed the old man's hand, he sighed,
Must this too be a dream?"

Afterwards, of the rolling prairie. "There was one of twenty miles in extent, not flat, but high and rolling, so that when you arrived at a high part, by gentle ascents, the view was beyond measure grand; as far as the eye could reach, nothing but the green, rolling plain, and at a vast distance, groves, all looking gentle and cultivated, yet all uninhabited. I think it would impress you, as it does me, that these scenes are truly sublime. I have a sensation of vastness which I have sought in vain among high mountains. Mountains crowd one sensation on another, till all is excitement, all is surprise, wonder, enchantment. Here is neither enchantment or disappointment, but expectation fully realized. I have always had an attachment for a plain. The Roman Campagna is a prairie. Peoria is in a most lovely situation. In fact I am so delighted that I am as full of superlatives as the Italian language. I could, however, find fault enough, if you ask what I dislike."

But no one did ask; it is not worth while where there is so much to admire. Yet the following is a good statement of the shadow side.

"As to the boasts about the rapid progress here, give me rather the firm fibre of a slow and knotty growth. I could not help thinking as much when I was talking to E. the other day, whom I met on board the boat. He quarrelled with Boston for its slowness; said it was a bad place for a young man. He could not make himself felt, could not see the effects of his exertions as he could here.—To be sure he could not. Here he comes, like a yankee farmer, with all the knowledge that our hard soil and laborious cultivation could give him, and what wonder if he is surprised at the work of his own hands, when he comes to such a soil as this. But he feeds not so many mouths, though he tills more acres. The plants he raises have not so exquisite a form, the vegetables so fine a flavor. His cultivation becomes more negligent, he is not so good a farmer. Is not this a true view? It strikes me continually. The traces of a man's hand in a new country are rarely productive of beauty. It is a cutting down of forest trees to make zigzag fences."

The most picturesque objects to be seen from Chicago on the inland side were the lines of Hoosier wagons. These rude farmers, the large first product of the soil, travel leisurely along, sleeping in their wagons by night, eating only what they bring with them. In the town they observe the same plan, and trouble no luxurious hotel for board and lodging. In the town they look like foreign peasantry, and contrast well with the many Germans, Dutch, and Irish. In the country it is very pretty to see them prepared to "camp out" at night, their horses taken out of harness, and they lounging under the trees, enjoying the evening meal.

On the lake side it is fine to see the great boats come panting in from their rapid and marvellous journey. Especially at night the motion of their lights is very majestic.

When the favorite boats, the Great Western and Illinois, are going out, the town is thronged with people from the south and farther west, to go in them. These moonlight nights I would hear the French rippling and fluttering familiarly amid the rude ups and downs of the Hoosier dialect.

At the hotel table were daily to be seen new faces, and new stories to be learned. And any one who has a large acquaintance may be pretty sure of meeting some of them here in the course of a few days.

MARIANA

Among those whom I met was Mrs. Z., the aunt of an old schoolmate, to whom I impatiently hastened, as soon as the meal was over, to demand news of Mariana. The answer startled me. Mariana, so full of life, was dead. That form, the most rich in energy and coloring of any I had ever seen, had faded from the earth. The circle of youthful associations had given way in the part, that seemed the strongest. What I now learned of the story of this life, and what was by myself remembered, may be bound together in this slight sketch.

At the boarding-school to which I was too early sent, a fond, a proud, and timid child, I saw among the ranks of the gay and graceful, bright or earnest girls, only one who interested my fancy or touched my young heart; and this was Mariana. She was, on the father's side, of Spanish Creole blood, but had been sent to the Atlantic coast, to receive a school education under the care of her aunt, Mrs. Z.

This lady had kept her mostly at home with herself, and Mariana had gone from her house to a day-school; but the aunt, being absent for a time in Europe, she had now been unfortunately committed for some time to the mercies of a boarding-school.

A strange bird she proved there,—a lonely swallow that could not make for itself a summer. At first, her schoolmates were captivated with her ways; her love of wild dances and sudden song, her freaks of passion and of wit. She was always new, always surprising, and, for a time, charming.

But, after awhile, they tired of her. She could never be depended on to join in their plans, yet she expected them to follow out hers with their whole strength. She was very loving, even infatuated in her own affections, and exacted from those who had professed any love for her, the devotion she was willing to bestow.

Yet there was a vein of haughty caprice in her character; a love of solitude, which made her at times wish to retire entirely, and at these times she would expect to be thoroughly understood, and let alone, yet to be welcomed back when she returned. She did not thwart others in their humors, but she never doubted of great indulgence from them.

Some singular habits she had which, when new, charmed, but, after acquaintance, displeased her companions. She had by nature the same habit and power of excitement that is described in the spinning dervishes of the East. Like them, she would spin until all around her were giddy, while her own brain, instead of being disturbed, was excited to great action. Pausing, she would declaim verse of others or her own; act many parts, with strange catch-words and burdens that seemed to act with mystical power on her own fancy, sometimes stimulating her to convulse the hearer with laughter, sometimes to melt him to tears. When her power began to languish, she would spin again till fired to recommence her singular drama, into which she wove figures from the scenes of her earlier childhood, her companions, and the dignitaries she sometimes saw, with fantasies unknown to life, unknown to heaven or earth.

This excitement, as may be supposed, was not good for her. It oftenest came on in the evening, and often spoiled her sleep. She would wake in the night, and cheat her restlessness by inventions that teazed, while they sometimes diverted her companions.

She was also a sleep-walker; and this one trait of her case did somewhat alarm her guardians, who, otherwise, showed the same profound stupidity as to this peculiar being, usual in the overseers of the young. They consulted a physician, who said she would outgrow it, and prescribed a milk diet.

Meantime, the fever of this ardent and too early stimulated nature was constantly increased by the restraints and narrow routine of the boarding school. She was always devising means to break in upon it. She had a taste which would have seemed ludicrous to her mates, if they had not felt some awe of her, from a touch of genius and power that never left her, for costume and fancy dresses, always some sash twisted about her, some drapery, something odd in the arrangement of her hair and dress, so that the methodical preceptress dared not let her go out without a careful scrutiny and remodelling, whose soberizing effects generally disappeared the moment she was in the free air.

At last, a vent for her was found in private theatricals. Play followed play, and in these and the rehearsals she found entertainment congenial with her. The principal parts, as a matter of course, fell to her lot; most of the good suggestions and arrangements came from her, and for a time she ruled masterly and shone triumphant.

During these performances the girls had heightened their natural bloom with artificial red; this was delightful to them—it was something so out of the way. But Mariana, after the plays were over, kept her carmine saucer on the dressing-table, and put on her blushes regularly as the morning.

When stared and jeered at, she at first said she did it because she thought it made her look prettier; but, after a while, she became quite petulant about it,—would make no reply to any joke, but merely kept on doing it.

This irritated the girls, as all eccentricity does the world in general, more than vice or malignity. They talked it over among themselves, till they got wrought up to a desire of punishing, once for all, this sometimes amusing, but so often provoking nonconformist.

Having obtained the leave of the mistress, they laid, with great glee, a plan one evening, which was to be carried into execution next day at dinner.

Among Mariana's irregularities was a great aversion to the meal-time ceremonial. So long, so tiresome she found it, to be seated at a certain moment, to wait while each one was served at so large a table, and one where there was scarcely any conversation; from day to day it became more heavy to her to sit there, or go there at all. Often as possible she excused herself on the ever-convenient plea of headache, and was hardly ever ready when the dinner-bell rang.

To-day it found her on the balcony, lost in gazing on the beautiful prospect. I have heard her say afterwards, she had rarely in her life been so happy,—and she was one with whom happiness was a still rapture. It was one of the most blessed summer days; the shadows of great white clouds empurpled the distant hills for a few moments only to leave them more golden; the tall grass of the wide fields waved in the softest breeze. Pure blue were the heavens, and the same hue of pure contentment was in the heart of Mariana.

Suddenly on her bright mood jarred the dinner bell. At first rose her usual thought, I will not, cannot go; and then the *must*, which daily life can always enforce, even upon the butterflies and birds, came, and she walked reluctantly to her room. She merely changed her dress, and never thought of adding the artificial rose to her cheek.

When she took her seat in the dining-hall, and was asked if she would be helped, raising her eyes, she saw the person who asked her was deeply rouged, with a bright glaring spot, perfectly round, in either cheek. She looked at the next, same apparition! She then slowly passed her eyes down the whole line, and saw the same, with a suppressed smile distorting every countenance. Catching the design at once, she deliberately looked along her own side of the table, at every schoolmate in turn; every one had joined in the trick. The teachers strove to be grave, but she saw they enjoyed the joke. The servants could not suppress a titter.

When Warren Hastings stood at the bar of Westminster Hall—when the Methodist preacher walked through a line of men, each of whom greeted him with a brickbat or a rotten egg, they had some preparation for the crisis, and it might not be very difficult to meet it with an impassive brow. Our little girl was quite unprepared to find herself in the midst of a world which despised her, and triumphed in her disgrace.

She had ruled, like a queen, in the midst of her companions; she had shed her animation through their lives, and loaded them with prodigal favors, nor once suspected that a powerful favorite might not be loved. Now, she felt that she had been but a dangerous plaything in the hands of those whose hearts she never had doubted.

Yet, the occasion found her equal to it, for Mariana had the kind of spirit, which, in a better cause, had made the Roman matron truly say of her death-wound, "It is not painful, Poetus." She did not blench—she did not change countenance. She swallowed her dinner with apparent composure. She made remarks to those near her, as if she had no eyes.

The wrath of the foe of course rose higher, and the moment they were freed from the restraints of the dining-room, they all ran off, gaily calling, and sarcastically laughing, with backward glances, at Mariana, left alone.

She went alone to her room, locked the door, and threw herself on the floor in strong convulsions. These had sometimes threatened her life, as a child, but of later years, she had outgrown them. School-hours came, and she was not there. A little girl, sent to her door, could get no answer. The teachers became alarmed, and broke it open. Bitter was their penitence and that of her companions at the state in which they found her. For some hours, terrible anxiety was felt; but, at last, nature, exhausted, relieved herself by a deep slumber.

From this Mariana rose an altered being. She made no reply to the expressions of sorrow from her companions, none to the grave and kind, but undiscerning comments of her teacher. She did not name the source of her anguish, and its poisoned dart sank deeply in. It was this thought which stung her so. What, not one, not a single one, in the hour of trial, to take my part, not one who refused to take part against me. Past words of love, and caresses, little heeded at the time, rose to her memory, and gave fuel to her distempered thoughts. Beyond the sense of universal perfidy, of burning resentment, she could not get. And Mariana, born for love, now hated all the world.

The change, however, which these feelings made in her conduct and appearance bore no such construction to the careless observer. Her gay freaks were quite gone, her wildness, her invention. Her dress was uniform, her manner much subdued. Her chief interest seemed now to lie in her studies, and in music. Her companions she never sought, but they, partly from uneasy remorseful feelings, partly that they really liked her much better now that she did not oppress and puzzle them, sought her continually. And here the black shadow comes upon her life, the only stain upon the history of Mariana.

They talked to her, as girls, having few topics, naturally do, of one another. And the demon rose within her, and spontaneously, without design, generally without words of positive falsehood, she became a genius of discord among them. She fanned those flames of envy and jealousy which a wise, true word from a third will often quench forever; by a glance, or a seemingly light reply, she planted the seeds of dissension, till there was scarce a peaceful affection, or sincere intimacy in the circle where she lived, and could not but rule, for she was one whose nature was to that of the others as fire to clay.

It was at this time that I came to the school, and first saw Mariana. Me she charmed at once, for I was a sentimental child, who, in my early ill health, had been indulged in reading novels, till I had no eyes for the common greens and browns of life. The heroine of one of these, "The Bandit's Bride," I immediately saw in Mariana. Surely the Bandit's Bride had just such hair,

68 SUMMER ON THE LAKES

and such strange, lively ways, and such a sudden flash of the eye. The Bandit's Bride, too, was born to be "misunderstood" by all but her lover. But Mariana, I was determined, should be more fortunate, for, until her lover appeared, I myself would be the wise and delicate being who could understand her.

It was not, however, easy to approach her for this purpose. Did I offer to run and fetch her handkerchief, she was obliged to go to her room, and would rather do it herself. She did not like to have people turn over for her the leaves of the music book as she played. Did I approach my stool to her feet, she moved away, as if to give me room. The bunch of wild flowers which I timidly laid beside her plate was left there.

After some weeks my desire to attract her notice really preyed upon me, and one day meeting her alone in the entry, I fell upon my knees, and kissing her hand, cried, "O Mariana, do let me love you, and try to love me a little." But my idol snatched away her hand, and, laughing more wildly than the Bandit's Bride was ever described to have done, ran into her room. After that day her manner to me was not only cold, but repulsive; I felt myself scorned, and became very unhappy.

Perhaps four months had passed thus, when, one afternoon, it became obvious that something more than common was brewing. Dismay and mystery were written in many faces of the older girls; much whispering was going on in corners.

In the evening, after prayers, the principal bade us stay; and, in a grave, sad voice, summoned forth Mariana to answer charges to be made against her.

Mariana came forward, and leaned against the chimney-piece. Eight of the older girls came forward, and preferred against her charges, alas, too well-founded, of calumny and falsehood.

My heart sank within me, as one after the other brought up their proofs, and I saw they were too strong to be resisted. I could not bear the thought of this second disgrace of my shining favorite. The first had been whispered to me, though the girls did not like to talk about it. I must confess, such is the charm of strength to softer natures, that neither of these crises could deprive Mariana of hers in my eyes.

At first, she defended herself with self-possession and eloquence. But when she found she could no more resist the truth, she suddenly threw herself down, dashing her head, with all her force, against the iron hearth, on which a fire was burning, and was taken up senseless.

The affright of those present was great. Now that they had perhaps killed her, they reflected it would have been as well, if they had taken warning from the former occasion, and approached very carefully a nature so capable of any extreme. After awhile she revived, with a faint groan, amid the sobs of her companions. I was on my knees by the bed, and held her cold hand. One of those most aggrieved took it from me to beg her pardon, and say it was impossible not to love her. She made no reply.

Neither that night, nor for several days, could a word be obtained from her, nor would she touch food; but, when it was presented to her, or any one drew near for any cause, she merely turned away her head, and gave no sign. The teacher saw that some terrible nervous affection had fallen upon her, that she grew more and more feverish. She knew not what to do.

Meanwhile a new revolution had taken place in the mind of the passionate, but nobly-tempered child. All these months nothing but the sense of injury had rankled in her heart. She had gone on in one mood, doing what the demon prompted, without scruple and without fear.

But, at the moment of detection, the tide ebbed, and the bottom of her soul lay revealed to her eye. How black, how stained and sad. Strange, strange that she had not seen before the baseness and cruelty of falsehood, the loveliness of truth. Now, amid the wreck, uprose the moral nature which never before had attained the ascendant. "But," she thought, "too late, sin is revealed to me in all its deformity, and, sin-defiled, I will not, cannot live. The mainspring of life is broken."

And thus passed slowly by her hours in that black despair of which only youth is capable. In older years men suffer more dull pain, as each sorrow that comes drops its leaden weight into the past, and, similar features of character bringing similar results, draws up a heavy burden buried in those depths. But only youth has energy, with fixed unwinking gaze, to contemplate grief, to hold it in the arms and to the heart, like a child which makes it wretched, yet is indubitably its own.

The lady who took charge of this sad child had never well understood her before, but had always looked on her with great tenderness. And now love seemed, when all around were in greatest distress, fearing to call in medical aid, fearing to do without it, to teach her where the only balm was to be found that could have healed this wounded spirit.

One night she came in, bringing a calming draught. Mariana was sitting, as usual, her hair loose, her dress the same robe they had put on her at first, her eyes fixed vacantly upon the whited wall. To the proffers and entreaties of her nurse she made no reply.

The lady burst into tears, but Mariana did not seem even to observe it.

The lady then said, "O my child, do not despair, do not think that one great fault can mar a whole life. Let me trust you, let me tell you the griefs of my sad life. I will tell to you, Mariana, what I never expected to impart to any one."

And so she told her tale: it was one of pain, of shame, borne, not for herself, but for one near and dear as herself. Mariana knew the lady, knew the pride and reserve of her nature; she had often admired to see how the cheek, lovely, but no longer young, mantled with the deepest blush of youth, and the blue eyes were cast down at any little emotion. She had understood the proud sensibility of the character. She fixed her eyes on those now raised to hers, bright with fast falling tears. She heard the story to the end, and then, without saying a word, stretched out her hand for the cup.

She returned to life, but it was as one who has passed through the valley of death. The heart of stone was quite broken in her. The fiery life fallen from flame to coal. When her strength was a little restored, she had all her companions summoned, and said to them; "I deserved to die, but a generous trust has called me back to life. I will be worthy of it, nor ever betray the truth, or resent injury more. Can you forgive the past?"

And they not only forgave, but, with love and earnest tears, clasped in their arms the returning sister. They vied with one another in offices of humble love to the humbled one; and, let it be recorded as an instance of the pure honor of which young hearts are capable, that these facts, known to forty persons, never, so far as I know, transpired beyond those walls.

It was not long after this that Mariana was summoned home. She went thither a wonderfully instructed being, though in ways those who had sent her forth to learn little dreamed of.

Never was forgotten the vow of the returning prodigal. Mariana could not resent, could not play false. The terrible crisis, which she so early passed through, probably prevented the world from hearing much of her. A wild fire was tamed in that hour of penitence at the boarding school, such as has oftentimes wrapped court and camp in its destructive glow.

But great were the perils she had yet to undergo, for she was one of those barks which easily get beyond soundings, and ride not lightly on the plunging billow.

Her return to her native climate seconded the effects of inward revolutions. The cool airs of the north had exasperated nerves too susceptible for their tension. Those of the south restored her to a more soft and indolent state. Energy gave place to feeling, turbulence to intensity of character.

At this time love was the natural guest, and he came to her under a form that might have deluded one less ready for delusion.

Sylvain was a person well proportioned to her lot in years, family, and fortune. His personal beauty was not great, but of a noble character. Repose marked his slow gesture, and the steady gaze of his large brown eye, but it was a repose that would give way to a blaze of energy when the occasion called. In his stature, expression, and heavy coloring, he might not unfitly be represented by the great magnolias that inhabit the forests of that climate. His voice, like everything about him, was rich and soft, rather than sweet or delicate.

Mariana no sooner knew him than she loved, and her love, lovely as she was, soon excited his. But, oh! it is a curse to woman to love first, or most. In so doing she reverses the natural relations, and her heart can never, never be satisfied with what ensues.

Mariana loved first, and loved most, for she had most force and variety to love with. Sylvain seemed, at first, to take her to himself, as the deep southern night might some fair star. But it proved not so.

Mariana was a very intellectual being, and she needed companionship. This she could only have with Sylvain, in the paths of passion and action. Thoughts he had none, and little delicacy of sentiment. The gifts she loved to prepare of such for him, he took with a sweet, but indolent smile; he held them lightly, and soon they fell from his grasp. He loved to have her near him, to feel the glow and fragrance of her nature, but cared not to explore the little secret paths whence that fragrance was collected.

Mariana knew not this for a long time. Loving so much, she imagined all the rest, and, where she felt a blank, always hoped that further communion would fill it up. When she found this could never be; that there was absolutely a whole province of her being to which nothing in his answered, she was too deeply in love to leave him. Often after passing hours together, beneath the southern moon, when, amid the sweet intoxication of mutual love, she still felt the desolation of solitude, and a repression of her finer powers, she had asked herself, can I give him up? But the heart always passionately answered, no! I may be miserable with him, but I cannot live without him.

And the last miserable feeling of these conflicts was, that if the lover, soon to be the bosom friend, could have dreamed of these conflicts, he would have laughed, or else been angry, even enough to give her up.

Ah weakness of the strong. Of these strong only where strength is weakness. Like others she had the decisions of life to make, before she had light by which to make them. Let none condemn her. Those who have not erred as fatally, should thank the guardian angel who gave them more time to prepare for judgment, but blame no children who thought at arm's length to find the moon. Mariana, with a heart capable of highest Eros, gave it to one who knew love only as a flower or plaything, and bound her heartstrings to one who parted his as lightly as the ripe fruit leaves the bough. The sequel could not fail. Many console themselves for the one great mistake with their children, with the world. This was not possible to Mariana. A few months of domestic life she still was almost happy. But Sylvain then grew tired. He wanted business and the world; of these she had no knowledge, for them no faculties. He wanted in her the head of his house; she to make her heart his home. No compromise was possible between natures of such unequal

MARIANA

poise, and which had met only on one or two points. Through all its stages she

> "felt
> The agonizing sense
> Of seeing love from passion melt
> Into indifference;
> The fearful shame that, day by day,
> Burns onward, still to burn,
> To have thrown her precious heart away,
> And met this black return,"

till death at last closed the scene. Not that she died of one downright blow on the heart. That is not the way such cases proceed. I cannot detail all the symptoms, for I was not there to watch them, and aunt Z. was neither so faithful an observer or narrator as I have shown myself in the school-day passages; but, generally, they were as follows.

Sylvain wanted to go into the world, or let it into his house. Mariana consented; but, with an unsatisfied heart, and no lightness of character, she played her part ill there. The sort of talent and facility she had displayed in early days, were not the least like what is called out in the social world by the desire to please and to shine. Her excitement had been muse-like, that of the improvisatrice, whose kindling fancy seeks to create an atmosphere round it, and makes the chain through which to set free its electric sparks. That had been a time of wild and exuberant life. After her character became more tender and concentrated, strong affection or a pure enthusiasm might still have called out beautiful talents in her. But in the first she was utterly disappointed. The second was not roused within her thought. She did not expand into various life, and remained unequal; sometimes too passive, sometimes too ardent, and not sufficiently occupied with what occupied those around her to come on the same level with them and embellish their hours.

Thus she lost ground daily with her husband, who, comparing her with the careless shining dames of society, wondered why he had found her so charming in solitude.

At intervals, when they were left alone, Mariana wanted to open her heart, to tell the thoughts of her mind. She was so conscious of secret riches within herself, that sometimes it seemed, could she but reveal a glimpse of them to the eye of Sylvain, he would be attracted near her again, and take a path where they could walk hand in hand. Sylvain, in these intervals, wanted an indolent repose. His home was his castle. He wanted no scenes too exciting there. Light jousts and plays were well enough, but no grave encounters. He liked to lounge, to sing, to read, to sleep. In fine, Sylvain became the kind, but preoccupied husband, Mariana, the solitary and wretched wife. He was off continually, with his male companions, on excursions or affairs of pleasure. At home Mariana found that neither her books nor music would console her.

She was of too strong a nature to yield without a struggle to so dull a fiend as despair. She looked into other hearts, seeking whether she could there find such home as an orphan asylum may afford. This she did rather because the chance came to her, and it seemed unfit not to seize the proffered plank, than in hope, for she was not one to double her stakes, but rather with Cassandra power to discern early the sure course of the game. And Cassandra whispered that she was one of those

> "Whom men love not, but yet regret,"

And so it proved. Just as in her childish days, though in a different form, it happened betwixt her and these companions. She could not be content to receive them quietly, but was stimulated to throw herself too much into the tie, into the hour, till she filled it too full for them. Like Fortunio, who sought to do homage to his friends by building a fire of cinnamon, not knowing that its perfume would be too strong for their endurance, so did Mariana. What she wanted to tell, they did not wish to hear; a little had pleased, so much overpowered, and they preferred the free air of the street, even, to the cinnamon perfume of her palace.

However, this did not signify; had they staid, it would not have availed her! It was a nobler road, a higher aim she needed now; this did not become clear to her.

She lost her appetite, she fell sick, had fever. Sylvain was alarmed, nursed her tenderly; she grew better. Then his care ceased, he saw not the mind's disease, but left her to rise into health and recover the tone of her spirits, as she might. More solitary than ever, she tried to raise herself, but she knew not yet enough. The weight laid upon her young life was a little too heavy for it. One long day she passed alone, and the thoughts and presages came too thick for her strength. She knew not what to do with them, relapsed into fever, and died.

Notwithstanding this weakness, I must ever think of her as a fine sample of womanhood, born to shed light and life on some palace home. Had she known more of God and the universe, she would not have given way where so many have conquered. But peace be with her; she now, perhaps, has entered into a larger freedom, which is knowledge. With her died a great interest in life to me. Since her I have never seen a Bandit's Bride. She, indeed, turned out to be only a merchant's.—Sylvain is married again to a fair and laughing girl, who will not die, probably, till their marriage grows a "golden marriage."

Aunt Z. had with her some papers of Mariana's, which faintly shadow forth the thoughts that engaged her in the last days. One of these seems to have been written when some faint gleam had been thrown across the path, only to make its darkness more visible. It seems to have been suggested by remembrance of the beautiful ballad, *Helen of Kirconnel Lee*, which once she loved to recite, and in tones that would not have sent a chill to the heart from which it came.

> "Death
> Opens her sweet white arms, and whispers Peace;
> Come, say thy sorrows in this bosom! This
> Will never close against thee, and my heart,
> Though cold, cannot be colder much than man's."

> "I wish I were where Helen lies,"
> A lover in the times of old,
>   Thus vents his grief in lonely sighs,
> And hot tears from a bosom cold.

> But, mourner for thy martyred love,
> Could'st thou but know what hearts must feel,
>   Where no sweet recollections move,
> Whose tears a desert fount reveal.

When "in thy arms burd Helen fell,"
She died, sad man, she died for thee,
  Nor could the films of death dispel
Her loving eye's sweet radiancy.

  Thou wert beloved, and she had loved,
Till death alone the whole could tell,
  Death every shade of doubt removed,
And steeped the star in its cold well.

  On some fond breast the parting soul
Relies,—earth has no more to give;
  Who wholly loves has known the whole,
The wholly loved doth truly live.

  But some, sad outcasts from this prize,
Wither down to a lonely grave,
  All hearts their hidden love despise,
And leave them to the whelming wave.

  They heart to heart have never pressed,
Nor hands in holy pledge have given,
    By father's love were ne'er caressed,
Nor in a mother's eye saw heaven.

  A flowerless and fruitless tree,
A dried up stream, a mateless bird,
  They live, yet never living be,
They die, their music all unheard.

  I wish I were where Helen lies,
For there I could not be alone;
  But now, when this dull body dies,
The spirit still will make its moan.

  Love passed me by, nor touched my brow;
Life would not yield one perfect boon;
  And all too late it calls me now,
O all too late, and all too soon.

  If thou couldst the dark riddle read
Which leaves this dart within my breast,

MARIANA

Then might I think thou lov'st indeed,
Then were the whole to thee confest.

Father, they will not take me home,
To the poor child no heart is free;
    In sleet and snow all night I roam;
Father,—was this decreed by thee?

I will not try another door,
To seek what I have never found;
    Now, till the very last is o'er,
Upon the earth I'll wander round.

I will not hear the treacherous call
That bids me stay and rest awhile,
    For I have found that, one and all,
They seek me for a prey and spoil.

They are not bad, I know it well;
I know they know not what they do;
    They are the tools of the dread spell
Which the lost lover must pursue.

In temples sometimes she may rest,
In lonely groves, away from men,
    There bend the head, by heats distrest,
Nor be by blows awoke again.

Nature is kind, and God is kind,
And, if she had not had a heart,
    Only that great discerning mind,
She might have acted well her part.

But oh this thirst, that none can still,
Save those unfounden waters free;
    The angel of my life should fill
And soothe me to Eternity!

It marks the defect in the position of woman that one like
Mariana should have found reason to write thus. To a man of
equal power, equal sincerity, no more!—many resources would
have presented themselves. He would not have needed to seek,

he would have been called by life, and not permitted to be quite wrecked through the affections only. But such women as Mariana are often lost, unless they meet some man of sufficiently great soul to prize them.

Van Artevelde's Elena, though in her individual nature unlike my Mariana, is like her in a mind whose large impulses are disproportioned to the persons and occasions she meets, and which carry her beyond those reserves which mark the appointed lot of woman. But, when she met Van Artevelde, he was too great not to revere her rare nature, without regard to the stains and errors of its past history; great enough to receive her entirely and make a new life for her; man enough to be a lover! But as such men come not so often as once an age, their presence should not be absolutely needed to sustain life.

At Chicago I read again Philip Van Artevelde, and certain passages in it will always be in my mind associated with the deep sound of the lake, as heard in the night. I used to read a short time at night, and then open the blind to look out. The moon would be full upon the lake, and the calm breath, pure light, and the deep voice harmonized well with the thought of the Flemish hero. When will this country have such a man? It is what she needs; no thin Idealist, no coarse Realist, but a man whose eye reads the heavens while his feet step firmly on the ground, and his hands are strong and dexterous for the use of human implements. A man religious, virtuous and—sagacious; a man of universal sympathies, but self-possessed; a man who knows the region of emotion, though he is not its slave; a man to whom this world is no mere spectacle, or fleeting shadow, but a great solemn game to be played with good heed, for its stakes are of eternal value, yet who, if his own play be true, heeds not what he loses by the falsehood of others. A man who hives from the past, yet knows that its honey can but moderately avail him; whose comprehensive eye scans the present, neither infatuated by its golden lures, nor chilled by its many ventures; who possesses prescience, as the wise man must, but not so far as to be driven mad to-day by the gift which discerns to-morrow. When there is such a man for America, the thought which urges her on will be expressed.

Now that I am about to leave Illinois, feelings of regret and admiration come over me, as in parting with a friend whom we have not had the good sense to prize and study, while hours of association, never perhaps to return, were granted. I have fixed my attention almost exclusively on the picturesque beauty of this region; it was so new, so inspiring. But I ought to have been more interested in the housekeeping of this magnificent state, in the education she is giving her children, in their prospects.

Illinois is, at present, a by-word of reproach among the nations, for the careless, prodigal course, by which, in early youth, she has endangered her honor. But you cannot look about you there, without seeing that there are resources abundant to retrieve, and soon to retrieve, far greater errors, if they are only directed with wisdom.

Might the simple maxim, that honesty is the best policy be laid to heart! Might a sense of the true aims of life elevate the tone of politics and trade, till public and private honor become identical! Might the western man in that crowded and exciting life which develops his faculties so fully for to-day, not forget that better part which could not be taken from him! Might the western woman take that interest and acquire that light for the education of the children, for which she alone has leisure!

This is indeed the great problem of the place and time. If the next generation be well prepared for their work, ambitious of good and skilful to achieve it, the children of the present settlers may be leaven enough for the mass constantly increasing by emigration. And how much is this needed where those rude foreigners can so little understand the best interests of the land they seek for bread and shelter. It would be a happiness to aid in this good work, and interweave the white and golden threads into the fate of Illinois. It would be a work worthy the devotion of any mind.

In the little that I saw, was a large proportion of intelligence, activity, and kind feeling; but, if there was much serious laying to heart of the true purposes of life, it did not appear in the tone of conversation.

Having before me the Illinois guide-book, I find there mentioned, as a "visionary," one of the men I should think of as able to be a truly valuable settler in a new and great country— Morris Birkbeck, of England. Since my return, I have read his journey to, and letters from, Illinois. I see nothing promised

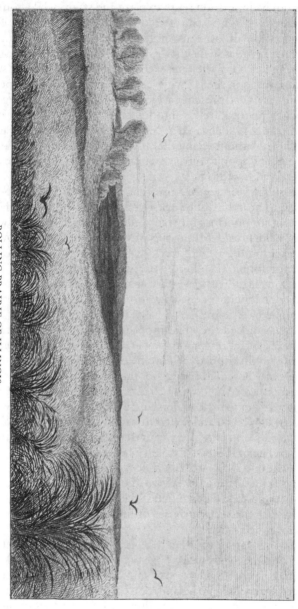

ROLLING PRAIRIE OF ILLINOIS

there that will not surely belong to the man who knows how to seek for it.

Mr. Birkbeck was an enlightened philanthropist, the rather that he did not wish to sacrifice himself to his fellow men, but to benefit them with all he had, and was, and wished. He thought all the creatures of a divine love ought to be happy and ought to be good, and that his own soul and his own life were not less precious than those of others; indeed, that to keep these healthy, was his only means of a healthy influence.

But his aims were altogether generous. Freedom, the liberty of law, not license; not indolence, work for himself and children and all men, but under genial and poetic influences;—these were his aims. How different from those of the new settlers in general! And into his mind so long ago shone steadily the two thoughts, now so prevalent in thinking and aspiring minds, of "Resist not evil," and "Every man his own priest, and the heart the only true church."

He has lost credit for sagacity from accidental circumstances. It does not appear that his position was ill chosen, or his means disproportioned to his ends, had he been sustained by funds from England, as he had a right to expect. But through the profligacy of a near relative, commissioned to collect these dues, he was disappointed of them, and his paper protested and credit destroyed in our cities, before he became aware of his danger.

Still, though more slowly and with more difficulty, he might have succeeded in his designs. The English farmer might have made the English settlement a model for good methods and good aims to all that region, had not death prematurely cut short his plans.

I have wished to say these few words, because the veneration with which I have been inspired for his character by those who knew him well, makes me impatient of this careless blame being passed from mouth to mouth and book to book. Success is no test of a man's endeavor, and Illinois will yet, I hope, regard this man, who knew so well what *ought* to be, as one of her true patriarchs, the Abraham of a promised land.

He was one too much before his time to be soon valued; but the time is growing up to him, and will understand his mild philanthropy and clear, large views.

I subjoin the account of his death, given me by a friend, as expressing, in fair picture, the character of the man.

"Mr. Birkbeck was returning from the seat of government, whither he had been on public business, and was accompanied by his son Bradford, a youth of sixteen or eighteen. It was necessary to cross a ford, which was rendered difficult by the swelling of the stream. Mr. B.'s horse was unwilling to plunge into the water, so his son offered to go first, and he followed. Bradford's horse had just gained footing on the opposite shore, when he looked back and perceived his father was dismounted, struggling in the water, and carried down by the current.

"Mr. Birkbeck could not swim; Bradford could; so he dismounted, and plunged into the stream to save his father. He got to him before he sank, held him up above water, and told him to take hold of his collar, and he would swim ashore with him. Mr. B. did so, and Bradford exerted all his strength to stem the current and reach the shore at a point where they could land; but, encumbered by his own clothing and his father's weight, he made no progress; and when Mr. B. perceived this, he, with his characteristic calmness and resolution, gave up his hold of his son, and, motioning to him to save himself, resigned himself to his fate. His son reached the shore, but was too much overwhelmed by his loss to leave it. He was found by some travellers, many hours after, seated on the margin of the stream, with his head in his hands, stupefied with grief.

"The body was found, and on the countenance was the sweetest smile; and Bradford said, 'just so he smiled upon me when he let go and pushed me away from him.'"

Many men can choose the right and best on a great occasion, but not many can, with such ready and serene decision, lay aside even life, when it is right and best. This little narrative touched my imagination in very early youth, and often has come up, in lonely vision, that face, serenely smiling above the current which bore him away to another realm of being.

Chapter V

WISCONSIN

A TERRITORY, not yet a state; still, nearer the acorn than we were.

It was very pleasant coming up. These large and elegant boats are so well arranged that every excursion may be a party of pleasure. There are many fair shows to see on the lake and its shores, almost always new and agreeable persons on board, pretty children playing about, ladies singing, (and if not very well, there is room to keep out of the way.) You may see a great deal here of Life, in the London sense, if you know a few people; or if you do not, and have the tact to look about you without seeming to stare.

We came to Milwaukie, where we were to pass a fortnight or more.

This place is most beautifully situated. A little river, with romantic banks, passes up through the town. The bank of the lake is here a bold bluff, eighty feet in height. From its summit, you enjoyed a noble outlook on the lake. A little narrow path wound along the edge of the lake below. I liked this walk much. Above me this high wall of rich earth, garlanded on its crest with trees, the long ripples of the lake coming up to my feet. Here, standing in the shadow, I could appreciate better its magnificent changes of color, which are the chief beauties of the lake-waters; but these are indescribable.

It was fine to ascend into the lighthouse, above this bluff, and watch from thence the thunder-clouds which so frequently rose over the lake, or the great boats coming in. Approaching the Milwaukie pier, they made a bend, and seemed to do obeisance in the heavy style of some dowager duchess entering a circle she wishes to treat with especial respect.

These boats come in and out every day, and still afford a cause for general excitement. The people swarm down to greet them, to receive and send away their packages and letters. To me they seemed such mighty messengers, to give, by their noble motion, such an idea of the power and fullness of life, that they were worthy to carry despatches from king to king. It must be very pleasant for those who have an active share in carrying on the affairs of this great and growing world to see them come in. It must be very pleasant to those who have dearly loved friends at the next station. To those who have neither business nor friends, it sometimes gives a desolating sense of insignificance.

The town promises to be, some time, a fine one, as it is so well situated; and they have good building material—a yellow brick, very pleasing to the eye. It seems to grow before you, and has indeed but just emerged from the thickets of oak and wild roses. A few steps will take you into the thickets, and certainly I never saw so many wild roses, or of so beautiful a red. Of such a color were the first red ones the world ever saw, when, says the legend, Venus flying to the assistance of Adonis, the rosebushes kept catching her to make her stay, and the drops of blood the thorns drew from her feet, as she tore herself away, fell on the white roses, and turned them this beautiful red.

I will here insert, though with no excuse, except that it came to memory at the time, this description of Titian's Venus and Adonis.

"This picture has that perfect balance of lines and forms that it would, (as was said of all Raphael's) 'seen at any distance have the air of an ornamental design.' It also tells its story at the first glance, though, like all beautiful works, it gains by study.

"On one side slumbers the little God of Love, as an emblem, I suppose, that only the love of man is worth embodying, for surely Cytherea's is awake enough. The quiver of Cupid, suspended to a tree, gives sportive grace to the scene which softens the tragedy of a breaking tie. The dogs of Adonis pull upon his hand; he can scarce forbear to burst from the detaining arms of Beauty herself, yet he waits a moment to coax her—to make an unmeaning promise. 'A moment, a moment, my love, and I will return; a moment only.' Adonis is not beautiful, except in his expression of eager youth. The Queen of Beauty does not choose Apollo. Venus herself is very beautiful; especially the body is lovely as can be; and the soft, imploring look, gives a conjugal delicacy to the face which purifies the whole picture. This Venus is not as fresh, as moving and breathing as Shakspeare's, yet lovelier to the mind if not to the sense.

MILWAUKIE   85

'Tis difficult to look at this picture without indignation, because it is, in one respect, so true. Why must women always try to detain and restrain what they love? Foolish beauty; let him go; it is thy tenderness that has spoiled him. Be less lovely—less feminine; abandon thy fancy for giving thyself wholly; cease to love so well, and any Hercules will spin among thy maids, if thou wilt. But let him go this time; thou canst not keep him. Sit there, by thyself, on that bank, and, instead of thinking how soon he will come back, think how thou may'st love him no better than he does thee, for the time has come."

It was soon after this moment that the poor Queen, hearing the frightened hounds, apprehended the rash huntsman's danger, and, flying through the woods, gave their hue to the red roses.

To return from the Grecian isles to Milwaukie. One day, walking along the river's bank in search of a waterfall to be seen from one ravine, we heard tones from a band of music, and saw a gay troop shooting at a mark, on the opposite bank. Between every shot the band played; the effect was very pretty.

On this walk we found two of the oldest and most gnarled hemlocks that ever afforded study for a painter. They were the only ones we saw; they seemed the veterans of a former race.

At Milwaukie, as at Chicago, are many pleasant people, drawn together from all parts of the world. A resident here would find great piquancy in the associations,—those he met having such dissimilar histories and topics. And several persons I saw evidently transplanted from the most refined circles to be met in this country. There are lures enough in the West for people of all kinds;—the enthusiast and the cunning man; the naturalist, and the lover who needs to be rich for the sake of her he loves.

The torrent of emigration swells very strongly towards this place. During the fine weather, the poor refugees arrive daily, in their national dresses, all travel-soiled and worn. The night they pass in rude shantees, in a particular quarter of the town, then walk off into the country—the mothers carrying their infants, the fathers leading the little children by the hand, seeking a home where their hands may maintain them.

One morning we set off in their track, and travelled a day's journey into this country,—fair, yet not, in that part which

I saw, comparable, in my eyes, to the Rock River region. It alternates rich fields, proper for grain, with oak openings, as they are called; bold, various and beautiful were the features of the scene, but I saw not those majestic sweeps, those boundless distances, those heavenly fields; it was not the same world.

Neither did we travel in the same delightful manner. We were now in a nice carriage, which must not go off the road, for fear of breakage, with a regular coachman, whose chief care was not to tire his horses, and who had no taste for entering fields in pursuit of wild flowers, or tempting some strange wood path in search of whatever might befall. It was pleasant, but almost as tame as New England.

But charming indeed was the place where we stopped. It was in the vicinity of a chain of lakes, and on the bank of the loveliest little stream, called the Bark river, which flowed in rapid amber brightness, through fields, and dells, and stately knolls, of most idylic beauty.

The little log cabin where we slept, with its flower garden in front, disturbed the scene no more than a stray lock on the fair cheek. The hospitality of that house I may well call princely; it was the boundless hospitality of the heart, which, if it has no Aladdin's lamp to create a palace for the guest, does him still higher service by the freedom of its bounty up to the very last drop of its powers.

Sweet were the sunsets seen in the valley of this stream, though here, and, I grieve to say, no less near the Rock River, the fiend, who has ever liberty to tempt the happy in this world, appeared in the shape of mosquitoes, and allowed us no bodily to enjoy our mental peace.

One day we ladies gave, under the guidance of our host, to visiting all the beauties of the adjacent lakes—Nomabbin, Silver, and Pine Lakes. On the shore of Nomabbin had formerly been one of the finest Indian villages. Our host said that, one day, as he was lying there beneath the bank, he saw a tall Indian standing at gaze on the knoll. He lay a long time, curious to see how long the figure would maintain its statue-like absorption. But, at last, his patience yielded, and, in moving, he made a slight noise. The Indian saw him, gave a wild, snorting sound of indignation and pain, and strode away.

What feelings must consume their heart at such moments! I scarcely see how they can forbear to shoot the white man where he stands.

But the power of fate is with the white man, and the Indian feels it. This same gentleman told of his travelling through the wilderness with an Indian guide. He had with him a bottle of spirit which he meant to give him in small quantities, but the Indian, once excited, wanted the whole at once. I would not, said Mr. ——, give it him, for I thought if he got really drunk, there was an end to his services as a guide. But he persisted, and at last tried to take it from me. I was not armed; he was, and twice as strong as I. But I knew an Indian could not resist the look of a white man, and I fixed my eye steadily on his. He bore it for a moment, then his eye fell; he let go the bottle. I took his gun and threw it to a distance. After a few moments' pause, I told him to go and fetch it, and left it in his hands. From that moment he was quite obedient, even servile, all the rest of the way.

This gentleman, though in other respects of most kindly and liberal heart, showed the aversion that the white man soon learns to feel for the Indian on whom he encroaches, the aversion of the injurer for him he has degraded. After telling the anecdote of his seeing the Indian gazing at the seat of his former home,

"A thing for human feelings the most trying,"

and which, one would think, would have awakened soft compassion—almost remorse—in the present owner of that fair hill, which contained for the exile the bones of his dead, the ashes of his hopes,—he observed, "They cannot be prevented from straggling back here to their old haunts. I wish they could. They ought not to be permitted to drive away *our* game." OUR game—just heavens!

The same gentleman showed, on a slight occasion, the true spirit of the sportsman, or, perhaps I might say of Man, when engaged in any kind of chase. Showing us some antlers, he said, "This one belonged to a majestic creature. But this other was the beauty. I had been lying a long time at watch, when at last I heard them come crackling along. I lifted my head cautiously, as they burst through the trees. The first was a magnificent fellow; but then I saw coming one, the prettiest, the most graceful I ever beheld—there was something so soft and beseeching in its look. I chose him at once; took aim, and shot him dead. You see the antlers are not very large; it was young, but the prettiest creature!"

In the course of this morning's drive, we visited the gentlemen on their fishing party. They hailed us gaily, and rowed ashore to show us what fine booty they had. No disappointment there, no dull work. On the beautiful point of land from which we first saw them, lived a contented woman, the only one I heard of out there. She was English, and said she had seen so much suffering in her own country that the hardships of this seemed as nothing to her. But the others—even our sweet and gentle hostess—found their labors disproportioned to their strength, if not to their patience; and, while their husbands and brothers enjoyed the country in hunting or fishing, they found themselves confined to a comfortless and laborious indoor life. But it need not be so long.

This afternoon, driving about on the banks of these lakes, we found the scene all of one kind of loveliness; wide, graceful woods, and then these fine sheets of water, with fine points of land jutting out boldly into them. It was lovely, but not striking or peculiar.

All woods suggest pictures. The European forest, with its long glades and green sunny dells, naturally suggested the figures of armed knight on his proud steed, or maiden, decked in gold and pearl, pricking along them on a snow white palfrey. The green dells, of weary Palmer sleeping there beside the spring with his head upon his wallet. Our minds, familiar with such figures, people with them the New England woods, wherever the sunlight falls down a longer than usual cart-track, wherever a cleared spot has lain still enough for the trees to look friendly, with their exposed sides cultivated by the light, and the grass to look velvet warm, and be embroidered with flowers. These western woods suggest a different kind of ballad. The Indian legends have, often, an air of the wildest solitude, as has the one Mr. Lowell has put into verse, in his late volume. But I did not see those wild woods; only such as suggest little romances of love and sorrow, like this:

WOODS

A maiden sat beneath the tree,
Tear-bedewed her pale cheeks be,
And she sigheth heavily.

From forth the wood into the light,
A hunter strides with carol light,
And a glance so bold and bright.

He careless stopped and eyed the maid;
"Why weepest thou?" he gently said,
"I love thee well; be not afraid."

He takes her hand, and leads her on;
She should have waited there alone,
For he was not her chosen one.

He leans her head upon his breast,
She knew 'twas not her home of rest,
But ah! she had been sore distrest.

The sacred stars looked sadly down;
The parting moon appeared to frown,
To see thus dimmed the diamond crown.

Then from the thicket starts a deer,
The huntsman, seizing on his spear,
Cries, "Maiden, wait thou for me here."

She sees him vanish into night,
She starts from sleep in deep affright,
For it was not her own true knight.

Though but in dream Gunhilda failed;
Though but a fancied ill assailed,
Though she but fancied fault bewailed.

Yet thought of day makes dream of night:
She is not worthy of the knight,
The inmost altar burns not bright.

If loneliness thou canst not bear,
Cannot the dragon's venom dare,
Of the pure meed thou shouldst despair.

INDIAN ENCAMPMENT

INDIAN ENCAMPMENT

Now sadder that lone maiden sighs,
Far bitterer tears profane her eyes,
Crushed in the dust her heart's flower lies.

On the bank of Silver Lake we saw an Indian encampment. A shower threatened us, but we resolved to try if we could not visit it before it came on. We crossed a wide field on foot, and found them amid the trees on a shelving bank; just as we reached them the rain began to fall in torrents, with frequent thunder claps, and we had to take refuge in their lodges. These were very small, being for temporary use, and we crowded the occupants much, among whom were several sick, on the damp ground, or with only a ragged mat between them and it. But they showed all the gentle courtesy which marks them towards the stranger, who stands in any need; though it was obvious that the visit, which inconvenienced them, could only have been caused by the most impertinent curiosity, they made us as comfortable as their extreme poverty permitted. They seemed to think we would not like to touch them: a sick girl in the lodge where I was, persisted in moving so as to give me the dry place; a woman with the sweet melancholy eye of the race, kept off the children and wet dogs from even the hem of my garment.

Without, their fires smouldered, and black kettles, hung over them on sticks, smoked and seethed in the rain. An old theatrical looking Indian stood with arms folded, looking up to the heavens, from which the rain dashed and the thunder reverberated; his air was French-Roman, that is, more romanesque than Roman. The Indian ponies, much excited, kept careering through the wood, around the encampment, and now and then halting suddenly, would thrust in their intelligent, though amazed, phizzes, as if to ask their masters when this awful pother would cease, and then, after a moment, rush and trample off again.

At last we got off, well wetted, but with a picturesque scene for memory. At a house where we stopped to get dry, they told us that this wandering band (of Pottawattamies,) who had returned on a visit, either from homesickness, or need of relief, were extremely destitute. The women had been there to see if they could barter their head bands with which they club their hair behind into a form not unlike a Grecian knot, for food. They seemed, indeed, to have neither food, utensils, clothes, nor bedding; nothing but the ground, the sky, and their own strength. Little wonder if they drove off the game!

Part of the same band I had seen in Milwaukie, on a begging dance. The effect of this was wild and grotesque. They wore much paint and feather head-dresses. "Indians without paint are poor coots," said a gentleman who had been a great deal with, and really liked, them; and I like the effect of the paint on them; it reminds of the gay fantasies of nature. With them in Milwaukie, was a chief, the finest Indian figure I saw, more than six feet in height, erect, and of a sullen, but grand gait and gesture. He wore a deep red blanket, which fell in large folds from his shoulders to his feet, did not join in the dance, but slowly strode about through the streets, a fine sight, not a French-Roman, but a real Roman. He looked unhappy, but listlessly unhappy, as if he felt it was of no use to strive or resist.

While in the neighborhood of these lakes, we visited also a foreign settlement of great interest. Here were minds, it seemed, to "comprehend the trusts," of their new life; and if they can only stand true to them, will derive and bestow great benefits therefrom.

But sad and sickening to the enthusiast who comes to these shores, hoping the tranquil enjoyment of intellectual blessings, and the pure happiness of mutual love, must be a part of the scene that he encounters at first. He has escaped from the heartlessness of courts, to encounter the vulgarity of a mob; he has secured solitude, but it is a lonely, a deserted solitude. Amid the abundance of nature he cannot, from petty, but insuperable obstacles, procure, for a long time, comforts, or a home.

But let him come sufficiently armed with patience to learn the new spells which the new dragons require, (and this can only be done on the spot,) he will not finally be disappointed of the promised treasure; the mob will resolve itself into men, yet crude, but of good dispositions, and capable of good character; the solitude will become sufficiently enlivened and home grow up at last from the rich sod.

In this transition state we found one of these homes. As we approached it seemed the very Eden which earth might still afford to a pair willing to give up the hackneyed pleasures of

THE COTTAGE

the world, for a better and more intimate communion with one another and with beauty: the wild road led through wide beautiful woods, to the wilder and more beautiful shores of the finest lake we saw. On its waters, glittering in the morning sun, a few Indians were paddling to and fro in their light canoes. On one of those fair knolls I have so often mentioned, stood the cottage, beneath trees which stooped as if they yet felt brotherhood with its roof tree. Flowers waved, birds fluttered round, all had the sweetness of a happy seclusion; all invited on entrance to cry, All hail ye happy ones! to those who inhabited it.

But on entrance to those evidently rich in personal beauty, talents, love, and courage, the aspect of things was rather sad. Sickness had been with them, death, care, and labor; these had not yet blighted them, but had turned their gay smiles grave. It seemed that hope and joy had given place to resolution. How much, too, was there in them, worthless in this place, which would have been so valuable elsewhere. Refined graces, cultivated powers, shine in vain before field laborers, as laborers are in this present world; you might as well cultivate heliotropes to present to an ox. Oxen and heliotropes are both good, but not for one another.

With them were some of the old means of enjoyment, the books, the pencil, the guitar; but where the wash-tub and the axe are so constantly in requisition, there is not much time and pliancy of hand for these.

In the inner room the master of the house was seated; he had been sitting there long, for he had injured his foot on ship-board, and his farming had to be done by proxy. His beautiful young wife was his only attendant and nurse, as well as a farm house-keeper; how well she performed hard and unaccustomed duties, the objects of her care shewed; everything that belonged to the house was rude but neatly arranged; the invalid, confined to an uneasy wooden chair, (they had not been able to induce any one to bring them an easy chair from the town,) looked as neat and elegant as if he had been dressed by the valet of a duke. He was of northern blood, with clear full blue eyes, calm features, a tempering of the soldier, scholar, and man of the world, in his aspect; whether that various intercourses had given himself that thorough-bred look never seen in Americans, or that it was inherited from a race who had known all these disciplines. He formed a great but pleasing contrast to his wife, whose glowing complexion and dark mellow eye bespoke an origin in some climate more familiar with the sun. He looked as if he could sit there a great while patiently, and live on his own mind, biding his time; she, as if she could bear anything for affection's sake, but would feel the weight of each moment as it passed.

Seeing the album full of drawings and verses which bespoke the circle of elegant and affectionate intercourse they had left behind, we could not but see that the young wife sometimes must need a sister, the husband a companion, and both must often miss that electricity which sparkles from the chain of congenial minds.

For man, a position is desirable in some degree proportioned to his education. Mr. Birkbeck was bred a farmer, but these were nurslings of the court and city; they may persevere, for an affectionate courage shone in their eyes, and, if so, become true lords of the soil, and informing geniuses to those around; then, perhaps, they will feel that they have not paid too dear for the tormented independence of the new settler's life. But, generally, damask roses will not thrive in the wood, and a ruder growth, if healthy and pure, we wish rather to see there.

I feel very differently about these foreigners from Americans; American men and women are inexcusable if they do not bring up children so as to be fit for vicissitudes; that is the meaning of our star, that here all men being free and equal, all should be fitted for freedom and an independence by his own resources wherever the changeful wave of our mighty stream may take him. But the star of Europe brought a different horoscope, and to mix destinies breaks the thread of both. The Arabian horse will not plough well, nor can the plough-horse be rode to play the jereed. But a man is a man wherever he goes, and something precious cannot fail to be gained by one who knows how to abide by a resolution of any kind, and pay the cost without a murmur.

Returning, the fine carriage at last fulfilled its threat of breaking down. We took refuge in a farm house. Here was a pleasant scene. A rich and beautiful estate, several happy families, who had removed together, and formed a natural community, ready to help and enliven one another. They were farmers at home, in western New York, and both men and women knew

THE SEERESS OF PREVORST 95

how to work. Yet even here the women did not like the change, but they were willing, "as it might be best for the young folks." Their hospitality was great, the housefull of women and pretty children seemed all of one mind.

Returning to Milwaukie much fatigued, I entertained myself for a day or two with reading. The book I had brought with me was in strong contrast with the life around me. Very strange was this vision of an exalted and sensitive existence, which seemed to invade the next sphere, in contrast with the spontaneous, instinctive life, so healthy and so near the ground I had been surveying. This was the German book entitled:

Die Seherin von Prevorst.—Eröffnungen über das innere Leben des Menschen und über das hereinragen einer Geisterwelt in die unsere. Mitgetheilt von Justinus Kerner.

The Seeress of Prevorst.—Revelations concerning the inward life of man, and the projection of a world of spirits into ours, communicated by Justinus Kerner.

This book, published in Germany some twelve years since, and which called forth there plenteous dews of admiration, as plenteous hail-storms of jeers and scorns, I never saw mentioned till some year or two since, in any English publication. Then a playful, but not sarcastic account of it, in the Dublin Magazine, so far excited my curiosity that I procured the book intending to read it so soon as I should have some leisure days, such as this journey has afforded.

Dr. Kerner, its author, is a man of distinction in his native land, both as a physician and a thinker, though always on the side of reverence, marvel, and mysticism. He was known to me only through two or three little poems of his in Catholic legends, which I much admired for the fine sense they showed of the beauty of symbols.

He here gives a biography, mental and physical, of one of the most remarkable cases of high nervous excitement that the age, so interested in such, yet affords, with all its phenomena of clairvoyance and susceptibility of magnetic influences. I insert some account of this biography at the request of many who have been interested by slight references to it. The book, a thick and heavy volume, written with true German patience, some would say clumsiness, has not, probably, and may not be translated into other languages. As to my own mental position on these subjects it may be briefly expressed by a dialogue between several persons who honor me with a portion of friendly confidence and of criticism, and myself expressed as *Free Hope*. The others may be styled *Old Church*, *Good Sense*, and *Self-Poise*.

Good Sense. I wonder you can take any interest in such observations or experiments. Don't you see how almost impossible it is to make them with any exactness, how entirely impossible to know anything about them unless made by yourself, when the least leaven of credulity, excited fancy, to say nothing of willing or careless imposture, spoils the whole loaf. Beside, allowing the possibility of some clear glimpses into a higher state of being, what do we want of it now? All around us lies what we neither understand nor use. Our capacities, our instincts for this our present sphere are but half developed. Let us confine ourselves to that till the lesson be learned; let us be completely natural, before we trouble ourselves with the supernatural. I never see any of these things but I long to get away and lie under a green tree and let the wind blow on me. There is marvel and charm enough in that for me.

Free Hope. And for me also. Nothing is truer than the Wordsworthian creed, on which Carlyle lays such stress, that we need only look on the miracle of every day, to sate ourselves with thought and admiration every day. But how are our faculties sharpened to do it? Precisely by apprehending the infinite results of every day.

Who sees the meaning of the flower uprooted in the ploughed field? The ploughman who does not look beyond its boundaries and does not raise his eyes from the ground? No—but the poet who sees that field in its relations with the universe, and looks oftener to the sky than on the ground. Only the dreamer shall understand realities, though, in truth, his dreaming must not be out of proportion to his waking!

The mind, roused powerfully by this existence, stretches of itself into what the French sage calls the "aromal state." From the hope thus gleaned it forms the hypothesis, under whose banner it collects its facts.

Long before these slight attempts were made to establish as a science what is at present called animal magnetism, always, in fact men were occupied more or less with this vital principle,

principle of flux and influx, dynamic of our mental mechanics, human phase of electricity. Poetic observation was pure, there was no quackery in its free course, as there is so often in this wilful tampering with the hidden springs of life, for it is tampering unless done in a patient spirit and with severe truth; yet it may be, by the rude or greedy miners, some good ore is unearthed. And some there are who work in the true temper, patient and accurate in trial, not rushing to conclusions, feeling there is a mystery, not eager to call it by name, till they can know it as a reality: such may learn, such may teach.

Subject to the sudden revelations, the breaks in habitual existence caused by the aspect of death, the touch of love, the flood of music, I never lived, that I remember, what you call a common natural day. All my days are touched by the supernatural, for I feel the pressure of hidden causes, and the presence, sometimes the communion, of unseen powers. It needs not that I should ask the clairvoyant whether "a spirit-world projects into ours." As to the specific evidence, I would not tarnish my mind by hasty reception. The mind is not, I know, a highway, but a temple, and its doors should not be carelessly left open. Yet it were sin, if indolence or coldness excluded what had a claim to enter; and I doubt whether, in the eyes of pure intelligence, an ill-grounded hasty rejection be not a greater sign of weakness than an ill-grounded and hasty faith.

I will quote, as my best plea, the saying of a man old in years, but not in heart, and whose long life has been distinguished by that clear adaptation of means to ends which gives the credit of practical wisdom. He wrote to his child, "I have lived too long, and seen too much to be *in*credulous." Noble the thought, no less so its frank expression, instead of saws of caution, mean advices, and other modern instances. Such was the romance of Socrates when he bade his disciples "sacrifice a cock to Æsculapius."

Old Church. You are always so quick-witted and voluble, Free Hope, you don't get time to see how often you err, and even, perhaps, sin and blaspheme. The Author of all has intended to confine our knowledge within certain boundaries, has given us a short span of time for a certain probation, for which our faculties are adapted. By wild speculation and intemperate curiosity we violate his will and incur dangerous, perhaps fatal,

98   SUMMER ON THE LAKES

consequences. We waste our powers, and, becoming morbid and visionary, are unfitted to obey positive precepts, and perform positive duties.

Free Hope. I do not see how it is possible to go further beyond the results of a limited human experience than those do who pretend to settle the origin and nature of sin, the final destiny of souls, and the whole plan of the causal spirit with regard to them. I think those who take your view, have not examined themselves, and do not know the ground on which they stand.

I acknowledge no limit, set up by man's opinion, as to the capacities of man. "Care is taken," I see it, "that the trees grow not up into heaven," but, to me it seems, the more vigorously they aspire the better. Only let it be a vigorous, not a partial or sickly aspiration. Let not the tree forget its root.

So long as the child insists on knowing where its dead parent is, so long as bright eyes weep at mysterious pressures, too heavy for the life, so long as that impulse is constantly arising which made the Roman emperor address his soul in a strain of such touching softness, vanishing from the thought, as the column of smoke from the eye, I know of no inquiry which the impulse of man suggests that is forbidden to the resolution of man to pursue. In every inquiry, unless sustained by a pure and reverent spirit, he gropes in the dark, or falls headlong.

Self-Poise. All this may be very true, but what is the use of all this straining? Far-sought is dear-bought. When we know that all is in each, and that the ordinary contains the extraordinary, why should we play the baby, and insist upon having the moon for a toy when a tin dish will do as well. Our deep ignorance is a chasm that we can only fill up by degrees, but the commonest rubbish will help us as well as shred silk. The God Brahma, while on earth, was set to fill up a valley, but he had only a basket given him in which to fetch earth for this purpose; so is it with us all. No leaps, no starts will avail us, by patient crystallization alone the equal temper of wisdom is attainable. Sit at home and the spirit-world will look in at your window with moonlit eyes; run out to find it, and rainbow and golden cup will have vanished and left you the beggarly child you were. The better part of wisdom is a sublime prudence, a pure and patient truth that will receive nothing it is not sure it can permanently lay to heart. Of our study there should be in proportion two-thirds of rejection to one of acceptance. And, amid the manifold infatuations and illusions of this world of emotion, a being capable of clear intelligence can do no better service than to hold himself upright, avoid nonsense, and do what chores lie in his way, acknowledging every moment that primal truth, which no fact exhibits, nor, if pressed by too warm a hope, will even indicate. I think, indeed, it is part of our lesson to give a formal consent to what is farcical, and to pick up our living and our virtue amid what is so ridiculous, hardly deigning a smile, and certainly not vexed. The work is done through all, if not by every one.

Free Hope. Thou art greatly wise, my friend, and ever respected by me, yet I find not in your theory or your scope, room enough for the lyric inspirations, or the mysterious whispers of life. To me it seems that it is madder never to abandon oneself, than often to be infatuated; better to be wounded, a captive, and a slave, than always to walk in armor. As to magnetism, that is only a matter of fancy. You sometimes need just such a field in which to wander vagrant, and if it bear a higher name, yet it may be that, in last result, the trance of Pythagoras might be classed with the more infantine transports of the Seeress of Prevorst.

What is done interests me more than what is thought and supposed. Every fact is impure, but every fact contains in it the juices of life. Every fact is a clod, from which may grow an amaranth or a palm.

Do you climb the snowy peaks from whence come the streams, where the atmosphere is rare, where you can see the sky nearer, from which you can get a commanding view of the landscape. I see great disadvantages as well as advantages in this dignified position. I had rather walk myself through all kinds of places, even at the risk of being robbed in the forest, half drowned at the ford, and covered with dust in the street.

I would beat with the living heart of the world, and understand all the moods, even the fancies or fantasies, of nature. I dare to trust to the interpreting spirit to bring me out all right at last—to establish truth through error.

SUMMER ON THE LAKES

Whether this be the best way is of no consequence, if it be the one individual character points out.

> For one, like me, it would be vain
> From glittering heights the eyes to strain;
> I the truth can only know,
> Tested by life's most fiery glow.
> Seeds of thought will never thrive
> Till dews of love shall bid them live.

Let me stand in my age with all its waters flowing round me. If they sometimes subdue, they must finally upbear me, for I seek the universal—and that must be the best.

The Spirit, no doubt, leads in every movement of my time: if I seek the How, I shall find it, as well as if I busied myself more with the Why.

Whatever is, is right, if only men are steadily bent to make it so, by comprehending and fulfilling its design.

May not I have an office, too, in my hospitality and ready sympathy? If I sometimes entertain guests who cannot pay with gold coin, with "fair rose nobles," that is better than to lose the chance of entertaining angels unawares.

You, my three friends, are held in heart-honor, by me. You, especially, Good-Sense, because where you do not go yourself, you do not object to another's going, if he will. You are really liberal. You, Old Church, are of use, by keeping unforgot the effigies of old religion, and reviving the tone of pure Spenserian sentiment, which this time is apt to stifle in its childish haste. But you are very faulty in censuring and wishing to limit others by your own standard. You, Self-Poise, fill a priestly office. Could but a larger intelligence of the vocations of others, and a tender sympathy with their individual natures be added, had you more of love, or more of apprehensive genius, (for either would give you the needed expansion and delicacy) you would command my entire reverence. As it is, I must at times deny and oppose you, and so must others, for you tend, by your influence, to exclude us from our full, free life. We must be content when you censure, and rejoiced when you approve; always admonished to good by your whole being, and sometimes by your judgment. And so I pass on to interest myself and others in the memoir of the Seherin von Prevorst.

THE SEERESS OF PREVORST

101

Aside from Löwenstein, a town of Wirtemberg, on mountains whose highest summit is more than eighteen hundred feet above the level of the sea, lies in romantic seclusion, surrounded on all sides by woods and hills, the hamlet of Prevorst.

Its inhabitants number about four hundred and fifty, most of whom support themselves by wood-cutting, and making charcoal, and collecting wood seed.

As is usual with those who live upon the mountains, these are a vigorous race, and generally live to old age without sickness. Diseases that infest the valley, such as ague, never touch them; but they are subject in youth to attacks upon the nerves, which one would not expect in so healthy a class. In a town situated near to, and like Prevorst, the children were often attacked with a kind of St. Vitus's dance. They would foresee when it would seize upon them, and, if in the field, would hasten home to undergo the paroxysms there. From these they rose, as from magnetic sleep, without memory of what had happened.

Other symptoms show the inhabitants of this region very susceptible to magnetic and sidereal influences.

On this mountain, and indeed in the hamlet of Prevorst, was, in 1801, a woman born, in whom a peculiar inner life discovered itself from early childhood. Frederica Hauffe, whose father was gamekeeper of this district of forest, was, as the position and solitude of her birthplace made natural, brought up in the most simple manner. In the keen mountain air and long winter cold, she was not softened by tenderness either as to dress or bedding, but grew up lively and blooming; and while her brothers and sisters, under the same circumstances, were subject to rheumatic attacks, she remained free from them. On the other hand, her peculiar tendency displayed itself in her dreams. If anything affected her painfully, if her mind was excited by reproof, she had instructive warning, or prophetic dreams.

While yet quite young, her parents let her go, for the advantages of instruction, to her grand-father, Johann Schmidgall, in Löwenstein.

Here were discovered in her the sensibility to magnetic and ghostly influences, which, the good Kerner assures us, her grand-parents deeply lamented, and did all in their power to repress. But, as it appears that her grandfather, also, had seen a ghost, and there were evidently legends in existence about the rooms in which the little Frederika saw ghosts, and spots where the presence of human bones caused her sudden shivering, we may be allowed to doubt whether indirect influence was not more powerful than direct repression upon these subjects.

There is the true German impartiality with regard to the scene of appearance for these imposing visiters; sometimes it is "a room in the Castle of Löwenstein, long disused," à la Radcliffe, sometimes "a deserted kitchen."

This "solemn, unhappy gift," brought no disturbance to the childish life of the maiden, she enjoyed life with more vivacity than most of her companions. The only trouble she had was the extreme irritability of the optic nerve, which, though without inflammation of the eyes, sometimes confined her to a solitary chamber. "This," says Dr. K. "was probably a sign of the development of the spiritual in the fleshly eye."

Sickness of her parents at last called her back to the lonely Prevorst, where, by trouble and watching beside sick beds, her feelings were too much excited, so that the faculty for prophetic dreams and the vision of spirits increased upon her.

From her seventeenth to her nineteenth year, when every outward relation was pleasant for her, this inward life was not so active, and she was distinguished from other girls of her circle only by the more intellectual nature, which displayed itself chiefly in the eyes, and by a greater liveliness which, however, never passed the bounds of grace and propriety.

She had none of the sentimentality so common at that age, and it can be proved that she had never an attachment, nor was disappointed in love, as has been groundlessly asserted.

In her nineteenth year, she was by her family betrothed to Herr H. The match was desirable on account of the excellence of the man, and the sure provision it afforded for her comfort through life.

But, whether from presentiment of the years of suffering that were before her, or from other hidden feelings, of which we only know with certainty that, if such there were, they were not occasioned by another attachment, she sank into a dejection, inexplicable to her family; passed whole days in weeping; scarcely slept for some weeks, and thus the life of feeling which had been too powerful in her childhood was called up anew in full force.

THE SEERESS OF PREVORST

On the day of her solemn betrothal, took place, also, the funeral of T., the preacher of Oberstenfeld, a man of sixty and more years, whose preaching, instruction, and character, (he was goodness itself,) had had great influence upon her life. She followed the dear remains, with others, to the church-yard. Her heart till then so heavy, was suddenly relieved and calmed, as she stood beside the grave. She remained there long, enjoying her new peace, and when she went away found herself tranquil, but indifferent to all the concerns of this world. Here began the period, not indeed as yet of sickness, but of her peculiar inward life, which knew afterward no pause.

Later, in somnambulic state, she spoke of this day in the following verses. The deceased had often appeared to her as a shape of light, protecting her from evil spirits.

(These are little simple rhymes; they are not worth translating into verse, though, in the original, they have a childish grace.)

> What was once so dark to me,
> I see now clearly.
>> In that day
> When I had given in marriage myself away,
>
> I stood quite immersed in thee,
> Thou angel figure above thy grave mound.
> Willingly would I have exchanged with thee,
> Willingly given up to thee my earthly luck,
> Which those around praised as the blessing of heaven.
>
> I prayed upon thy grave
> For one blessing only,
>> That the wings of this angel
>> Might henceforward
>> On the hot path of life,
>> Waft around me the peace of heaven.
> There standest thou, angel, now; my prayer was heard.

She was, in consequence of her marriage, removed to Kürnbach, a place on the borders of Würtemberg and Baden. Its position is low, gloomy, shut in by hills; opposite in all the influences of earth and atmosphere to those of Prevorst and its vicinity.

Those of electrical susceptibility are often made sick or well by change of place. Papponi, (of whom Amoretti writes,) a man of such susceptibility, was cured of convulsive attacks by change of place. Pennet could find repose while in one part of Calabria, only by wrapping himself in an oil-cloth mantle, thus, as it were, isolating himself. That great sense of sidereal and imponderable influences, which afterward manifested itself so clearly in the Seherin, probably made this change of place very unfavorable to her. Later, it appeared, that the lower she came down from the hills, the more she suffered from spasms, but on the heights her tendency to the magnetic state was the greatest.

But also mental influences were hostile to her. Already withdrawn from the outward life, she was placed, where, as consort and housekeeper to a laboring man, the calls on her care and attention were incessant. She was obliged hourly to forsake her inner home, to provide for an outer, which did not correspond with it.

She bore this seven months, though flying to solitude, whenever outward relations permitted. But longer it was not possible to conceal the inward verity by an outward action, "the body sank beneath the attempt, and the spirit took refuge in the inner circle."

One night she dreamed that she awoke and found the dead body of the preacher T. by her side; that at the same time her father, and two physicians were considering what should be done for her in a severe sickness. She called out that "the dead friend would help her; she needed no physician." Her husband, hearing her cry out in sleep, woke her.

This dream was presage of a fever, which seized her next morning. It lasted fourteen days with great violence, and was succeeded by attacks of convulsion and spasm. This was the beginning of that state of bodily suffering and mental exaltation in which she passed the remaining seven years of her life.

She seems to have been very injudiciously treated in the first stages of her illness. Bleeding was resorted to, as usual in cases of extreme suffering where the nurses know not what else to do, and, as usual, the momentary relief was paid for by an increased nervousness, and capacity for suffering.

THE SEERESS OF PREVORST

Magnetic influences from other persons were of frequent use to her, but they were applied without care as to what characters and constitutions were brought into connexion with hers, and were probably in the end just as injurious to her as the loss of blood. At last she became so weak, so devoid of all power in herself, that her life seemed entirely dependent on artificial means and the influence of other men.

There is a singular story of a woman in the neighborhood, who visited her once or twice, apparently from an instinct that she should injure her, and afterwards, interfered in the same way, and with the same results, in the treatment of her child.

This demoniacal impulse and power, which were ascribed to the Canidias of ancient superstition, may be seen subtly influencing the members of every-day society. We see persons led, by an uneasy impulse, towards the persons and the topics where they are sure they can irritate and annoy. This is constantly observable among children, also in the closest relations between grown up people who have not yet the government of themselves, neither are governed by the better power.

There is also an interesting story of a quack who treated her with amulets, whose parallel may be found in the action of such persons in common society. It is an expression of the power that a vulgar and self-willed nature will attain over one delicate, poetical, but not yet clear within itself; outwardly it yields to a power which it inwardly disclaims.

A touching little passage is related of a time in the first years, when she seemed to be better, so much so as to receive an evening visit from some female friends. They grew merry and began to dance; she remained sad and thoughtful. When they stopped, she was in the attitude of prayer. One of her intimates, observing this, began to laugh. This affected her so much, that she became cold and rigid like a corpse. For some time they did not hear her breathe, and, when she did, it was with a rattling noise. They applied mustard poultices, and used foot and hand baths; she was brought back to life, but to a state of great suffering.

She recognized as her guardian spirit, who sometimes magnetized her or removed from her neighborhood substances that were hurtful to her, her grand-mother; thus coinciding with the popular opinion that traits reappear in the third generation.

Now began still greater wonders; the second sight, numerous and various visits from spirits and so forth.

The following may be mentioned in connection with theories and experiments current among ourselves.

"A friend, who was often with her at this time, wrote to me (Kerner): When I, with my finger, touch her *on the forehead between the eyebrows*, she says each time something that bears upon the state of my soul. Some of these sentences I record.

'Keep thy soul so that thou mayst bear it in thy hands.'

'When thou comest into a world of bustle and folly, hold the Lord fast in thy heart.'

'If any seek to veil from thee thy true feeling, pray to God for grace.'

'Permit not thyself to stifle the light that springs up within thyself.'

'Think often of the cross of Jesus; go forth and embrace it.'

'As the dove found a resting-place in Noah's ark, so wilt thou, also, find a resting-place which God has appointed for thee.'"

When she was put under the care of Kerner, she had been five years in this state, and was reduced to such weakness, that she was, with difficulty, sustained from hour to hour.

He thought at first it would be best to take no notice of her magnetic states and directions, and told her he should not, but should treat her with regard to her bodily symptoms, as he would any other invalid.

"At this time she fell every evening into magnetic sleep, and gave orders about herself; to which, however, those round her no longer paid attention.

"I was now called in. I had never seen this woman, but had heard many false or perverted accounts of her condition. I must confess that I shared the evil opinion of the world as to her illness; that I advised to pay no attention to her magnetic situation, and the orders she gave in it; in her spasms, to forbear the laying of hands upon her; to deny her the support of persons of stronger nerves; in short, to do all possible to draw her out of the magnetic state, and to treat her with attention, but with absolutely none but the common medical means.

THE SEERESS OF PREVORST 107

"These views were shared by my friend, Dr. Off, of Löwenstein, who continued to treat her accordingly. But without good results. Hemorrhage, spasms, night-sweats continued. Her gums were scorbutically affected, and bled constantly; she lost all her teeth. Strengthening remedies affected her like being drawn up from her bed by force; she sank into a fear of all men, and a deadly weakness. Her death was to be wished, but it came not. Her relations, in despair, not knowing themselves what they could do with her, brought her, almost against my will, to me at Weinsberg.

"She was brought hither an image of death, perfectly emaciated, unable to raise herself. Every three or four minutes, a teaspoonful of nourishment must be given her, else she fell into faintness or convulsion. Her somnambulic situation alternated with fever, hemorrhage, and night-sweats. Every evening, about seven o'clock, she fell into magnetic sleep. She then spread out her arms, and found herself, from that moment, in a clairvoyant state; but only when she brought them back upon her breast, did she begin to speak. (Kerner mentions that her child, too, slept with its hands and feet crossed.) In this state her eyes were shut, her face calm and bright. As she fell asleep, the first night after her arrival, she asked for me, but I bade them tell her that I now, and in future, should speak to her only when awake.

"After she awoke, I went to her and declared, in brief and earnest terms, that I should pay no attention to what she said in sleep, and that her somnambulic state, which had lasted so long to the grief and trouble of her family, must now come to an end. This declaration I accompanied by an earnest appeal, designed to awaken a firm will in her to put down the excessive activity of brain that disordered her whole system. Afterwards, no address was made to her on any subject when in her sleep-waking state. She was left to lie unheeded. I pursued a homœopathic treatment of her case. But the medicines constantly produced effects opposite to what I expected. She now suffered less from spasm and somnambulism, but with increasing marks of weakness and decay. All seemed as if the end of her sufferings drew near. It was too late for the means I wished to use. Affected so variously and powerfully by magnetic means in the first years of her illness, she had now no life more, so thoroughly was the force of her own organization exhausted, but what she borrowed from others. In her now more infrequent magnetic trance, she was always seeking the true means of her cure. It was touching to see how, retiring within herself, she sought for help. The physician who had aided her so little with his drugs, must often stand abashed before this inner physician, perceiving it to be far better skilled than himself."

After some weeks forbearance, Kerner did ask her in her sleep what he should do for her. She prescribed a magnetic treatment, which was found of use. Afterwards, she described a machine, of which there is a drawing in this book, which she wished to have made for her use; it was so, and she derived benefit from it. She had indicated such a machine in the early stages of her disease, but at that time no one attended to her. By degrees she grew better under this treatment, and lived at Weinsberg, nearly two years, though in a state of great weakness, and more in the magnetic and clairvoyant than in the natural human state.

How his acquaintance with her affected the physician, he thus expresses:

"During those last months of her abode on the earth, there remained to her only the life of a sylph. I have been interested to record, not a journal of her sickness, but the mental phenomena of such an almost disembodied life. Such may cast light on the period when also our Psyche may unfold her wings, free from bodily bonds, and the hindrances of space and time. I give facts; each reader may interpret them in his own way.

"The manuals of animal magnetism and other writings have proposed many theories by which to explain such. All these are known to me. I shall make no reference to them, but only, by use of parallel facts here and there, show that the phenomena of this case recall many in which there is nothing marvellous, but which are manifestly grounded in our common existence. Such apparitions cannot too frequently, if only for moments, flash across that common existence, as electric lights from the higher world.

"Frau H. was, previous to my magnetic treatment, in so deep a somnambulic life, that she was, in fact, never rightly awake, even when she seemed to be; or rather, let us say, she was at all times more awake than others are; for it is strange to term sleep this state which is just that of the clearest wakefulness. Better to say she was immersed in the inward state.

"In this state and the consequent excitement of the nerves, she had almost wholly lost organic force, and received it only by transmission from those of stronger condition, principally from their eyes and the ends of the fingers. The atmosphere and nerve communications of others, said she, bring me the life which I need; they do not feel it; these effusions on which I live, would flow from them and be lost, if my nerves did not attract them; only in this way can I live.

"She often assured us that others did not suffer by loss of what they imparted to her; but it cannot be denied that persons were weakened by constant intercourse with her, suffered from contraction in the limbs, trembling, &c. They were weakened also in the eyes and pit of the stomach. From those related to her by blood, she could draw more benefit than from others, and, when very weak, from them only; probably on account of a natural affinity of temperament. She could not bear to have around her nervous and sick persons; those from whom she could gain nothing made her weaker.

"Even so it is remarked that flowers soon lose their beauty near the sick, and suffer peculiarly under the contact or care of some persons.

"Other physicians, beside myself, can vouch that the presence of some persons affected her as a pabulum vitæ, while, if left with certain others or alone, she was sure to grow weaker.

"From the air, too, she seemed to draw a peculiar ethereal nourishment of the same sort; she could not remain without an open window in the severest cold of winter.*

"The spirit of things, about which we have no perception, was sensible to her, and had influence on her; she showed this sense of the spirit of metals, plants, animals, and men. Imponderable existences, such as the various colors of the ray, showed distinct influences upon her. The electric fluid was visible and sensible to her when it was not to us. Yea! what is incredible! even the written words of men she could discriminate by touch."[†]

---

* Near us, this last winter, a person who suffered, and finally died, from spasms like those of the Seherin, also found relief from having the windows open, while the cold occasioned great suffering to his attendants.

[†] Facts of the same kind are asserted of late among ourselves, and believed, though "incredible."

These experiments are detailed under their several heads in the book.

From her eyes flowed a peculiar spiritual light which impressed even those who saw her for a very short time. She was in each relation more spirit than human.

Should we compare her with anything human, we would say she was as one detained at the moment of dissolution, betwixt life and death; and who is better able to discern the affairs of the world that lies before, than that behind him.

She was often in situations when one who had, like her, the power of discerning spirits, would have seen her own free from the body, which at all times enveloped it only as a light veil. She saw herself often out of the body; saw herself double. She would say, "I seem out of myself, hover above my body, and think of it as something apart from myself. But it is not a pleasant feeling, because I still sympathize with my body. If only my soul were bound more firmly to the nerve-spirit, it might be bound more closely with the nerves themselves; but the bond of my nerve-spirit is always becoming looser."

She makes a distinction between spirit as the pure intelligence; soul, the ideal of this individual man; and nerve-spirit, the dynamic of his temporal existence. Of this feeling of double identity, an invalid, now wasting under nervous disease, often speaks to me. He has it when he first awakes from sleep. Blake, the painter, whose life was almost as much a series of trances as that of our Seherin, in his designs of the Resurrection, represents spirits as rising from, or hovering over, their bodies in the same way.

Often she seemed quite freed from her body, and to have no more sense of its weight.

As to artificial culture, or dressing, (dressur,) Frau H. had nothing of it. She had learned no foreign tongue, neither history, nor geography, nor natural philosophy, nor any other of those branches now imparted to those of her sex in their schools. The Bible and hymn-book were, especially in the long years of her sickness, her only reading: her moral character was throughout blameless; she was pious without fanaticism. Even her long suffering, and the peculiar manner of it, she recognized as the grace of God; as she expresses in the following verses:

THE SEERESS OF PREVORST   III

Great God! how great is thy goodness,
To me thou hast given faith and love,
Holding me firm in the distress of my sufferings.

In the darkness of my sorrow,
I was so far led away,
As to beg for peace in speedy death.

But then came to me the mighty strong faith;
Hope came; and came eternal love;
They shut my earthly eyelids.
When, O bliss!

Dead lies my bodily frame,
But in the inmost mind a light burns up,
Such as none knows in the waking life.
Is it a light? no! but a sun of grace!

Often in the sense of her sufferings, while in the magnetic trance, she made prayers in verse, of which this is one:

Father, hear me!
Hear my prayer and supplication.
Father, I implore thee,
Let not thy child perish!
Look on my anguish, my tears.

Shed hope into my heart, and still its longing,
Father, on thee I call; have pity!
Take something from me, the sick one, the poor one.

Father, I leave thee not,
Though sickness and pain consume me.
If I the spring's light,
See only through the mist of tears,
Father, I leave thee not.

These verses lose their merit of a touching simplicity in an unrhymed translation; but they will serve to show the habitual temper of her mind.

"As I was a maker of verses," continues Dr. Kerner, "it was easy to say, Frau H. derived this talent from my magnetic influence; but she made these little verses before she came under my care." Not without deep significance was Apollo distinguished as being at once the God of poesy, of prophecy, and the medical art. Sleep-waking develops the powers of seeing, healing, and poesy. How nobly the ancients understood the inner life; how fully is it indicated in their mysteries?

I know a peasant maiden, who cannot write, but who, in the magnetic state, speaks in measured verse.

Galen was indebted to his nightly dreams for a part of his medical knowledge.

The calumnies spread about Frau H. were many and gross; this she well knew. As one day she heard so many of these as to be much affected by them, we thought she would express her feelings that night in the magnetic sleep, but she only said "they can affect my body, but not my spirit." Her mind, raised above such assaults by the consciousness of innocence, maintained its tranquillity and dwelt solely on spiritual matters.

Once in her sleep-waking she wrote thus:

> When the world declares of me
> Such cruel ill in calumny,
> And to your ears it finds a way,
> Do you believe it, yea or nay?

I answered:

> To us thou seemest true and pure,
> Let others view it as they will;
> We have our assurance still
> If our own sight can make us sure.

People of all kinds, to my great trouble, were always pressing to see her. If we refused them access to the sick room, they avenged themselves by the invention of all kinds of falsehoods.

She met all with an equal friendliness, even when it cost her bodily pain, and those who defamed her, she often defended. There came to her both good and bad men. She felt the evil in men clearly, but would not censure; lifted up a stone to cast at no sinner, but was rather likely to awake, in the faulty beings she suffered near her, faith in a spiritual life which might make them better.

Years before she was brought to me, the earth, with its atmosphere, and all that is about and upon it, human beings not excepted, was no more for her. She needed, not only a magnetizer, not only a love, an earnestness, an insight, such as scarce lies within the capacity of any man, but also what no mortal could bestow upon her, another heaven, other means of nourishment, other air than that of this earth. She belonged to the world of spirits, living here herself, as more than half spirit. She belonged to the state after death, into which she had advanced more than half way.

It is possible she might have been brought back to an adaptation for this world in the second or third year of her malady; but, in the fifth, no mode of treatment could have effected this. But by care she was aided to a greater harmony and clearness of the inward life; she enjoyed at Weinsberg, as she after said, the richest and happiest days of this life, and to us her abode here remains a point of light.

As to her outward form, we have already said it seemed but a thin veil about her spirit. She was little, her features of an oriental cast, her eye had the penetrating look of a seer's eye, which was set off by the shade of long dark eyelashes. She was a light flower that only lived on rays.

Eschenmayer writes thus of her in his "Mysteries."

"Her natural state was a mild, friendly earnestness, always disposed to prayer and devotion; her eye had a highly spiritual expression, and remained, notwithstanding her great sufferings, always bright and clear. Her look was penetrating, would quickly change in the conversation, seem to give forth sparks, and remain fixed on some one place,—this was a token that some strange apparition fettered it,—then would she resume the conversation. When I first saw her, she was in a situation which showed that her bodily life could not long endure, and that recovery to the common natural state was quite impossible. Without visible derangement of the functions, her life seemed only a wick glimmering in the socket. She was, as Kerner truly describes her, like one arrested in the act of dying and detained in the body by magnetic influences. Spirit and soul seemed often divided, and the spirit to have taken up its abode in other regions, while the soul was yet bound to the body."

I have given these extracts as being happily expressive of the relation between the physician and the clairvoyant, also of her character.

It seems to have been one of singular gentleness, and grateful piety, simple and pure, but not at all one from which we should expect extraordinary development of brain in any way; yet the excitement of her temperament from climate, scenery, the influence of traditions which evidently flowed round her, and a great constitutional impressibility did develop in her brain the germs both of poetic creation and science.

I say poetic creation, for, to my mind, the ghosts she saw were projections of herself into objective reality. The Hades she imagines is based in fact, for it is one of souls, who, having neglected their opportunities for better life, find themselves left forlorn, helpless, seeking aid from beings still ignorant and prejudiced, perhaps much below themselves in natural powers. Having forfeited their chance of direct access to God, they seek mediation from the prayers of men. But in the coloring and dress* of these ghosts, as also in their manner and mode of speech, there is a great deal which seems merely fanciful—local and peculiar.

To me, these interviews represent only prophecies of her mind; yet, considered in this way, they are, if not ghostly, spiritual facts of high beauty, and which cast light on the state of the soul after its separation from the body. Her gentle patience with them, her steady reference to a higher cause, her pure joy, when they became white in the light of happiness obtained through aspiration, are worthy of a more than half enfranchised angel.

As to the stories of mental correspondence and visits to those still engaged in this world, such as are told of her presentiment of her father's death, and connexion with him in the last moments, these are probably pure facts. Those who have sufficient strength of affection to be easily disengaged

---

*The women ghosts all wear veils, put on the way admired by the Italian poets, of whom, however, she could know nothing.

from external impressions and habits, and who dare trust their mental impulses are familiar with such.

Her invention of a language seems a simply natural motion of the mind when left to itself. The language we habitually use is so broken, and so hackneyed by ages of conventional use, that, in all deep states of being, we crave one simple and primitive in its stead. Most persons make one more or less clear from looks, tones, and symbols:—this woman, in the long leisure of her loneliness, and a mind bent upon itself, attempted to compose one of letters and words. I look upon it as no gift from without, but a growth from her own mind.

Her invention of a machine, of which she made a drawing, her power of drawing correctly her life-circle, and sun-circle, and the mathematical feeling she had of her existence, in correspondent sections of the two, are also valuable as mental facts. These figures describe her history and exemplify the position of mathematics toward the world of creative thought.

Every fact of mental existence ought to be capable of similar demonstration. I attach no especial importance to her circles:— we all live in such; all who observe themselves have the same sense of exactness and harmony in the revolutions of their destiny. But few attend to what is simple and invariable in the motions of their minds, and still fewer seek out means clearly to express them to others.

Gœthe has taken up these facts in his Wanderjahre, where he speaks of his Macaria; also, one of these persons who are compensated for bodily infirmity by a more concentrated and acute state of mind, and consequent accesses of wisdom, as being bound to a star. When she was engaged by a sense of these larger revolutions, she seemed to those near her on the earth, to be sick; when she was, in fact, lower, but better adapted to the details and variations of an earthly life, these said she was well. Macaria knew the sun and life circles, also, the lives of spirit and soul, as did the forester's daughter of Prevorst.

Her power of making little verses was one of her least gifts. Many excitable persons possess this talent at versification, as all may possess it. It is merely that a certain exaltation of feeling raises the mode of expression with it, in the same way as song differs from speech. Verses of this sort do not necessarily demand the high faculties that constitute the poet,—the creative powers. Many verses, good ones, are personal or national merely. Ballads, hymns, love-lyrics, have often no claim differing from those of common prose speech, to the title of poems, except a greater keenness and terseness of expression.

The verses of this Seherin are of the simplest character, the natural garb for the sighs or aspirations of a lonely heart. She uses the shortest words, the commonest rhymes, and the verses move us by their nature and truth alone.

The most interesting of these facts to me, are her impressions from minerals and plants. Her impressions coincide with many ancient superstitions.

The hazel woke her immediately and gave her more power, therefore the witch with her hazel wand, probably found herself superior to those around her. We may also mention, in reference to witchcraft, that Dr. K. asserts that, in certain moods of mind, she had no weight, but was upborne upon water, like cork, thus confirming the propriety, and justice of our forefathers' ordeal for witchcraft!

The laurel produced on her the highest magnetic effect, therefore the Sibyls had good reasons for wearing it on their brows.

"The laurel had on her, as on most sleep-wakers, a distinguished magnetic effect. We thus see why the priestess at Delphi, previous to uttering her oracles, shook a laurel tree, and then seated herself on a tripod covered with laurel boughs. In the temple of Æsculapius, and others, the laurel was used to excite sleep and dream."

From grapes she declared impressions, which corresponded with those caused by the wines made from them. Many kinds were given her, one after the other, by the person who raised them, and who gives a certificate as to the accuracy of her impressions, and his belief that she could not have derived them from any cause, but that of the touch.

She prescribed vegetable substances to be used in her machine, (as a kind of vapor bath,) and with good results to herself.

She enjoyed contact with minerals, deriving from those she liked a sense of concentrated life. Her impressions of the precious stones, corresponded with many superstitions of the ancients, which led to the preference of certain gems for amulets, on which they had engraved talismanic figures.

The ancients, in addition to their sense of the qualities that distinguish the diamond above all gems, venerated it as a talisman against wild beasts, poison, and evil spirits, thus expressing the natural influence of what is so enduring, bright, and pure. Townshend, speaking of the effect of gems on one of his sleep-wakers, said, she loved the diamond so much that she would lean her forehead towards it, whenever it was brought near her.

It is observable that these sleep-wakers, in their prescriptions, resemble the ancient sages, who culled only simples for the sick. But if they have this fine sense, also, for the qualities of animal and mineral substances, there is no reason why they should not turn bane to antidote, and prescribe at least homeopathic doses of poison, to restore the diseased to health.

The Seherin ascribed different states to the right and left sides of every body, even of the lady moon. The left is most impressible. Query: Is this the reason why the left hand has been, by the custom of nations, so almost disused, because the heart is on the left side?

She also saw different sights in the left from the right eye. In the left, the bodily state of the person; in the right, his real or destined self, how often unknown to himself, almost always obscured or perverted by his present ignorance or mistake. She had also the gift of second sight. She saw the coffins of those about to die. She saw in mirrors, cups of water; in soap-bubbles, the coming future.

We are here reminded of many beautiful superstitions and legends; of the secret pool in which the daring may, at mid-moon of night, read the future; of the magic globe, on whose pure surface Britomart sees her future love, whom she must seek, arrayed in knightly armor, through a difficult and hostile world.

> A looking-glass, right wondrously aguized,
> Whose virtues through the wyde world soon were solemnized.
> It vertue had to show in perfect sight,
> Whatever thing was in the world contayned,
> Betwixt the lowest earth and hevens hight;
> So that it to the looker appertayned,
> Whatever foe had wrought, or friend had fayned,

SUMMER ON THE LAKES

Herein discovered was, ne ought mote pas,
  Ne ought in secret from the same remayned;
Forthy it round and hollow shaped was,
Like to the world itselfe, and seemed a World of Glas.
Faerie Queene, Book III.

Such mirrors had Cornelius Agrippa and other wizards. The soap-bubble is such a globe; only one had need of second sight or double sight to see the pictures on so transitory a mirror. Perhaps it is some vague expectation of such wonders, that makes us so fond of blowing them in childish years. But, perhaps, it is rather as a prelude to the occupation of our lives, blowing bubbles where all things may be seen, that, "to the looker appertain," if we can keep them long enough or look quick enough.

In short, were this biography of no other value, it would be most interesting as showing how the floating belief of nations, always no doubt shadowing forth in its imperfect fashion the poetic facts with their scientific exposition, is found to grow up anew in a simple, but high-wrought nature.

The fashioning spirit, working upwards from the clod to man, proffers as its last, highest essay, the brain of man. In the lowest zoöphyte it aimed at this; some faint rudiments may there be discerned: but only in man has it perfected that immense galvanic battery that can be loaded from above, below, and around;—that engine, not only of perception, but of conception and consecutive thought,—whose right hand is memory, whose life is idea, the crown of nature, the platform from which spirit takes wing.

Yet, as gradation is the beautiful secret of nature, and the fashioning spirit, which loves to develop and transcend, loves no less to moderate, to modulate, and harmonize, it did not mean by thus drawing man onward to the next state of existence, to destroy his fitness for this. It did not mean to destroy his sympathies with the mineral, vegetable, and animal realms, of whose components he is in great part composed; which were the preface to his being, of whom he is to take count, whom he should govern as a reasoning head of a perfectly arranged body. He was meant to be the historian, the philosopher, the poet, the king of this world, no less than the prophet of the next.

THE SEERESS OF PREVORST 119

These functions should be in equipoise, and when they are not, when we see excess either on the natural (so called as distinguished from the spiritual,) or the spiritual side, we feel that the law is transgressed. And, if it be the greatest sorrow to see brain merged in body, to see a man more hands or feet than head, so that we feel he might, with propriety, be on all fours again, or even crawl like the serpent; it is also sad to see the brain, too much excited on some one side, which we call madness, or even unduly and prematurely, so as to destroy in its bloom, the common human existence of the person, as in the case before us, and others of the poetical and prophetical existence.

We would rather minds should foresee less and see more surely, that death should ensue by gentler gradation, and the brain be the governor and interpreter, rather than the destroyer, of the animal life. But, in cases like this, where the animal life is prematurely broken up, and the brain prematurely exercised, we may as well learn what we can from it, and believe that the glimpses thus caught, if not as precious as the full view, are bright with the same light, and open to the same scene.

There is a family character about all the German ghosts. We find the same features in these stories as in those related by Jung Stilling and others. They bear the same character as the pictures by the old masters, of a deep and simple piety. She stands before as, this piety, in a full, high-necked robe, a simple, hausfrauish cap, a clear, straightforward blue eye. These are no terrible, gloomy ghosts with Spanish mantle or Italian dagger. We feel quite at home with them, and sure of their good faith.

To the Seherin, they were a real society, constantly inspiring good thoughts. The reference to them in these verses, written in her journal shortly before her death, is affecting, and shows her deep sense of their reality. She must have felt that she had been a true friend to them, by refusing always, as she did, requests she thought wrong, and referring them to a Saviour.

> Farewell, my friends,
> All farewell,
> God bless you for your love—
> Bless you for your goodness.
>   All farewell!

And you, how shall I name you?
    Who have so saddened me,
I will name you also—Friends;
You have been discipline to me.
    Farewell! farewell!

Farewell! you my dear ones,
Soon will you know*
How hard have been my sufferings
    In the Pilgrim land.
        Farewell!

    Let it not grieve you,
That my woes find an end;
    Farewell, dear ones,
Till the second meeting;
    Farewell! Farewell!

In this journal her thoughts dwell much upon those natural ties which she was not permitted to enjoy. She thought much of her children, and often fancied she had saw the one who had died, growing in the spirit land. Any allusion to them called a sweet smile on her face when in her trance.

Other interesting poems are records of these often beautiful visions, especially of that preceding her own death; the address to her life-circle, the thought of which is truly great, (this was translated in the Dublin Magazine,) and descriptions of her earthly state as an imprisonment. The story of her life, though stained like others, by partialities, and prejudices, which were not justly distinguished from what was altogether true and fair, is a poem of so pure a music, presents such gentle and holy images, that we sympathize fully in the love and gratitude Kerner and his friends felt towards her, as the friend of their best life. She was a St. Theresa in her way.

His address to her, with which his volume closes, may thus be translated in homely guise. In the original it has no merit,

---

* The physician thought she here referred to the examination of her body that would take place after her death. The brain was found to be sound, though there were marks of great disease elsewhere.

THE SEERESS OF PREVORST 121

except as uttering his affectionate and reverent feeling towards his patient, the peasant girl,—"the sick one, the poor one." But we like to see how, from the mouths of babes and sucklings, praise may be so perfected as to command this reverence from the learned and worldly-wise.

> Farewell; the debt I owe thee
>   Ever in heart I bear;
> My soul sees, since I know thee,
>   The spirit depths so clear.
>
> Whether in light or shade,
>   Thy soul now dwelling hath;
> Be, if my faith should fade,
>   The guide upon my path.
>
> Livest thou in mutual power,
>   With spirits blest and bright,
> O be, in death's dark hour,
>   My help to heaven's light.
>
> Upon thy grave is growing,
>   The plant by thee beloved,*
> St. Johns-wort golden glowing,
>   Like St. John's thoughts of love.
>
> Witness of sacred sorrow,
>   Whene'er thou meet'st my eye,
> O flower, from thee I borrow,
>   Thoughts for eternity.
>
> Farewell! the woes of earth
>   No more my soul affright;
> Who knows their temporal birth
>   Can easy bear their weight.

I do confess this is a paraphrase, not a translation, also, that in the other extracts, I have taken liberties with the original for the sake of condensation, and clearness. What I have written

---

* She received great benefit from decoctions of this herb, and often prescribed it to others.

must be received as a slight and conversational account of the work.

Two or three other remarks, I had forgotten, may come in here.

The glances at the spirit-world have none of that large or universal significance, none of that value from philosophical analogy, that is felt in any picture by Swedenborg, or Dante, of permanent relations. The mind of the forester's daughter was exalted and rapidly developed; still the wild cherry tree bore no orange; she was not transformed into a philosophic or poetic organization.

Yet many of her untaught notions remind of other seers of a larger scope. She, too, receives this life as one link in a long chain; and thinks that immediately after death, the meaning of the past life will appear to us as one word.

She tends to a belief in the aromal state, and in successive existences on this earth; for behind persons she often saw another being, whether their form in the state before or after this, I know not; behind a woman a man, equipped for fight, and so forth. Her perception of character, even in cases of those whom she saw only as they passed her window, was correct.

Kerner aims many a leaden sarcasm at those who despise his credulity. He speaks of those sages as men whose brain is a glass table, incapable of receiving the electric spark, and who will not believe, because, in their mental isolation, they are incapable of feeling these facts.

Certainly, I think he would be dull, who could see no meaning or beauty in the history of the forester's daughter of Prevorst. She lived but nine-and-twenty years, yet, in that time, had traversed a larger portion of the field of thought than all her race before, in their many and long lives.

Of the abuses to which all these magical implements are prone, I have an instance, since leaving Milwaukie, in the journal of a man equally sincere, but not equally inspired, led from Germany hither by signs and wonders, as a commissioned agent of Providence, who, indeed, has arranged every detail of his life with a minuteness far beyond the promised care of the sparrow. He props himself by spiritual aid from a maiden now in this country, who was once an attendant on the Seeress, and who seems to have caught from her the contagion of trance, but not its revelations.

Do not blame me that I have written so much about Germany and Hades, while you were looking for news of the West. Here, on the pier, I see disembarking the Germans, the Norwegians, the Swedes, the Swiss. Who knows how much of old legendary lore, of modern wonder, they have already planted amid the Wisconsin forests? Soon, soon their tales of the origin of things, and the Providence which rules them, will be so mingled with those of the Indian, that the very oak trees will not know them apart,—will not know whether itself be a Runic, a Druid, or a Winnebago oak.

Some seeds of all growths that have ever been known in this world might, no doubt, already be found in these Western wilds, if we had the power to call them to life.

I saw, in the newspaper, that the American Tract Society boasted of their agents' having exchanged, at a Western cabin door, tracts for the Devil on Two Sticks, and then burnt that more entertaining than edifying volume. No wonder, though, they study it there. Could one but have the gift of reading the dreams dreamed by men of such various birth, various history, various mind, it would afford much more extensive amusement than did the chambers of one Spanish city!

Could I but have flown at night through such mental experiences, instead of being shut up in my little bedroom at the Milwaukie boarding house, this chapter would have been worth reading. As it is, let us hasten to a close.

Had I been rich in money, I might have built a house, or set up in business, during my fortnight's stay at Milwaukie, matters move on there at so rapid a rate. But, being only rich in curiosity, I was obliged to walk the streets and pick up what I could in casual intercourse. When I left the street, indeed, and walked on the bluffs, or sat beside the lake in their shadow, my mind was rich in dreams congenial to the scene, some time to be realized, though not by me.

A boat was left, keel up, half on the sand, half in the water, swaying with each swell of the lake. It gave a picturesque grace to that part of the shore, as the only image of inaction—only object of a pensive character to be seen. Near this I sat, to dream my dreams and watch the colors of the lake, changing hourly, till the sun sank. These hours yielded impulses, wove webs, such as life will not again afford.

Returning to the boarding house, which was also a boarding school, we were sure to be greeted by gay laughter.

This school was conducted by two girls of nineteen and seventeen years; their pupils were nearly as old as themselves; the relation seemed very pleasant between them. The only superiority—that of superior knowledge—was sufficient to maintain authority—all the authority that was needed to keep daily life in good order.

In the West, people are not respected merely because they are old in years; people there have not time to keep up appearances in that way; when they cease to have a real advantage in wisdom, knowledge, or enterprise, they must stand back, and let those who are oldest in character "go ahead," however few years they may count. There are no banks of established respectability in which to bury the talent there; no napkin of precedent in which to wrap it. What cannot be made to pass current, is not esteemed coin of the realm.

To the windows of this house, where the daughter of a famous "Indian fighter," i. e. fighter against the Indians, was learning French and the piano, came wild, tawny figures, offering for sale their baskets of berries. The boys now, instead of brandishing the tomahawk, tame their hands to pick raspberries.

Here the evenings were much lightened by the gay chat of one of the party, who, with the excellent practical sense of mature experience, and the kindest heart, united a naiveté and innocence such as I never saw in any other who had walked so long life's tangled path. Like a child, she was everywhere at home, and like a child, received and bestowed entertainment from all places, all persons. I thanked her for making me laugh, as did the sick and poor, whom she was sure to find out in her briefest sojourn in any place, for more substantial aid. Happy are those who never grieve, and so often aid and enliven their fellow men!

This scene, however, I was not sorry to exchange for the much celebrated beauties of the Island of Mackinaw.

Chapter VI

MACKINAW

LATE AT NIGHT we reached this island, so famous for its beauty, and to which I proposed a visit of some length. It was the last week in August, when a large representation from the Chippewa and Ottowa tribes are here to receive their annual payments from the American government. As their habits make travelling easy and inexpensive to them, neither being obliged to wait for steamboats, or write to see whether hotels are full, they come hither by thousands, and those thousands in families, secure of accommodation on the beach, and food from the lake, to make a long holiday out of the occasion. There were near two thousand encamped on the island already, and more arriving every day.

As our boat came in, the captain had some rockets let off. This greatly excited the Indians, and their yells and wild cries resounded along the shore. Except for the momentary flash of the rockets, it was perfectly dark, and my sensations as I walked with a stranger to a strange hotel, through the midst of these shrieking savages, and heard the pants and snorts of the departing steamer, which carried away all my companions, were somewhat of the dismal sort; though it was pleasant, too, in the way that everything strange is; everything that breaks in upon the routine that so easily incrusts us.

I had reason to expect a room to myself at the hotel, but found none, and was obliged to take up my rest in the common parlor and eating-room, a circumstance which ensured my being an early riser.

With the first rosy streak, I was out among my Indian neighbors, whose lodges honey-combed the beautiful beach, that curved away in long, fair outline on either side the house. They were already on the alert, the children creeping out from beneath the blanket door of the lodge; the women pounding corn in their rude mortars, the young men playing on their pipes. I had been much amused, when the strain proper to the Winnebago courting flute was played to me on another instrument, at any one fancying it a melody; but now, when I heard the notes in their true tone and time, I thought it not unworthy comparison, in its graceful sequence, and the light flourish, at the close, with the sweetest bird-songs; and this, like the bird-song, is only practised to allure a mate. The Indian, become a citizen and a husband, no more thinks of playing the flute than one of the "settled down" members of our society would of choosing the "purple light of love" as dye-stuff for a surtout.

Mackinaw has been fully described by able pens, and I can only add my tribute to the exceeding beauty of the spot and its position. It is charming to be on an island so small that you can sail round it in an afternoon, yet large enough to admit of long secluded walks through its gentle groves. You can go round it in your boat; or, on foot, you can tread its narrow beach, resting, at times, beneath the lofty walls of stone, richly wooded, which rise from it in various architectural forms. In this stone, caves are continually forming, from the action of the atmosphere; one of these is quite deep, and with a fragment left at its mouth, wreathed with little creeping plants, that looks, as you sit within, like a ruined pillar.

The arched rock surprised me, much as I had heard of it, from the perfection of the arch. It is perfect whether you look up through it from the lake, or down through it to the transparent waters. We both ascended and descended, no very easy matter, the steep and crumbling path, and rested at the summit, beneath the trees, and at the foot upon the cool mossy stones beside the lapsing wave. Nature has carefully decorated all this architecture with shrubs that take root within the crevices, and small creeping vines. These natural ruins may vie for beautiful effect with the remains of European grandeur, and have, beside, a charm as of a playful mood in nature.

The sugar-loaf rock is a fragment in the same kind as the pine rock we saw in Illinois. It has the same air of a helmet, as seen from an eminence at the side, which you descend by a long and steep path. The rock itself may be ascended by the bold and agile. Half way up is a niche, to which those, who are neither, can climb by a ladder. A very handsome young officer

ARCHED ROCK FROM THE WATER

and lady who were with us did so, and then, facing round, stood there side by side, looking in the niche, if not like saints or angels wrought by pious hands in stone, as romantically, if not as holily, worthy the gazer's eye.

The woods which adorn the central ridge of the island are very full in foliage, and, in August, showed the tender green and pliant leaf of June elsewhere. They are rich in beautiful mosses and the wild raspberry.

From Fort Holmes, the old fort, we had the most commanding view of the lake and straits, opposite shores, and fair islets. Mackinaw, itself, is best seen from the water. Its peculiar shape is supposed to have been the origin of its name, Michilimackinac, which means the Great Turtle. One person whom I saw, wished to establish another etymology, which he fancied to be more refined; but, I doubt not, this is the true one, both because the shape might suggest such a name, and that the existence of an island in this commanding position, which did so, would seem a significant fact to the Indians. For Henry gives the details of peculiar worship paid to the Great Turtle, and the oracles received from this extraordinary Apollo of the Indian Delphos.

It is crowned most picturesquely, by the white fort, with its gay flag. From this, on one side, stretches the town. How pleasing a sight, after the raw, crude, staring assemblage of houses, everywhere else to be met in this country, an old French town, mellow in its coloring, and with the harmonious effect of a slow growth, which assimilates, naturally, with objects round it. The people in its streets, Indian, French, half-breeds, and others, walked with a leisure step, as of those who live a life of taste and inclination, rather than of the hard press of business, as in American towns elsewhere.

On the other side, along the fair, curving beach, below the white houses scattered on the declivity, clustered the Indian lodges, with their amber brown matting, so soft, and bright of hue, in the late afternoon sun. The first afternoon I was there, looking down from a near height, I felt that I never wished to see a more fascinating picture. It was an hour of the deepest serenity; bright blue and gold, rich shadows. Every moment the sunlight fell more mellow. The Indians were grouped and scattered among the lodges; the women preparing food, in the kettle or frying-pan, over the many small fires; the children, half-naked, wild as little goblins, were playing both in and out of the water. Here and there lounged a young girl, with a baby at her back, whose bright eyes glanced, as if born into a world of courage and of joy, instead of ignominious servitude and slow decay. Some girls were cutting wood, a little way from me, talking and laughing, in the low musical tone, so charming in the Indian women. Many bark canoes were upturned upon the beach, and, by that light, of almost the same amber as the lodges. Others, coming in, their square sails set, and with almost arrowy speed, though heavily laden with dusky forms, and all the apparatus of their household. Here and there a sail-boat glided by, with a different, but scarce less pleasing motion.

It was a scene of ideal loveliness, and these wild forms adorned it, as looking so at home in it. All seemed happy, and they were happy that day, for they had no firewater to madden them, as it was Sunday, and the shops were shut.

From my window, at the boarding house, my eye was constantly attracted by these picturesque groups. I was never tired of seeing the canoes come in, and the new arrivals set up their temporary dwellings. The women ran to set up the tent-poles, and spread the mats on the ground. The men brought the chests, kettles, &c.; the mats were then laid on the outside, the cedar boughs strewed on the ground, the blanket hung up for a door, and all was completed in less than twenty minutes. Then they began to prepare the night meal, and to learn of their neighbors the news of the day.

The habit of preparing food out of doors, gave all the gipsy charm and variety to their conduct. Continually I wanted Sir Walter Scott to have been there. If such romantic sketches were suggested to him, by the sight of a few gipsies, not a group near one of these fires but would have furnished him material for a separate canvass. I was so taken up with the spirit of the scene, that I could not follow out the stories suggested by these weather-beaten, sullen, but eloquent figures.

They talked a great deal, and with much variety of gesture, so that I often had a good guess at the meaning of their discourse. I saw that, whatever the Indian may be among the whites, he is anything but taciturn with his own people. And he often would declaim, or narrate at length, as indeed it is obvious, that these tribes possess great power that way, if only from the fables taken from their stores, by Mr. Schoolcraft.

I liked very much to walk or sit among them. With the women I held much communication by signs. They are almost invariably coarse and ugly, with the exception of their eyes, with a peculiarly awkward gait, and forms bent by burthens. This gait, so different from the steady and noble step of the men, marks the inferior position they occupy. I had heard much eloquent contradiction of this. Mrs. Schoolcraft had maintained to a friend, that they were in fact as nearly on a par with their husbands as the white woman with hers. "Although," said she, "on account of inevitable causes, the Indian woman is subjected to many hardships of a peculiar nature, yet her position, compared with that of the man, is higher and freer than that of the white woman. Why will people look only on one side? They either exalt the Red man into a Demigod or degrade him into a beast. They say that he compels his wife to do all the drudgery, while he does nothing but hunt and amuse himself; forgetting that, upon his activity and power of endurance as a hunter, depends the support of his family; that this is labor of the most fatiguing kind, and that it is absolutely necessary that he should keep his frame unbent by burdens and unworn by toil, that he may be able to obtain the means of subsistence. I have witnessed scenes of conjugal and parental love in the Indian's wigwam from which I have often, often thought the educated white man, proud of his superior civilization, might learn an useful lesson. When he returns from hunting, worn out with fatigue, having tasted nothing since dawn, his wife, if she is a good wife, will take off his moccasons and replace them with dry ones, and will prepare his game for their repast, while his children will climb upon him, and he will caress them with all the tenderness of a woman; and in the evening the Indian wigwam is the scene of the purest domestic pleasures. The father will relate for the amusement of the wife, and for the instruction of the children, all the events of the day's hunt, while they will treasure up every word that falls, and thus learn the theory of the art, whose practice is to be the occupation of their lives."

Mrs. Grant speaks thus of the position of woman amid the Mohawk Indians:

"Lady Mary Montague says, that the court of Vienna was the paradise of old women, and that there is no other place in the world where a woman past fifty excites the least interest. Had her travels extended to the interior of North America, she would have seen another instance of this inversion of the common mode of thinking. Here a woman never was of consequence, till she had a son old enough to fight the battles of his country. From that date she held a superior rank in society; was allowed to live at ease, and even called to consultations on national affairs. In savage and warlike countries, the reign of beauty is very short, and its influence comparatively limited. The girls in childhood had a very pleasing appearance; but excepting their fine hair, eyes, and teeth, every external grace was soon banished by perpetual drudgery, carrying burdens too heavy to be borne, and other slavish employments considered beneath the dignity of the men. These walked before erect and graceful, decked with ornaments which set off to advantage the symmetry of their well-formed persons, while the poor women followed, meanly attired, bent under the weight of the children and utensils, which they carried everywhere with them, and disfigured and degraded by ceaseless toils. They were very early married, for a Mohawk had no other servant but his wife, and, whenever he commenced hunter, it was requisite he should have some one to carry his load, cook his kettle, make his moccasons, and, above all, produce the young warriors who were to succeed him in the honors of the chase and of the tomahawk. Wherever man is a mere hunter, woman is a mere slave. It is domestic intercourse that softens man, and elevates woman; and of that there can be but little, where the employments and amusements are not in common; the ancient Caledonians honored the fair; but then it is to be observed, they were fair huntresses, and moved in the light of their beauty to the hill of roes; and the culinary toils were entirely left to the rougher sex. When the young warrior made his appearance, it softened the cares of his mother, who well knew that, when he grew up, every deficiency in tenderness to his wife would be made up in superabundant duty and affection to her. If it were possible to carry filial veneration to excess, it was done here; for all other charities were absorbed in it. I wonder this system of depressing the sex in their early years, to exalt them when all their juvenile attractions were flown, and when mind alone can distinguish them, has not occurred to our modern reformers. The Mohawks took good care not to admit their women to share their prerogatives, till they approved themselves good wives and mothers."

The observations of women upon the position of woman are always more valuable than those of men; but, of these two, Mrs. Grant's seems much nearer the truth than Mrs. Schoolcraft's, because, though her opportunities for observation did not bring her so close, she looked more at both sides to find the truth.

Carver, in his travels among the Winnebagoes, describes two queens, one nominally so, like Queen Victoria; the other invested with a genuine royalty, springing from her own conduct.

In the great town of the Winnebagoes, he found a queen presiding over the tribe, instead of a sachem. He adds, that, in some tribes, the descent is given to the female line in preference to the male, that is, a sister's son will succeed to the authority, rather than a brother's son.

The position of this Winnebago queen, reminded me forcibly of Queen Victoria's.

"She sat in the council, but only asked a few questions, or gave some trifling directions in matters relative to the state, for women are never allowed to sit in their councils, except they happen to be invested with the supreme authority, and then it is not customary for them to make any formal speeches, as the chiefs do. She was a very ancient woman, small in stature, and not much distinguished by her dress from several young women that attended her. These, her attendants, seemed greatly pleased whenever I showed any tokens of respect to their queen, especially when I saluted her, which I frequently did to acquire her favor."

The other was a woman, who being taken captive, found means to kill her captor, and make her escape, and the tribe were so struck with admiration at the courage and calmness she displayed on the occasion, as to make her chieftainess in her own right.

Notwithstanding the homage paid to women, and the consequence allowed her in some cases, it is impossible to look upon the Indian women, without feeling that they *do* occupy a lower place than women among the nations of European civilization. The habits of drudgery expressed in their form and gesture, the soft and wild but melancholy expression of their eye, reminded me of the tribe mentioned by Mackenzie, where the women destroy their female children, whenever they have a good opportunity; and of the eloquent reproaches addressed by the Paraguay woman to her mother, that she had not, in the same way, saved her from the anguish and weariness of her lot.

More weariness than anguish, no doubt, falls to the lot of most of these women. They inherit submission, and the minds of the generality accommodate themselves more or less to any posture. Perhaps they suffer less than their white sisters, who have more aspiration and refinement, with little power of self-sustenance. But their place is certainly lower, and their share of the human inheritance less.

Their decorum and delicacy are striking, and show that when these are native to the mind, no habits of life make any difference. Their whole gesture is timid, yet self-possessed. They used to crowd round me, to inspect little things I had to show them, but never press near; on the contrary, would reprove and keep off the children. Anything they took from my hand, was held with care, then shut or folded, and returned with an air of lady-like precision. They would not stare, however curious they might be, but cast sidelong glances.

A locket that I wore, was an object of untiring interest; they seemed to regard it as a talisman. My little sun-shade was still more fascinating to them; apparently they had never before seen one. For an umbrella they entertain profound regard, probably looking upon it as the most luxurious superfluity a person can possess, and therefore a badge of great wealth. I used to see an old squaw, whose sullied skin and coarse, tanned locks, told that she had braved sun and storm, without a doubt or care, for sixty years at the least, sitting gravely at the door of her lodge, with an old green umbrella over her head, happy for hours together in the dignified shade. For her happiness pomp came not, as it so often does, too late; she received it with grateful enjoyment.

One day, as I was seated on one of the canoes, a woman came and sat beside me, with her baby in its cradle set up at her feet. She asked me by a gesture, to let her take my sun-shade, and then to show her how to open it. Then she put it into her baby's hand, and held it over its head, looking at me the while with a sweet, mischievous laugh, as much as to say, "you carry a thing that is only fit for a baby;" her pantomime was very pretty. She, like the other women, had a glance, and shy, sweet expression in the eye; the men have a steady gaze.

That noblest and loveliest of modern Preux, Lord Edward Fitzgerald, who came through Buffalo to Detroit and Mackinaw, with Brant, and was adopted into the Bear tribe by the name of Eghnidal, was struck, in the same way, by the delicacy of manners in the women. He says, "Notwithstanding the life they lead, which would make most women rough and masculine, they are as soft, meek and modest, as the best brought up girls in England. Somewhat coquettish too! Imagine the manners of Mimi in a poor *squaw*, that has been carrying packs in the woods all her life."

McKenney mentions that the young wife, during the short bloom of her beauty, is an object of homage and tenderness to her husband. One Indian woman, the Flying Pigeon, a beautiful, an excellent woman, of whom he gives some particulars, is an instance of the power uncommon characters will always exert of breaking down the barriers custom has erected round them. She captivated by her charms, and inspired with reverence for her character, her husband and son. The simple praise with which the husband indicates the religion, the judgment, and the generosity he saw in her, are as satisfying as Count Zinzendorf's more labored eulogium on his "noble consort." The conduct of her son, when, many years after her death, he saw her picture at Washington, is unspeakably affecting. Catlin gives anecdotes of the grief of a chief for the loss of a daughter, and the princely gifts he offers in exchange for her portrait, worthy not merely of European, but of Troubadour sentiment. It is also evident that, as Mrs. Schoolcraft says, the women have great power at home. It can never be otherwise, men being dependent upon them for the comfort of their lives. Just so among ourselves, wives who are neither esteemed nor loved by their husbands, have great power over their conduct by the friction of every day, and over the formation of their opinions by the daily opportunities so close a relation affords, of perverting testimony and instilling doubts. But these sentiments should not come in brief flashes, but burn as a steady flame, then there would be more women worthy to inspire them. This power is good for nothing, unless the woman be wise to use it aright. Has the Indian, has the white woman, as noble a feeling of life and its uses, as religious a self-respect, as worthy a field of thought and action, as man? If not, the white woman, the Indian woman, occupies an inferior position to that of man. It is not so much a question of power, as of privilege.

The men of these subjugated tribes, now accustomed to drunkenness and every way degraded, bear but a faint impress of the lost grandeur of the race. They are no longer strong, tall, or finely proportioned. Yet as you see them stealing along a height, or striding boldly forward, they remind you of what *was* majestic in the red man.

On the shores of lake Superior, it is said, if you visit them at home, you may still see a remnant of the noble blood. The Pillagers—(Pilleurs)—a band celebrated by the old travellers, are still existant there.

"Still some, 'the eagles of their tribe,' may rush."

I have spoken of the hatred felt by the white man for the Indian: with white women it seems to amount to disgust, to loathing. How I could endure the dirt, the peculiar smell of the Indians, and their dwellings, was a great marvel in the eyes of my lady acquaintance; indeed, I wonder why they did not quite give me up, as they certainly looked on me with great distaste for it. "Get you gone, you Indian dog," was the felt, if not the breathed, expression towards the hapless owners of the soil. All their claims, all their sorrows quite forgot, in abhorrence of their dirt, their tawny skins, and the vices the whites have taught them.

A person who had seen them during great part of a life, expressed his prejudices to me with such violence, that I was no longer surprised that the Indian children threw sticks at him, as he passed. A lady said, "do what you will for them, they will be ungrateful. The savage cannot be washed out of them. Bring up an Indian child and see if you can attach it to you." The next moment, she expressed, in the presence of one of those children whom she was bringing up, loathing at the odor left by one of her people, and one of the most respected, as he passed through the room. When the child is grown she will consider it basely ungrateful not to love her, as it certainly will not; and this will be cited as an instance of the impossibility of attaching the Indian.

Whether the Indian could, by any efforts of love and intelligence from the white man, have been civilized and made a valuable ingredient in the new state, I will not say; but this we are sure of; the French Catholics, at least, did not harm them, nor disturb their minds merely to corrupt them. The French they loved. But the stern Presbyterian, with his dogmas and his task-work, the city circle and the college, with their niggard concessions and unfeeling stare, have never tried the experiment. It has not been tried. Our people and our government have sinned alike against the first-born of the soil, and if they are the fated agents of a new era, they have done nothing—have invoked no god to keep them sinless while they do the hest of fate.

Worst of all, when they invoke the holy power only to mask their iniquity; when the felon trader, who, all the week, has been besotting and degrading the Indian with rum mixed with red pepper, and damaged tobacco, kneels with him on Sunday before a common altar, to tell the rosary which recalls the thought of him crucified for love of suffering men, and to listen to sermons in praise of "purity"!!

My savage friends, cries the old fat priest, you must, above all things, aim at *purity*.

Oh, my heart swelled when I saw them in a Christian church. Better their own dog-feasts and bloody rites than such mockery of that other faith.

"The dog," said an Indian, "was once a spirit; he has fallen for his sin, and was given by the Great Spirit, in this shape, to man, as his most intelligent companion. Therefore we sacrifice it in highest honor to our friends in this world,—to our protecting geniuses in another."

There was religion in that thought. The white man sacrifices his own brother, and to Mammon, yet he turns in loathing from the dog-feast.

RECEPTION OF INDIAN CHIEFS 137

"You say," said the Indian of the South to the missionary, "that Christianity is pleasing to God. How can that be?—Those men at Savannah are Christians."

Yes! slave-drivers and Indian traders are called Christians, and the Indian is to be deemed less like the Son of Mary than they! Wonderful is the deceit of man's heart!

I have not, on seeing something of them in their own haunts, found reason to change the sentiments expressed in the following lines, when a deputation of the Sacs and Foxes visited Boston in 1837, and were, by one person at least, received in a dignified and courteous manner.

Governor Everett Receiving the Indian Chiefs,

NOVEMBER, 1837.

Who says that Poesy is on the wane,
And that the Muses tune their lyres in vain?
'Mid all the treasures of romantic story,
When thought was fresh and fancy in her glory,
Has ever Art found out a richer theme,
More dark a shadow, or more soft a gleam,
Than fall upon the scene, sketched carelessly,
In the newspaper column of to-day?

American romance is somewhat stale.
Talk of the hatchet, and the faces pale,
Wampum and calumets and forests dreary,
Once so attractive, now begins to weary.
Uncas and Magawisca please us still,
Unreal, yet idealized with skill;
But every poetaster scribbling witling,
From the majestic oak his stylus whittling,
Has helped to tire us, and to make us fear
The monotone in which so much we hear
Of "stoics of the wood," and "men without a tear."

Yet Nature, ever buoyant, ever young,
If let alone, will sing as erst she sung;
The course of circumstance gives back again
The Picturesque, erewhile pursued in vain;
Shows us the fount of Romance is not wasted—
The lights and shades of contrast not exhausted.

Shorn of his strength, the Samson now must sue
   For fragments from the feast his fathers gave,
The Indian dare not claim what is his due,
   But as a boon his heritage must crave;
His stately form shall soon be seen no more
Through all his father's land, th' Atlantic shore,
Beneath the sun, to *us* so kind, *they* melt,
More heavily each day our rule is felt;
The tale is old,—we do as mortals must:
Might makes right here, but God and Time are just.

So near the drama hastens to its close,
On this last scene awhile your eyes repose;
The polished Greek and Scythian meet again,
The ancient life is lived by modern men—
The savage through our busy cities walks,—
He in his untouched grandeur silent stalks.
Unmoved by all our gaieties and shows,
Wonder nor shame can touch him as he goes;
He gazes on the marvels we have wrought,
But knows the models from whence all was brought;
In God's first temples he has stood so oft,
And listened to the natural organ loft—
Has watched the eagle's flight, the muttering thunder heard,
Art cannot move him to a wondering word;
Perhaps he sees that all this luxury
Brings less food to the mind than to the eye;
Perhaps a simple sentiment has brought
More to him than your arts had ever taught.
What are the petty triumphs *Art* has given,
To eyes familiar with the naked heaven?

All has been seen—dock, railroad, and canal,
Fort, market, bridge, college, and arsenal,
Asylum, hospital, and cotton mill,
The theatre, the lighthouse, and the jail.
The Braves each novelty, reflecting, saw,
And now and then growled out the earnest *yaw*.
And now the time is come, 'tis understood,
When, having seen and thought so much, a *talk* may do
      some good.

A well-dressed mob have thronged the sight to greet,
And motley figures throng the spacious street;

RECEPTION OF INDIAN CHIEFS

Majestical and calm through all they stride,
Wearing the blanket with a monarch's pride;
The gazers stare and shrug, but can't deny
Their noble forms and blameless symmetry.

If the Great Spirit their morale has slighted,
And wigwam smoke their mental culture blighted,
Yet the physique, at least, perfection reaches,
In wilds where neither Combe nor Spursheim teaches;
Where whispering trees invite man to the chase,
And bounding deer allure him to the race.

Would thou hadst seen it! That dark, stately band,
Whose ancestors enjoyed all this fair land,
Whence they, by force or fraud, were made to flee,
Are brought, the white man's victory to see.
Can kind emotions in their proud hearts glow,
As through these realms, now decked by Art, they go?
The church, the school, the railroad and the mart—
Can these a pleasure to their minds impart?
All once was theirs—earth, ocean, forest, sky—
How can they joy in what now meets the eye?
Not yet Religion has unlocked the soul,
Nor Each has learned to glory in the Whole!

Must they not think, so strange and sad their lot,
That they by the Great Spirit are forgot?
From the far border to which they are driven,
They might look up in trust to the clear heaven;
But *here*—what tales doth every object tell
Where Massasoit sleeps—where Philip fell!

We take our turn, and the Philosopher
Sees through the clouds a hand which cannot err,
An unimproving race, with all their graces
And all their vices, must resign their places;
And Human Culture rolls its onward flood
Over the broad plains steeped in Indian blood.

Such thoughts steady our faith; yet there will rise
Some natural tears into the calmest eyes—
Which gaze where forest princes haughty go,
Made for a gaping crowd a raree show.

SUMMER ON THE LAKES

But *this* a scene seems where, in courtesy,
The pale face with the forest prince could vie,
For One presided, who, for tact and grace,
In any age had held an honored place,—
In Beauty's own dear day, had shone a polished Phidian vase!

Oft have I listened to his accents bland,
    And owned the magic of his silvery voice,
In all the graces which life's arts demand,
    Delighted by the justness of his choice,
Not his the stream of lavish, fervid thought,—
The rhetoric by passion's magic wrought;
Not his the massive style, the lion port,
Which with the granite class of mind assort;
But, in a range of excellence his own,
With all the charms to soft persuasion known,
Amid our busy people we admire him—"elegant and lone."

He scarce needs words, so exquisite the skill
Which modulates the tones to do his will,
That the mere sound enough would charm the ear,
And lap in its Elysium all who hear.
The intellectual paleness of his cheek,
    The heavy eyelids and slow, tranquil smile,
The well cut lips from which the graces speak,
    Fit him alike to win or to beguile;
Then those words so well chosen, fit, though few,
Their linked sweetness as our thoughts pursue,
We deem them spoken pearls, or radiant diamond dew.

And never yet did I admire the power
    Which makes so lustrous every threadbare theme—
Which won for Lafayette one other hour,
    And e'en on July Fourth could cast a gleam—
As now, when I behold him play the host,
With all the dignity which red men boast—
With all the courtesy the whites have lost;—
Assume the very hue of savage mind,
Yet in rude accents show the thought refined;—
Assume the naiveté of infant age,
And in such prattle seem still more a sage;
The golden mean with tact unerring seized,
A courtly critic shone, a simple savage pleased;

The stoic of the woods his skill confessed,
As all the Father answered in his breast,
To the sure mark the silver arrow sped,
The man without a tear a tear has shed;
And thou hadst wept, hadst thou been there, to see
How true one sentiment must ever be,
In court or camp, the city or the wild,
To rouse the Father's heart, you need but name his Child.

'Twas a fair scene—and acted well by all;
So here's a health to Indian braves so tall—
Our Governor and Boston people all!

I will copy the admirable speech of Governor Everett on that occasion, as I think it the happiest attempt ever made to meet the Indian in his own way, and catch the tone of his mind. It was said, in the newspapers, that Keokuck did actually shed tears when addressed as a father. If he did not with his eyes, he well might in his heart.

EVERETT'S SPEECH

Chiefs and warriors of the Sauks and Foxes, you are welcome to our hall of council.

Brothers! you have come a long way from home to visit your white brethren; we rejoice to take you by the hand.

Brothers! we have heard the names of your chiefs and warriors; our brothers, who have travelled into the West, have told us a great deal of the Sauks and Foxes; we rejoice to see you with our own eyes, and take you by the hand.

Brothers! we are called the Massachusetts. This is the name of the red men that once lived here. Their wigwams filled yonder field; their council fire was kindled on this spot. They were of the same great race as the Sauks and Misquakuiks.

Brothers! when our fathers came over the great waters, they were a small band. The red man stood upon the rock by the seaside, and saw our fathers. He might have pushed them into the water and drowned them. But he stretched out his arm to our fathers and said, "Welcome, white men!" Our fathers were hungry, and the red men gave them corn and venison. Our fathers were cold, and the red man wrapped them up in his blanket. We are now numerous and powerful, but we remember the kindness of the red man to our fathers. Brothers, you are welcome; we are glad to see you.

Brothers! our faces are pale, and your faces are dark; but our hearts are alike. The Great Spirit has made his children of different colors, but he loves them all.

Brothers! you dwell between the Mississippi and the Missouri. They are mighty rivers. They have one branch far East in the Alleghanies, and the other far West in the Rocky Mountains; but they flow together at last into one great stream, and run down together into the sea. In like manner, the red man dwells in the West, and the white man in the East, by the great waters; but they are all one branch, one family; it has many branches and one head.

Brothers! as you entered our council house, you beheld the image of our great Father Washington. It is a cold stone—it cannot speak. But he was the friend of the red man, and bade his children live in peace with their red brethren. He is gone to the world of spirits. But his words have made a very deep print in our hearts, like the step of a strong buffalo on the soft clay of the prairie.

Brother! I perceive your little son between your knees. God preserve his life, my brother. He grows up before you like the tender sapling by the side of the mighty oak. May the oak and the sapling flourish a long time together. And when the mighty oak is fallen to the ground, may the young tree fill its place in the forest, and spread out its branches over the tribe like the parent trunk.

Brothers! I make you a short talk, and again bid you welcome to our council hall.

Not often have they been addressed with such intelligence and tact. The few who have not approached them with sordid rapacity, but from love to them, as men, and souls to be redeemed, have most frequently been persons intellectually too narrow, too straightly bound in sects or opinions, to throw themselves into the character or position of the Indians, or impart to them anything they can make available. The Christ shown them by these missionaries, is to them but a new and more powerful Manito; the signs of the new religion, but the fetiches that have aided the conquerors.

Here I will copy some remarks made by a discerning observer, on the methods used by the missionaries, and their natural results.

"Mr. —— and myself had a very interesting conversation, upon the subject of the Indians, their character, capabilities, &c. After ten years' experience among them, he was forced to acknowledge, that the results of the missionary efforts had produced nothing calculated to encourage. He thought that there was an intrinsic disability in them, to rise above, or go beyond the sphere in which they had so long moved. He said, that even those Indians who had been converted, and who had adopted the habits of civilization, were very little improved in their real character; they were as selfish, as deceitful, and as indolent, as those who were still heathens. They had repaid the kindnesses of the missionaries with the basest ingratitude, killing their cattle and swine, and robbing them of their harvests, which they wantonly destroyed. He had abandoned the idea of effecting any general good to the Indians. He had conscientious scruples, as to promoting an enterprise so hopeless, as that of missions among the Indians, by sending accounts to the east, that might induce philanthropic individuals to contribute to their support. In fact, the whole experience of his intercourse with them, seemed to have convinced him of the irremediable degradation of the race. Their fortitude under suffering, he considered the result of physical and mental insensibility; their courage, a mere animal excitement, which they found it necessary to inflame, before daring to meet a foe. They have no constancy of purpose; and are, in fact, but little superior to the brutes, in point of moral development. It is not astonishing, that one looking upon the Indian character, from Mr. ——'s point of view, should entertain such sentiments. The object of his intercourse with them was, to make them apprehend the mysteries of a theology, which, to the most enlightened, is an abstruse, metaphysical study; and it is not singular they should prefer their pagan superstitions, which address themselves more directly to the senses. Failing in the attempt to christianize, before civilizing them, he inferred, that, in the intrinsic degradation of their faculties, the obstacle was to be found."

Thus the missionary vainly attempts, by once or twice holding up the cross, to turn deer and tigers into lambs; vainly attempts to convince the red man that a heavenly mandate takes from him his broad lands. He bows his head, but does not at heart acquiesce. He cannot. It is not true; and if it were, the descent of blood through the same channels, for centuries, had formed habits of thought not so easily to be disturbed.

Amalgamation would afford the only true and profound means of civilization. But nature seems, like all else, to declare, that this race is fated to perish. Those of mixed blood fade early, and are not generally a fine race. They lose what is best in either type, rather than enhance the value of each, by mingling. There are exceptions, one or two such I know of, but this, it is said, is the general rule.

A traveller observes, that the white settlers, who live in the woods, soon become sallow, lanky, and dejected; the atmosphere of the trees does not agree with Caucasian lungs; and it is, perhaps, in part, an instinct of this, which causes the hatred of the new settlers towards trees. The Indian breathed the atmosphere of the forests freely; he loved their shade. As they are effaced from the land, he fleets too; a part of the same manifestation, which cannot linger behind its proper era.

The Chippewas have lately petitioned the state of Michigan, that they may be admitted as citizens; but this would be vain, unless they could be admitted, as brothers, to the heart of the white man. And while the latter feels that conviction of superiority, which enabled our Wisconsin friend to throw away the gun, and send the Indian to fetch it, he had need to be very good, and very wise, not to abuse his position. But the white man, as yet, is a half-tamed pirate, and avails himself, as much as ever, of the maxim, "Might makes right." All that civilization does for the generality, is to cover up this with a veil of subtle evasions and chicane, and here and there to rouse the individual mind to appeal to heaven against it.

I have no hope of liberalizing the missionary, of humanizing the sharks of trade, of infusing the conscientious drop into the flinty bosom of policy, of saving the Indian from immediate degradation, and speedy death. The whole sermon may be preached from the text, "Needs be that offences must come, yet wo them by whom they come." Yet, ere they depart, I wish there might be some masterly attempt to reproduce, in art or literature, what is proper to them, a kind of beauty and grandeur, which few of the every-day crowd have hearts to feel, yet which ought to leave in the world its monuments, to inspire the thought of genius through all ages. Nothing in this kind has been done masterly; since it was Clevengers's ambition, 'tis pity he had not opportunity to try fully his powers. We hope some other mind may be bent upon it, ere too late.

At present the only lively impress of their passage through the world is to be found in such books as Catlin's and some stories told by the old travellers, of which I purpose a brief account.

First, let me give another brief tale of the power exerted by the white man over the savage in a trying case, but, in this case, it was righteous, was moral power.

"We were looking over McKenney's trip to the Lakes, and, on observing the picture of Key-way-no-wut, or the Going Cloud, Mr. B. observed 'Ah, that is the fellow I came near having a fight with,' and he detailed at length the circumstances. This Indian was a very desperate character, and whom all the Leech lake band stood in fear of. He would shoot down any Indian who offended him, without the least hesitation, and had become quite the bully of that part of the tribe. The trader at Leech lake warned Mr. B. to beware of him, and said that he once, when he (the trader) refused to give up to him his stock of wild rice, went and got his gun and tomahawk, and shook the tomahawk over his head, saying '*Now*, give me your wild rice.' The trader complied with his exaction, but not so did Mr. B. in the adventure which I am about to relate. Key-way-no-wut came frequently to him with furs, wishing him to give for them cotton cloth, sugar, flour, &c. Mr. B. explained to him that he could not trade for furs, as he was sent there as a teacher, and that it would be like putting his hand into the fire to do so, as the traders would inform against him, and he would be sent out of the country. At the same time, he *gave* him the articles which he wished. Key-way-no-wut found this a very convenient way of getting what he wanted, and followed up this sort of game, until, at last, it became insupportable.

One day the Indian brought a very large otter skin, and said 'I want to get for this ten pounds of sugar, and some flour and cloth,' adding, 'I am not like other Indians, *I* want to pay for what I get.' Mr. B. found that he must either be robbed of all he had by submitting to these exactions, or take a stand at once. He thought, however, he would try to avoid a scrape, and told his customer he had not so much sugar to spare. 'Give me then,' said he, 'what you can spare,' and Mr. B. thinking to make him back out, told him he would give him five pounds of sugar for his skin. 'Take it,' said the Indian. He left the skin, telling Mr. B. to take good care of it. Mr. B. took it at once to the trader's store, and related the circumstance, congratulating himself that he had got rid of the Indian's exactions. But, in about a month, Key-way-no-wut appeared bringing some dirty Indian sugar, and said 'I have brought back the sugar that I borrowed of you, and I want my otter skin back.' Mr. B. told him, 'I *bought* an otter skin of you, but if you will return the other articles you have got for it, perhaps I can get it for you.' 'Where is the skin?' said he very quickly, 'what have you done with it?' Mr. B. replied it was in the trader's store, where he (the Indian) could not get it. At this information he was furious, laid his hands on his knife and tomahawk, and commanded Mr. B. to bring it at once. Mr. B. found this was the crisis, where he must take a stand or be 'rode over rough shod' by this man; his wife, who was present was much alarmed, and begged he would get the skin for the Indian, but he told her that 'either he or the Indian would soon be master of his house, and if she was afraid to see it decided which was to be so, she had better retire.' He turned to Key-way-no-wut, and addressed him in a stern voice as follows: 'I will *not* give you the skin. How often have you come to my house, and I have shared with you what I had. I gave you tobacco when you were well, and medicine when you were sick, and you never went away from my wigwam with your hands empty. And this is the way you return my treatment to you. I had thought you were a man and a chief, but you are not, you are nothing but an old woman. Leave this house, and never enter it again.' Mr. B. said he expected the Indian would attempt his life when he said this, but that he had placed himself in a position so that he could defend himself, and he looked straight into the Indian's eye, and like other wild beasts he quailed before the glance of mental and moral courage. He calmed down at once, and soon began to make apologies. Mr. B. then told him kindly, but firmly, that, if he wished to walk in the same path with him, he must walk as straight as the crack on the floor before them; adding that he would not walk with anybody who would jostle him by walking so crooked as he had done. He was perfectly tamed, and Mr. B. said he never had any more trouble with him."

The conviction here livingly enforced of the superiority on the side of the white man, was thus expressed by the Indian orator at Mackinaw while we were there. After the customary compliments about sun, dew, &c., "This," said he, "is the difference between the white and the red man; the white man looks to the future and paves the way for posterity." This is a statement uncommonly refined for an Indian; but one of the gentlemen present, who understood the Chippeway, vouched for it as a literal rendering of his phrases; and he did indeed touch the vital point of difference. But the Indian, if he understands, cannot make use of his intelligence. The fate of his people is against it, and Pontiac and Philip have no more chance, than Julian in the times of old.

Now that I am engaged on this subject, let me give some notices of writings upon it, read either at Mackinaw or since my return.

Mrs. Jameson made such good use of her brief visit to these regions, as leaves great cause to regret she did not stay longer and go farther; also, that she did not make more use of her acquaintance with, indeed, adoption by, the Johnson family. Mr. Johnson seems to have been almost the only white man who knew how to regard with due intelligence and nobleness, his connexion with the race. Neither French or English, of any powers of sympathy, or poetical apprehension, have lived among the Indians without high feelings of enjoyment. Perhaps no luxury has been greater, than that experienced by the persons, who, sent either by trade or war, during the last century, into these majestic regions, found guides and shelter amid the children of the soil, and recognized in a form so new and of such varied, yet simple, charms, the tie of brotherhood.

But these, even Sir William Johnston, whose life, surrounded by the Indians in his castle on the Mohawk, is described with such vivacity by Mrs. Grant, have been men better fitted to enjoy and adapt themselves to this life, than to observe and record it. The very faculties that made it so easy for them to live in the present moment, were likely to unfit them for keeping its chronicle. Men, whose life is full and instinctive, care little for the pen. But the father of Mrs. Schoolcraft seems to have taken pleasure in observation and comparison, and to have imparted the same tastes to his children. They have enough of European culture to have a standard, by which to judge their native habits and inherited lore.

By the premature death of Mrs. Schoolcraft was lost a mine of poesy, to which few had access, and from which Mrs. Jameson would have known how to coin a series of medals for the history of this ancient people. We might have known in clear outline, as now we shall not, the growths of religion and philosophy, under the influences of this climate and scenery, from such suggestions as nature and the teachings of the inward mind presented.

Now we can only gather that they had their own theory of the history of this globe; had perceived a gap in its genesis, and tried to fill it up by the intervention of some secondary power, with moral sympathies. They have observed the action of fire and water upon this earth; also that the dynasty of animals has yielded to that of man. With these animals they have profound sympathy, and are always trying to restore to them their lost honors. On the rattlesnake, the beaver, and the bear, they seem to look with a mixture of sympathy and veneration, as on their fellow settlers in these realms. There is something that appeals powerfully to the imagination in the ceremonies they observe, even in case of destroying one of these animals. I will say more of this by-and-by.

The dog they cherish as having been once a spirit of high intelligence; and now in its fallen and imprisoned state, given to man as his special companion. He is therefore to them a sacrifice of peculiar worth: whether to a guardian spirit or a human friend. Yet nothing would be a greater violation than giving the remains of a sacrificial feast to the dogs, or even suffering them to touch the bones.

Similar inconsistencies may be observed in the treatment of the dog by the white man. He is the most cherished companion in the familiar walks of many men; his virtues form the theme of poetry and history; the nobler races present grand traits, and are treated with proportionate respect. Yet the epithets dog and hound, are there set apart to express the uttermost contempt.

Goethe, who abhorred dogs, has selected that animal for the embodiment of the modern devil, who, in earlier times, chose rather the form of the serpent.

There is, indeed, something that peculiarly breaks in on the harmony of nature, in the bark of the dog, and that does not at all correspond with the softness and sagacity observable in his eye. The baying the moon, I have been inclined to set down as an unfavorable indication; but, since Fourier has found out that the moon is dead, and "no better than carrion;" and the Greeks have designated her as Hecate, the deity of suicide and witchcraft, the dogs are perhaps in the right.

They have among them the legend of the carbuncle, so famous in oriental mythos. Adair states that they believe this fabulous gem may be found on the spot where the rattlesnake has been destroyed.

If they have not the archetypal man, they have the archetypal animal, "the grandfather of all beavers;" to them, who do not know the elephant, this is the symbol of wisdom, as the rattlesnake and bear of power.

I will insert here a little tale about the bear, which has not before appeared in print, as representing their human way of looking on these animals, even when engaged in their pursuit. To me such stories give a fine sense of the lively perceptions and exercise of fancy, enjoyed by them in their lives of woodcraft:

MUCKWA, OR THE BEAR

A young Indian, who lived a great while ago, when he was quite young killed a bear; and the tribe from that circumstance called him Muckwa. As he grew up he became an expert hunter, and his favorite game was the bear, many of which he killed. One day he started off to a river far remote from the lodges of his tribe, and where berries and grapes were very plenty, in pursuit of bears. He hunted all day but found nothing; and just at night he came to some lodges which he thought to be those of some of his tribe. He approached the largest of them, lifted the curtain at its entrance, and went in, when he perceived the inmates to be bears, who were seated around the fire smoking. He said nothing, but seated himself also and smoked the pipe which they offered him, in silence. An old grey bear, who was the chief, ordered supper to be brought for him, and after he had eaten it, addressed him as follows: "My son, I am glad to see you come among us in a friendly manner. You have been a great hunter, and all the she-bears of our tribe tremble when they hear your name. But cease to trouble us, and come and live with me; we have a very pleasant life, living upon the fruits of the earth; and in the winter, instead of being obliged to hunt and travel through the deep snow, we sleep soundly until the sun unchains the streams, and makes the tender buds put forth for our subsistence. I will give you my daughter for a wife, and we will live happily together." Muckwa was inclined to accept the old bear's offer; but when he saw the daughter, who came and took off his wet moccasons, and gave him dry ones, he thought that he had never seen any Indian woman so beautiful. He accepted the offer of the chief of the bears, and lived with his wife very happily for some time. He had by her two sons, one of whom was like an Indian, and the other like a bear. When the bear-child was oppressed with heat, his mother would take him into the deep cool caves, while the Indian-child would shiver with cold, and cry after her in vain. As the autumn advanced, the bears began to go out in search of acorns, and then the she-bear said to Muckwa, "Stay at home here and watch our house, while I go to gather some nuts." She departed and was gone for some days with her people. By-and-by Muckwa became tired of staying at home, and thought that he would go off to a distance and resume his favorite bear-hunting. He accordingly started off, and at last came to a grove of lofty oaks, which were full of large acorns. He found signs of bear, and soon espied a fat she-bear on the top of a tree. He shot at her with a good aim, and she fell, pierced by his unerring arrow. He went up to her, and found it was his sister-in-law, who reproached him with his cruelty, and told him to return to his own people. Muckwa returned quietly home, and pretended not to have left his lodge. However, the old chief understood, and was disposed to kill him in revenge; but his wife found means to avert her father's anger. The winter season now coming on, Muckwa prepared to accompany his wife into winter quarters; they selected a large tamarack tree, which was hollow, and lived there comfortably until a party of hunters discovered their retreat. The she-bear told Muckwa to remain quietly in the tree, and that she would decoy off the hunters. She came out of the hollow, jumped from a bough of the tree, and escaped unharmed, although the hunters shot after her. Some time after, she returned to the tree, and told Muckwa that he had better go back to his own people. "Since you have lived among us," said she, "we have nothing but ill-fortune; you have killed my sister; and now your friends have followed your footsteps to our retreats to kill us. The Indian and the bear cannot live in the same lodge, for the Master of Life has appointed for them different habitations." So Muckwa returned with his son to his own people; but he never after would shoot a she-bear, for fear that he should kill his wife.

I admire this story for the *savoir faire*, the nonchalance, the Vivian Greyism of Indian life. It is also a poetical expression of the sorrows of unequal relations; those in which the Master of Life was not consulted. Is it not pathetic; the picture of the mother carrying off the child that was like herself into the deep, cool caves, while the other, shivering with cold, cried after her in vain? The moral, too, of Muckwa's return to the bear lodges, thinking to hide his sin by silence, while it was at once discerned by those connected with him, is fine.

We have a nursery tale, of which children never weary, of a little boy visiting a bear house and holding intercourse with them on terms as free as Muckwa did. So, perhaps, the child of Norman-Saxon blood, no less than the Indian, finds some pulse of the Orson in his veins.

As they loved to draw the lower forms of nature up to them, divining their histories, and imitating their ways, in their wild dances and paintings; even so did they love to look upward and people the atmosphere that enfolds the earth, with fairies and manitoes. The sister, obliged to leave her brother on the earth, bids him look up at evening, and he will see her painting her face in the west.

All places, distinguished in any way by nature, aroused the feelings of worship, which, however ignorant, are always elevating. See as instances in this kind, the stories of Nanabojou, and the Winnebago Prince, at the falls of St. Anthony.

As with the Greeks, beautiful legends grow up which express the aspects of various localities. From the distant sand-banks in the lakes, glittering in the sun, come stories of enchantresses combing, on the shore, the long golden hair of a beautiful daughter. The Lorelei of the Rhine, with her syren song, and the sad events that follow, is found on the lonely rocks of Lake Superior.

The story to which I now refer, may be found in a book called Life on the Lakes, or, a Trip to the Pictured Rocks. There are two which purport to be Indian tales; one is simply a romantic narrative, connected with a spot at Mackinaw, called Robinson's Folly. This, no less than the other, was unknown to those persons I saw on the island; but as they seem entirely beyond the powers of the person who writes them down, and the other one has the profound and original meaning of Greek tragedy, I believe they must be genuine legends.

The one I admire is the story of a young warrior, who goes to keep, on these lonely rocks, the fast which is to secure him vision of his tutelary spirit. There the loneliness is broken by the voice of sweet music from the water. The Indian knows well that to break the fast, which is the crisis of his life, by turning his attention from seeking the Great Spirit, to any lower object, will deprive him through life of heavenly protection, probably call down the severest punishment.

But the temptation is too strong for him; like the victims of the Lorelei, he looks, like them beholds a maiden of unearthly beauty, to him the harbinger of earthly wo.

The development of his fate, that succeeds; of love, of heart-break, of terrible revenge, which back upon itself recoils, may vie with anything I have ever known of stern tragedy, is altogether unlike any other form, and with all the peculiar expression we see lurking in the Indian eye. The demon is not frightful and fantastic, like those that haunt the German forest; but terribly human, as if of full manhood, reared in the shadow of the black forests. An Indian sarcasm vibrates through it, which, with Indian fortitude, defies the inevitable torture.

The Indian is steady to that simple creed, which forms the basis of all this mythology; that there is a God, and a life beyond

OLD ADAIR

153

this; a right and wrong which each man can see, betwixt which each man should choose; that good brings with it its reward and vice its punishment. Their moral code, if not refined as that of civilized nations, is clear and noble in the stress laid upon truth and fidelity. And all unprejudiced observers bear testimony that the Indians, until broken from their old anchorage by intercourse with the whites, who offer them, instead, a religion of which they furnish neither interpretation nor example, were singularly virtuous, if virtue be allowed to consist in a man's acting up to his own ideas of right.

Old Adair, who lived forty years among the Indians; not these tribes, indeed, but the southern Indians, does great justice to their religious aspiration. He is persuaded that they are Jews, and his main object is to identify their manifold ritual, and customs connected with it, with that of the Jews. His narrative contains much that is worthless, and is written in the most tedious manner of the folios. But his devotion to the records of ancient Jewry, has really given him power to discern congenial traits elsewhere, and for the sake of what he has expressed of the noble side of Indian character, we pardon him our having to wade through so many imbecilities.

An infidel, he says, is, in their language, "one who has shaken hands with the accursed speech;" a religious man, "one who has shaken hands with the beloved speech." If this be a correct definition, we could wish Adair more religious.

He gives a fine account of their methods of purification. These show a deep reliance on the sustaining Spirit. By fasting and prayer they make ready for all important decisions and actions. Even for the war path, on which he is likely to endure such privations, the brave prepares by a solemn fast. His reliance is on the spirit in which he goes forth.

We may contrast with the opinion of the missionary, as given on a former page, the testimony of one, who knew them as Adair did, to their heroism under torture.

He gives several stories, illustrative both of their courage, fortitude, and resource in time of peril, of which I will cite only the two first.

"The Shawano Indians took a Muskohge warrior, known by the name of 'Old Scrany;' they bastinadoed him in the usual manner, and condemned him to the fiery torture. He underwent a great deal, without showing any concern; his countenance and behavior were as if he suffered not the least pain, and was formed beyond the common laws of nature. He told them, with a bold voice, that he was a very noted warrior, and gained most of his martial preferments at the expense of their nation, and was desirous of showing them in the act of dying that he was still as much their superior, as when he headed his gallant countrymen against them. That, although he had fallen into their hands, in forfeiting the protection of the divine power, by some impurity or other, yet he had still so much virtue remaining, as would enable him to punish himself more exquisitely than all their despicable, ignorant crowd could possibly do, if they gave him liberty by untying him, and would hand to him one of the red hot gun-barrels out of the fire. The proposal, and his method of address, appeared so exceedingly bold and uncommon, that his request was granted. Then he suddenly seized one end of the red hot barrel, and, brandishing it from side to side, he found his way through the armed and surprised multitude, and leaped down a prodigious steep and high bank into a branch of the river, dived through it, ran over a small island, passed the other branch amidst a shower of bullets, and, though numbers of his eager enemies were in close pursuit of him, he got to a bramble swamp, and in that naked, mangled condition, reached his own country. He proved a sharp thorn in their side afterwards, to the day of his death.

"The Shawano also captivated a warrior of the Anantooiah, and put him to the stake, according to their usual cruel solemnities. Having unconcernedly suffered much sharp torture, he told them with scorn, they did not know how to punish a noted enemy, therefore he was willing to teach them, and would confirm the truth of his assertion, if they allowed him the opportunity. Accordingly he requested of them a pipe and some tobacco, which was given him; as soon as he lighted it, he sat down, naked as he was, on the women's burning torches, that were within his circle, and continued smoking his pipe without the least discomposure. On this a head warrior leaped up, and said they had seen, plain enough, that he was a warrior, and not afraid of dying; nor should he have died, but that he was both spoiled by the fire, and devoted to it by their laws; however, though he was a very dangerous enemy, and his nation a treacherous people, it should appear they paid a regard to bravery, even in one, who was marked over the body with war streaks at the cost of many lives of their beloved kindred. And then, by way of favor, he, with his friendly tomahawk, put an end to all his pains: though this merciful but bloody instrument was ready some minutes before it gave the blow, yet, I was assured, the spectators could not perceive the sufferer to change, either his posture, or his steady, erect countenance in the least."

Some stories as fine, but longer, follow. In reference to which Adair says, "The intrepid behavior of these red stoics, their surprising contempt of and indifference to life or death, instead of lessening, helps to confirm our belief of that supernatural power, which supported the great number of primitive martyrs, who sealed the christian faith with their blood. The Indians have as much belief and expectation of a future state, as the greater part of the Israelites seem to have. But the christians of the first centuries, may justly be said to exceed even the most heroic American Indians, for they bore the bitterest persecution with steady patience, in imitation of their divine leader Messiah, in full confidence of divine support and of a glorious recompense of reward; and, instead of even wishing for revenge on their cruel enemies and malicious tormentors, (which is the chief principle that actuates the Indians,) they not only forgave them, but, in the midst of their tortures, earnestly prayed for them, with composed countenances, sincere love, and unabated fervor. And not only men of different conditions, but the delicate women and children suffered with constancy, and died praying for their tormentors: the Indian women and children, and their young men untrained to war, are incapable of displaying the like patience and magnanimity."

Thus impartially looks the old trader. I meant to have inserted other passages, that of the encampment at Yowanne, and the horse race to which he challenged them, to show how well he could convey in his garrulous fashion the whole presence of Indian life. That of Yowanne, especially, takes my fancy much, by its wild and subtle air, and the old-nurse fashion in which every look and gesture is detailed. His enjoyment, too, at outwitting the Indians in their own fashion is contagious. There is a fine history of a young man driven by a presentiment to run upon his death. But I find, to copy these stories, as they stand, would half fill this little book, and compression would spoil them, so I must wait some other occasion.

The story, later, of giving an Indian liquid fire to swallow, I give at full length, to show how a kindhearted man and one well disposed towards them, can treat them, and view his barbarity as a joke. It is not then so much wonder, if the trader, with this same feeling that they may be treated, (as however brutes should not be,) brutally, mixes red pepper and damaged tobacco with the rum, intending in their fever to fleece them of all they possess.

Like Murray and Henry, he has his great Indian chief, who represents what the people should be, as Pericles and Phocion what the Greek people should be. If we are entitled to judge by its best fruits of the goodness of the tree, Adair's Red Shoes, and Henry's Wawatam, should make us respect the first possessors of our country, and doubt whether we are in all ways worthy to fill their place. Of the whole tone of character, judgment may be formed by what is said of the death of Red Shoes.

"This chief, by his several transcendent qualities had arrived at the highest pitch of the red glory. . . .

"He was murdered, for the sake of a French reward, by one of his own countrymen. He had the misfortune to be taken very sick on the road, and to lodge apart from the camp, according to their custom. A Judas, tempted by the high reward of the French for killing him, officiously pretended to take great care of him. While Red Shoes kept his face toward him, the barbarian had such feelings of awe and pity that he had not power to perpetrate his wicked design; but when he turned his back, then gave the fatal shot. In this manner fell this valuable brave man, by hands that would have trembled to attack him on an equality."

Adair, with all his sympathy for the Indian, mixes quite unconsciously some white man's views of the most decided sort. For instance, he recommends that the tribes be stimulated as much as possible to war with each other, that they may the more easily and completely be kept under the dominion of the whites, and he gives the following record of brutality as quite a jocose and adroit procedure.

"I told him, on his importuning me further, that I had a full bottle of the water of *ane hoome*, 'bitter ears,' meaning long pepper, of which he was ignorant. We were of opinion that his eager thirst for liquor, as well as his ignorance of the burning quality of the pepper, would induce the bacchanal to try it. He accordingly applauded my generous disposition, and said his heart had all along told him I would not act beneath the character I bore among his country people. The bottle was brought, I laid it on the table, and then told him, as he was spitting very much, (a general custom among the Indians when they are eager for anything,) if I drank it all at one sitting it would cause me to spit in earnest, as I used it only when I ate, and then very moderately; but though I loved it, if his heart was very poor for it, I should be silent, and not the least grudge him for pleasing his mouth. He said, 'your heart is honest, indeed; I thank you, for it is good to my heart, and makes it greatly to rejoice.' Without any further ceremony he seized the bottle, uncorked it, and swallowed a large quantity of the burning liquid, till he was nearly strangled. He gasped for a considerable time, and as soon as he recovered his breath, he said *Hah*, and soon after kept stroking his throat with his right hand. When the violence of this burning draught was pretty well over, he began to flourish away in praise of the strength of the liquor and bounty of the giver. He then went to his companion and held the liquor to his mouth according to custom, till he took several hearty swallows. This Indian seemed rather more sensible of its fiery quality than the other, for it suffocated him for a considerable time; but as soon as he recovered his breath, he tumbled about the floor like a drunken person. In this manner they finished the whole bottle, into which two others had been decanted. The burning liquor so highly inflamed their bodies, that one of the Choctaws, to cool his inward parts, drank water till he almost burst; the other, rather than bear the ridicule of the people, and the inward fire that distracted him, drowned himself the second night after in a broad and shallow clay hole. . . . .

"There was an incident similar, which happened among the Cherokees. When all the liquor was expended the Indians went home, leading with them, at my request, those that were drunk.

One, however, soon came back, and earnestly importuned me for more Nawahti, which signifies both physic and spirituous liquor. They, as they are now become great liars, suspect all others of being infected with their own disposition and principles. The more I excused myself, the more anxious he grew, so as to become offensive. I then told him I had only one quarter of a bottle of strong physic, which sick people might drink in small quantities, for the cure of inward pains: and, laying it down before him, I declared I did not on any account choose to part with it, but as his speech had become very long and troublesome, he might do just as his heart directed him concerning it. He took it up, saying, his heart was very poor for physic, but he would cure it, and make it quite straight. The bottle contained three gills of strong spirits of turpentine, which, in a short time he drank off. Such a quantity would have demolished me or any white person. The Indians, in general, are either capable of suffering exquisite pain longer than we are, or of showing more constancy and composure in their torments. The troublesome visiter soon tumbled down and foamed prodigiously. I then sent for some of his relations to carry him home. They came; I told them he drank greedily, and too much of the physic. They said, it was his usual custom, when the red people bought the English physic. They gave him a decoction of proper herbs and roots, the next day sweated him, repeated the former draught, and he got well. As these turpentine spirits did not inebriate him, but only inflamed his intestines, he well remembered the burning quality of my favorite physic, and cautioned the rest from ever teasing me for any physic I had concealed in any sort of bottles for my own use; otherwise they might be sure it would spoil them like the eating of fire."

We are pleased to note that the same white man, who so resolutely resisted the encroachments of Key-way-no-wut, devised a more humane expedient in a similar dilemma.

"Mr. B. told me that, when he first went into the Indian country, they got the taste of his peppermint, and, after that, colics prevailed among them to an alarming extent, till Mrs. B. made a strong decoction of flagroot, and gave them in place of their favorite medicine. This effected, as might be supposed, a radical cure."

I am inclined to recommend Adair to the patient reader, if such may be found in these United States, with the assurance that, if he will have tolerance for its intolerable prolixity and dryness, he will find, on rising from the book, that he has partaken of an infusion of real Indian bitters, such as may not be drawn from any of the more attractive memoirs on the same subject.

Another book of interest, from its fidelity and candid spirit, though written without vivacity, and by a person neither of large mind nor prepared for various inquiry, is Carver's Travels, "for three years throughout the interior parts of America, for more than five thousand miles."

He set out from Boston in "June, 1786, and proceeded, by way of Albany and Niagara, to Michilimackinac, a fort situated between the Lakes Huron and Michigan, and distant from Boston 1300 miles."

It is interesting to follow his footsteps in these localities, though they be not bold footsteps.

He mentions the town of the Sacs, on the Wisconsin, as the largest and best built he saw, "composed of ninety houses, each large enough for several families. These are built of hewn plank, neatly jointed, and covered with bark so compactly as to keep out the most penetrating rains. Before the doors are placed comfortable sheds, in which the inhabitants sit, when the weather will permit, and smoke their pipes. The streets are regular and spacious. In their plantations, which lie adjacent to their houses, and which are neatly laid out, they raise great quantities of Indian corn, beans and melons."

Such settlements compare very well with those which were found on the Mohawk. It was of such that the poor Indian was thinking, whom our host saw gazing on the shore of Nomabbin lake.

He mentions the rise and fall of the lake-waters, by a tide of three feet, once in seven years,—a phenomenon not yet accounted for.

His view of the Indian character is truly impartial. He did not see it so fully drawn out by circumstances as Henry did, (of whose narrative we shall presently speak,) but we come to similar results from the two witnesses. They are in every feature Romans, as described by Carver, and patriotism their leading impulse. He deserves the more credit for the justice he is able to do them, that he had undergone the terrors of death at their hands, when present at the surrender of one of the forts, and had seen them in that mood which they express by drinking the blood and eating the hearts of their enemies, yet is able to understand the position of their minds, and allow for their notions of duty.

No selfish views, says he, influence their advice, or obstruct their consultations.

Let me mention here the use they make of their vapor baths. "When about to decide on some important measure, they go into them, thus cleansing the skin and carrying off any peccant humors, so that the body may, as little as possible, impede the mind by any ill conditions."

They prepare the bath for one another when any arrangement is to be made between families, on the opposite principle to the whites, who make them drunk before bargaining with them. The bath serves them instead of a cup of coffee, to stimulate the thinking powers.

He mentions other instances of their kind of delicacy, which, if different from ours, was, perhaps, more rigidly observed.

Lovers never spoke of love till the daylight was quite gone.

"If an Indian goes to visit any particular person in a family, he mentions for whom his visit is intended, and the rest of the family, immediately retiring to the other end of the hut or tent, are careful not to come near enough to interrupt them during the whole of the conversation."

In cases of divorce, which was easily obtained, the advantage rested with the woman. The reason given is indeed contemptuous toward her, but a chivalric direction is given to the contempt.

"The children of the Indians are always distinguished by the name of the mother, and, if a woman marries several husbands, and has issue by each of them, they are called after her. The reason they give for this is, that, 'as their offspring are indebted to the father for the soul, the invisible part of their essence, and to the mother for their corporeal and apparent part, it is most rational that they should be distinguished by the name of the latter, from whom they indubitably derive their present being.'"

This is precisely the division of functions made by Ovid, as the father sees Hercules perishing on the funeral pyre.

> "Nec nisi materna Vulcanum parte potentem
> Sentiet. Æternum est a me quod traxit et expers
> Atque immune necis, nullaqe domabile flamma."

He is not enough acquainted with natural history to make valuable observations. He mentions, however, as did my friend, the Indian girl, that those splendid flowers, the Wickapee and the root of the Wake-Robin, afford valuable medicines. Here, as in the case of the Lobelia, nature has blazoned her drug in higher colors than did ever quack doctor.

He observes some points of resemblance between the Indians and Tartars, but they are trivial, and not well considered. He mentions that the Tartars have the same custom, with some of these tribes, of shaving all the head except a tuft on the crown. Catlin says this is intended to afford a convenient means by which to take away the scalp; for they consider it a great disgrace to have the foeman neglect this, as if he considered the conquest, of which the scalp is the certificate, no addition to his honors.

"The Tartars," he says, "had a similar custom of sacrificing the dog; and among the Kamschatkans was a dance resembling the dog-dance of our Indians."

My friend, who joined me at Mackinaw, happened, on the homeward journey, to see a little Chinese girl, who had been sent over by one of the missions, and observed that, in features, complexion, and gesture, she was a counterpart to the little Indian girls she had just seen playing about on the lake shore.

The parentage of these tribes is still an interesting subject of speculation, though, if they be not created for this region, they have become so assimilated to it as to retain little trace of any other. To me it seems most probable, that a peculiar race was bestowed on each region, as the lion on one latitude and the white bear on another. As man has two natures—one, like that of the plants and animals, adapted to the uses and enjoyments of this planet, another, which presages and demands a higher sphere—he is constantly breaking bounds, in proportion as the mental gets the better of the mere instinctive existence. As yet, he loses in harmony of being what he gains in height

SUMMER ON THE LAKES

and extension; the civilized man is a larger mind, but a more imperfect nature than the savage.

It is pleasant to meet, on the borders of these two states, one of those persons who combines some of the good qualities of both; not, as so many of these adventurers do, the rapaciousness and cunning of the white, with the narrowness and ferocity of the savage, but the sentiment and thoughtfulness of the one, with the boldness, personal resource, and fortitude of the other.

Such a person was Alexander Henry, who left Quebec in 1760, for Mackinaw and the Sault St. Marie, and remained in those regions, of which he has given us a most lively account, sixteen years.

His visit to Mackinaw was premature; the Indians were far from satisfied; they hated their new masters. From the first, the omens were threatening, and before many months passed, the discontent ended in the seizing of the fort at Mackinaw and massacre of its garrison; on which occasion Henry's life was saved by a fine act of Indian chivalry.

Wawatam, a distinguished chief, had found himself drawn, by strong affinity, to the English stranger. He had adopted him as a brother, in the Indian mode. When he found that his tribe had determined on the slaughter of the whites, he obtained permission to take Henry away with him, if he could. But not being able to prevail on him, as he could not assign the true reasons, he went away deeply saddened, but not without obtaining a promise that his brother should not be injured. The reason he was obliged to go, was, that his tribe felt his affections were so engaged, that his self-command could not be depended on to keep their secret. Their promise was not carefully observed, and, in consequence of the baseness of a French Canadian in whose house Henry took refuge,—baseness such as has not, even by their foes, been recorded of any Indian, his life was placed in great hazard. But Wawatam returned in time to save him. The scene in which he appears, accompanied by his wife—who seems to have gone hand in hand with him in this matter—lays down all his best things in a heap, in the middle of the hall, as a ransom for the captive, and his little, quiet speech, are as good as the Iliad. They have the same simplicity, the same lively force and tenderness.

Henry goes away with his adopted brother, and lives for some time among the tribe. The details of this life are truly interesting. One time he is lost for several days while on the chase. The description of these weary, groping days, the aspect of natural objects and of the feelings thus inspired, and the mental change after a good night's sleep, form a little episode worthy the epic muse. He stripped off the entire bark of a tree for a coverlet in the snow-storm, going to sleep with "the most distracted thoughts in the world, while the wolves around seemed to know the distress to which he was reduced;" but he waked in the morning another man, clear-headed, able to think out the way to safety.

When living in the lodge, he says: "At one time much scarcity of food prevailed. We were often twenty-four hours without eating; and when in the morning we had no victuals for the day before us, the custom was to black our faces with grease and charcoal, and exhibit, through resignation, a temper as cheerful as in the midst of plenty." This wise and dignified proceeding reminds one of a charming expression of what is best in French character, as described by Rigolette, in the Mysteries of Paris, of the household of Père Cretu and Ramonette.

He bears witness to much virtue among them. Their superstitions, as described by him, seem childlike and touching. He gives with much humor, traits that show their sympathy with the lower animals, such as I have mentioned. He speaks of them as, on the whole, taciturn, because their range of topics is so limited, and seems to have seen nothing of their talent for narration. Catlin, on the contrary, describes them as lively and garrulous, and says, that their apparent taciturnity among the whites is owing to their being surprised at what they see, and unwilling, from pride, to show that they are so, as well as that they have little to communicate on their side, that they think will be valuable.

After peace was restored, and Henry lived long at Mackinaw and the Sault St. Marie, as a trader, the traits of his biography and intercourse with the Indians, are told in the same bold and lively style. I wish I had room for many extracts, as the book is rare.

He made a journey one winter on snow shoes, to Prairie du Chien, which is of romantic interest as displaying his character. His companions could not travel nearly so fast as he did, and detained him on the way. Provisions fell short; soon they were ready to perish of starvation. Apprehending this, on a long journey, in the depth of winter, broken by no hospitable station, Henry had secreted some chocolate. When he saw his companions ready to lie down and die, he would heat water, boil in it a square of this, and give them. By the heat of the water and the fancy of nourishment, they would be revived, and induced to proceed a little further. At last they saw antlers sticking up from the ice, and found the body of an elk, which had sunk in and been frozen there, and thus preserved to save their lives. On this "and excellent soup" made from bones they found they were sustained to their journey's end; thus furnishing, says Henry, one other confirmation of the truth, that "despair was not made for man;" this expression, and his calm consideration for the Canadian woman that was willing to betray him to death, denote the two sides of a fine character.

He gives an interesting account of the tribe called "The Weepers," on account of the rites with which they interrupt their feasts in honor of their friends.

He gives this humorous notice of a chief, called "The Great Road."

"The chief, to whose kindly reception we were so much indebted, was of a complexion rather darker than that of the Indians in general. His appearance was greatly injured by the condition of his hair, and this was the result of an extraordinary superstition.

"The Indians universally fix upon a particular object as sacred to themselves—as the giver of prosperity and as their preserver from evil. The choice is determined either by a dream or some strong predilection of fancy, and usually falls upon an animal, part of an animal, or something else which is to be met with by land, or by water; but the Great Road had made choice of his hair, placing, like Samson, all his safety in this portion of his proper substance! His hair was the fountain of all his happiness; it was his strength and his weapon—his spear and his shield. It preserved him in battle, directed him in the chase, watched over him in the march, and gave length of days to his wives and children. Hair, of a quality like this, was not to be profaned by the touch of human hands. I was assured that it never had been cut nor combed from his childhood upward, and that when any part of it fell from his head, he treasured that part with care; meanwhile, it did not escape all care, even while growing on the head, but was in the especial charge of a spirit, who dressed it while the owner slept. The spirit's style of hair-dressing was peculiar, the hair being matted into ropes, which spread in all directions."

I insert the following account of a visit from some Indians to him at Mackinaw, with a design to frighten him, and one to Carver, for the same purpose, as very descriptive of Indian manners:

"At two o'clock in the afternoon, the Chippeways came to my house, about sixty in number, and headed by Mina-va-va-na, their chief. They walked in single file, each with his tomahawk in one hand, and scalping knife in the other. Their bodies were naked, from the waist upwards, except in a few examples, where blankets were thrown loosely over the shoulders. Their faces were painted with charcoal, worked up with grease; their bodies with white clay in patterns of various fancies. Some had feathers thrust through their noses, and their heads decorated with the same. It is unnecessary to dwell on the sensations with which I beheld the approach of this uncouth, if not frightful, assemblage.

"Looking out, I saw about twenty naked young Indians, the most perfect in their shape, and by far the handsomest I had ever seen, coming towards me, and dancing as they approached to the music of their drums. At every ten or twelve yards they halted, and set up their yells and cries.

"When they reached my tent I asked them to come in, which, without deigning to make me any answer, they did. As I observed they were painted red and black, as they are when they go against an enemy, and perceived that some parts of the war-dance were intermixed with their other movements, I doubted not but they were set on by the hostile chief who refused my salutation. I therefore determined to sell my life as dearly as possible. To this purpose I received them sitting on my chest, with my gun and pistols beside me; and ordered my men to keep a watchful eye on them, and be also on their guard.

"The Indians being entered, they continued their dance alternately, singing at the same time of their heroic exploits, and the superiority of their race over every other people. To enforce their language, though it was uncommonly nervous and expressive, and such as would of itself have carried terror to the firmest heart; at the end of every period they struck their war-clubs against the poles of my tent with such violence, that I expected every moment it would have tumbled upon us. As each of them in dancing round passed by me, they placed their right hands over their eyes, and coming close to me, looked me steadily in the face, which I could not construe into a token of friendship. My men gave themselves up for lost; and I acknowledge for my own part, that I never found my apprehensions more tumultuous on any occasion."

He mollified them, however, in the end by presents.

It is pity that Lord Edward Fitzgerald did not leave a detailed account of his journey through the wilderness, where he was pilot of an unknown course for twenty days, as Murray and Henry have of theirs. There is nothing more interesting than to see the civilized man thus thrown wholly on himself and his manhood, and *not* found at fault.

McKenney and Hall's book upon the Indians is a valuable work. The portraits of the chiefs alone would make a history, and they are beautifully colored.

Most of the anecdotes may be found again in Drake's Book of the Indians; which will afford a useful magazine to their future historian.

I shall, however, cite a few of them, as especially interesting to myself.

Of Guess, the inventor of the Cherokee alphabet, it was observable in the picture, and observed in the text, that his face had an oriental cast. The same, we may recall, was said of that of the Seeress of Prevorst, and the circumstance presents pleasing analogies. Intellect dawning through features still simple and national, presents very different apparitions from the "expressive" and "historical" faces of a broken and cultured race, where there is always more to divine than to see.

Of the picture of the Flying Pigeon, the beautiful and excellent woman mentioned above, a keen observer said, "If you cover the forehead, you would think the face that of a Madonna, but the forehead is still savage; the perceptive faculties look so sharp, and the forehead not moulded like a European forehead." This is very true; in her the moral nature was most developed, and the effect of a higher growth upon her face is entirely different from that upon Guess.

His eye is inturned, while the proper Indian eye gazes steadily, as if on a distant object. That is half the romance of it, that it makes you think of dark and distant places in the forest.

Guess always preferred inventing his implements to receiving them from others: and, when considered as mad by his tribe, while bent on the invention of his alphabet, contented himself with teaching it to his little daughter; an unimpeachable witness.

Red Jacket's face, too, is much more intellectual than almost any other. But, in becoming so, it loses nothing of the peculiar Indian stamp, but only carries these traits to their perfection. Irony, discernment, resolution, and a deep smouldering fire, that disdains to flicker where it cannot blaze, may there be read. Nothing can better represent the sort of unfeelingness the whites have towards the Indians, than their conduct towards his remains. He had steadily opposed the introduction of white religion, or manners, among the Indians. He believed that for them to break down the barriers was to perish. On many occasions he had expressed this with all the force of his eloquence. He told the preachers, "if the Great Spirit had meant your religion for the red man, he would have given it to them. What they (the missionaries) tell us, we do not understand; and the light they ask for us, makes the straight and plain path trod by our fathers dark and dreary."

When he died, he charged his people to inter him themselves. "Dig my grave yourselves, and let not the white man pursue me there." In defiance of this last solemn request, and the invariable tenor of his life, the missionaries seized the body and performed their service over it, amid the sullen indignation of his people, at what, under the circumstances, was sacrilege.

Of Indian religion a fine specimen is given in the conduct of one of the war chiefs, who, on an important occasion, made a vow to the sun of entire renunciation in case he should be crowned with success. When he was so, he first went through a fast, and sacrificial dance, involving great personal torment, and lasting several days; then, distributing all his property, even his lodges, and mats, among the tribe, he and his family took up their lodging upon the bare ground, beneath the bare sky.

The devotion of the Stylites and the hair-cloth saints, is in act, though not in motive, less noble, because this great chief proposed to go on in common life, where he had lived as a prince—a beggar.

The memoir by Corn Plant of his early days is beautiful.

Very fine anecdotes are told of two of the Western chiefs, father and son, who had the wisdom to see the true policy toward the whites, and steadily to adhere to it.

A murder having taken place in the jurisdiction of the father, he delivered himself up, with those suspected, to imprisonment. One of his companions chafed bitterly under confinement. He told the chief, if they ever got out, he would kill him, and did so. The son, then a boy, came in his rage and sorrow, to this Indian, and insulted him in every way. The squaw, angry at this, urged her husband "to kill the boy at once." But he only replied with "the joy of the valiant," "He will be a great Brave," and then delivered himself up to atone for his victim, and met his death with the noblest Roman composure.

This boy became rather a great chief than a great brave, and the anecdotes about him are of signal beauty and significance.

There is a fine story of an old mother, who gave herself to death instead of her son. The son, at the time, accepted the sacrifice, seeing, with Indian coolness, that it was better she should give up her few solitary and useless days, than he a young existence full of promise. But he could not abide by this view, and after suffering awhile all the anguish of remorse, he put himself solemnly to death in the presence of the tribe, as the only atonement he could make. His young wife stood by, with her child in her arms, commanding her emotions, as he desired, for, no doubt, it seemed to her also, a sacred duty.

But the finest story of all is that of Petalesharro, in whose tribe at the time, and not many years since, the custom of offering human sacrifices still subsisted. The fire was kindled, the victim, a young female captive, bound to the stake, the tribe assembled round. The young brave darted through them, snatched the girl from her peril, placed her upon his horse, and both had vanished before the astonished spectators had thought to interpose.

He placed the girl in her distant home, and then returned. Such is the might of right, when joined with courage, that none ventured a word of resentment or question. His father, struck by truth, endeavored, and with success, to abolish the barbarous custom in the tribe. On a later occasion, Petalesharro again offered his life, if required, but it was not.

This young warrior visiting Washington, a medal was presented him in honor of these acts. His reply deserves sculpture: "When I did it, I knew not that it was good. I did it in ignorance. This medal makes me know that it was good."

The recorder, through his playful expressions of horror at a declaration so surprising to the civilized Good, shows himself sensible to the grand simplicity of heroic impulse it denotes. Were we, too, so good, as to need a medal to show us that we are!

The half-breed and half-civilized chiefs, however handsome, look vulgar beside the pure blood. They have the dignity of neither race.

The death of Oseola, (as described by Catlin,) presents a fine picture in the stern, warlike kind, taking leave with kindness, as a private friend, of the American officers; but, as a foe in national regards, he raised himself in his dying bed, and painted his face with the tokens of eternal enmity.

The historian of the Indians should be one of their own race, as able to sympathize with them, and possessing a mind as enlarged and cultivated as John Ross, and with his eye turned to the greatness of the past, rather than the scanty promise of the future. Hearing of the wampum belts, supposed to have been sent to our tribes by Montezuma, on the invasion of the Spaniard, we feel that an Indian who could glean traditions familiarly from the old men, might collect much that we could interpret.

Still, any clear outline, even of a portion of their past, is not to be hoped, and we shall be well contented if we can have a collection of genuine fragments, that will indicate as clearly their life, as a horse's head from the Parthenon the genius of Greece.

Such, to me, are the stories I have cited above. And even European sketches of this greatness, distant and imperfect though they be, yet convey the truth, if made in a sympathizing spirit. Adair's Red Shoes, Murray's old man, Catlin's noble Mandan chief, Henry's Wa-wa-tam, with what we know of Philip, Pontiac, Tecumseh and Red Jacket, would suffice to give the ages a glimpse at what was great in Indian life and Indian character.

We hope, too, there will be a national institute, containing all the remains of the Indians,—all that has been preserved by official intercourse at Washington, Catlin's collection, and a picture gallery as complete as can be made, with a collection of skulls from all parts of the country. To this should be joined the scanty library that exists on the subject.

I have not mentioned Mackenzie's Travels. He is an accurate observer, but sparing in his records, because his attention was wholly bent on his own objects. This circumstance gives a heroic charm to his scanty and simple narrative. Let what will happen, or who will go back, he cannot; he must find the sea, along those frozen rivers, through those starving countries, among tribes of stinted men, whose habitual interjection was "edui, it is hard, uttered in a querulous tone," distrusted by his followers, deserted by his guides, on, on he goes, till he sees the sea, cold, lowering, its strand bristling with foes; but he does see it.

His few observations, especially on the tribes who lived on fish, and held them in such superstitious observance, give a lively notion of the scene.

A little pamphlet has lately been published, giving an account of the massacre at Chicago, which I wish much I had seen while there, as it would have imparted an interest to spots otherwise barren. It is written with animation, and in an excellent style, telling just what we want to hear, and no more. The traits given of Indian generosity are as characteristic as those of Indian cruelty. A lady, who was saved by a friendly chief holding her under the waters of the lake, while the balls were whizzing around, received also, in the heat of the conflict, a reviving draught from a squaw, who saw she was exhausted; and, as she lay down, a mat was hung up between her and the scene of butchery, so that she was protected from the sight, though she could not be from sounds, full of horror.

I have not wished to write sentimentally about the Indians, however moved by the thought of their wrongs and speedy extinction. I know that the Europeans who took possession of this country, felt themselves justified by their superior civilization and religious ideas. Had they been truly civilized or Christianized, the conflicts which sprang from the collision of the two races, might have been avoided; but this cannot be expected in movements made by masses of men. The mass has never yet been humanized, though the age may develop a human thought.

Since those conflicts and differences did arise, the hatred which sprang, from terror and suffering, on the European side, has naturally warped the whites still farther from justice.

The Indian, brandishing the scalps of his friends and wife, drinking their blood and eating their hearts, is by him viewed as a fiend, though, at a distant day, he will no doubt be considered as having acted the Roman or Carthaginian part of heroic and patriotic self-defence, according to the standard of right and motives prescribed by his religious faith and education. Looked at by his own standard, he is virtuous when he most injures his enemy, and the white, if he be really the superior in enlargement of thought, ought to cast aside his inherited prejudices enough to see this,—to look on him in pity and brotherly goodwill, and do all he can to mitigate the doom of those who survive his past injuries.

In McKenney's book, is proposed a project for organizing the Indians under a patriarchal government, but it does not look feasible, even on paper. Could their own intelligent men be left to act unimpeded in their behalf, they would do far better for them than the white thinker, with all his general knowledge. But we dare not hope the designs of such will not always be frustrated by the same barbarous selfishness they were in Georgia. There was a chance of seeing what might have been done, now lost forever.

Yet let every man look to himself how far this blood shall be required at his hands. Let the missionary, instead of preaching to the Indian, preach to the trader who ruins him, of the dreadful account which will be demanded of the followers of Cain, in a sphere where the accents of purity and love come on the ear more decisively than in ours. Let every legislator take the subject to heart, and if he cannot undo the effects of past sin, try for that clear view and right sense that may save us from sinning still more deeply. And let every man and every woman, in their private dealings with the subjugated race, avoid all share in embittering, by insult or unfeeling prejudice, the captivity of Israel.

Chapter VII

SAULT ST. MARIE

NINE DAYS I PASSED ALONE at Mackinaw, except for occasional visits from kind and agreeable residents at the fort, and Mr. and Mrs. A. Mr. A., long engaged in the fur-trade, is gratefully remembered by many travellers. From Mrs. A., also, I received kind attentions, paid in the vivacious and graceful manner of her nation.

The society at the boarding house entertained, being of a kind entirely new to me. There were many traders from the remote stations, such as La Pointe, Arbre Croche,—men who had become half wild and wholly rude, by living in the wild; but good-humored, observing, and with a store of knowledge to impart, of the kind proper to their place.

There were two little girls here, that were pleasant companions for me. One gay, frank, impetuous, but sweet and winning. She was an American, fair, and with bright brown hair. The other, a little French Canadian, used to join me in my walks, silently take my hand, and sit at my feet when I stopped in beautiful places. She seemed to understand without a word; and I never shall forget her little figure, with its light, but pensive motion, and her delicate, grave features, with the pale, clear complexion and soft eye. She was motherless, and much left alone by her father and brothers, who were boatmen. The two little girls were as pretty representatives of Allegro and Penseroso, as one would wish to see.

I had been wishing that a boat would come in to take me to the Sault St. Marie, and several times started to the window at night in hopes that the pant and dusky-red light crossing the waters belonged to such an one; but they were always boats for Chicago or Buffalo, till, on the 28th of August, Allegro, who shared my plans and wishes, rushed in to tell me that the General Scott had come, and, in this little steamer, accordingly, I set off the next morning.

174   SUMMER ON THE LAKES

I was the only lady, and attended in the cabin by a Dutch girl and an Indian woman. They both spoke English fluently, and entertained me much by accounts of their different experiences.

The Dutch girl told me of a dance among the common people at Amsterdam, called the shepherd's dance. The two leaders are dressed as shepherd and shepherdess; they invent to the music all kinds of movements, descriptive of things that may happen in the field, and the rest were obliged to follow. I have never heard of any dance which gave such free play to the fancy as this. French dances merely describe the polite movements of society; Spanish and Neapolitan, love; the beautiful Mazurkas, &c., are warlike or expressive of wild scenery. But in this one is great room both for fun and fancy.

The Indian was married, when young, by her parents, to a man she did not love. He became dissipated, and did not maintain her. She left him, taking with her their child; for whom and herself she earns a subsistence by going as chambermaid in these boats. Now and then, she said, her husband called on her, and asked if he might live with her again; but she always answered, no. Here she was far freer than she would have been in civilized life.

I was pleased by the nonchalance of this woman, and the perfectly national manner she had preserved after so many years of contact with all kinds of people. The two women, when I left the boat, made me presents of Indian work, such as travellers value, and the manner of the two was characteristic of their different nations. The Indian brought me hers, when I was alone, looked bashfully down when she gave it, and made an almost sentimental little speech. The Dutch girl brought hers in public, and, bridling her short chin with a self-complacent air, observed she had *bought* it for me. But the feeling of affectionate regard was the same in the minds of both.

Island after island we passed, all fairly shaped and clustering friendly, but with little variety of vegetation.

In the afternoon the weather became foggy, and we could not proceed after dark. That was as dull an evening as ever fell.

The next morning the fog still lay heavy, but the captain took me out in his boat on an exploring expedition, and we found the remains of the old English fort on Point St. Joseph's. All around was so wholly unmarked by anything but stress of wind and weather, the shores of these islands and their woods so like one another, wild and lonely, but nowhere rich and majestic, that there was some charm in the remains of the garden, the remains even of chimneys and a pier. They gave feature to the scene.

Here I gathered many flowers, but they were the same as at Mackinaw.

The captain, though he had been on this trip hundreds of times, had never seen this spot, and never would, but for this fog, and his desire to entertain me. He presented a striking instance how men, for the sake of getting a living, forget to live. It is just the same in the most romantic as the most dull and vulgar places. Men get the harness on so fast, that they can never shake it off, unless they guard against this danger from the very first. In Chicago, how many men, who never found time to see the prairies or learn anything unconnected with the business of the day, or about the country they were living in!

So this captain, a man of strong sense and good eyesight, rarely found time to go off the track or look about him on it. He lamented, too, that there had been no call which induced him to develop his powers of expression, so that he might communicate what he had seen, for the enjoyment or instruction of others.

This is a common fault among the active men, the truly living, who could tell what life is. It should not be so. Literature should not be left to the mere literati—eloquence to the mere orator. Every Cæsar should be able to write his own commentary. We want a more equal, more thorough, more harmonious development, and there is nothing to hinder from it the men of this country, except their own supineness, or sordid views.

When the weather did clear, our course up the river was delightful. Long stretched before us the island of St. Joseph's, with its fair woods of sugar maple. A gentleman on board, who belongs to the Fort at the Sault, said their pastime was to come in the season of making sugar, and pass some time on this island,—the days at work, and the evening in dancing and other amusements.

I wished to extract here Henry's account of this, for it was just the same sixty years ago as now, but have already occupied too much room with extracts. Work of this kind done in the open air, where everything is temporary, and every utensil prepared on the spot, gives life a truly festive air. At such times, there is labor and no care—energy with gaiety, gaiety of the heart.

I think with the same pleasure of the Italian vintage, the Scotch harvest-home, with its evening dance in the barn, the Russian cabbage-feast even, and our huskings and hop-gatherings—the hop-gatherings where the groups of men and girls are pulling down and filling baskets with the gay festoons, present as graceful pictures as the Italian vintage.

I should also like to insert Henry's descriptions of the method of catching trout and white fish, the delicacies of this region, for the same reason as I want his account of the Gens de Terre, the savages among savages, and his tales, dramatic, if not true, of cannibalism.

I have no less grieved to omit Carver's account of the devotion of a Winnebago prince at the Falls of St. Anthony, which he describes with a simplicity and intelligence, that are very pleasing.

I take the more pleasure in both Carver and Henry's power of appreciating what is good in the Indian character, that both had run the greatest risk of losing their lives during their intercourse with the Indians, and had seen them in their utmost exasperation, with all its revolting circumstances.

I wish I had a thread long enough to string on it all these beads that take my fancy; but, as I have not, I can only refer the reader to the books themselves, which may be found in the library of Harvard College, if not elsewhere.

How pleasant is the course along a new river, the sight of new shores; like a life, would but life flow as fast, and upbear us with as full a stream. I hoped we should come in sight of the rapids by daylight; but the beautiful sunset was quite gone, and only a young moon trembling over the scene, when we came within hearing of them.

I sat up long to hear them merely. It was a thoughtful hour. These two days, the 29th and 30th August, are memorable in my life; the latter is the birth-day of a near friend. I pass them alone, approaching Lake Superior; but I shall not enter into that truly wild and free region; shall not have the canoe voyage, whose daily adventure, with the camping out at night beneath the stars, would have given an interlude of such value to my existence. I shall not see the Pictured Rocks, their chapels and urns. It did not depend on me; it never has, whether such things shall be done or not.

My friends! may they see, and do, and be more, especially those who have before them a greater number of birthdays, and of a more healthy and unfettered existence:

To Edith, on Her Birthday

If the same star our fates together bind,
Why are we thus divided, mind from mind?
If the same law one grief to both impart,
How could'st thou grieve a trusting mother's heart?

Our aspiration seeks a common aim,
Why were we tempered of such differing frame?
—But 'tis too late to turn this wrong to right;
Too cold, too damp, too deep, has fallen the night.

And yet, the angel of my life replies,
Upon that night a Morning Star shall rise,
Fairer than that which ruled the temporal birth,
Undimmed by vapors of the dreamy earth;

It says, that, where a heart thy claim denies,
Genius shall read its secret ere it flies;
The earthly form may vanish from thy side,
Pure love will make thee still the spirit's bride.

And thou, ungentle, yet much loving child,
Whose heart still shows the "untamed haggard wild,"
A heart which justly makes the highest claim,
Too easily is checked by transient blame;

Ere such an orb can ascertain its sphere,
The ordeal must be various and severe;
My prayers attend thee, though the feet may fly,
I hear thy music in the silent sky.

I should like, however, to hear some notes of earthly music to-night. By the faint moonshine I can hardly see the banks;

how they look I have no guess, except that there are trees, and, now and then, a light lets me know there are homes with their various interests. I should like to hear some strains of the flute from beneath those trees, just to break the sound of the rapids.

> When no gentle eyebeam charms;
> No fond hope the bosom warms;
> Of thinking the lone mind is tired—
> Nought seems bright to be desired;
>
> Music, be thy sails unfurled,
> Bear me to thy better world;
> O'er a cold and weltering sea,
> Blow thy breezes warm and free;
>
> By sad sighs they ne'er were chilled,
> By sceptic spell were never stilled;
> Take me to that far-off shore,
> Where lovers meet to part no more;
> There doubt, and fear and sin are o'er,
> The star of love shall set no more.

With the first light of dawn I was up and out, and then was glad I had not seen all the night before; it came upon me with such power in its dewy freshness. O! they are beautiful indeed, these rapids! The grace is so much more obvious than the power. I went up through the old Chippeway burying ground to their head, and sat down on a large stone to look. A little way off was one of the home lodges, unlike in shape to the temporary ones at Mackinaw, but these have been described by Mrs. Jameson. Women, too, I saw coming home from the woods, stooping under great loads of cedar boughs, that were strapped upon their backs. But in many European countries women carry great loads, even of wood, upon their backs. I used to hear the girls singing and laughing as they were cutting down boughs at Mackinaw; this part of their employment, though laborious, gives them the pleasure of being a great deal in the free woods.

I had ordered a canoe to take me down the rapids, and presently I saw it coming, with the two Indian canoe-men in pink calico shirts, moving it about with their long poles, with a grace and dexterity worthy fairy land. Now and then they cast the scoop-net; all looked just as I had fancied, only far prettier.

When they came to me, they spread a mat in the middle of the canoe; I sat down, and in less than four minutes we had descended the rapids, a distance of more than three quarters of a mile. I was somewhat disappointed in this being no more of an exploit than I found it. Having heard such expressions used as of "darting," or, "shooting down," these rapids, I had fancied there was a wall of rock somewhere, where descent would somehow be accomplished, and that there would come some one gasp of terror and delight, some sensation entirely new to me; but I found myself in smooth water, before I had time to feel anything but the buoyant pleasure of being carried so lightly through this surf amid the breakers. Now and then the Indians spoke to one another in a vehement jabber, which, however, had no tone that expressed other than pleasant excitement. It is, no doubt, an act of wonderful dexterity to steer amid these jagged rocks, when one rude touch would tear a hole in the birch canoe; but these men are evidently so used to doing it, and so adroit, that the silliest person could not feel afraid. I should like to have come down twenty times, that I might have had leisure to realize the pleasure. But the fog which had detained us on the way, shortened the boat's stay at the Sault, and I wanted my time to walk about.

While coming down the rapids, the Indians caught a white-fish for my breakfast; and certainly it was the best of breakfasts. The white-fish I found quite another thing caught on this spot, and cooked immediately, from what I had found it at Chicago or Mackinaw. Before, I had had the bad taste to prefer the trout, despite the solemn and eloquent remonstrances of the Habitués, to whom the superiority of white-fish seemed a cardinal point of faith.

I am here reminded that I have omitted that indispensable part of a travelling journal, the account of what we found to eat. I cannot hope to make up, by one bold stroke, all my omissions of daily record; but that I may show myself not destitute of the common feelings of humanity, I will observe that he whose affections turn in summer towards vegetables, should not come to this region, till the subject of diet be better understood; that of fruit, too, there is little yet, even at the best hotel tables; that the prairie chickens require no praise from me, and that the trout and white-fish are worthy the transparency of the lake waters.

In this brief mention I by no means mean to give myself an air of superiority to the subject. If a dinner in the Illinois woods, on dry bread and drier meat, with water from the stream that flowed hard by, pleased me best of all, yet at one time, when living at a house where nothing was prepared for the table fit to touch, and even the bread could not be partaken of without a headach in consequence, I learnt to understand and sympathize with the anxious tone in which fathers of families, about to take their innocent children into some scene of wild beauty, ask first of all, "Is there a good table?" I shall ask just so in future. Only those whom the Powers have furnished small travelling cases of ambrosia, can take exercise all day, and be happy without even bread morning or night.

Our voyage back was all pleasure. It was the fairest day. I saw the river, the islands, the clouds to the greatest advantage.

On board was an old man, an Illinois farmer, whom I found a most agreeable companion. He had just been with his son, and eleven other young men, on an exploring expedition to the shores of lake Superior. He was the only old man of the party, but he had enjoyed, most of any, the journey. He had been the counsellor and playmate, too, of the young ones. He was one of those parents,—why so rare?—who understand and live a new life in that of their children, instead of wasting time and young happiness in trying to make them conform to an object and standard of their own. The character and history of each child may be a new and poetic experience to the parent, if he will let it. Our farmer was domestic, judicious, solid; the son, inventive, enterprising, superficial, full of follies, full of resources, always liable to failure, sure to rise above it. The father conformed to, and learnt from, a character he could not change, and won the sweet from the bitter.

His account of his life at home, and of his late adventures among the Indians, was very amusing, but I want talent to write it down. I have not heard the slang of these people intimately enough. There is a good book about Indiana, called the New

Purchase, written by a person who knows the people of the country well enough to describe them in their own way. It is not witty, but penetrating, valuable for its practical wisdom and good-humored fun.

There were many sportsman stories told, too, by those from Illinois and Wisconsin. I do not retain any of these well enough, nor any that I heard earlier, to write them down, though they always interested me from bringing wild, natural scenes before the mind. It is pleasant for the sportsman to be in countries so alive with game; yet it is so plenty that one would think shooting pigeons or grouse would seem more like slaughter, than the excitement of skill to a good sportsman. Hunting the deer is full of adventure, and needs only a Scrope to describe it to invest the western woods with *historic* associations.

How pleasant it was to sit and hear rough men tell pieces out of their own common lives, in place of the frippery talk of some fine circle with its conventional sentiment, and timid, second-hand criticism. Free blew the wind, and boldly flowed the stream, named for Mary mother mild.

A fine thunder shower came on in the afternoon. It cleared at sunset, just as we came in sight of beautiful Mackinaw, over which a rainbow bent in promise of peace.

I have always wondered, in reading travels, at the childish joy travellers felt at meeting people they knew, and their sense of loneliness when they did not, in places where there was everything new to occupy the attention. So childish, I thought, always to be longing for the new in the old, and the old in the new. Yet just such sadness I felt, when I looked on the island, glittering in the sunset, canopied by the rainbow, and thought no friend would welcome me there; just such childish joy I felt, to see unexpectedly on the landing, the face of one whom I called friend.

The remaining two or three days were delightfully spent, in walking or boating, or sitting at the window to see the Indians go. This was not quite so pleasant as their coming in, though accomplished with the same rapidity; a family not taking half an hour to prepare for departure, and the departing canoe a beautiful object. But they left behind, on all the shore, the blemishes of their stay—old rags, dried boughs, fragments of

MACKINAW BEACH

INDIANS
183

food, the marks of their fires. Nature likes to cover up and gloss over spots and scars, but it would take her some time to restore that beach to the state it was in before they came.

S. and I had a mind for a canoe excursion, and we asked one of the traders to engage us two good Indians, that would not only take us out, but be sure and bring us back, as we could not hold converse with them. Two others offered their aid, beside the chief's son, a fine looking youth of about sixteen, richly dressed in blue broadcloth, scarlet sash and leggins, with a scarf of brighter red than the rest, tied around his head, its ends falling gracefully on one shoulder. They thought it, apparently, fine amusement to be attending two white women; they carried us into the path of the steamboat, which was going out, and paddled with all their force,—rather too fast, indeed, for there was something of a swell on the lake, and they sometimes threw water into the canoe. However, it flew over the waves, light as a sea-gull. They would say, "Pull away," and "Ver' warm," and, after these words, would laugh gaily. They enjoyed the hour, I believe, as much as we.

The house where we lived belonged to the widow of a French trader, an Indian by birth, and wearing the dress of her country. She spoke French fluently, and was very ladylike in her manners. She is a great character among them. They were all the time coming to pay her homage, or to get her aid and advice; for she is, I am told, a shrewd woman of business. My companion carried about her sketch-book with her, and the Indians were interested when they saw her using her pencil, though less so than about the sun-shade. This lady of the tribe wanted to borrow the sketches of the beach, with its lodges and wild groups, "to show to the *savages*," she said.

Of the practical ability of the Indian women, a good specimen is given by McKenney, in an amusing story of one who went to Washington, and acted her part there in the "first circles," with a tact and sustained dissimulation worthy of Cagliostro. She seemed to have a thorough love of intrigue for its own sake, and much dramatic talent. Like the chiefs of her nation, when on an expedition among the foe, whether for revenge or profit, no impulses of vanity or wayside seductions had power to turn her aside from carrying out her plan as she had originally projected it.

Although I have little to tell, I feel that I have learnt a great deal of the Indians, from observing them even in this broken and degraded condition. There is a language of eye and motion which cannot be put into words, and which teaches what words never can. I feel acquainted with the soul of this race; I read its nobler thought in their defaced figures. There *was* a greatness, unique and precious, which he who does not feel will never duly appreciate the majesty of nature in this American continent.

I have mentioned that the Indian orator, who addressed the agents on this occasion, said, the difference between the white man and the red man is this: "the white man no sooner came here, than he thought of preparing the way for his posterity; the red man never thought of this." I was assured this was exactly his phrase; and it defines the true difference. We get the better because we do

"Look before and after."

But, from the same cause, we

"Pine for what is not."

The red man, when happy, was thoroughly happy; when good, was simply good. He needed the medal, to let him know that he *was* good.

These evenings we were happy, looking over the old-fashioned garden, over the beach, over the waters and pretty island opposite, beneath the growing moon; we did not stay to see it full at Mackinaw. At two o'clock, one night, or rather morning, the Great Western came snorting in, and we must go; and Mackinaw, and all the north-west summer, is now to me no more than picture and dream;—

"A dream within a dream."

These last days at Mackinaw have been pleasanter than the "lonesome" nine, for I have recovered the companion with whom I set out from the East, one who sees all, prizes all, enjoys much, interrupts never.

At Detroit we stopped for half a day. This place is famous in our history, and the unjust anger at its surrender is still

GENERAL HULL

expressed by almost every one who passes there. I had always shared the common feeling on this subject; for the indignation at a disgrace to our arms that seemed so unnecessary, has been handed down from father to child, and few of us have taken the pains to ascertain where the blame lay. But now, upon the spot, having read all the testimony, I felt convinced that it should rest solely with the government, which, by neglecting to sustain General Hull, as he had a right to expect they would, compelled him to take this step, or sacrifice many lives, and of the defenceless inhabitants, not of soldiers, to the cruelty of a savage foe, for the sake of his reputation.

I am a woman, and unlearned in such affairs; but, to a person with common sense and good eyesight, it is clear, when viewing the location, that, under the circumstances, he had no prospect of successful defence, and that to attempt it would have been an act of vanity, not valor.

I feel that I am not biased in this judgment by my personal relations, for I have always heard both sides, and, though my feelings had been moved by the picture of the old man sitting down, in the midst of his children, to a retired and despoiled old age, after a life of honor and happy intercourse with the public, yet tranquil, always secure that justice must be done at last, I supposed, like others, that he deceived himself, and deserved to pay the penalty for failure to the responsibility he had undertaken. Now on the spot, I change, and believe the country at large must, ere long, change from this opinion. And I wish to add my testimony, however trifling its weight, before it be drowned in the voice of general assent, that I may do some justice to the feelings which possessed me here and now.

A noble boat, the Wisconsin, was to be launched this afternoon, the whole town was out in many-colored array, the band playing. Our boat swept round to a good position, and all was ready but—the Wisconsin, which could not be made to stir. This was quite a disappointment. It would have been an imposing sight.

In the boat many signs admonished that we were floating eastward. A shabbily dressed phrenologist laid his hand on every head which would bend, with half-conceited, half-sheepish expression, to the trial of his skill. Knots of people gathered here and there to discuss points of theology. A bereaved lover

SUMMER ON THE LAKES

was seeking religious consolation in — Butler's Analogy, which he had purchased for that purpose. However, he did not turn over many pages before his attention was drawn aside by the gay glances of certain damsels that came on board at Detroit, and, though Butler might afterwards be seen sticking from his pocket, it had not weight to impede him from many a feat of lightness and liveliness. I doubt if it went with him from the boat. Some there were, even, discussing the doctrines of Fourier. It seemed pity they were not going to, rather than from, the rich and free country where it would be so much easier, than with us, to try the great experiment of voluntary association, and show, beyond a doubt, that "an ounce of prevention is worth a pound of cure," a maxim of the "wisdom of nations," which has proved of little practical efficacy as yet.

Better to stop before landing at Buffalo, while I have yet the advantage over some of my readers.

The Book to the Reader

WHO OPENS, AS AMERICAN READERS OFTEN DO,
AT THE END, WITH DOGGEREL SUBMISSION

To see your cousin in her country home,
If at the time of blackberries you come,
"Welcome, my friends," she cries with ready glee,
"The fruit is ripened, and the paths are free.
But, madam, you will tear that handsome gown;
The little boy be sure to tumble down;
And, in the thickets where they ripen best,
The matted ivy, too, its bower has drest.
And then, the thorns your hands are sure to rend,
Unless with heavy gloves you will defend;
Amid most thorns the sweetest roses blow,
Amid most thorns the sweetest berries grow."

If, undeterred, you to the fields must go,
    You tear your dresses and you scratch your hands;
But, in the places where the berries grow,
    A sweeter fruit the ready sense commands,

THE BOOK TO THE READER

Of wild, gay feelings, fancies springing sweet—
Of bird-like pleasures, fluttering and fleet.

Another year, you cannot go yourself,
   To win the berries from the thickets wild,
And housewife skill, instead, has filled the shelf
   With blackberry jam, "by best receipts compiled,—
Not made with country sugar, for too strong
The flavors that to maple juice belong;
But foreign sugar, nicely mixed 'to suit
The taste,' spoils not the fragrance of the fruit."

"'Tis pretty good," half-tasting, you reply,
"I scarce should know it from fresh blackberry.
But the best pleasure such a fruit can yield,
Is to be gathered in the open field;
If only as an article of food,
Cherry or crab-apple are quite as good;
And, for occasions of festivity,
West India sweetmeats you had better buy."

Thus, such a dish of homely sweets as these
In neither way may chance the taste to please.

Yet try a little with the evening-bread;
Bring a good needle for the spool of thread;
Take fact with fiction, silver with the lead,
And, at the mint, you can get gold instead;
In fine, read me, even as you would be read.

WOMAN IN THE
NINETEENTH CENTURY

*"Frei durch Vernunft, stark durch Gesetze,
Durch Sanftmuth gross, und reich durch Schätze,
Die lange Zeit dein Busen dir verschwieg."*

---

*"I meant the day-star should not brighter rise,
Nor lend like influence from its lucent seat;
I meant she should be courteous, facile, sweet,
Free from that solemn vice of greatness, pride;
I meant each softest virtue there should meet,
Fit in that softer bosom to reside;
Only a (heavenward and instructed) soul
I purposed her, that should, with even powers,
The rock, the spindle, and the shears control
Of destiny, and spin her own free hours."*

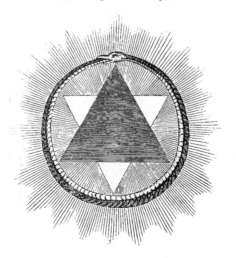

Preface

THE FOLLOWING ESSAY is a reproduction, modified and expanded, of an article published in "The Dial, Boston, July, 1843," under the title of "The Great Lawsuit. Man versus Men: Woman versus Women."

This article excited a good deal of sympathy, and still more interest. It is in compliance with wishes expressed from many quarters, that it is prepared for publication in its present form.

Objections having been made to the former title, as not sufficiently easy to be understood, the present has been substituted as expressive of the main purpose of the essay; though, by myself, the other is preferred, partly for the reason others do not like it, *i. e.*, that it requires some thought to see what it means, and might thus prepare the reader to meet me on my own ground. Beside, it offers a larger scope, and is, in that way, more just to my desire. I meant, by that title, to intimate the fact that, while it is the destiny of Man, in the course of the Ages, to ascertain and fulfil the law of his being, so that his life shall be seen, as a whole, to be that of an angel or messenger, the action of prejudices and passions, which attend, in the day, the growth of the individual, is continually obstructing the holy work that is to make the earth a part of heaven. By Man I mean both man and woman: these are the two halves of one thought. I lay no especial stress on the welfare of either. I believe that the development of the one cannot be effected without that of the other. My highest wish is that this truth should be distinctly and rationally apprehended, and the conditions of life and freedom recognized as the same for the daughters and the sons of time; twin exponents of a divine thought.

I solicit a sincere and patient attention from those who open the following pages at all. I solicit of women that they will lay it to heart to ascertain what is for them the liberty of law. It is for this, and not for any, the largest, extension of partial privileges that I seek. I ask them, if interested by these suggestions, to search their own experience and intuitions for better, and fill up with fit materials the trenches that hedge them in. From men I ask a noble and earnest attention to any thing that can be offered on this great and still obscure subject, such as I have met from many with whom I stand in private relations.

And may truth, unpolluted by prejudice, vanity, or selfishness, be granted daily more and more, as the due inheritance, and only valuable conquest for us all!

November, 1844.

Woman in the Nineteenth Century

"Frailty, thy name is WOMAN."
"The Earth waits for her Queen."

THE CONNECTION BETWEEN THESE QUOTATIONS may not be obvious, but it is strict. Yet would any contradict us, if we made them applicable to the other side, and began also

> Frailty, thy name is MAN.
> The Earth waits for its King.

Yet man, if not yet fully installed in his powers, has given much earnest of his claims. Frail he is indeed, how frail! how impure! Yet often has the vein of gold displayed itself amid the baser ores, and Man has appeared before us in princely promise worthy of his future.

If, oftentimes, we see the prodigal son feeding on the husks in the fair field no more his own, anon, we raise the eyelids, heavy from bitter tears, to behold in him the radiant apparition of genius and love, demanding not less than the all of goodness, power and beauty. We see that in him the largest claim finds a due foundation. That claim is for no partial sway, no exclusive possession. He cannot be satisfied with any one gift of life, any one department of knowledge or telescopic peep at the heavens. He feels himself called to understand and aid nature, that she may, through his intelligence, be raised and interpreted; to be a student of, and servant to, the universe-spirit; and king of his planet, that as an angelic minister, he may bring it into conscious harmony with the law of that spirit.

In clear triumphant moments, many times, has rung through the spheres the prophecy of his jubilee, and those moments, though past in time, have been translated into eternity by thought; the bright signs they left hang in the heavens, as single stars or constellations, and, already, a thickly sown radiance consoles the wanderer in the darkest night. Other heroes since Hercules have fulfilled the zodiac of beneficent labors, and then given up their mortal part to the fire without a murmur; while no God dared deny that they should have their reward

> Siquis tamen, Hercule, siquis
> Forte Deo doliturus erit, data præmia nollet,
> Sed meruise dari sciet, invitus que probabit,
> Assensere Dei.

Sages and lawgivers have bent their whole nature to the search for truth, and thought themselves happy if they could buy, with the sacrifice of all temporal ease and pleasure, one seed for the future Eden. Poets and priests have strung the lyre with the heartstrings, poured out their best blood upon the altar, which, reared anew from age to age shall at last sustain the flame pure enough to rise to highest heaven. Shall we not name with as deep a benediction those who, if not so immediately, or so consciously, in connection with the eternal truth, yet, led and fashioned by a divine instinct, serve no less to develope and interpret the open secret of love passing into life, energy creating for the purpose of happiness; the artist whose hand, drawn by a pre-existent harmony to a certain medium, moulds it to forms of life more highly and completely organized than are seen elsewhere, and, by carrying out the intention of nature, reveals her meaning to those who are not yet wise enough to divine it; the philosopher who listens steadily for laws and causes, and from those obvious, infers those yet unknown; the historian who, in faith that all events must have their reason and their aim, records them, and thus fills archives from which the youth of prophets may be fed. The man of science dissects the statements, tests the facts, and demonstrates order, even where he cannot its purpose.

Lives, too, which bear none of these names, have yielded tones of no less significance. The candlestick set in a low place has given light as faithfully, where it was needed, as that upon the hill. In close alleys, in dismal nooks, the Word has been read as distinctly, as when shown by angels to holy men in the dark prison. Those who till a spot of earth scarcely larger than is wanted for a grave, have deserved that the sun should shine upon its sod till violets answer.

So great has been, from time to time, the promise, that, in all ages, men have said the gods themselves came down to dwell with them; that the All-Creating wandered on the earth to taste, in a limited nature, the sweetness of virtue; that the All-Sustaining incarnated himself to guard, in space and time, the destinies of this world; that heavenly genius dwelt among the shepherds, to sing to them and teach them how to sing. Indeed

"Der stets den Hirten gnadig sich bewies."

"He has constantly shown himself favorable to shepherds."

And the dwellers in green pastures and natural students of the stars were selected to hail, first among men, the holy child, whose life and death were to present the type of excellence, which has sustained the heart of so large a portion of mankind in these later generations.

Such marks have been made by the footsteps of *man*, (still alas! to be spoken of as the *ideal* man,) wherever he has passed through the wilderness of *men*, and whenever the pigmies stepped in one of those they felt dilate within the breast somewhat that promised nobler stature and purer blood. They were impelled to forsake their evil ways of decrepit scepticism, and covetousness of corruptible possessions. Conviction flowed in upon them. They, too, raised the cry; God is living, now, to-day; and all beings are brothers, for they are his children. Simple words enough, yet which only angelic nature, can use or hear in their full free sense.

These were the triumphant moments, but soon the lower nature took its turn, and the era of a truly human life was postponed.

Thus is man still a stranger to his inheritance, still a pleader, still a pilgrim. Yet his happiness is secure in the end. And now, no more a glimmering consciousness, but assurance begins to be felt and spoken, that the highest ideal man can form of his own powers, is that which he is destined to attain. Whatever the soul knows how to seek, it cannot fail to obtain. This is the law and the prophets. Knock and it shall be opened, seek and ye shall find. It is demonstrated; it is a maxim. Man no longer paints his proper nature in some form and says, "Prometheus had it; it is God-like;" but "Man must have it; it is human." However disputed by many, however ignorantly used, or falsified by those who do receive it, the fact of an universal, unceasing revelation has been too clearly stated in words to be lost sight of in thought, and sermons preached from the text, "Be ye perfect," are the only sermons of a pervasive and deep-searching influence.

But, among those who meditate upon this text, there is a great difference of view, as to the way in which perfection shall be sought.

Through the intellect, say some. Gather from every growth of life its seed of thought; look behind every symbol for its law; if thou canst *see* clearly, the rest will follow.

Through the life, say others. Do the best thou knowest to-day. Shrink not from frequent error in this gradual fragmentary state. Follow thy light for as much as it will show thee, be faithful as far as thou canst, in hope that faith presently will lead to sight. Help others, without blaming their need of thy help. Love much and be forgiven.

It needs not intellect, needs not experience, says a third. If you took the true way, your destiny would be accomplished in a purer and more natural order. You would not learn through facts of thought or action, but express through them the certainties of wisdom. In quietness yield thy soul to the causal soul. Do not disturb thy apprenticeship by premature effort; neither check the tide of instruction by methods of thy own. Be still, seek not, but wait in obedience. Thy commission will be given.

Could we indeed say what we want, could we give a description of the child that is lost, he would be found. As soon as the soul can affirm clearly that a certain demonstration is wanted, it is at hand. When the Jewish prophet described the Lamb, as the expression of what was required by the coming era, the time drew nigh. But we say not, see not as yet, clearly, what we would. Those who call for a more triumphant expression of love, a love that cannot be crucified, show not a perfect sense of what has already been given. Love has already been expressed, that made all things new, that gave the worm its place and

WOMAN IN THE NINETEENTH CENTURY 197

ministry as well as the eagle; a love to which it was alike to descend into the depths of hell, or to sit at the right hand of the Father.

Yet, no doubt, a new manifestation is at hand, a new hour in the day of man. We cannot expect to see any one sample of completed being, when the mass of men still lie engaged in the sod, or use the freedom of their limbs only with wolfish energy. The tree cannot come to flower till its root be free from the cankering worm, and its whole growth open to air and light. While any one is base, none can be entirely free and noble. Yet something new shall presently be shown of the life of man, for hearts crave, if minds do not know how to ask it.

Among the strains of prophecy, the following, by an earnest mind of a foreign land, written some thirty years ago, is not yet outgrown; and it has the merit of being a positive appeal from the heart, instead of a critical declaration what man should *not* do.

"The ministry of man implies, that he must be filled from the divine fountains which are being engendered through all eternity, so that, at the mere name of his master, he may be able to cast all his enemies into the abyss; that he may deliver all parts of nature from the barriers that imprison them; that he may purge the terrestrial atmosphere from the poisons that infect it; that he may preserve the bodies of men from the corrupt influences that surround, and the maladies that afflict them; still more, that he may keep their souls pure from the malignant insinuations which pollute, and the gloomy images that obscure them; that he may restore its serenity to the Word, which false words of men fill with mourning and sadness; that he may satisfy the desires of the angels, who await from him the development of the marvels of nature; that, in fine, his world may be filled with God, as eternity is."*

Another attempt we will give, by an obscure observer of our own day and country, to draw some lines of the desired image. It was suggested by seeing the design of Crawford's Orpheus, and connecting with the circumstance of the American, in his garret at Rome, making choice of this subject, that of Americans here at home, showing such ambition to represent the character,

* St. Martin.

by calling their prose and verse "Orphic sayings"—"Orphics." We wish we could add that they have shown that musical apprehension of the progress of nature through her ascending gradations which entitled them so to do, but their attempts are frigid, though sometimes grand; in their strain we are not warmed by the fire which fertilized the soil of Greece.

Orpheus was a law-giver by theocratic commission. He understood nature, and made her forms move to his music. He told her secrets in the form of hymns, nature as seen in the mind of God. His soul went forth toward all beings, yet could remain sternly faithful to a chosen type of excellence. Seeking what he loved, he feared not death nor hell, neither could any shape of dread daunt his faith in the power of the celestial harmony that filled his soul.

It seemed significant of the state of things in this country, that the sculptor should have represented the seer at the moment when he was obliged with his hand to shade his eyes.

> Each Orpheus must to the depths descend,
> For only thus the Poet can be wise,
>   Must make the sad Persephone his friend,
> And buried love to second life arise;
>   Again his love must lose through too much love,
> Must lose his life by living life too true,
>   For what he sought below is passed above,
> Already done is all that he would do;
>   Must tune all being with his single lyre,
> Must melt all rocks free from their primal pain,
>   Must search all nature with his one soul's fire,
> Must bind anew all forms in heavenly chain.
>   If he already sees what he must do,
> Well may he shade his eyes from the far-shining view.

A better comment could not be made on what is required to perfect man, and place him in that superior position for which he was designed, than by the interpretation of Bacon upon the legends of the Syren coast. When the wise Ulysses passed, says he, he caused his mariners to stop their ears with wax, knowing there was in them no power to resist the lure of that voluptuous song. But he, the much experienced man, who wished to be experienced in all, and use all to the service of wisdom, desired to hear the song that he might understand its meaning. Yet, distrusting his own power to be firm in his better purpose, he caused himself to be bound to the mast, that he might be kept secure against his own weakness. But Orpheus passed unfettered, so absorbed in singing hymns to the gods that he could not even hear those sounds of degrading enchantment.

Meanwhile not a few believe, and men themselves have expressed the opinion, that the time is come when Eurydice is to call for an Orpheus, rather than Orpheus for Eurydice: that the idea of Man, however imperfectly brought out, has been far more so than that of Woman, that she, the other half of the same thought, the other chamber of the heart of life, needs now to take her turn in the full pulsation, and that improvement in the daughters will best aid in the reformation of the sons of this age.

It should be remarked that, as the principle of liberty is better understood, and more nobly interpreted, a broader protest is made in behalf of Woman. As men become aware that few men have had a fair chance, they are inclined to say that no women have had a fair chance. The French Revolution, that strangely disguised angel, bore witness in favor of woman, but interpreted her claims no less ignorantly than those of man. Its idea of happiness did not rise beyond outward enjoyment, unobstructed by the tyranny of others. The title it gave was citoyen, citoyenne, and it is not unimportant to woman that even this species of equality was awarded her. Before, she could be condemned to perish on the scaffold for treason, not as a citizen, but as a subject. The right with which this title then invested a human being, was that of bloodshed and license. The Goddess of Liberty was impure. As we read the poem addressed to her not long since, by Beranger, we can scarcely refrain from tears as painful as the tears of blood that flowed when "such crimes were committed in her name." Yes! man, born to purify and animate the unintelligent and the cold, can, in his madness, degrade and pollute no less the fair and the chaste. Yet truth was prophesied in the ravings of that hideous fever, caused by long ignorance and abuse. Europe is conning a valued lesson from the blood-stained page. The same tendencies, farther unfolded, will bear good fruit in this country.

Yet, by men in this country, as by the Jews, when Moses was leading them to the promised land, every thing has been done that inherited depravity could do, to hinder the promise of heaven from its fulfilment. The cross here as elsewhere, has been planted only to be blasphemed by cruelty and fraud. The name of the Prince of Peace has been profaned by all kinds of injustice toward the Gentile whom he said he came to save. But I need not speak of what has been done towards the red man, the black man. Those deeds are the scoff of the world; and they have been accompanied by such pious words that the gentlest would not dare to intercede with "Father, forgive them, for they know not what they do."

Here, as elsewhere, the gain of creation consists always in the growth of individual minds, which live and aspire, as flowers bloom and birds sing, in the midst of morasses; and in the continual development of that thought, the thought of human destiny, which is given to eternity adequately to express, and which ages of failure only seemingly impede. Only seemingly, and whatever seems to the contrary, this country is as surely destined to elucidate a great moral law, as Europe was to promote the mental culture of man.

Though the national independence be blurred by the servility of individuals, though freedom and equality have been proclaimed only to leave room for a monstrous display of slave-dealing and slave-keeping; though the free American so often feels himself free, like the Roman, only to pamper his appetites and his indolence through the misery of his fellow beings, still it is not in vain, that the verbal statement has been made, "All men are born free and equal." There it stands, a golden certainty wherewith to encourage the good, to shame the bad. The new world may be called clearly to perceive that it incurs the utmost penalty, if it reject or oppress the sorrowful brother. And, if men are deaf, the angels hear. But men cannot be deaf. It is inevitable that an external freedom, an independence of the encroachments of other men, such as has been achieved for the nation, should be so also for every member of it. That which has once been clearly conceived in the intelligence cannot fail sooner or later to be acted out. It has become a law as irrevocable as that of the Medes in their ancient dominion; men will privately sin against it, but the law, as expressed by a leading mind of the age,

WOMAN IN THE NINETEENTH CENTURY 201

> "Tutti fatti a sembianza d'un Solo,
> Figli tutti d'un solo riscatto,
> In qual'ora, in qual parte del suolo
> Trascorriamo quest' aura vital,
> Siam fratelli, siam stretti ad un patto:
> Maladetto colui che lo infrange,
> Che s'innalza sul fiacco che piange
> Che contrista uno spirto immortal."*

> "All made in the likeness of the One,
>   All children of one ransom,
> In whatever hour, in whatever part of the soil,
>   We draw this vital air,
> We are brothers; we must be bound by one compact,
>   Accursed he who infringes it,
> Who raises himself upon the weak who weep,
>   Who saddens an immortal spirit."

This law cannot fail of universal recognition. Accursed be he who willingly saddens an immortal spirit, doomed to infamy in later, wiser ages, doomed in future stages of his own being to deadly penance, only short of death. Accursed be he who sins in ignorance, if that ignorance be caused by sloth.

We sicken no less at the pomp than the strife of words. We feel that never were lungs so puffed with the wind of declamation, on moral and religious subjects, as now. We are tempted to implore these "word-heroes," these word-Catos, word-Christs, to beware of cant† above all things; to remember that hypocrisy is the most hopeless as well as the meanest of crimes, and that those must surely be polluted by it, who do not reserve a part of their morality and religion for private use. Landor says that he cannot have a great deal of mind who cannot afford to let the larger part of it lie fallow, and what is true of genius is not less so of virtue. The tongue is a valuable member, but should appropriate but a

---

* Manzoni.

† Dr. Johnson's one piece of advice should be written on every door; "Clear your mind of cant." But Byron, to whom it was so acceptable, in clearing away the noxious vine, shook down the building. Sterling's emendation is worthy of honor:

> "Realize your cant, not cast it off."

small part of the vital juices that are needful all over the body. We feel that the mind may "grow black and rancid in the smoke" even "of altars." We start up from the harangue to go into our closet and shut the door. There inquires the spirit, "Is this rhetoric the bloom of healthy blood or a false pigment artfully laid on?" And yet again we know where is so much smoke, must be some fire; with so much talk about virtue and freedom, must be mingled some desire for them; that it cannot be in vain that such have become the common topics of conversation among men, rather than schemes for tyranny and plunder, that the very newspapers see it best to proclaim themselves Pilgrims, Puritans, Heralds of Holiness. The king that maintains so costly a retinue cannot be a mere boast, or Carabbas fiction. We have waited here long in the dust; we are tired and hungry, but the triumphal procession must appear at last.

Of all its banners, none has been more steadily upheld, and under none have more valor and willingness for real sacrifices been shown, than that of the champions of the enslaved African. And this band it is, which, partly from a natural following out of principles, partly because many women have been prominent in that cause, makes, just now, the warmest appeal in behalf of woman.

Though there has been a growing liberality on this subject, yet society at large is not so prepared for the demands of this party, but that they are and will be for some time, coldly regarded as the Jacobins of their day.

"Is it not enough," cries the irritated trader, "that you have done all you could to break up the national union, and thus destroy the prosperity of our country, but now you must be trying to break up family union, to take my wife away from the cradle and the kitchen hearth to vote at polls, and preach from a pulpit? Of course, if she does such things, she cannot attend to those of her own sphere. She is happy enough as she is. She has more leisure than I have, every means of improvement, every indulgence."

"Have you asked her whether she was satisfied with these *indulgences*?"

"No, but I know she is. She is too amiable to wish what would make me unhappy, and too judicious to wish to step beyond

WOMAN IN THE NINETEENTH CENTURY   203

the sphere of her sex. I will never consent to have our peace disturbed by any such discussions."

"'Consent—you?' it is not consent from you that is in question, it is assent from your wife."

"Am not I the head of my house?"

"You are not the head of your wife. God has given her a mind of her own."

"I am the head and she the heart."

"God grant you play true to one another then. I suppose I am to be grateful that you did not say she was only the hand. If the head represses no natural pulse of the heart, there can be no question as to your giving your consent. Both will be of one accord, and there needs but to present any question to get a full and true answer. There is no need of precaution, of indulgence, or consent. But our doubt is whether the heart does consent with the head, or only obeys its decrees with a passiveness that precludes the exercise of its natural powers, or a repugnance that turns sweet qualities to bitter, or a doubt that lays waste the fair occasions of life. It is to ascertain the truth, that we propose some liberating measures."

Thus vaguely are these questions proposed and discussed at present. But their being proposed at all implies much thought and suggests more. Many women are considering within themselves, what they need that they have not, and what they can have, if they find they need it. Many men are considering whether women are capable of being and having more than they are and have, *and*, whether, if so, it will be best to consent to improvement in their condition.

This morning, I open the Boston "Daily Mail," and find in its "poet's corner," a translation of Schiller's "Dignity of Woman." In the advertisement of a book on America, I see in the table of contents this sequence, "Republican Institutions. American Slavery. American Ladies."

I open the "*Deutsche Schnellpost*," published in New-York, and find at the head of a column, *Juden-und Frauen-emancipation in Ungarn*. Emancipation of Jews and Women in Hungary.

The past year has seen action in the Rhode-Island legislature, to secure married women rights over their own property, where men showed that a very little examination of the subject could teach them much; an article in the Democratic Review on the same subject more largely considered, written by a woman, impelled, it is said, by glaring wrong to a distinguished friend having shown the defects in the existing laws, and the state of opinion from which they spring; and an answer from the revered old man, J. Q. Adams, in some respects the Phocion of his time, to an address made him by some ladies. To this last I shall again advert in another place.

These symptoms of the times have come under my view quite accidentally: one who seeks, may, each month or week, collect more.

The numerous party, whose opinions are already labelled and adjusted too much to their mind to admit of any new light, strive, by lectures on some model-woman of bride-like beauty and gentleness, by writing and lending little treatises, intended to mark out with precision the limits of woman's sphere, and woman's mission, to prevent other than the rightful shepherd from climbing the wall, or the flock from using any chance to go astray.

Without enrolling ourselves at once on either side, let us look upon the subject from the best point of view which to-day offers. No better, it is to be feared, than a high house-top. A high hill-top, or at least a cathedral spire, would be desirable.

It may well be an Anti-Slavery party that pleads for woman, if we consider merely that she does not hold property on equal terms with men; so that, if a husband dies without making a will, the wife, instead of taking at once his place as head of the family, inherits only a part of his fortune, often brought him by herself, as if she were a child, or ward only, not an equal partner.

We will not speak of the innumerable instances in which profligate and idle men live upon the earnings of industrious wives; or if the wives leave them, and take with them the children, to perform the double duty of mother and father, follow from place to place, and threaten to rob them of the children, if deprived of the rights of a husband, as they call them, planting themselves in their poor lodgings, frightening them into paying tribute by taking from them the children, running into debt at the expense of these otherwise so overtasked helots. Such instances count up by scores within my own memory. I have

WOMAN IN THE NINETEENTH CENTURY 205

seen the husband who had stained himself by a long course of low vice, till his wife was wearied from her heroic forgiveness, by finding that his treachery made it useless, and that if she would provide bread for herself and her children, she must be separate from his ill fame. I have known this man come to instal himself in the chamber of a woman who loathed him and say she should never take food without his company. I have known these men steal their children whom they knew they had no means to maintain, take them into dissolute company, expose them to bodily danger, to frighten the poor woman, to whom, it seems, the fact that she alone had borne the pangs of their birth, and nourished their infancy, does not give an equal right to them. I do believe that this mode of kidnapping, and it is frequent enough in all classes of society, will be by the next age viewed as it is by Heaven now, and that the man who avails himself of the shelter of men's laws to steal from a mother her own children, or arrogate any superior right in them, save that of superior virtue, will bear the stigma he deserves, in common with him who steals grown men from their mother land, their hopes, and their homes.

I said, we will not speak of this now, yet I have spoken, for the subject makes me feel too much. I could give instances that would startle the most vulgar and callous, but I will not, for the public opinion of their own sex is already against such men, and where cases of extreme tyranny are made known, there is private action in the wife's favor. But she ought not to need this, nor, I think, can she long. Men must soon see that, on their own ground, that woman is the weaker party, she ought to have legal protection, which would make such oppression impossible. But I would not deal with "atrocious instances" except in the way of illustration, neither demand from men a partial redress in some one matter, but go to the root of the whole. If principles could be established, particulars would adjust themselves aright. Ascertain the true destiny of woman, give her legitimate hopes, and a standard within herself; marriage and all other relations would by degrees be harmonized with these.

But to return to the historical progress of this matter. Knowing that there exists in the minds of men a tone of feeling towards women as towards slaves, such as is expressed in the common phrase, "Tell that to women and children," that the infinite soul can only work through them in already ascertained limits; that the gift of reason, man's highest prerogative, is allotted to them in much lower degree; that they must be kept from mischief and melancholy by being constantly engaged in active labor, which is to be furnished and directed by those better able to think, &c. &c.; we need not multiply instances, for who can review the experience of last week without recalling words which imply, whether in jest or earnest, these views or views like these; knowing this, can we wonder that many reformers think that measures are not likely to be taken in behalf of women, unless their wishes could be publicly represented by women?

That can never be necessary, cry the other side. All men are privately influenced by women; each has his wife, sister, or female friends, and is too much biased by these relations to fail of representing their interests, and, if this is not enough, let them propose and enforce their wishes with the pen. The beauty of home would be destroyed, the delicacy of the sex be violated, the dignity of halls of legislation degraded by an attempt to introduce them there. Such duties are inconsistent with those of a mother; and then we have ludicrous pictures of ladies in hysterics at the polls, and senate chambers filled with cradles.

But if, in reply, we admit as truth that woman seems destined by nature rather for the inner circle, we must add that the arrangements of civilized life have not been, as yet, such as to secure it to her. Her circle, if the duller, is not the quieter. If kept from "excitement," she is not from drudgery. Not only the Indian squaw carries the burdens of the camp, but the favorites of Louis the Fourteenth accompany him in his journeys, and the washerwoman stands at her tub and carries home her work at all seasons, and in all states of health. Those who think the physical circumstances of woman would make a part in the affairs of national government unsuitable, are by no means those who think it impossible for the negresses to endure field work, even during pregnancy, or the sempstresses to go through their killing labors.

As to the use of the pen, there was quite as much opposition to woman's possessing herself of that help to free agency, as there is now to her seizing on the rostrum or the desk; and she is likely to draw, from a permission to plead her cause that way, opposite inferences to what might be wished by those who now grant it.

As to the possibility of her filling with grace and dignity, any such position, we should think those who had seen the great actresses, and heard the Quaker preachers of modern times, would not doubt, that woman can express publicly the fulness of thought and creation, without losing any of the peculiar beauty of her sex. What can pollute and tarnish is to act thus from any motive except that something needs to be said or done. Women could take part in the processions, the songs, the dances of old religion; no one fancied their delicacy was impaired by appearing in public for such a cause.

As to her home, she is not likely to leave it more than she now does for balls, theatres, meetings for promoting missions, revival meetings, and others to which she flies, in hope of an animation for her existence, commensurate with what she sees enjoyed by men. Governors of ladies' fairs are no less engrossed by such a change, than the Governor of the state by his; presidents of Washingtonian societies no less away from home than presidents of conventions. If men look straitly to it, they will find that, unless their lives are domestic, those of the women will not be. A house is no home unless it contain food and fire for the mind as well as for the body. The female Greek, of our day, is as much in the street as the male to cry, What news? We doubt not it was the same in Athens of old. The women, shut out from the market place, made up for it at the religious festivals. For human beings are not so constituted that they can live without expansion. If they do not get it one way, they must another, or perish.

As to men's representing women fairly at present, while we hear from men who owe to their wives not only all that is comfortable or graceful, but all that is wise in the arrangement of their lives, the frequent remark, "You cannot reason with a woman," when from those of delicacy, nobleness, and poetic culture, the contemptuous phrase "women and children," and that in no light sally of the hour, but in works intended to give a permanent statement of the best experiences, when not one man, in the million, shall I say? no, not in the hundred million, can rise above the belief that woman was made *for man*, when

208   WOMAN IN THE NINETEENTH CENTURY

such traits as these are daily forced upon the attention, can we feel that man will always do justice to the interests of woman? Can we think that he takes a sufficiently discerning and religious view of her office and destiny, *ever* to do her justice, except when prompted by sentiment, accidentally or transiently, that is, for the sentiment will vary according to the relations in which he is placed. The lover, the poet, the artist, are likely to view her nobly. The father and the philosopher have some chance of liberality; the man of the world, the legislator for expediency, none.

Under these circumstances, without attaching importance, in themselves, to the changes demanded by the champions of woman, we hail them as signs of the times. We would have every arbitrary barrier thrown down. We would have every path laid open to woman as freely as to man. Were this done and a slight temporary fermentation allowed to subside, we should see crystallizations more pure and of more various beauty. We believe the divine energy would pervade nature to a degree unknown in the history of former ages, and that no discordant collision, but a ravishing harmony of the spheres would ensue.

Yet, then and only then, will mankind be ripe for this, when inward and outward freedom for woman as much as for man shall be acknowledged as a right, not yielded as a concession. As the friend of the negro assumes that one man cannot by right, hold another in bondage, so should the friend of woman assume that man cannot, by right, lay even well-meant restrictions on woman. If the negro be a soul, if the woman be a soul, appareled in flesh, to one Master only are they accountable. There is but one law for souls, and if there is to be an interpreter of it, he must come not as man, or son of man, but as son of God.

Were thought and feeling once so far elevated that man should esteem himself the brother and friend, but nowise the lord and tutor of woman, were he really bound with her in equal worship, arrangements as to function and employment would be of no consequence. What woman needs is not as a woman to act or rule, but as a nature to grow, as an intellect to discern, as a soul to live freely and unimpeded, to unfold such powers as were given her when we left our common home. If fewer talents were given her, yet if allowed the free and full employment of these, so that she may render back to the giver his own with

MIRANDA 209

usury, she will not complain; nay I dare to say she will bless and rejoice in her earthly birth-place, her earthly lot. Let us consider what obstructions impede this good era, and what signs give reason to hope that it draws near.

I was talking on this subject with Miranda, a woman, who, if any in the world could, might speak without heat and bitterness of the position of her sex. Her father was a man who cherished no sentimental reverence for woman, but a firm belief in the equality of the sexes. She was his eldest child, and came to him at an age when he needed a companion. From the time she could speak and go alone, he addressed her not as a plaything, but as a living mind. Among the few verses he ever wrote was a copy addressed to this child, when the first locks were cut from her head, and the reverence expressed on this occasion for that cherished head, he never belied. It was to him the temple of immortal intellect. He respected his child, however, too much to be an indulgent parent. He called on her for clear judgment, for courage, for honor and fidelity; in short, for such virtues as he knew. In so far as he possessed the keys to the wonders of this universe, he allowed free use of them to her, and by the incentive of a high expectation, he forbade, as far as possible, that she should let the privilege lie idle.

Thus this child was early led to feel herself a child of the spirit. She took her place easily, not only in the world of organized being, but in the world of mind. A dignified sense of self-dependence was given as all her portion, and she found it a sure anchor. Herself securely anchored, her relations with others were established with equal security. She was fortunate in a total absence of those charms which might have drawn to her bewildering flatteries, and in a strong electric nature, which repelled those who did not belong to her, and attracted those who did. With men and women her relations were noble, affectionate without passion, intellectual without coldness. The world was free to her, and she lived freely in it. Outward adversity came, and inward conflict, but that faith and self-respect had early been awakened which must always lead at last, to an outward serenity and an inward peace.

Of Miranda I had always thought as an example, that the restraints upon the sex were insuperable only to those who think them so, or who noisily strive to break them. She had taken a course of her own, and no man stood in her way. Many of her acts had been unusual, but excited no uproar. Few helped, but none checked her, and the many men, who knew her mind and her life, showed to her confidence, as to a brother, gentleness as to a sister. And not only refined, but very coarse men approved and aided one in whom they saw resolution and clearness of design. Her mind was often the leading one, always effective.

When I talked with her upon these matters, and had said very much what I have written, she smilingly replied: "and yet we must admit that I have been fortunate, and this should not be. My good father's early trust gave the first bias, and the rest followed of course. It is true that I have had less outward aid, in after years, than most women, but that is of little consequence. Religion was early awakened in my soul, a sense that what the soul is capable to ask it must attain, and that, though I might be aided and instructed by others, I must depend on myself as the only constant friend. This self dependence, which was honored in me, is deprecated as a fault in most women. They are taught to learn their rule from without, not to unfold it from within.

"This is the fault of man, who is still vain, and wishes to be more important to woman than, by right, he should be."

"Men have not shown this disposition toward you," I said.

"No! because the position I early was enabled to take was one of self-reliance. And were all women as sure of their wants as I was, the result would be the same. But they are so overloaded with precepts by guardians, who think that nothing is so much to be dreaded for a woman as originality of thought or character, that their minds are impeded by doubts till they lose their chance of fair free proportions. The difficulty is to get them to the point from which they shall naturally develope self-respect, and learn self-help.

"Once I thought that men would help to forward this state of things more than I do now. I saw so many of them wretched in the connections they had formed in weakness and vanity. They seemed so glad to esteem women whenever they could.

"'The soft arms of affection,' said one of the most discerning spirits, 'will not suffice for me, unless on them I see the steel bracelets of strength.'"

But early I perceived that men never, in any extreme of despair, wished to be women. On the contrary they were ever ready to taunt one another at any sign of weakness, with,

"Art thou not like the women, who"—

The passage ends various ways, according to the occasion and rhetoric of the speaker. When they admired any woman they were inclined to speak of her as "above her sex." Silently I observed this, and feared it argued a rooted scepticism, which for ages had been fastening on the heart, and which only an age of miracles could eradicate. Ever I have been treated with great sincerity; and I look upon it as a signal instance of this, that an intimate friend of the other sex said, in a fervent moment, that I "deserved in some star to be a man." He was much surprised when I disclosed my view of my position and hopes, when I declared my faith that the feminine side, the side of love, of beauty, of holiness, was now to have its full chance, and that, if either were better, it was better now to be a woman, for even the slightest achievement of good was furthering an especial work of our time. He smiled incredulous. "She makes the best she can of it," thought he. "Let Jews believe the pride of Jewry, but I am of the better sort, and know better."

Another used as highest praise, in speaking of a character in literature, the words "a manly woman."

So in the noble passage of Ben Jonson:

"I meant the day-star should not brighter ride,
    Nor shed like influence from its lucent seat;
I meant she should be courteous, facile, sweet,
    Free from that solemn vice of greatness, pride;
I meant each softest virtue there should meet,
    Fit in that softer bosom to abide,
Only a learned and a *manly* soul,
    I purposed her, that should with even powers,
The rock, the spindle, and the shears control
    Of destiny, and spin her own free hours."

"Methinks," said I, "you are too fastidious in objecting to this. Jonson in using the word 'manly' only meant to heighten the picture of this, the true, the intelligent fate, with one of the deeper colors." "And yet," said she, "so invariable is the use of this word where a heroic quality is to be described, and I feel so sure that persistence and courage are the most womanly no less than the most manly qualities, that I would exchange these words for others of a larger sense at the risk of marring the fine tissue of the verse. Read, 'a heavenward and instructed soul,' and I should be satisfied. Let it not be said, wherever there is energy or creative genius, 'She has a masculine mind.'"

This by no means argues a willing want of generosity toward woman. Man is as generous toward her, as he knows how to be.

Wherever she has herself arisen in national or private history, and nobly shone forth in any form of excellence, men have received her, not only willingly, but with triumph. Their encomiums indeed, are always, in some sense, mortifying; they show too much surprise. Can this be you? he cries to the transfigured Cinderella; well I should never have thought it, but I am very glad. We will tell every one that you have "*surpassed your sex.*"

In every-day life the feelings of the many are stained with vanity. Each wishes to be lord in a little world, to be superior at least over one; and he does not feel strong enough to retain a life-long ascendancy over a strong nature. Only a Theseus could conquer before he wed the Amazonian Queen. Hercules wished rather to rest with Dejanira, and received the poisoned robe, as a fit guerdon. The tale should be interpreted to all those who seek repose with the weak.

But not only is man vain and fond of power, but the same want of development, which thus affects him morally, prevents his intellectually discerning the destiny of woman. The boy wants no woman, but only a girl to play ball with him, and mark his pocket handkerchief.

Thus, in Schiller's Dignity of Woman, beautiful as the poem is, there is no "grave and perfect man," but only a great boy to be softened and restrained by the influence of girls. Poets, the elder brothers of their race, have usually seen farther; but what can you expect of every-day men, if Schiller was not more prophetic as to what women must be? Even with Richter, one foremost thought about a wife was that she would "cook him something good." But as this is a delicate subject, and we are in constant danger of being accused of slighting what are called "the functions," let me say in behalf of Miranda and myself, that we have high respect for those who cook something good, who create and preserve fair order in houses, and prepare therein the shining raiment for worthy inmates, worthy guests. Only these "functions" must not be a drudgery, or enforced necessity, but a part of life. Let Ulysses drive the beeves home while Penelope there piles up the fragrant loaves; they are both well employed if these be done in thought and love, willingly. But Penelope is no more meant for a baker or weaver solely, than Ulysses for a cattle-herd.

The sexes should not only correspond to and appreciate, but prophesy to one another. In individual instances this happens. Two persons love in one another the future good which they aid one another to unfold. This is imperfectly or rarely done in the general life. Man has gone but little way; now he is waiting to see whether woman can keep step with him, but instead of calling out, like a good brother, "you can do it, if you only think so," or impersonally; "any one can do what he tries to do;" he often discourages with school-boy brag: "Girls can't do that; girls can't play ball." But let any one defy their taunts, break through and be brave and secure, they rend the air with shouts.

This fluctuation was obvious in a narrative I have lately seen, the story of the life of Countess Emily Plater, the heroine of the last revolution in Poland. The dignity, the purity, the concentrated resolve, the calm, deep enthusiasm, which yet could, when occasion called, sparkle up a holy, an indignant fire, make of this young maiden the figure I want for my frontispiece. Her portrait is to be seen in the book, a gentle shadow of her soul. Short was the career—like the maid of Orleans, she only did enough to verify her credentials, and then passed from a scene on which she was, probably, a premature apparition.

When the young girl joined the army where the report of her exploits had preceded her, she was received in a manner that marks the usual state of feeling. Some of the officers were disappointed at her quiet manners; that she had not the air and tone of a stage-heroine. They thought she could not have acted heroically unless in buskins; had no idea that such deeds only showed the habit of her mind. Others talked of the delicacy of her sex, advised her to withdraw from perils and dangers, and had no comprehension of the feelings within her breast that made this impossible. The gentle irony of her reply to these self-constituted tutors, (not one of whom showed himself her equal in conduct or reason,) is as good as her indignant reproof at a later period to the general, whose perfidy ruined all.

But though, to the mass of these men, she was an embarrassment and a puzzle, the nobler sort viewed her with a tender enthusiasm worthy of her. "Her name," said her biographer, "is known throughout Europe. I paint her character that she may be as widely loved."

With pride, he shows her freedom from all personal affections; that, though tender and gentle in an uncommon degree, there was no room for a private love in her consecrated life. She inspired those who knew her with a simple energy of feeling like her own. We have seen, they felt, a woman worthy the name, capable of all sweet affections, capable of stern virtue.

It is a fact worthy of remark, that all these revolutions in favor of liberty have produced female champions that share the same traits, but Emily alone has found a biographer. Only a near friend could have performed for her this task, for the flower was reared in feminine seclusion, and the few and simple traits of her history before her appearance in the field could only have been known to the domestic circle. Her biographer has gathered them up with a brotherly devotion.

No! man is not willingly ungenerous. He wants faith and love, because he is not yet himself an elevated being. He cries, with sneering skepticism, Give us a sign. But if the sign appears, his eyes glisten, and he offers not merely approval, but homage.

The severe nation which taught that the happiness of the race was forfeited through the fault of a woman, and showed its thought of what sort of regard man owed her, by making him accuse her on the first question to his God; who gave her to the patriarch as a handmaid, and by the Mosaical law, bound her to allegiance like a serf; even they greeted, with solemn rapture, all great and holy women as heroines, prophetesses, judges in Israel; and if they made Eve listen to the serpent, gave Mary as a bride to the Holy Spirit. In other nations it has been the same down to our day. To the woman who could conquer, a triumph was awarded. And not only those whose strength was recommended to the heart by association with goodness and beauty, but those who were bad, if they were steadfast and strong, had their claims allowed. In any age a Semiramis, an Elizabeth of England, a Catharine of Russia, makes her place good, whether in a large or small circle. How has a little wit, a little genius, been celebrated in a woman! What an intellectual triumph was that of the lonely Aspasia, and how heartily acknowledged! She, indeed, met a Pericles. But what annalist, the rudest of men, the most plebeian of husbands, will spare from his page one of the few anecdotes of Roman women—Sappho! Eloisa! The names are of threadbare celebrity. Indeed they were not more suitably met in their own time than the Countess Colonel Plater on her first joining the army. They had much to mourn, and their great impulses did not find due scope. But with time enough, space enough, their kindred appear on the scene. Across the ages, forms lean, trying to touch the hem of their retreating robes. The youth here by my side cannot be weary of the fragments from the life of Sappho. He will not believe they are not addressed to himself, or that he to whom they were addressed could be ungrateful. A recluse of high powers devotes himself to understand and explain the thought of Eloisa; he asserts her vast superiority in soul and genius to her master; he curses the fate that cast his lot in another age than hers. He could have understood her: he would have been to her a friend, such as Abelard never could. And this one woman he could have loved and reverenced, and she, alas! lay cold in her grave hundreds of years ago. His sorrow is truly pathetic. These responses that come too late to give joy are as tragic as any thing we know, and yet the tears of later ages glitter as they fall on Tasso's prison bars. And we know how elevating to the captive is the security that somewhere an intelligence must answer to his.

The man habitually most narrow towards women will be flushed, as by the worst assault on Christianity, if you say it has made no improvement in her condition. Indeed, those most opposed to new acts in her favor, are jealous of the reputation of those which have been done.

We will not speak of the enthusiasm excited by actresses, improvisatrici, female singers, for here mingles the charm of beauty and grace; but female authors, even learned women, if not insufferably ugly and slovenly, from the Italian professor's daughter, who taught behind the curtain, down to Mrs. Carter and Madame Dacier, are sure of an admiring audience, and what is far better, chance to use what they have learned, and to learn more, if they can once get a platform on which to stand.

But how to get this platform, or how to make it of reasonably easy access is the difficulty. Plants of great vigor will almost always struggle into blossom, despite impediments. But there should be encouragement, and a free genial atmosphere for those of more timid sort, fair play for each in its own kind. Some are like the little, delicate flowers which love to hide in the dripping mosses, by the sides of mountain torrents, or in the shade of tall trees. But others require an open field, a rich and loosened soil, or they never show their proper hues.

It may be said that man does not have his fair play either; his energies are repressed and distorted by the interposition of artificial obstacles. Ay, but he himself has put them there; they have grown out of his own imperfections. If there *is* a misfortune in woman's lot, it is in obstacles being interposed by men, which do *not* mark her state; and, if they express her past ignorance, do not her present needs. As every man is of woman born, she has slow but sure means of redress, yet the sooner a general justness of thought makes smooth the path, the better.

Man is of woman born, and her face bends over him in infancy with an expression he can never quite forget. Eminent men have delighted to pay tribute to this image, and it is an hacknied observation, that most men of genius boast some remarkable development in the mother. The rudest tar brushes off a tear with his coat-sleeve at the hallowed name. The other day, I met a decrepit old man of seventy, on a journey, who challenged the stage-company to guess where he was going. They guessed aright, "To see your mother." "Yes," said he, "she is ninety-two, but has good eye-sight still, they say. I have not seen her these forty years, and I thought I could not die in peace without." I should have liked his picture painted as a companion piece to that of a boisterous little boy, whom I saw attempt to declaim at a school exhibition—

> "O that those lips had language. Life has passed
> With me but roughly since I heard thee last."

He got but very little way before sudden tears shamed him from the stage.

Some gleams of the same expression which shone down upon his infancy, angelically pure and benign, visit man again with hopes of pure love, of a holy marriage. Or, if not before, in the eyes of the mother of his child they again are seen, and dim fancies pass before his mind, that woman may not have been born for him alone, but have come from heaven, a commissioned soul, a messenger of truth and love; that she can only make for him a home in which he may lawfully repose, in so far as she is

"True to the kindred points of Heaven and home."

In gleams, in dim fancies, this thought visits the mind of common men. It is soon obscured by the mists of sensuality, the dust of routine, and he thinks it was only some meteor, or ignis fatuus that shone. But, as a Rosicrucian lamp, it burns unwearied, though condemned to the solitude of tombs; and to its permanent life, as to every truth, each age has in some form borne witness. For the truths, which visit the minds of careless men only in fitful gleams, shine with radiant clearness into those of the poet, the priest, and the artist.

Whatever may have been the domestic manners of the ancients, the idea of woman was nobly manifested in their mythologies and poems, where she appears as Sita in the Ramayana, a form of tender purity, as the Egyptian Isis,* of divine wisdom never yet surpassed. In Egypt, too, the Sphynx, walking the earth with lion tread, looked out upon its marvels in the calm, inscrutable beauty of a virgin's face, and the Greek could only add wings to the great emblem. In Greece, Ceres and Proserpine, significantly termed "the great goddesses," were seen seated, side by side. They needed not to rise for any worshipper or any change; they were prepared for all things, as those initiated to their mysteries knew. More obvious is the meaning of these three forms, the Diana, Minerva, and Vesta. Unlike in the expression of their beauty, but alike in this,—that each was self-sufficing. Other forms were only accessories and

---

* For an adequate description of the Isis, see Appendix A.

illustrations, none the complement to one like these. Another might, indeed, be the companion, and the Apollo and Diana set off one another's beauty. Of the Vesta, it is to be observed, that not only deep-eyed, deep-discerning Greece, but ruder Rome, who represents the only form of good man, (the always busy warrior,) that could be indifferent to woman, confided the permanence of its glory to a tutelary goddess, and her wisest legislator spoke of meditation as a nymph.

Perhaps in Rome the neglect of woman was a reaction on the manners of Etruria, where the priestess Queen, warrior Queen, would seem to have been so usual a character.

An instance of the noble Roman marriage, where the stern and calm nobleness of the nation was common to both, we see in the historic page through the little that is told us of Brutus and Portia. Shakspeare has seized on the relation in its native lineaments, harmonizing the particular with the universal; and, while it is conjugal love, and no other, making it unlike the same relation, as seen in Cymbeline, or Othello, even as one star differeth from another in glory.

> "By that great vow
> Which did incorporate and make us one,
> Unfold to me, yourself, your half,
> Why you are heavy.   *   *   *
> Dwell I but in the suburbs
> Of your good pleasure? If it be no more,
> Portia is Brutus' harlot, not his wife."

Mark the sad majesty of his tone in answer. Who would not have lent a life-long credence to that voice of honor?

> "You are my true and honorable wife,
> As dear to me as are the ruddy drops
> That visit this sad heart."

It is the same voice that tells the moral of his life in the last words—

> "Countrymen,
> My heart doth joy, that yet in all my life,
> I found no man but he was true to me."

It was not wonderful that it should be so.

Shakspeare, however, was not content to let Portia rest her plea for confidence on the essential nature of the marriage bond;

> "I grant I am a woman; but withal,
> A woman that lord Brutus took to wife.
> I grant I am a woman; but withal,
> A woman well reputed—Cato's daughter.
> Think you I am *no stronger than my sex*,
> Being so fathered and so husbanded?"

And afterwards in the very scene where Brutus is suffering under that "insupportable and touching loss," the death of his wife, Cassius pleads—

> "Have you not love enough to bear with me,
> When that rash humor which my mother gave me
> Makes me forgetful?
> *Brutus* Yes, Cassius; and henceforth,
> When you are over-earnest with your Brutus,
> He'll think your mother chides and leave you so."

As indeed it was a frequent belief among the ancients, as with our Indians, that the *body* was inherited from the mother, the *soul* from the father. As in that noble passage of Ovid, already quoted, where Jupiter, as his divine synod are looking down on the funeral pyre of Hercules, thus triumphs—

> Nic nisi *maternâ* Vulcanum parte potentem.
> Sentiet. Aeternum est, à me quod traxit, et expers
> At que immune necis, nullaque domabile flamma
> Idque ego defunctum terrâ cœlestibus oris
> Accipiam, cunctisque meum lætabile factum
> Dis fore confido.

> "The part alone of gross *maternal* frame
> Fire shall devour, while that from me he drew
> Shall live immortal and its force renew;
> That, when he's dead, I'll raise to realms above;
> Let all the powers the righteous act approve."

It is indeed a god speaking of his union with an earthly woman, but it expresses the common Roman thought as to marriage, the same which permitted a man to lend his wife to a friend, as if she were a chattel.

"She dwelt but in the suburbs of his good pleasure."

Yet the same city as I have said leaned on the worship of Vesta, the Preserver, and in later times was devoted to that of Isis. In Sparta, thought, in this respect as in all others, was expressed in the characters of real life, and the women of Sparta were as much Spartans as the men. The citoyen, citoyenne of France was here actualized. Was not the calm equality they enjoyed as honorable as the devotion of chivalry? They intelligently shared the ideal life of their nation.

Like the men they felt

"Honor gone, all's gone,
Better never have been born."

They were the true friends of men. The Spartan, surely, would not think that he received only his body from his mother. The sage, had he lived in that community, could not have thought the souls of "vain and foppish men will be degraded after death, to the forms of women, and, if they do not there make great efforts to retrieve themselves, will become birds."

(By the way it is very expressive of the hard intellectuality of the merely *mannish* mind, to speak thus of birds, chosen always by the *feminine* poet as the symbols of his fairest thoughts.)

We are told of the Greek nations in general, that woman occupied there an infinitely lower place than man. It is difficult to believe this when we see such range and dignity of thought on the subject in the mythologies, and find the poets producing such ideals as Cassandra, Iphiginia, Antigone, Macaria, where Sibylline priestesses told the oracle of the highest god, and he could not be content to reign with a court of fewer than nine muses. Even victory wore a female form.

But whatever were the facts of daily life, I cannot complain of the age and nation, which represents its thought by such a symbol as I see before me at this moment. It is a zodiac of the busts of gods and goddesses, arranged in pairs. The circle

WOMAN IN GREECE

breathes the music of a heavenly order. Male and female heads are distinct in expression, but equal in beauty, strength and calmness. Each male head is that of a brother and a king— each female of a sister and a queen. Could the thought, thus expressed, be lived out, there would be nothing more to be desired. There would be unison in variety, congeniality in difference.

Coming nearer our own time, we find religion and poetry no less true in their revelations. The rude man, just disengaged from the sod, the Adam, accuses woman to his God, and records her disgrace to their posterity. He is not ashamed to write that he could be drawn from heaven by one beneath him, one made, he says, from but a small part of himself. But in the same nation, educated by time, instructed by a succession of prophets, we find woman in as high a position as she has ever occupied. No figure that has ever arisen to greet our eyes has been received with more fervent reverence than that of the Madonna. Heine calls her the *Dame du Comptoir* of the Catholic church, and this jeer well expresses a serious truth.

And not only this holy and significant image was worshipped by the pilgrim, and the favorite subject of the artist, but it exercised an immediate influence on the destiny of the sex. The empresses who embraced the cross, converted sons and husbands. Whole calendars of female saints, heroic dames of chivalry, binding the emblem of faith on the heart of the best-beloved, and wasting the bloom of youth in separation and loneliness, for the sake of duties they thought it religion to assume, with innumerable forms of poesy, trace their lineage to this one. Nor, however imperfect may be the action, in our day, of the faith thus expressed, and though we can scarcely think it nearer this ideal, than that of India or Greece was near their ideal, is it in vain that the truth has been recognized, that woman is not only a part of man, bone of his bone, and flesh of his flesh, born that men might not be lonely, but that women are in themselves possessors of and possessed by immortal souls. This truth undoubtedly received a greater outward stability from the belief of the church that the earthly parent of the Saviour of souls was a woman.

222   WOMAN IN THE NINETEENTH CENTURY

The assumption of the Virgin, as painted by sublime artists, Petrarch's Hymn to the Madonna,* cannot have spoken to the world wholly without result, yet, oftentimes those who had ears heard not.

See upon the nations the influence of this powerful example. In Spain look only at the ballads. Woman in these is "very woman;" she is the betrothed, the bride, the spouse of man, there is on her no hue of the philosopher, the heroine, the savante, but she looks great and noble; why? because she is also, through her deep devotion, the betrothed of heaven. Her upturned eyes have drawn down the light that casts a radiance round her. See only such a ballad as that of "Lady Teresa's Bridal."

Where the Infanta, given to the Moorish bridegroom, calls down the vengeance of Heaven on his unhallowed passion, and thinks it not too much to expiate by a life in the cloister, the involuntary stain upon her princely youth.[†] It was this constant sense of claims above those of earthly love or happiness that made the Spanish lady who shared this spirit, a guerdon to be won by toils and blood and constant purity, rather than a chattel to be bought for pleasure and service.

Germany did not need to *learn* a high view of woman; it was inborn in that race. Woman was to the Teuton warrior his priestess, his friend, his sister, in truth, a wife. And the Christian statues of noble pairs, as they lie above their graves in stone, expressing the meaning of all the by-gone pilgrimage by hands folded in mutual prayer, yield not a nobler sense of the place and powers of woman, than belonged to the altvater day. The holy love of Christ which summoned them, also, to choose "the better part, that which could not be taken from them," refined and hallowed in this nation a native faith, thus showing that it was not the warlike spirit alone that left the Latins so barbarous in this respect.

But the Germans, taking so kindly to this thought, did it the more justice. The idea of woman in their literature is expressed both to a greater height and depth than elsewhere.

I will give as instances the themes of three ballads.

* Appendix, B.
† Appendix, C.

One is upon a knight who had always the name of the Virgin on his lips. This protected him all his life through, in various and beautiful modes, both from sin and other dangers, and, when he died, a plant sprang from his grave, which so gently whispered the Ave Maria that none could pass it by with an unpurified heart.

Another is one of the legends of the famous Drachenfels. A maiden, one of the earliest converts to Christianity, was carried by the enraged populace to this dread haunt of "the dragon's fabled brood," to be their prey. She was left alone, but unafraid, for she knew in whom she trusted. So, when the dragons came rushing towards her, she showed them a crucifix and they crouched reverently at her feet. Next day the people came, and seeing these wonders, are all turned to the faith which exalts the lowly.

The third I have in mind is another of the Rhine legends. A youth is sitting with the maid he loves on the shore of an isle, her fairy kingdom, then perfumed by the blossoming grape vines, which draped its bowers. They are happy; all blossoms with them, and life promises its richest wine. A boat approaches on the tide; it pauses at their feet. It brings, perhaps, some joyous message, fresh dew for their flowers, fresh light on the wave. No! it is the usual check on such great happiness. The father of the Count departs for the crusade; will his son join him, or remain to rule their domain, and wed her he loves? Neither of the affianced pair hesitate a moment. "I must go with my father." "Thou must go with thy father." It was one thought, one word. "I will be here again," he said, "when these blossoms have turned to purple grapes." "I hope so," she sighed, while the prophetic sense said "no."

And there she waited, and the grapes ripened, and were gathered into the vintage, and he came not. Year after year passed thus, and no tidings; yet still she waited.

He, meanwhile, was in a Moslem prison. Long he languished there without hope, till, at last, his patron saint appeared in vision and announced his release, but only on condition of his joining the monastic order for the service of the saint.

And so his release was effected, and a safe voyage home given. And once more he sets sail upon the Rhine. The maiden, still watching beneath the vines, sees at last the object of all this

224 WOMAN IN THE NINETEENTH CENTURY

patient love approach. Approach, but not to touch the strand to which she, with outstretched arms, has rushed. He dares not trust himself to land, but in low, heart-broken tones, tells her of heaven's will; and that he, in obedience to his vow, is now on his way to a convent on the river bank, there to pass the rest of his earthly life in the service of the shrine. And then he turns his boat, and floats away from her and hope of any happiness in this world, but urged, as he believes, by the breath of heaven.

The maiden stands appalled, but she dares not murmur, and cannot hesitate long. She also bids them prepare her boat. She follows her lost love to the convent gate, requests an interview with the abbot, and devotes her Elysian isle, where vines had ripened their ruby fruit in vain for her, to the service of the monastery where her love was to serve. Then, passing over to the nunnery opposite, she takes the veil, and meets her betrothed at the altar; and for a life long union, if not the one they had hoped in earlier years.

Is not this sorrowful story of a lofty beauty? Does it not show a sufficiently high view of woman, of marriage? This is commonly the chivalric, still more the German view.

Yet, wherever there was a balance in the mind of man of sentiment, with intellect, such a result was sure. The Greek Xenophon has not only painted as a sweet picture of the domestic woman, in his Economics, but in the Cyropedia has given, in the picture of Panthea, a view of woman which no German picture can surpass, whether lonely and quiet with veiled lids, the temple of a vestal loveliness, or with eyes flashing, and hair flowing to the free wind, cheering on the hero to fight for his God, his country, or whatever name his duty might bear at the time. This picture I shall copy by and by. Yet Xenophon grew up in the same age with him who makes Iphigenia say to Achilles—

> "Better a thousand women should perish than one man cease to see the light."

This was the vulgar Greek sentiment. Xenophon, aiming at the ideal man, caught glimpses of the ideal woman also. From the figure of a Cyrus, the Pantheas stand not afar. They do not in thought; they would not in life.

WOMAN HAD ALWAYS HER SHARE OF POWER 225

I could swell the catalogue of instances far beyond the reader's patience. But enough have been brought forward to show that, though there has been great disparity betwixt the nations as between individuals in their culture on this point, yet the idea of woman has always cast some rays and often been forcibly represented.

Far less has woman to complain that she has not had her share of power. This, in all ranks of society, except the lowest, has been hers to the extent that vanity would crave, far beyond what wisdom would accept. In the very lowest, where man, pressed by poverty, sees in woman only the partner of toils and cares, and cannot hope, scarcely has an idea of, a comfortable home, he often maltreats her, and is less influenced by her. In all ranks, those who are gentle and uncomplaining, too candid to intrigue, too delicate to encroach, suffer much. They suffer long, and are kind; verily, they have their reward. But wherever man is sufficiently raised above extreme poverty or brutal stupidity, to care for the comforts of the fireside, or the bloom and ornament of life, woman has always power enough, if she choose to exert it, and is usually disposed to do so, in proportion to her ignorance and childish vanity. Unacquainted with the importance of life and its purposes, trained to a selfish coquetry and love of petty power, she does not look beyond the pleasure of making herself felt at the moment, and governments are shaken and commerce broken up to gratify the pique of a female favorite. The English shopkeeper's wife does not vote, but it is for her interest that the politician canvasses by the coarsest flattery. France suffers no woman on her throne, but her proud nobles kiss the dust at the feet of Pompadour and Dubarry; for such flare in the lighted foreground where a Roland would modestly aid in the closet. Spain, (that same Spain which sang of Ximena and the Lady Teresa,) shuts up her women in the care of duennas, and allows them no book but the Breviary, but the ruin follows only the more surely from the worthless favorite of a worthless queen. Relying on mean precautions, men indeed cry peace, peace, where there is no peace.

It is not the transient breath of poetic incense that women want; each can receive that from a lover. It is not life-long sway; it needs but to become a coquette, a shrew, or a good cook, to be sure of that. It is not money, nor notoriety, nor the badges of authority that men have appropriated to themselves. If demands, made in their behalf, lay stress on any of these particulars, those who make them have not searched deeply into the need. It is for that which at once includes these and precludes them; which would not be forbidden power, lest there be temptation to steal and misuse it; which would not have the mind perverted by flattery from a worthiness of esteem. It is for that which is the birthright of every being capable to receive it,—the freedom, the religious, the intelligent freedom of the universe, to use its means; to learn its secret as far as nature has enabled them, with God alone for their guide and their judge.

Ye cannot believe it, men; but the only reason why women ever assume what is more appropriate to you, is because you prevent them from finding out what is fit for themselves. Were they free, were they wise fully to develop the strength and beauty of woman; they would never wish to be men, or manlike. The well-instructed moon flies not from her orbit to seize on the glories of her partner. No; for she knows that one law rules, one heaven contains, one universe replies to them alike. It is with women as with the slave.

> "Vor dem Sklaven, wenn er die Kette bricht,
> Vor dem freien Menschen erzittert nicht."

Tremble not before the free man, but before the slave who has chains to break.

In slavery, acknowledged slavery, women are on a par with men. Each is a work-tool, an article of property, no more! In perfect freedom, such as is painted in Olympus, in Swedenborg's angelic state, in the heaven where there is no marrying nor giving in marriage, each is a purified intelligence, an enfranchised soul,—no less!

> Jene himmlische Gestalten
> Sie fragen nicht nach Mann und Weib,
> Und keine kleider, keine Falten
> Umgeben den verklarten Leib.

The child who sang this was a prophetic form, expressive of the longing for a state of perfect freedom, pure love. She could

ELIZABETH, ISABELLA AND MARINA

not remain here, but was transplanted to another air. And it may be that the air of this earth will never be so tempered that such can bear it long. But, while they stay, they must bear testimony to the truth they are constituted to demand.

That an era approaches which shall approximate nearer to such a temper than any has yet done, there are many tokens, indeed so many, that only a few of the most prominent can here be enumerated.

The reigns of Elizabeth of England and Isabella of Castile foreboded this era. They expressed the beginning of the new state, while they forwarded its progress. These were strong characters and in harmony with the wants of their time. One showed that this strength did not unfit a woman for the duties of a wife and a mother, the other that it could enable her to live and die alone, a wide energetic life, a courageous death. Elizabeth is certainly no pleasing example. In rising above the weakness, she did not lay aside the weaknesses ascribed to her sex; but her strength must be respected now, as it was in her own time.

Elizabeth and Mary Stuart seem types, moulded by the spirit of the time, and placed upon an elevated platform to show to the coming ages, woman such as the conduct and wishes of man in general is likely to make her, lovely even to allurement, quick in apprehension and weak in judgment, with grace and dignity of sentiment, but no principle; credulous and indiscreet, yet artful; capable of sudden greatness or of crime, but not of a steadfast wisdom, or self-restraining virtue; and woman half-emancipated and jealous of her freedom, such as she has figured before and since in many a combative attitude, mannish, not equally manly, strong and prudent more than great or wise; able to control vanity, and the wish to rule through coquetry and passion, but not to resign these dear deceits, from the very foundation, as unworthy a being capable of truth and nobleness. Elizabeth, taught by adversity, put on her virtues as armor, more than produced them in a natural order from her soul. The time and her position called on her to act the wise sovereign, and she was proud that she could do so, but her tastes and inclinations would have led her to act the weak woman. She was without magnanimity of any kind.

228   WOMAN IN THE NINETEENTH CENTURY

We may accept as an omen for ourselves, that it was Isabella who furnished Columbus with the means of coming hither. This land must pay back its debt to woman, without whose aid it would not have been brought into alliance with the civilized world.

A graceful and meaning figure is that introduced to us by Mr. Prescott, in the Conquest of Mexico, in the Indian girl Marina, who accompanied Cortes, and was his interpreter in all the various difficulties of his career. She stood at his side, on the walls of the besieged palace, to plead with her enraged countrymen. By her name he was known in New Spain, and, after the conquest, her gentle intercession was often of avail to the conquered. The poem of the Future may be read in some features of the story of "Malinche."

The influence of Elizabeth on literature was real, though, by sympathy with its finer productions, she was no more entitled to give name to an era than Queen Anne. It was simply that the fact of having a female sovereign on the throne affected the course of a writer's thoughts. In this sense, the presence of a woman on the throne always makes its mark. Life is lived before the eyes of men, by which their imaginations are stimulated as to the possibilities of woman. "We will die for our King, Maria Theresa," cry the wild warriors, clashing their swords, and the sounds vibrate through the poems of that generation. The range of female character in Spenser alone might content us for one period. Britomart and Belphœbe have as much room on the canvass as Florimel; and where this is the case, the haughtiest amazon will not murmur that Una should be felt to be the fairest type.

Unlike as was the English Queen to a fairy queen, we may yet conceive that it was the image of *a* queen before the poet's mind, that called up this splendid court of women. Shakspeare's range is also great; but he has left out the heroic characters, such as the Macaria of Greece, the Britomart of Spenser. Ford and Massinger have, in this respect, soared to a higher flight of feeling than he. It was the holy and heroic woman they most loved, and if they could not paint an Imogen, a Desdemona, a Rosalind, yet, in those of a stronger mould, they showed a higher ideal, though with so much less poetic power to embody it, than we see in Portia or Isabella. The simple truth of Cordelia,

ENGLISH IDEALS

229

indeed, is of this sort. The beauty of Cordelia is neither male nor female; it is the beauty of virtue.

The ideal of love and marriage rose high in the mind of all the Christian nations who were capable of grave and deep feeling. We may take as examples of its English aspect, the lines,

> "I could not love thee, dear, so much,
> Loved I not honor more."

Or the address of the Commonwealth's man to his wife, as she looked out from the Tower window to see him for the last time, on his way to the scaffold. He stood up in the cart, waved his hat, and cried, "To Heaven, my love, to Heaven, and leave you in the storm?"

Such was the love of faith and honor, a love which stopped, like Colonel Hutchinson's, "on this side idolatry," because it was religious. The meeting of two such souls Donne describes as giving birth to an "abler soul."

Lord Herbert wrote to his love,

> "Were not our souls immortal made,
> Our equal loves can make them such."

In the "Broken Heart" of Ford, Penthea, a character which engages my admiration even more deeply than the famous one of Calanthe, is made to present to the mind the most beautiful picture of what these relations should be in their purity. Her life cannot sustain the violation of what she so clearly felt.

Shakspeare, too, saw that, in true love as in fire, the utmost ardor is coincident with the utmost purity. It is a true lover that exclaims in the agony of Othello,

> "If thou art false, O then Heaven mocks itself."

The son, framed like Hamlet, to appreciate truth in all the beauty of relations, sinks into deep melancholy, when he finds his natural expectations disappointed. He has no mother. She to whom he gave the name, disgraces from his heart's shrine all the sex.

> "Frailty, thy name is woman."

It is because a Hamlet could find cause to say so, that I have put the line, whose stigma has never been removed, at the head of my work. But, as a lover, surely a Hamlet would not have so far mistook, as to have finished with such a conviction. He would have felt the faith of Othello, and that faith could not, in his more dispassionate mind, have been disturbed by calumny.

In Spain, this thought is arrayed in a sublimity, which belongs to the sombre and passionate genius of the nation. Calderon's Justina resists all the temptation of the Demon, and raises her lover, with her, above the sweet lures of mere temporal happiness. Their marriage is vowed at the stake; their souls are liberated together by the martyr flame into "a purer state of sensation and existence."

In Italy, the great poets wove into their lives an ideal love which answered to the highest wants. It included those of the intellect and the affections, for it was a love of spirit for spirit. It was not ascetic, or superhuman, but, interpreting all things, gave their proper beauty to details of the common life, the common day; the poet spoke of his love, not as a flower to place in his bosom, or hold carelessly in his hand, but as a light towards which he must find wings to fly, or "a stair to heaven." He delighted to speak of her, not only as the bride of his heart, but the mother of his soul; for he saw that, in cases where the right direction had been taken, the greater delicacy of her frame, and stillness of her life, left her more open to spiritual influx than man is. So he did not look upon her as betwixt him and earth, to serve his temporal needs, but, rather, betwixt him and heaven, to purify his affections and lead him to wisdom through love. He sought, in her, not so much the Eve, as the Madonna.

In these minds the thought, which gleams through all the legends of chivalry, shines in broad intellectual effulgence, not to be misinterpreted, and their thought is reverenced by the world, though it lies so far from the practice of the world as yet, so far, that it seems as though a gulf of death yawned between.

Even with such men, the practice was, often, widely different from the mental faith. I say mental, for if the heart were thoroughly alive with it, the practice could not be dissonant. Lord Herbert's was a marriage of convention, made for him at fifteen; he was not discontented with it, but looked only to the advantages it brought of perpetuating his family on the basis of a great fortune. He paid, in act, what he considered a dutiful attention to the bond; his thoughts travelled elsewhere; and while forming a high ideal of the companionship of minds in marriage, he seems never to have doubted that its realization must be postponed to some other state of being. Dante, almost immediately after the death of Beatrice, married a lady chosen for him by his friends, and Boccaccio, in describing the miseries that attended, in this case,

"The form of an union where union is none,"

speaks as if these were inevitable to the connection, and the scholar and poet, especially, could expect nothing but misery and obstruction in a domestic partnership with woman.

Centuries have passed since, but civilized Europe is still in a transition state about marriage; not only in practice, but in thought. It is idle to speak with contempt of the nations where polygamy is an institution, or seraglios a custom, when practices far more debasing haunt, well nigh fill, every city and every town. And so far as union of one with one is believed to be the only pure form of marriage, a great majority of societies and individuals are still doubtful whether the earthly bond must be a meeting of souls, or only supposes a contract of convenience and utility. Were woman established in the rights of an immortal being, this could not be. She would not, in some countries, be given away by her father, with scarcely more respect for her feelings than is shown by the Indian chief, who sells his daughter for a horse, and beats her if she runs away from her new home. Nor, in societies where her choice is left free, would she be perverted, by the current of opinion that seizes her, into the belief that she must marry, if it be only to find a protector, and a home of her own.

Neither would man, if he thought the connection of permanent importance, form it so lightly. He would not deem it a trifle, that he was to enter into the closest relations with another soul, which, if not eternal in themselves, must eternally affect his growth.

232   WOMAN IN THE NINETEENTH CENTURY

Neither, did he believe woman capable of friendship,* would he, by rash haste, lose the chance of finding a friend in the person who might, probably, live half a century by his side. Did love, to his mind, stretch forth into infinity, he would not miss his chance of its revelations, that he might, the sooner, rest from his weariness by a bright fireside, and secure a sweet and graceful attendant "devoted to him alone." Were he a step higher, he would not carelessly enter into a relation where he might not be able to do the duty of a friend, as well as a protector from external ill, to the other party, and have a being in his power pining for sympathy, intelligence and aid, that he could not give.

What deep communion, what real intercourse is implied by the sharing the joys and cares of parentage, when any degree of equality is admitted between the parties! It is true that, in a majority of instances, the man looks upon his wife as an adopted child, and places her to the other children in the relation of nurse or governess, rather than of parent. Her influence with them is sure, but she misses the education which should enlighten that influence, by being thus treated. It is the order of nature that children should complete the education, moral and mental, of parents, by making them think what is needed for the best culture of human beings, and conquer all faults and impulses that interfere with their giving this to these dear objects, who represent the world to them. Father and mother should assist one another to learn what is required for this sublime priesthood of nature. But, for this, a religious recognition of equality is required.

Where this thought of equality begins to diffuse itself, it is shown in four ways.

The household partnership. In our country, the woman looks for a "smart but kind" husband; the man for a "capable, sweet-tempered" wife.

The man furnishes the house; the woman regulates it. Their relation is one of mutual esteem, mutual dependence. Their talk is of business, their affection shows itself by practical kindness. They know that life goes more smoothly and cheerfully to each for the other's aid; they are grateful and content. The

* See Appendix D, Spinoza's view.

MADAME ROLAND 233

wife praises her husband as a "good provider;" the husband, in return, compliments her as a "capital housekeeper." This relation is good, as far as it goes.

Next comes a closer tie, which takes the two forms, either of mutual idolatry, or of intellectual companionship. The first, we suppose, is to no one a pleasing subject of contemplation. The parties weaken and narrow one another; they lock the gate against all the glories of the universe, that they may live in a cell together. To themselves they seem the only wise, to all others steeped in infatuation; the gods smile as they look forward to the crisis of cure; to men, the woman seems an unlovely syren; to women, the man an effeminate boy.

The other form, of intellectual companionship, has become more and more frequent. Men engaged in public life, literary men, and artists, have often found in their wives companions and confidants in thought no less than in feeling. And as the intellectual development of woman has spread wider and risen higher, they have, not unfrequently, shared the same employment. As in the case of Roland and his wife, who were friends in the household and in the nation's councils, read, regulated home affairs, or prepared public documents together, indifferently.

It is very pleasant, in letters begun by Roland, and finished by his wife, to see the harmony of mind, and the difference of nature; one thought, but various ways of treating it.

This is one of the best instances of a marriage of friendship. It was only friendship, whose basis was esteem; probably neither party knew love, except by name.

Roland was a good man, worthy to esteem, and be esteemed; his wife as deserving of admiration, as able to do without it. Madame Roland is the fairest specimen we have yet of her class, as clear to discern her aim, as valiant to pursue it, as Spenser's Britomart; austerely set apart from all that did not belong to her, whether as woman or as mind. She is an antetype of a class to which the coming time will afford a field, the Spartan matron, brought by the culture of the age of Books to intellectual consciousness and expansion.

Self-sufficingness, strength, and clear-sightedness were, in her, combined with a power of deep and calm affection. She, too, would have given a son or husband the device for his shield, "Return with it or upon it;" and this, not because she loved little, but much. The page of her life is one of unsullied dignity.

Her appeal to posterity is one against the injustice of those who committed such crimes in the name of Liberty. She makes it in behalf of herself and her husband. I would put beside it, on the shelf, a little volume, containing a similar appeal from the verdict of contemporaries to that of mankind, made by Godwin in behalf of his wife, the celebrated, the, by most men, detested, Mary Wolstonecraft. In his view, it was an appeal from the injustice of those who did such wrong in the name of virtue.

Were this little book interesting for no other cause, it would be so for the generous affection evinced under the peculiar circumstances. This man had courage to love and honor this woman in the face of the world's sentence, and of all that was repulsive in her own past history. He believed he saw of what soul she was, and that the impulses she had struggled to act out were noble, though the opinions to which they had led might not be thoroughly weighed. He loved her, and he defended her for the meaning and tendency of her inner life. It was a good fact.

Mary Wolstonecraft, like Madame Dudevant, (commonly known as George Sand,) in our day, was a woman whose existence better proved the need of some new interpretation of woman's rights, than any thing she wrote. Such beings as these, rich in genius, of most tender sympathies, capable of high virtue and a chastened harmony, ought not to find themselves, by birth, in a place so narrow, that, in breaking bonds, they become outlaws. Were there as much room in the world for such, as in Spenser's poem for Britomart, they would not run their heads so wildly against the walls, but prize their shelter rather. They find their way, at last, to light and air, but the world will not take off the brand it has set upon them. The champion of the Rights of Woman found, in Godwin, one who would plead that cause like a brother. He who delineated with such purity of traits the form of woman in the Marguerite, of whom the weak St. Leon could never learn to be worthy, a pearl indeed whose price was above rubies, was not false in life to the faith by which he had hallowed his romance. He acted as he wrote, like a brother.

GEORGE SAND

This form of appeal rarely fails to touch the basest man. "Are you acting towards other women in the way you would have men act towards your sister?" George Sand smokes, wears male attire, wishes to be addressed as "Mon frère;"—perhaps, if she found those who were as brothers, indeed, she would not care whether she were brother or sister.*

---

* Since writing the above, I have read with great satisfaction, the following sonnets addressed to George Sand by a woman who has precisely the qualities that the author of Simon and Indiana lacks. It is such a woman, so unblemished in character, so high in aim, and pure in soul, that should address this other, as noble in nature, but clouded by error, and struggling with circumstances. It is such women that will do such justice. They are not afraid to look for virtue and reply to aspiration, among those who have *not* "dwelt in decencies forever." It is a source of pride and happiness to read this address from the heart of Elizabeth Barrett.

To George Sand

A DESIRE

Thou large-brained woman and large-hearted man,
    Self-called George Sand! whose soul, amid the lions
    Of thy tumultuous senses moans defiance,
And answers roar for roar, as spirits can:
I would some mild miraculous thunder ran
    Above the applauded circus, in appliance
    Of thine own nobler nature's strength and science,
        Drawing two pinions, white as wings of swan,
From the strong shoulders, to amaze the place
    With holier light! that thou to woman's claim,
And man's might join, beside, the angel's grace
Of a pure genius sanctified from blame;
Till child and maiden pressed to thine embrace,
    To kiss upon thy lips a stainless fame.

To the Same

A RECOGNITION

True genius, but true woman! dost deny
    Thy woman's nature with a manly scorn,
    And break away the gauds and armlets worn
    By weaker women in captivity?
Ah, vain denial! that revolted cry
    Is sobbed in by a woman's voice forlorn:—

236   WOMAN IN THE NINETEENTH CENTURY

We rejoice to see that she, who expresses such a painful contempt for men in most of her works, as shows she must have known great wrong from them, depicting in "La Roche Mauprat," a man raised by the workings of love, from the depths of savage sensualism, to a moral and intellectual life. It was love for a pure object, for a steadfast woman, one of those who, the Italian said, could make the stair to heaven.

This author, beginning like the many in assault upon bad institutions, and external ills, yet deepening the experience through comparative freedom, sees at last, that the only efficient remedy must come from individual character. These bad institutions, indeed, it may always be replied, prevent individuals from forming good character, therefore we must remove them. Agreed, yet keep steadily the higher aim in view. Could you clear away all the bad forms of society, it is vain, unless the individual begin to be ready for better. There must be a parallel movement in these two branches of life. And all the rules left by Moses availed less to further the best life than the living example of one Messiah.

Still, still the mind of the age struggles confusedly with these problems, better discerning as yet the ill it can no longer bear, than the good by which it may supersede it. But women, like Sand, will speak now and cannot be silenced; their characters and their eloquence alike foretell an era when such as they shall easier learn to lead true lives. But though such forebode, not such shall be the parents of it.* Those who would reform the world must show that they do not speak in the heat of wild impulse; their lives must be unstained by passionate error; they

---

> Thy woman's hair, my sister, all unshorn,
>   Floats back dishevelled strength in agony,
> Disproving thy man's name, and while before
>   The world thou burnest in a poet-fire,
> We see thy woman-heart beat evermore
>   Through the large flame. Beat purer, heart, and higher,
> Till God unsex thee on the spirit-shore;
>   To which alone unsexing, purely aspire.

This last sonnet seems to have been written after seeing the picture of Sand, which represents her in a man's dress, but with long loose hair, and an eye whose mournful fire is impressive even in the caricatures.

* Appendix, E.

must be severe lawgivers to themselves. They must be religious students of the divine purpose with regard to man, if they would not confound the fancies of a day with the requisitions of eternal good. Their liberty must be the liberty of law and knowledge. But, as to the transgressions against custom which have caused such outcry against those of noble intention, it may be observed, that the resolve of Eloisa to be only the mistress of Abelard, was that of one who saw in practice around her, the contract of marriage made the seal of degradation. Shelley feared not to be fettered, unless so to be was to be false. Wherever abuses are seen, the timid will suffer; the bold will protest. But society has a right to outlaw them till she has revised her law; and this she must be taught to do, by one who speaks with authority, not in anger or haste.

If Godwin's choice of the calumniated authoress of the "Rights of Woman," for his honored wife, be a sign of a new era, no less so is an article to which I have alluded some pages back, published five or six years ago in one of the English Reviews, where the writer, in doing full justice to Eloisa, shows his bitter regret that she lives not now to love him, who might have known better how to prize her love than did the egotistical Abelard.

These marriages, these characters, with all their imperfections, express an onward tendency. They speak of aspiration of soul, of energy of mind, seeking clearness and freedom. Of a like promise are the tracts lately published by Goodwyn Barmby, (the European Pariah, as he calls himself,) and his wife Catharine. Whatever we may think of their measures, we see in them wedlock; the two minds are wed by the only contract that can permanently avail, of a common faith and a common purpose.

We might mention instances, nearer home, of minds, partners in work and in life, sharing together, on equal terms, public and private interests, and which wear not, on any side, the aspect of offence shown by those last-named: persons who steer straight onward, yet, in our comparatively free life, have not been obliged to run their heads against any wall. But the principles which guide them might, under petrified and oppressive institutions, have made them warlike, paradoxical, and in some sense, Pariahs. The phenomena are different, the law is the same, in all these cases. Men and women have been obliged to build up their house anew from the very foundation. If they found stone ready in the quarry, they took it peaceably, otherwise they alarmed the country by pulling down old towers to get materials.

These are all instances of marriage as intellectual companionship. The parties meet mind to mind, and a mutual trust is produced, which can buckler them against a million. They work together for a common purpose, and, in all these instances, with the same implement, the pen. The pen and the writing-desk furnish forth as naturally the retirement of woman as of man.

A pleasing expression, in this kind, is afforded by the union in the names of the Howitts. William and Mary Howitt we heard named together for years, supposing them to be brother and sister; the equality of labors and reputation, even so, was auspicious; more so, now we find them man and wife. In his late work on Germany, Howitt mentions his wife, with pride, as one among the constellation of distinguished English-women, and in a graceful simple manner.

Our pleasure, indeed, in this picture, is marred by the vulgar apparition which has of late displaced the image, which we had from her writings cherished of a pure and gentle Quaker poetess. The surprise was painful as that of the little sentimentalist in the tale of "L'Amie Inconnue" when she found her correspondent, the poetess, the "adored Araminta," scolding her servants in Welsh, and eating toasted cheese and garlic. Still, we cannot forget what we have thought of the partnership in literature and affection between the Howitts, the congenial pursuits and productions, the pedestrian tours where the married pair showed that marriage, on a wide enough basis, does not destroy the "inexhaustible" entertainment which lovers found in one another's company.

In naming these instances, I do not mean to imply that community of employment is essential to union of husband and wife, more than to the union of friends. Harmony exists in difference, no less than in likeness, if only the same key-note govern both parts. Woman the poem, man the poet! Woman the heart, man the head! Such divisions are only important when they are never to be transcended. If nature is never bound down, nor the voice of inspiration stifled, that is enough. We are pleased that women should write and speak, if they feel the need of it, from having something to tell; but silence for ages would be no misfortune, if that silence be from divine command, and not from man's tradition.

While Goetz Von Berlichingen rides to battle, his wife is busy in the kitchen; but difference of occupation does not prevent that community of inward life, that perfect esteem, with which he says—

"Whom God loves, to him gives he such a wife."

Manzoni thus dedicates his "Adelchi."

"To his beloved and venerated wife, Enrichetta Luigia Blondel, who, with conjugal affection and maternal wisdom, has preserved a virgin mind, the author dedicates this 'Adelchi,' grieving that he could not, by a more splendid and more durable monument, honor the dear name, and the memory of so many virtues."

The relation could not be fairer, or more equal, if she, too, had written poems. Yet the position of the parties might have been the reverse as well; the woman might have sung the deeds, given voice to the life of the man, and beauty would have been the result, as we see, in pictures of Arcadia, the nymph singing to the shepherds, or the shepherd, with his pipe, alluring the nymphs; either makes a good picture. The sounding lyre requires, not muscular strength, but energy of soul to animate the hand which would control it. Nature seems to delight in varying the arrangements, as if to show that she will be fettered by no rule, and we must admit the same varieties that she admits.

The fourth and highest grade of marriage union, is the religious, which may be expressed as pilgrimage towards a common shrine. This includes the others: home sympathies and household wisdom, for these pilgrims must know how to assist each other along the dusty way; intellectual communion, for how sad it would be on such a journey to have a companion to whom you could not communicate thoughts and aspirations as they sprang to life; who would have no feeling for the prospects that open, more and more glorious as we advance;

240 WOMAN IN THE NINETEENTH CENTURY

who would never see the flowers that may be gathered by the most industrious traveller. It must include all these. Such a fellow-pilgrim Count Zinzendorf seems to have found in his Countess, of whom he thus writes:

"Twenty-five years' experience has shown me that just the help-mate whom I have, is the only one that could suit my vocation. Who else could have so carried through my family affairs? Who lived so spotlessly before the world? Who so wisely aided me in my rejection of a dry morality? Who so clearly set aside the Pharisaism which, as years passed, threatened to creep in among us? Who so deeply discerned as to the spirits of delusion, which sought to bewilder us? Who would have governed my whole economy so wisely, richly, and hospitably, when circumstances commanded? Who have taken indifferently the part of servant or mistress, without, on the one side, affecting an especial spirituality; on the other, being sullied by any worldly pride? Who, in a community where all ranks are eager to be on a level, would, from wise and real causes, have known how to maintain inward and outward distinctions? Who, without a murmur, have seen her husband encounter such dangers by land and sea? Who undertaken with him, and *sustained* such astonishing pilgrimages? Who, amid such difficulties, always held up her head and supported me? Who found such vast sums of money, and acquitted them on her own credit? And, finally, who, of all human beings, could so well understand and interpret to others my inner and outer being as this one, of such nobleness in her way of thinking, such great intellectual capacity, and free from the theological perplexities that enveloped me!"

Let any one peruse, with all their power, the lineaments of this portrait, and see if the husband had not reason, with this air of solemn rapture and conviction, to challenge comparison? We are reminded of the majestic cadence of the line whose feet step in the just proportions of Humanity,

"Daughter of God and Man, accomplished Eve!"

An observer* adds this testimony:

---

* Spangenberg.

"We may, in many marriages, regard it as the best arrangement, if the man has so much advantage over his wife, that she can, without much thought of her own, be, by him, led and directed as by a father. But it was not so with the Count and his consort. She was not made to be a copy; she was an original; and, while she loved and honored him, she thought for herself, on all subjects, with so much intelligence, that he could and did look on her as sister and friend also."

Compare with this refined specimen of a religiously civilized life, the following imperfect sketch of a North American Indian, and we shall see that the same causes will always produce the same results. The Flying Pigeon (Ratchewaine) was the wife of a barbarous chief, who had six others, but she was his only true wife, because the only one of a strong and pure character, and, having this, inspired a veneration, as like as the mind of the man permitted, to that inspired by the Countess Zinzendorf. She died when her son was only four years old, yet left on his mind a feeling of reverent love worthy the thought of Christian chivalry. Grown to manhood, he shed tears on seeing her portrait.

THE FLYING PIGEON

"Ratchewaine was chaste, mild, gentle in her disposition, kind, generous, and devoted to her husband. A harsh word was never known to proceed from her mouth; nor was she ever known to be in a passion. Mahaskah used to say of her, after her death, that her hand was shut, when those, who did not want, came into her presence; but when the really poor came in, it was like a strainer full of holes, letting all she held in it pass through. In the exercise of generous feeling she was uniform. It was not indebted for its exercise to whim, or caprice, or partiality. No matter of what nation the applicant for her bounty was, or whether at war or peace with her nation; if he were hungry, she fed him; if naked, she clothed him; and if houseless, she gave him shelter. The continued exercise of this generous feeling kept her poor. And she has been known to give away her last blanket—all the honey that was in the lodge, the last bladder of bear's oil, and the last piece of dried meat.

"She was scrupulously exact in the observance of all the religious rites which her faith imposed upon her. Her conscience

242   WOMAN IN THE NINETEENTH CENTURY

is represented to have been extremely tender. She often feared that her acts were displeasing to the Great Spirit, when she would blacken her face, and retire to some lone place, and fast and pray."

To these traits should be added, but for want of room, anecdotes which show the quick decision and vivacity of her mind. Her face was in harmony with this combination. Her brow is as ideal and the eyes and lids as devout and modest as the Italian pictures of the Madonna, while the lower part of the face has the simplicity and childish strength of the Indian race. Her picture presents the finest specimen of Indian beauty we have ever seen.

Such a woman is the sister and friend of all beings, as the worthy man is their brother and helper.

With like pleasure we survey the pairs wedded on the eve of missionary effort. They, indeed, are fellow pilgrims on a well-made road, and whether or no they accomplish all they hope for the sad Hindoo, or the nearer savage, we feel that, in the burning waste, their love is like to be a healing dew, in the forlorn jungle, a tent of solace to one another. They meet, as children of one Father, to read together one book of instruction.

We must insert in this connection the most beautiful picture presented by ancient literature of wedded love under this noble form.

It is from the romance in which Xenophon, the chivalrous Greek, presents his ideal of what human nature should be.

The generals of Cyrus had taken captive a princess, a woman of unequalled beauty, and hastened to present her to the prince as the part of the spoil he would think most worthy of his acceptance.

Cyrus visits the lady, and is filled with immediate admiration by the modesty and majesty with which she receives him. He finds her name is Panthea, and that she is the wife of Abradatus, a young king whom she entirely loves. He protects her as a sister, in his camp, till he can restore her to her husband.

After the first transports of joy at this re-union, the heart of Panthea is bent on showing her love and gratitude to her magnanimous and delicate protector. And as she has nothing so precious to give as the aid of Abradatus, that is what she most wishes to offer. Her husband is of one soul with her in this, as in all things.

The description of her grief and self-destruction, after the death which ensued upon this devotion, I have seen quoted, but never that of their parting when she sends him forth to battle. I shall copy both. If they have been read by any of my readers, they may be so again with profit in this connexion, for never were the heroism of a true woman, and the purity of love, in a true marriage, painted in colors more delicate or more lively.

"The chariot of Abradatus, that had four perches and eight horses, was completely adorned for him; and when he was going to put on his linen corslet, which was a sort of armor used by those of his country, Panthea brought him a golden helmet, and arm-pieces, broad bracelets for his wrists, a purple habit that reached down to his feet, and hung in folds at the bottom, and a crest dyed of a violet color. These things she had made unknown to her husband, and by taking the measure of his armor. He wondered when he saw them, and inquired thus of Panthea: 'And have you made me these arms, woman, by destroying your own ornaments?' 'No, by Jove,' said Panthea, 'not what is the most valuable of them; for it is you, if you appear to others to be what I think you, that will be my greatest ornament.' And, saying that, she put on him the armor, and, though she endeavored to conceal it, the tears poured down her cheeks. When Abradatus, who was before a man of fine appearance, was set out in those arms, he appeared the most beautiful and noble of all, especially, being likewise so by nature. Then, taking the reins from the driver, he was just preparing to mount the chariot, when Panthea, after she had desired all that were there to retire, thus said:

"'O Abradatus! if ever there was a woman who had a greater regard to her husband than to her own soul, I believe you know that I am such an one; what need I therefore speak of things in particular? for I reckon that my actions have convinced you more than any words I can now use. And yet, though I stand thus affected towards you, as you know I do, I swear by this friendship of mine and yours, that I certainly would rather choose to be put under ground jointly with you, approving yourself a brave man, than to live with you in disgrace and

244 WOMAN IN THE NINETEENTH CENTURY

shame; so much do I think you and myself worthy of the noblest things. Then I think that we both lie under great obligations to Cyrus, that, when I was a captive, and chosen out for himself, he thought fit to treat me neither as a slave, nor, indeed, as a woman of mean account, but he took and kept me for you, as if I were his brother's wife. Besides, when Araspes, who was my guard, went away from him, I promised him, that, if he would allow me to send for you, you would come to him, and approve yourself a much better and more faithful friend than Araspes.'

"Thus she spoke; and Abradatus being struck with admiration at her discourse, laying his hand gently on her head, and lifting up his eyes to heaven, made this prayer: 'Do thou, O greatest Jove! grant me to appear a husband worthy of Panthea, and a friend worthy of Cyrus, who has done us so much honor!'

"Having said this, he mounted the chariot by the door of the driver's seat; and, after he had got up, when the driver shut the door, Panthea, who had now no other way to salute him, kissed the seat of the chariot. The chariot then moved, and she, unknown to him, followed, till Abradatus turning about, and seeing her, said: 'Take courage, Panthea! Fare you happily and well, and now go your ways.' On this her women and servants carried her to her conveyance, and, laying her down, concealed her by throwing the covering of a tent over her. The people, though Abradatus and his chariot made a noble spectacle, were not able to look at him till Panthea was gone."

After the battle—

"Cyrus calling to some of his servants, 'Tell me, said he, has any one seen Abradatus? for I admire that he now does not appear.' One replied, 'My sovereign, it is because he is not living, but died in the battle as he broke in with his chariot on the Egyptians. All the rest, except his particular companions, they say, turned off when they saw the Egyptians' compact body. His wife is now said to have taken up his dead body, to have placed it in the carriage that she herself was conveyed in, and to have brought it hither to some place on the river Pactolus, and her servants are digging a grave on a certain elevation. They say that his wife, after setting him out with all the ornaments she has, is sitting on the ground with his head on her knees.'

PANTHEA

Cyrus, hearing this, gave himself a blow on the thigh, mounted his horse at a leap, and taking with him a thousand horse, rode away to this scene of affliction; but gave orders to Gadatas and Gobryas to take with them all the rich ornaments proper for a friend and an excellent man deceased, and to follow after him; and whoever had herds of cattle with him, he ordered them to take both oxen, and horses, and sheep in good number, and to bring them away to the place where, by inquiry, they should find him to be, that he might sacrifice these to Abradatus.

"As soon as he saw the woman sitting on the ground, and the dead body there lying, he shed tears at the afflicting sight, and said: 'Alas! thou brave and faithful soul, hast thou left us, and art thou gone?' At the same time he took him by the right hand, and the hand of the deceased came away, for it had been cut off, with a sword, by the Egyptians. He, at the sight of this, became yet much more concerned than before. The woman shrieked out in a lamentable manner, and, taking the hand from Cyrus, kissed it, fitted it to its proper place again, as well as she could, and said, 'The rest, Cyrus, is in the same condition, but what need you see it? And I know that I was not one of the least concerned in these his sufferings, and, perhaps, you were not less so, for I, fool that I was! frequently exhorted him to behave in such a manner as to appear a friend to you, worthy of notice; and I know he never thought of what he himself should suffer, but of what he should do to please you. He is dead, therefore,' said she, 'without reproach, and I, who urged him on, sit here alive.' Cyrus, shedding tears for some time in silence, then spoke—'He has died, woman, the noblest death; for he has died victorious! do you adorn him with these things that I furnish you with.' (Gobryas and Gadatas were then come up and had brought rich ornaments in great abundance with them.) 'Then,' said he, 'be assured that he shall not want respect and honor in all other things: but, over and above, multitudes shall concur in raising him a monument that shall be worthy of us, and all the sacrifices shall be made him that are proper to be made in honor of a brave man. You shall not be left destitute, but, for the sake of your modesty and every other virtue, I will pay you all other honors, as well as place those about you who will conduct you wherever you please. Do you but make it known to

246 WOMAN IN THE NINETEENTH CENTURY

me where it is that you desire to be conveyed to.' And Panthea replied, 'Be confident, Cyrus,' said she, 'I will not conceal from you to whom it is that I desire to go.'

"He, having said this, went away with great pity for her that she should have lost such a husband, and for the man that he should have left such a wife behind him, never to see her more. Panthea then gave orders for her servants to retire, 'Till such time,' said she, 'as I shall have lamented my husband, as I please.' Her nurse she bid to stay, and gave orders that, when she was dead, she would wrap her and her husband up in one mantle together. The nurse, after having repeatedly begged her not to do this, and meeting with no success, but observing her to grow angry, sat herself down, breaking out into tears. She, being before-hand provided with a sword, killed herself, and, laying her head down on her husband's breast, she died. The nurse set up a lamentable cry, and covered them both as Panthea had directed.

"Cyrus, as soon as he was informed of what the woman had done, being struck with it, went to help her if he could. The servants, three in number, seeing what had been done, drew their swords and killed themselves, as they stood at the place where she had ordered them. And the monument is now said to have been raised by continuing the mount on to the servants; and on a pillar above, they say, the names of the man and woman were written in Syriac letters.

"Below were three pillars, and they were inscribed thus, 'Of the servants.' Cyrus, when he came to this melancholy scene, was struck with admiration of the woman, and, having lamented over her, went away. He took care, as was proper, that all the funeral rites should be paid them in the noblest manner, and the monument, they say, was raised up to a very great size."

These be the ancients, who, so many assert had no idea of the dignity of woman, or of marriage. Such love Xenophon could paint as subsisting between those who after death "would see one another never more." Thousands of years have passed since, and with the reception of the cross, the nations assume the belief that those who part thus, may meet again and forever, if spiritually fitted to one another, as Abradatus and Panthea were, and yet do we see such marriages among them? If at all, how often?

THE WIFE INFLUENCES THE HUSBAND 247

I must quote two more short passages from Xenophon, for he is a writer who pleases me well.

Cyrus receiving the Armenians whom he had conquered.

"'Tigranes,' said he, 'at what rate would you purchase the regaining of your wife?' Now Tigranes happened to be *but lately married*, and had a very great love for his wife," (that clause perhaps sounds *modern*.)

"Cyrus," said he, "I would ransom her at the expense of my life."

"Take then your own to yourself," said he.   *   *   *

When they came home, one talked of Cyrus' wisdom, another of his patience and resolution, another of his mildness. One spoke of his beauty and the smallness of his person, and, on that, Tigranes asked his wife, "And do you, Armenian dame, think Cyrus handsome?" "Truly," said she, "I did not look at him." "At whom, then, did you look?" said Tigranes. "At him who said that, to save me from servitude, he would ransom me at the expense of his own life."

From the Banquet.—

Socrates, who observed her with pleasure, said, "This young girl has confirmed me in the opinion I have had, for a long time, that the female sex are nothing inferior to ours, excepting only in strength of body, or, perhaps, in steadiness of judgment."

In the Economics, the manner in which the husband gives counsel to his young wife, presents the model of politeness and refinement. Xenophon is thoroughly the gentleman, gentle in breeding and in soul. All the men he describes are so, while the shades of manner are distinctly marked. There is the serene dignity of Socrates, with gleams of playfulness thrown across its cool religious shades, the princely mildness of Cyrus, and the more domestic elegance of the husband in the Economics.

There is no way that men sin more against refinement, as well as discretion, than in their conduct towards their wives. Let them look at the men of Xenophon. Such would know how to give counsel, for they would know how to receive it. They would feel that the most intimate relations claimed most, not least, of refined courtesy. They would not suppose that confidence justified carelessness, nor the reality of affection want of delicacy in the expression of it.

248   WOMAN IN THE NINETEENTH CENTURY

Such men would be too wise to hide their affairs from the wife and then expect her to act as if she knew them. They would know that if she is expected to face calamity with courage, she must be instructed and trusted in prosperity, or, if they had failed in wise confidence such as the husband shows in the Economics, they would be ashamed of anger or querulous surprise at the results that naturally follow.

Such men would not be exposed to the bad influence of bad wives, for all wives, bad or good, loved or unloved, inevitably influence their husbands, from the power their position not merely gives, but necessitates, of coloring evidence and infusing feelings in hours when the patient, shall I call him? is off his guard. Those who understand the wife's mind, and think it worth while to respect her springs of action, know better where they are. But to the bad or thoughtless man who lives carelessly and irreverently so near another mind, the wrong he does daily back upon himself recoils. A Cyrus, an Abradatus knows where he stands.

But to return to the thread of my subject.

Another sign of the times is furnished by the triumphs of female authorship. These have been great and constantly increasing. Women have taken possession of so many provinces for which men had pronounced them unfit, that though these still declare there are some inaccessible to them, it is difficult to say just *where* they must stop.

The shining names of famous women have cast light upon the path of the sex, and many obstructions have been removed. When a Montague could learn better than her brother, and use her lore afterward to such purpose, as an observer, it seemed amiss to hinder woman from preparing themselves to see, or from seeing all they could, when prepared. Since Somerville has achieved so much, will any young girl be prevented from seeking a knowledge of the physical sciences, if she wishes it? De Stael's name was not so clear of offence; she could not forget the woman in the thought; while she was instructing you as a mind, she wished to be admired as a woman; sentimental tears often dimmed the eagle glance. Her intellect too, with all its splendor, trained in a drawing-room, fed on flattery, was tainted and flawed; yet its beams make the obscurest school-house in New-England warmer and lighter to the little rugged girls,

SCHOOL-INSTRUCTION 249

who are gathered together on its wooden bench. They may never through life hear her name, but she is not the less their benefactress.

The influence has been such, that the aim certainly is, now, in arranging school instruction for girls, to give them as fair a field as boys. As yet, indeed, these arrangements are made with little judgment or reflection; just as the tutors of Lady Jane Grey, and other distinguished women of her time, taught them Latin and Greek, because they knew nothing else themselves, so now the improvement in the education of girls is to be made by giving them young men as teachers, who only teach what has been taught themselves at college, while methods and topics need revision for these new subjects, which could better be made by those who had experienced the same wants. Women are, often, at the head of these institutions, but they have, as yet, seldom been thinking women, capable to organize a new whole for the wants of the time, and choose persons to officiate in the departments. And when some portion of instruction is got of a good sort from the school, the far greater proportion which is infused from the general atmosphere of society contradicts its purport. Yet books and a little elementary instruction are not furnished, in vain. Women are better aware how great and rich the universe is, not so easily blinded by narrowness or partial views of a home circle. "Her mother did so before her," is no longer a sufficient excuse. Indeed, it was never received as an excuse to mitigate the severity of censure, but was adduced as a reason, rather, why there should be no effort made for reformation.

Whether much or little has been done or will be done, whether women will add to the talent of narration, the power of systematizing, whether they will carve marble, as well as draw and paint, is not important. But that it should be acknowledged that they have intellect which needs developing, that they should not be considered complete, if beings of affection and habit alone, is important.

Yet even this acknowledgment, rather conquered by woman than proffered by man, has been sullied by the usual selfishness. So much is said of women being better educated, that they may become better companions and mothers *for men*. They should be fit for such companionship, and we have mentioned, with satisfaction, instances where it has been established. Earth knows no fairer, holier relation than that of a mother. It is one which, rightly understood, must both promote and require the highest attainments. But a being of infinite scope must not be treated with an exclusive view to any one relation. Give the soul free course, let the organization, both of body and mind, be freely developed, and the being will be fit for any and every relation to which it may be called. The intellect, no more than the sense of hearing, is to be cultivated merely that she may be a more valuable companion to man, but because the Power who gave a power, by its mere existence, signifies that it must be brought out towards perfection.

In this regard of self-dependence, and a greater simplicity and fulness of being, we must hail as a preliminary the increase of the class contemptuously designated as old maids.

We cannot wonder at the aversion with which old bachelors and old maids have been regarded. Marriage is the natural means of forming a sphere, of taking root on the earth; it requires more strength to do this without such an opening; very many have failed, and their imperfections have been in every one's way. They have been more partial, more harsh, more officious and impertinent than those compelled by severer friction to render themselves endurable. Those, who have a more full experience of the instincts, have a distrust, as to whether they can be thoroughly human and humane, such as is hinted in the saying, "Old maids' and bachelors' children are well cared for," which derides at once their ignorance and their presumption.

Yet the business of society has become so complex, that it could now scarcely be carried on without the presence of these despised auxiliaries; and detachments from the army of aunts and uncles are wanted to stop gaps in every hedge. They rove about, mental and moral Ishmaelites, pitching their tents amid the fixed and ornamented homes of men.

In a striking variety of forms, genius of late, both at home and abroad, has paid its tribute to the character of the Aunt, and the Uncle, recognizing in these personages the spiritual parents, who had supplied defects in the treatment of the busy or careless actual parents.

They also gain a wider, if not so deep experience. Those who are not intimately and permanently linked with others, are

OLD BACHELORS AND OLD MAIDS

thrown upon themselves, and, if they do not there find peace and incessant life, there is none to flatter them that they are not very poor and very mean.

A position which so constantly admonishes, may be of inestimable benefit. The person may gain, undistracted by other relationships, a closer communion with the one. Such a use is made of it by saints and sybils. Or she may be one of the lay sisters of charity, a Canoness, bound by an inward vow! Or the useful drudge of all men, the Martha, much sought, little prized! Or the intellectual interpreter of the varied life she sees; the Urania of a half-formed world's twilight.

Or she may combine all these. Not "needing to care that she may please a husband," a frail and limited being, her thoughts may turn to the centre, and she may, by steadfast contemplation entering into the secret of truth and love, use it for the use of all men, instead of a chosen few, and interpret through it all the forms of life. It is possible, perhaps, to be at once a priestly servant, and a loving muse.

Saints and geniuses have often chosen a lonely position in the faith that if, undisturbed by the pressure of near ties, they would give themselves up to the inspiring spirit, it would enable them to understand and reproduce life better than actual experience could.

How many old maids take this high stand, we cannot say: it is an unhappy fact, that too many who have come before the eye are gossips rather, and not always good-natured gossips. But if these abuse, and none make the best of their vocation, yet it has not failed to produce some good results. It has been seen by others, if not by themselves, that beings, likely to be left alone, need to be fortified and furnished within themselves, and education and thought have tended more and more to regard these beings as related to absolute Being, as well as to other men. It has been seen that, as the breaking of no bond ought to destroy a man, so ought the missing of none to hinder him from growing. And thus a circumstance of the time, which springs rather from its luxury than its purity, has helped to place women on the true platform.

Perhaps the next generation, looking deeper into this matter, will find that contempt is put upon old maids, or old women at all, merely because they do not use the elixir which would

252   WOMAN IN THE NINETEENTH CENTURY

keep them always young. Under its influence a gem brightens yearly which is only seen to more advantage through the fissures Time makes in the casket.* No one thinks of Michael Angelo's Persican Sibyl, or St. Theresa, or Tasso's Leonora, or the Greek Electra, as an old maid, more than of Michael Angelo or Canova as old bachelors, though all had reached the period in life's course appointed to take that degree.

See a common woman at forty; scarcely has she the remains of beauty, of any soft poetic grace which gave her attraction as woman, which kindled the hearts of those who looked on her to sparkling thoughts, or diffused round her a roseate air of gentle love. See her, who was, indeed, a lovely girl, in the coarse full-blown dahlia flower of what is commonly called matron-beauty, fat, fair, and forty, showily dressed, and with manners as broad and full as her frill or satin cloak. People observe, "how well she is preserved;" "she is a fine woman still," they say. This woman, whether as a duchess in diamonds, or one of our city dames in mosaics, charms the poet's heart no more, and would look much out of place kneeling before the Madonna. She "does well the honors of her house," "leads society," is, in short, always spoken and thought of upholstery-wise.

Or see that care-worn face, from which every soft line is blotted, those faded eyes from which lonely tears have driven the flashes of fancy, the mild white beam of a tender enthusiasm. This woman is not so ornamental to a tea party; yet she would please better, in picture. Yet surely she, no more than the other, looks as a human being should at the end of forty years. Forty years! have they bound those brows with no garland? shed in the lamp no drop of ambrosial oil?

Not so looked the Iphigenia in Aulis. Her forty years had seen her in anguish, in sacrifice, in utter loneliness. But those pains were borne for her father and her country; the sacrifice she had made pure for herself and those around her. Wandering alone at night in the vestal solitude of her imprisoning grove, she has looked up through its "living summits" to the stars, which shed down into her aspect their own lofty melody. At forty she would not misbecome the marble.

---

* Appendix, F.

THE BETROTHED OF THE SUN 253

Not so looks the Persica. She is withered, she is faded; the drapery that enfolds her has, in its dignity an angularity, too, that tells of age, of sorrow, of a stern composure to the *must*. But her eye, that torch of the soul, is untamed, and in the intensity of her reading, we see a soul invincibly young in faith and hope. Her age is her charm, for it is the night of the Past that gives this beacon fire leave to shine. Wither more and more, black Chrysalid! thou dost but give the winged beauty time to mature its splendors.

Not so looked Victoria Colonna, after her life of a great hope, and of true conjugal fidelity. She had been, not merely a bride, but a wife, and each hour had helped to plume the noble bird. A coronet of pearls will not shame her brow; it is white and ample, a worthy altar for love and thought.

Even among the North American Indians, a race of men as completely engaged in mere instinctive life as almost any in the world, and where each chief, keeping many wives as useful servants, of course looks with no kind eye on celibacy in woman, it was excused in the following instance mentioned by Mrs. Jameson. A woman dreamt in youth that she was betrothed to the Sun. She built her a wigwam apart, filled it with emblems of her alliance, and means of an independent life. There she passed her days, sustained by her own exertions, and true to her supposed engagement.

In any tribe, we believe, a woman, who lived as if she was betrothed to the Sun, would be tolerated, and the rays which made her youth blossom sweetly, would crown her with a halo in age.

There is, on this subject, a nobler view than heretofore, if not the noblest, and improvement here must coincide with that in the view taken of marriage.

We must have units before we can have union, says one of the ripe thinkers of the times.

If larger intellectual resources begin to be deemed needful to woman, still more is a spiritual dignity in her, or even the mere assumption of it, looked upon with respect. Joanna Southcote and Mother Anne Lee are sure of a band of disciples; Ecstatica, Dolorosa, of enraptured believers who will visit them in their lowly huts, and wait for days to revere them in their trances. The foreign noble traverses land and sea to hear a few words from the lips of the lowly peasant girl, whom he believes especially visited by the Most High. Very beautiful, in this way, was the influence of the invalid of St. Petersburg, as described by De Maistre.

Mysticism, which may be defined as the brooding soul of the world, cannot fail of its oracular promise as to woman. "The mothers"—"The mother of all things," are expressions of thought which lead the mind towards this side of universal growth. Whenever a mystical whisper was heard, from Behmen down to St. Simon, sprang up the thought, that, if it be true, as the legend says, that humanity withers through a fault committed by and a curse laid upon woman, through her pure child, or influence, shall the new Adam, the redemption, arise. Innocence is to be replaced by virtue, dependence by a willing submission, in the heart of the Virgin Mother of the new race.

The spiritual tendency is towards the elevation of woman, but the intellectual by itself is not so. Plato sometimes seems penetrated by that high idea of love, which considers man and woman as the two-fold expression of one thought. This the angel of Swedenborg, the angel of the coming age, cannot surpass, but only explain more fully. But then again Plato, the man of intellect, treats woman in the Republic as property, and, in the Timæus, says that man, if he misuse the privileges of one life, shall be degraded into the form of woman, and then, if he do not redeem himself, into that of a bird. This, as I said above, expresses most happily how anti-poetical is this state of mind. For the poet, contemplating the world of things, selects various birds as the symbols of his most gracious and ethereal thoughts, just as he calls upon his genius, as muse, rather than as God. But the intellect, cold, is ever more masculine than feminine; warmed by emotion, it rushes towards mother earth, and puts on the forms of beauty.

The electrical, the magnetic element in woman has not been fairly brought out at any period. Every thing might be expected from it; she has far more of it than man. This is commonly expressed by saying that her intuitions are more rapid and more correct. You will often see men of high intellect absolutely stupid in regard to the atmospheric changes, the fine invisible links which connect the forms of life around them, while common women, if pure and modest, so that a vulgar self do not overshadow the mental eye, will seize and delineate these with unerring discrimination.

Women who combine this organization with creative genius, arc very commonly unhappy at present. They see too much to act in conformity with those around them, and their quick impulses seem folly to those who do not discern the motives. This is an usual effect of the apparition of genius, whether in man or woman, but is more frequent with regard to the latter, because a harmony, an obvious order and self-restraining decorum, is most expected from her.

Then women of genius, even more than men, are likely to be enslaved by an impassioned sensibility. The world repels them more rudely, and they are of weaker bodily frame.

Those, who seem overladen with electricity, frighten those around them. "When she merely enters the room, I am what the French call *herissé*," said a man of petty feelings and worldly character of such a woman, whose depth of eye and powerful motion announced the conductor of the mysterious fluid.

Wo to such a woman who finds herself linked to such a man in bonds too close. It is the cruellest of errors. He will detest her with all the bitterness of wounded self-love. He will take the whole prejudice of manhood upon himself, and to the utmost of his power imprison and torture her by its imperious rigors.

Yet, allow room enough, and the electric fluid will be found to invigorate and embellish, not destroy life. Such women are the great actresses, the songsters. Such traits we read in a late searching, though too French analysis of the character of Mademoiselle Rachel, by a modern La Rochefoucoult. The Greeks thus represent the muses; they have not the golden serenity of Apollo; they are *over*-flowed with thought; there is something tragic in their air. Such are the Sibyls of Guercino, the eye is over-full of expression, dilated and lustrous; it seems to have drawn the whole being into it.

Sickness is the frequent result of this over-charged existence. To this region, however misunderstood, or interpreted with presumptuous carelessness, belong the phenomena of magnetism, or mesmerism, as it is now often called, where the trance of the Ecstatica purports to be produced by the agency of one human being on another, instead of, as in her case, direct from the spirit.

WOMAN IN THE NINETEENTH CENTURY

The worldling has his sneer at this as at the services of religion. "The churches can always be filled with women." "Show me a man in one of your magnetic states, and I will believe."

Women are, indeed, the easy victims both of priestcraft and self-delusion, but this would not be, if the intellect was developed in proportion to the other powers. They would, then, have a regulator, and be more in equipoise, yet must retain the same nervous susceptibility, while their physical structure is such as it is.

It is with just that hope, that we welcome every thing that tends to strengthen the fibre and develope the nature on more sides. When the intellect and affections are in harmony; when intellectual consciousness is calm and deep; inspiration will not be confounded with fancy.

> Then, "she who advances
>   With rapturous, lyrical glances,
>   Singing the song of the earth, singing
>   Its hymn to the Gods,"

will not be pitied, as a madwoman, nor shrunk from as unnatural.

The Greeks, who saw every thing in forms, which we are trying to ascertain as law, and classify as cause, embodied all this in the form of Cassandra. Cassandra was only unfortunate in receiving her gift too soon. The remarks, however, that the world still makes in such cases, are well expressed by the Greek dramatist.

In the Trojan Dames, there are fine touches of nature with regard to Cassandra. Hecuba shows that mixture of shame and reverence that prosaic kindred always do towards the inspired child, the poet, the elected sufferer for the race.

When the herald announces that Cassandra is chosen to be the mistress of Agamemnon, Hecuba answers, with indignation, betraying the pride and faith she involuntarily felt in this daughter.

Hec. "The maiden of Phoebus, to whom the golden haired
    Gave as a privilege a virgin life!
Tal. Love of the inspired maiden hath pierced him.
Hec. Then cast away, my child, the sacred keys, and from thy person
    The consecrated garlands which thou wearest."

SEERESS OF PREVORST

Yet, when a moment after, Cassandra appears, singing, wildly, her inspired song, Hecuba calls her, "My *frantic* child."
Yet how graceful she is in her tragic *raptus*, the chorus shows.

> *Chor.* "How sweetly at thy house's ills thou smil'st,
> Chanting what, haply, thou wilt not show true."

If Hecuba dares not trust her highest instinct about her daughter, still less can the vulgar mind of the herald Talthybius, a man not without feeling, but with no princely, no poetic blood, abide the wild prophetic mood which insults all his prejudices.

> *Tal.* "The venerable, and that accounted wise,
> Is nothing better than that of no repute,
> For the greatest king of all the Greeks,
> The dear son of Atreus, is possessed with the love
> Of this madwoman. I, indeed, am poor,
> Yet, I would not receive her to my bed."

The royal Agamemnon could see the beauty of Cassandra, HE was not afraid of her prophetic gifts.

The best topic for a chapter on this subject in the present day, would be the history of the Seeress of Prevorst, the best observed subject of magnetism in our present times, and who, like her ancestresses of Delphos, was roused to ecstacy or phrenzy by the touch of the laurel.

I observe in her case, and in one known to me here, that, what might have been a gradual and gentle disclosure of remarkable powers, was broken and jarred into disease by an unsuitable marriage. Both these persons were unfortunate in not understanding what was involved in this relation, but acted ignorantly as their friends desired. They thought that this was the inevitable destiny of woman. But when engaged in the false position, it was impossible for them to endure its dissonances, as those of less delicate perceptions can, and the fine flow of life was checked and sullied. They grew sick, but, even so, learnt and disclosed more than those in health are wont to do.

In such cases, worldlings sneer, but reverent men learn wondrous news, either from the person observed, or by thoughts caused in themselves by the observation. Fenelon learns from Guyon, Kerner, from his Seeress, what we fain would know.

But to appreciate such disclosures one must be a child, and here the phrase, "women and children" may, perhaps, be interpreted aright, that only little children shall enter into the kingdom of heaven.

All these motions of the time, tides that betoken a waxing moon, overflow upon our land. The world, at large, is readier to let woman learn and manifest the capacities of her nature than it ever was before, and here is a less encumbered field and freer air than any where else. And it ought to be so; we ought to pay for Isabella's jewels.

The names of nations are feminine—religion, virtue, and victory are feminine. To those who have a superstition, as to outward reigns, it is not without significance that the name of the queen of our mother-land should at this crisis be Victoria—Victoria the First. Perhaps to us it may be given to disclose the era thus outwardly presaged.

Another Isabella too at this time ascends the throne. Might she open a new world to her sex! But, probably, these poor little women are, least of any, educated to serve as examples or inspirers for the rest. The Spanish queen is younger; we know of her that she sprained her foot the other day, dancing in her private apartments; of Victoria, that she reads aloud, in a distinct voice and agreeable manner, her addresses to parliament on certain solemn days, and, yearly, that she presents to the nation some new prop of royalty. These ladies have, very likely, been trained more completely to the puppet life than any other. The queens, who have been queens indeed, were trained by adverse circumstances to know the world around them and their own powers.

It is moving, while amusing, to read of the Scottish peasant measuring the print left by the queen's foot as she walks, and priding himself on its beauty. It is so natural to wish to find what is fair and precious in high places, so astonishing to find the Bourbon a glutton, or the Guelph a dullard or gossip.

In our own country, women are, in many respects, better situated than men. Good books are allowed, with more time to read them. They are not so early forced into the bustle of life, nor so weighed down by demands for outward success. The perpetual changes, incident to our society, make the blood circulate freely

THE BRIBE IS NOT THE PRIZE

through the body politic, and, if not favorable at present to the grace and bloom of life, they are so to activity, resource, and would be to reflection, but for a low materialist tendency, from which the women are generally exempt in themselves, though its existence, among the men, has a tendency to repress their impulses and make them doubt their instincts, thus, often, paralyzing their action during the best years.

But they have time to think, and no traditions chain them, and few conventionalities compared with what must be met in other nations. There is no reason why they should not discover that the secrets of nature are open, the revelations of the spirit waiting for whoever will seek them. When the mind is once awakened to this consciousness, it will not be restrained by the habits of the past, but fly to seek the seeds of a heavenly future.

Their employments are more favorable to meditation than those of men.

Woman is not addressed religiously here, more than elsewhere. She is told she should be worthy to be the mother of a Washington, or the companion of some good man. But in many, many instances, she has already learnt that all bribes have the same flaw; that truth and good are to be sought solely for their own sakes. And, already, an ideal sweetness floats over many forms, shines in many eyes.

Already deep questions are put by young girls on the great theme: What shall I do to enter upon the eternal life?

Men are very courteous to them. They praise them often, check them seldom. There is chivalry in the feeling towards "the ladies," which gives them the best seats in the stage-coach, frequent admission, not only to lectures of all sorts, but to courts of justice, halls of legislature, reform conventions. The newspaper editor "would be better pleased that the Lady's Book should be filled up exclusively by ladies. It would then, indeed, be a true gem, worthy to be presented by young men to the mistresses of their affections." Can gallantry go further?

In this country is venerated, wherever seen, the character which Goethe spoke of an Ideal, which he saw actualized in his friend and patroness, the Grand Duchess Amelia. "The excellent woman is she, who, if the husband dies, can be a father to the children." And this, if read aright, tells a great deal.

Women who speak in public, if they have a moral power, such as has been felt from Angelina Grimke and Abby Kelly; that is, if they speak for conscience' sake, to serve a cause which they hold sacred, invariably subdue the prejudices of their hearers, and excite an interest proportionate to the aversion with which it had been the purpose to regard them.

A passage in a private letter so happily illustrates this, that it must be inserted here.

Abby Kelly in the Town-House of ———.

"The scene was not unheroic—to see that woman, true to humanity and her own nature, a centre of rude eyes and tongues, even gentlemen feeling licensed to make part of a species of mob around a female out of her sphere. As she took her seat in the desk amid the great noise, and in the throng, full, like a wave, of something to ensue, I saw her humanity in a gentleness and unpretension, tenderly open to the sphere around her, and, had she not been supported by the power of the will of genuineness and principle, she would have failed. It led her to prayer, which, in woman especially, is childlike; sensibility and will going to the side of God and looking up to him; and humanity was poured out in aspiration.

"She acted like a gentle hero, with her mild decision and womanly calmness. All heroism is mild and quiet and gentle, for it is life and possession, and combativeness and firmness show a want of actualness. She is as earnest, fresh, and simple as when she first entered the crusade. I think she did much good, more than the men in her place could do, for woman feels more as being and reproducing, this brings the subject more into home relations. Men speak through, and mostly from intellect, and this addresses itself in others, which creates and is combative."

Not easily shall we find elsewhere, or before this time, any written observations on the same subject, so delicate and profound.

The late Dr. Channing, whose enlarged and tender and religious nature, shared every onward impulse of his time, though his thoughts followed his wishes with a deliberative caution, which belonged to his habits and temperament, was greatly interested in these expectations for women. His own treatment of them was absolutely and thoroughly religious. He regarded them as souls, each of which had a destiny of its own,

KINMONT AND SHELLEY

261

incalculable to other minds, and whose leading it must follow, guided by the light of a private conscience. He had sentiment, delicacy, kindness, taste; but they were all pervaded and ruled by this one thought, that all beings had souls, and must vindicate their own inheritance. Thus all beings were treated by him with an equal, and sweet, though solemn, courtesy. The young and unknown, the woman and the child, all felt themselves regarded with an infinite expectation, from which there was no reaction to vulgar prejudice. He demanded of all he met, to use his favorite phrase, "great truths."

His memory, every way dear and reverend, is, by many, especially cherished for this intercourse of unbroken respect.

At one time, when the progress of Harriet Martineau through this country, Angelina Grimke's appearance in public, and the visit of Mrs. Jameson had turned his thoughts to this subject, he expressed high hopes as to what the coming era would bring to woman. He had been much pleased with the dignified courage of Mrs. Jameson in taking up the defence of her sex, in a way from which women usually shrink, because, if they express themselves on such subjects with sufficient force and clearness to do any good, they are exposed to assaults whose vulgarity makes them painful. In intercourse with such a woman, he had shared her indignation at the base injustice, in many respects, and in many regions, done to the sex; and been led to think of it far more than ever before. He seemed to think that he might some time write upon the subject. That his aid is withdrawn from the cause is a subject of great regret, for, on this question as on others, he would have known how to sum up the evidence and take, in the noblest spirit, middle ground. He always furnished a platform on which opposing parties could stand, and look at one another under the influence of his mildness and enlightened candor.

Two younger thinkers, men both, have uttered noble prophecies, auspicious for woman. Kinmont, all whose thoughts tended towards the establishment of the reign of love and peace, thought that the inevitable means of this would be an increased predominance given to the idea of woman. Had he lived longer, to see the growth of the peace party, the reforms in life and medical practice which seek to substitute water for wine and drugs, pulse for animal food, he would have been confirmed in his view of the way in which the desired changes are to be effected.

In this connection, I must mention Shelley, who, like all men of genius, shared the feminine development, and, unlike many, knew it. His life was one of the first pulse-beats in the present reform-growth, He, too, abhorred blood and heat, and, by his system and his song, tended to reinstate a plant-like gentleness in the development of energy. In harmony with this, his ideas of marriage were lofty, and, of course, no less so of woman, her nature, and destiny.

For woman, if, by a sympathy as to outward condition she is led to aid the enfranchisement of the slave, must be no less so, by inward tendency, to favor measures which promise to bring the world more thoroughly and deeply into harmony with her nature. When the lamb takes place of the lion as the emblem of nations, both women and men will be as children of one spirit, perpetual learners of the word and doers thereof, not hearers only.

A writer in the New-York Pathfinder, in two articles headed "Femality," has uttered a still more pregnant word than any we have named. He views woman truly from the soul, and not from society, and the depth and leading of his thoughts are proportionably remarkable. He views the feminine nature as a harmonizer of the vehement elements, and this has often been hinted elsewhere; but what he expresses most forcibly is the lyrical, the inspiring, and inspired apprehensiveness of her being.

This view being identical with what I have before attempted to indicate, as to her superior susceptibility to magnetic or electric influence, I will now try to express myself more fully.

There are two aspects of woman's nature, represented by the ancients as Muse and Minerva. It is the former to which the writer in the Pathfinder looks. It is the latter which Wordsworth has in mind, when he says—

"With a placid brow,
Which woman ne'er should forfeit, keep thy vow."

The especial genius of woman I believe to be electrical in movement, intuitive in function, spiritual in tendency. She

EXCEPTIONS TO EVERY RULE

excels not so easily in classification, or re-creation, as in an instinctive seizure of causes, and a simple breathing out of what she receives that has the singleness of life, rather than the selecting and energizing of art.

More native is it to her to be the living model of the artist than to set apart from herself any one form in objective reality; more native to inspire and receive the poem, than to create it. In so far as soul is in her completely developed, all soul is the same; but as far as it is modified in her as woman, it flows, it breathes, it sings, rather than deposits soil, or finishes work, and that which is especially feminine flushes, in blossom, the face of earth, and pervades, like air and water, all this seeming solid globe, daily renewing and purifying its life. Such may be the especially feminine element, spoken of as Femality. But it is no more the order of nature that it should be incarnated pure in any form, than that the masculine energy should exist unmingled with it in any form.

Male and female represent the two sides of the great radical dualism. But, in fact, they are perpetually passing into one another. Fluid hardens to solid, solid rushes to fluid. There is no wholly masculine man, no purely feminine woman.

History jeers at the attempts of physiologists to bind great original laws by the forms which flow from them. They make a rule; they say from observation, what can and cannot be. In vain! Nature provides exceptions to every rule. She sends women to battle, and sets Hercules spinning; she enables women to bear immense burdens, cold, and frost; she enables the man, who feels maternal love, to nourish his infant like a mother. Of late she plays still gayer pranks. Not only she deprives organizations, but organs, of a necessary end. She enables people to read with the top of the head, and see with the pit of the stomach. Presently she will make a female Newton, and a male Syren.

Man partakes of the feminine in the Apollo, woman of the masculine as Minerva.

What I mean by the Muse is the unimpeded clearness of the intuitive powers which a perfectly truthful adherence to every admonition of the higher instincts would bring to a finely organized human being. It may appear as prophecy or as poesy. It enabled Cassandra to foresee the results of actions passing round her; the Seeress to behold the true character of the person through the mask of his customary life. (Sometimes she saw a feminine form behind the man, sometimes the reverse.) It enabled the daughter of Linnæus to see the soul of the flower exhaling from the flower.* It gave a man, but a poet man, the power of which he thus speaks: "Often in my contemplation of nature, radiant intimations, and as it were sheaves of light appear before me as to the facts of cosmogony in which my mind has, perhaps, taken especial part." He wisely adds, "but it is necessary with earnestness to verify the knowledge we gain by these flashes of light." And none should forget this. Sight must be verified by life before it can deserve the honors of piety and genius. Yet sight comes first, and of this sight of the world of causes, this approximation to the region of primitive motions, women I hold to be especially capable. Even without equal freedom with the other sex, they have already shown themselves so, and should these faculties have free play, I believe they will open new, deeper and purer sources of joyous inspiration than have as yet refreshed the earth.

Let us be wise and not impede the soul. Let her work as she will. Let us have one creative energy, one incessant revelation. Let it take what form it will, and let us not bind it by the past to man or woman, black or white. Jove sprang from Rhea, Pallas from Jove. So let it be.

If it has been the tendency of these remarks to call woman rather to the Minerva side,—if I, unlike the more generous writer, have spoken from society no less than the soul,—let it be pardoned! It is love that has caused this, love for many incarcerated souls, that might be freed, could the idea of religious self-dependence be established in them, could the weakening habit of dependence on others be broken up.

Proclus teaches that every life has, in its sphere, a totality or wholeness of the animating powers of the other spheres; having only, as its own characteristic, a predominance of some one power. Thus Jupiter comprises, within himself, the other

---

* The daughter of Linnaeus states, that, while looking steadfastly at the red lily, she saw its spirit hovering above it, as a red flame. It is true, this, like many fair spirit-stories, may be explained away as an optical illusion, but its poetic beauty and meaning would, even then, make it valuable, as an illustration of the spiritual fact.

PROCLUS TEACHES WELL

twelve powers, which stand thus: The first triad is *demiurgic or fabricative*, i. e., Jupiter, Neptune, Vulcan; the second, *defensive*, Vesta, Minerva, Mars; the third, *vivific*, Ceres, Juno, Diana; and the fourth, Mercury, Venus, Apollo, *elevating and harmonic*. In the sphere of Jupiter, energy is predominant—with Venus, beauty; but each comprehends and apprehends all the others.

When the same community of life and consciousness of mind begins among men, humanity will have, positively and finally, subjugated its brute elements and Titanic childhood; criticism will have perished; arbitrary limits and ignorant censure be impossible; all will have entered upon the liberty of law, and the harmony of common growth.

Then Apollo will sing to his lyre what Vulcan forges on the anvil, and the Muse weave anew the tapestries of Minerva.

It is, therefore, only in the present crisis that the preference is given to Minerva. The power of continence must establish the legitimacy of freedom, the power of self-poise the perfection of motion.

Every relation, every gradation of nature is incalculably precious, but only to the soul which is poised upon itself, and to whom no loss, no change, can bring dull discord, for it is in harmony with the central soul.

If any individual live too much in relations, so that he becomes a stranger to the resources of his own nature, he falls, after a while, into a distraction, or imbecility, from which he can only be cured by a time of isolation, which gives the renovating fountains time to rise up. With a society it is the same. Many minds, deprived of the traditionary or instinctive means of passing a cheerful existence, must find help in self-impulse, or perish. It is therefore that, while any elevation, in the view of union, is to be hailed with joy, we shall not decline celibacy as the great fact of the time. It is one from which no vow, no arrangement, can at present save a thinking mind. For now the rowers are pausing on their oars; they wait a change before they can pull together. All tends to illustrate the thought of a wise cotemporary. Union is only possible to those who are units. To be fit for relations in time, souls, whether of man or woman, must be able to do without them in the spirit.

It is therefore that I would have woman lay aside all thought, such as she habitually cherishes, of being taught and led by men.

I would have her, like the Indian girl, dedicate herself to the Sun, the Sun of Truth, and go no where if his beams did not make clear the path. I would have her free from compromise, from complaisance, from helplessness, because I would have her good enough and strong enough to love one and all beings, from the fulness, not the poverty of being.

Men, as at present instructed, will not help this work, because they also are under the slavery of habit. I have seen with delight their poetic impulses. A sister is the fairest ideal, and how nobly Wordsworth, and even Byron, have written of a sister.

There is no sweeter sight than to see a father with his little daughter. Very vulgar men become refined to the eye when leading a little girl by the hand. At that moment the right relation between the sexes seems established, and you feel as if the man would aid in the noblest purpose, if you ask him in behalf of his little daughter. Once two fine figures stood before me, thus. The father of very intellectual aspect, his falcon eye softened by affection as he looked down on his fair child, she the image of himself, only more graceful and brilliant in expression. I was reminded of Southey's Kehama; when lo, the dream was rudely broken. They were talking of education, and he said,

"I shall not have Maria brought too forward. If she knows too much, she will never find a husband; superior women hardly ever can."

"Surely," said his wife, with a blush, "you wish Maria to be as good and wise as she can, whether it will help her to marriage or not."

"No," he persisted, "I want her to have a sphere and a home, and some one to protect her when I am gone."

It was a trifling incident, but made a deep impression. I felt that the holiest relations fail to instruct the unprepared and perverted mind. If this man, indeed, could have looked at it on the other side, he was the last that would have been willing to have been taken himself for the home and protection he could give, but would have been much more likely to repeat the tale of Alcibiades with his phials.

But men do *not* look at both sides, and women must leave off asking them and being influenced by them, but retire within themselves, and explore the groundwork of life till they find their peculiar secret. Then, when they come forth again, renovated and baptized, they will know how to turn all dross to gold, and will be rich and free though they live in a hut, tranquil, if in a crowd. Then their sweet singing shall not be from passionate impulse, but the lyrical overflow of a divine rapture, and a new music shall be evolved from this many-chorded world.

Grant her, then, for a while, the armor and the javelin. Let her put from her the press of other minds and meditate in virgin loneliness. The same idea shall re-appear in due time as Muse, or Ceres, the all-kindly patient Earth-Spirit.

Among the throng of symptoms which denote the present tendency to a crisis in the life of woman, which resembles the change from girlhood with its beautiful instincts, but unharmonized thoughts, its blind pupilage and restless seeking, to self-possessed, wise, and graceful womanhood, I have attempted to select a few.

One of prominent interest is the unison of three male minds, upon the subject, which, for width of culture, power of self-concentration and dignity of aim, take rank as the prophets of the coming age, while their histories and labors are rooted in the past.

Swedenborg came, he tells us, to interpret the past revelation and unfold a new. He announces the new church that is to prepare the way for the New Jerusalem, a city built of precious stones, hardened and purified by secret processes in the veins of earth through the ages.

Swedenborg approximated to that harmony between the scientific and poetic lives of mind, which we hope from the perfected man. The links that bind together the realms of nature, the mysteries that accompany her births and growths, were unusually plain to him. He seems a man to whom insight was given at a period when the mental frame was sufficiently matured to retain and express its gifts.

His views of woman are, in the main, satisfactory. In some details, we may object to them as, in all his system, there are still remains of what is arbitrary and seemingly groundless; fancies that show the marks of old habits, and a nature as yet

268   WOMAN IN THE NINETEENTH CENTURY

not thoroughly leavened with the spiritual leaven. At least so it seems to me now. I speak reverently, for I find such reason to venerate Swedenborg, from an imperfect knowledge of his mind, that I feel one more perfect might explain to me much that does not now secure my sympathy.

His idea of woman is sufficiently large and noble to interpose no obstacle to her progress. His idea of marriage is consequently sufficient. Man and woman share an angelic ministry, the union is from one to one, permanent and pure.

As the New Church extends its ranks, the needs of woman must be more considered.

Quakerism also establishes woman on a sufficient equality with man. But though the original thought of Quakerism is pure, its scope is too narrow, and its influence, having established a certain amount of good and made clear some truth, must, by degrees, be merged in one of wider range.* The mind of Swedenborg appeals to the various nature of man and allows room for æsthetic culture and the free expression of energy.

As apostle of the new order, of the social fabric that is to rise from love, and supersede the old that was based on strife, Charles Fourier comes next, expressing, in an outward order, many facts of which Swedenborg saw the secret springs. The mind of Fourier, though grand and clear, was, in some respects, superficial. He was a stranger to the highest experiences. His eye was fixed on the outward more than the inward needs of man. Yet he, too, was a seer of the divine order, in its musical expression, if not in its poetic soul. He has filled one department of instruction for the new era, and the harmony in action, and freedom for individual growth he hopes shall exist; and if the methods he proposes should not prove the true ones, yet his fair propositions shall give many hints, and make room for the inspiration needed for such.

He, too, places woman on an entire equality with man, and wishes to give to one as to the other that independence which must result from intellectual and practical development.

---

* In worship at stated periods, in daily expression, whether by word or deed, the Quakers have placed woman on the same platform with man. Can any one assert that they have reason to repent this?

FOURIER'S VIEW

Those who will consult him for no other reason, might do so to see how the energies of woman may be made available in the pecuniary way. The object of Fourier was to give her the needed means of self help, that she might dignify and unfold her life for her own happiness, and that of society. The many, now, who see their daughters liable to destitution, or vice to escape from it, may be interested to examine the means, if they have not yet soul enough to appreciate the ends he proposes.

On the opposite side of the advancing army, leads the great apostle of individual culture, Goethe. Swedenborg makes organization and union the necessary results of solitary thought. Fourier, whose nature was, above all, constructive, looked to them too exclusively. Better institutions, he thought, will make better men. Goethe expressed, in every way, the other side. If one man could present better forms, the rest could not use them till ripe for them.

Fourier says, As the institutions, so the men! All follies are excusable and natural under bad institutions.

Goethe thinks, As the man, so the institutions! There is no excuse for ignorance and folly. A man can grow in any place, if he will.

Ay! but Goethe, bad institutions are prison walls and impure air that make him stupid, so that he does not will.

And thou, Fourier, do not expect to change mankind at once, or even "in three generations" by arrangement of groups and series, or flourish of trumpets for attractive industry. If these attempts are made by unready men, they will fail.

Yet we prize the theory of Fourier no less than the profound suggestion of Goethe. Both are educating the age to a clearer consciousness of what man needs, what man can be, and better life must ensue.

Goethe, proceeding on his own track, elevating the human being in the most imperfect states of society, by continual efforts at self-culture, takes as good care of women as of men. His mother, the bold, gay Frau Aja, with such playful freedom of nature; the wise and gentle maiden, known in his youth, over whose sickly solitude "the Holy Ghost brooded as a dove;" his sister, the intellectual woman *par excellence*: the Duchess Amelia; Lili, who combined the character of the woman of the world with the lyrical sweetness of the shepherdess, on whose

270   WOMAN IN THE NINETEENTH CENTURY

chaste and noble breast flowers and gems were equally at home; all these had supplied abundant suggestions to his mind, as to the wants and the possible excellencies of woman. And, from his poetic soul, grew up forms new and more admirable than life has yet produced, for whom his clear eye marked out paths in the future.

In Faust, we see the redeeming power, which, at present, upholds woman, while waiting for a better day, in Margaret. The lovely little girl, pure in instinct, ignorant in mind, is misled and profaned by man abusing her confidence.* To the Mater *Dolorosa* she appeals for aid. It is given to the soul, if not against outward sorrow; and the maiden, enlightened by her sufferings, refusing to receive temporal salvation by the aid of an evil power, obtains the eternal in its stead.

In the second part, the intellectual man, after all his manifold strivings, owes to the interposition of her whom he had betrayed *his* salvation. She intercedes, this time herself a glorified spirit, with the Mater *Gloriosa*.

Leonora, too, is woman, as we see her now, pure, thoughtful, refined by much acquaintance with grief.

Iphigenia he speaks of in his journals as his "daughter," and she is the daughter† whom a man will wish, even if he has chosen his wife from very mean motives. She is the virgin, steadfast soul, to whom falsehood is more dreadful than any other death.

But it is to Wilhelm Meister's Apprenticeship and Wandering Years that I would especially refer, as these volumes contain the sum of the Sage's observations during a long life, as to what

---

* As Faust says, her only fault was a "Kindly delusion,"—"ein guter wahn."
† Goethe was as false to his ideas in practice, as Lord Herbert. And his punishment was the just and usual one of connections formed beneath the standard of right, from the impulses of the baser self. Iphigenia was the worthy daughter of his mind, but the son, child of his degrading connection in actual life, corresponded with that connection. This son, on whom Goethe vainly lavished so much thought and care, was like his mother, and like Goethe's attachment for his mother, "This young man," says a late well informed writer, (M. Henri Blaze,) "Wieland, with good reason, called the son of the servant, *der Sohn der Magd*. He inherited from his father only his name and his *physique*."

THE TRUE FELICITY 271

man should do, under present circumstances, to obtain mastery over outward, through an initiation into inward life, and severe discipline of faculty.

As Wilhelm advances in the upward path he becomes acquainted with better forms of woman by knowing how to seek, and how to prize them when found. For the weak and immature man will, often, admire a superior woman, but he will not be able to abide by a feeling, which is too severe a tax on his habitual existence. But, with Wilhelm, the gradation is natural and expresses ascent in the scale of being. At first he finds charm in Mariana and Philina, very common forms of feminine character, not without redeeming traits, no less than charms, but without wisdom or purity. Soon he is attended by Mignon, the finest expression ever yet given to what I have called the lyrical element in woman. She is a child, but too full-grown for this man; he loves, but cannot follow her; yet is the association not without an enduring influence. Poesy has been domesticated in his life, and, though he strives to bind down her heavenward impulse, as art or apothegm, these are only the tents, beneath which he may sojourn for a while, but which may be easily struck, and carried on limitless wanderings.

Advancing into the region of thought, he encounters a wise philanthropy in Natalia, (instructed, let us observe, by an *uncle*,) practical judgment and the outward economy of life in Theresa, pure devotion in the Fair Saint.

Farther and last he comes to the house of Macaria, the soul of a star, *i. e.* a pure and perfected intelligence embodied in feminine form, and the centre of a world whose members revolve harmoniously round her. She instructs him in the archives of a rich human history, and introduces him to the contemplation of the heavens.

From the hours passed by the side of Mariana to these with Macaria, is a wide distance for human feet to traverse. Nor has Wilhelm travelled so far, seen and suffered so much in vain. He now begins to study how he may aid the next generation; he sees objects in harmonious arrangement, and from his observations deduces precepts by which to guide his course as a teacher and a master, "help-full, comfort-full."

272   WOMAN IN THE NINETEENTH CENTURY

In all these expressions of woman, the aim of Goethe is satisfactory to me. He aims at a pure self-subsistence, and free development of any powers with which they may be gifted by nature as much for them as for men. They are units, addressed as souls. Accordingly the meeting between man and woman, as represented by him, is equal and noble, and, if he does not depict marriage, he makes it possible.

In the Macaria, bound with the heavenly bodies in fixed revolutions, the centre of all relations, herself unrelated, he expresses the Minerva side of feminine nature. It was not by chance that Goethe gave her this name. Macaria, the daughter of Hercules, who offered herself as a victim for the good of her country, was canonized by the Greeks, and worshipped as the Goddess of true Felicity. Goethe has embodied this Felicity as the Serenity that arises from Wisdom, a Wisdom, such as the Jewish wise man venerated, alike instructed in the designs of heaven, and the methods necessary to carry them into effect upon earth.

Mignon is the electrical, inspired, lyrical nature. And wherever it appears we echo in our aspirations that of the child,

> "So let me seem until I be:—
> Take not the *white robe* away."
> *   *   *   *   *
> "Though I lived without care and toil,
> Yet felt I sharp pain enough,
> Make me again forever young."

All these women, though we see them in relations, we can think of as unrelated. They all are very individual, yet seem, nowhere, restrained. They satisfy for the present, yet arouse an infinite expectation.

The economist Theresa, the benevolent Natalia, the fair Saint, have chosen a path, but their thoughts are not narrowed to it. The functions of life to them are not ends, but suggestions.

Thus, to them, all things are important, because none is necessary. Their different characters have fair play, and each is beautiful in its minute indications, for nothing is enforced or conventional, but every thing, however slight, grows from the essential life of the being.

Mignon and Theresa wear male attire when they like, and it is graceful for them to do so, while Macaria is confined to her arm-chair behind the green curtain, and the Fair Saint could not bear a speck of dust on her robe.

All things are in their places in this little world, because all is natural and free, just as "there is room for everything out of doors." Yet all is rounded in by natural harmony, which will always arise where Truth and Love are sought in the light of Freedom.

Goethe's book bodes an era of freedom like its own of "extraordinary generous seeking," and new revelations. New individualities shall be developed in the actual world, which shall advance upon it as gently as the figures come out upon his canvass.

I have indicated on this point the coincidence between his hopes and those of Fourier, though his are directed by an infinitely higher and deeper knowledge of human nature. But, for our present purpose, it is sufficient to show how surely these different paths have conducted to the same end two earnest thinkers. In some other place I wish to point out similar coincidences between Goethe's model school and the plans of Fourier, which may cast light upon the page of prophecy.

Many women have observed that the time drew nigh for a better care of the sex, and have thrown out hints that may be useful. Among these may be mentioned—

Miss Edgeworth, who, although restrained by the habits of her age and country, and belonging more to the eighteenth than the nineteenth century, has done excellently as far as she goes. She had a horror of sentimentalism, and the love of notoriety, and saw how likely women, in the early stages of culture, were to aim at these. Therefore she bent her efforts to recommending domestic life. But the methods she recommends are such as will fit a character for any position to which it may be called. She taught a contempt of falsehood, no less in its most graceful, than in its meanest apparitions; the cultivation of a clear, independent judgment, and adherence to its dictates; habits of various and liberal study and employment, and a capacity for friendship. Her standard of character is the same for both sexes. Truth, honor, enlightened benevolence, and aspiration after knowledge. Of poetry, she knows nothing, and her religion consists in honor and loyalty to obligations once assumed, in short, in "the great idea of duty which holds us upright." Her whole tendency is practical.

Mrs. Jameson is a sentimentalist, and, therefore, suits us ill in some respects, but she is full of talent, has a just and refined perception of the beautiful, and a genuine courage when she finds it necessary. She does not appear to have thought out, thoroughly, the subject on which we are engaged, and her opinions, expressed as opinions, are sometimes inconsistent with one another. But from the refined perception of character, admirable suggestions are given in her "Women of Shakspeare," and "Loves of the Poets."

But that for which I most respect her is the decision with which she speaks on a subject which refined women are usually afraid to approach, for fear of the insult and scurril jest they may encounter; but on which she neither can nor will restrain the indignation of a full heart. I refer to the degradation of a large portion of women into the sold and polluted slaves of men, and the daring with which the legislator and man of the world lifts his head beneath the heavens, and says "this must be; it cannot be helped; it is a necessary accompaniment of *civilization*."

So speaks the *citizen*. Man born of woman, the father of daughters, declares that he will and must buy the comforts and commercial advantages of his London, Vienna, Paris, New-York, by conniving at the moral death, the damnation, so far as the action of society can insure it, of thousands of women for each splendid metropolis.

O men! I speak not to you. It is true that your wickedness (for you must not deny that, at least, nine thousand out of the ten fall through the vanity you have systematically flattered, or the promises you have treacherously broken;) yes, it is true that your wickedness is its own punishment. Your forms degraded and your eyes clouded by secret sin; natural harmony broken and fineness of perception destroyed in your mental and bodily organization; God and love shut out from your hearts by the foul visitants you have permitted there; incapable of pure marriage; incapable of pure parentage; incapable of worship; oh wretched men, your sin is its own punishment! You have lost the world in losing yourselves. Who ruins another has admitted the worm to the root of his own tree, and the fuller ye fill the cup of evil, the deeper must be your own bitter draught. But I speak not to you—you need to teach and warn one another. And more than one voice rises in earnestness. And all that *women* say to the heart that has once chosen the evil path, is considered prudery, or ignorance, or perhaps, a feebleness of nature which exempts from similar temptations.

But to you, women, American women, a few words may not be addressed in vain. One here and there may listen.

You know how it was in the Oriental clime. One man, if wealth permitted, had several wives and many hand-maidens. The chastity and equality of genuine marriage, with "the thousand decencies that flow," from its communion, the precious virtues that gradually may be matured, within its enclosure, were unknown.

But this man did not wrong according to his light. What he did, he might publish to God and Man; it was not a wicked secret that hid in vile lurking-places and dens, like the banquets of beasts of prey. Those women were not lost, not polluted in their own eyes, nor those of others. If they were not in a state of knowledge and virtue, they were at least in one of comparative innocence.

You know how it was with the natives of this continent. A chief had many wives whom he maintained and who did his household work; those women were but servants, still they enjoyed the respect of others and their own. They lived together in peace. They knew that a sin against what was in their nation esteemed virtue, would be as strictly punished in man as in woman.

Now pass to the countries where marriage is between one and one. I will not speak of the Pagan nations, but come to those which own the Christian rule. We all know what that enjoins; there is a standard to appeal to.

See now, not the mass of the people, for we all know that it is a proverb and a bitter jest to speak of the "down-trodden million." We know that, down to our own time, a principle never had so fair a chance to pervade the mass of the people, but that we must solicit its illustration from select examples.

Take the Paladin, take the Poet. Did *they* believe purity more impossible to man than to woman? Did they wish woman to believe that man was less amenable to higher motives, that pure aspirations would not guard him against bad passions, that honorable employments and temperate habits would not keep him free from slavery to the body. O no! Love was to them a part of heaven, and they could not even wish to receive its happiness, unless assured of being worthy of it. Its highest happiness to them was, that it made them wish to be worthy. They courted probation. They wished not the title of knight, till the banner had been upheld in the heats of battle, amid the rout of cowards.

I ask of you, young girls—I do not mean *you*, whose heart is that of an old coxcomb, though your locks have not yet lost their sunny tinge. Not of you whose whole character is tainted with vanity, inherited or taught, who have early learnt the love of coquettish excitement, and whose eyes rove restlessly in search of a "conquest" or a "beau." You who are ashamed *not* to be seen by others the mark of the most contemptuous flattery or injurious desire. To such I do not speak. But to thee, maiden, who, if not so fair, art yet of that unpolluted nature which Milton saw when he dreamed of Comus and the Paradise. Thou, child of an unprofaned wedlock, brought up amid the teachings of the woods and fields, kept fancy-free by useful employment and a free flight into the heaven of thought, loving to please only those whom thou wouldst not be ashamed to love; I ask of thee, whose cheek has not forgotten its blush nor thy heart its lark-like hopes, if he whom thou mayst hope the Father will send thee, as the companion of life's toils and joys, is not to thy thought pure? Is not manliness to thy thought purity, *not* lawlessness? Can his lips speak falsely? Can he do, in secret, what he could not avow to the mother that bore him? O say, dost thou not look for a heart free, open as thine own, all whose thoughts may be avowed, incapable of wronging the innocent, or still farther degrading the fallen. A man, in short, in whom brute nature is entirely subject to the impulses of his better self.

Yes! it was thus that thou didst hope, for I have many, many times seen the image of a future life, of a destined spouse, painted on the tablets of a virgin heart.

It might be that she was not true to these hopes. She was taken into what is called "the world," froth and scum as it mostly is on the social caldron. There, she saw fair woman carried in the waltz close to the heart of a being who appeared to her

MAN IS NOT OF SATYR-DESCENT 277

a Satyr. Being warned by a male friend that he was in fact of that class, and not fit for such familiar nearness to a chaste being, the advised replied that "women should know nothing about such things." She saw one fairer given in wedlock to a man of the same class. "Papa and mamma said that all men were faulty, at some time in their lives; they had a great many temptations. Frederick would be so happy at home; he would not want to do wrong." She turned to the married women; they, oh tenfold horror! laughed at her supposing "men were like women." Sometimes, I say, she was not true and either sadly accommodated herself to "woman's lot," or acquired a taste for satyr-society, like some of the Nymphs, and all the Bacchanals of old. But to these who could not and would not accept a mess of pottage, or a Circe cup, in lieu of their birthright, and to these others who have yet their choice to make, I say, Courage! I have some words of cheer for you. A man, himself of unbroken purity, reported to me the words of a foreign artist, that "the world would never be better till men subjected themselves to the same laws they had imposed on women;" that artist, he added, was true to the thought. The same was true of Canova, the same of Beethoven. "Like each other demi-god, they kept themselves free from stain," and Michael Angelo, looking over here from the loneliness of his century, might meet some eyes that need not shun his glance.

In private life, I am assured by men who are not so sustained and occupied by the worship of pure beauty, that a similar consecration is possible, is practiced. That many men feel that no temptation can be too strong for the will of man, if he invokes the aid of the Spirit instead of seeking extenuation from the brute alliances of his nature. In short, what the child fancies is really true, though almost the whole world declares it a lie. Man is a child of God; and if he seek His guidance to keep the heart with diligence, it will be so given that all the issues of life may be pure. Life will then be a temple.

> The temple round
> Spread green the pleasant ground;
> The fair colonnade
> Be of pure marble pillars made;
> Strong to sustain the roof,

Time and tempest proof,
Yet, amidst which, the lightest breeze
Can play as it please;
The audience hall
Be free to all
Who revere
The Power worshipped here,
Sole guide of youth
Unswerving Truth:
In the inmost shrine
Stands the image divine,
Only seen
By those whose deeds have worthy been—
Priestlike clean.
Those, who initiated are,
Declare,
As the hours
Usher in varying hopes and powers;
It changes its face,
It changes its age,
Now a young beaming Grace,
Now Nestorian Sage:
But, to the pure in heart,
This shape of primal art
In age is fair,
In youth seems wise,
Beyond compare,
Above surprise;
What it teaches native seems
Its new lore our ancient dreams;
Incense rises from the ground,
Music flows around;
Firm rest the feet below, clear gaze the eyes above,
When Truth to point the way through Life assumes the
wand of Love;
But, if she cast aside the robe of green,
Winter's silver sheen,
White, pure as light,
Makes gentle shroud as worthy weed as bridal robe had been.*

* (*As described by the historian.*)

The temple of Juno is like what the character of woman should be.
Columns! graceful decorums, attractive yet sheltering.

We are now in a transition state, and but few steps have yet been taken. From polygamy, Europe passed to the marriage *de convenance*. This was scarcely an improvement. An attempt was then made to substitute genuine marriage, (the mutual choice of souls inducing a permanent union,) as yet baffled on every side by the haste, the ignorance, or the impurity of man.

Where man assumes a high principle to which he is not yet ripened; it will happen, for a long time, that the few will be nobler than before; the many worse. Thus now. In the country of Sidney and Milton, the metropolis is a den of wickedness, and a stye of sensuality; in the country of Lady Russell, the custom of English Peeresses, of selling their daughters to the highest bidder, is made the theme and jest of fashionable novels by unthinking children who would stare at the idea of sending them to a Turkish slave dealer, though the circumstances of the bargain are there less degrading, as the will and thoughts of the person sold are not so degraded by it, and it is not done in defiance of an acknowledged law of right in the land and the age.

I must here add that I do not believe there ever was put upon record more depravation of man, and more despicable frivolity of thought and aim in woman, than in the novels which purport to give the picture of English fashionable life, which are read with such favor in our drawing rooms, and give the tone to the manners of some circles. Compared with the hard-hearted cold folly there described, crime is hopeful, for it, at least, shows some power remaining in the mental constitution.

To return: Attention has been awakened among men to the stains of celibacy, and the profanations of marriage. They begin to write about it and lecture about it. It is the tendency now to endeavor to help the erring by showing them the physical law. This is wise and excellent; but forget not the better half. Cold bathing and exercise will not suffice to keep a life pure, without an inward baptism and noble and exhilarating employment for the thoughts and the passions. Early marriages are desirable, but if, (and the world is now so out of joint that there are a

---

Porch! noble inviting aspect of the life.
Kaos! receives the worshippers. See here the statue of the Divinity.
Ophistodomos! Sanctuary where the most precious possessions were kept safe from the hand of the spoiler and the eye of the world.

280 WOMAN IN THE NINETEENTH CENTURY

hundred thousand chances to one against it,) a man does not early, or at all, find the person to whom he can be united in the marriage of souls, will you give him in the marriage *de convenance*, or if not married, can you find no way for him to lead a virtuous and happy life? Think of it well, ye who think yourselves better than pagans, for many of *them* knew this sure way.*

To you, women of America, it is more especially my business to address myself on this subject, and my advice may be classed under three heads:

Clear your souls from the taint of vanity.

Do not rejoice in conquests, either that your power to allure may be seen by other women, or for the pleasure of rousing passionate feelings that gratify your love of excitement.

It must happen, no doubt, that frank and generous women will excite love they do not reciprocate, but, in nine cases out of ten, the woman has, half consciously, done much to excite. In this case she shall not be held guiltless, either as to the unhappiness or injury to the lover. Pure love, inspired by a worthy object, must ennoble and bless, whether mutual or not; but that which is excited by coquettish attraction of any grade of refinement, must cause bitterness and doubt, as to the reality of human goodness, so soon as the flush of passion is over. And that you may avoid all taste for these false pleasures

> "Steep the soul
> In one pure love, and it will last thee long."

The love of truth, the love of excellence, which, whether you clothe them in the person of a special object or not, will have

---

* The Persian sacred books, the Desatir, describe the great and holy prince Ky Khosrou, as being "an angel, and the son of an angel," one to whom the Supreme says, "Thou art not absent from before me for one twinkling of an eye. I am never out of thy heart. And I am contained in nothing but in thy heart, and in a heart like thy heart. And I am nearer unto thee than thou art to thyself." This Prince had in his Golden Seraglio three ladies of surpassing beauty, and all four, in this royal monastery, passed their lives, and left the world, as virgins.

The Persian people had no scepticism when the history of such a mind was narrated. They were Catholics.

THE OLD MAN ELOQUENT 281

power to save you from following Duessa, and lead you in the green glades where Una's feet have trod.

It was on this one subject that a venerable champion of good, the last representative of the spirit which sanctified the revolution and gave our country such a sunlight of hope in the eyes of the nations, the same who lately in Boston offered anew to the young men the pledge taken by the young men of his day, offered, also, his counsel, on being addressed by the principal of a girl's school, thus:

REPLY OF MR. ADAMS

Mr. Adams was so deeply affected by the address of Miss Foster, as to be for some time inaudible. When heard, he spoke as follows:

"This is the first instance in which a lady has thus addressed me personally; and I trust that all the ladies present will be able sufficiently to enter into my feelings to know, that I am more affected by this honor, than by any other I could have received.

"You have been pleased, Madam, to allude to the character of my father, and the history of my family, and their services to the country. It is indeed true, that from the existence of the Republic as an independent nation, my father and myself have been in the public service of the country, almost without interruption. I came into the world, as a person having personal responsibilities, with the Declaration of Independence, which constituted us a nation. I was a child at that time, and had then perhaps the greatest of blessings that can be bestowed on man—a mother who was anxious and capable to form her children to what they ought to be. From that mother I derived whatever instruction—religious especially, and moral—has pervaded a long life; I will not say perfectly, and as it ought to be; but I will say, because it is justice only to the memory of her whom I revere, that if, in the course of my life, there has been any imperfection, or deviation from what she taught me, the fault is mine, and not hers.

"With such a mother, and such other relations with the sex, of sister, wife, and daughter, it has been the perpetual instruction of my life to love and revere the female sex. And in order to carry that sentiment of love and reverence to its highest degree

282 WOMAN IN THE NINETEENTH CENTURY

of perfection, I know of nothing that exists in human society better adapted to produce that result, than institutions of the character that I have now the honor to address.

"I have been taught, as I have said, through the course of my life, to love and to revere the female sex; but I have been taught, also—and that lesson has perhaps impressed itself on my mind even more strongly, it may be, than the other—I have been taught not to flatter them. It is not unusual in the intercourse of man with the other sex—and especially for young men—to think, that the way to win the hearts of ladies is by flattery.—To love and to revere the sex, is what I think the duty of man; but *not to flatter them*; and this I would say to the young ladies here; and if they, and others present, will allow me, with all the authority which nearly four score years may have with those who have not yet attained one score—I would say to them what I have no doubt they say to themselves, and are taught here, not to take the flattery of men as proof of perfection.

"I am now, however, I fear, assuming too much of a character that does not exactly belong to me. I therefore conclude, by assuring you, Madam, that your reception of me has affected me, as you perceive, more than I can express in words; and that I shall offer my best prayers, till my latest hour, to the Creator of us all, that this institution especially, and all others of a similar kind, designed to form the female mind to wisdom and virtue, may prosper to the end of time."

It will be interesting to add here the character of Mr. Adams's mother, as drawn by her husband, the first John Adams, in a family letter* written just before his death.

"I have reserved for the last the life of Lady Russell. This I have not yet read, because I read it more than forty years ago. On this hangs a tale which you ought to know and communicate it to your children. I bought the life and letters of Lady Russell, in the year 1775, and sent it to your grandmother, with an express intent and desire, that she should consider it a mirror in which to contemplate herself; for, at that time, I thought it extremely probable, from the daring and dangerous career I was determined to run, that she would one day find herself in the situation of Lady Russell, her husband without a head.

* Journal and Correspondence of Miss Adams, vol. i. p. 246.

This lady was more beautiful than Lady Russell, had a brighter genius, more information, a more refined taste, and, at least, her equal in the virtues of the heart; equal fortitude and firmness of character, equal resignation to the will of Heaven, equal in all the virtues and graces of the christian life. Like Lady Russell, she never, by word or look, discouraged me from running all hazards for the salvation of my country's liberties; she was willing to share with me, and that her children should share with us both, in all the dangerous consequences we had to hazard."

Will a woman who loves flattery or an aimless excitement, who wastes the flower of her mind on transitory sentiments, ever be loved with a love like that, when fifty years trial have entitled to the privileges of "the golden marriage?"

Such was the love of the iron-handed warrior for her, not his hand-maid, but his help-meet:

"Whom God loves, to him gives he such a wife."

I find the whole of what I want in this relation, in the two epithets by which Milton makes Adam address *his* wife.

In the intercourse of every day he begins:

> "Daughter of God and man, *accomplished* Eve."*

In a moment of stronger feeling,

> "Daughter of God and man, IMMORTAL Eve."

What majesty in the cadence of the line; what dignity, what reverence in the attitude, both of giver and receiver!

The woman who permits, in her life, the alloy of vanity; the woman who lives upon flattery, coarse or fine, shall never be thus addressed. She is *not* immortal as far as her will is concerned, and every woman who does so creates miasma, whose spread is indefinite. The hand, which casts into the waters of life a stone of offence, knows not how far the circles thus caused, may spread their agitations.

A little while since, I was at one of the most fashionable places of public resort. I saw there many women, dressed without

---

* See Appendix, H.

regard to the season or the demands of the place, in apery, or, as it looked, in mockery of European fashions. I saw their eyes restlessly courting attention. I saw the way in which it was paid, the style of devotion, almost an open sneer, which it pleased those ladies to receive from men whose expression marked their own low position in the moral and intellectual world. Those women went to their pillows with their heads full of folly, their hearts of jealousy, or gratified vanity: those men, with the low opinion they already entertained of woman confirmed. These were American *ladies*; i. e., they were of that class who have wealth and leisure to make full use of the day, and confer benefits on others. They were of that class whom the possession of external advantages makes of pernicious example to many, if these advantages be misused.

Soon after, I met a circle of women, stamped by society as among the most degraded of their sex. "How," it was asked of them, "did you come here?" for, by the society that I saw in the former place, they were shut up in a prison. The causes were not difficult to trace: love of dress, love of flattery, love of excitement. They had not dresses like the other ladies, so they stole them; they could not pay for flattery by distinctions, and the dower of a worldly marriage, so they paid by the profanation of their persons. In excitement, more and more madly sought from day to day, they drowned the voice of conscience.

Now I ask you, my sisters, if the women at the fashionable house be not answerable for those women being in the prison?

As to position in the world of souls, we may suppose the women of the prison stood fairest, both because they had misused less light, and because loneliness and sorrow had brought some of them to feel the need of better life, nearer truth and good. This was no merit in them, being an effect of circumstance, but it was hopeful. But you, my friends, (and some of you I have already met,) consecrate yourselves without waiting for reproof, in free love and unbroken energy, to win and to diffuse a better life. Offer beauty, talents, riches, on the altar; thus shall ye keep spotless your own hearts, and be visibly or invisibly the angels to others.

I would urge upon those women who have not yet considered this subject, to do so. Do not forget the unfortunates who

LIFT UP THE FALLEN

dare not cross your guarded way. If it do not suit you to act with those who have organized measures of reform, then hold not yourself excused from acting in private. Seek out these degraded women, give them tender sympathy, counsel, employment. Take the place of mothers, such as might have saved them originally.

If you can do little for those already under the ban of the world, and the best considered efforts have often failed, from a want of strength in those unhappy ones to bear up against the sting of shame and the prejudices of the world, which makes them seek oblivion again in their old excitements, you will at least leave a sense of love and justice in their hearts that will prevent their becoming utterly imbittered and corrupt. And you may learn the means of prevention for those yet uninjured. There will be found in a diffusion of mental culture, simple tastes, best taught by your example, a genuine self-respect, and above all, what the influence of man tends to hide from woman, the love and fear of a divine, in preference to a human tribunal.

But suppose you save many who would have lost their bodily innocence (for as to mental, the loss of that is incalculably more general,) through mere vanity and folly; there still remain many, the prey and spoil of the brute passions of man. For the stories frequent in our newspapers outshame antiquity, and vie with the horrors of war.

As to this, it must be considered that, as the vanity and proneness to seduction of the imprisoned women represented a general degradation in their sex; so do these acts a still more general and worse in the male. Where so many are weak it is natural there should be many lost, where legislators admit that ten thousand prostitutes are a fair proportion to one city, and husbands tell their wives that it is folly to expect chastity from men, it is inevitable that there should be many monsters of vice.

I must in this place mention, with respect and gratitude, the conduct of Mrs. Child in the case of Amelia Norman. The action and speech of this lady was of straight-forward nobleness, undeterred by custom or cavil from duty towards an injured sister. She showed the case and the arguments the counsel against the prisoner had the assurance to use in their true light to the public. She put the case on the only ground of religion

286   WOMAN IN THE NINETEENTH CENTURY

and equity. She was successful in arresting the attention of many who had before shrugged their shoulders, and let sin pass as necessarily a part of the company of men. They begin to ask whether virtue is not possible, perhaps necessary, to man as well as to woman. They begin to fear that the perdition of a woman must involve that of a man. This is a crisis. The results of this case will be important.

In this connection I must mention Eugene Sue, the French novelist, several of whose works have been lately transplanted among us, as having the true spirit of reform as to women. Like every other French writer, he is still tainted with the transmissions of the old regime. Still falsehood may be permitted for the sake of advancing truth, evil as the way to good. Even George Sand, who would trample on every graceful decorum, and every human law for the sake of a sincere life, does not see that she violates it by making her heroines able to tell falsehoods in a good cause. These French writers need ever to be confronted by the clear perception of the English and German mind, that the only good man, consequently the only good reformer, is he

> "Who bases good on good alone, and owes
> To virtue every triumph that he knows."

Still, Sue has the heart of a reformer, and especially towards women, he sees what they need, and what causes are injuring them. From the histories of Fleur de Marie and La Louve, from the lovely and independent character of Rigolette, from the distortion given to Matilda's mind, by the present views of marriage, and from the truly noble and immortal character of the "hump-backed Sempstress" in the "Wandering Jew," may be gathered much that shall elucidate doubt and direct inquiry on this subject. In reform, as in philosophy, the French are the interpreters to the civilized world. Their own attainments are not great, but they make clear the past, and break down barriers to the future.

Observe that the good man of Sue is pure as Sir Charles Grandison.

Apropos to Sir Charles, women are accustomed to be told by men that the reform is to come *from them*. "You," say the men, "must frown upon vice, you must decline the attentions of the corrupt, you must not submit to the will of your husband when it seems to you unworthy, but give the laws in marriage, and redeem it from its present sensual and mental pollutions."

This seems to us hard. Men have, indeed, been, for more than a hundred years, rating women for countenancing vice. But at the same time, they have carefully hid from them its nature, so that the preference often shown by women for bad men, arises rather from a confused idea that they are bold and adventurous, acquainted with regions which women are forbidden to explore, and the curiosity that ensues, than a corrupt heart in the woman. As to marriage it has been inculcated on women for centuries, that men have not only stronger passions than they, but of a sort that it would be shameful for them to share or even understand. That, therefore, they must "confide in their husbands," i. e., submit implicitly to their will. That the least appearance of coldness or withdrawal, from whatever cause, in the wife is wicked, because liable to turn her husband's thoughts to illicit indulgence; for a man is so constituted that he must indulge his passions or die!

Accordingly a great part of women look upon men as a kind of wild beasts, but "suppose they are all alike;" the unmarried are assured by the married that, "if they knew men as they do," i. e., by being married to them, "they would not expect continence or self-government from them."

I might accumulate illustrations on this theme, drawn from acquaintance with the histories of women, which would startle and grieve all thinking men, but I forbear. Let Sir Charles Grandison preach to his own sex, or if none there be, who feels himself able to speak with authority from a life unspotted in will or deed, let those who are convinced of the practicability and need of a pure life, as the foreign artist was, advise the others, and warn them by their own example, if need be.

The following passage from a female writer on female affairs, expresses a prevalent way of thinking on this subject.

"It may be that a young woman, exempt from all motives of vanity, determines to take for a husband a man who does not inspire her with a very decided inclination. Imperious circumstances, the evident interest of her family, or the danger of a suffering celibacy, may explain such a resolution. If, however,

288   WOMAN IN THE NINETEENTH CENTURY

she were to endeavor to surmount a personal repugnance, we should look upon this as *injudicious*. Such a rebellion of nature marks the limit that the influence of parents, or the self-sacrifice of the young girl, should never pass. *We shall be told that this repugnance is an affair of the imagination*; it may be so; but imagination is a power which it is temerity to brave; and its antipathy is more difficult to conquer than its preference."*

Among ourselves, the exhibition of such a repugnance from a woman who had been given in marriage "by advice of friends," was treated by an eminent physician as sufficient proof of insanity. If he had said sufficient cause for it, he would have been nearer right.

It has been suggested by men who were pained by seeing bad men admitted, freely, to the society of modest women, thereby encouraged to vice by impunity, and corrupting the atmosphere of homes; that there should be a senate of the matrons in each city and town, who should decide what candidates were fit for admission to their houses and the society of their daughters.[†]

Such a plan might have excellent results, but it argues a moral dignity and decision, which does not yet exist, and needs to be induced by knowledge and reflection. It has been the tone to keep women ignorant on these subjects, or when they were not, to command that they should seem so. "It is indelicate," says the father or husband, "to inquire into the private character of such an one. It is sufficient that I do not think him unfit to visit you." And so, this man, who would not tolerate these pages in his house, "unfit for family reading," because they speak plainly, introduces there a man whose shame is written on his brow, as well as the open secret of the whole town, and, presently, if *respectable* still, and rich enough, gives him his daughter to wife. The mother affects ignorance, "supposing he is no worse than most men." The daughter *is* ignorant; something in the mind of the new spouse seems strange to her, but she supposes it is "woman's lot" not to be perfectly happy in her affections; she has always heard, "men could not understand women," so she weeps alone, or takes to dress and the duties of the house.

---

* Madame Necker de Saussure.
† See Goethe's Tasso. "A synod of good women should decide,"—if the golden age is to be restored.

The husband, of course, makes no avowal, and dreams of no redemption.

"In the heart of every young woman," says the female writer, above quoted, addressing herself to the husband, "depend upon it, there is a fund of exalted ideas; she conceals, represses, without succeeding in smothering them. *So long as these ideas in your wife are directed to* YOU, *they are, no doubt, innocent,* but take care that they be not accompanied with *too much* pain. In other respects, also, spare her delicacy. Let all the antecedent parts of your life, if there are such, which would give her pain, be concealed from her; *her happiness and her respect for you would suffer from this misplaced confidence.* Allow her to retain that flower of purity, *which should distinguish her in your eyes from every other woman.*" We should think so, truly, under this canon. Such a man must esteem purity an exotic that could only be preserved by the greatest care. Of the degree of mental intimacy possible, in such a marriage, let every one judge for himself!

On this subject, let every woman, who has once begun to think, examine herself, see whether she does not suppose virtue possible and necessary to man, and whether she would not desire for her son a virtue which aimed at a fitness for a divine life, and involved, if not asceticism, that degree of power over the lower self, which shall "not exterminate the passions, but keep them chained at the feet of reason." The passions, like fire, are a bad master; but confine them to the hearth and the altar, and they give life to the social economy, and make each sacrifice meet for heaven.

When many women have thought upon this subject, some will be fit for the Senate, and one such Senate in operation would affect the morals of the civilized world.

At present I look to the young. As preparatory to the Senate, I should like to see a society of novices, such as the world has never yet seen, bound by no oath, wearing no badge. In place of an oath they should have a religious faith in the capacity of man for virtue; instead of a badge, should wear in the heart a firm resolve not to stop short of the destiny promised him as a son of God. Their service should be action and conservatism, not of old habits, but of a better nature, enlightened by hopes that daily grow brighter.

290　WOMAN IN THE NINETEENTH CENTURY

If sin was to remain in the world, it should not be by their connivance at its stay, or one moment's concession to its claims.

They should succor the oppressed, and pay to the upright the reverence due in hero-worship by seeking to emulate them. They would not denounce the willingly bad, but they could not be with them, for the two classes could not breathe the same atmosphere.

They would heed no detention from the time-serving, the worldly and the timid.

They could love no pleasures that were not innocent and capable of good fruit.

I saw, in a foreign paper, the title now given to a party abroad, "Los Exaltados." Such would be the title now given these children by the world: Los Exaltados, Las Exaltadas; but the world would not sneer always, for from them would issue a virtue by which it would, at last, be exalted too.

I have in my eye a youth and a maiden whom I look to as the nucleus of such a class. They are both in early youth, both as yet uncontaminated, both aspiring, without rashness, both thoughtful, both capable of deep affection, both of strong nature and sweet feelings, both capable of large mental development. They reside in different regions of earth, but their place in the soul is the same. To them I look, as, perhaps, the harbingers and leaders of a new era, for never yet have I known minds so truly virgin, without narrowness or ignorance.

When men call upon women to redeem them, they mean such maidens. But such are not easily formed under the present influences of society. As there are more such young men to help give a different tone, there will be more such maidens.

The English novelist, D'Israeli, has, in his novel of the "Young Duke," made a man of the most depraved stock be redeemed by a woman who despises him when he has only the brilliant mask of fortune and beauty to cover the poverty of his heart and brain, but knows how to encourage him when he enters on a better course. But this woman was educated by a father who valued character in women.

Still there will come now and then, one who will, as I hope of my young Exaltada, be example and instruction to the rest. It was not the opinion of woman current among Jewish men that formed the character of the mother of Jesus.

LOVE PARTS NOT WITH IDUNA 291

Since the sliding and backsliding men of the world, no less than the mystics declare that, as through woman man was lost, so through woman must man be redeemed, the time must be at hand. When she knows herself indeed as "accomplished," still more as "immortal Eve," this may be.

As an immortal, she may also know and inspire immortal love, a happiness not to be dreamed of under the circumstances advised in the last quotation. Where love is based on concealment, it must, of course, disappear when the soul enters the scene of clear vision!

And, without this hope, how worthless every plan, every bond, every power!

"The giants," said the Scandinavian Saga, "had induced Loke, (the spirit that hovers between good and ill,) to steal for them Iduna, (Goddess of Immortality,) and her apples of pure gold. He lured her out, by promising to show, on a marvellous tree he had discovered, apples beautiful as her own, if she would only take them with her for a comparison. Thus, having lured her beyond the heavenly domain, she was seized and carried away captive by the powers of misrule.

As now the gods could not find their friend Iduna, they were confused with grief; indeed they began visibly to grow old and gray. Discords arose, and love grew cold. Indeed, Odur, spouse of the goddess of love and beauty, wandered away and returned no more. At last, however, the gods, discovering the treachery of Loke, obliged him to win back Iduna from the prison in which she sat mourning. He changed himself into a falcon, and brought her back as a swallow, fiercely pursued by the Giant King, in the form of an eagle. So she strives to return among us, light and small as a swallow. We must welcome her form as the speck on the sky that assures the glad blue of Summer. Yet one swallow does not make a summer. Let us solicit them in flights and flocks!

Returning from the future to the present, let us see what forms Iduna takes, as she moves along the declivity of centuries to the valley where the lily flower may concentrate all its fragrance.

It would seem as if this time were not very near to one fresh from books, such as I have of late been—no: *not* reading, but sighing over. A crowd of books having been sent me since my friends knew me to be engaged in this way, on Woman's

292   WOMAN IN THE NINETEENTH CENTURY

"Sphere," Woman's "Mission," and Woman's "Destiny," I believe that almost all that is extant of formal precept has come under my eye. Among these I read with refreshment, a little one called "The Whole Duty of Woman," "indited by a noble lady at the request of a noble lord," and which has this much of nobleness, that the view it takes is a religious one. It aims to fit woman for heaven, the main bent of most of the others is to fit her to please, or, at least, not to disturb a husband.

Among these I select as a favorable specimen, the book I have already quoted, "The Study* of the Life of Woman, by Madame Necker de Saussure, of Geneva, translated from the French." This book was published at Philadelphia, and has been read with much favor here. Madame Necker is the cousin of Madame de Stael, and has taken from her works the motto prefixed to this.

"Cette vie n'a quelque prix que si elle sert a' l'education morale de notre cœur."

Mde. Necker is, by nature, capable of entire consistency in the application of this motto, and, therefore, the qualifications she makes, in the instructions given to her own sex, show forcibly the weight which still paralyzes and distorts the energies of that sex.

The book is rich in passages marked by feeling and good suggestions, but taken in the whole the impression it leaves is this:

Woman is, and *shall remain* inferior to man and subject to his will, and, in endeavoring to aid her, we must anxiously avoid any thing that can be misconstrued into expression of the contrary opinion, else the men will be alarmed, and combine to defeat our efforts.

The present is a good time for these efforts, for men are less occupied about women than formerly. Let us, then, seize upon the occasion, and do what we can to make our lot tolerable. But we must sedulously avoid encroaching on the territory of man. If we study natural history, our observations may be made useful, by some male naturalist; if we draw well, we may make our services acceptable to the artists. But our names must not

---

* This title seems to be incorrectly translated from the French. I have not seen the original.

be known, and, to bring these labors to any result, we must take some man for our head, and be his hands.

The lot of woman is sad. She is constituted to expect and need a happiness that cannot exist on earth. She must stifle such aspirations within her secret heart, and fit herself, as well as she can, for a life of resignations and consolations.

She will be very lonely while living with her husband. She must not expect to open her heart to him fully, or that, after marriage, he will be capable of the refined service of love. The man is not born for the woman, only the woman for the man. "Men cannot understand the hearts of women." The life of woman must be outwardly a well-intentioned, cheerful dissimulation of her real life.

Naturally, the feelings of the mother, at the birth of a female child, resemble those of the Paraguay woman, described by Southey as lamenting in such heart-breaking tones that her mother did not kill her the hour she was born. "Her mother, who knew what the life of a woman must be;"—or those women seen at the north by Sir A. Mackenzie, who performed this pious duty towards female infants whenever they had an opportunity.

"After the first delight, the young mother experiences feelings a little different, according as the birth of a son or a daughter has been announced.

"Is it a son? A sort of glory swells at this thought the heart of the mother; she seems to feel that she is entitled to gratitude. She has given a citizen, a defender to her country. To her husband an heir of his name, to herself a protector. And yet the contrast of all these fine titles with this being, so humble, soon strikes her. At the aspect of this frail treasure, opposite feelings agitate her heart; she seems to recognize in him *a nature superior to her own*, but subjected to a low condition, and she honors a future greatness in the object of extreme compassion. Somewhat of that respect and adoration for a feeble child, of which some fine pictures offer the expression in the features of the happy Mary, seem reproduced with the young mother who has given birth to a son.

"Is it a daughter? There is usually a slight degree of regret; so deeply rooted is the idea of the superiority of man in happiness and dignity, and yet, as she looks upon this child, she is more and more *softened* towards it—a deep sympathy—a sentiment

294 WOMAN IN THE NINETEENTH CENTURY

of identity with this delicate being takes possession of her; an extreme pity for so much weakness, a more pressing need of prayer stirs her heart. Whatever sorrows she may have felt, she dreads for her daughter; but she will guide her to become much wiser, much better than herself. And then the gayety, the frivolity of the young woman have their turn. This little creature is a flower to cultivate, a doll to decorate."

Similar sadness at the birth of a daughter I have heard mothers express not unfrequently.

As to this living so entirely for men, I should think when it was proposed to women they would feel, at least, some spark of the old spirit of races allied to our own. If he is to be my bridegroom *and lord*, cries Brunhilda,* he must first be able to pass through fire and water. I will serve at the banquet, says the Walkyrie, but only him who, in the trial of deadly combat, has shown himself a hero.

If women are to be bond-maids, let it be to men superior to women in fortitude, in aspiration, in moral power, in refined sense of beauty! You who give yourselves "to be supported," or because "one must love something," are they who make the lot of the sex such that mothers are sad when daughters are born.

It marks the state of feeling on this subject that it was mentioned, as a bitter censure on a woman who had influence over those younger than herself. "She makes those girls want to see heroes?"

"And will that hurt them?"

"Certainly; how *can* you ask? They will find none, and so they will never be married."

"*Get* married" is the usual phrase, and the one that correctly indicates the thought, but the speakers, on this occasion, were persons too outwardly refined to use it. They were ashamed of the word, but not of the thing. Madame Necker, however, sees good possible in celibacy.

Indeed, I know not how the subject could be better illustrated, than by separating the wheat from the chaff in Madame Necker's book; place them in two heaps and then summon the reader to choose; giving him first a near-sighted glass to examine the two; it might be a christian, an astronomical, or an artistic glass,

---

* See the Nibelungen Lays.

any kind of good glass to obviate acquired defects in the eye. I would lay any wager on the result.

But time permits not here a prolonged analysis. I have given the clues for fault-finding.

As a specimen of the good take the following passage, on the phenomena of what I have spoken of, as the lyrical or electric element in woman.

"Women have been seen to show themselves poets in the most pathetic pantomimic scenes, where all the passions were depicted full of beauty; and these poets used a language unknown to themselves, and the performance once over, their inspiration was a forgotten dream. Without doubt there is an interior development to beings so gifted, but their sole mode of communication with us is their talent. They are, in all besides, the inhabitants of another planet."

Similar observations have been made by those who have seen the women at Irish wakes, or the funeral ceremonies of modern Greece or Brittany, at times when excitement gave the impulse to genius; but, apparently, without a thought that these rare powers belonged to no other planet, but were a high development of the growth of this, and might by wise and reverent treatment, be made to inform and embellish the scenes of every day. But, when woman has her fair chance, they will do so, and the poem of the hour will vie with that of the ages. I come now with satisfaction to my own country, and to a writer, a female writer, whom I have selected as the clearest, wisest, and kindliest, who has as yet, used pen here on these subjects. This is Miss Sedgwick.

Miss Sedgwick, though she inclines to the private path, and wishes that, by the cultivation of character, might should vindicate right, sets limits nowhere, and her objects and inducements are pure. They are the free and careful cultivation of the powers that have been given, with an aim at moral and intellectual perfection. Her speech is moderate and sane, but never palsied by fear or sceptical caution.

Herself a fine example of the independent and beneficent existence that intellect and character can give to woman, no less than man, if she know how to seek and prize it; also that the intellect need not absorb or weaken, but rather will refine and invigorate the affections, the teachings of her practical good

296 WOMAN IN THE NINETEENTH CENTURY

sense come with great force, and cannot fail to avail much. Every way her writings please me both as to the means and the ends. I am pleased at the stress she lays on observance of the physical laws, because the true reason is given. Only in a strong and clean body can the soul do its message fitly.

She shows the meaning of the respect paid to personal neatness both in the indispensable form of cleanliness, and of that love of order and arrangement, that must issue from a true harmony of feeling.

The praises of cold water seem to me an excellent sign in the age. They denote a tendency to the true life. We are now to have, as a remedy for ills, not orvietan, or opium, or any quack medicine, but plenty of air and water, with due attention to warmth and freedom in dress, and simplicity of diet.

Every day we observe signs that the natural feelings on these subjects are about to be reinstated, and the body to claim care as the abode and organ of the soul, not as the tool of servile labor, or the object of voluptuous indulgence.

A poor woman who had passed through the lowest grades of ignominy, seemed to think she had never been wholly lost, "for," said she, "I would always have good under-clothes;" and, indeed, who could doubt that this denoted the remains of private self-respect in the mind?

A woman of excellent sense said, "it might seem childish, but to her one of the most favorable signs of the times, was that the ladies had been persuaded to give up corsets."

Yes! let us give up all artificial means of distortion. Let life be healthy, pure, all of a piece. Miss Sedgwick, in teaching that domestics must have the means of bathing as much as their mistresses, and time, too, to bathe, has symbolized one of the most important of human rights.

Another interesting sign of the time is the influence exercised by two women, Miss Martineau and Miss Barrett, from their sick rooms. The lamp of life which, if it had been fed only by the affections, depended on precarious human relations, would scarce have been able to maintain a feeble glare in the lonely prison, now shines far and wide over the nations, cheering fellow sufferers and hallowing the joy of the healthful.

These persons need not health or youth, or the charms of personal presence, to make their thoughts available. A few more

THE O'CONNELL MASS

such, and old woman* shall not be the synonyme for imbecility, nor old maid a term of contempt, nor woman be spoken of as a reed shaken in the wind.

It is time, indeed, that men and women both should cease to grow old in any other way than as the tree does, full of grace and honor. The hair of the artist turns white, but his eye shines clearer than ever, and we feel that age brings him maturity, not decay. So would it be with all were the springs of immortal refreshment but unsealed within the soul, then like these women they would see, from the lonely chamber window, the glories of the universe; or, shut in darkness, be visited by angels.

I now touch on my own place and day, and, as I write, events are occurring that threaten the fair fabric approached by so long an avenue. Week before last the Gentile was requested to aid the Jew to return to Palestine, for the Millennium, the reign of the Son of Mary, was near. Just now, at high and solemn mass, thanks were returned to the Virgin for having delivered O'Connell from unjust imprisonment, in requital of his having consecrated to her the league formed in behalf of Liberty on Tara's Hill. But, last week brought news which threatens that a cause identical with the enfranchisement of Jews, Irish, women, ay, and of Americans in general, too, is in danger, for the choice of the people threatens to rivet the chains of slavery and the leprosy of sin permanently on this nation, through the annexation of Texas!

Ah! if this should take place, who will dare again to feel the throb of heavenly hope, as to the destiny of this country? The noble thought that gave unity to all our knowledge, harmony to all our designs;—the thought that the progress of history had brought on the era, the tissue of prophecies pointed out the spot, where humanity was, at last, to have a fair chance to know itself, and all men be born free and equal for the eagle's flight, flutters as if about to leave the breast, which, deprived of it, will have no more a nation, no more a home on earth.

Women of my country!—Exaltadas! if such there be,—Women of English, old English nobleness, who understand the courage of Boadicea, the sacrifice of Godiva, the power of Queen Emma to tread the red hot iron unharmed. Women who

---

* An apposite passage is quoted in Appendix F.

share the nature of Mrs. Hutchinson, Lady Russell, and the mothers of our own revolution: have you nothing to do with this? You see the men, how they are willing to sell shamelessly, the happiness of countless generations of fellow-creatures, the honor of their country, and their immortal souls, for a money market and political power. Do you not feel within you that which can reprove them, which can check, which can convince them? You would not speak in vain; whether each in her own home, or banded in unison.

Tell these men that you will not accept the glittering baubles, spacious dwellings, and plentiful service, they mean to offer you through these means. Tell them that the heart of women demands nobleness and honor in man, and that, if they have not purity, have not mercy, they are no longer fathers, lovers, husbands, sons of yours.

This cause is your own, for as I have before said, there is a reason why the foes of African slavery seek more freedom for women; but put it not upon that ground, but on the ground of right.

If you have a power, it is a moral power. The films of interest are not so close around you as around the men. If you will but think, you cannot fail to wish to save the country from this disgrace. Let not slip the occasion, but do something to lift off the curse incurred by Eve.

You have heard the women engaged in the abolition movement accused of boldness, because they lifted the voice in public, and lifted the latch of the stranger. But were these acts, whether performed judiciously or no, *so* bold as to dare before God and man to partake the fruits of such offence as this?

You hear much of the modesty of your sex. Preserve it by filling the mind with noble desires that shall ward off the corruptions of vanity and idleness. A profligate woman, who left her accustomed haunts and took service in a New-York boarding-house, said "she had never heard talk so vile at the Five Points, as from the ladies at the boarding-house." And why? Because they were idle; because, having nothing worthy to engage them, they dwelt, with unnatural curiosity, on the ill they dared not go to see.

It will not so much injure your modesty to have your name, by the unthinking, coupled with idle blame, as to have upon

THE HEMISPHERES

your soul the weight of not trying to save a whole race of women from the scorn that is put upon *their* modesty.

Think of this well! I entreat, I conjure you, before it is too late. It is my belief that something effectual might be done by women, if they would only consider the subject, and enter upon it in the true spirit, a spirit gentle, but firm, and which feared the offence of none, save One who is of purer eyes than to behold iniquity.

And now I have designated in outline, if not in fulness, the stream which is ever flowing from the heights of my thought.

In the earlier tract, I was told, I did not make my meaning sufficiently clear. In this I have consequently tried to illustrate it in various ways, and may have been guilty of much repetition. Yet, as I am anxious to leave no room for doubt, I shall venture to retrace, once more, the scope of my design in points, as was done in old-fashioned sermons.

Man is a being of two-fold relations, to nature beneath, and intelligences above him. The earth is his school, if not his birth-place: God his object: life and thought, his means of interpreting nature, and aspiring to God.

Only a fraction of this purpose is accomplished in the life of any one man. Its entire accomplishment is to be hoped only from the sum of the lives of men, or man considered as a whole.

As this whole has one soul and one body, any injury or obstruction to a part, or to the meanest member, affects the whole. Man can never be perfectly happy or virtuous, till all men are so.

To address man wisely, you must not forget that his life is partly animal, subject to the same laws with nature.

But you cannot address him wisely unless you consider him still more as soul, and appreciate the conditions and destiny of soul.

The growth of man is two-fold, masculine and feminine.

As far as these two methods can be distinguished they are so as

Energy and Harmony.

Power and Beauty.

Intellect and Love.

Or by some such rude classification, for we have not language primitive and pure enough to express such ideas with precision.

WOMAN IN THE NINETEENTH CENTURY

These two sides are supposed to be expressed in man and woman, that is, as the more and less, for the faculties have not been given pure to either, but only in preponderance. There are also exceptions in great number, such as men of far more beauty than power, and the reverse. But as a general rule, it seems to have been the intention to give a preponderance on the one side, that is called masculine, and on the other, one that is called feminine.

There cannot be a doubt that, if these two developments were in perfect harmony, they would correspond to and fulfil one another, like hemispheres, or the tenor and bass in music.

But there is no perfect harmony in human nature; and the two parts answer one another only now and then, or, if there be a persistent consonance, it can only be traced, at long intervals, instead of discoursing an obvious melody.

What is the cause of this?

Man, in the order of time, was developed first; as energy comes before harmony; power before beauty.

Woman was therefore under his care as an elder. He might have been her guardian and teacher.

But as human nature goes not straight forward, but by excessive action and then reaction in an undulated course, he misunderstood and abused his advantages, and became her temporal master instead of her spiritual sire.

On himself came the punishment. He educated woman more as a servant than a daughter, and found himself a king without a queen.

The children of this unequal union showed unequal natures, and, more and more, men seemed sons of the hand-maid, rather than princes.

At last there were so many Ishmaelites that the rest grew frightened and indignant. They laid the blame on Hagar, and drove her forth into the wilderness.

But there were none the fewer Ishmaelites for that.

At last men became a little wiser, and saw that the infant Moses was, in every case, saved by the pure instincts of woman's breast. For, as too much adversity is better for the moral nature than too much prosperity, woman, in this respect, dwindled less than man, though in other respects, still a child in leading strings.

THE NEW DODONA!

So man did her more and more justice, and grew more and more kind.

But yet, his habits and his will corrupted by the past, he did not clearly see that woman was half himself, that her interests were identical with his, and that, by the law of their common being, he could never reach his true proportions while she remained in any wise shorn of hers.

And so it has gone on to our day; both ideas developing, but more slowly than they would under a clearer recognition of truth and justice, which would have permitted the sexes their due influence on one another, and mutual improvement from more dignified relations.

Wherever there was pure love, the natural influences were, for the time, restored.

Wherever the poet or artist gave free course to his genius, he saw the truth, and expressed it in worthy forms, for these men especially share and need the feminine principle. The divine birds need to be brooded into life and song by mothers.

Wherever religion (I mean the thirst for truth and good, not the love of sect and dogma,) had its course, the original design was apprehended in its simplicity, and the dove presaged sweetly from Dodona's oak.

I have aimed to show that no age was left entirely without a witness of the equality of the sexes in function, duty and hope.

Also that, when there was unwillingness or ignorance, which prevented this being acted upon, women had not the less power for their want of light and noble freedom. But it was power which hurt alike them and those against whom they made use of the arms of the servile; cunning, blandishment, and unreasonable emotion.

That now the time has come when a clearer vision and better action are possible. When man and woman may regard one another as brother and sister, the pillars of one porch, the priests of one worship.

I have believed and intimated that this hope would receive an ampler fruition, than ever before, in our own land.

And it will do so if this land carry out the principles from which sprang our national life.

I believe that, at present, women are the best helpers of one another.

302   WOMAN IN THE NINETEENTH CENTURY

Let them think; let them act; till they know what they need.

We only ask of men to remove arbitrary barriers. Some would like to do more. But I believe it needs for woman to show herself in her native dignity, to teach them how to aid her; their minds are so encumbered by tradition.

When Lord Edward Fitzgerald travelled with the Indians, his manly heart obliged him at once, to take the packs from the squaws and carry them. But we do not read that the red men followed his example, though they are ready enough to carry the pack of the white woman, because she seems to them a superior being.

Let woman appear in the mild majesty of Ceres, and rudest churls will be willing to learn from her.

You ask, what use will she make of liberty, when she has so long been sustained and restrained?

I answer; in the first place, this will not be suddenly given. I read yesterday a debate of this year on the subject of enlarging women's rights over property. It was a leaf from the class-book that is preparing for the needed instruction. The men learned visibly as they spoke. The champions of woman saw the fallacy of arguments, on the opposite side, and were startled by their own convictions. With their wives at home, and the readers of the paper, it was the same. And so the stream flows on; thought urging action, and action leading to the evolution of still better thought.

But, were this freedom to come suddenly, I have no fear of the consequences. Individuals might commit excesses, but there is not only in the sex a reverence for decorums and limits inherited and enhanced from generation to generation, which many years of other life could not efface, but a native love, in woman as woman, of proportion, of "the simple art of not too much," a Greek moderation, which would create immediately a restraining party, the natural legislators and instructors of the rest, and would gradually establish such rules as are needed to guard, without impeding, life.

The Graces would lead the choral dance, and teach the rest to regulate their steps to the measure of beauty.

But if you ask me what offices they may fill; I reply—any. I do not care what case you put; let them be sea-captains, if

IT WAS THE MAN'S NOTION

you will. I do not doubt there are women well fitted for such an office, and, if so, I should be glad to see them in it, as to welcome the maid of Saragossa, or the maid of Missolonghi, or the Suliote heroine, or Emily Plater.

I think women need, especially at this juncture, a much greater range of occupation than they have, to rouse their latent powers. A party of travellers lately visited a lonely hut on a mountain. There they found an old woman that told them she and her husband had lived there forty years. "Why," they said, "did you choose so barren a spot? She "did not know; *it was the man's notion.*"

And, during forty years, she had been content to act, without knowing why, upon "the man's notion." I would not have it so.

In families that I know, some little girls like to saw wood, others to use carpenters' tools. Where these tastes are indulged, cheerfulness and good humor are promoted. Where they are forbidden, because "such things are not proper for girls," they grow sullen and mischievous.

Fourier had observed these wants of women, as no one can fail to do who watches the desires of little girls, or knows the ennui that haunts grown women, except where they make to themselves a serene little world by art of some kind. He, therefore, in proposing a great variety of employments, in manufactures or the care of plants and animals, allows for one third of woman, as likely to have a taste for masculine pursuits, one third of men for feminine.

Who does not observe the immediate glow and serenity that is diffused over the life of women, before restless or fretful, by engaging in gardening, building, or the lowest department of art. Here is something that is not routine, something that draws forth life toward the infinite.

I have no doubt, however, that a large proportion of women would give themselves to the same employments as now, because there are circumstances that must lead them. Mothers will delight to make the nest soft and warm. Nature would take care of that; no need to clip the wings of any bird that wants to soar and sing, or finds in itself the strength of pinion for a migratory flight unusual to its kind. The difference would be that *all* need not be constrained to employements, for which *some* are unfit.

I have urged upon the sex self-subsistence in its two forms of self-reliance and self-impulse, because I believe them to be the needed means of the present juncture.

I have urged on woman independence of man, not that I do not think the sexes mutually needed by one another, but because in woman this fact has led to an excessive devotion, which has cooled love, degraded marriage, and prevented either sex from being what it should be to itself or the other.

I wish woman to live, *first* for God's sake. Then she will not make an imperfect man her god, and thus sink to idolatry. Then she will not take what is not fit for her from a sense of weakness and poverty. Then, if she finds what she needs in man embodied, she will know how to love, and be worthy of being loved.

By being more a soul, she will not be less woman, for nature is perfected through spirit.

Now there is no woman, only an overgrown child.

That her hand may be given with dignity, she must be able to stand alone. I wish to see men and women capable of such relations as are depicted by Landor in his Pericles and Aspasia, where grace is the natural garb of strength, and the affections are calm, because deep. The softness is that of a firm tissue, as when

> "The gods approve
> The depth, but not the tumult of the soul,
> A fervent, not ungovernable love."

A profound thinker has said, "no married woman can represent the female world, for she belongs to her husband. The idea of woman must be represented by a virgin."

But that is the very fault of marriage, and of the present relation between the sexes, that the woman does belong to the man, instead of forming a whole with him. Were it otherwise, there would be no such limitation to the thought.

Woman, self-centred, would never be absorbed by any relation; it would be only an experience to her as to man. It is a vulgar error that love, *a* love to woman is her whole existence;

she also is born for Truth and Love in their universal energy. Would she but assume her inheritance, Mary would not be the only virgin mother. Not Manzoni alone would celebrate in his wife the virgin mind with the maternal wisdom and conjugal affections. The soul is ever young, ever virgin.

And will not she soon appear? The woman who shall vindicate their birthright for all women; who shall teach them what to claim, and how to use what they obtain? Shall not her name be for her era Victoria, for her country and life Virginia? Yet predictions are rash; she herself must teach us to give her the fitting name.

An idea not unknown to ancient times has of late been revived, that, in the metamorphoses of life, the soul assumes the form, first of man, then of woman, and takes the chances, and reaps the benefits of either lot. Why then, say some, lay such emphasis on the rights or needs of woman? What she wins not, as woman, will come to her as man.

That makes no difference. It is not woman, but the law of right, the law of growth, that speaks in us, and demands the perfection of each being in its kind, apple as apple, woman as woman. Without adopting your theory I know that I, a daughter, live through the life of man; but what concerns me now is, that my life be a beautiful, powerful, in a word, a complete life in its kind. Had I but one more moment to live, I must wish the same.

Suppose, at the end of your cycle, your great world-year, all will be completed, whether I exert myself or not (and the supposition is *false*,) but suppose it true, am I to be indifferent about it? Not so! I must beat my own pulse true in the heart of the world; for *that* is virtue, excellence, health.

Thou, Lord of Day! didst leave us to-night so calmly glorious, not dismayed that cold winter is coming, not postponing thy beneficence to the fruitful summer! Thou didst smile on thy day's work when it was done, and adorn thy down-going as thy up-rising, for thou art loyal, and it is thy nature to give life, if thou canst, and shine at all events!

I stand in the sunny noon of life. Objects no longer glitter in the dews of morning, neither are yet softened by the shadows of evening. Every spot is seen, every chasm revealed. Climbing the dusty hill, some fair effigies that once stood for symbols of human destiny have been broken; those I still have with me, show defects in this broad light. Yet enough is left, even by experience, to point distinctly to the glories of that destiny; faint, but not to be mistaken streaks of the future day. I can say with the bard,

"Though many have suffered shipwreck, still beat noble hearts."

Always the soul says to us all: Cherish your best hopes as a faith, and abide by them in action. Such shall be the effectual fervent means to their fulfilment,

> For the Power to whom we bow
> Has given its pledge that, if not now,
> They of pure and stedfast mind,
> By faith exalted, truth refined,
> *Shall* hear all music loud and clear,
> Whose first notes they ventured here.
> Then fear not thou to wind the horn,
> Though elf and gnome thy courage scorn;
> Ask for the Castle's King and Queen;
> Though rabble rout may rush between,
> Beat thee senseless to the ground,
> In the dark beset thee round;
> Persist to ask and it will come,
> Seek not for rest in humbler home;
> So shalt thou see what few have seen,
> The palace home of King and Queen.

15th November, 1844.

Appendix

A

Apparition of the goddess Isis to her votary, from Apuleius. "Scarcely had I closed my eyes, when behold (I saw in a dream) a divine form emerging from the middle of the sea, and raising a countenance venerable, even to the gods themselves. Afterwards, the whole of the most splendid image seemed to stand before me, having gradually shaken off the sea. I will endeavor to explain to you its admirable form, if the poverty of human language will but afford me the power of an appropriate narration; or if the divinity itself, of the most luminous form, will supply me with a liberal abundance of fluent diction. In the first place, then, her most copious and long hairs, being gradually intorted, and promiscuously scattered on her divine neck, were softly defluous. A multiform crown, consisting of various flowers, bound the sublime summit of her head. And in the middle of the crown, just on her forehead, there was a smooth orb resembling a mirror, or rather a white refulgent light, which indicated that she was the moon. Vipers rising up after the manner of furrows, environed the crown on the right hand and on the left, and Cerealian ears of corn were also extended from above. Her garment was of many colors, and woven from the finest flax, and was at one time lucid with a white splendor, at another yellow from the flower of crocus, and at another flaming with a rosy redness. But that which most excessively dazzled my sight, was a very black robe, fulgid with a dark splendor, and which, spreading round and passing under her right side, and ascending to her left shoulder, there rose protuberant, like the centre of a shield, the dependent part of her robe falling in many folds, and having small knots of fringe, gracefully flowing in its extremities. Glittering stars were dispersed through the embroidered border of the robe, and through the whole of its surface, and the full moon, shining in the middle of the stars, breathed forth flaming fires. A crown, wholly consisting of flowers and fruits of every kind, adhered

WOMAN IN THE NINETEENTH CENTURY

with indivisible connexion to the border of conspicuous robe, in all its undulating motions.

"What she carried in her hands also consisted of things of a very different nature. Her right hand bore a brazen rattle, through the narrow lamina of which, bent like a belt, certain rods passing, produced a sharp triple sound through the vibrating motion of her arm. An oblong vessel, in the shape of a boat, depended from her left hand, on the handle of which, in that part which was conspicuous, an asp raised its erect head and largely swelling neck. And shoes, woven from the leaves of the victorious palm tree, covered her immortal feet. Such, and so great a goddess, breathing the fragrant odour of the shores of Arabia the happy, deigned thus to address me."

The foreign English of the translator, Thomas Taylor, gives the description the air of being, itself, a part of the Mysteries. But its majestic beauty requires no formal initiation to be enjoyed.

B

I give this, in the original, as it does not bear translation. Those who read Italian will judge whether it is not a perfect description of a perfect woman.

Lodi e Preghiere a Maria

Vergine bella che di sol vestita,
Coronata di stelle, al sommo Sole
   Piacesti si, che'n te sua luce ascose;
Amor mi spinge a dir di te parole:
   Ma non so 'ncominciar senza tu' aita,
E di Colui che amando in te si pose.
   Invoco lei che ben sempre rispose,
Chi la chiamò con fede.
   Vergine, s'a mercede
Miseria extrema dell' smane cose
   Giammai ti volse, al mio prego t'inchina:
Soccorri alla mia guerra;
   Bench' i' sia terra, e tu del ciel Regina.

APPENDIX

Vergine saggia, e del bel numero una
Delle beate vergini prudenti;
   Anzi la prima, e con più chiara lampa;
O saldo scudo dell' afflitte gente
   Contra colpi di Morte e di Fortuna,
Sotto' l qual si trionfa, non pur scampa:
   O refrigerio alcieco ardor ch' avvampa
Qui fra mortali sciocchi,
   Vergine, que' begli occhi
Che vider tristi la spietata stampa
   Ne' dolci membri del tuo caro figlio,
Volgi al mio dubbio stato;
   Che sconsigliato a te vien per consiglio.

Vergine pura, d'ogni parte intera,
Del tuo parto gentil figliuola e madre;
   Che allumi questa vita, e l'altra adorni;
Per te il tuo Figlio e quel del sommo Padre,
   O finestra del ciel lucente altera,
Venne a salvarne in su gli estremi giorni,
   E fra tutt' i terreni altri soggiorni
Sola tu fusti eletta,
   Vergine benedetta;
Che 'l pianto d' Eva in allegrezza torni';
   Fammi; che puoi; della sua grazia degno,
Senza fine o beata,
   Già coronata nel superno regno.

Vergine santa d'ogni grazia piena;
Che per vera e altissima umiltate
   Salisti al ciel, onde miei preghi ascolti;
Tu partoristi il fonte di pietate,
   E di giustizia il Sol, che rasserena
Il secol pien d'errori oscuri e folti:
   Tre dolci e cari nomi ha' in te raccolti,
Madre, Figliuola, e Sposa;
   Vergine gloriosa,
Donna del Re che nostri lacci ha sciolti,
   E fatto 'l mondo libero e felice;
Nelle cui sante piaghe
   Prego ch'appaghe il cor, vera beatrice.

Vergine sola al mondo senza esempio,
Che 'l ciel di tue bellezze innamorasti,
   Cui nè prima fu simil, nè seconda;
Santi pensieri, atti pietosi e casti
   Al vero Dio sacrato, e vivo tempio
Fecero in tua virginita feconda.
   Per te può la mia vita esser gioconda,
S' a' tuoi preghi, o MARIA
   Vergine dolce, e pia,
Ove 'l fallo abbondò, la grazia abbonda.
   Con le ginocchia della mente inchine
Prego che sia mia scorta;
   E la mia torta via drizzi a buon fine.

Vergine chiara, e stabile in eterno,
Di questo tempestoso mare stella;
   D'ogni fedel nocchier fidata guida;
Pon mente in che terribile procella
   I mi ritrovo sol senza governo,
Ed ho gia' da vicin l'ultime strida:
   Ma pur' in te l'anima mia si fida;
Peccatrice; i' nol nego,
   Vergine: ma te prego
Che 'l tuo nemico del mia mal non rida:
   Ricorditi che fece il peccar nostro
Prender Dio, per scamparne,
   Umana carne al tuo virginal christro.

Vergine, quante lagrime ho già sparte,
Quante lusinghe, e quanti preghi indarno,
   Pur per mia pena, e per mio grave danno!
Da poi ch' i nacqui in su la riva d' Arno;
   Cercando or questa ed or quell altra parte,
Non è stata mia vita altro ch' affanno.
   Mortal bellezza, atti, e parole m' hanno
Tutta ingombrata l'alma.
   Vergine sacra, ed alma,
Non tardar; ch' i' non forse all' ultim 'ann,
   I di miei piu correnti che saetta,
Fra miserie e peccati
   Sonsen andati, e sol Morte n'aspetta.

APPENDIX

Vergine, tale è terra, e posto ha in doglia
Lo mio cor; che vivendo in pianto il tenne;
   E di mille miei mali un non sapea;
E per saperlo, pur quel che n'avvenne,
   Fora avvenuto: ch' ogni altra sua voglia
Era a me morte, ed a lei fama rea
   Or tu, donna del ciel, tu nostra Dea,
Se dir lice, e conviensi;
   Vergine d'alti sensi,
Tu vedi il tutto; e quel che non potea
   Far altri, è nulla a e la tua gran virtute;
Pon fine al mio dolore;
   Ch'a te onore ed a me fia salute.

Vergine, in cui ho tutta mia speranza
Che possi e vogli al gran bisogno aitarme;
   Non mi lasciare in su l'estremo passo:
Non guardar me, ma chi degnò crearme;
   No'l mio valor, ma l'alta sua sembianza;
Che in me ti mova a curar d'uorm si basso.
   Medusa, e l'error mio io han fatto un sasso
D'umor vano stillante;
   Vergine, tu di sante
Lagrime, e pie adempi 'l mio cor lasso;
   Ch' almen l'ultimo pianto sia divoto,
      Senza terrestro limo;
Come fu'l primo non d'insania voto.

Vergine umana, e nemica d'orgoglio,
Del comune principio amor t'induca;
   Miserere d' un cor contrito umile;
Che se poca mortal terra caduca
   Amar con si mirabil fede soglio;
Che devro far di te cosa gentile?
   Se dal mio stato assai misero, e vile
Per le tue man resurgo,
   Vergine; è' sacro, e purgo
Al tuo nome e pens ieri e'ngegno, e stile;
   La lingua, e'l cor, le lagrime, e i sospiri,
Scorgimi al miglior guado;
   E prendi in grado i cangiati desiri.

WOMAN IN THE NINETEENTH CENTURY

> Il di s'appressa, e non pote esser lunge;
>   Si corre il tempo, e vola,
> Vergine unica, e sola;
>   E'l cor' or conscienza, or morte punge.
> Raccommandami al tuo Figliuol, verace
>   Uomo, e verace Dio;
> Ch' accolga 'l mio spirto ultimo in pace.

As the Scandinavian represented Frigga the Earth, or World mother, knowing all things, yet never herself revealing them, though ready to be called to counsel by the gods. It represents her in action, decked with jewels and gorgeously attended. But, says the Mythos, when she ascended the throne of Odin, her consort (Haaven) she left with mortals, her friend, the Goddess of Sympathy, to protect them in her absence.

Since, Sympathy goes about to do good. Especially she devotes herself to the most valiant and the most oppressed. She consoled the Gods in some degree even for the death of their darling Baldur. Among the heavenly powers she has no consort.

C

"The Wedding of the Lady Theresa"

FROM LOCKHART'S SPANISH BALLADS

> "'Twas when the fifth Alphonso in Leon held his sway,
>   King Abdalla of Toledo an embassy did send;
> He asked his sister for a wife, and in an evil day
>   Alphonso sent her, for he feared Abdalla to offend;
> He feared to move his anger, for many times before
> He had received in danger much succor from the Moor.

> Sad heart had fair Theresa, when she their paction knew;
>   With streaming tears she heard them tell she 'mong the
>   Moors must go;
> That she, a Christian damsel, a Christian firm and true,
>   Must wed a Moorish husband, it well might cause her wo;
> But all her tears and all her prayers they are of small avail;
>   At length she for her fate prepares, a victim sad and pale.

> The king hath sent his sister to fair Toledo town,
>   Where then the Moor Abdalla his royal state did keep;

APPENDIX

When she drew near, the Moslem from his golden throne came
 down,
 And courteously received her, and bade her cease to weep;
With loving words he pressed her to come his bower within;
With kisses he caressed her, but still she feared the sin.

'Sir King, Sir King, I pray thee,'—'twas thus Theresa spake,
 'I pray thee, have compassion, and do to me no wrong;
For sleep with thee I may not, unless the vows I break,
 Whereby I to the holy church of Christ my Lord belong;
For thou hast sworn to serve Mahoun, and if this thing should be,
The curse of God it must bring down upon thy realm and thee.

'The angel of Christ Jesu, to whom my heavenly Lord
 Hath given my soul in keeping, is ever by my side;
If thou dost me dishonor, he will unsheath his sword,
 And smite thy body fiercely, at the crying of thy bride;
Invisible he standeth; his sword like fiery flame,
Will penetrate thy bosom, the hour that sees my shame.'

The Moslem heard her with a smile; the earnest words she said,
 He took for bashful maiden's wile, and drew her to his bower:
In vain Theresa prayed and strove,—she pressed Abdalla's bed,
 Perforce received his kiss of love, and lost her maiden flower.
A woful woman there she lay, a loving lord beside,
And earnestly to God did pray, her succor to provide.

The angel of Christ Jesu her sore complaint did hear,
 And plucked his heavenly weapon from out his sheath unseen,
He waved the brand in his right hand, and to the King came near,
 And drew the point o'er limb and joint, beside the weeping
 Queen:
A mortal weakness from the stroke upon the King did fall;
He could not stand when daylight broke, but on his knees must
 crawl.

Abdalla shuddered inly, when he this sickness felt,
 And called upon his barons, his pillow to come nigh;
'Rise up,' he said 'my liegemen,' as round his bed they knelt,
 'And take this Christian lady, else certainly I die;
Let gold be in your girdles, and precious stones beside,
 And swiftly ride to Leon, and render up my bride.'

314   WOMAN IN THE NINETEENTH CENTURY

When they were come to Leon, Theresa would not go
   Into her brother's dwelling, where her maiden years were spent;
But o'er her downcast visage a white veil she did throw,
   And to the ancient nunnery of Las Huelgas went.
There, long, from worldly eyes retired, a holy life she led;
There she, an aged saint, expired; there sleeps she with the dead."

D

The following extract from Spinoza is worthy of attention, as expressing the view which a man of the largest intellectual scope may take of woman, if that part of his life to which her influence appeals, has been left unawakened.

He was a man of the largest intellect, of unsurpassed reasoning powers, yet he makes a statement false to history, for we well know how often men and women have ruled together without difficulty, and one in which very few men even at the present day, I mean men who are thinkers, like him, would acquiesce.

I have put in contrast with it three expressions of the latest literature.

1st. From the poems of W. E. Channing, a poem called "Reverence," equally remarkable for the deep wisdom of its thought and the beauty of its utterance, and containing as fine a description of one class of women as exists in literature.

In contrast with this picture of woman, the happy Goddess of Beauty, the wife, the friend, "the summer queen," I add one by the author of "Festus," of a woman of the muse, the sybil kind, which seems painted from living experience.

And thirdly, I subjoin Eugene Sue's description of a wicked, but able woman of the practical sort, and appeal to all readers whether a species that admits of three such varieties is so easily to be classed away, or kept within prescribed limits, as Spinoza, and those who think like him, believe.

SPINOZA. TRACTATUS POLITICI, DE DEMOCRATIA, CAPUT XI

"Perhaps some one will here ask, whether the supremacy of man over woman is attributable to nature or custom? For if it be human institutions alone to which this fact is owing, there is no reason why we should exclude women from a share in government. Experience, however, most plainly teaches that it is woman's weakness which places her under the authority of man. Since it has nowhere happened that men and women ruled together; but wherever men and women are found the world over, there we see the men ruling and the women ruled, and in this order of things men and women live together in peace and harmony. The Amazons, it is true, are reputed formerly to have held the reins of government, but they drove men from their dominions; the male of their offspring they invariably destroyed, permitting their daughters alone to live. Now if women were by nature upon an equality with men, if they equalled men in fortitude, in genius (qualities which give to men might, and consequently, right) it surely would be the case, that among the numerous and diverse nations of the earth, some would be found where both sexes ruled conjointly, and others where the men were ruled by the women, and so educated as to be mentally inferior: since this state of things no where exists, it is perfectly fair to infer that the rights of women are not equal to those of men; but that women must be subordinate, and therefore cannot have an equal, far less a superior place in the government. If, too, we consider the passions of men—how the love men feel towards women is seldom any thing but lust and impulse, and much less a reverence for qualities of soul than an admiration of physical beauty, observing, too, how men are afflicted when their sweethearts favor other wooers, and other things of the same character,—we shall see at a glance that it would be, in the highest degree, detrimental to peace and harmony, for men and women to possess an equal share in government."

"Reverence"

"As an ancestral heritage revere
All learning, and all thought. The painter's fame
Is thine, whate'er thy lot, who honorest grace.
And need enough in this low time, when they,
Who seek to captivate the fleeting notes
Of heaven's sweet beauty, must despair almost,
So heavy and obdurate show the hearts
Of their companions. Honor kindly then

Those who bear up in their so generous arms
The beautiful ideas of matchless forms;
For were these not portrayed, our human fate,—
Which is to be all high, majestical,
To grow to goodness with each coming age,
Till virtue leap and sing for joy to see
So noble, virtuous men,—would brief decay;
And the green, festering slime, oblivious, haunt
About our common fate. Oh honor them!

But what to all true eyes has chiefest charm,
And what to every breast where beats a heart
Framed to one beautiful emotion,—to
One sweet and natural feeling, lends a grace
To all the tedious walks of common life,
This is fair woman,—woman, whose applause
Each poet sings,—woman the beautiful.
Not that her fairest brow, or gentlest form
Charm us to tears; not that the smoothest cheek,
Where ever rosy tints have made their home,
So rivet us on her; but that she is
The subtle, delicate grace,—the inward grace,
For words too excellent; the noble, true,
The majesty of earth; the summer queen:
In whose conceptions nothing but what's great
Has any right. And, O! her love for him,
Who does but his small part in honoring her;
Discharging a sweet office, sweeter none,
Mother and child, friend, counsel and repose;—
Nought matches with her, nought has leave with her
To highest human praise. Farewell to him
Who reverences not with an excess
Of faith the beauteous sex; all barren he
Shall live a living death of mockery.

Ah! had but words the power, what could we say
Of woman! We, rude men, of violent phrase,
Harsh action, even in repose inwardly harsh;
Whose lives walk blustering on high stilts, removed
From all the purely gracious influence
Of mother earth. To single from the host
Of angel forms one only, and to her
Devote our deepest heart and deepest mind

APPENDIX

Seems almost contradiction. Unto her
We owe our greatest blessings, hours of cheer,
Gay smiles, and sudden tears, and more than these
A sure perpetual love. Regard her as
She walks along the vast still earth; and see!
Before her flies a laughing troop of joys,
And by her side treads old experience,
With never-failing voice admonitory;
The gentle, though infallible, kind advice,
The watchful care, the fine regardfulness,
Whatever mates with what we hope to find,
All consummate in her—the summer queen.

To call past ages better than what now
Man is enacting on life's crowded stage,
Cannot improve our worth; and for the world
Blue is the sky as ever, and the stars
Kindle their crystal flames at soft-fallen eve
With the same purest lustre that the east
Worshipped. The river gently flows through fields
Where the broad-leaved corn spreads out, and loads
Its ear as when the Indian tilled the soil.
The dark green pine,—green in the winter's cold,
Still whispers meaning emblems, as of old;
The cricket chirps, and the sweet, eager birds
In the sad woods crowd their thick melodies;
But yet, to common eyes, life's poetry
Something has faded, and the cause of this
May be that man, no longer at the shrine
Of woman, kneeling with true reverence,
In spite of field, wood, river, stars and sea
Goes most disconsolate. A babble now,
A huge and wind-swelled babble, fills the place
Of that great adoration which of old
Man had for woman. In these days no more
Is love the pith and marrow of man's fate.

Thou who in early years feelest awake
To finest impulses from nature's breath,
And in thy walk hearest such sounds of truth
As on the common ear strike without heed,
Beware of men around thee. Men are foul,
With avarice, ambition and deceit;

WOMAN IN THE NINETEENTH CENTURY

The worst of all, ambition. This is life
Spent in a feverish chase for selfish ends,
Which has no virtue to redeem its toil
But one long, stagnant hope to raise the self.
The miser's life to this seems sweet and fair;
Better to pile the glittering coin, than seek
To overtop our brothers and our loves.
Merit in this? Where lies it, though thy name
Ring over distant lands, meeting the wind
Even on the extremest verge of the wide world.
Merit in this? Better be hurled abroad
On the vast whirling tide, than in thyself
Concentred, feed upon thy own applause.
Thee shall the good man yield no reverence;
But, while the idle, dissolute crowd are loud
In voice to send thee flattery, shall rejoice
That he has scaped thy fatal doom, and known
How humble faith in the good soul of things
Provides amplest enjoyment. O my brother,
If the Past's counsel any honor claim
From thee, go read the history of those
Who a like path have trod, and see a fate
Wretched with fears, changing like leaves at noon,
When the new wind sings in the white birch wood.
Learn from the simple child the rule of life,
And from the movements of the unconscious tribes
Of animal nature, those that bend the wing
Or cleave the azure tide, content to be,
What the great frame provides,—freedom and grace.
Thee, simple child, do the swift winds obey,
And the white waterfalls with their bold leaps
Follow thy movements. Tenderly the light
Thee watches, girding with a zone of radiance,
And all the swinging herbs love thy soft steps."

Description of Angela, from "Festus"

"I loved her for that she was beautiful,
    And that to me she seemed to be all nature
    And all varieties of things in one;
    Would set at night in clouds of tears, and rise
    All light and laughter in the morning; fear
    No petty customs nor appearances,

APPENDIX

But think what others only dreamed about;
And say what others did but think; and do
What others would but say; and glory in
What others dared but do; it was these which won me;
And that she never schooled within her breast
One thought or feeling, but gave holiday
To all; and that she told me all her woes
And wrongs and ills; and so she made them mine
In the communion of love; and we
Grew like each other, for we loved each other;
She, mild and generous as the sun in spring;
And I, like earth, all budding out with love.

    *   *   *

The beautiful are never desolate:
For some one alway loves them; God or man;
If man abandons, God Himself takes them:
And thus it was. She whom I once loved died,
The lightning loathes its cloud; the soul its clay.
Can I forget that hand I took in mine,
Pale as pale violets; that eye, where mind
And matter met alike divine?—ah, no!
May God that moment judge me when I do!
Oh! she was fair; her nature once all spring
And deadly beauty, like a maiden sword,
Startlingly beautiful. I see her now!
Wherever thou art thy soul is in my mind;
Thy shadow hourly lengthens o'er my brain
And peoples all its pictures with thyself;
Gone, not forgotten; passed, not lost; thou wilt shine
In heaven like a bright spot in the sun!
She said she wished to die, and so she died,
For, cloudlike, she poured out her love, which was
Her life, to freshen this parched heart. It was thus;
I said we were to part, but she said nothing;
There was no discord; it was music ceased,
Life's thrilling, bursting, bounding joy. She sate,
Like a house-god, her hands fixed on her knee,
And her dark hair lay loose and long behind her,
Through which her wild bright eye flashed like a flint;
She spake not, moved not, but she looked the more,
As if her eye were action, speech, and feeling.
I felt it all, and came and knelt beside her,
The electric touch solved both our souls together;
Then came the feeling which unmakes, undoes;

Which tears the sealike soul up by the roots,
And lashes it in scorn against the skies.

     *   *   *

It is the saddest and the sorest sight,
One's own love weeping. But why call on God?
But that the feeling of the boundless bounds
All feeling; as the welkin does the world;
It is this which ones us with the whole and God.
Then first we wept; then closed and clung together;
And my heart shook this building of my breast
Like a live engine booming up and down:
She fell upon me like a snow-wreath thawing.
Never were bliss and beauty, love and wo,
Ravelled and twined together into madness,
As in that one wild hour to which all else
The past, is but a picture. That alone
Is real, and forever there in front.

     *   *   *

    *   *   * After that I left her,
And only saw her once again alive."

—

"Mother Saint Perpetua, the superior of the convent, was a tall woman, of about forty years, dressed in dark gray serge, with a long rosary hanging at her girdle; a white mob cap, with a long black veil, surrounded her thin wan face with its narrow hooded border. A great number of deep transverse wrinkles plowed her brow, which resembled yellowish ivory in color and substance. Her keen and prominent nose was curved like the hooked beak of a bird of prey; her black eye was piercing and sagacious; her face was at once intelligent, firm, and cold.

"For comprehending and managing the material interests of the society, Mother Saint Perpetua could have vied with the shrewdest and most wily lawyer. When women are possessed of what is called *business talent*, and when they apply thereto the sharpness of perception, the indefatigable perseverance, the prudent dissimulation, and above all, the correctness and rapidity of judgment at first sight, which are peculiar to them, they arrive at prodigious results.

"To mother Saint Perpetua, a woman of a strong and solid head, the vast monied business of the society was but child's

APPENDIX

play. None better than she understood how to buy depreciated properties, to raise them to their original value, and sell them to advantage; the average purchase of rents, the fluctuations of exchange, and the current prices of shares in all the leading speculations, were perfectly familiar to her. Never had she directed her agents to make a single false speculation, when it had been the question how to invest funds, with which good souls were constantly endowing the society of Saint Mary. She had established in the house a degree of order, of discipline, and, above all, of economy, that were indeed remarkable; the constant aim of all her exertions being, not to enrich herself, but the community over which she presided; for the spirit of association, when it is directed to an object of *collective selfishness*, gives to corporations all the faults and vices of individuals."

E

The following is an extract from a letter addressed to me by one of the monks of the 19th century. A part I have omitted, because it does not express my own view, unless with qualifications which I could not make, except by full discussion of the subject.

"Woman in the 19th century should be a pure, chaste, holy being.

"This state of being in woman is no more attained by the expansion of her intellectual capacity, than by the augmentation of her physical force.

"Neither is it attained by the increase or refinement of her love for man, or for any object whatever, or for all objects collectively; but

"This state of being is attained by the reference of all her powers and all her actions to the source of Universal Love, whose constant requisition is a pure, chaste and holy life.

"So long as woman looks to man (or to society) for that which she needs, she will remain in an indigent state, for he himself is indigent of it, and as much needs it as she does.

"So long as this indigence continues, all unions or relations constructed between man and woman are constructed in indigence, and can produce only indigent results or unhappy consequences.

322 WOMAN IN THE NINETEENTH CENTURY

"The unions now constructing, as well as those in which the parties constructing them were generated, being based on self-delight, or lust, can lead to no more happiness in the 20th, than is found in the 19th century.

"It is not amended institutions, it is not improved education, it is not another selection of individuals for union, that can meliorate the sad result, but the *basis* of the union must be changed.

"If in the natural order Woman and Man would adhere strictly to physiological or natural laws, in physical chastity, a most beautiful amendment of the human race, and human condition, would in a few generations adorn the world.

"Still, it belongs to Woman in the spiritual order, to devote herself wholly to her eternal husband, and become the Free Bride of the One who alone can elevate her to her true position, and reconstruct her a pure, chaste, and holy being."

F

I have mislaid an extract from "The Memoirs of an American Lady" which I wished to use on this subject, but its import is, briefly, this:

Observing of how little consequence the Indian women are in youth, and how much in age, because in that trying life, good counsel and sagacity are more prized than charms, Mrs. Grant expresses a wish that Reformers would take a hint from observation of this circumstance.

In another place she says: "The misfortune of our sex is, that young women are not regarded as the material from which old women must be made."

I quote from memory, but believe the weight of the remark is retained.

G

Euripides   Sophocles

As many allusions are made in the foregoing pages to characters of women drawn by the Greek dramatists, which may not be familiar to the majority of readers, I have borrowed from the papers of Miranda, some notes upon them. I trust the girlish tone of apostrophizing rapture may be excused. Miranda was very young at the time of writing, compared with her present mental age. *Now*, she would express the same feelings, but in a worthier garb—if she expressed them at all.

Iphigenia! Antigone! you were worthy to live! *We* are fallen on evil times, my sisters! our feelings have been checked; our thoughts questioned; our forms dwarfed and defaced by a bad nurture. Yet hearts, like yours, are in our breasts, living, if unawakened; and our minds are capable of the same resolves. You, we understand at once, those who stare upon us pertly in the street, we cannot—could never understand.

You knew heroes, maidens, and your fathers were kings of men. You believed in your country, and the gods of your country. A great occasion was given to each, whereby to test her character.

You did not love on earth; for the poets wished to show us the force of woman's nature, virgin and unbiassed. You were women; not wives, or lovers, or mothers. Those are great names, but we are glad to see *you* in untouched flower.

Were brothers so dear, then, Antigone? We have no brothers. We see no men into whose lives we dare look steadfastly, or to whose destinies we look forward confidently. We care not for their urns; what inscription could we put upon them? They live for petty successes; or to win daily the bread of the day. No spark of kingly fire flashes from their eyes.

None! are there *none*?

It is a base speech to say it. Yes! there are some such; we have sometimes caught their glances. But rarely have they been rocked in the same cradle as we, and they do not look upon us much; for the time is not yet come.

Thou art so grand and simple! we need not follow thee; thou dost not need our love.

But, sweetest Iphigenia; who knew *thee*, as to me thou art known. I was not born in vain, if only for the heavenly tears I have shed with thee. She will be grateful for them. I have understood her wholly; as a friend should, better than she understood herself.

With what artless art the narrative rises to the crisis. The conflicts in Agamemnon's mind, and the imputations of

324   WOMAN IN THE NINETEENTH CENTURY

Menelaus give us, at once, the full image of him, strong in will and pride, weak in virtue, weak in the noble powers of the mind that depend on imagination. He suffers, yet it requires the presence of his daughter to make him feel the full horror of what he is to do.

> "Ah me! that breast, those cheeks, those golden tresses!"

It is her beauty, not her misery, that makes the pathos. This is noble. And then, too, the injustice of the gods, that she, this creature of unblemished loveliness, must perish for the sake of a worthless woman. Even Menelaus feels it, the moment he recovers from his wrath.

> "What hath she to do,
> The virgin daughter, with my Helena!
>   *   *   Its former reasonings now
> My soul foregoes.   *   *   *   *
>   For it is not just
> That thou shouldst groan, but my affairs go pleasantly,
> That those of thy house should die, and mine see the light."

Indeed the overwhelmed aspect of the king of men might well move him.

> *Men.* "Brother, give me to take thy right hand,
> *Aga.*   I give it, *for* the victory is thine, and I am wretched.
>   I am, indeed, ashamed to drop the tear,
>   And not to drop the tear I am ashamed."

How beautifully is Iphigenia introduced; beaming more and more softly on us with every touch of description. After Clytemnestra has given Orestes (then an infant,) out of the chariot, she says:

> "Ye females, in your arms,
> Receive her, for she is of tender age.
> Sit here by my feet, my child,
> By thy mother, Iphigenia, and show
> These strangers how I am blessed in thee,
> And here address thee to thy father.

Iphi.   Oh mother, should I run, wouldst thou be angry?
And embrace my father breast to breast?"

With the same sweet timid trust she prefers the request to himself, and as he holds her in his arms, he seems as noble as Guido's Archangel; as if he never could sink below the trust of such a being!

The Achilles, in the first scene, is fine. A true Greek hero; not too good; all flushed with the pride of youth; but capable of god-like impulses. At first, he thinks only of his own wounded pride, (when he finds Iphigenia has been decoyed to Aulis under the pretext of becoming his wife;) but the grief of the queen soon makes him superior to his arrogant chafings. How well he says:—

> "*Far as a young man may*, I will repress
> So great a wrong."

By seeing him here, we understand why he, not Hector, was the hero of the Iliad. The beautiful moral nature of Hector was early developed by close domestic ties, and the cause of his country. Except in a purer simplicity of speech and manner, he might be a modern and a christian. But Achilles is cast in the largest and most vigorous mould of the earlier day: his nature is one of the richest capabilities, and therefore less quickly unfolds its meaning. The impression it makes at the early period is only of power and pride; running as fleetly with his armor on, as with it off; but sparks of pure lustre are struck, at moments, from the mass of ore. Of this sort is his refusal to see the beautiful virgin he has promised to protect. None of the Grecians must have the right to doubt his motives. How wise and prudent, too, the advice he gives as to the queen's conduct! He will not show himself, unless needed. His pride is the farthest possible remote from vanity. His thoughts are as free as any in our own time.

> "The prophet? what is he? a man
> Who speaks 'mong many falsehoods, but few truths,
> Whene'er chance leads him to speak true; when false,
> The prophet is no more."

326 WOMAN IN THE NINETEENTH CENTURY

Had Agamemnon possessed like clearness of sight, the virgin would not have perished, but also, Greece would have had no religion and no national existence.

When, in the interview with Agamemnon, the Queen begins her speech, in the true matrimonial style, dignified though her gesture be, and true all she says, we feel that truth, thus sauced with taunts, will not touch his heart, nor turn him from his purpose. But when Iphigenia begins her exquisite speech, as with the breathings of a lute,

> "Had I, my father, the persuasive voice
>   Of Orpheus, &c.
>   Compel me not
> What is beneath to view. I was the first
> To call thee father; me thou first didst call
> Thy child: I was the first that on thy knees
> Fondly caressed thee, and from thee received
> The fond caress: this was thy speech to me:—
> 'Shall I, my child, e'er see thee in some house
> Of splendor, happy in thy husband, live
> And flourish, as becomes my dignity?'
> My speech to thee was, leaning 'gainst thy cheek,
> (Which with my hand I now caress:) 'And what
> Shall I then do for thee? shall I receive
> My father when grown old, and in my house
> Cheer him with each fond office, to repay
> The careful nurture which he gave my youth?'
> These words are in my memory deep impressed,
> Thou hast forgot them and will kill thy child."

Then she adjures him by all the sacred ties, and dwells pathetically on the circumstance which had struck even Menelaus.

> "If Paris be enamored of his bride,
>   His Helen, what concerns it me? and how
> Comes he to my destruction?
>   Look upon me;
>   Give me a smile, give me a kiss, my father;
> That if my words persuade thee not, in death
> I may have this memorial of thy love."

APPENDIX 327

Never have the names of father and daughter been uttered with a holier tenderness than by Euripides, as in this most lovely passage, or in the "Suppliants," after the voluntary death of Evadne; Iphis says

> "What shall this wretch now do? Should I return
> To my own house?—sad desolation there
> I shall behold, to sink my soul with grief.
> Or go I to the house of Capaneus?
> That was delightful to me, when I found
> My daughter there; but she is there no more:
> Oft would she kiss my cheek, with fond caress
> Oft soothe me. To a father, waxing old,
> Nothing is dearer than a daughter! sons
> Have spirits of higher pitch, but less inclined
> To sweet endearing fondness. Lead me then,
> Instantly lead me to my house, consign
> My wretched age to darkness, there to pine
> And waste away.
>   Old age,
> Struggling with many griefs, O how I hate thee!"

But to return to Iphigenia,—how infinitely melting is her appeal to Orestes, whom she holds in her robe.

> "My brother, small assistance canst thou give
> Thy friends; yet for thy sister with thy tears
> Implore thy father that she may not die:
> Even infants have a sense of ills; and see,
> My father! silent though he be, he sues
> To thee: be gentle to me; on my life
> Have pity: thy two children by this beard
> Entreat thee, thy dear children: one is yet
> An infant, one to riper years arrived."

The mention of Orestes, then an infant, all through, though slight, is of a domestic charm that prepares the mind to feel the tragedy of his after lot. When the Queen says

> "Dost thou sleep,
> My son? The rolling chariot hath subdued thee;
> Wake to thy sister's marriage happily."

328   WOMAN IN THE NINETEENTH CENTURY

We understand the horror of the doom which makes this cherished child a parricide. And so when Iphigenia takes leave of him after her fate is by herself accepted.

Iphi. "To manhood train Orestes,
Cly. Embrace him, for thou ne'er shalt see him more.
Iphi. (*To Orestes.*) Far as thou couldst, thou didst assist thy friends."

We know not how to blame the guilt of the maddened wife and mother. In her last meeting with Agamemnon, as in her previous expostulations and anguish, we see that a straw may turn the balance, and make her his deadliest foe. Just then, came the suit of Ægisthus, then, when every feeling was uprooted or lacerated in her heart.

Iphigenia's moving address has no further effect than to make her father turn at bay and brave this terrible crisis. He goes out, firm in resolve; and she and her mother abandon themselves to a natural grief.

Hitherto nothing has been seen in Iphigenia, except the young girl, weak, delicate, full of feeling and beautiful as a sunbeam on the full green tree. But, in the next scene, the first impulse of that passion which makes and unmakes us, though unconfessed even to herself, though hopeless and unreturned, raises her at once into the heroic woman, worthy of the goddess who demands her.

Achilles appears to defend her, whom all others clamorously seek to deliver to the murderous knife. She sees him, and fired with thoughts, unknown before, devotes herself at once for the country which has given birth to such a man.

> "To be too fond of life
> Becomes not me; nor for myself alone,
> But to all Greece, a blessing didst thou bear me.
> Shall thousands, when their country's injured, lift
> Their shields; shall thousands grasp the oar, and dare,
> Advancing bravely 'gainst the foe, to die
> For Greece? And shall my life, my single life,
> Obstruct all this? Would this be just? What word
> Can we reply? Nay more, it is not right
> That he with all the Grecians should contest
> In fight, should die, *and for a woman*. No:

APPENDIX

More than a thousand women is one man
Worthy to see the light of day.
   *   *   *   for Greece I give my life.
Slay me; demolish Troy: for these shall be
Long time my monuments, my children these,
My nuptials and my glory."

This sentiment marks woman, when she loves enough to feel what a creature of glory and beauty a true *man* would be, as much in our own time as that of Euripides. Cooper makes the weak Hetty say to her beautiful sister:

"Of course, I don't compare you with Harry. A handsome man is always far handsomer than any woman." True, it was the sentiment of the age, but it was the first time Iphigenia had felt it. In Agamemnon she saw *her father*, to him she could prefer her claim. In Achilles she saw *a man*, the crown of creation, enough to fill the world with his presence, were all other beings blotted from its spaces.*

The reply of Achilles is as noble. Here is his bride, he feels it now, and all his vain vauntings are hushed.

"Daughter of Agamemnon, highly blessed
Some god would make me, if I might attain
Thy nuptials. Greece in thee I happy deem,
And thee in Greece.   *   *
   *   *   * in thy thought
Revolve this well; death is a dreadful thing."

How sweet is her reply, and then the tender modesty with which she addresses him here and elsewhere as "*stranger.*"

"Reflecting not on any, thus I speak:
Enough of wars and slaughters from the charms
Of Helen rise; but die not thou for me,
O Stranger, nor distain thy sword with blood,
But let me save my country if I may."

---

* Men do not often reciprocate this pure love.

"Her prentice han' she tried on man,
And then she made the lasses o',"

Is a fancy, not a feeling, in their more frequently passionate and strong, than noble or tender natures.

330 WOMAN IN THE NINETEENTH CENTURY

> *Achilles.* "O glorious spirit! nought have I 'gainst this
> To urge, since such thy will, for what thou sayst
> Is generous. Why should not the truth be spoken?"

But feeling that human weakness may conquer yet, he goes to wait at the altar, resolved to keep his promise of protection thoroughly.

In the next beautiful scene she shows that a few tears might overwhelm her in his absence. She raises her mother beyond weeping them, yet her soft purity she cannot impart.

> *Iphi.* "My father, and thy husband do not hate:
> *Cly.* For thy dear sake fierce contests must he bear.
> *Iphi.* For Greece reluctant me to death he yields;
> *Cly.* Basely, with guile unworthy Atreus' son."

This is truth incapable of an answer and Iphigenia attempts none.

She begins the hymn which is to sustain her,

> "Lead me; mine the glorious fate,
> To o'erturn the Phrygian state."

After the sublime flow of lyric heroism, she suddenly sinks back into the tenderer feeling of her dreadful fate.

> "O my country, where these eyes
> Opened on Pelasgic skies!
> O ye virgins, once my pride,
> In Mycenæ who abide!
> CHORUS.
> Why of Perseus name the town,
> Which Cyclopean ramparts crown?
> IPHIGENIA.
> Me you rear'd a beam of light,
> Freely now I sink in night."

Freely; as the messenger afterwards recounts it.

> *   *   *
> "Imperial Agamemnon, when he saw
> His daughter, as a victim to the grave,

APPENDIX 331

> Advancing, groan'd, and bursting into tears,
> Turned from the sight his head, before his eyes,
> Holding his robe. The virgin near him stood,
> And thus addressed him: 'Father, I to thee
> Am present; for my country, and for all
> The land of Greece, I freely give myself
> A victim: to the altar let them lead me,
> Since such the oracle. If aught on me
> Depends, be happy, and obtain the prize
> Of glorious conquest, and revisit safe
> Your country. Of the Grecians, for this cause,
> Let no one touch me; with intrepid spirit
> Silent will I present my neck.' She spoke,
> And all that heard revered the noble soul
> And virtue of the virgin."

How quickly had the fair bud bloomed up into its perfection. Had she lived a thousand years, she could not have surpassed this. Goethe's Iphigenia, the mature woman, with its myriad delicate traits, never surpasses, scarcely equals what we know of her in Euripides.

Can I appreciate this work in a translation? I think so, impossible as it may seem to one who can enjoy the thousand melodies, and words in exactly the right place and cadence of the original. They say you can see the Apollo Belvidere in a plaster cast, and I cannot doubt it, so great the benefit conferred on my mind, by a transcript thus imperfect. And so with these translations from the Greek. I can divine the original through this veil, as I can see the movements of a spirited horse by those of his coarse grasscloth muffler. Beside, every translator who feels his subject is inspired, and the divine Aura informs even his stammering lips.

Iphigenia is more like one of the women Shakspeare loved than the others; she is a tender virgin, ennobled and strengthened by sentiment more than intellect, what they call a woman *par excellence.*

Macaria is more like one of Massinger's women. She advances boldly, though with the decorum of her sex and nation:

> *Macaria.* "Impute not boldness to me that I come
> Before you, strangers; this my first request
> I urge; for silence and a chaste reserve

332   WOMAN IN THE NINETEENTH CENTURY

> Is woman's genuine praise, and to remain
> Quiet within the house. But I come forth,
> Hearing thy lamentations, Iolaus:
> Though charged with no commission, yet perhaps,
> I may be useful."   *   *

Her speech when she offers herself as the victim, is reasonable, as one might speak to-day. She counts the cost all through. Iphigenia is too timid and delicate to dwell upon the loss of earthly bliss, and the due experience of life, even as much as Jeptha's daughter did, but Macaria is explicit, as well befits the daughter of Hercules.

> "Should *these* die, myself
> Preserved, of prosperous future could I form
> One cheerful hope?
> A poor forsaken virgin who would deign
> To take in marriage? Who would wish for sons
> From one so wretched? Better then to die,
> Than bear such undeserved miseries:
> One less illustrious this might more beseem.
>   *   *   *
> I have a soul that unreluctantly
> Presents itself, and I proclaim aloud
> That for my brothers and myself I die.
> I am not fond of life, but think I gain
> An honorable prize to die with glory."

Still nobler when Iolaus proposes rather that she shall draw lots with her sisters.

> "*By lot* I will not die, for to such death
>   No thanks are due, or glory—name it not.
>   If you accept me, if my offered life
>   Be grateful to you, willingly I give it
>   For these, but by constraint I will not die."

Very fine are her parting advice and injunctions to them all:

> "Farewell! revered old man, farewell! and teach
>   These youths in all things to be wise, like thee,
>   Naught will avail them more."

APPENDIX

Macaria has the clear Minerva eye: Antigone's is deeper, and more capable of emotion, but calm. Iphigenia's, glistening, gleaming with angel truth, or dewy as a hidden violet.

I am sorry that Tennyson, who spoke with such fitness of all the others in his "Dream of fair women," has not of Iphigenia. Of her alone he has not made a fit picture, but only of the circumstances of the sacrifice. He can never have taken to heart this work of Euripides, yet he was so worthy to feel it. Of Jeptha's daughter, he has spoken as he would of Iphigenia, both in her beautiful song, and when

> "I heard Him, for He spake, and grief became
> A solemn scorn of ills.
>
> It comforts me in this one thought to dwell
> That I subdued me to my father's will;
> Because the kiss he gave me, ere I fell,
> Sweetens the spirit still.
>
> Moreover it is written, that my race
> Hewed Ammon, hip and thigh from Arroer
> Or Arnon unto Minneth. Here her face
> Glow'd as I look'd on her.
>
> She locked her lips; she left me where I stood;
> "Glory to God," she sang, and past afar,
> Thridding the sombre boskage of the woods,
> Toward the morning-star."

In the "Trojan dames" there are fine touches of nature with regard to Cassandra. Hecuba shows that mixture of shame and reverence, that prose kindred always do, towards the inspired child, the poet, the elected sufferer for the race.

When the herald announces that she is chosen to be the mistress of Agamemnon, Hecuba answers indignant, and betraying the involuntary pride and faith she felt in this daughter.

> "The virgin of Apollo, whom the God,
> Radiant with golden locks, allowed to live
> In her pure vow of maiden chastity?
> *Tal.* With love the raptured virgin smote his heart.

334 WOMAN IN THE NINETEENTH CENTURY

> *Hec.* Cast from thee, O my daughter, cast away
>   Thy sacred wand, rend off the honored wreaths,
>   The splendid ornaments that grace thy brows."

Yet the moment Cassandra appears, singing wildly her inspired song, Hecuba calls her

> "My *frantic* child."

Yet how graceful she is in her tragic phrenzy, the chorus shows—

> "How sweetly at thy house's ills thou smil'st,
>   Chanting what haply thou wilt not show true?"

But if Hecuba dares not trust her highest instinct about her daughter, still less can the vulgar mind of the herald (a man not without tenderness of heart, but with no princely, no poetic blood,) abide the wild prophetic mood which insults his prejudices both as to country and decorums of the sex. Yet Agamemnon, though not a noble man, is of large mould and could admire this strange beauty which excited distaste in common minds.

> *Tel.* "What commands respect, and is held high
>   As wise, is nothing better than the mean
>   Of no repute: for this most potent king
>   Of all the Grecians, the much honored son
>   Of Atreus, is enamored with his prize,
>   This frantic raver. I am a poor man,
>   Yet would I not receive her to my bed."

Cassandra answers with a careless disdain,

> "This is a busy slave."

With all the lofty decorum of manners among the ancients, how free was their intercourse, man to man, how full the mutual understanding between prince and "busy slave!" Not here in adversity only, but in the pomp of power, it was so. Kings were approached with ceremonious obeisance, but not hedged round with etiquette, they could see and know their fellows.

APPENDIX

The Andromache here is just as lovely as that of the Iliad.

To her child whom they are about to murder, the same that was frightened at the "glittering plume."

> "Dost thou weep,
> My son? Hast thou a sense of thy ill fate?
> Why dost thou clasp me with thy hands, why hold
> My robes, and shelter thee beneath my wings,
> Like a young bird? No more my Hector comes,
> Returning from the tomb; he grasps no more
> His glittering spear, bringing protection to thee."
>   *   *   *
>   *   *   "O soft embrace,
> And to thy mother dear. O fragrant breath!
> In vain I swathed thy infant limbs, in vain
> I gave thee nurture at this breast, and toiled,
> Wasted with care. *If ever*, now embrace,
> Now clasp thy mother; throw thine arms around
> My neck and join thy cheek, thy lips to mine."

As I look up I meet the eyes of Beatrice Cenci. Beautiful one, these woes, even, were less than thine, yet thou seemest to understand them all. Thy clear melancholy gaze says, they, at least, had known moments of bliss, and the tender relations of nature had not been broken and polluted from the very first. Yes! the gradations of wo are all but infinite: only good can be infinite.

Certainly the Greeks knew more of real home intercourse, and more of woman than the Americans. It is in vain to tell me of outward observances. The poets, the sculptors always tell the truth. In proportion as a nation is refined, women *must* have an ascendancy, it is the law of nature.

Beatrice! thou wert not "fond of life," either, more than those princesses. Thou wert able to cut it down in the full flower of beauty, as an offering to *the best* known to thee. Thou wert not so happy as to die for thy country or thy brethren, but thou wert worthy of such an occasion.

In the days of chivalry woman was habitually viewed more as an ideal, but I do not know that she inspired a deeper and more home-felt reverence than Iphigenia in the breast of Achilles, or Macaria in that of her old guardian, Iolaus.

WOMAN IN THE NINETEENTH CENTURY

We may, with satisfaction, add to these notes the words to which Haydn has adapted his magnificent music in "The Creation."

"In native worth and honor clad, with beauty, courage, strength adorned, erect to heaven, and tall, he stands, a Man!—the lord and king of all! The large and arched front sublime of wisdom deep declares the seat, and in his eyes with brightness shines the soul, the breath and image of his God. With fondness leans upon his breast the partner for him formed, a woman fair, and graceful spouse. Her softly smiling virgin looks, of flowery spring the mirror, bespeak him love, and joy and bliss."

Whoever has heard this music must have a mental standard as to what man and woman should be. Such was marriage in Eden, when "erect to heaven *he* stood," but since, like other institutions, this must be not only reformed, but revived, may be offered as a picture of something intermediate,—the seed of the future growth,—

H

The Sacred Marriage

And has another's life as large a scope?
It may give due fulfilment to thy hope,
And every portal to the unknown may ope.

If, near this other life, thy inmost feeling
Trembles with fateful prescience of revealing
The future Deity, time is still concealing.

If thou feel thy whole force drawn more and more
To launch that other bark on seas without a shore;
And no still secret must be kept in store;

If meannesses that dim each temporal deed,
The dull decay that mars the fleshly weed,
And flower of love that seems to fall and leave no seed—

Hide never the full presence from thy sight
Of mutual aims and tasks, ideals bright,
Which feed their roots to-day on all this seeming blight.

APPENDIX

Twin stars that mutual circle in the heaven,
Two parts for spiritual concord given,
Twin Sabbaths that inlock the Sacred Seven;

Still looking to the centre for the cause,
Mutual light giving to draw out the powers,
And learning all the other groups by cognizance of one
    another's laws:

The parent love the wedded love includes,
The one permits the two their mutual moods,
The two each other know mid myriad multitudes;

With child-like intellect discerning love,
And mutual action energizing love,
In myriad forms affiliating love.

A world whose seasons bloom from pole to pole,
A force which knows both starting-point and goal,
A Home in Heaven,—the Union in the Soul.

SHORT PUBLISHED WORKS

VIEW OF THE LUNATIC ASYLUM AND MAD HOUSE, ON BLACKWELL'S ISLAND, NEW YORK.

NEW ENGLAND SHORT
PUBLISHED WORKS
1839–1844

Translator's Preface

from Conversations with Goethe in the
Last Years of His Life

THIS book cannot fail to interest all who are desirous to understand the character and opinions of Goethe, or the state of literary society in Germany. The high opinion which Goethe entertained of Eckermann's fidelity, judgment, and comprehension of himself, is sufficiently proved, by his appointing him editor of his Posthumous Works. The light in which this book is regarded by the distinguished circle of which Goethe was the glory, may be seen by a reference to the first volume of Mrs. Jameson's late work, "Winter Studies and Summer Rambles in Canada."

It is, obviously, a most faithful record. Perhaps there is no instance in which one mind has been able to give out what it received from another, so little colored by its own substance. It is true that the simple reverence, and thorough subordination to the mind of Goethe, which make Eckermann so transparent a medium, prevent his being of any value as an interpreter. Never was satellite more completely in harmony with his ruling orb. He is merely the sounding-board to the various notes played by the master's hand; and what we find here is, to all intents and purposes, not conversation, but monologue. A finer book might be made by selections from Goethe's miscellanies; but here some subjects are brought forward on which he never wrote. The journal form gives an ease and life to the discussion, and what is wanting in fulness and beauty is made up to us by the pleasure we always take in the unpremeditated flow of thought, and in seeing what topics come up naturally with such a person as Goethe.

341

An imperial genius must have not only willing subjects, but good instruments. Eckermann has all the merit of an intelligent minister and a discreet secretary. He is ruled and modelled, but not blinded, by Goethe. When we look at the interesting sketch of his youthful struggles, and see what obligations he owed to Goethe, as well before as after their personal acquaintance, we cannot blame him for his boundless gratitude to the sun which chased away so many clouds from his sky. He seems, indeed, led onward to be the foster-child and ready helper of this great man, and could not so well have filled this place, if he had kept sufficiently aloof to satisfy our pride. I say *our* pride, because we are jealous for minds which we see in this state of subordination. We feel it too dangerous to what is most valuable in character; and, rare as independence is, we cannot but ask it from all who live in the light of genius.

Still, our feeling towards Eckermann is not only kindly, but respectful. He is not ridiculous, like Boswell, for no vanity or littleness sullies his sincere enthusiasm. In these sober and enlightened days, we rebel against man-worship, even though it be hero-worship. But how could this person, so rich in natural gifts, so surrounded by what was bright, beautiful, and courtly, and at so high a point of culture, fail to be overpowering to an obscure youth, whose abilities he had been the chief means of unfolding? It could not be otherwise than that Eckermann should sit at his feet, and live on his bounty. Enough for the disciple to know how to use what he received with thoughtful gratitude. That Goethe also knew how to receive is evident from his correspondences with Zelter, Schiller, and Meyer,— relations which show him in a better light than this with Eckermann, because the parties were on more equal terms.

Those letters, or the substance of them, will, some time, be published here. Meanwhile, the book before us has merits which they do not possess. It paints Goethe to us as he was in the midst of his family, and in his most careless or weary hours. Under such circumstances, whatever may be thought of his views, (and they are often still less suited to our public than to that of Germany,) his courteous grace, his calm wisdom and reliance on the harmony of his faith with his nature, must be felt, by the unprejudiced reader, to be beautiful and rare.

PREFACE TO *CONVERSATIONS WITH GOETHE* 343

And here it may not be amiss to give some intimation (more my present limits do not permit) of the grounds on which Goethe is, to myself, an object of peculiar interest and constant study.

I hear him much assailed by those among us who know him, some few in his own language, but most from translations of "Wilhelm Meister" and "Faust." These, his two great works, in which he proposed to himself the enigma of life, and solved it after his own fashion, were, naturally enough, selected, in preference to others, for translating. This was, for all but the translators, unfortunate, because these two, above all others, require a knowledge of the circumstances and character from which they rose, to ascertain their scope and tendency.

It is sneeringly said, "Those persons who are so fanatical for German literature always say, if you object to any of their idols, that you are not capable of appreciating them." And it is truly, though oftentimes too impatiently, said. The great movement in German literature is too recent to be duly estimated, even by those most interested to examine it. The waves have scarce yet ebbed from this new continent, and those who are visiting its shores, see so much that is new and beautiful, that of their many obligations to the phenomenon, the chief is, as yet, that of the feeling of fresh creative life at work there. No wonder that they feel vexed at those who declare, from an occasional peep through a spy-glass, that they see no new wonders for geology; that they can botanize all the flowers, and find nothing worthy of fresh attempts at classification; and that there are no birds except a few sea-gulls. Would these hasty critics but recollect how long it was before similar movements in Italy, Spain, France, and England, found their proper place in the thoughts of other nations, they would not think fifty years' investigation too much for fifty years' growth, and would no longer provoke the ire of those who are lighting their tapers at the German torch. Meanwhile it is silly to be in a pet always; and disdainful answers have been recognized as useless since Solomon's time, or earlier. What could have been the reason they were not set aside, while that wise prince lived, once for all?

The objections usually made, though not without a foundation in truth, are such as would answer themselves on a more thorough acquaintance with the subject. In France and

England there has seemed an approximation, of late, to juster views. Yet, in a recent number of "Blackwood's Magazine," has appeared an article as ignorant (and that is a strong word) as any thing that has ever been written about Goethe.

The objections, so far as I know them, may be resolved into these classes—

He is not a Christian;
He is not an Idealist;
He is not a Democrat;
He is not Schiller.

If by Christian be meant the subordination of the intellectual to the spiritual, I shall not deny that with Goethe the reverse was the case. He sought always for unity; but the want with him was chiefly one of the intellect. A creative activity was his law. He was far from insensible to spiritual beauty in the human character. He has imbodied it in its finest forms; but he merely put it in, what seemed to him, its place, as the keystone of the social arch, and paints neither that nor any other state with partiality. Such was his creed as a writer. "I paint," he seems to say, "what I have seen; choose from it, or take it all, as you will or can." In his love of form Goethe was a Greek; constitutionally, and by the habit of his life, averse to the worship of sorrow. His God was rather the creative and upholding than the paternal spirit; his religion, that all his powers must be unfolded; his faith, "that nature could not dispense with Immortality." In the most trying occasions of his life, he referred to "the great Idea of Duty which alone can hold us upright." Renunciation, the power of sacrificing the temporary for the permanent, is a leading idea in one of his great works, "Wilhelm Meister." The thought of the Catholic Dante is repeated in his other great work, ("Faust,") where Margaret, by her innocence of heart, and the resolute aversion to the powers of darkness, which her mind, in its most shattered state, does not forget, redeems not only her own soul, but that of her erring lover. The virgin Ottilia, who immolates herself to avoid the possibility of spotting her thoughts with passion, gives to that much-abused book (*Die Wahlverwandtschaften*) the pathetic moral of the pictures of the Magdalen. His two highest female characters, Natalia and Makaria, are representations of beneficence and heavenly wisdom. Iphigenia, by her

PREFACE TO *CONVERSATIONS WITH GOETHE* 345

steadfast truth, hallows all about her, and disarms the powers of hell. Such traits as these may be accumulated; yet it remains not the less true that Goethe was not what is called a spiritual writer. Those who cannot draw their moral for themselves had best leave his books alone; they require the power as life does. This advantage only does he give, or intend to give you, of looking at life brought into a compass convenient to your eye, by a great observer and artist, and at times when you can look uninterrupted by action, undisturbed by passion.

He was not an Idealist; that is to say, he thought not so much of what might be as what is. He did not seek to alter or exalt Nature, but merely to select from her rich stores. Here, indeed, even as an artist, he would always have stopped short of the highest excellence, if he had not at times been inspired beyond his knowledge and his will. Had his views been different, his peculiar powers of minute, searching, and extended observation would have been much injured; as, instead of looking at objects with the single aim of ascertaining their properties, he would have examined them only to gain from them what most favored his plans. I am well satisfied that "he went the way that God and Nature called him."

He was an Aristocrat. And, in the present day, hostility arises instinctively against one who does not believe in the people, and whose tastes are in favor of a fixed external gradation. My sympathies are with the great onward movement now obvious throughout the civilized world; my hope is that we may make a fair experiment whether men can be educated to rule themselves, and communities be trusted to choose their own rulers. This is, it seems, the present tendency of the Ages; and, had I influence, I would not put a straw in the way. Yet a minority is needed to keep these liberals in check, and make them pause upon their measures long enough to know what they are doing; for, as yet, the caldron of liberty has shown a constant disposition to overboil. The artist and literary man is naturally thrown into this body, by his need of repose, and a firm ground to work in his proper way. Certainly Goethe by nature belonged on that side; and no one, who can understand the structure of his mind, instead of judging him by his outward relations, will impute to him unworthy motives, or think he could, being what he was, hold other opinions. And is not this all which is important? The gates that keep out the water while the ship is building have their place also, as well as the ship itself, or the wind which fills the sails. To be sincere, consistent, and intelligent in what one believes is what is important; a higher power takes care of the rest.

In reply to those who object to him that he is not Schiller, it may be remarked that Shakspeare was not Milton, nor Ariosto Tasso. It was, indeed, unnecessary that there should be two Schillers, one being sufficient to represent a certain class of thoughts and opinions. It would be well if the admirers of Schiller would learn from him to admire and profit by his friend and coadjutor, as he himself did.

Schiller was wise enough to judge each nature by its own law, great enough to understand greatness of an order different from his own. He was too well aware of the value of the more beautiful existences to quarrel with the rose for not being a lily, the eagle for not being a swan.

I am not fanatical as to the benefits to be derived from the study of German literature. I suppose, indeed, that there lie the life and learning of the century, and that he who does not go to those sources can have no just notion of the workings of the spirit in the European world these last fifty years or more; but my tastes are often displeased by German writers, even by Goethe—of German writers the most English and most Greek. To cultivate the tastes, we must go to another school; but I wish that we could learn from the Germans habits of more liberal criticism, and leave this way of judging from comparison or personal predilections. If we must draw parallels, we ought to be sure that we are capable of a love for all greatness as fervent as that of Plutarch's time. Perhaps it may be answered that the comparison between Goethe and Schiller began in Germany: it did so, but arose there from circumstances with which we have nothing to do. Generally, the wise German criticises with the positive degree, and is well aware of the danger in using the comparative.

For the rest, no one who has a higher aim in reading German books than mere amusement; no one who knows what it is to become acquainted with a literature as literature, in its history of mutual influences, diverse yet harmonious tendencies, can leave aside either Schiller or Goethe; but far, far least the latter.

PREFACE TO *CONVERSATIONS WITH GOETHE* 347

It would be leaving Augustus Cæsar out of the history of Rome because he was not Brutus.

Having now confessed to what Goethe is not, I would indicate, as briefly as possible, what, to me, he is.

Most valuable as a means of balancing the judgment and suggesting thought from his antagonism to the spirit of the age. He prefers the perfecting of the few to the slight improvement of the many. He believes more in man than men, effort than success, thought than action, nature than providence. He does not insist on my believing with him. I would go up often into this fortress, and look from its battlements, to see how goes the fight below. I need not fear to be detained. He knows himself too well to ask any thing of another except to know him.

As one of the finest lyric poets of modern times. Bards are also prophets; and woe to those who refuse to hear the singer, to tender him the golden cup of homage. Their punishment is in their fault.

As the best writer of the German language, who has availed himself of all its advantages of richness and flexibility, and added to them a degree of lightness, grace, clearness, and precision, beyond any other writer of his time; who has, more than any other, tended to correct the fantastic, cumbrous, centipede style indigenous to Germany.

As a critic, on art and literature, not to be surpassed in independence, fairness, powers of sympathy, and largeness of view.

As almost the finest observer of his time of human nature, and almost as much so of external nature. He has great delicacy of penetration, and a better tact at selecting objects than almost any who has looked at the time of which I am a child. Could I omit to study this eighty years' journal of my parent's life, traced from so commanding a position, by so sure a hand, and one informed by so keen and cultivated an eye? Where else shall we find so large a mirror, or one with so finely decorated a frame?

As a mind which has known how to reconcile individuality of character with universality of thought; a mind which, whatever be its faults, ruled and relied on itself alone; a nature which knew its law, and revolved on its proper axis, unrepenting, never bustling, always active, never stagnant, always calm.

348   NEW ENGLAND SHORT PUBLISHED WORKS

A distinguished critic speaks of Goethe as the conqueror of his century. I believe I do not take so admiring a view of the character of Goethe as this, his only competent English critic. I refer to Mr. Carlyle. But so far as attaining the object he himself proposed, a choice of aim, a "wise limitation," and unwearied constancy in the use of means; so far as leaving behind the limbo of self-questioning uncertainty in which most who would fain think as well as act are wading, and bringing his life into an uninterrupted harmony with his thought, he did indeed conquer. He knew both what he sought and how to seek it—a great matter!

I am not a blind admirer of Goethe. I have felt what others feel, and seen what others see. I, too, have been disturbed by his aversion to pain and isolation of heart. I also have looked in vain for the holy and heroic elements. Nor do I believe that any degree of objectivity is inconsistent with a partiality for what is noblest in individual characters. Shakspeare is a proof to the contrary. As a critic, he does not treat subjects masterly. He does not give you, at once, a central point, and make you feel the root of the matter; but you must read his essays as aggregates of thoughts, rather clustering round than unfolding the subject. In his later years, he lost his architectural vigor; and his works are built up like the piles in Piranesi's "Visions" of galleries and balconies connected only by cobweb ladders. Many of his works I feel to be fragmentary and inadequate. I am even disposed to deny him the honors most generally awarded him—those of the artist. I think he had the artist's eye, and the artist's hand, but not the artist's love of structure.

But I will stop here, and wait till the time when I shall have room to substantiate my charges. I flatter myself I have now found fault enough to prove me a worthy critic, after the usual fashion. Mostly, I prefer levelling upwards, in the way recommended by Goethe in speaking of the merchants he met while travelling.

While it is so undesirable that any man should receive what he has not examined, a far more frequent danger is that of flippant irreverence. Not all that the heavens contain is obvious to the unassisted eye of the careless spectator. Few men are great, almost as few able to appreciate greatness. The critics have written little upon the "Iliad," in all these ages, which

PREFACE TO *CONVERSATIONS WITH GOETHE* 349

Alexander would have thought worth keeping with it in his golden box. Nor Shakspeare, nor Dante, nor Calderon, has as yet found a sufficient critic, though Coleridge and the Schlegels have lived since they did. The greatness of Goethe his nation has felt for more than half a century; the world is beginning to feel it, but time may not yet have ripened his critic; especially as the grand historical standing point is the only one from which a comprehensive view could be taken of him.

Meanwhile, it is safer to take off the hat and shout *Vivat!* to the conqueror who may become a permanent sovereign, than to throw stones and mud from the gutter. The star shines, and that it is with no borrowed light, his foes are his voucher. And every planet is a portent to the world; but whether for good or ill, only he can know who has science for many calculations. Not he who runs can read these books, or any books of any worth. I am content to describe him in the terms Hamlet thought sufficiently honorable to him he honored most:—

> "He was a man, *take him for all in all*,
> We shall not look upon his like again."

As such, worth our study;—and more to us than elder great men, because of our own day, and busied most with those questions which lie nearest us.

With regard to the manner in which the task of translation has been performed, I have been under some disadvantages, which should be briefly mentioned. I thought the book would be an easy one to translate, as, for a book of table-talk, so much greater liberty would be allowed, and so much less care demanded, than for a classical work, or one of science. But the wide range of topics, and the use of coterie technics, have made it more difficult, and less fit for the amusement of leisure hours, than was expected. Some of these technics I have used as they stood, such as *motiv*, *grandiose*, and *apprehensiv*, the last-named of which I do not understand; the first, Mrs. Jameson has explained, in a note to the "Winter Studies." Generally, my acquaintance with Goethe's works, on the same subjects, makes me confident that I have the thought.

Then I was unexpectedly obliged, by ill health, to dictate a considerable part of it. I was not accustomed to this way of getting thoughts put upon paper, and do not feel as well satisfied with these pages as with those written by my own hand. I have, however, looked them over so carefully, that I think there can be no inaccuracies of consequence.

But, besides,—it being found that the two German volumes would not, by any means, make two, yet were too much for one of the present series,—it seemed necessary, in some way, to compress or curtail the book. For this purpose, passages have been omitted relating to Goethe's theory of colors. These contain accounts of experiments made by Eckermann, and remarks of Goethe's suggested by them. As the *Farbenlehre* is scarcely known here, I thought these would not now be interesting, and that, if the work to which they refer should by and by be translated, they might to better advantage be inserted in an appendix. And I was glad to dispense with them, because I have no clear understanding of the subject, and could not have been secure of doing them justice.

I have also omitted Eckermann's meagre record of his visit to Italy, some discussions about a novel of Goethe's, not yet translated, which would scarcely be intelligible to those who have not read it, and occasionally other passages, which seemed to me expletive, or so local as to be uninteresting. I have also frequently condensed Eckermann's remarks, and sometimes, though more rarely, those of his patron.

I am aware that there is a just prejudice against paraphrastic or mutilated translations, and that, in this delicate process, I have laid myself open to much blame. But I have done it with such care, that I feel confident the substance of the work, and its essential features, will be found here, and hope, if so, that any who may be acquainted with the original, and regret omissions, will excuse them. These two rules have been observed,—not to omit even such details as snuffing the candles and walking to the stove, (given by the good Eckermann with that truly German minuteness which, many years ago, so provoked the wit of Mr. Jeffrey,) when they seem needed to finish out the picture, either of German manners, or Goethe's relations to his friends or household. Neither has any thing been omitted which would cast either light or shade on his character. I am sure that nothing has been softened or extenuated, and believe

PREFACE TO *CONVERSATIONS WITH GOETHE* 351

that Goethe's manners, temper, and opinions, wear here the same aspect that they do in the original.

I have a confidence that the translation is, in the truest sense, faithful, and trust that those who find the form living and symmetrical, will not be inclined severely to censure some change in the cut or make of the garment in which it is arrayed.

JAMAICA PLAINS, May 23, 1839.

A Short Essay on Critics

An essay on Criticism were a serious matter; for, though this age be emphatically critical, the writer would still find it necessary to investigate the laws of criticism as a science, to settle its conditions as an art. Essays entitled critical are epistles addressed to the public through which the mind of the recluse relieves itself of its impressions. Of these the only law is, "Speak the best word that is in thee." Or they are regular articles, got up to order by the literary hack writer, for the literary mart, and the only law is to make them plausible. There is not yet deliberate recognition of a standard of criticism, though we hope the always strengthening league of the republic of letters must ere long settle laws on which its Amphictyonic council may act. Meanwhile let us not venture to write on criticism, but by classifying the critics imply our hopes, and thereby our thoughts.

First, there are the subjective class, (to make use of a convenient term, introduced by our German benefactors.) These are persons to whom writing is no sacred, no reverend employment. They are not driven to consider, not forced upon investigation by the fact, that they are deliberately giving their thoughts an independent existence, and that it may live to others when dead to them. They know no agonies of conscientious research, no timidities of self-respect. They see no Ideal beyond the present hour, which makes its mood an uncertain tenure. How things affect them now they know; let the future, let the whole take care of itself. They state their impressions as they rise, of other men's spoken, written, or acted thoughts. They never dream of going out of themselves to seek the motive, to trace the law of another nature. They never dream that there are statures which cannot be measured from their point of view. They love, they like, or they hate; the book is detestable, immoral, absurd, or admirable, noble, of a most approved scope;—these statements they make with authority, as those who bear the evangel of pure taste and accurate judgment, and need be tried before no human synod. To them it seems that their present position commands the universe.

352

A SHORT ESSAY ON CRITICS

Thus the essays on the works of others, which are called criticisms, are often, in fact, mere records of impressions. To judge of their value you must know where the man was brought up, under what influences,—his nation, his church, his family even. He himself has never attempted to estimate the value of these circumstances, and find a law or raise a standard above all circumstances, permanent against all influence. He is content to be the creature of his place, and to represent it by his spoken and written word. He takes the same ground with the savage, who does not hesitate to say of the product of a civilization on which he could not stand, "It is bad," or "It is good."

The value of such comments is merely reflex. They characterize the critic. They give an idea of certain influences on a certain act of men in a certain time or place. Their absolute, essential value is nothing. The long review, the eloquent article by the man of the nineteenth century are of no value by themselves considered, but only as samples of their kind. The writers were content to tell what they felt, to praise or to denounce without needing to convince us or themselves. They sought not the divine truths of philosophy, and she proffers them not, if unsought.

Then there are the apprehensive. These can go out of themselves and enter fully into a foreign existence. They breathe its life; they live in its law; they tell what it meant, and why it so expressed its meaning. They reproduce the work of which they speak, and make it better known to us in so far as two statements are better than one. There are beautiful specimens in this kind. They are pleasing to us as bearing witness of the genial sympathies of nature. They have the ready grace of love with somewhat of the dignity of disinterested friendship. They sometimes give more pleasure than the original production of which they treat, as melodies will sometimes ring sweetlier in the echo. Besides there is a peculiar pleasure in a true response; it is the assurance of equipoise in the universe. These, if not true critics, come nearer the standard than the subjective class, and the value of their work is ideal as well as historical.

Then there are the comprehensive, who must also be apprehensive. They enter into the nature of another being and judge his work by its own law. But having done so, having ascertained his design and the degree of his success in fulfilling it, thus measuring his judgment, his energy, and skill, they do also know how to put that aim in its place, and how to estimate its relations. And this the critic can only do who perceives the analogies of the universe, and how they are regulated by an absolute, invariable principle. He can see how far that work expresses this principle as well as how far it is excellent in its details. Sustained by a principle, such as can be girt within no rule, no formula, he can walk around the work, he can stand above it, he can uplift it, and try its weight. Finally he is worthy to judge it.

Critics are poets cut down, says some one by way of jeer; but, in truth, they are men with the poetical temperament to apprehend, with the philosophical tendency to investigate. The maker is divine; the critic sees this divine, but brings it down to humanity by the analytic process. The critic is the historian who records the order of creation. In vain for the maker, who knows without learning it, but not in vain for the mind of his race.

The critic is beneath the maker, but is his needed friend. What tongue could speak but to an intelligent ear, and every noble work demands its critic. The richer the work, the more severe would be its critic; the larger its scope, the more comprehensive must be his power of scrutiny. The critic is not a base caviller, but the younger brother of genius. Next to invention is the power of interpreting invention; next to beauty the power of appreciating beauty.

And of making others appreciate it; for the universe is a scale of infinite gradation, and below the very highest, every step is explanation down to the lowest. Religion, in the two modulations of poetry and music, descends through an infinity of waves to the lowest abysses of human nature. Nature is the literature and art of the divine mind; human literature and art the criticism on that; and they, too, find their criticism within their own sphere.

The critic, then, should be not merely a poet, not merely a philosopher, not merely an observer, but tempered of all three. If he criticize the poem, he must want nothing of what constitutes the poet, except the power of creating forms and speaking in music. He must have as good an eye and as fine a sense; but if he had as fine an organ for expression also, he would make the poem instead of judging it. He must be inspired by the

A SHORT ESSAY ON CRITICS

philosopher's spirit of inquiry and need of generalization, but he must not be constrained by the hard cemented masonry of method to which philosophers are prone. And he must have the organic acuteness of the observer, with a love of ideal perfection, which forbids him to be content with mere beauty of details in the work or the comment upon the work.

There are persons who maintain, that there is no legitimate criticism, except the reproductive; that we have only to say what the work is or is to us, never what it is not. But the moment we look for a principle, we feel the need of a criterion, of a standard; and then we say what the work is *not*, as well as what it *is*; and this is as healthy though not as grateful and gracious an operation of the mind as the other. We do not seek to degrade but to classify an object by stating what it is not. We detach the part from the whole, lest it stand between us and the whole. When we have ascertained in what degree it manifests the whole, we may safely restore it to its place, and love or admire it there ever after.

The use of criticism in periodical writing is to sift, not to stamp a work. Yet should they not be "sieves and drainers for the use of luxurious readers," but for the use of earnest inquirers, giving voice and being to their objections, as well as stimulus to their sympathies. But the critic must not be an infallible adviser to his reader. He must not tell him what books are not worth reading, or what must be thought of them when read, but what he read in them. Wo to that coterie where some critic sits despotic, intrenched behind the infallible "We." Wo to that oracle who has infused such soft sleepiness, such a gentle dulness into his atmosphere, that when he opes his lips no dog will bark. It is this attempt at dictatorship in the reviewers, and the indolent acquiescence of their readers, that has brought them into disrepute. With such fairness did they make out their statements, with such dignity did they utter their verdicts, that the poor reader grew all too submissive. He learned his lesson with such docility, that the greater part of what will be said at any public or private meeting can be foretold by any one who has read the leading periodical works for twenty years back. Scholars sneer at and would fain dispense with them altogether; and the public, grown lazy and helpless by this constant use of props and stays, can now scarce brace itself even to get through a magazine article, but reads in the daily paper laid beside the breakfast plate a short notice of the last number of the long established and popular review, and thereupon passes its judgment and is content.

Then the partisan spirit of many of these journals has made it unsafe to rely upon them as guide-books and expurgatory indexes. They could not be content merely to stimulate and suggest thought, they have at last become powerless to supersede it.

From these causes and causes like these, the journals have lost much of their influence. There is a languid feeling about them, an inclination to suspect the justice of their verdicts, the value of their criticisms. But their golden age cannot be quite past. They afford too convenient a vehicle for the transmission of knowledge; they are too natural a feature of our time to have done all their work yet. Surely they may be redeemed from their abuses, they may be turned to their true uses. But how?

It were easy to say what they should *not* do. They should not have an object to carry or a cause to advocate, which obliges them either to reject all writings which wear the distinctive traits of individual life, or to file away what does not suit them, till the essay, made true to their design, is made false to the mind of the writer. An external consistency is thus produced, at the expense of all salient thought, all genuine emotion of life, in short, and living influences. Their purpose may be of value, but by such means was no valuable purpose ever furthered long. There are those, who have with the best intention pursued this system of trimming and adaptation, and thought it well and best to

"Deceive their country for their country's good."

But their country cannot long be so governed. It misses the pure, the full tone of truth; it perceives that the voice is modulated to coax, to persuade, and it turns from the judicious man of the world, calculating the effect to be produced by each of his smooth sentences to some earnest voice which is uttering thoughts, crude, rash, ill-arranged it may be, but true to one human breast, and uttered in full faith, that the God of Truth will guide them aright.

A SHORT ESSAY ON CRITICS

And here, it seems to me, has been the greatest mistake in the conduct of these journals. A smooth monotony has been attained, an uniformity of tone, so that from the title of a journal you can infer the tenor of all its chapters. But nature is ever various, ever new, and so should be her daughters, art and literature. We do not want merely a polite response to what we thought before, but by the freshness of thought in other minds to have new thought awakened in our own. We do not want stores of information only, but to be roused to digest these into knowledge. Able and experienced men write for us, and we would know what they think, as they think it not for us but for themselves. We would live with them, rather than be taught by them how to live; we would catch the contagion of their mental activity, rather than have them direct us how to regulate our own. In books, in reviews, in the senate, in the pulpit, we wish to meet thinking men, not schoolmasters or pleaders. We wish that they should do full justice to their own view, but also that they should be frank with us, and, if now our superiors, treat us as if we might some time rise to be their equals. It is this true manliness, this firmness in his own position, and this power of appreciating the position of others, that alone can make the critic our companion and friend. We would converse with him, secure that he will tell us all his thought, and speak as man to man. But if he adapts his work to us, if he stifles what is distinctively his, if he shows himself either arrogant or mean, or, above all, if he wants faith in the healthy action of free thought, and the safety of pure motive, we will not talk with him, for we cannot confide in him. We will go to the critic who trusts Genius and trusts us, who knows that all good writing must be spontaneous, and who will write out the bill of fare for the public as he read it for himself,—

> "Forgetting vulgar rules, with spirit free
> To judge each author by his own intent,
> Nor think one standard for all minds is meant."

Such an one will not disturb us with personalities, with sectarian prejudices, or an undue vehemence in favor of petty plans or temporary objects. Neither will he disgust us by smooth obsequious flatteries and an inexpressive, lifeless gentleness. He will be free and make free from the mechanical and distorting influences we hear complained of on every side. He will teach us to love wisely what we before loved well, for he knows the difference between censoriousness and discernment, infatuation and reverence; and, while delighting in the genial melodies of Pan, can perceive, should Apollo bring his lyre into audience, that there may be strains more divine than those of his native groves.

F.

A Record of Impressions
PRODUCED BY THE EXHIBITION OF MR. ALLSTON'S PICTURES
IN THE SUMMER OF 1839

––––––––––

This is a record of impressions. It does not aspire to the dignity of criticism. The writer is conscious of an eye and taste, not sufficiently exercised by study of the best works of art, to take the measure of one who has a claim to be surveyed from the same platform. But, surprised at finding that an exhibition intended to promote thought and form the tastes of our public, has called forth no expression* of what it was to so many, who almost daily visited it; and believing that comparison and discussion of the impressions of individuals is the best means to ascertain the sum of the whole, and raise the standard of taste, I venture to offer what, if not true in itself, is at least true to the mind of one observer, and may lead others to reveal more valuable experiences.

Whether the arts can ever be at home among us; whether the desire now manifested to cultivate them be not merely one of our modes of imitating older nations; or whether it springs from a need of balancing the bustle and care of daily life by the unfolding of our calmer and higher nature, it is at present difficult to decide. If the latter, it is not by unthinking repetition of the technics of foreign connoisseurs, or by a servile reliance on the judgment of those, who assume to have been formed by a few hasty visits to the galleries of Europe, that we shall effect an object so desirable, but by a faithful recognition of the feelings naturally excited by works of art, not indeed flippant, as if our raw, uncultivated nature was at once competent to appreciate those finer manifestations of nature, which slow growths of ages and peculiar aspects of society have occasionally brought out, to testify to us what we may and should be. We know it is not so; we know that if such works are to be assimilated at all by those who are not under the influences that produced them, it

––––––––––

* Since the above was written, we see an article on the Exhibition in the North American Review for April, 1840.

360 NEW ENGLAND SHORT PUBLISHED WORKS

must be by gradually educating us to their own level. But it is not blind faith that will educate us, that will open the depths and clear the eye of the mind, but an examination which cannot be too close, if made in the spirit of reverence and love.

It was as an essay in this kind that the following pages were written. They are pages of a journal, and their form has not been altered, lest any attempt at a more fair and full statement should destroy that freshness and truth of feeling, which is the chief merit of such.

July, 1839.

On the closing of the Allston exhibition, where I have spent so many hours, I find myself less a gainer than I had expected, and feel that it is time to look into the matter a little, with such a torch or penny rush candle as I can command.

I have seen most of these pictures often before; the Beatrice and Valentine when only sixteen. The effect they produced upon me was so great, that I suppose it was not possible for me to avoid expecting too large a benefit from the artist.

The calm and meditative cast of these pictures, the ideal beauty that shone *through* rather than *in* them, and the harmony of coloring were as unlike anything else I saw, as the Vicar of Wakefield to Cooper's novels. I seemed to recognise in painting that self-possessed elegance, that transparent depth, which I most admired in literature; I thought with delight that such a man as this had been able to grow up in our bustling, reasonable community, that he had kept his foot upon the ground, yet never lost sight of the rose-clouds of beauty floating above him. I saw, too, that he had not been troubled, but possessed his own soul with the blandest patience; and I hoped, I scarce know what, probably the *mot d'enigme* for which we are all looking. How the poetical mind can live and work in peace and good faith! how it may unfold to its due perfection in an unpoetical society!

From time to time I have seen other of these pictures, and they have always been to me sweet silvery music, rising by its clear tone to be heard above the din of life; long forest glades glimmering with golden light, longingly eyed from the window of some crowded drawing room.

EXHIBITION OF ALLSTON'S PICTURES   361

But now, seeing so many of them together, I can no longer be content merely to feel, but must judge these works. I must try to find the centre, to measure the circumference; and I fare somewhat as I have done, when I have seen in periodicals detached thoughts by some writer, which seemed so full of meaning and suggestion, that I would treasure them up in my memory, and think about them, till I had made a picture of the author's mind, which his works when I found them collected would not justify. Yet the great writer would go beyond my hope and abash my fancy; should not the great painter do the same?

Yet, probably, I am too little aware of the difficulties the artist encounters, before he can produce anything excellent, fully to appreciate the greatness he has shown. Here, as elsewhere, I suppose the first question should be, What ought we to expect under the circumstances?

There is no poetical ground-work ready for the artist in our country and time. Good deeds appeal to the understanding. Our religion is that of the understanding. We have no old established faith, no hereditary romance, no such stuff as Catholicism, Chivalry afforded. What is most dignified in the Puritanic modes of thought is not favorable to beauty. The habits of an industrial community are not propitious to delicacy of sentiment.

He, who would paint human nature, must content himself with selecting fine situations here and there; and he must address himself, not to a public which is not educated to prize him, but to the small circle within the circle of men of taste.

If, like Wilkie or Newton, he paints direct from nature, only selecting and condensing, or choosing lights and draperies, I suppose he is as well situated now as he could ever have been; but if, like Mr. Allston, he aims at the Ideal, it is by no means the same. He is in danger of being sentimental and picturesque, rather than spiritual and noble. Mr. Allston has not fallen into these faults; and if we can complain, it is never of blemish or falsity, but of inadequacy. Always he has a high purpose in what he does, never swerves from his aim, but sometimes fails to reach it.

The Bible, familiar to the artist's youth, has naturally furnished subjects for his most earnest efforts. I will speak of four pictures on biblical subjects, which were in this exhibition.

362 NEW ENGLAND SHORT PUBLISHED WORKS

Restoring the dead man by the touch of the Prophet's Bones. I should say there was a want of artist's judgment in the very choice of the subject.

In all the miracles where Christ and the Apostles act a part, and which have been favorite subjects with the great painters, poetical beauty is at once given to the scene by the moral dignity, the sublime exertion of faith on divine power in the person of the main actor. He is the natural centre of the picture, and the emotions of all present grade from and cluster round him. So in a martyrdom, however revolting or oppressive the circumstances, there is room in the person of the sufferer for a similar expression, a central light which shall illuminate and dignify all round it.

But a miracle effected by means of a relique, or dry bones, has the disagreeable effect of mummery. In this picture the foreground is occupied by the body of the patient in that state of deadly rigidity and pallor so offensive to the sensual eye. The mind must reason the eye out of an instinctive aversion, and force it to its work,—always an undesirable circumstance.

In such a picture as that of the Massacre of the Innocents, painful as the subject is, the beauty of forms in childhood, and the sentiment of maternal love, so beautiful even in anguish, charm so much as to counterpoise the painful emotions. But here, not only is the main figure offensive to the sensual eye, thus violating one principal condition of art; it is incapable of any expression at such a time beyond that of physical anguish during the struggle of life suddenly found to re-demand its dominion. Neither can the assistants exhibit any emotions higher than those of surprise, terror, or, as in the case of the wife, an overwhelming anxiety of suspense.

The grouping and coloring of this picture are very good, and the individual figures managed with grace and discrimination, though without much force.

The subjects of the other three pictures are among the finest possible, grand no less than beautiful, and of the highest poetical interest. They present no impediment to the manifestation of genius. Let us look first at Jeremiah in prison dictating to Baruch.

The strength and dignity of the Jew physique, and the appropriateness of the dress, allowed fair play to the painter's

EXHIBITION OF ALLSTON'S PICTURES 363

desire to portray inspiration manifesting itself by a suitable organ. As far as the accessories and grouping of the figures nothing can be better. The form of the prophet is brought out in such noble relief, is in such fine contrast to the pale and feminine sweetness of the scribe at his feet, that for a time you are satisfied. But by and by you begin to doubt, whether this picture is not rather imposing than majestic. The dignity of the prophet's appearance seems to lie rather in the fine lines of the form and drapery, than in the expression of the face. It was well observed by one who looked on him, that, if the eyes were cast down, he would become an ordinary man. This is true, and the expression of the bard must not depend on a look or gesture, but beam with mild electricity from every feature. Allston's Jeremiah is not the mournfully indignant bard, but the robust and stately Jew, angry that men will not mark his word and go his way. But Baruch is admirable! His overwhelmed yet willing submission, the docile faith which turns him pale, and trembles almost tearful in his eye, are given with infinite force and beauty. The *coup d'œil* of this picture is excellent, and it has great merit, but not the highest.

Miriam. There is hardly a subject which, for the combination of the sublime with the beautiful, could present greater advantages than this. Yet this picture also, with all its great merits, fails to satisfy our highest requisitions.

I could wish the picture had been larger, and that the angry clouds and swelling sea did not need to be looked for as they do. For the whole attention remains so long fixed on the figure of Miriam, that you cannot for some time realize who she is. You merely see this bounding figure, and the accessories are so kept under, that it is difficult to have the situation full in your mind, and feel that you see not merely a Jewish girl dancing, but the representative of Jewry rescued and triumphant! What a figure this might be! The character of Jewish beauty is so noble and profound! This maiden had been nurtured in a fair and highly civilized country, in the midst of wrong and scorn indeed, but beneath the shadow of sublime institutions. In a state of abject bondage, in a catacomb as to this life, she had embalmed her soul in the memory of those days, when God walked with her fathers, and did for their sakes such mighty works. Amid all the pains and penances of slavery, the memory of Joseph, the presence of Moses, exalt her soul to the highest pitch of national pride. The chords had of late been strung to their greatest tension, by the series of prodigies wrought in behalf of the nation of which her family is now the head. Of these the last and grandest had just taken place before her eyes.

Imagine the stately and solemn beauty with which such nurture and such a position might invest the Jewish Miriam. Imagine her at the moment when her soul would burst at last the shackles in which it had learned to move freely and proudly, when her lips were unsealed, and she was permitted before her brother, deputy of the Most High, and chief of their assembled nation, to sing the song of deliverance. Realize this situation, and oh, how far will this beautiful picture fall short of your demands!

The most unimaginative observers complain of a want of depth in the eye of Miriam. For myself, I make the same complaint, as much as I admire the whole figure. How truly is she upborne, what swelling joy and pride in every line of her form! And the face, though inadequate, is not false to the ideal. Its beauty is mournful, and only wants the heroic depth, the cavernous flame of eye, which should belong to such a face in such a place.

The Witch of Endor is still more unsatisfactory. What a tragedy was that of the stately Saul, ruined by his perversity of will, despairing, half mad, refusing to give up the sceptre which he feels must in a short time be wrenched from his hands, degrading himself to the use of means he himself had forbid as unlawful and devilish, seeking the friend and teacher of his youth by means he would most of all men disapprove. The mournful significance of the crisis, the stately aspect of Saul as celebrated in the history, and the supernatural events which had filled his days, gave authority for investing him with that sort of beauty and majesty proper to archangels ruined. What have we here? I don't know what is generally thought about the introduction of a ghost on canvass, but it is to me as ludicrous as the introduction on the stage of the ghost in Hamlet (*in his nightgown*) as the old play book direction was. The effect of such a representation seems to me unattainable in a picture. There cannot be due distance and shadowy softness.

Then what does the picture mean to say? In the chronicle, the witch, surprised and affrighted at the apparition, reproaches the king, "Why hast thou deceived me? for thou art Saul."

EXHIBITION OF ALLSTON'S PICTURES   365

But here the witch (a really fine figure, fierce and *prononcé* as that of a Norna should be) seems threatening the king, who is in an attitude of theatrical as well as degrading dismay. To me this picture has no distinct expression, and is wholly unsatisfactory, maugre all its excellences of detail.

In fine, the more I have looked at these pictures, the more I have been satisfied that the grand historical style did not afford the scope most proper to Mr. Allston's genius. The Prophets and Sibyls are for the Michael Angelos. The Beautiful is Mr. Allston's dominion. There he rules as a Genius, but in attempts such as I have been considering, can only show his appreciation of the stern and sublime thoughts he wants force to reproduce.

But on his own ground we can meet the painter with almost our first delight.

A certain bland delicacy enfolds all these creations as an atmosphere. Here is no effort, they have floated across the painter's heaven on the golden clouds of phantasy.

These pictures (I speak here only of figures, of the landscapes a few words anon) are almost all in repose. The most beautiful are Beatrice, The Lady reading a Valentine, The Evening Hymn, Rosalie, The Italian Shepherd Boy, Edwin, Lorenzo and Jessica. The excellence of these pictures is subjective and even feminine. They tell us the painter's ideal of character. A graceful repose, with a fitness for moderate action. A capacity of emotion, with a habit of reverie. Not one of these beings is in a state of *epanchement*, not one is, or perhaps could be, thrown off its equipoise. They are, even the softest, characterized by entire though unconscious self-possession.

While looking at them would be always coming up in my mind the line,

> "The genius loci, feminine and fair."

Grace, grace always.

Mr. Allston seems to have an exquisite sensibility to color, and a great love for drapery. The last sometimes leads him to direct our attention too much to it, and sometimes the accessories are made too prominent; we look too much at shawls, curtains, rings, feathers, and carcanets.

366 NEW ENGLAND SHORT PUBLISHED WORKS

I will specify two of these pictures, which seem to me to indicate Mr. Allston's excellences as well as any.

The Italian shepherd boy is seated in a wood. The form is almost nude, and the green glimmer of the wood gives the flesh the polished whiteness of marble. He is very beautiful, this boy; and the beauty, as Mr. Allston loves it best, has not yet unfolded all its leaves. The heart of the flower is still a perfumed secret. He sits as if he could sit there forever, gracefully lost in reverie, steeped, if we may judge from his mellow brown eye, in the present loveliness of nature, in the dimly anticipated ecstasies of love.

Every part of nature has its peculiar influence. On the hill top one is roused, in the valley soothed, beside the waterfall absorbed. And in the wood, who has not, like this boy, walked as far as the excitement of exercise would carry him, and then, with "blood listening in his frame," and heart brightly awake, seated himself on such a bank. At first he notices everything, the clouds doubly soft, the sky deeper blue, as seen shimmering through the leaves, the fyttes of golden light seen through the long glades, the skimming of a butterfly ready to light on some starry wood-flower, the nimble squirrel peeping archly at him, the flutter and wild notes of the birds, the whispers and sighs of the trees,— gradually he ceases to mark any of these things, and becomes lapt in the Elysian harmony they combine to form. Who has ever felt this mood understands why the observant Greek placed his departed great ones in groves. While during this trance he hears the harmonies of Nature, he seems to become her and she him; it is truly the mother in the child, and the Hamadryads look out with eyes of tender twilight approbation from their beloved and loving trees. Such an hour lives for us again in this picture.

Mr. Allston has been very fortunate in catching the shimmer and glimmer of the woods, and tempering his greens and browns to their peculiar light.

Beatrice. This is spoken of as Dante's Beatrice, but I should think can scarcely have been suggested by the Divine Comedy. The painter merely having in mind how the great Dante loved a certain lady called Beatrice, embodied here his own ideal of a poet's love.

The Beatrice of Dante was, no doubt, as pure, as gentle, as high-bred, but also possessed of much higher attributes than this fair being.

EXHIBITION OF ALLSTON'S PICTURES 367

How fair, indeed, and not unmeet for a poet's love. But there lies in her no germ of the celestial destiny of Dante's saint. What she is, what she can be, it needs no Dante to discover.

She is not a lustrous, bewitching beauty, neither is she a high and poetic one. She is not a concentrated perfume, nor a flower, nor a star; yet somewhat has she of every creature's best. She has the golden mean, without any touch of the mediocre. She can venerate the higher, and compassionate the lower, and do to all honor due with most grateful courtesy and nice tact. She is velvet-soft, her mild and modest eyes have tempered all things round her, till no rude sound invades her sphere; yet, if need were, she could resist with as graceful composure as she can favor or bestow.

No vehement emotion shall heave that bosom, and the tears shall fall on those cheeks more like dew than rain. Yet are her feelings delicate, profound, her love constant and tender, her resentment calm but firm.

Fair as a maid, fairer as a wife, fairest as a lady mother and ruler of a household, she were better suited to a prince than a poet. Even if no prince could be found worthy of her, I would not wed her to a poet, if he lived in a cottage. For her best graces demand a splendid setting to give them their due lustre, and she should rather enhance than cause her environment.

There are three pictures in the comic kind, which are good. It is genteel comedy, not rich, easily taken in and left, but having the lights and shades well marked. They show a gentlemanlike playfulness. In Catharine and Petruchio, the Gremio is particularly good, and the tear-distained Catharine, whose head, shoulder, knee, and foot seem to unite to spell the word *Pout*, is next best.

The Sisters—a picture quite unlike those I have named—does not please me much, though I should suppose the execution remarkably good. It is not in repose nor in harmony, nor is it rich in suggestion, like the others. It aims to speak, but says little, and is not beautiful enough to fill the heart with its present moment. To me it makes a break in the chain of thought the other pictures had woven.

Scene from Gil Blas—also unlike the other in being perfectly objective, and telling all its thought at once. It is a fine painting.

368　NEW ENGLAND SHORT PUBLISHED WORKS

Mother and Child. A lovely little picture. But there is to my taste an air of got up naiveté and delicacy in it. It seems selected, arranged by "an intellectual effort." It did not flow into the artist's mind like the others. But persons of better taste than I like it better than I do!

Jews—full of character. Isaac is too dignified and sad; gold never rusted the soul of the man that owned that face.

The Landscapes. At these I look with such unalloyed delight, that I have been at moments tempted to wish that the artist had concentrated his powers on this department of art, in so high a degree does he exhibit the attributes of the master. A power of sympathy, which gives each landscape a perfectly individual character. Here the painter is merged in his theme, and these pictures affect us as parts of nature, so absorbed are we in contemplating them, so difficult is it to remember them as pictures. How the clouds float! how the trees live and breathe out their mysterious souls in the peculiar attitude of every leaf. Dear companions of my life, whom yearly I know better, yet into whose heart I can no more penetrate than see your roots, while you live and grow. I feel what you have said to this painter; I can in some degree appreciate the power he has shown in repeating here the gentle oracle.

The soul of the painter is in these landscapes, but not his character. Is not that the highest art? Nature and the soul combined; the former freed from slight crudities or blemishes, the latter from its merely human aspect.

These landscapes are too truly works of art, their language is too direct, too lyrically perfect to be translated into this of words, without doing them an injury.

To those, who confound praise with indiscriminate eulogium, and who cannot understand the mind of one, whose highest expression of admiration is a close scrutiny, perhaps the following lines will convey a truer impression, than the foregoing remarks, of the feelings of the writer. They were suggested by a picture painted by Mr. Allston for a gentleman of Boston, which has never yet been publicly exhibited. It is of the same class with his Rosalie and Evening Hymn, pictures which were not particularized in the above record, because they inspired no thought except of their excelling beauty, which draws the heart into itself.

EXHIBITION OF ALLSTON'S PICTURES　369

These two sonnets may be interesting, as showing how similar trains of thought were opened in the minds of two observers.

"To-day I have been to see Mr. Allston's new picture of The Bride, and am more convinced than ever of the depth and value of his genius, and of how much food for thought his works contain. The face disappointed me at first by its want of beauty. Then I observed the peculiar expression of the eyes, and that of the lids, which tell such a tale, as well as the strange complexion, all heightened by the color of the background, till the impression became very strong. It is the story of the lamp of love, lighted, even burning with full force in a being that cannot yet comprehend it. The character is domestic, far more so than that of the ideal and suffering Rosalie, of which, nevertheless, it reminds you.

To W. Allston, on Seeing His 'Bride'

Weary and slow and faint with heavy toil,
The fainting traveller pursues his way,
O'er dry Arabian sands the long, long day,
Where at each step floats up the dusty soil;
And when he finds a green and gladsome isle,
And flowing water in that plain of care,
And in the midst a marble fountain fair,
To tell that others suffered too erewhile,
And then appeased their thirst, and made this fount
To them a sad remembrance, but a joy
To all who follow—his tired spirits mount
At such dim-visioned company—so I
Drink of thy marble source, and do not count
Weary the way in which thou hast gone by.

　　　　　　　　　　　　　　　　　　J.

To Allston's Picture, 'The Bride'

Not long enough we gaze upon that face,
Not pure enough the life with which we live,
To be full tranced by that softest grace,
To win all pearls those lucid depths can give;
Here Phantasy has borrowed wings of Even,
And stolen Twilight's latest, sacred hues,

A Soul has visited the woman's heaven,
Where palest lights a silver sheen diffuse,
To see aright the vision which he saw,
We must ascend as high upon the stair,
Which leads the human thought to heavenly law,
And see the flower bloom in its natal air;
Thus might we read aright the lip and brow,
Where Thought and Love beam too subduing for our senses now.

O.

The Magnolia of Lake Pontchartrain

THE stars tell all their secrets to the flowers, and, if we only knew how to look around us, we should not need to look above. But man is a plant of slow growth, and great heat is required to bring out his leaves. He must be promised a boundless futurity, to induce him to use aright the present hour. In youth, fixing his eyes on those distant worlds of light, he promises himself to attain them, and there find the answer to all his wishes. His eye grows keener as he gazes, a voice from the earth calls it downward, and he finds all at his feet.

I was riding on the shore of Lake Pontchartrain, musing on an old English expression, which I had only lately learned to interpret. "He was fulfilled of all nobleness." Words so significant charm us like a spell long before we know their meaning. This I had now learned to interpret. Life had ripened from the green bud, and I had seen the difference, wide as from earth to heaven, between nobleness, and the fulfilment of nobleness.

A fragrance beyond anything I had ever known came suddenly upon the air and interrupted my meditation. I looked around me, but saw no flower from which it could proceed. There is no word for it; exquisite and delicious have lost all meaning now. It was of a full and penetrating sweetness, too keen and delicate to be cloying. Unable to trace it, I rode on, but the remembrance of it pursued me. I had a feeling that I must forever regret my loss, my want, if I did not return and find the poet of the lake, which could utter such a voice. In earlier days I might have disregarded such a feeling; but now I have learned to prize the monitions of my nature as they deserve, and learn sometimes what is not for sale in the market-place. So I turned back and rode to and fro at the risk of abandoning the object of my ride.

I found her at last, the Queen of the South, singing to herself in her lonely bower. Such should a sovereign be, most regal when alone; for then there is no disturbance to prevent the full consciousness of power. All occasions limit, a kingdom is but an occasion, and no sun ever saw itself adequately reflected on sea or land.

Nothing at the south had affected me like the Magnolia. Sickness and sorrow, which have separated me from my kind, have requited my loss by making known to me the loveliest dialect of the divine language. "Flowers," it has been truly said, "are the only positive present made us by nature." Man has not been ungrateful, but consecrated the gift to adorn the darkest and brightest hours. If it is ever perverted, it is to be used as a medicine, and even this vexes me. But no matter for that. We have pure intercourse with these purest creations; we love them for their own sake, for their beauty's sake. As we grow beautiful and pure, we understand them better. With me knowledge of them is a circumstance, a habit of my life, rather than a merit. I have lived with them, and with them almost alone, till I have learned to interpret the slightest signs by which they manifest their fair thoughts. There is not a flower in my native region, which has not for me a tale, to which every year is adding new incidents, yet the growths of this new climate brought me new and sweet emotions, and, above all others, was the Magnolia a revelation. When I first beheld her, a stately tower of verdure, each cup, an imperial vestal, full-displayed to the eye of day, yet guarded from the too hasty touch even of the wind by its graceful decorums of firm, glistening, broad, green leaves, I stood astonished as might a lover of music, who after hearing in all his youth only the harp or the bugle, should be saluted on entering some vast cathedral by the full peal of its organ.

After I had recovered from my first surprise, I became acquainted with the flower, and found all its life in harmony. Its fragrance, less enchanting than that of the rose, excited a pleasure more full of life, and which could longer be enjoyed without satiety. Its blossoms, if plucked from their home, refused to retain their dazzling hue, but drooped and grew sallow, like princesses captive in the prison of a barbarous foe.

But there was something quite peculiar in the fragrance of this tree; so much so, that I had not at first recognised the Magnolia. Thinking it must be of a species I had never yet seen, I alighted, and leaving my horse, drew near to question it with eyes of reverent love.

"Be not surprised," replied those lips of untouched purity, "stranger, who alone hast known to hear in my voice a tone more deep and full than that of my beautiful sisters. Sit down, and listen to my tale, nor fear, that I will overpower thee by too much sweetness. I am indeed of the race you love, but in it I stand alone. In my family I have no sister of the heart, and though my root is the same as that of the other virgins of our royal house, I bear not the same blossom, nor can I unite my voice with theirs in the forest choir. Therefore I dwell here alone, nor did I ever expect to tell the secret of my loneliness. But to all that ask there is an answer, and I speak to thee.

"Indeed, we have met before, as that secret feeling of home, which makes delight so tender, must inform thee. The spirit that I utter once inhabited the glory of the most glorious climates. I dwelt once in the orange tree."

"Ah?" said I! "then I did not mistake. It is the same voice I heard in the saddest season of my youth, a time described by the prophetic bard.

> 'Sconosciuto pur cammina avanti
> Per quella via ch'è piu deserta e sola,
>   E rivolgendo in se quel che far deggia,
>   In gran tempesta di pensieri on deggia.'

"I stood one evening on a high terrace in another land, the land where 'the plant man has grown to greatest size.' It was an evening, whose unrivalled splendor demanded perfection in man, answering to that he found in nature, a sky 'black-blue,' deep as eternity, stars of holiest hope, a breeze promising rapture in every breath. To all I might have answered, applying still farther the prophecy,

> 'Una ombra oscura al mondo toglie.
>   I varj aspetti e i color tinge in negro.'

"I could not long endure this discord between myself and such beauty, I retired within my window, and lit the lamp. Its rays fell on an orange tree, full clad in its golden fruit and bridal blossoms. How did we talk together then, fairest friend; thou didst tell me all; and yet thou knowest, that even then, had

I asked any part of thy dower, it would have been to bear the sweet fruit, rather than the sweeter blossoms. My wish had been expressed by another.

> 'O that I were an orange tree,
> That busy plant!
> Then should I ever laden be
> And never want
> Some fruit for him that dresseth me.'

"Thou didst seem to me the happiest of all spirits in wealth of nature, in fulness of utterance. How is it that I find thee now in another habitation?"

"How is it, Man, that thou art now content that thy life bears no golden fruit?"

"It is," I replied, "that I have at last, through privation, been initiated into the secret of peace. Blighted without, unable to find myself in other forms of nature, I was driven back upon the centre of my being, and there found all being. For the wise, the obedient child from one point can draw all lines, and in one germ read all the possible disclosures of successive life."

"Even so," replied the flower, "and ever for that reason am I trying to simplify my being. How happy I was in the 'spirit's dower when first it was wed,' I told thee in that earlier day. But after a while I grew weary of that fulness of speech, I felt a shame at telling all I knew and challenging all sympathies. I was never silent. I was never alone. I had a voice for every season, for day and night. On me the merchant counted, the bride looked to me for her garland, the nobleman for the chief ornament of his princely hall, and the poor man for his wealth. All sang my praises, all extolled my beauty, all blessed my beneficence. And, for a while, my heart swelled with pride and pleasure. But as years passed, my mood changed. The lonely moon rebuked me as she hid from the wishes of man, nor would return till her due change was passed. The inaccessible sun looked on me with the same ray as on all others; my endless profusion could not bribe him to one smile sacred to me alone. The mysterious wind passed me by to tell its secret to the solemn pine. And the nightingale sang to the rose, rather than me, though she was often silent, and buried herself yearly in the dark earth.

THE MAGNOLIA OF LAKE PONTCHARTRAIN   375

"I had no mine or thine, I belonged to all, I could never rest, I was never at one. Painfully I felt this want, and from every blossom sighed entreaties for some being to come and satisfy it. With every bud I implored an answer, but each bud only produced—an orange.

"At last this feeling grew more painful and thrilled my very root. The earth trembled at the touch with a pulse so sympathetic, that ever and anon it seemed, could I but retire and hide in that silent bosom for one calm winter, all would be told me, and tranquillity, deep as my desire, be mine. But the law of my being was on me, and man and nature seconded it. Ceaselessly they called on me for my beautiful gifts; they decked themselves with them, nor cared to know the saddened heart of the giver. O how cruel they seemed at last, as they visited and despoiled me, yet never sought to aid me, or even paused to think that I might need their aid; yet I would not hate them. I saw it was my seeming riches that bereft me of sympathy. I saw they could not know what was hid beneath the perpetual veil of glowing life. I ceased to expect aught from them, and turned my eyes to the distant stars. I thought, could I but hoard from the daily expenditure of my juices, till I grew tall enough, I might reach those distant spheres, which looked so silent and consecrated, and there pause a while from these weary joys of endless life, and in the lap of winter, find my spring.

"But not so was my hope to be fulfilled. One starlight night I was looking, hoping, when a sudden breeze came up. It touched me, I thought, as if it were a cold white beam from those stranger worlds. The cold gained upon my heart, every blossom trembled, every leaf grew brittle, and the fruit began to seem unconnected with the stem. Soon I lost all feeling, and morning found the pride of the garden black, stiff, and powerless.

"As the rays of the morning sun touched me, consciousness returned, and I strove to speak, but in vain. Sealed were my fountains and all my heart-beats still. I felt that I had been that beauteous tree, but now only was—what—I knew not; yet I was, and the voices of men said, It is dead; cast it forth and plant another in the costly vase. A mystic shudder of pale joy then separated me wholly from my former abode.

"A moment more and I was before the queen and guardian of the flowers. Of this being I cannot speak to thee in any language now possible betwixt us. For this is a being of another order from thee, an order whose presence thou mayst feel, nay, approach step by step, but which cannot be known till thou art it, nor seen nor spoken of till thou hast passed through it.

"Suffice it to say, that it is not such a being as men love to paint, a fairy,—like them, only lesser and more exquisite than they, a goddess, larger and of statelier proportion, an angel,—like still, only with an added power. Man never creates, he only recombines the lines and colors of his own existence; only a deific fancy could evolve from the elements the form that took me home.

"Secret, radiant, profound ever, and never to be known, was she; many forms indicate and none declare her. Like all such beings she was feminine. All the secret powers are 'Mothers.' There is but one paternal power.

"She had heard my wish while I looked at the stars, and in the silence of fate prepared its fulfilment. 'Child of my most communicative hour,' said she, 'the full pause must not follow such a burst of melody. Obey the gradations of nature, nor seek to retire at once into her utmost purity of silence. The vehemence of thy desire at once promises and forbids its gratification. Thou wert the keystone of the arch and bound together the circling year; thou canst not at once become the base of the arch, the centre of the circle. Take a step inward, forget a voice, lose a power; no longer a bounteous sovereign, become a vestal priestess and bide thy time in the Magnolia.'

"Such is my history, friend of my earlier day. Others of my family, that you have met, were formerly the religious lily, the lonely dahlia, fearless decking the cold autumn, and answering the shortest visits of the sun with the brightest hues, the narcissus, so wrapt in self-contemplation, that it could not abide the usual changes of a life. Some of these have perfume, others not, according to the habit of their earlier state, for as spirits change, they still bear some trace, a faint reminder of their latest step upwards or inwards. I still speak with somewhat of my former exuberance, and over-ready tenderness to the dwellers on this shore, but each star sees me purer, of deeper thought, and more capable of retirement into my own heart. Nor shall I again detain a wanderer, luring him from afar, nor shall I again subject myself to be questioned by an alien spirit to tell the tale of my being in words that divide it from itself. Farewell stranger, and believe that nothing strange can meet me more. I have atoned by confession; further penance needs not, and I feel the Infinite possess me more and more. Farewell, to meet again in prayer, in destiny, in harmony, in elemental power."

The Magnolia left me, I left not her, but must abide forever in the thought to which the clue was found in the margin of that lake of the South.

Leila
"In a deep vision's intellectual scene."

I HAVE often but vainly attempted to record what I know of Leila. It is because she is a mystery, which can only be indicated by being reproduced. Had a Poet or Artist met her, each glance of her's would have suggested some form of beauty, for she is one of those rare beings who seem a key to all nature. Mostly those we know seem struggling for an individual existence. As the procession passes an observer like me, one seems a herald, another a basket-bearer, another swings a censer, and oft-times even priest and priestess suggest the ritual rather than the Divinity. Thinking of these men your mind dwells on the personalities at which they aim. But if you looked on Leila she was rather as the *fetiche* which to the mere eye almost featureless, to the thought of the pious wild man suggests all the elemental powers of nature, with their regulating powers of conscience and retribution. The eye resting on Leila's eye, felt that it never reached the heart. Not as with other men did you meet a look which you could define as one of displeasure, scrutiny, or tenderness. You could not turn away, carrying with you some distinct impression, but your glance became a gaze from a perception of a boundlessness, of depth below depth, which seemed to say "in this being (couldst thou but rightly apprehend it) is the clasp to the chain of nature." Most men, as they gazed on Leila were pained; they left her at last baffled and well-nigh angry. For most men are bound in sense, time, and thought. They shrink from the overflow of the infinite; they cannot a moment abide in the coldness of abstractions; the weight of an idea is too much for their lives. They cry, "O give me a form which I may clasp to the living breast, fuel for the altars of the heart, a weapon for the hand." And who can blame them; it is almost impossible for time to bear this sense of eternity. Only the Poet, who is so happily organized as continually to relieve himself by reproduction, can bear it without falling into a kind of madness. And men called Leila mad, because they felt she made them so. But I, Leila, could look on thee;—to my restless spirit thou didst bring a kind of peace, for thou wert a bridge between me and the infinite; thou didst arrest the step, and the eye as the veil hanging before the Isis. Thy nature seemed large enough for boundless suggestion. I did not love thee, Leila, but the desire for love was soothed in thy presence. I would fain have been nourished by some of thy love, but all of it I felt was only for the all.

We grew up together with name and home and parentage. Yet Leila ever seemed to me a spirit under a mask, which she might throw off at any instant. That she did not, never dimmed my perception of the unreality of her existence among us. She *knows* all, and *is* nothing. She stays here, I suppose, as a reminder to man of the temporary nature of his limitations. For she ever transcends sex, age, state, and all the barriers behind which man entrenches himself from the assaults of Spirit. You look on her, and she is the clear blue sky, cold and distant as the Pole-star; suddenly this sky opens and flows forth a mysterious wind that bears with it your last thought beyond the verge of all expectation, all association. Again, she is the mild sunset, and puts you to rest on a love-couch of rosy sadness, when on the horizon swells up a mighty sea and rushes over you till you plunge on its waves, affrighted, delighted, quite freed from earth.

When I cannot look upon her living form, I avail myself of the art magic. At the hour of high moon, in the cold silent night, I seek the centre of the park. My daring is my vow, my resolve my spell. I am a conjurer, for Leila is the vasty deep. In the centre of the park, perfectly framed in by solemn oaks and pines, lies a little lake, oval, deep, and still it looks up steadily as an eye of earth should to the ever promising heavens which are so bounteous, and love us so, yet never give themselves to us. As that lake looks at Heaven, so look I on Leila. At night I look into the lake for Leila.

If I gaze steadily and in the singleness of prayer, she rises and walks on its depths. Then know I each night a part of her life; I know where she passes the midnight hours.

In the day she lives among men; she observes their deeds, and gives them what they want of her, justice or love. She is unerring in speech or silence, for she is disinterested, a pure victim, bound to the altar's foot; God teaches her what to say.

In the night she wanders forth from her human investment, and travels amid those tribes, freer movers in the game of spirit and matter, to whom man is a supplement. I know not then whether she is what men call dreaming, but her life is true, full, and more single than by day.

I have seen her among the Sylphs' faint florescent forms that hang in the edges of life's rainbows. She is very fair, thus, Leila; and I catch, though edgewise, and sharp-gleaming as a sword, that bears down my sight, the peculiar light which she will be when she finds the haven of herself. But sudden is it, and whether king or queen, blue or yellow, I never can remember; for Leila is too deep a being to be known in smile or tear. Ever she passes sudden again from these hasty glories and tendernesses into the back-ground of being, and should she ever be detected it will be in the central secret of law. Breathless is my ecstasy as I pursue her in this region. I grasp to detain what I love, and swoon and wake and sigh again. On all such beauty transitoriness has set its seal. This sylph nature pierces through the smile of childhood. There is a moment of frail virginity on which it has set its seal, a silver star which may at any moment withdraw and leave a furrow on the brow it decked. Men watch these slender tapers which seem as if they would burn out next moment. They say that such purity is the seal of death. It is so; the condition of this ecstasy is, that it seems to die every moment, and even Leila has not force to die often; the electricity accumulates many days before the wild one comes, which leads to these sylph nights of tearful sweetness.

After one of these, I find her always to have retreated into the secret veins of earth. Then glows through her whole being the fire that so baffles men, as she walks on the surface of earth; the blood-red, heart's-blood-red of the carbuncle. She is, like it, her own light, and beats with the universal heart, with no care except to circulate as the vital fluid; it would seem waste then for her to rise to the surface. There in these secret veins of earth she thinks herself into fine gold, or aspires for her purest self, till she interlaces the soil with veins of silver. She disdains not to retire upon herself in the iron ore. She knows that fires are preparing on upper earth to temper this sternness of her silent self. I venerate her through all this in awed silence. I wait upon her steps through the mines. I light my little torch and follow her through the caves where despair clings by the roof, as she trusts herself to the cold rushing torrents, which never saw the sun nor heard of the ocean. I know if she pauses, it will be to diamond her nature, transcending generations. Leila! thou hast never yet, I believe, penetrated to the central ices, nor felt the whole weight of earth. But thou searchest and searchest. Nothing is too cold, too heavy, nor too dark for the faith of the being whose love so late smiled and wept itself into the rainbow, and was the covenant of an only hope. Am I with thee on thy hours of deepest search? I think not, for still thou art an abyss to me, and the star which glitters at the bottom, often withdraws into newer darknesses. O draw me, Star, I fear not to follow; it is my eye and not my heart which is weak. Show thyself for longer spaces. Let me gaze myself into religion, then draw me down,—down.

As I have wished this, most suddenly Leila bursts up again in the fire. She greets the sweet moon with a smile so haughty, that the heavenly sky grows timid, and would draw back; but then remembering that the Earth also is planetary, and bound in one music with all its spheres, it leans down again and listens softly what this new, strange voice may mean. And it seems to mean wo, wo! for, as the deep thought bursts forth, it shakes the thoughts in which time was resting; the cities fall in ruins; the hills are rent asunder; and the fertile valleys ravaged with fire and water. Wo, wo! but the moon and stars smile denial, and the echo changes the sad, deep tone into divinest music. Wait thou, O Man, and walk over the hardened lava to fresh wonders. Let the chain be riven asunder; the gods will give a pearl to clasp it again.

Since these nights, Leila, Saint of Knowledge, I have been fearless, and utterly free. There are to me no requiems more, death is a name, and the darkest seeming hours sing Te Deum.

See with the word the form of earth transfused to stellar clearness, and the Angel Leila showers down on man balm and blessing. One downward glance from that God-filled eye, and violets clothe the most ungrateful soil, fruits smile healthful along the bituminous lake, and the thorn glows with a crown of amaranth. Descend, thou of the silver sandals, to thy weary son; turn hither that swan-guided car. Not mine but thine, Leila. The rivers of bliss flow forth at thy touch, and the shadow of sin falls separate from the form of light. Thou art now pure ministry, one arrow from the quiver of God; pierce to the centre of things, and slay Dagon for evermore. Then shall be no more sudden smiles, nor tears, nor searchings in secret caves, nor slow growths of centuries. But floating, hovering, brooding, strong-winged bliss shall fill eternity, roots shall not be clogged with earth, but God blossom into himself for evermore.

Straight at the wish the arrows divine of my Leila ceased to pierce. Love retired back into the bosom of chaos, and the Holy Ghost descended on the globes of matter. Leila, with wild hair scattered to the wind, bare and often bleeding feet, opiates and divining rods in each over-full hand, walked amid the habitations of mortals as a Genius, visited their consciences as a Demon.

At her touch all became fluid, and the prison walls grew into Edens. Each ray of particolored light grew populous with beings struggling into divinity. The redemption of matter was interwoven into the coronal of thought, and each serpent form soared into a Phenix.

Into my single life I stooped and plucked from the burning my divine children. And ever, as I bent more and more with an unwearied benignity, an elected pain like that of her, my wild-haired Genius; more beauteous forms, unknown before to me, nay, of which the highest God had not conscience as shapes, were born from that suddenly darting flame, which had threatened to cleave the very dome of my being. And Leila, she, the moving principle; O, who can speak of the immortal births of her unshrinking love. Each surge left Venus Urania at her feet; from each abjured blame, rose floods of solemn incense, that strove in vain to waft her to the sky. And I heard her voice, which ever sang, "I shrink not from the baptism, from slavery let freedom, from parricide piety, from death let birth be known."

Could I but write this into the words of earth, the secret of moral and mental alchymy would be discovered, and all Bibles have passed into one Apocalypse; but not till it has all been lived can it be written.

Meanwhile cease not to whisper of it, ye pines, plant here the hope from age to age; blue dome, wait as tenderly as now;

cease not, winds, to bear the promise from zone to zone; and thou, my life, drop the prophetic treasure from the bud of each day,—Prophecy.

Of late Leila kneels in the dust, yea, with her brow in the dust. I know the thought that is working in her being. To be a child, yea, a human child, perhaps man, perhaps woman, to bear the full weight of accident and time, to descend as low as ever the divine did, she is preparing. I also kneel. I would not avail myself of all this sight. I cast aside my necromancy, and yield all other prowess for the talisman of humility. But Leila, wondrous circle, who hast taken into thyself all my thought, shall I not meet thee on the radius of human nature? I will be thy fellow pilgrim, and we will learn together the bliss of gratitude.

Should this ever be, I shall seek the lonely lake no more, for in the eye of Leila I shall find not only the call to search, but the object sought. Thou hast taught me to recognise all powers; now let us be impersonated, and traverse the region of forms together. *Together*, CAN that be, thinks Leila, can one be with any but God? Ah! it is so, but only those who have known the one can know the two. Let us pass out into nature, and she will give us back to God yet wiser, and worthier, than when clinging to his footstool as now. "Have I ever feared," said Leila. Never! but the hour is come for still deeper trust. Arise! let us go forth!

Yuca Filamentosa

"The Spirit builds his house, in the least flowers,—
A beautiful mansion. How the colours live,
Intricately delicate. Every night
An angel for this purpose from the heavens,
With his small urn of ivory-like hue, drops
A globular world of the purest element
In the flower's midst, feeding its tender soul
With lively inspiration. I wonder
That a man wants knowledge; is there not here
Spread in amazing wealth, a form too rare,
A soul so inward, that with an open heart
Tremulous and tender, we all must fear,
Not to see near enough, of these deep thoughts?"—MS.

OFTEN, as I looked up to the moon, I had marvelled to see how calm she was in her loneliness. The correspondences between the various parts of this universe are so perfect, that the ear, once accustomed to detect them, is always on the watch for an echo. And it seemed that the earth must be peculiarly grateful to the orb whose light clothes every feature of her's with beauty. Could it be that she answers with a thousand voices to each visit from the sun, who with unsparing scrutiny reveals all her blemishes, yet never returns one word to the flood of gentleness poured upon her by the sovereign of the night?

I was sure there must be some living hieroglyphic to indicate that class of emotions which the moon calls up. And I perceived that the all-perceiving Greeks had the same thought, for they tell us that Diana loved once and was beloved again.

In the world of gems, the pearl and opal answered to the moonbeam, but where was the Diana-flower?—Long I looked for it in vain. At last its discovery was accidental, and in the quarter where I did not expect it.

For several years I had kept in my garden two plants of the Yuca Filamentosa, and bestowed upon them every care without being repaid by a single blossom. Last June, I observed with pleasure that one was preparing to flower. From that time I watched it eagerly, though provoked at the slowness with which it unfolded its buds.

A few days after, happening to look at the other, which had not by any means so favorable an exposure, I perceived flower-buds on that also. I was taking my walk as usual at sunset, and, as I returned, the slender crescent of the young moon greeted me, rising above a throne of clouds, clouds of pearl and opal.

Soon, in comparing the growth of my two plants, I was struck by a singular circumstance. The one, which had budded first, seemed to be waiting for the other, which, though, as I said before, least favorably placed of the two, disclosed its delicate cups with surprising energy.

At last came the night of the full moon, and they burst into flower together. That was indeed a night of long-sought melody.

The day before, looking at them just ready to bloom, I had not expected any farther pleasure from the fulfilment of their promise, except the gratification of my curiosity. The little greenish bells lay languidly against the stem; the palmetto-shaped leaves which had, as it were, burst asunder to give way to the flower-stalk, leaving their edges rough with the filaments from which the plant derives its name, looked ragged and dull in the broad day-light.

But now each little bell had erected its crest to meet the full stream of moonlight, and the dull green displayed a reverse of silvery white. The filaments seemed a robe, also of silver, but soft and light as gossamer. Each feature of the plant was now lustrous and expressive in proportion to its former dimness, and the air of tender triumph, with which it raised its head towards the moon, as if by worship to thank her for its all, spoke of a love, bestowed a loveliness beyond all which I had heretofore known of beauty.

As I looked on this flower my heart swelled with emotions never known but once before. Once, when I saw in woman what is most womanly, the love of a seraph shining through death. I expected to see my flower pass and melt as she did in the celestial tenderness of its smile.

I longed to have some other being share a happiness which seemed to me so peculiar and so rare, and called Alcmeon from the house. The heart and mind of Alcmeon are not without vitality, but have never been made interpreters between nature and the soul. He is one who could travel amid the magnificent displays of the tropical climates, nor even look at a flower, nor do I believe he ever drew a thought from the palm tree more than the poplar.

But the piercing sweetness of this flower's look in its nuptial hour conquered even his obtuseness. He stood before it a long time, sad, soft, and silent. I believe he realized the wants of his nature more than ever he had done before, in the course of what is called a life.

Next day I went out to look at the plants, and all the sweet glory had vanished. Dull, awkward, sallow stood there in its loneliness the divinity of the night before.—Oh Absence!—Life was in the plant; birds sang and insects hovered around; the blue sky bent down lovingly, the sun poured down nobly over it,—but the friend, to whom the key of its life had been given in the order of nature, had begun to decline from the ascendant, had retired into silence, and the faithful heart had no language for any other.

At night the flowers were again as beautiful as before.—Fate! let me never murmur more. There is an hour of joy for every form of being, an hour of rapture for those that wait most patiently.—Queen of night!—Humble Flower!—how patient were ye, the one in the loneliness of bounty,—the other in the loneliness of poverty. The flower brooded on her own heart; the moon never wearied of filling her urn, for those she could not love as children. Had the eagle waited for her, she would have smiled on him as serenely as on the nightingale. Admirable are the compensations of nature. As that flower, in its own season, imparted a dearer joy than all my lilies and roses, so does the Aloes in its concentrated bliss know all that has been diffused over the hundred summers through which it kept silent.— Remember the Yuca; wait and trust; and either Sun or Moon, according to thy fidelity, will bring thee to love and to know.

from *Bettine Brentano and Her Friend Günderode*

BETTINE BRENTANO's letters to Goethe, published under the title of Goethe's Correspondence with a Child, are already well known among us and met with a more cordial reception from readers in general than could have been expected. Even those who are accustomed to measure the free movements of art by the conventions that hedge the path of daily life, who, in great original creations, seek only intimations of the moral character borne by the author in his private circle, and who, had they been the contemporaries of Shakspeare, would have been shy of visiting the person who took pleasure in the delineation of a Falstaff;—even those whom Byron sneers at as "the garrison people," suffered themselves to be surprised in their intrenchments, by the exuberance and wild, youthful play of Bettine's genius, and gave themselves up to receive her thoughts and feelings in the spirit which led her to express them. They felt that here was one whose only impulse was to *live*,—to unfold and realize her nature, and they forgot to measure what she did by her position in society.

There have been a few exceptions of persons who judged the work unworthily, who showed entire insensibility to its fulness of original thought and inspired fidelity to nature, and vulgarized by their impure looks the innocent vagaries of youthful idolatry. But these have been so few that, this time, the vulgar is not the same with the mob, but the reverse.

If such was its reception from those long fettered by custom, and crusted over by artificial tastes, with what joy was it greeted by those of free intellect and youthful eager heart. So very few printed books are in any wise a faithful transcript of life, that the possession of one really sincere made an era in many minds, unlocking tongues that had long been silent as to what was dearest and most delicate in their experiences, or most desired for the future, and making the common day and common light rise again to their true value, since it was seen how fruitful they

388   NEW ENGLAND SHORT PUBLISHED WORKS

had been to this one person. The meteor playing in our sky diffused there an electricity and a light, which revealed unknown attractions in seemingly sluggish substances, and lured many secrets from the dim recesses in which they had been cowering for years, unproductive, cold, and silent.

Yet, while we enjoyed this picture of a mind tuned to its highest pitch by the desire of daily ministering to an idolized object; while we were enriched by the results of the Child's devotion to him, hooted at by the Philistines as the "Old Heathen," but to her poetic apprehension "Jupiter, Apollo, all in one," we must feel that the relation in which she stands to Goethe is not a beautiful one. Idolatries are natural to youthful hearts noble enough for a passion beyond the desire for sympathy or the instinct of dependence, and almost all aspiring natures can recall a period when some noble figure, whether in life or literature, stood for them at the gate of heaven, and represented all the possible glories of nature and art. This worship is, in most instances, a secret worship; the still, small voice constantly rising in the soul to bid them harmonize the discords of the world, and distill beauty from imperfection, for another of kindred nature has done so. This figure whose achievements they admire is their St. Peter, holding for them the keys of Paradise, their model, their excitement to fulness and purity of life, their external conscience. When this devotion is silent, or only spoken out through our private acts, it is most likely to make the stair to heaven, and lead men on till suddenly they find the golden gate will open at their own touch, and they need neither mediator nor idol more. The same course is observable in the religion of nations, where the worship of Persons rises at last into free thought in the minds of Philosophers.

But when this worship is expressed, there must be singular purity and strength of character on the part both of Idol and Idolater, to prevent its degenerating into a mutual excitement of vanity, or mere infatuation.

"Thou art the only one worthy to inspire me," cries one.

"Thou art the only one capable of understanding my inspiration," smiles back the other.

And clouds of incense rise to hide from both the free breath of heaven!

But if the idol stands there, grim and insensible, the poor votary will oftentimes redouble his sacrifices with passionate fervor, till the scene becomes as sad a farce as that of Juggernaut, and all that is dignified in human nature lies crushed and sullied by one superstitious folly.

An admiration restrained by self-respect; (I do not mean pride, but a sense that one's own soul is, after all, a regal power and a precious possession, which, if not now of as apparent magnificence, is of as high an ultimate destiny as that of another) honors the admirer no less than the admired. But humility is not groveling weakness, neither does bounty consist in prodigality; and the spendthrifts of the soul deserve to famish on husks for many days; for, if they had not wandered so far from the Father, he would have given them bread.

In short we are so admirably constituted, that excess anywhere must lead to poverty somewhere; and though he is mean and cold, who is incapable of free abandonment to a beautiful object, yet if there be not in the mind a counterpoising force, which draws us back to the centre in proportion as we have flown from it, we learn nothing from our experiment, and are not vivified but weakened by our love.

Something of this we feel with regard to Bettine and Goethe. The great poet of her nation, and representative of half a century of as high attainment as mind has ever made, was magnet strong enough to draw out the virtues of many beings as rich as she. His greatness was a household word, and the chief theme of pride in the city of her birth. To her own family he had personally been well known in all the brilliancy of his dawn. She had grown up in the atmosphere he had created. Seeing him up there on the mountain, he seemed to her all beautiful and majestic in the distant rosy light of its snow-peaks. Add a nature, like one of his own melodies, as subtle, as fluent, and as productive of minute flowers and mosses, we could not wonder if one so fitted to receive him, had made of her whole life a fair sculptured pedestal for this one figure.

All this would be well, or rather, not ill, if he were to her only an object of thought; but when the two figures are brought into open relation with one another; it is too unequal. Were Bettine, indeed, a child, she might bring her basket of flowers and strew them in his path without expecting even a smile in return. But to say nothing of the reckoning by years, which the curious have made, we constantly feel that she is not a child. She is so indeed when compared with him as to maturity of growth, but she is not so in their relation, and the degree of knowledge she shows of life and thought compels us to demand some conscious dignity of her as a woman. The great art where to stop is not evinced in all passages. Then Goethe is so cold, so repulsive, diplomatic, and courteously determined not to compromise himself. Had he assumed truly the paternal attitude, he might have been far more gentle and tender, he might have fostered all the beauteous blossoms of this young fancy, without ever giving us a feeling of pain and inequality. But he does not; there is an air as of an elderly guardian flirting cautiously with a giddy, inexperienced ward, or a Father Confessor, who, instead of through the holy office raising and purifying the thoughts of the devotee, uses it to gratify his curiosity. We cannot accuse him of playing with her feelings. He never leads her on. She goes herself, following the vision which gleams before her. "I will not," he says, "wile the little bird from its nest," and he does not. But he is willing to make a tool of this fresh, fervent being; he is unrelenting as ever in this. What she offers from the soul the artist receives,—to use artistically. Indeed we see, that he enjoyed as we do the ceaseless bee-like hum of gathering from a thousand flowers, but only with the cold pleasure of an observer; there is no genuine movement of a grateful sensibility. We often feel that Bettine should perceive this, and that it should have modified the nature of her offerings. For now there is nothing kept sacred, and no balance of beauty maintained in her life. Impatiently she has approached where she was not called, and the truth and delicacy of spiritual affinities has been violated. She has followed like a slave where she might as a pupil. Observe this, young idolaters. Have you chosen a bright particular star for the object of your vespers? you will not see it best or revere it best by falling prostrate in the dust; but stand erect, though with upturned brow and face pale with devotion.

An ancient author says, "it is the punishment of those who have honored their kings as gods to be expelled from the gods," and we feel this about Bettine, that her boundless abandonment to one feeling must hinder for a time her progress and that her maturer years are likely to lag slowly after the fiery haste of her youth. She lived so long, not for truth, but for a human object, that the plant must have fallen into the dust when its prop was withdrawn, and lain there long before it could economize its juices enough to become a tree where it had been a vine.

We also feel as if she became too self-conscious in the course of this intimacy. There being no response from the other side to draw her out naturally, she hunts about for means to entertain a lordly guest, who brings nothing to the dinner, but a silver fork. Perhaps Goethe would say his questions and answers might be found in his books; that if she knew what he was, she knew what to bring. But the still human little maiden wanted to excite surprise at least if not sympathy by her gifts, and her simplicity was perverted in the effort. We see the fanciful about to degenerate into the fantastic, freedom into lawlessness, and are reminded of the fate of Euphorion in Goethe's great Rune.

Thus we follow the course of this intimacy with the same feelings as the love of Tasso, and, in the history of fiction, of Werther, and George Douglas, as also those of Sappho, Eloisa, and Mlle. de L'Espinasse. There is a hollowness in the very foundation, and we feel from the beginning,

"It will not, nor it cannot come to good."

Yet we cannot but be grateful to circumstances, even if not in strict harmony with our desires, to which we owe some of the most delicate productions of literature, those few pages it boasts which are genuine transcripts of private experience. They are mostly tear-stained;—by those tears have been kept living on the page those flowers, which the poets present to us only when distilled into essences. The few records in this kind that we possess remind us of the tapestries woven by prisoners and exiles, pathetic heir-looms, in noble families.

Of these letters to Goethe some have said they were so pure a product, so free from any air of literature, as to make the reader feel he had never seen a genuine book before.

Another, "She seems a spirit in a mask of flesh, to each man's heart revealing his secret wishes and the vast capacities of the narrowest life."

But the letters to Goethe are not my present subject; and those before me with the same merits give us no cause however trifling for regret. They are letters which passed between Bettine, and the Canoness Günderode, the friend to whom she was devoted several years previous to her acquaintance with Goethe.

The readers of the Correspondence with a Child will remember the history of this intimacy, and of the tragedy with which it closed, as one of the most exquisite passages in the volumes. The filling out of the picture is not unworthy the outline there given.

Günderode was a Canoness in one of the orders described by Mrs. Jameson, living in the house of her order, but mixing freely in the world at her pleasure. But as she was eight or ten years older than her friend, and of a more delicate and reserved nature, her letters describe a narrower range of outward life. She seems to have been intimate with several men of genius and high cultivation, especially in philosophy, as well as with Bettine; these intimacies afforded stimulus to her life, which passed, at the period of writing, either in her little room with her books and her pen, or in occasional visits to her family and to beautiful country-places.

Bettine, belonging to a large and wealthy family of extensive commercial connexions, and seeing at the house of grandmother Me. La Roche, most of the distinguished literati of the time, as well as those noble and princely persons who were proud to do honor to letters, if they did not professedly cultivate them, brings before us a much wider circle. The letters would be of great interest, if only for the distinct pictures they present of the two modes of life; and the two beautiful figures which animate and portray these modes of life are in perfect harmony with them.

I have been accustomed to distinguish the two as Nature and Ideal. Bettine, hovering from object to object, drawing new tides of vital energy from all, living freshly alike in man and tree, loving the breath of the damp earth as well as that of the flower which springs from it, bounding over the fences of society as easily as over the fences of the field, intoxicated with the apprehension of each new mystery, never hushed into silence by the highest, flying and singing like the bird, sobbing with the hopelessness of an infant, prophetic, yet astonished at the fulfilment of each prophecy, restless, fearless, clinging to love, yet unwearied in experiment—is not this the pervasive vital force, cause of the effect which we call nature?

And Günderode, in the soft dignity of each look and gesture, whose lightest word has the silvery spiritual clearness of an angel's lyre, harmonizing all objects into their true relations, drawing from every form of life its eternal meaning, checking, reproving, and clarifying all that was unworthy by her sadness at the possibility of its existence. Does she not meet the wild, fearless bursts of the friendly genius, to measure, to purify, to interpret, and thereby to elevate? As each word of Bettine's calls to enjoy and behold, like a free breath of mountain air, so each of Günderode's comes like the moonbeam to transfigure the landscape, to hush the wild beatings of the heart and dissolve all the sultry vapors of day into the pure dewdrops of the solemn and sacred night.

The action of these two beings upon one another, as representing classes of thoughts, is thus of the highest poetical significance. As persons, their relation is not less beautiful. An intimacy between two young men is heroic. They call one another to combat with the wrongs of life; they buckler one another against the million; they encourage each other to ascend the steeps of knowledge; they hope to aid one another in the administration of justice, and the diffusion of prosperity. As the life of man is to be active, they have still more the air of brothers in arms than of fellow students. But the relation between two young girls is essentially poetic. What is more fair than to see little girls, hand in hand, walking in some garden, laughing, singing, chatting in low tones of mystery, cheek to cheek and brow to brow. Hermia and Helena, the nymphs gathering flowers in the vale of Enna, sister Graces and sister Muses rise to thought, and we feel how naturally the forms of women are associated in the contemplation of beauty and the harmonies of affection. The correspondence between very common-place girls is interesting, if they are not foolish sentimentalists, but healthy natures with a common groundwork of real life. There is a fluent tenderness, a native elegance in the arrangement of trifling incidents, a sincere childlike sympathy in aspirations that mark the destiny of woman. She should be the poem, man the poet.

The relation before us presents all that is lovely between woman and woman, adorned by great genius and beauty on both sides. The advantage in years, the higher culture, and greater harmony of Günderode's nature is counterbalanced, by the ready springing impulse, richness, and melody of the other.

And not only are these letters interesting as presenting this view of the interior of German life, and of an ideal relation realized, but the high state of culture in Germany which presented to the thoughts of those women themes of poesy and philosophy as readily, as to the English or American girl come the choice of a dress, the last concert or assembly, has made them expressions of the noblest aspiration, filled them with thoughts and oftentimes deep thoughts on the great subjects. Many of the poetical fragments from the pen of Günderode are such as would not have been written, had she not been the contemporary of Schelling and Fichte, yet are they native and original, the atmosphere of thought reproduced in the brilliant and delicate hues of a peculiar plant. This transfusion of such energies as are manifested in Goethe, Kant, and Schelling into these private lives is a creation not less worthy our admiration, than the forms which the muse has given them to bestow on the world through their immediate working by their chosen means. These are not less the children of the genius than his statue or the exposition of his method. Truly, as regards the artist, the immortal offspring of the Muse,

"Loves where (art) has set its seal,"

are objects of clearer confidence than the lives on which he has breathed; they are safe as the poet tells us death alone can make the beauty of the actual; they will ever bloom as sweet and fair as now, ever thus radiate pure light, nor degrade the prophecy of high moments, by compromise, fits of inanity, or folly, as the living poems do. But to the universe, which will give time and room to correct the bad lines in those living poems, it is given to wait as the artist with his human feelings cannot, though secure that a true thought never dies, but once gone forth must work and live forever.

We know that cant and imitation must always follow a bold expression of thought in any wise, and reconcile ourself as well as we can to those insects called by the very birth of the rose to prey upon its sweetness. But pleasure is unmingled, where thought has done its proper work and fertilized while it modified each being in its own kind. Let him who has seated himself beneath the great German oak, and gazed upon the growth of poesy, of philosophy, of criticism, of historic painting, of the drama, till the life of the last fifty years seems well worth man's living, pick up also these little acorns which are dropping gracefully on the earth, and carry them away to be planted in his own home, for in each fairy form may be read the story of the national tree, the promise of future growths as noble.

The talisman of this friendship may be found in Günderode's postscript to one of her letters, "If thou findest Muse, write soon again," I have hesitated whether this might not be, "if thou findest Musse (leisure) write soon again;" then had the letters wound up like one of our epistles here in America. But, in fine, I think there can be no mistake. They waited for the Muse. Here the pure products of public and private literature are on a par. That inspiration which the poet finds in the image of the ideal man, the man of the ages, of whom nations are but features, and Messiahs the voice, the friend finds in the thought of his friend, a nature in whose positive existence and illimitable tendencies he finds the mirror of his desire, and the spring of his conscious growth. For those who write in the spirit of sincerity, write neither to the public nor the individual, but to the soul made manifest in the flesh, and publication or correspondence only furnish them with the occasion for bringing their thoughts to a focus.

The day was made rich to Bettine and her friend by hoarding its treasures for one another. If we have no object of the sort, we cannot live at all in the day, but thoughts stretch out into eternity and find no home. We feel of these two that they were enough to one another to be led to indicate their best thoughts, their fairest visions, and therefore theirs was a true friendship. They needed not "descend to meet."

NEW YORK SHORT PUBLISHED WORKS 1844–1846

Emerson's Essays

ESSAYS: SECOND SERIES. By R. W. EMERSON. Boston. James Monroe and Company, 1844.

At the distance of three years this volume follows the first series of Essays, which have already made to themselves a circle of readers, attentive, thoughtful, more and more intelligent, and this circle is a large one if we consider the circumstances of this country, and of England, also, at this time.

In England it would seem there are a larger number of persons waiting for an invitation to calm thought and sincere intercourse than among ourselves. Copies of Mr. Emerson's first published little volume called "Nature," have there been sold by thousands in a short time, while one edition has needed seven years to get circulated here. Several of his Orations and Essays from "The Dial" have also been republished there, and met with a reverent and earnest response.

We suppose that while in England the want of such a voice is as great as here, a larger number are at leisure to recognize that want; a far larger number have set foot in the speculative region and have ears refined to appreciate these melodious accents.

Our people, heated by a partisan spirit, necessarily occupied in these first stages by bringing out the material resources of the land, not generally prepared by early training for the enjoyment of books that require attention and reflection, are still more injured by a large majority of writers and speakers, who lend all their efforts to flatter corrupt tastes and mental indolence, instead of feeling it their prerogative and their duty to admonish the community of the danger and arouse it to nobler energy. The aim of the writer or lecturer is not to say the best he knows in as few and well-chosen words as he can, making it his first aim to do justice to the subject. Rather he seeks to beat out a thought as thin as possible, and to consider what the audience will be most willing to receive.

398 NEW YORK SHORT PUBLISHED WORKS

The result of such a course is inevitable. Literature and Art must become daily more degraded; Philosophy cannot exist. A man who feels within his mind some spark of genius, or a capacity for the exercise of talent, should consider himself as endowed with a sacred commission. He is the natural priest, the shepherd of the people. He must raise his mind as high as he can toward the heaven of truth, and try to draw up with him those less gifted by nature with ethereal lightness. If he does not so, but rather employs his powers to flatter them in their poverty, and to hinder aspiration by useless words, and a mere seeming of activity, his sin is great, he is false to God, and false to man.

Much of this sin indeed is done ignorantly. The idea that literature calls men to the genuine hierarchy is almost forgotten. One, who finds himself able, uses his pen, as he might a trowel, solely to procure himself bread, without having reflected on the position in which he thereby places himself.

Apart from the troop of mercenaries, there is one, still larger, of those who use their powers merely for local and temporary ends, aiming at no excellence other than may conduce to these. Among these, rank persons of honor and the best intentions, but they neglect the lasting for the transient, as a man neglects to furnish his mind that he may provide the better for the house in which his body is to dwell for a few years.

When these sins and errors are prevalent, and threaten to become more so, how can we sufficiently prize and honor a mind which is quite pure from such? When, as in the present case, we find a man whose only aim is the discernment and interpretation of the spiritual laws by which we live and move and have our being, all whose objects are permanent, and whose every word stands for a fact.

If only as a representative of the claims of individual culture in a nation which tends to lay such stress on artificial organization and external results, Mr. Emerson would be invaluable here. History will inscribe his name as a father of the country, for he is one who pleads her cause against herself.

If New-England may be regarded as a chief mental focus to the New World, and many symptoms seem to give her this place, as to other centres the characteristics of heart and lungs to the body politic; if we may believe, as the writer does believe, that what is to be acted out in the country at large is, most frequently, first indicated there, as all the phenomena of the nervous system in the fantasies of the brain, we may hail as an auspicious omen the influence Mr. Emerson has there obtained, which is deep-rooted, increasing, and, over the younger portion of the community, far greater than that of any other person.

His books are received there with a more ready intelligence than elsewhere, partly because his range of personal experience and illustration applies to that region, partly because he has prepared the way for his books to be read by his great powers as a speaker.

The audience that waited for years upon the lectures, a part of which is incorporated into these volumes of Essays, was never large, but it was select, and it was constant. Among the hearers were some, who though, attracted by the beauty of character and manner, they were willing to hear the speaker through, always went away discontented. They were accustomed to an artificial method, whose scaffolding could easily be retraced, and desired an obvious sequence of logical inferences. They insisted there was nothing in what they had heard, because they could not give a clear account of its course and purport. They did not see that Pindar's odes might be very well arranged for their own purpose, and yet not bear translating into the methods of Mr. Locke.

Others were content to be benefitted by a good influence without a strict analysis of its means. "My wife says it is about the elevation of human nature, and so it seems to me;" was a fit reply to some of the critics. Many were satisfied to find themselves excited to congenial thought and nobler life, without an exact catalogue of the thoughts of the speaker.

Those who believed no truth could exist, unless encased by the burrs of opinion, went away utterly baffled. Sometimes they thought he was on their side, then presently would come something on the other. He really seemed to believe there were two sides to every subject, and even to intimate higher ground from which each might be seen to have an infinite number of sides or bearings, an impertinence not to be endured! The partisan heard but once and returned no more.

But some there were, simple souls, whose life had been, perhaps, without clear light, yet still a search after truth for its own sake, who were able to receive what followed on the suggestion of a subject in a natural manner, as a stream of thought. These recognized, beneath the veil of words, the still small voice of conscience, the vestal fires of lone religious hours, and the mild teachings of the summer woods.

The charm of the elocution, too, was great. His general manner was that of the reader, occasionally rising into direct address or invocation in passages where tenderness or majesty demanded more energy. At such times both eye and voice called on a remote future to give a worthy reply. A future which shall manifest more largely the universal soul as it was then manifest to this soul. The tone of the voice was a grave body tone, full and sweet rather than sonorous, yet flexible and haunted by many modulations, as even instruments of wood and brass seem to become after they have been long played on with skill and taste; how much more so the human voice! In the more expressive passages it uttered notes of silvery clearness, winning, yet still more commanding. The words uttered in those tones, floated awhile above us, then took root in the memory like winged seed.

In the union of an even rustic plainness with lyric inspirations, religious dignity with philosophic calmness, keen sagacity in details with boldness of view, we saw what brought to mind the early poets and legislators of Greece—men who taught their fellows to plow and avoid moral evil, sing hymns to the gods and watch the metamorphosis of nature. Here in civic Boston was such a man—one who could see man in his original grandeur and his original childishness, rooted in simple nature, raising to the heavens the brow and eyes of a poet.

And these lectures seemed not so much lectures as grave didactic poems, theogonies, perhaps, adorned by odes when some Power was in question whom the poet had best learned to serve, and with eclogues wisely portraying in familiar tongue the duties of man to man and "harmless animals."

Such was the attitude in which the speaker appeared to that portion of the audience who have remained permanently attached to him.—They value his words as the signets of reality; receive his influence as a help and incentive to a nobler discipline than the age, in its general aspect, appears to require; and do

EMERSON'S ESSAYS

not fear to anticipate the verdict of posterity in claiming for him the honors of greatness, and, in some respects, of a Master.

In New-England he thus formed for himself a class of readers, who rejoice to study in his books what they already know by heart. For, though the thought has become familiar, its beautiful garb is always fresh and bright in hue.

A similar circle of like-minded the books must and do form for themselves, though with a movement less directly powerful, as more distant from its source.

The Essays have also been obnoxious to many charges. To that of obscurity, or want of perfect articulation. Of "Euphuism," as an excess of fancy in proportion to imagination, and an inclination, at times, to subtlety at the expense of strength, has been styled. The human heart complains of inadequacy, either in the nature or experience of the writer, to represent its full vocation and its deeper needs. Sometimes it speaks of this want as "under-development" or a want of expansion which may yet be remedied; sometimes doubts whether "in this mansion there be either hall or portal to receive the loftier of the Passions." Sometimes the soul is deified at the expense of nature, then again nature at that of man, and we are not quite sure that we can make a true harmony by balance of the statements.—This writer has never written one good work, if such a work be one where the whole commands more attention than the parts. If such an one be produced only where, after an accumulation of materials, fire enough be applied to fuse the whole into one new substance. This second series is superior in this respect to the former, yet in no one essay is the main stress so obvious as to produce on the mind the harmonious effect of a noble river or a tree in full leaf. Single passages and sentences engage our attention too much in proportion. These essays, it has been justly said, tire like a string of mosaics or a house built of medals. We miss what we expect in the work of the great poet, or the great philosopher, the liberal air of all the zones: the glow, uniform yet various in tint, which is given to a body by free circulation of the heart's blood from the hour of birth. Here is, undoubtedly, the man of ideas, but we want the ideal man also; want the heart and genius of human life to interpret it, and here our satisfaction is not so perfect. We doubt this friend raised himself too early to the perpendicular and did not lie along the ground long enough to hear the secret whispers of our parent life. We could wish he might be thrown by conflicts on the lap of mother earth, to see if he would not rise again with added powers.

All this we may say, but it cannot excuse us from benefitting by the great gifts that have been given, and assigning them their due place.

Some painters paint on a red ground. And this color may be supposed to represent the ground-work most immediately congenial to most men, as it is the color of blood and represents human vitality. The figures traced upon it are instinct with life in its fulness and depth.

But other painters paint on a gold ground. And a very different, but no less natural, because also a celestial beauty, is given to their works who choose for their foundation the color of the sunbeam, which nature has preferred for her most precious product, and that which will best bear the test of purification, gold.

If another simile may be allowed, another no less apt is at hand. Wine is the most brilliant and intense expression of the powers of earth.—It is her potable fire, her answer to the sun. It exhilarates, it inspires, but then it is liable to fever and intoxicate too the careless partaker.

Mead was the chosen drink of the Northern gods. And this essence of the honey of the mountain bee was not thought unworthy to revive the souls of the valiant who had left their bodies on the fields of strife below.

Nectar should combine the virtues of the ruby wine, the golden mead, without their defects or dangers.

Two high claims our writer can vindicate on the attention of his contemporaries. One from his sincerity. You have his thought just as it found place in the life of his own soul. Thus, however near or relatively distant its approximation to absolute truth, its action on you cannot fail to be healthful. It is a part of the free air.

He belongs to that band of whom there may be found a few in every age, and who now in known human history may be counted by hundreds, who worship the one God only, the God of Truth. They worship, not saints, nor creeds, nor churches, nor reliques, nor idols in any form. The mind is kept open to truth, and life only valued as a tendency toward it. This must be illustrated by acts and words of love, purity and intelligence. Such are the salt of the earth; let the minutest crystal of that salt be willingly by us held in solution.

The other is through that part of his life, which, if sometimes obstructed or chilled by the critical intellect, is yet the prevalent and the main source of his power. It is that by which he imprisons his hearer only to free him again as a "liberating God" (to use his own words). But indeed let us use them altogether, for none other, ancient or modern, can more worthily express how, making present to us the courses and destinies of nature, he invests himself with her serenity and animates us with her joy.

"Poetry was all written before time was, and whenever we are so finely organized that we can penetrate into that region where the air is music, we hear those primal warblings, and attempt to write them down, but we lose ever and anon a word, or a verse, and substitute something of our own, and thus miswrite the poem. The men of more delicate ear write down these cadences more faithfully, and these transcripts, though imperfect, become the songs of the nations."

"As the eyes of Lyncæus were said to see through the earth, so the poet turns the world to glass, and shows us all things in their right series and procession. For, through that better perception, he stands one step nearer to things, and sees the flowing or metamorphosis; perceives that thought is multiform; that within the form of every creature is a force impelling it to ascend into a higher form; and following with his eyes the life, uses the forms which express that life, and so the speech flows with the flowing of nature."

Thus have we in a brief and unworthy manner indicated some views of these books. The only true criticism of these, or any good books, may be gained by making them the companions of our lives. Does every accession of knowledge or a juster sense of beauty make us prize them more? Then they are good, indeed, and more immortal than mortal. Let that test be applied to these; essays which will lead to great and complete poems— somewhere. *

French Novelists of the Day
BALZAC   GEORGE SAND   EUGENE SUE

THE thirteenth number of the "Wandering Jew," just published
by Winchester, has delivered us from our anxieties as to the
objects of Jesuit persecution, though by a *coup de main* clumsier
than is usual even with Sue. Now, we have matters arranged
for a few months more of contest with the Society of Jesus,
but we think our author must depend for interest during the
last volume, no longer on the conduct of the plot, but on the
portraiture of characters.

It is cheering to know how great is the influence such
a writer as Sue exerts, from his energy of feeling on some
subjects of moral interest. It is true that he has also much
talent and a various experience of life; but writers who far
surpass him here, as we think Balzac does, wanting this heart
of faith, have no influence, except merely on the tastes of their
readers.

We hear much lamentation among good people at the
introduction of so many French novels among us, corrupting,
they say, our youth by pictures of decrepit vice and prurient
crime, such as would never, otherwise, be dreamed of here, and
corrupting it the more that such knowledge is so precocious—
for the same reason that a boy may be more deeply injured by
initiation into wickedness than a man, for he is not only robbed
of his virtue, but prevented from developing the strength
that might restore it. But it is useless to bewail what is the
inevitable result of the movement of our time. Europe must
pour her corruptions, no less than her riches, on our shores,
both in the form of books and of living men. She cannot, if
she would, check the tide which bears them hitherward; no
defences are possible, on our vast extent of shore, that can
preclude their ingress. We have exulted in premature and hasty
growth; we must brace ourselves to bear the evils that ensue.
Our only hope lies in rousing, in our own community, a soul
of goodness, a wise aspiration, that shall give us strength to
assimilate this unwholesome food to better substance, or cast
off its contaminations. A mighty sea of life swells within our

FRENCH NOVELISTS OF THE DAY

nation, and, if there be salt enough, foreign bodies shall not have power to breed infection there.

We have had some opportunity to observe that the worst works offered are rejected. On the steamboats we have seen translations of vile books, bought by those who did not know from the names of their authors what to expect, torn, after a cursory glance at their contents, and scattered to the winds. Not even the all but all-powerful desire to get one's money's worth, since it had once been paid, could contend against the blush of shame that rose on the cheek of the reader.

It would be desirable for our people to know something of these writers and of the position they occupy abroad; for the nature of their circulation, rather than its extent, might be the guide both to translator and buyer. The object of the first is generally money—of the last, amusement. But the merest mercenary might prefer to pass his time in translating a good book, and our imitation of Europe does not yet go so far that the American milliner can be depended on to copy any thing from the Parisian grisette, except her cap.

One of the most unexceptionable and attractive writers of modern France is DE VIGNY. His life has been passed in the Army, but many years of peace have given him time for literary culture, while his acquaintance with the traditions of the Army, from the days of its dramatic achievements under Bonaparte, supply the finest materials both for narrative and reflection. His tales are written with infinite grace, refined sensibility, and a dignified view. His treatment of a subject shows that closeness of grasp and clearness of sight which are rarely attained by one who is not at home in active as well as thoughtful life. He has much penetration, too, and has touched some of the most delicate springs of human action. His works have been written in hours of leisure; this has diminished their number but given him many advantages over the thousands of professional writers that fill the coffee houses of Paris by day, and its garrets by night. We wish he were more read here in the original: with him would be found good French, and the manners, thoughts and feelings of a cosmopolite gentleman. We have seen, with pleasure, one or two of his tales translated into the pages of the Democratic Review.

406 NEW YORK SHORT PUBLISHED WORKS

But the three who have been and will be most read here, as they occupy the first rank in their own country, are BALZAC, GEORGE SAND and EUGENE SUE.

BALZAC has been a very fruitful writer, and as he is fond of juggler's tricks of every description, and holds nothing earnest or sacred, he is vain of the wonderful celerity with which some of his works, and those quite as good as any, have been written. They seem to have been conceived, composed and written down with that degree of speed with which it is possible to lay pen to paper. Indeed, we think he cannot be surpassed in the ready and sustained command of his resources. His almost unsurpassed quickness and fidelity of eye, both as to the disposition of external objects, and the symptoms of human passion, combined with a strong memory, have filled his mind with materials, and we doubt not that if his thoughts could be put into writing with the swiftness of thought, he would give us one of his novels every week in the year.

Here end our praises of Balzac; what he is, as a man, in daily life, we know not. He must originally have had a heart, or he could not read so well the hearts of others; perhaps there are still private ties that touch him. But as a writer, never was the modern Mephistopheles, "the spirit that denieth," more worthily represented than by Balzac.

He combines the spirit of the man of science, with that of the amateur collector. He delights to analyze, to classify; there is no anomaly too monstrous, no specimen too revolting, to ensure his ardent, but passionless scrutiny. But then—he has taste and judgment to know what is fair, rare and exquisite. He takes up such an object carefully and puts it in a good light. But he has no hatred for what is loathsome, no contempt for what is base, no love for what is lovely, no faith in what is noble. To him there is no virtue and no vice; men and women are more or less finely organized; noble and tender conduct is more agreeable than the reverse, because it argues better health; that is all.

Nor is this from an intellectual calmness, nor from an unusual power of analyzing motives, and penetrating delusions merely; neither is it mere indifference. There is a touch of the demon, also, in Balzac; the cold but gayly familiar demon, and the smile of the amateur yields easily to a sneer, as he delights to show you on what foul juices the fair flower was fed. He is a thorough

FRENCH NOVELISTS OF THE DAY 407

and willing materialist. The trance of Religion is congestion of the brain; the joy of the Poet the thrilling of the blood in the rapture of sense; and every good not only rises from, but hastens back into, the jaws of death and nothingness: a rainbow arch above a pestilential chaos!

Thus Balzac, with all his force and fulness of talent, never rises one moment into the region of genius. For genius is, in its nature, positive and creative, and cannot exist where there is no heart to believe in realities. Neither can he have a permanent influence on a nature which is not thoroughly corrupt. He might for a while stagger an ingenuous mind which had not yet thought for itself. But this could not last. His unbelief makes his thought too shallow. He has not that power which a mind, only in part sophisticated, may retain, where the heart still beats warmly, though it sometimes beats amiss. Write, paint, argue, as you will, where there is a sound spot in any human being, he cannot be made to believe that this present bodily frame is more than a temporary condition of his being, though one to which he may have become shamefully enslaved by fault of inheritance, education, or his own carelessness.

Taken in his own way, we know no modern tragedies more powerful than Balzac's "Eugenie Grandet," "Sweet Pea," "Search after the Absolute," "Father Goriot." See there goodness, aspiration, the loveliest instincts, stifled, strangled by fate, in the form of our own brute nature.—The fate of the ancient Prometheus was happiness to that of these who must pay for ever having believed there was divine fire in Heaven, by agonies of despair, and conscious degradation, unknown to those who began by believing man to be the most richly endowed of brutes—no more!

Balzac is admirable in his description of look, tone, gesture. He has a keen sense of whatever is peculiar to the individual. Nothing in modern romance surpasses the death-scene of Father Goriot, the Parisian Lear, in the almost immortal life with which the parental instincts are displayed. And with equal precision and delicacy of shading he will paint the slightest by play in the manners of some young girl.

"Seraphitus" is merely a specimen of his great powers of intellectual transposition. Amid his delight at the botanical riches of the new and elevated region in which he is traveling, we catch, if only by echo, the hem and chuckle of the French materialist.

No more of him!—We leave him to his suicidal work.

An entirely opposite character, in every leading trait, yet bearing traces of the same influences, is the celebrated GEORGE SAND. It is probably known to a great proportion of readers that this writer is a woman, who writes under the name of and frequently assumes the dress and manners of a man. It is also known that she has not only broken the marriage bond, and, since that, formed other connections independent of the civil or ecclesiastical sanction, but that she first rose into notice through works which systematically assailed the present institution of marriage and the social bonds which are connected with it.

No facts are more adapted to startle every feeling of our community; but, since the works of Sand are read here, notwithstanding, and cannot fail to be so while they exert so important an influence abroad, it would be well they should be read intelligently, as to the circumstances of their birth, and their tendency.

George Sand we esteem to be a person of strong passions, but of original nobleness and a love of right sufficient to guide them all to the service of worthy aims. But she fell upon evil times. She was given in marriage according to the fashion of the old regime; she was taken from a convent where she had heard a great deal about the law of God and the example of Jesus, into a society where no vice was proscribed, if it would wear the cloak of hypocrisy. She found herself impatient of deception, and loudly called by passion: she yielded; but she could not do so, as others did, sinning against what she owned to be the rule of right, and the will of Heaven. She protested; she examined; she assailed. She "hacked into the roots of things," and the bold sound of her axe called around her every foe that finds a home amid the growths of civilization. Still she persisted. "If it be real," thought she, "it cannot be destroyed; as to what is false, the sooner it goes the better; and I, for one, had rather perish beneath its fall than wither in its shade."

SCHILLER puts into the mouth of Mary Stuart these words as her only plea: "The world knows the worst of me; and I may boast that, though I have erred, I am better than my

FRENCH NOVELISTS OF THE DAY

reputation." Sand may say the same. All is open, noble; the free descriptions, the sophistry of passion are, at least, redeemed by a desire for truth as strong as ever beat in any heart. To the weak or unthinking the reading of such books may not be desirable, for only those who take exercise as men can digest strong meat. But to any one able to understand the position and circumstances, we believe this reading cannot fail of bringing good impulses, valuable suggestions, and it is quite free from that subtle miasma which taints so large a portion of French literature, not less since the Revolution than before. This we say to the foreign reader. To her own country Sand is a boon precious and prized, both as a warning and a leader, for which none there can be ungrateful. She has dared to probe its festering wounds, and if they be not past all surgery, she is one who, most of any, helps toward a cure.

Would, indeed, the surgeon had come with quite clean hands! A woman of Sand's genius, as free, as bold, and pure from even the suspicion of error, might have filled an apostolic station among her people. *Then* with what force had come her cry, "If it be false, give it up; *but*, if it be true, keep to it—one or the other!"

But we have read all we wish to say upon this subject, lately uttered just from the quarter we could wish. It is such a woman, so unblemished in character, so high in aim, and pure in soul, that should address this other, as noble in nature, but clouded by error, and struggling with circumstances. It is such women that will do such justice. They are not afraid to look for virtue and reply to aspiration, among those who have not "dwelt in decencies for ever." It is a source of pride and happiness to read this address from the heart of Elizabeth Barrett:

To George Sand

A DESIRE

Thou large-brained woman and large-hearted man,
   Self called George Sand! whose soul, amid the lions
   Of thy tumultuous senses moans defiance,
And answers roar for roar, as spirits can:
I would some mild miraculous thunder ran
   Above th' applauded circus, in appliance
   Of thine own nobler nature's strength and science,

Drawing two pinions, white as wings of swan,
From the strong shoulders, to amaze the place
   With holier light! that thou to woman's claim,
And man's, might join, beside, the angel's grace
   Of a pure genius sanctified from blame;
Till child and maiden pressed to thine embrace,
   To kiss upon thy lips a stainless fame.

To the Same

A RECOGNITION

True genius, but true woman! dost deny
   Thy woman's nature with a manly scorn,
And break away the gauds and armlets worn
   By weaker women in captivity?
Ah, vain denial! that revolted cry
   Is sobbed in by a woman's voice forlorn:—
Thy woman's hair, my sister, all unshorn,
   Floats back disheveled strength in agony,
Disproving thy man's name, and while before
   The world thou burnest in a poet-fire,
We see thy woman-heart beat evermore
   Through the large flame. Beat purer, heart, and higher,
Till God unsex thee on the spirit shore;
   To which alone unsexing, purely aspire.

This last sonnet seems to have been written after seeing the picture of Sand, which represents her in a man's dress, but with long, loose hair, and an eye whose mournful fire is impressive even in the caricatures.

For some years Sand has quitted her post of assailant. She has seen that it is better to seek some form of life worthy to supersede the old, than rudely to destroy it, heedless of the future. Her force is bending towards philanthropic measures. She does not appear to possess much of the constructive faculty, and, though her writings command a great pecuniary compensation, and have a wide sway, it is rather for their tendency than their thought. She has reached no commanding point of view from which she may give orders to the advanced corps. She is still at work with others in the trench, though she works with more force than almost any.

FRENCH NOVELISTS OF THE DAY   411

In power, indeed, Sand bears the palm above any of the Novelists. She is vigorous in conception, often great in the apprehension and the contrast of characters. She knows passion, as has been well hinted, at a *white* heat, when all the lower particles are remoulded by its power. Her descriptive talent is very great, and her poetic feeling exquisite. She wants but little of being a poet, but that little indispensable. Yet she keeps us always hovering on the borders of the enchanted fields. She has, to a signal degree, that power of exact transcript from her own mind of which almost all writers fail. There is no veil, no half-plastic integument between us and the thought. We vibrate perfectly with it.

This is her chief charm, and, next to it, is one in which we know no French writer that resembles her, except Rousseau, though he, indeed, is vastly her superior in it. This is, of concentrated glow. Her nature glows beneath the words, like fire beneath the ashes, deep;—deep!

Her best works are unequal; in many parts written hastily, or carelessly, or with flagging spirits. They all promise far more than they perform; the work is not done masterly; she has not reached that point where a writer sits at the helm of his own genius. Sometimes she plies the oar; sometimes she drifts. But what greatness she has is genuine; there is no tinsel of any kind, no drapery carefully adjusted or chosen gesture about her. May Heaven lead her, at last, to the full possession of her best self, in harmony with the higher laws of life!

We are not acquainted with all her works, but among those we know, mention "La Roche Mauprat," "André," "Jacques," "Les Sept Cordes de la Lyre" and "Les Maitres Mosaistes," as representing her higher inspirations, her sincerity in expression, and her dramatic powers. They are full of faults; still they show also her scope and aim with some fairness, which those readers who chance at first on such of her books as "Leone Lioni," may fail to find, or even such as "Simon" and "Spiridion," though into the imperfect web of these are woven threads of pure gold. Such is the first impression made by the girl Fiamma, as she appears before us, so noble, with the words "E l'onore;" such the thought in "Spiridion" of making the apparition the reward of virtue.

The work she is now publishing, "Consuelo," with its sequel "Baroness de Rudolstadt" exhibit her genius poised on a firmer pedestal, breathing a serener air. Still it is faulty in conduct, and shows some obliquity of vision. She has not reached the Interpreter's house yet. But when she does, she will have clues to guide many a pilgrim whom one less tried, less tempted than herself, could not help on the way.

EUGENE SUE is a writer of far inferior powers, on the whole, to Sand, though he possesses some brilliant talents that she wants. His aims and modes are more external than her's; he is not so deeply acquainted with his own nature, or with that of any other person. Like her, he began life in a corrupt society— struggled, doubted, half despaired; erred, apparently, himself, and feared there was no virtue and no truth; but is conquering now.

We observe, in a late notice of Sue, that he began to write at quite mature age, at the suggestion of a friend. We should think it was so; that he was by nature intended for a practical man, rather than a writer. He paints all his characters from the practical point of view.

As an observer, when free from exaggeration, he has as good an eye as Balzac, but he is far more rarely thus free, for, in temperament, he is unequal and sometimes muddy. But then he has the heart and faith that Balzac wants, yet is less enslaved by emotion than Sand, therefore he has made more impression on his time and place than either. We refer now to his later works; though his earlier show much talent, yet his progress, both as a writer and thinker, has been so considerable that those of the last few years entirely eclipse his earlier essays.

These latter works are the "Mysteries of Paris," "Matilda," and the "Wandering Jew," which is now in course of publication. In these, he has begun and is continuing a crusade against the evils of a corrupt civilization which are inflicting such woes and wrongs upon his contemporaries.

Sue, however, does not merely assail, but would build up. His anatomy is not intended to injure the corpse, or, like that of Balzac, to entertain the intellect merely. Earnestly he hopes to learn from it the remedies for disease and the conditions of health. Sue is a Socialist. He believes he sees the means by which the heart of mankind may be made to beat with one great hope,

FRENCH NOVELISTS OF THE DAY 413

one love; and instinct with this thought, his tales of horror are not tragedies.

This is the secret of the deep interest he has awakened in this country that he shares a hope which is, half unconsciously to herself, stirring all her veins. It is not so warmly out-spoken as in other lands, both because no such pervasive ills as yet call loudly for redress, and because private conservatism is here great, in proportion to the absence of authorized despotism. We are not disposed to quarrel with this; it is well for the value of new thoughts to be tested by a good deal of resistance. Opposition, if it does not preclude free discussion, is of use in educating men to know what they want. Only by intelligent men, exercised by thought and tried in virtue, can such measures as Sue proposes be carried out; and when such Associates present themselves in sufficient numbers, we have no fear but the cause of Association, in its grander forms, will have fair play in America.

As a writer, Sue shows his want of a high kind of imagination by his unshrinking portraiture of physical horrors. We do not believe any man could look upon some things he describes and live. He is very powerful in his description of the workings of animal nature; especially when he speaks of them in animals merely, they have the simplicity of the lower kind with the more full expression of human nature. His pictures of women are of rare excellence, and it is observable that the more simple and pure the character is, the more justice he does to it. This shows that, whatever his career may have been, his heart is uncontaminated. Men he does not describe so well, and fails entirely when he aims at one grand and simple enough for a great moral agent. His conceptions are strong, but in execution he is too melodramatic. Just compare *his* "Wandering Jew" with that of Beranger. The latter is as diamond compared with charcoal. Then, like all those writers who write in numbers that come out weekly or monthly, he abuses himself and his subject; he often *must*; the arrangement is false and mechanical.

The attitude of Sue is at this moment imposing, as he stands, pen in hand—this his only weapon against an innumerable host of foes, the champion of poverty, innocence and humanity, against superstition, selfishness and prejudice. When his works are forgotten, and for all their strong points and brilliant decorations, they may ere long be forgotten, still the writer's name shall be held in imperishable honor as the teacher of the ignorant, the guardian of the weak, a true Tribune for the people of his own time.

To sum up this imperfect account of their merits, I see De Vigny, a retiring figure, the gentleman, the solitary thinker, but, in his way, the efficient foe of false honor, and superstitious prejudice. Balzac is the heartless surgeon, probing the wounds and describing the delirium of suffering men for the amusement of his students. Sand a grand, fertile, aspiring, but, in some measure, distorted and irregular nature. Sue a bold and glittering crusader, with endless ballads jingling in the silence of the night before the battle. They are much right and a good deal wrong; for instance, all, even Sand, who would lay down her life for the sake of truth, will let their virtuous characters practice stratagems, falsehood, and violence; in fact, do evil for the sake of good. They still show this taint of the old regime, and no wonder! La belle France has worn rouge so long that the purest mountain air will not, at once, or soon, restore the natural hues to her complexion. But they are fine figures, and all ruled by the onward spirit of the time. Led by that spirit, I see them moving on the troubled waters; they do not sink, and I trust they will find their way to the coasts where the new era will introduce new methods, in a spirit of nobler activity, wiser patience, and holier faith than the world has yet seen.

Will Balzac also see that shore, or has he only broken away the bars that hindered others from setting sail? We do not know. When we read an expression of such lovely innocence as the letter of the little country maidens to their Parisian brother (in Father Goriot), we hope; but presently we see him sneering behind the mask, and we fear. Let Frenchmen speak to this. They know best what disadvantages a Frenchman suffers under, and whether it is possible Balzac be still alive, except in his eyes. Those, we know, are well alive.

To read these or any foreign works fairly, the reader must understand the national circumstances under which they were written. To use them worthily, he must know how to interpret them for the use of the Universe. *

Review

ETHEROLOGY; OR THE PHILOSOPHY OF MESMERISM AND PHRENOLOGY; Including a New Philosophy of Sleep and of Consciousness, with a Review of the Pretensions of Neurology and Phreno-Magnetism: By J. STANLEY GRIMES, Counsellor at Law, formerly President of the Western Phrenological Society, Professor of Medical Jurisprudence in the Castleton Medical College, and author of A New System of Phrenology. New-York: Saxton & Miles, 205 Broadway. 1845.

MAN is always trying to get charts and directions for the supersensual element in which he finds himself involuntarily moving. Sometimes, indeed, for long periods, a life of continual activity in supplying bodily wants or warding off bodily dangers will make him inattentive to the circumstances of this other life. Then, in an interval of leisure, he will start to find himself pervaded by the power of this more subtle and searching energy, and will turn his thoughts, with new force, to scrutinize its nature and its promises.

At such times a corps is formed of workmen, furnished with various implements for the work. Some collect facts from which they hope to build up a theory; others propose theories by whose light they hope to detect valuable facts; a large number are engaged in circulating reports of these labors; a larger in attempting to prove them invalid and absurd. These last are of some use by shaking the canker-worms from the trees; all are of use in elucidating truth.

Such a course of study has the civilized world been engaged in for some years back with regard to what is called Animal Magnetism. We say the civilized world, because, though a large portion of the learned and intellectual, to say nothing of the thoughtless and the prejudiced, view such researches as folly, yet we believe that those prescient souls, those minds more deeply alive, which are the heart of this and the parents of the next era, all, more or less, consciously or unconsciously, share the belief in such an agent as is understood by the largest definition of Animal Magnetism; that is, a means by which influence and thought may be communicated from one being to another, independent of the usual organs, and with a completeness and precision rarely attained through these.

For ourselves, since we became conscious at all of our connexion with the two forms of being called the spiritual and material, we have perceived the existence of such an agent, and should have no doubts on the subject, if we had never heard one human voice in correspondent testimony with our perceptions. The existence of such an agent we know, have tested some of its phenomena, but of its law and its analysis find ourselves nearly as ignorant as in earliest childhood. And we must confess that the best writers we have read seem to us about equally ignorant. We derive pleasure and profit in very unequal degrees from their statements, in proportion to their candor, clearness of perception, severity of judgment, and largeness of view. If they possess these elements of wisdom, their statements are valuable as affording materials for the true theory, but theories proposed by them affect us, as yet, only as partially sustained hypotheses. Too many among them are stained by faults which must prevent their coming to any valuable results, sanguine haste, jealous vanity, a lack of that profound devotion which alone can win Truth from her cold well, careless classification, abrupt generalizations. We see, as yet, no writer great enough for the patient investigation, in a spirit liberal yet severely true, which the subject demands. We see no man of Shakspearean, Newtonian incapability of deceiving himself or others.

However, no such man is needed, and we believe that it is pure democracy to rejoice that, in this department as in others, it is no longer some one great genius that concentrates within himself the vital energy of his time. It is many working together who do the work. The waters spring up in every direction, as little rills, each of which does its work. We see a movement corresponding with this in the region of exact science, and we have no doubt that in the course of fifty years a new circulation will be comprehended as clearly as the circulation of the blood is now.

In metaphysics, in phrenology, in animal magnetism, in electricity, in chemistry, the tendency is the same, even when conclusions seem most dissonant. The mind presses nearer home to the seat of consciousness the more intimate law and rule of life, and old limits become fluid beneath the fire of thought.

ETHEROLOGY

We are learning much, and it will be a grand music, that shall be played on this organ of many pipes.

With regard to Mr. Grimes's book, in the first place, we do not possess sufficient knowledge of the subject to criticise it thoroughly; and secondly, if we did, it could not be done in narrow limits.—To us his classification is unsatisfactory, his theory inadequate, his point of view uncongenial. We disapprove of the spirit in which he himself criticises other disciples in this science who have, we believe, made some good observations, with many failures, though, like himself, they do not hold themselves lowly as disciples enough to suit us.—For we do not believe there is any man, *yet*, who is entitled to give himself the air of having taken a degree on this subject. We do not want the tone of qualification or mincing apology. We want no mock modesty, but its reality, which is the almost sure attendant on greatness. What a lesson it would be for this country if a body of men could be at work together in that harmony which would not fail to ensue on a *disinterested* love of discovering truth, and with that patience and exactness in experiment without which no machine was ever invented worthy a patent. The most superficial, go-ahead, hit-or-miss American knows that no machine was ever perfected without this patience and exactness; and let no one hope to achieve victories in the realm of mind at a cheaper rate than in that of matter!

In speaking thus of Mr. Grimes's book, we can still cordially recommend it to the perusal of our readers. Its statements are full and sincere. The writer has abilities which only need to be used with more thoroughness and a higher aim to guide him to valuable attainments. It appears from notices affixed to his book that he has commanded an unusual share of attention, in a field where he has many competitors, and we think his book would win for him the same. It will bestow on those who do not find in it positive instruction, information and suggestion enough to requite a careful perusal. The best criticism on this as on other such works is to associate it as a manual with our own inquiries.

It will be the best justice to Mr. Grimes after what we have said of our impression as to the tone of his work to publish the following extracts from his own preface:

"When the doctrines of Phreno-Magnetism and Neurology were announced, and were making converts by thousands, and multitudes of new organs were daily discovered by these means, so that my private science was threatened with an overwhelming inundation, I was forced to take up this subject in earnest. About every friend I met asked my opinion of the new doctrines and new organs, and seemed surprized at my skepticism. This has led me to the determination of publishing this volume, that I may thus at once justify myself, and vindicate what seem to me the true principles of Phrenology. If I am mistaken in any of the propositions which I have assumed, there will be enough to correct me, and I shall acknowledge the correction with gratitude.   *   *   *   *   *

"There has [have?] been so many new doctrines advanced within a short time, both on the subject of Phrenology and Mesmerism, that I must necessarily assume the office of a critic in speaking of the performances of others. I am aware that I shall be liable to the charge of arrogance; but, at the present time, scarcely any two Phrenologians nor Mesmerologists can be found who agree; any one, therefore, who treats upon both these subjects at once, with the design of producing an harmonious system, must seem to assume that he is wiser than all others, and capable of filling the chair of the grand-master of the fraternity. No modesty of expression nor respectfulness of style can shield him from this imputation. Under these circumstances I have deemed it best to 'speak right straight on' regardless of the apparent egotism, and to 'utter my thoughts with entire independence of everything but truth and justice.'"

Mr. Grimes's work opens with an introduction which he calls "Synopsis of Etherology," and whoever reads that will be likely to find his interest so far awakened as to give fair attention to the book.

In this connection we will relate a passage from personal experience to us powerfully expressive of the nature of this higher agent in the intercourse of minds:

Some years ago the writer went, unexpectedly, into a house where a blind girl, thought at that time to have attained an extraordinary degree of clairvoyance, lay in a trance of somnambulism.—The writer was not invited there, nor known to the party, but accompanied a gentleman who was.

The Somnambulist was in a very happy state. On her lips was the satisfied smile, and her features expressed the gentle elevation incident to the state. The writer had never seen any one

ETHEROLOGY 419

in it, and had formed no image or opinion on the subject. She was agreeably impressed by the Somnambulist, but on listening to the details of her observations on a distant place, thought she had really no vision, but was merely led or impressed by the mind of the person who held her hand.

After awhile, the writer was beckoned forward, and her hand given to the blind girl. The latter instantly dropped it with an expression of pain, and complained that she should have been brought in contact with a person so sick, and suffering at that moment under violent nervous headach. This really was the case, but no one present could have been aware of it.

After a while, the Somnambulist seemed penitent and troubled. She asked again for the hand she had rejected, and, while holding it, attempted to magnetize the sufferer. She seemed touched by profound pity, spoke most intelligently of the disorder of health and its causes, and gave advice, which, if followed at that time, the writer has every reason to believe would have remedied the ill.

Not only no other person present, but the person advised also, had no adequate idea then of the extent to which health was affected, nor saw fully till some time after the justice of what was said by the Somnambulist. There is every reason to believe that neither she, nor the persons who had the care of her, knew even the name of the person whom she so affectionately wished to help.

Several years after, the writer in visiting an asylum for the blind saw this girl seated there.—She was no longer a somnambulist, though, from a nervous disease, very susceptible to magnetic influences. I went to her among a crowd of strangers and shook hands with her as several others had done. I then asked, "Do you not know me?" She answered "No." "Do you not remember ever to have met me?" She tried to recollect, but still said "No." I then addressed a few remarks to her about her situation there, but she seemed preoccupied, and, while I turned to speak with some one else, wrote with a pencil these words which she gave me at parting:

> "The ills that Heaven decrees
> The brave with courage bear."

420   NEW YORK SHORT PUBLISHED WORKS

Others may explain this as they will, to me it was a token that the same affinity that had acted before, gave the same knowledge; for the writer was at the time ill in the same way as before. It also seemed to indicate that the somnambulic trance was only a form of the higher development, the sensibility to more subtle influences, in the terms of Mr. Grimes, a susceptibility to Etherium. The blind girl perhaps never knew who the writer was, but saw my true state more clearly than any other person did, and I have kept those penciled lines written in the stiff round character proper to the blind, as a talisman of "Credenciveness", as the book before me styles it, credulity as the world at large does, and, to my own mind, as one of the clues granted during this earthly life to the mysteries of future states of being and more rapid and complete modes of intercourse between mind and mind. *

Our City Charities

VISIT TO BELLEVUE ALMS HOUSE, TO THE FARM SCHOOL, THE ASYLUM FOR THE INSANE, AND PENITENTIARY ON BLACKWELL'S ISLAND.

The aspect of Nature was sad; what is worse, it was dull and dubious, when we set forth on these visits. The sky was leaden and lowering, the air unkind and piercing, the little birds sat mute and astonished at the departure of the beautiful days which had lured them to premature song. It was a suitable day for such visits. The pauper establishments that belong to a great city take the place of the skeleton at the banquets of old. They admonish us of stern realities, which must bear the same explanation as the frequent blight of Nature's bloom. They should be looked at by all, if only for their own sakes, that they may not sink listlessly into selfish ease, in a world so full of disease. They should be looked at by all who wish to enlighten themselves as to the means of aiding their fellow-creatures in any way, public or private. For nothing can really be done till the right principles are discovered, and it would seem they still need to be discovered or elucidated, so little is done, with a

OUR CITY CHARITIES 421

great deal of desire in the heart of the community to do what is right. Such visits are not yet calculated to encourage and exhilarate, as does the story of the Prodigal Son; they wear a grave aspect and suit the grave mood of a *cold* Spring day.

At the Alms House there is every appearance of kindness in the guardians of the poor, and there was a greater degree of cleanliness and comfort than we had expected. But the want of suitable and sufficient employment is a great evil. The persons who find here either a permanent or temporary refuge have scarcely any occupation provided except to raise vegetables for the establishment, and prepare clothing for themselves. The men especially have the most vagrant, degraded air, and so much indolence must tend to confirm them in every bad habit. We were told that, as they are under no strict discipline, their labor at the various trades could not be made profitable; yet surely the means of such should be provided, even at some expense. Employments of various kinds must be absolutely needed, if only to counteract the bad effects of such a position. Every establishment in aid of the poor should be planned with a view to their education. There should be instruction, both practical and in the use of books, openings to a better intercourse than they can obtain from their miserable homes, correct notions as to cleanliness, diet, and fresh air. A great deal of pains would be lost in their case, as with all other arrangements for the good of the many, but here and there the seed would fall into the right places, and some members of the down-trodden million, rising a little from the mud, would raise the whole body with them.

As we saw old women enjoying their dish of gossip and their dish of tea, and mothers able for a while to take care in peace of their poor little children, we longed and hoped for that genius, who shall teach how to make, of these establishments, places of rest and instruction, not of degradation.

The causes which make the acceptance of public charity so much more injurious to the receiver than that of private are obvious, but surely not such that the human mind which has just invented the magnetic telegraph and Anastatic printing, may not obviate them. A deeper religion at the heart of Society would devise such means. Why should it be that the poor may still feel themselves men; paupers not? The poor man does not feel himself injured but benefitted by the charity of the doctor who gives him back the bill he is unable to pay, because the doctor is acting from intelligent sympathy—from love. Let Society do the same. She might raise the man, who is accepting her bounty, instead of degrading him.

Indeed, it requires great nobleness and faith in human nature, and God's will concerning it, for the officials not to take the tone toward these under their care, which their vices and bad habits prompt, but which must confirm them in the same. Men treated with respect are reminded of self-respect, and if there is a sound spot left in the character, the healthy influence spreads.

We were sorry to see mothers with their newborn infants exposed to the careless scrutiny of male visitors. In the hospital, those who had children scarce a day old were not secure from the gaze of the stranger. This cannot be pleasant to them, and, if they have not refinement to dislike it, those who have should teach it to them. But we suppose there is no woman who has so entirely lost sight of the feelings of girlhood as not to dislike the scrutiny of strangers at a time which is sacred, if any in life is. Women they may like to see, even strangers, if they can approach them with delicacy.

In the yard of the hospital, we saw a little Dutch girl, a dwarf, who would have suggested a thousand poetical images and fictions to the mind of Victor Hugo or Sir Walter Scott. She had been brought here to New-York, as we understood, by some showman and then deserted, so that this place was her only refuge. No one could communicate with her or know her feelings, but she showed what they were, by running to the gate whenever it was opened, though treated with familiar kindness and seeming pleased by it. She had a large head, ragged dark hair, a glowering wizard eye, an uncouth yet pleasant smile, like an old child;—she wore a gold ring, and her complexion was as yellow as gold, if not as bright; altogether she looked like a gnome, more than any attempt we have ever known to embody in Art that fabled inhabitant of the mines and secret caves of earth.

From the Alms House we passed in an open boat to the Farm School. We were unprepared to find this, as we did, only a school upon a small farm, instead of one in which study is associated with labor. The children are simply taken care of and taught the common English branches till they are twelve years old,

OUR CITY CHARITIES

423

when they are bound out to various kinds of work. We think this plan very injudicious. It is bad enough for the children of rich parents, not likely in after life to bear a hard burden, and who are, at any rate, supplied with those various excitements required to develope the character in the earliest years; it is bad enough, we say, for these to have no kind of useful labor mingled with their plays and studies. Even those children would expand more, and be more variously called forth, and better prepared for common life, if another course were pursued. But, in schools like this at the farm, where the children, on leaving it, will be at once called on for adroitness and readiness of mind and body, and where the absence of natural ties and the various excitements that rise from them inevitably give to life a mechanical routine calculated to cramp and chill the character, it would be peculiarly desirable to provide various occupations, and such as are calculated to prepare for common life. As to economy of time, there is never time lost, by mingling other pursuits with the studies of children; they have vital energy enough for many things at once, and learn more from books when their attention is quickened by other kinds of culture.

Some of these children were pretty, and they were healthy and well-grown, considering the general poverty or vice of the class from which they were taken. That terrible scourge, opthalmia, disfigured many among them. This disease, from some cause not yet detected, has been prevalent here for many years. We trust it may yield to the change of location next summer. There is not water enough here to give the children decent advantages as to bathing. This, too, will be remedied by the change. The Principal, who has been almost all his life connected with this establishment and that at Bellevue, seemed to feel a lively interest in his charge. He has arranged the dormitories with excellent judgment, both as to ventilation and neatness. This, alone, is a great advantage these children have over those of poor families living at home. They may pass the night in healthy sleep, and have thereby a chance for innocent and active days.

We saw with pleasure the little children engaged in the kind of drill they so much enjoy, of gesticulation regulated by singing. It was also pretty to see the babies sitting in a circle and the nurses in the midst feeding them, alternately, with a spoon. It

424   NEW YORK SHORT PUBLISHED WORKS

seemed like a nest full of little birds, each opening its bill as the parent returns from her flight.

Hence we passed to the Asylum for the Insane. Only a part of this building is completed, and it is well known that the space is insufficient. Twice as many are inmates here as can be properly accommodated. A tolerable degree, however, of order and cleanliness is preserved. We could not but observe the vast difference between the appearance of the insane here and at Bloomingdale, or other Institutions where the number of attendants and nature of the arrangements permit them to be the objects of individual treatment; that is, where the wants and difficulties of each patient can be distinctly and carefully attended to. At Bloomingdale, the shades of character and feeling were nicely kept up, decorum of manners preserved, and the insane showed in every way that they felt no violent separation betwixt them and the rest of the world, and might easily return to it. The eye, though bewildered, seemed lively, and the tongue prompt. But *here*, insanity appeared in its more stupid, wild, or despairing forms. They crouched in corners; they had no eye for the stranger, no heart for hope, no habitual expectation of light. Just as at the Farm School, where the children show by their unformed features and mechanical movements that they are treated by wholesale, so do these poor sufferers. It is an evil incident to public establishments, and which only a more intelligent public attention can obviate.

One figure we saw, here also, of high poetical interest. It was a woman seated on the floor, in the corner of her cell, with a shawl wrapped gracefully around her head and chest, like a Nun's veil. Her hair was grey, her face attenuated and very pallid, her eyes large, open, fixed and bright with a still fire. She never moved them nor ceased chanting the service of the Church. She was a Catholic, who became insane while preparing to be a Nun. She is surely a Nun now in her heart; and a figure from which a painter might study for some of the most consecrated subjects.

Passing to the Penitentiary, we entered on one of the gloomiest scenes that deforms this great metropolis. Here are the twelve hundred, who receive the punishment due to the vices of so large a portion of the rest. And under what circumstances! Never was punishment treated more simply as

OUR CITY CHARITIES

425

a social convenience, without regard to pure right, or a hope of reformation.

Public attention is now so far awake to the state of the Penitentiary that it cannot be long, we trust, before proper means of classification are devised, a temporary asylum provided for those who leave this purgatory, even now, unwilling to return to the inferno from which it has for a time kept them, and means presented likely to lead some, at least, among the many, who seem hardened, to better views and hopes. It must be that the more righteous feeling which has shown itself in regard to the prisons at Sing Sing and elsewhere, must take some effect as to the Penitentiary also. The present Superintendant enters into the necessity of such improvements, and, should he remain there, will do what he can to carry them into effect.

The want of proper matrons, or any matrons, to take the care so necessary for the bodily or mental improvement or even decent condition of the seven hundred women assembled here, is an offence that cries aloud. It is impossible to take the most cursory survey of this assembly of women; especially it is impossible to see them in the Hospital, where the circumstances are a little more favorable, without seeing how many there are in whom the feelings of innocent childhood are not dead, who need only good influences and steady aid to raise them from the pit of infamy and wo into which they have fallen. And, if there was not one that could be helped, at least Society owes them the insurance of a decent condition while here. We trust that interest on this subject will not slumber.

The recognized principles of all such institutions which have any higher object than the punishment of fault, (and we believe few among us are so ignorant as to avow that as the only object, though they may, from want of thought, act as if it were,) are—Classification as the first step, that the bad may not impede those who wish to do well; 2d. Instruction, practical, oral, and by furnishing books which may open entirely new hopes and thoughts to minds oftener darkened than corrupted; 3d. A good Sanitary system, which promotes self-respect, and, through health and purity of body, the same in mind.

In visiting the Tombs the other day, we found the air in the upper galleries unendurable, and felt great regret that those confined there should be constantly subjected to it. Give the free breath of Heaven to all who are still permitted to breathe.—We cannot, however, wonder at finding this barbarity in a prison, having been subjected to it at the most fashionable places of public resort. Dr. Griscom has sent us his excellent lecture on the health of New-York, which we recommend to all who take a vital interest in the city where they live, and have intellect to discern that a cancer on the body must in time affect the head and heart also. We thought, while reading, that it was not surprising typhus fever and opthalmia should be bred in the cellars, while the families of those who live in palaces breathe such infected air at public places, and receive their visitors on New Year's day by candle-light. (That was a sad omen for the New Year—did they mean to class themselves among those who love darkness rather than light?)

We hope to see the two thousand poor people, and the poor children, better situated in their new abode, when we visit them again. The Insane Asylum will gain at once by enlargement of accommodations; but more attendance is also necessary, and, for that purpose, the best persons should be selected. We saw, with pleasure, tame pigeons walking about among the most violent of the insane, but we also saw two attendants with faces brutal and stolid. Such a charge is too delicate to be intrusted to any but excellent persons. Of the Penitentiary we shall write again. All criticism, however imperfect, should be welcome. There is no reason why New-York should not become a model for other States in these things. There is wealth enough, intelligence, and good desire enough, and *surely, need enough.* If she be not the best cared for city in the world, she threatens to surpass in corruption London and Paris. Such bane as is constantly poured into her veins demands powerful antidotes.

But nothing effectual can be achieved while both measures and men are made the sport of political changes. It is a most crying and shameful evil, which does not belong to our institutions, but is a careless distortion of them, that the men and measures are changed in these institutions with changes from Whig to Democrat, from Democrat to Whig. Churches, Schools, Colleges, the care of the Insane, and suffering Poor, should be preserved from the uneasy tossings of this delirium. The Country, the State, should look to it that only those fit for such officers should be chosen for such, apart from all considerations of political party.

Let this be thought of; for without an absolute change in this respect no permanent good whatever can be effected; and farther, let not economy but utility be the rule of expenditure, for, here, parsimony is the worst prodigality. *

Prevalent Idea That Politeness Is Too Great a Luxury to Be Given to the Poor

A FEW days ago, a lady, crossing in one of the ferry boats that ply from this city, saw a young boy, poorly dressed, sitting with an infant in his arms on one of the benches. She observed that the child looked sickly and coughed. This, as the day was raw, made her anxious in its behalf, and she went to the boy and asked whether he was alone there with the baby, and if he did not think the cold breeze dangerous for it. He replied that he was sent out with the child to take care of it, and that his father said the fresh air from the water would do it good.

While he made this simple answer, a number of persons had collected around to listen, and one of them, a well-dressed woman, addressed the boy in a string of such questions and remarks as these:

"What is your name? Where do you live? Are you telling us the truth? It's a shame to have that baby out in such weather; you'll be the death of it. (To the bystanders:) I would go and see his mother and tell her about it, if I was sure he had told us the truth about where he lived. How do you expect to get back? Here, (in the rudest voice,) somebody says you have not told the truth as to where you live."

The child, whose only offence consisted in taking care of the little one in public, and answering when he was spoken to, began to shed tears at the accusations thus grossly preferred against him. The bystanders stared at both; but among them all there was not one with sufficiently clear notions of propriety and moral energy to say to this impudent questioner, "Woman! do you suppose, because you wear a handsome shawl, and that boy a patched jacket, that you have any right to speak to him at all, unless he wishes it, far less to prefer against him those rude accusations. Your vulgarity is unendurable; leave the place or alter your manner."

Many such instances have we seen of insolent rudeness or more insolent affability founded on no apparent grounds, except an apparent difference in pecuniary position, for no one can suppose in such cases the offending party has really enjoyed the benefit of refined education and society, but all present let them pass as matters of course. It was sad to see how the poor would endure—mortifying to see how the purse-proud dared offend. An excellent man who was, in his early years, a missionary to the poor, used to speak afterwards with great shame of the manner in which he had conducted himself towards them.—"When I recollect," said he, "the freedom with which I entered their houses, inquired into all their affairs, commented on their conduct and disputed their statements I wonder I was never horsewhipped and feel that I ought to have been; it would have done me good, for I needed as severe a lesson on the universal obligations of politeness in its only genuine form of respect for man as man, and delicate sympathy with each in his peculiar position."

Charles Lamb, who was indeed worthy to be called a human being from those refined sympathies, said, "You call him a gentleman: does his washerwoman find him so?" We may say, if she did so, she found him a *man*, neither treating her with vulgar abruptness, nor giving himself airs of condescending liveliness, but treating her with that genuine respect which a feeling of equality inspires.

To doubt the veracity of another is an insult which in most *civilized* communities must in the so-called higher classes be atoned for by blood, but, in those same communities, the same men will, with the utmost lightness, doubt the truth of one who wears a ragged coat, and thus do all they can to injure and degrade him by assailing his self-respect, and breaking the feeling of personal honor—a wound to which hurts a man as a wound to its bark does a tree.

Then how rudely are favors conferred, just as a bone is thrown to a dog. A gentleman indeed will not do *that* without accompanying signs of sympathy and regard. Just as this woman said, "If you have told the truth I will go and see your mother," are many acts performed on which the actors pride themselves as kind and charitable.

All men might learn from the French in these matters. That people, whatever be their faults, are really well-bred, and many

LIFE OF FREDERICK DOUGLASS

acts might be quoted from their romantic annals, where gifts were given from rich to poor with a graceful courtesy, equally honorable and delightful to the giver and the receiver.

In Catholic countries there is more courtesy, for charity is there a duty, and must be done for God's sake; there is less room for a man to give himself the Pharisaical tone about it. A rich man is not so surprised to find himself in contact with a poor one; nor is the custom of kneeling on the open pavement, the silk robe close to the beggar's rags, without profit. The separation by pews, even on the day when all meet nearest, is as bad for the manners as the soul.

Blessed be he or she who has passed through this world, not only with an open purse and willingness to render the aid of mere outward benefits, but with an open eye and open heart, ready to cheer the downcast, and enlighten the dull by words of comfort and looks of love. The wayside charities are the most valuable both as to sustaining hope and diffusing knowledge, and none can render them who has not an expansive nature, a heart alive to affection, and some true notion, however imperfectly developed, of the nature of human brotherhood.

Such an one can never sauce the given meat with taunts, freeze the bread by a cold glance of doubt, or plunge the man who asked for his hand deeper back into the mud by any kind of rudeness.

In the little instance with which we begun, no help *was* asked, unless by the sight of the timid little boy's old jacket. But the license which this seemed to the well-clothed woman to give to rudeness was so characteristic of a deep fault now existing, that a volume of comments might follow and a host of anecdotes be drawn from almost any one's experience in exposition of it. Those few words, perhaps, may awaken thought in those who have drawn tears from others' eyes through an ignorance brutal, but not hopelessly so, if they are willing to rise above it. *

Review

NARRATIVE OF THE LIFE OF FREDERICK DOUGLASS, AN AMERICAN SLAVE. Written by him self. Boston: Published at the Anti-Slavery Office No. 25 Cornhill. 1845.

430   NEW YORK SHORT PUBLISHED WORKS

FREDERICK DOUGLASS has been for some time a prominent member of the Abolition party. He is said to be an excellent speaker—can speak from a thorough personal experience—and has upon the audience, beside, the influence of a strong character and uncommon talents. In the book before us he has put into the story of his life the thoughts, the feelings and the adventures that have been so affecting through the living voice; nor are they less so from the printed page. He has had the courage to name the persons, times and places, thus exposing himself to obvious danger, and setting the seal on his deep convictions as to the religious need of speaking the whole truth. Considered merely as a narrative, we have never read one more simple, true, coherent, and warm with genuine feeling. It is an excellent piece of writing, and on that score to be prized as a specimen of the powers of the Black Race, which Prejudice persists in disputing. We prize highly all evidence of this kind, and it is becoming more abundant. The Cross of the Legion of Honor has just been conferred in France on Dumas and Souliè, both celebrated in the paths of light literature. Dumas, whose father was a General in the French Army, is a Mulatto; Souliè, a Quadroon. He went from New-Orleans, where, though to the eye a white man, yet, as known to have African blood in his veins, he could never have enjoyed the privileges due to a human being. Leaving the Land of Freedom, he found himself free to develope the powers that God had given.

Two wise and candid thinkers,—the Scotchman, Kinmont, prematurely lost to this country, of which he was so faithful and generous a student, and the late Dr. Channing,—both thought that the African Race had in them a peculiar element, which, if it could be assimilated with those imported among us from Europe, would give to genius a development, and to the energies of character a balance and harmony beyond what has been seen heretofore in the history of the world. Such an element is indicated in their lowest estate by a talent for melody, a ready skill at imitation and adaptation, an almost indestructible elasticity of nature. It is to be remarked in the writings both of Souliè and Dumas, full of faults but glowing with plastic life and fertile in invention. The same torrid energy and saccharine fulness may be felt in the writings of this Douglass, though his life being one of action or resistance, was less favorable to *such* powers than one of a more joyous flow might have been.

The book is prefaced by two communications,—one from Garrison, and one from Wendell Phillips. That from the former is in his usual over-emphatic style. His motives and his course have been noble and generous. We look upon him with high respect, but he has indulged in violent invective and denunciation till he has spoiled the temper of his mind. Like a man who has been in the habit of screaming himself hoarse to make the deaf hear, he can no longer pitch his voice on a key agreeable to common ears. Mr. Phillips's remarks are equally decided, without this exaggeration in the tone. Douglass himself seems very just and temperate. We feel that his view, even of those who have injured him most, may be relied upon. He knows how to allow for motives and influences. Upon the subject of Religion, he speaks with great force, and not more than our own sympathies can respond to. The inconsistencies of Slaveholding professors of religion cry to Heaven. We are not disposed to detest, or refuse communion with them. Their blindness is but one form of that prevalent fallacy which substitutes a creed for a faith, a ritual for a life. We have seen too much of this system of atonement not to know that those who adopt it often began with good intentions, and are, at any rate, in their mistakes worthy of the deepest pity. But that is no reason why the truth should not be uttered, trumpet-tongued, about the thing. "Bring no more vain oblations"; sermons must daily be preached anew on that text. Kings, five hundred years ago, built Churches with the spoils of War; Clergymen to-day command Slaves to obey a Gospel which they will not allow them to read, and call themselves Christians amid the curses of their fellow men.—The world ought to get on a little faster than that, if there be really any principle of improvement in it. The Kingdom of Heaven may not at the beginning have dropped seed larger than a mustard-seed, but even from that we had a right to expect a fuller growth than can be believed to exist, when we read such a book as this of Douglass. Unspeakably affecting is the fact that he never saw his mother at all by day-light.

432   NEW YORK SHORT PUBLISHED WORKS

"I do not recollect of ever seeing my mother by the light of day. She was with me in the night. She would lie down with me, and get me to sleep, but long before I waked she was gone."

The following extract presents a suitable answer to the hacknied argument drawn by the defender of Slavery from the songs of the Slave, and is also a good specimen of the powers of observation and manly heart of the writer. We wish that every one may read his book and see what a mind might have been stifled in bondage,—what a man may be subjected to the insults of spendthrift dandies, or the blows of mercenary brutes, in whom there is no whiteness except of the skin, no humanity except in the outward form, and of whom the Avenger will not fail yet to demand—"Where is thy brother?" *

"The Home Plantation of Colonel Lloyd wore the appearance of a country village. All the mechanical operations for all the farms were performed here. The shoemaking and mending, the blacksmithing, cartwrighting, coopering, weaving and grain grinding, were all performed by the slaves on the Home Plantation. The whole place wore a business-like aspect very unlike the neighboring farms. The number of houses, too, conspired to give it advantage over the neighboring farms. It was called by the slaves the *Great House Farm*. Few privileges were esteemed higher, by the slaves of the out-farms, than that of being selected to do errands at the Great House Farm. It was associated in their minds with greatness. A Representative could not be prouder of his election to a seat in the American Congress, than a slave on one of the out-farms would be of his election to do errands at the Great House Farm. They regarded it as evidence of great confidence reposed in them by their overseers; and it was on this account, as well as a constant desire to be out of the field from under the driver's lash, that they esteemed it a high privilege, one worth careful living for. He was called the smartest and most trusty fellow, who has this honor conferred upon him the most frequently. The competitors for this office sought as diligently to please their overseers, as the office-seekers in the political parties seek to please and deceive the People. The same traits of character might be seen in Col. Lloyd's slaves, as are seen in the slaves of the political parties.

"The slaves selected to go to the Great House Farm, for the monthly allowance for themselves and their fellow slaves, were peculiarly enthusiastic. While on their way, they would make the dense old woods for miles around, reverberate with their wild songs, revealing at once the highest joy and the deepest sadness. They would compose and sing as they went along, consulting neither time nor tune. The thought that came up, came out—if not in the word, in the sound;—and as frequently in the one as in the other. They would sometimes sing the most pathetic sentiment in the most rapturous tone, and the most rapturous sentiment in the most pathetic tone. Into all their songs they would manage to weave something of the Great House Farm. Especially would they do this when leaving home. They would then sing most exultingly the following words:

'I am going away to the Great House Farm!
O, yea! O, yea! O!'

This they would sing, as a chorus, to words which to many would seem unmeaning jargon, but which nevertheless, were full of meaning to themselves. I have sometimes thought that the mere hearing of those songs would do more to impress some minds with the horrible character of Slavery, than the reading of whole volumes of philosophy on the subject could do.

"I did not, when a slave, understand the deep meaning of those rude and apparently incoherent songs. I was myself within the circle; so that I neither saw nor heard as those without might see and hear. They told a tale of wo which was then altogether beyond my feeble comprehension; they were tones loud, long and deep; they breathed the prayer and complaint of souls boiling over with the bitterest anguish. Every tone was a testimony against Slavery, and a prayer to God for deliverance from chains. The hearing of those wild notes always depressed my spirit, and filled me with ineffable sadness. I have frequently found myself in tears while hearing them. The mere recurrence to those songs, even now, afflicts me; and while I am writing these lines, an expression of feeling has already found its way down my cheek. To those songs I trace my first glimmering conception of the dehumanizing character of Slavery. I can never get rid of that conception. Those songs still follow me, to deepen my hatred of slavery, and quicken my sympathies for my brethren in bonds. If any one wishes to be impressed with the soul-killing effects of Slavery, let them go to Col. Lloyd's Plantation, and, on allowance day, place himself in the deep pine woods, and there let him, in silence, analyze the sounds that shall pass through the chambers of his soul,—and if he is not thus impressed, it will only be because 'there is no flesh in his obdurate heart.'

"I have often been utterly astonished, since I came to the North, to find persons who could speak of the singing among slaves as evidence of their contentment and happiness. It is impossible to conceive of a greater mistake. Slaves sing most when they are most unhappy. The songs of the slave represent the sorrows of his heart, and he is relieved by them, only as an aching heart is relieved by its tears. At least, such is my experience. I have often sung to drown my sorrow, but seldom to express my happiness. Crying for joy, and singing for joy, were alike uncommon to me while in the jaws of Slavery. The singing of a man cast away upon a desolate island might be as appropriately considered as evidence of contentment and happiness, as the singing of a slave; the songs of the one and of the other are prompted by the same emotion."

The Irish Character

In one of the eloquent passages quoted in The Tribune of Wednesday under the head "Spirit of the Irish Press," we find these words:

> "Domestic love, almost morbid from external suffering, prevents him (the Irishman) from becoming a fanatic and a misanthrope, and reconciles him to life."

This recalled to our mind the many touching instances known to us of such traits among the Irish we have seen here. We have seen instances of morbidness like this. A girl sent

THE IRISH CHARACTER   435

"home," after she was well established herself, for a young brother of whom she was particularly fond. He came, and, shortly after, died. She was so overcome by his loss, that she took poison and died. The great poet of serious England says, and we believe it to be his serious thought though laughingly said, "Men have died and worms have eaten them, but not for love." Whether or no death may follow from the loss of a lover or a child, we believe that among no people but the Irish would it upon loss of a young brother.

Another poor young woman, in the flower of her youth, denied herself, not only every pleasure, but almost the necessaries of life, to save the sum she thought ought to be hers before sending to Ireland for a widowed mother. Just as she was on the point of doing so, she heard that her mother had died fifteen months before. The keenness and persistence of her grief defy description. With a delicacy of feeling which shewed the native poetry of the Irish mind she dwelt, most of all, upon the thought that while she was working and pinching and dreaming of happiness with her mother, it was, indeed, but a dream, and that cherished parent lay still and cold in the ground. She felt fully the cruel cheat of fate. "Och, and she was dead all those times I was a thinking on her!" was the deepest note of her lament.

They are able, however, to make the sacrifice even of these intense family affections in a worthy cause. We knew a woman who postponed sending for her only child, whom she had left in Ireland, for years, while she maintained a sick friend who had none else to help her.

The poetry of which I have spoken shows itself even here, where they are separated from old romantic associations, and begin the new life in the new world by doing all its drudgery. We know flights of poetry repeated to us by those present at their wakes—passages of natural eloquence from the lamentations for the dead, more beautiful than those recorded in the annals of Britany or Roumelia.

It is the same genius, so exquisitely mournful, tender, and glowing too with the finest enthusiasm, that makes their national music, in these respects, the finest in the world. It is the music of the harp; its tones are deep and thrilling. It is the harp so beautifully described in "The harp of Tara's halls," a

436   NEW YORK SHORT PUBLISHED WORKS

song whose simple pathos is unsurpassed. A feeling was never more adequately embodied.

It is the genius which will enable Emmet's appeal to draw tears from the remotest generations, however much they may be strangers to the circumstances which called it forth. It is the genius which beamed in chivalrous loveliness through each act of Lord Edward Fitzgerald,—the genius which, ripened by English culture, favored by suitable occasions, has shed such glory on the land which has done all it could to quench it on the parent hearth.

When we consider all the fire which glows so untameably in Irish veins, the character of her people, considering the circumstances—almost miraculous in its goodness—we cannot forbear, notwithstanding all the temporary ills they aid in here, to give them all a welcome to our shores. Those ills we need not enumerate; they are known to all, and we rank among them what others would not, that by their ready service to do all the hard work they make it easier for the rest of the population to grow effeminate and help the country to grow too fast. But that is her destiny, to grow too fast; it is useless talking against it. Their extreme ignorance, their blind devotion to a priesthood, their pliancy in the hands of demagogues threaten continuance of these ills; yet, on the other hand, we must regard them as a most valuable element in the new race. They are looked upon with contempt for their want of aptitude at learning new things, their ready and ingenious lying, their eye-service. These are the faults of an oppressed race which must require the aid of better circumstances through two or three generations to eradicate. Their virtues are their own;—they are many, genuine, and deeply rooted. Can an impartial observer fail to admire their truth to domestic ties, their power of generous bounty and more generous gratitude, their indefatigable good humor, (for ages of wrong, which have driven them to so many acts of desperation, could never sour their blood at its source) their ready wit, their elasticity of nature. They are at bottom one of the best nations of the world.—Would they were welcomed here, not to work merely, but to intelligent sympathy and efforts, both patient and ardent for the education of their children. No sympathy could be better deserved, no efforts wiselier timed. Future Burkes and Currans would know how to give thanks for them, and Fitzgeralds rise upon the soil, which boasts the magnolia with its kingly stature and majestical white blossoms, to the same lofty and pure beauty. Will you not believe it, merely because that bog-bred youth you solaced in the mud-hole tells you lies and drinks to cheer him in those endless diggings? You are short-sighted, my friend; you do not look to the future, you will not turn your head to see what may have been the influences of the past; you have not examined your own breast to see whether the monitor there had not commanded you to do your part to counteract these influences, and yet the Irishman appeals to you eye to eye. He is very personal himself; he expects a personal interest from you. Nothing has been able to destroy this hope, which is the fruit of his nature. We were much touched by O'Connell's direct address to the Queen as "Lady," but she did not listen, and we fear few ladies and gentlemen will, till the prayers of destiny compels them. *

Review

TALES: By EDGAR A. POE. Wiley & Putnam's Library of American Books. No. II.

MR. Poe's tales need no aid of newspaper comment to give them popularity; they have secured it. We are glad to see them given to the public in this neat form, so that thousands more may be entertained by them without injury to their eye-sight.

No form of literary activity has so terribly degenerated among us as the tale. Now that every body who wants a new hat or bonnet takes this way to earn one from the magazines or annuals, we are inundated with the very flimsiest fabrics ever spun by mortal brain. Almost every person of feeling or fancy could supply a few agreeable and natural narratives, but when, instead of using their materials spontaneously, they set to work, with geography in hand, to find unexplored nooks of wild scenery in which to locate their Indians, or interesting farmers' daughters, or with some abridgement of history to hunt up monarchs or heroes yet unused to become the subjects of their crude coloring, the sale-work produced is a sad affair

438 NEW YORK SHORT PUBLISHED WORKS

indeed and "gluts the market" to the sorrow both of buyers and lookers-on.

In such a state of things, the writings of Mr. Poe are a refreshment, for they are the fruit of genuine observations and experience, combined with an invention, which is not "making up," as children call *their* way of contriving stories, but a penetration into the causes of things which leads to original but credible results. His narrative proceeds with vigor, his colors are applied with discrimination, and where the effects are fantastic they are not unmeaningly so.

The "Murders of the Rue Morgue" especially made a great impression upon those who did not know its author and were not familiar with his mode of treatment. Several of his stories make us wish he would enter the higher walk of the metaphysical novel, and, taking a mind of the self-possessed and deeply marked sort that suits him, give us a deeper and longer acquaintance with its life and the springs of its life than is possible in the compass of these tales.

As Mr. Poe is a professed critic, and of all the band the most unsparing to others, we are surprized to find some inaccuracies in the use of words, such as these "he had with him many books, but rarely *employed* them."—"His results have, in truth, the *whole air* of intuition."

The degree of skill shown in the management of revolting or terrible circumstances makes the pieces that have such subjects more interesting than the others. Even the failures are those of an intellect of strong fibre and well-chosen aim. *

The Wrongs of American Women
The Duty of American Women

THE same day brought us a copy of Mr. Burdett's little book, in which the sufferings and difficulties that beset the large class of women who must earn their subsistence in a city like New-York are delineated with so much simplicity, feeling and exact adherence to the facts—and a printed circular containing proposals for immediate practical adoption of the plan more fully described in a book published some weeks since under the title "The Duty of American Women to their Country," which

THE WRONGS OF AMERICAN WOMEN 439

was ascribed alternately to Mrs. Stone and Miss Catherine Beecher, but of which we understand both those ladies decline the responsibility. The two matters seemed linked with one another by natural piety. Full acquaintance with the wrong must call forth all manner of inventions for its redress.

The Circular, in showing the vast want that already exists of good means for instructing the children of this nation, especially in the West, states also the belief that among women, as being less immersed in other cares and toils, from the preparation it gives for their task as mothers, and from the necessity in which a great proportion stand of earning a subsistence somehow, at least during the years which precede marriage, if they *do* marry, must the number of teachers wanted be found, which is estimated already at *sixty thousand.*

We cordially sympathize with these views.

Much has been written about Woman's keeping within her sphere, which is defined as the domestic sphere. As a little girl she is to learn the lighter family duties, while she acquires that limited acquaintance with the realm of literature and science that will enable her to superintend the instruction of children in their earliest years. It is not generally proposed that she should be sufficiently instructed and developed to understand the pursuits or aims of her future husband; she is not to be a helpmeet to him, in the way of companionship or counsel, except in the care of his house and children. Her youth is to be passed partly in learning to keep house and the use of the needle, partly in the social circle where her manners may be formed, ornamental accomplishments perfected and displayed, and the husband found who shall give her the domestic sphere for which exclusively she is to be prepared.

Were the destiny of Woman thus exactly marked out, did she invariably retain the shelter of a parent's or a guardian's roof till she married, did marriage give her a sure home and protector, were she never liable to be made a widow, or, if so, sure of finding immediate protection from a brother or new husband, so that she might never be forced to stand alone one moment, and were her mind given for this world only, with no faculties capable of eternal growth and infinite improvement, we would still demand for her a far wider and more generous culture than is proposed by those who so anxiously define her

NEW YORK SHORT PUBLISHED WORKS

sphere. We would demand it that she might not ignorantly or frivolously thwart the designs of her husband, that she might be the respected friend of her sons no less than her daughters, that she might give more refinement, elevation and attraction to the society which is needed to give the characters of *men* polish and plasticity—no less so than to save them from vicious and sensual habits. But the most fastidious critic on the departure of Woman from her sphere, can scarcely fail to see at present that a vast proportion of the sex, if not the better half, do not, CANNOT, have this domestic sphere. Thousands and scores of thousands in this country no less than in Europe are obliged to maintain themselves alone. Far greater numbers divide with their husbands the care of earning a support for the family. In England, now, the progress of society has reached so admirable a pitch that the position of the sexes is frequently reversed, and the husband is obliged to stay at home and "mind the house and bairns" while the wife goes forth to the employment she alone can secure.

We readily admit that the picture of this is most painful—that Nature made entirely an opposite distribution of functions between the sexes. We believe the natural order to be the best, and that, if it could be followed in an enlightened spirit, it would bring to Woman all she wants, no less for her immortal than her mortal destiny. We are not surprised that men, who do not look deeply or carefully at causes or tendencies, should be led by disgust at the hardened, hackneyed characters which the present state of things too often produces in women to such conclusions as they are. We, no more than they, delight in the picture of the poor woman digging in the mines in her husband's clothes. We, no more than they, delight to hear their voices shrilly raised in the market-place, whether of apples or celebrity. But we see that at present they must do as they do for bread. Hundreds and thousands must step out of that hallowed domestic sphere, with no choice but to work or steal, or belong to men, not as wives, but as the wretched slaves of sensuality.

And this transition state, with all its revolting features, indicates, we do believe, the approach of a nobler era than the world has yet known. We trust that by the stress and emergencies of the present and coming time, the minds of women will be formed to more reflection and higher purposes than

THE WRONGS OF AMERICAN WOMEN 441

heretofore—their latent powers developed, their characters strengthened and eventually beautified and harmonized. Should the state of society then be such that each may remain, as Nature seems to have intended, the tutelary genius of a home, while men manage the out-door business of life, both may be done with a wisdom, a mutual understanding and respect unknown at present. Men will be no less the gainers by this than women, finding in pure and more religious marriages the joys of friendship and love combined—in their mothers and daughters better instruction, sweeter and nobler companionship, and in society at large an excitement to their finer powers and feelings unknown at present except in the region of the fine arts.

Blest be the generous, the wise among them who seek to forward hopes like these, instead of struggling against the fiat of Providence and the march of Fate to bind down rushing Life to the standard of the Past. Such efforts are vain, but those who make them are unhappy and unwise.

It is not, however, to such that we address ourselves, but to those who seek to make the best of things as they are, while they also strive to make them better. Such persons will have seen enough of the state of things in London, Paris, New-York, and manufacturing regions every where, to feel that there is an imperative necessity for opening more avenues of employment to women, and fitting them better to enter them, rather than keeping them back. Women have invaded many of the trades and some of the professions. Sewing, to the present killing extent, they cannot long bear. Factories seem likely to afford them permanent employment. In the culture of fruit, flowers and vegetables, even in the sale of them, we rejoice to see them engaged. In domestic service they will be aided, but can never be supplanted, by machinery. As much room as there is here for woman's mind and woman's labor will always be filled. A few have usurped the martial province, but these must always be few; the nature of woman is opposed to war. It is natural enough to see "Female Physicians," and we believe that the lace cap and work-bag are as much at home here as the wig and gold-headed cane. In the priesthood they have from all time shared more or less—in many eras more than at the present. We believe there has been no female lawyer, and probably will be none. The pen, many of the fine arts they have made their own, and, in the more refined countries of the world, as writers, as musicians, as painters, as actors, women occupy as advantageous ground as men. Writing and music may be esteemed professions for them more than any other.

But there are two others where the demand must invariably be immense, and for which they are naturally better fitted than men, for which we should like to see them better prepared and better rewarded than they are. These are the professions of nurse to the sick and of teacher. The first of these professions we have warmly desired to see dignified. It is a noble one, now most unjustly regarded in the light of menial service. It is one which no menial, no servile nature can fitly occupy. We were rejoiced when an intelligent lady of Massachusetts made the refined heroine of a little romance select that calling. This lady (Mrs. George Lee) has looked on society with unusual largeness of spirit and healthiness of temper. She is well acquainted with the world of conventions, but sees beneath it the world of nature. She is a generous writer and unpretending, as the generous are wont to be. We do not recall the name of the tale, but the circumstance above mentioned marks its temper. We hope to see the time when the refined and cultivated will choose this profession and learn it, not only through experience under the direction of the doctor, but by acquainting themselves with the laws of matter and of mind, so that all they do shall be intelligently done, and afford them the means of developing intelligence as well as the nobler, tenderer feelings of humanity; for even the last part of the benefit they cannot receive if their work be done in a selfish or mercenary spirit.

The other profession is that of teacher, for which women are peculiarly adapted by their nature, superiority in tact, quickness of sympathy, gentleness, patience, and a clear and animated manner in narration or description. To form a good teacher should be added to this sincere modesty combined with firmness, liberal views with a power and will to liberalize them still further, a good method and habits of exact and thorough investigation. In the two last requisites women are generally deficient, but there are now many shining examples to prove that if they are immethodical and superficial as teachers it is because it is the custom so to teach them, and that when aware of these faults they can and will correct them.

THE WRONGS OF AMERICAN WOMEN 443

The profession is of itself an excellent one for the improvement of the teacher during that interim between youth and maturity when the mind needs testing, tempering, and to review and rearrange the knowledge it has acquired. The natural method of doing this for one's self is to attempt teaching others; those years also are the best of the practical teacher. The teacher should be near the pupil both in years and feelings—no oracle, but the elder brother or sister of the pupil. More experience and years form the lecturer and the director of studies, but injure the powers as to familiar teaching.

These are just the years of leisure in the lives even of those women who are to enter the domestic sphere, and this calling most of all compatible with a constant progress as to qualifications for that.

Viewing the matter thus it may well be seen that we should hail with joy the assurance that sixty thousand *female* teachers are wanted, and more likely to be, and that a plan is projected which looks wise, liberal and generous, to afford the means of those whose hearts answer to this high calling obeying their dictates.

The plan is to have Cincinnati for a central point, where teachers shall be for a short time received, examined and prepared for their duties. By mutual agreement and coöperation of the various sects funds are to be raised and teachers provided according to the wants and tendencies of the various locations now destitute. What is to be done for them centrally, is for suitable persons to examine into their various kinds of fitness, communicate some general views whose value has been tested, and counsel adapted to the difficulties and advantages of their new positions. The Central Committee are to have the charge of raising funds and finding teachers and places where teachers are wanted.

The passage of thoughts, teachers and funds will be from East to West, the course of sunlight upon this earth.

The plan is offered as the most extensive and pliant means of doing a good and preventing ill to this nation, by means of a national education, whose normal school shall have an invariable object in the search after truth and the diffusion of the means of knowledge, while its form shall be plastic according to the wants of the time. This normal school promises to have good

444 NEW YORK SHORT PUBLISHED WORKS

effects, for it proposes worthy aims through simple means, and the motive for its formation and support seems to be disinterested philanthropy.

It promises to eschew the bitter spirit of sectarianism and proselytism, else we, for one party, could have nothing to do with it. Men, no doubt, have been oftentimes kept from absolute famine by the wheat with which such tares are mingled; but we believe the time is come when a purer and more generous food is to be offered to the people at large. We believe the aim of all education to be to rouse the mind to action, show it the means of discipline and of information: then leave it free, with God, Conscience, and the love of Truth for its guardians and teachers. Wo be to those who sacrifice these aims of universal and eternal value to the propagation of a set of opinions. But on this subject we can accept such doctrine as is offered by Rev. Calvin Stowe, one of the committee, in the following passage:

"In judicious practice, I am persuaded there will seldom be any very great difficulty, especially if there be excited in the community anything like a whole-hearted honesty and enlightened sincerity in the cause of public instruction.

"It is all right for people to suit their own taste and convictions in respect to sect; and by fair means and at proper times to teach their children and those under their influence to prefer the denominations which they prefer; but farther than this no one has any right to go. It is all wrong to hazard the well being of the soul, to jeopardize great public interests for the sake of advancing the interests of a sect. People must learn to practise some self-denial, on Christian principles, in respect to their denominational preferences, as well as in respect to other things, before pure Religion can ever gain a complete victory over every form of human selfishness."

The persons who propose themselves to the examination and instruction of the teachers at Cincinnati, till the plan shall be sufficiently under weigh to provide regularly for the office, are Mrs. Stowe and Miss Catherine Beecher, ladies well known to fame, as possessing unusual qualifications for the task.

As to finding abundance of teachers, who that reads this little book of Mr. Burdett's, or the account of the compensation of female labor in New-York, and the hopeless, comfortless, useless, pernicious lives those who have even the advantage of getting work must live with the sufferings and almost inevitable degradation to which those who cannot are exposed, but must long to match such as are capable of this better profession, and among the multitude there must be many who are or could be made so, from their present toils and make them free and the means of freedom and growth to others.

To many books on such subjects, among others to "Woman in the Nineteenth Century," the objection has been made that they exhibit ills without specifying any practical means for their remedy. The writer of the last named essay does indeed think that it contains one great rule which, if laid to heart, would prove a practical remedy for many ills, and of such daily and hourly efficacy in the conduct of life that any extensive observance of it for a single year would perceptibly raise the tone of thought, feeling and conduct throughout the civilized world. But to those who ask not only such a principle, but an external method for immediate use, we say, here is one proposed that looks noble and promising, the proposers offer themselves to the work with heart and hand, with time and purse: Go ye and do likewise.

Those who wish details as to this plan, will find them in the "Duty of American Women to their Country," published by Harper & Brothers, Cliff-st. The publishers may, probably, be able to furnish also the Circular to which we have referred. At a leisure day we shall offer some suggestions and remarks as to the methods and objects there proposed. *

Review

POEMS. By HENRY WADSWORTH LONGFELLOW; with Illustrations by D. HUNTINGTON. Philadelphia: Carey & Hart, Chesnut-st. 1845.

POETRY is not a superhuman or supernatural gift. It is, on the contrary, the fullest and therefore most completely natural expression of what is human.—It is that of which the rudiments lie in every human breast, but developed to a more complete existence than the obstructions of daily life permit, clothed in an adequate form, domesticated in nature by the use of apt images, the perception of grand analogies, and set to the music of the spheres for the delight of all who have ears to hear. We have uttered these remarks, which may, to many of our readers, seem truisms, for the sake of showing that our definition of poetry is large enough to include all kinds of excellence. It includes not only the great bards, but the humblest minstrels. The great bards bring to light the more concealed treasures, gems which centuries have been employed in forming and which it is their office to reveal, polish and set for the royal purposes of man; the wandering minstrel with his lighter but beautiful office calls the attention of men to the meaning of the flowers, which also is hidden from the careless eye, though they have grown and bloomed in full sight of all who chose to look. All the poets are the priests of Nature, though the greatest are also the prophets of the manhood of man.—For, when fully grown, the life of man must be all poetry; each of his thoughts will be a key to the treasures of the universe; each of his acts a revelation of beauty, his language will be music, and his habitual presence will overflow with more energy and inspire with a nobler rapture than do the fullest strains of lyric poetry now.

Meantime we need poets; men more awakened to the wonders of life and gifted more or less with a power to express what they see, and to all who possess, in any degree, those requisites we offer and we owe welcome and tribute, whether the place of their song be in the Pantheon, from which issue the grand decrees of immortal thought, or by the fireside, where hearts need kindling and eyes need clarifying by occasional drops of nectar in their tea.

But this—this alone we claim, and can welcome none who cannot present this title to our hearing; that the vision be genuine, the expression spontaneous. No imposition upon our young fellow citizens of pinchbeck for gold! they must have the true article, and pay the due intellectual price, or they will wake from a life-long dream of folly to find themselves beggars.

And never was a time when satirists were more needed to scourge from Parnassus the magpies who are devouring the food scattered there for the singing birds. There will always be a good deal of mock poetry in the market with the genuine; it grows up naturally as tares among the wheat, and, while there is a fair proportion preserved, we abstain from severe weeding lest the

POEMS BY LONGFELLOW 447

two come up together; but when the tares have almost usurped the field, it is time to begin and see if the field cannot be freed from them and made ready for a new seed-time.

The rules of versification are now understood and used by those who have never entered into that soul from which metres grow as acorns from the oak, shapes as characteristic of the parent tree, containing in like manner germs of limitless life for the future. And as to the substance of these jingling rhymes, and dragging, stumbling rhythms, we might tell of bombast, or still worse, an affected simplicity, sickly sentiment, or borrowed dignity; but it is sufficient to comprise all in this one censure. The writers did not write because they felt obliged to relieve themselves of the swelling thought within, but as an elegant exercise which may win them rank and reputation above the crowd. Their lamp is not lit by the sacred and inevitable lightning from above, but carefully fed by their own will to be seen of men.

There are very few now rhyming in England, not obnoxious to this censure, still fewer in our America. For such no laurel blooms. May the friendly poppy soon crown them and grant us stillness to hear the silver tones of genuine music, for, if such there be, they are at present almost stifled by these fifes and gongs.

Yet there is a middle class, composed of men of little original poetic power, but of much poetic taste and sensibility, whom we would not wish to have silenced. They do no harm but much good, (if only their minds are not confounded with those of a higher class,) by educating in others the faculties dominant in themselves. In this class we place the writer at present before us.

We must confess to a coolness toward Mr. Longfellow, in consequence of the exaggerated praises that have been bestowed upon him. When we see a person of moderate powers receive honors which should be reserved for the highest, we feel somewhat like assailing him and taking from him the crown which should be reserved for grander brows. And yet this is, perhaps, ungenerous. It may be that the management of publishers, the hyperbole of paid or undiscerning reviewers, or some accidental cause which gives a temporary interest to productions beyond what they would permanently command, have raised such an one to a place as much above his wishes as

NEW YORK SHORT PUBLISHED WORKS

his claims, and which he would rejoice, with honorable modesty, to vacate at the approach of one worthier. We the more readily believe this of Mr. Longfellow, as one so sensible to the beauties of other writers and so largely indebted to them, *must* know his own comparative rank better than his readers have known it for him.

And yet so much adulation is dangerous. Mr. Longfellow, so lauded on all hands—now able to collect his poems which have circulated so widely in previous editions, and been paid for so handsomely by the handsomest annuals, in this beautiful volume, illustrated by one of the most distinguished of our younger artists—has found a flatterer in that very artist. The portrait which adorns this volume is not merely flattered or idealized, but there is an attempt at adorning it by expression thrown into the eyes with just that which the original does not possess, whether in face or mind. We have often seen faces whose usually coarse and heavy lineaments were harmonized at times into beauty by the light that rises from the soul into the eyes. The intention Nature had with regard to the face and its wearer, usually eclipsed beneath bad habits or a bad education, is then disclosed and we see what hopes Death has in store for that soul. But here the enthusiasm thrown into the eyes only makes the rest of the face look more weak, and the idea suggested is the anomalous one of a Dandy Pindar.

Such is not the case with Mr. Longfellow himself. He is never a Pindar, though he is sometimes a Dandy even in the clean and elegantly ornamented streets and trim gardens of his verse. But he is still more a man of cultivated taste, delicate though not deep feeling, and some, though not much, poetic force.

Mr. Longfellow has been accused of plagiarism. We have been surprised that any one should have been anxious to fasten special charges of this kind upon him, when we had supposed it so obvious that the greater part of his mental stores were derived from the works of others. He has no style of his own growing out of his own experiences and observations of nature. Nature with him, whether human or external, is always seen through the windows of literature. There are in his poems sweet and tender passages descriptive of his personal feelings, but very few showing him as an observer, at first hand, of the passions within, or the landscape without.

POEMS BY LONGFELLOW 449

This want of the free breath of nature, this perpetual borrowing of imagery, this excessive, because superficial, culture which he has derived from an acquaintance with the elegant literature of many nations and men out of proportion to the experience of life within himself, prevent Mr. Longfellow's verses from ever being a true refreshment to ourselves. He says in one of his most graceful verses:

> From the cool cisterns of the midnight air
>   My spirit drank repose;
> The fountain of perpetual peace flows there,
>   From those deep cisterns flows.

Now this is just what we cannot get from Mr. Longfellow. No solitude of the mind reveals to us the deep cisterns.

Let us take, for example of what we do not like, one of his worst pieces, the Prelude to the Voices of the Night—

> Beneath some patriarchal tree
>   I lay upon the ground;
> His hoary arms uplifted be,
>   And all the broad leaves over me
>   Clapped their little hands in glee
>   With one continuous sound.

What an unpleasant mixture of images! Such never rose in a man's mind, as he lay on the ground and looked up to the tree above him. The true poetry for this stanza would be to give us an image of what was in the writer's mind as he lay there and looked up. But this idea of the leaves clapping their little hands with glee is taken out of some book; or, at any rate, is a book thought and not one that came in the place, and jars entirely with what is said of the tree uplifting its hoary arms. Then take this other stanza from a man whose mind *should* have grown up in familiarity with the American *genius loci*.

> Therefore at Pentecost, which brings
>   The Spring clothed like a bride,
> When nestling buds unfold their wings,
> And bishop's caps have golden rings,
> Musing upon many things,
>   I sought the woodlands wide.

450   NEW YORK SHORT PUBLISHED WORKS

Musing upon many things—ay! and upon many books too, or we should have nothing of Pentecost or bishop's caps with their golden rings. For ourselves, we have not the least idea what bishop's caps are;—are they flowers?—or what? Truly, the schoolmaster was abroad in the woodlands that day! As to the conceit of the wings of the buds, it is a false image, because one that cannot be carried out. Such will not be found in the poems of poets; with such the imagination is all compact, and their works are not dead mosaics, with substances inserted merely because pretty, but living growths, homogeneous and satisfactory throughout.

Such instances could be adduced every where throughout the poems, depriving us of any clear pleasure from any one piece, and placing his poems beside such as these of Bryant in the same light as that of the prettiest *made* shell, beside those whose every line and hue tells a history of the action of winds and waves and the secrets of one class of organizations.

But, do we, therefore esteem Mr. Longfellow a wilful or conscious plagiarist? By no means. It is his misfortune that other men's thoughts are so continually in his head as to overshadow his own. The order of fine development is for the mind the same as the body, to take in just so much food as will sustain it in its exercise and assimilate with its growth. If it is so assimilated— if it becomes a part of the skin, hair and eyes of the man, it is his own, no matter whether he pick it up in the wood, or borrow from the dish of a fellow man, or receive it in the form of manna direct from Heaven. "Do you ask the genius" said Goethe "to give an account of what he has taken from others. As well demand of the hero an account of the beeves and loaves which have nourished him to such martial stature."

But Mr. Longfellow presents us, not with a new product in which all the old varieties are melted into a fresh form, but rather with a tastefully arranged Museum, between whose glass cases are interspersed neatly potted rose trees, geraniums and hyacinths, grown by himself with aid of in-door heat. Still we must acquit him of being a willing or conscious plagiarist. Some objects in the collection are his own; as to the rest, he has the merit of appreciation, and a reärrangement, not always judicious, but the result of feeling on his part.

POEMS BY LONGFELLOW 451

Such works as Mr. Longfellow's we consider injurious only if allowed to usurp the place of better things. The reason of his being overrated here, is because through his works breathes the air of other lands with whose products the public at large is but little acquainted. He will do his office, and a desirable one, of promoting a taste for the literature of these lands before his readers are aware of it. As a translator he shows the same qualities as in his own writings; what is forcible and compact he does not render adequately, grace and sentiment he appreciates and reproduces. Twenty years hence when he stands upon his own merits, he will rank as a writer of elegant, if not always accurate taste, of great imitative power, and occasional felicity in an original way, where his feelings are really stirred. He has touched no subject where he has not done somewhat that is pleasing, though also his poems are much marred by ambitious failings. As instances of his best manner we would mention "The Reaper and the Flowers," "Lines to the Planet Mars," "A Gleam of Sunshine," and "The Village Blacksmith." His two ballads are excellent imitations, yet in them is no spark of fire. In "Nuremberg" are charming passages. Indeed the whole poem is one of the happiest specimens of Mr. L.'s poetic feeling, taste and tact in making up a rosary of topics and images.— Thinking it may be less known than most of the poems we will quote it. The engraving which accompanies it of the rich old architecture is a fine gloss on its contents.

Nuremberg

In the valley of the Pegnitz, where across broad meadow lands
Rise the blue Franconian mountains, Nuremberg, the ancient,
    stands.

Quaint old town of toil and traffic—quaint old town of art and
    song—
Memories haunt thy pointed gables, like the rooks that round them
    throng;

Memories of the Middle Ages, when the Emperors, rough and
    bold,
Had their dwelling in thy castle, time-defying, centuries old;

And thy brave and thrifty burghers boasted in their uncouth
    rhyme,
That their great imperial city stretched its hand through every clime.

In the court-yard of the castle, bound with many an iron band,
Stands the mighty linden, planted by Queen Cunigunde's hand.

On the square the oriel window, where in old heroic days,
Sat the poet Melchior, singing Kaiser Maximilian's praise.

Every where I see around me rise the wondrous world of Art—
Fountains wrought with richest sculpture, standing in the common
    mart;

And above cathedral doorways, saints and bishops carved in stone,
By a former age commissioned as apostles to our own.

In the church of sainted Sebald sleeps enshrined his holy dust,
And in bronze the Twelve Apostles guard from age to age their trust;

In the church of sainted Lawrence stands a Pix of sculpture rare,
Like the foamy sheaf of fountains, rising through the painted air.

Here, when Art was still Religion, with a simple reverent heart,
Lived and labored Albert Durer, the Evangelist of Art;

Hence in silence and in sorrow, toiling still with busy hand,
Like an emigrant he wandered, seeking for the Better Land.

Emigravit is the inscription on the tomb-stone where he lies;
Dead he is not, but departed, for the Artist never dies.

Fairer seems the ancient city, and the sunshine seems more fair,
That he once has trod its pavement—that he once has breathed its
    air!

Through these streets so broad and stately, these obscure and
    dismal lanes,
Walked of yore the Master-singers, chanting rude poetic strains.

From remote and sunless suburbs came they to the friendly guild,
Building nests in Fame's great temple, as in spouts the swallows
    build.

POEMS BY LONGFELLOW   453

As the weaver plied the shuttle, wove he too the mystic rhyme,
And the smith his iron measures hammered to the anvil's chime;

Thanking God, whose boundless wisdom makes the flowers of
        poesy bloom
In the forge's dust and cinders—in the tissues of the loom.

Here Hans Sachs, the cobbler-poet, laureate of the gentle craft,
Wisest of the Twelve Wise Masters, in huge folios sang and laughed.

But his house is now an ale-house, with a nicely sanded floor,
And a garland in the window, and his face above the door;

Painted by some humble artist, as in Adam Paschman's song,
As the old man, gray and dove-like, with his great beard white and
        long.

And at night the swart mechanic comes to drown his cank and care,
Quaffing ale from pewter tankards in the master's antique chair.

Vanished is the ancient splendor, and before my dreamy eye
Wave these mingling shapes and figures, like a faded tapestry.

Not thy Councils, not thy Kaisers, win for thee the world's regard;
But thy painter, Albert Durer, and Hans Sachs, thy cobbler bard.

Thus, oh, Nuremberg! a wanderer from a region far away,
As he paced thy streets and court-yards, sang in thought his careless
        lay;

Gathering from the pavement's crevice, as a flow'ret of the soil,
The nobility of labor, the long pedigree of toil.

This image of the thought gathered like a flower from the
crevice of the pavement, is truly natural and poetical.

Here is another image which came into the mind of the
writer as he looked at the subject of his verse, and which pleases
accordingly. It is from one of the new poems, addressed to
Driving Cloud, "chief of the mighty Omahaws."

Wrapt in thy scarlet blanket I see thee stalk through the city's
Narrow and populous streets, as once by the margin of rivers
Stalked those birds unknown, that have left us only their foot-prints.

454   NEW YORK SHORT PUBLISHED WORKS

What, in a few short years, will remain of thy race but the
foot-prints?

Here is another very graceful and natural simile:

> A feeling of sadness and longing,
>   That is not akin to pain,
> And resembles sorrow only
>   As the mist resembles rain.

Another—

> I will forget her! All dear recollections,
> Pressed in my heart like flowers within a book,
> Shall be torn out and scattered to the winds.

The Drama from which this is taken is an elegant exercise
of the pen, after the fashion of the best models. Plan, figures,
all are academical. It is a faint reflex of the actions and passions
of men, tame in the conduct and lifeless in the characters, but
not heavy, and containing good meditative passages.

And now farewell to the handsome book, with its Preciosos
and Preciosas, its Vikings and knights, and cavaliers, its flowers
of all climes, and wild flowers of none. We have not wished to
depreciate those writings below their current value more than
truth absolutely demands. We have not forgotten that, if a man
cannot himself sit at the feet of the Muse, it is much if he prizes
those who may; it makes him a teacher to the people. Neither
have we forgotten that Mr. Longfellow has a genuine respect
for his pen, never writes carelessly, nor when he does not wish
to, nor for money alone. Nor are we intolerant to those who
prize hot-house bouquets beyond all the free beauty of nature;
that helps the gardener and has its uses. But still let us not
forget—Excelsior!! *

Review

THE POETICAL WORKS OF PERCY BYSSHE SHELLEY: First Amerian
Edition, (complete,) with some remarks on the Poetical Faculty
and its Influence on Human Destiny; embracing a Biographical and

Critical Notice, by G. G. FOSTER. New-York: J. S. Redfield, Clinton Hall.

WE are very glad to see this handsome copy of Shelley ready for those who have long been vainly inquiring at all the book-stores for such an one.

In Europe the fame of Shelley has risen superior to the clouds that darkened its earlier days, hiding this true image from his fellow men,—and from his own sad eyes oftentimes the common light of day. As a thinker, men have learnt to pardon what they consider errors in opinion for the sake of singular nobleness, purity and love in his main tendency or spirit. As a poet, the many faults of his works having been acknowledged, there is room and place to admire his far more numerous and exquisite beauties.

The heart of the man few, who have hearts of their own, refuse to reverence, and many, even of devoutest Christians would not refuse the book which contains Queen Mab as a Christmas gift.—For it has been recognized that the founder of the Christian Church would have suffered one to come unto him, who was in faith and love so truly what he sought in a disciple, without regard to the form his doctrine assumed.

The qualities of his poetry have often been analyzed, and the severer critics, impatient of his exuberance, or unable to use their accustomed spectacles in the golden mist that broods over all he has done, deny him high honors, but the soul of aspiring youth, untrammeled by the canons of taste, and untamed by scholarly discipline, swells into rapture at his lyric sweetness, finds ambrosial refreshment from his plenteous fancies, catches fire at his daring thought, and melts into boundless weeping at his tender sadness,—the sadness of a soul betrothed to an Ideal unattainable in this present sphere.

For ourselves we dispute not with the *doctrinaires* or the critics. We cannot speak dispassionately of an influence that has been so dear to us. Nearer than the nearest companions of life actual has Shelley been to us. Many other great ones have shone upon us, and all who ever did so shine are still resplendent in our firmament, for our mental life has not been broken and contradictory, but thus far we "see what we foresaw." But Shelley seemed to us an incarnation of what was sought in the

456   NEW YORK SHORT PUBLISHED WORKS

sympathies and desires of instinctive life, a light of dawn, and a foreshowing of the weather of this day.

When still in childish years fell in our way the "Hymn to Intellectual Beauty." In a green meadow, skirted by a rich wood, watered by a lovely rivulet, made picturesque by a mill a little farther down, sat a party of young persons gayer than and almost as inventive as those that told the tales recorded by Boccaccio. They were passing a few days in a scene of deep seclusion there uncared for by tutor or duenna, and with no bar of routine to check the pranks of their gay, childish fancies. Every day they assumed parts which through the waking hours must be acted out. One day it was the characters in one of Richardson's novels, and most solemnly we "my deared" each other with richest brocade of affability, and interchanged in long stiff phrase our sentimental secrets and prim opinions. But to-day we sought relief in personating birds or insects, and now it was the Libellula who, tired of wild flitting and darting, rested on the grassy bank and read aloud the "Hymn to Intellectual Beauty" torn by chance from the leaf of a foreign magazine.

It was one of these chances which we ever remember as the interposition of some good angel in our fate. Solemn tears marked the change of mood in our little party, and with the words

"Have I not kept my vow?"

began a chain of thoughts, whose golden links still bind the years together.

Two or three years after it was frosty Christmas as now;— the trees cracked with their splendid burden of ice, the old wooden country house was banked up with high drifts of the beautiful snow, when the Libellula became the owner of Shelley's poems. It was her Christmas box, and for three days and three nights she ceased not to extract its sweets, and how familiar still in memory every object seen from the chair in which she sat enchanted there three days, memorable to her as those of July to the French nation. The fire, the position of the lamp, the variegated shadows of that alcoved room, the stars winter bright, up to which she looked with such a feeling of

THE POETICAL WORKS OF SHELLEY   457

congeniality from the contemplation of this starry soul,—O could but a De Quincey describe those days in which the bridge between the real and ideal rose unbroken! He would not do it, though, as *Suspiria de Profundis*, but as sighs of joy upon the mountain hight.

The poems we read then are what every one still reads, the "Julian and Maddalo" with its profound revelations of the inward life,—"Alastor," the soul sweeping like a breeze through nature,—and some of the minor poems, "Queen Mab," the "Prometheus" and other more formal works we have not been able to read much. It was not when he tried to express opinions which the wrongs of the world had put into his head, but when he abandoned himself to the feelings which nature had implanted in his own breast that Shelley seemed to us so full of inspiration, and it is so still.

In reply to all that can be urged against him by people whom we do not wish to abuse, for surely "they know not what they do," we are wont simply to refer to the fact that he was the only man who redeemed the human race from suspicion to the embittered soul of Byron. "Why," said Byron, "he is a man who would willingly die for others. *I am sure of it.*"

Yes! balance that against all the ill you can think of him, that he was a man able to live wretched for the sake of speaking sincerely what he supposed to be truth, willing to die for the good of his fellows.

Mr. Foster has spoken well of him as a man:

"First, of the man, Shelley—of his sad experience of life—his fierce and bitter struggles with the storm which his own electric nature gathered about him—his weary battle, single handed, with a world in arms—there is little to be said in words; but that little is pregnant with deep meaning: it is the memoir of a hero and a prophet—a hero without outward and visible deeds of heroism—a prophet 'without honor in his own country,' or earnest audience any where on earth— who poured out the inspirations with which his soul was fraught, whether men would listen or no, and because he was impelled by a divine instinct, and could not forbear.

"Of Shelley's personal character, it is enough to say that it was wholly pervaded by the same unbounded and unquestioning love for his fellow men—the same holy and fervid hope in their ultimate virtue and happiness—the same scorn of baseness and hatred of oppression—which beam forth in all his writings with a pure and constant light. The theory which he wrote was the practice which his whole life exemplified. Noble, kind, generous, passionate, tender, with a courage greater than the courage of the chief of warriors, for it could *endure*—these were the qualities in which his life was embalmed."

Believing the poems are not generally known as it has so long been difficult to obtain copies, we make more words of ours superfluous by copious extracts. Take first what came to us first, and is in truth the Credo of the poet:

Hymn to Intellectual Beauty

The awful shadow of some unseen Power
   Floats, tho' unseen, among us; visiting
   This various world with as inconstant wing
As Summer winds that creep from flower to flower;
Like moonbeams that behind some piny mountain shower,
   It visits with inconstant glance
   Each human heart and countenance;
Like hues and harmonies of evening,
   Like clouds in starlight widely spread,
   Like memory of music fled,
   Like aught that for its grace may be
Dear, and yet dearer for its mystery.——

Spirit of BEAUTY, that dost consecrate
   With thine own hues all thou dost shine upon
   Of human thought or form, where art thou gone?
Why dost thou pass away, and leave our state,
This dim vast vale of tears, vacant and desolate?
   Ask why the sunlight not for ever
   Weaves rainbows o'er yon mountain river;
Why aught should fall and fade that once is shown;
   Why fear and dream and death and birth
   Cast on the daylight of this earth
   Such gloom, why Man has such a scope
For love and hate, despondency and hope?

No voice from some sublimer world hath ever
   To sage or poet these responses given:
   Therefore the names of Demon, Ghost and Heaven
Remain the records of their vain endeavor:

THE POETICAL WORKS OF SHELLEY 459

Frail spells, whose uttered charm might not avail to sever,
  From all we hear and all we see,
  Doubt, chance and mutability.
Thy light alone, like mist o'er mountains driven,
  Or music by the night wind sent
  Through strings of some still instrument,
  Or moonlight on a midnight stream,
Gives grace and truth to Life's unquiet dream.

Love, Hope and Self-Esteem, like clouds, depart
  And come, for some uncertain moments lent.
  Man were immortal and omnipotent,
Didst thou, unknown and awful as thou art,
Keep with thy glorious train firm state within his heart,
  Thou messenger of sympathies
  That wax and wane in lovers' eyes;
Thou, that to human thought art nourishment,
  Like darkness to a dying flame!
  Depart not as thy shadow came;
  Depart not, lest the grave should be,
Like life and fear, a dark reality.

While yet a boy I sought for ghosts, and sped
  Through many a listening chamber, cave and ruin,
  And starlight wood, with fearful steps pursuing
Hopes of high talk with the departed dead.
I called on poisonous names with which our youth is fed:
  I was not heard; I saw them not;
  When musing deeply on the lot
Of life, at that sweet time when winds are wooing
  All vital things that wake to bring
  News of birds and blossoming,
  Sudden, thy shadow fell on me;
I shrieked, and clasped my hands in ecstasy!

I vowed that I would dedicate my powers
  To thee and thine: have I not kept the vow?
  With beating heart and streaming eyes, even now
I call the phantoms of a thousand hours
Each from his voiceless grave: they have in visioned bowers
  Of studious Zeal or Love's delight
  Outwatched with me the envious Night:
They know that never joy illumed my brow,

460 NEW YORK SHORT PUBLISHED WORKS

Unlinked with hope that thou wouldst free
This world from its dark slavery,
That thou, O awful LOVELINESS,
Wouldst live whate'er these words can not express.

The day becomes more solemn and serene
When noon is past: there is a harmony
In Autumn, and a lustre in its sky,
Which through the Summer is not heard nor seen
As if it could not be, as if it had not been!
Thus let thy power, which like the truth
Of nature on my passive youth
Descended, to my onward life supply
Its calm, to one who worships thee,
And every form containing thee,
Whom, SPIRIT fair, thy spells did bind
To fear himself, and love all human kind.

The following is happily expressive of his mild sweet grace:

Lines to a Critic

Honey from silkworms who can gather,
Or silk from the yellow bee?
The grass may grow in winter weather
As soon as hate in me.

Hate men who cant, and men who pray,
And men who rail like thee;
An equal passion to repay
They are not coy like me.

Or seek some slave of power and gold,
To be thy dear heart's mate;
Thy love will move that bigot cold,
Sooner than me thy hate.

A passion like the one I prove
Can not divided be;
I hate thy want of truth and love:
How should I then hate thee?

December, 1817.

THE POETICAL WORKS OF SHELLEY   461

Here is one of his Æolian Melodies:

The Past

Wilt thou forget the happy hours
Which we buried in Love's sweet bowers,
Heaping over their corpses cold
Blossoms and leaves, instead of mould?
Blossoms which were the joys that fell,
And leaves, the hopes that yet remain.

Forget the dead, the past? O yet
There are ghosts that may take revenge for it;
Memories that make the heart a tomb,
Regrets which glide through the spirit's gloom,
And with ghastly whispers tell
That joy, once lost, is pain.

The Hymns to Apollo and to Pan are among the finest specimens of his genius, and form a beautiful contrast one to the other:

Hymn of Apollo

The sleepless Hours who watch me as I lie,
    Curtained with star-enwoven tapestries,
From the broad moonlight of the sky,
    Fanning the busy dreams from my dim eyes—
Waken me when their mother, the grey Dawn,
Tells them that dreams and that the Moon is gone.

Then I arise, and climbing Heaven's blue dome,
    I walk over the mountains and the waves,
Leaving my robe upon the ocean foam;
    My footsteps pave the clouds with fire; the caves
Are filled with my bright presence, and the air
Leaves the green earth to my embraces bare.

The sunbeams are my shafts, with which I kill
    Deceit, that loves the night and fears the day;
All men who do or even imagine ill
    Fly me, and from the glory of my ray
Good minds and open actions take new might,
Until diminished by the reign of Night.

462 NEW YORK SHORT PUBLISHED WORKS

I feed the clouds, the rainbows and the flowers,
   With their ethereal colors; the Moon's globe
And the pure stars in their eternal bowers
   Are cinctured with my power as with a robe;
Whatever lamps on earth or heaven may shine,
Are portions of one power, which is mine.

I stand at noon upon the peak of heaven,
   Then with unwilling steps I wander down
Into the clouds of the Atlantic even;
   For grief that I depart they weep and frown:
What look is more delightful than the smile
With which I soothe them from the Western Isle?

I am the eye with which the Universe
   Beholds itself and knows itself divine;
All harmony of instrument or verse,
   All prophecy, all medicine are mine,
All light of Art or Nature; to my song
Victory and Praise in their own right belong.

Hymn of Pan

From the forests and highlands
    We come, we come;
From the river-girt islands,
    Where loud waves are dumb
      Listening to my sweet pipings.
The wind in the reeds and the rushes,
   The bees on the bells of thyme,
The birds on the myrtle-bushes,
   The cicale above in the lime,
And the lizards below in the grass,
Were as silent as ever old Tmolus* was,
      Listening to my sweet pipings.

Liquid Peneus was flowing,
    And all dark Tempe lay

---

*This and the former poem were written at the request of a friend, to be inserted in a Drama on the subject of Midas. Apollo and Pan contended before Tmolus for the prize in Music.

THE POETICAL WORKS OF SHELLEY

In Pelion's shadow, outgrowing
    The light of the dying day,
        Speeded with my sweet pipings.
The Sileni and Sylvans and Fauns,
    And the Nymphs of the woods and waves,
To the edge of the moist river-lawns,
    And the brink of the dewy caves,
And all that did then attend and follow,
Were silent with love, as you now, Apollo,
        With envy of my sweet pipings.

I sang of the dancing stars,
    I sang of the dædal Earth,
And of Heaven—and the giant wars,
    And Love and Death and Birth,
        And then I changed my pipings,
Singing how down the vale of Menalus
    I pursued a maiden and clasped a reed:
Gods and men, we are all deluded thus!
    It breaks in our bosom and then we bleed:
All wept, as I think both ye now would,
If envy or age had not frozen your blood,
        At the sorrow of my sweet pipings.

The opening of "Lines written among the Euganean Hills" and "Stanzas" p. 635 are among the profoundest as expressive of his mental struggles, and the latter is almost overpowering from the tearful depths it discloses. The sufferings of Shelley were those of a body in which the brain had been prematurely developed, a seeming gain of life always atoned for by a dreadful price of frequent dejection and morbid suffering which slower and more healthy natures cannot understand, of a heart overflowing with love, persecuted by hate of those it longed to serve, of a soul whose sight outwent that of its Age, and was therefore continually grieved by the shortcomings of others and its own. Still;—after life's fitful fever, he surely sleeps not, but transplanted to some congenial sphere grows and blooms free from canker, blight or frost. Even in his saddest hour he was sure of it.

The crane o'er seas and forests seeks her home;
No bird so wild but has its quiet nest,

464   NEW YORK SHORT PUBLISHED WORKS

> Whence it no more would roam;
> The sleepless billows on the ocean's breast,
> Burst like a bursting heart, and die in peace,
>   And thus at length find rest,
> Doubtless there *is* a place of peace,—

Such an one thou didst find, and now when thy life and its strivings lie before the world at sufficient distance for both motive and result to be seen, hard must be the heart indeed and Pharisaically seared the conscience of him who will dare to cast a stone at the monument of Shelley.

As to intellectual appreciation of the poems, what is said by Shelley himself of the way of regarding the imaginary author of one of them may apply to the whole.

"He had fitted up the ruins of an old building, where it was his hope to have realized a scheme of life suited perhaps to that happier and better world of which he is an inhabitant, but hardly practicable in this. His life was singular—less on account of the romantic vicissitudes which diversified it than the ideal tinge which it received from his own character and feelings. The present poem, like the 'Vita Nuova' of Dante, is sufficiently intelligible to a certain class of readers without a matter-of-fact history of the circumstances to which it relates; and to a certain other class it must ever remain incomprehensible from a defect of a common organ of perception for the ideas of which it treats. Not but that *gran vergogna sarebbe a colui, che rimasse cosa sotto veste di figura, o di colore rettorico: e domandato non sapesse denudare le sue parole da cotal veste, in guisa che avessero verace intendimento*." (Shame would it be indeed to the writer, if he took shelter under the garb of figures or the colors of rhetoric, and could not, on fitting occasion, lay bare the true meaning of his words.)

No such shame rests on Shelley. The web of his imagination was sometimes spun out to such delicate and filmy tissue that common hands could not touch without tearing it, but its lightest thread is vital with the life-blood of immortal Ideas.

On his monument might be placed this inscription, from his own verse:

> High, spirit-wingéd heart! who didst for ever
> Beat thine unfeeling bars with vain endeavor,

1st January, 1846

Till those bright plumes of thought, in which arrayed,
It over-soared this low and worldly shade,
Lay shattered; and thy panting, wounded breast
Stained with dear blood its unmaternal nest!
We weep vain tears: blood would less bitter be,
Yet poured forth gladlier, could it profit thee.

*

1st January, 1846

THE New Year dawns, and its appearance is hailed by a flutter of festivity. Men and women run from house to house, scattering gifts, smiles, and congratulations. It is a custom that seems borrowed from a better day, unless indeed it be a prophecy that such must come.

For why so much congratulation? A year has passed; we are nearer by a twelvemonth to the term of this earthly probation. It is a solemn thought, and though the consciousness of having hallowed the days by our best endeavor, and of having much occasion to look to the Ruling Power of all with grateful benediction, must, in cases where such feelings are unalloyed, bring joy, one would think it must even then be a grave joy, and one that would disincline to this loud gayety in welcoming a new year; another year,—in which we may, indeed, strive forward in a good spirit, and find our strivings blest, but must surely expect trials, temptations and disappointments from without, frailty, short coming or convulsion in ourselves.

If it be appropriate to a reflective habit of mind to ask with each night-fall the Pythagorean questions, how much more so at the close of the year!

> What hast thou done that's worth the doing?
> And what pursued that's worth pursuing?
> What sought thou knewest thou shouldst shun?
> What done thou shouldst have left undone?

The intellectual man will also ask, What new truths have been opened to me, or what facts presented that will lead to the discovery of truths?—The poet and the lover—What new forms of beauty have been presented for my delight, and as

466   NEW YORK SHORT PUBLISHED WORKS

memorable illustrations of the Divine presence,—unceasing, but oftentimes unfelt by our sluggish natures.

Are there many men who fail sometimes to ask themselves questions to this depth? who do not care to know whether they have done right or forborne to do wrong; whether their spirits have been enlightened by Truth or kindled by Beauty?

Yes! strange to say, there are many who, despite the natural aspirations of the soul and the revelations showered upon the world, think only whether they have made money, whether the world thinks more highly of them than it did in bygone years— whether wife and children have been in good bodily health, and what those who call to pay their respects and drink the New Year's coffee, will think of their carpets, new also.

How often is it that the rich man thinks even of that proposed by Dickens as the noblest employment of the season, making the poor happy in the way he likes best for himself, by distribution of turkey and plum pudding. Some, indeed, adorn the day with this much grace, though we doubt whether it be oftenest those who could each, with ease, make that one day a glimpse of comfort to a thousand who pass the other winter days in shivering poverty. But some such there are who go about to the dark and frosty dwellings, giving the "mite" where and when it is most needed. We knew a lady, all whose riches consisted in her good head and two hands, widow of an eminent lawyer, but keeping boarders for a livelihood, engaged in that hardest of occupations, with her house full and hands full, she yet found time to make and bake for New Year's day a hundred pies—and not the pie from which being eaten issued the famous four-and-twenty blackbirds gave more cause for merriment or was a fitter "dish to set before the King."

God bless his Majesty, the *good* King, who on such a day cares for the least as much as the greatest, and like Henry IV. proposes it as a worthy aim of his endeavor that "every poor man shall have his chicken in the pot." This does not seem, on superficial survey, such a wonderful boon to crave for creatures made in God's own likeness, yet is it one that no King could ever yet bestow on his subjects, if we except the King of Cockaigne. Our maker of the hundred pies is the best prophet we have seen as yet of such a blissful state.

1ST JANUARY, 1846   467

But mostly to him who hath is given in material as well as in spiritual things, and we fear the pleasures of this day are arranged almost wholly in reference to the beautiful, the healthy, the wealthy, the witty, and that but few banquets are prepared for the halt, the blind, and the sorrowful. But where they are, of a surety water turns to wine by inevitable Christ-power; no aid of miracle need be invoked. As for thoughts which should make an epoch of the period, we suppose the number of those to be in about the same proportion to the number of minds capable of thought that the pearls now existent bear to the oysters still subsistent.

Can we make pearls from our oyster-bed? At least, let us open some of the shells and try.

Dear Public and Friends! we wish you a happy New Year. We trust that the year past has given earnest of such an one in so far as having taught you somewhat how to deserve and to appreciate it.

For ourselves the months have brought much, though, perhaps, superficial instruction. Its scope has been chiefly Love and Hope for all human beings, and among others for thyself.

We have seen many fair poesies of human life, in which, however, the tragic thread has not been wanting. We have seen the exquisite developments of childhood and sunned the heart in its smiles. But also we have seen the evil star looming up that threatened cloud and wreck to its future years. We have seen beings of some precious gifts lost irrecoverably as regards this present life from inheritance of a bad organization and unfortunate circumstances of early years. We have seen the victims of vice lying in the gutter, companied by vermin, trampled upon by sensuality and ignorance. We have seen those who wished not to rise, and those who strove to do so, but fell back through weakness. Sadder and more ominous still, we have seen the good man—in many impulses and acts of most pure, most liberal, and undoubted goodness—we have seen a spot of base indulgence, a fibre of brutality, canker in a vital part this fine plant, and, while we could not withdraw love and esteem for the good we could not doubt, have wept secretly in the corner for the ill we could not deny. We have seen two deaths; one of the sinner, early cut down—one of the just, full of years and honor—*both* were calm; both professed their reliance on the wisdom of a Heavenly Father. We have seen the beauteous shows of nature in undisturbed succession, holy moonlight on the snows, loving moonlight on the summer fields, the stars which disappoint never and bless ever, the flowing waters which soothe and stimulate, a garden of roses calling for Queens among women, Poets and Heroes among men. We have seen a desire to answer to this call, and Genius brought rich wine, but spilt it on the way from its careless, fickle gait, and Virtue tainted with a touch of the peacock, and Philosophy, never enjoying, always seeking, who had got together all the materials for the crowning experiment, but there was no love to kindle the fire under the furnace, and the precious secret is not precipitated yet, for the pot will not boil to make the gold through your

> Double, double,
> Toil and trouble,

if Love do not fan the fire.

We have seen the decay of friendships unable to endure the light of an ideal hope—have seen, too, their resurrection in a faith and hope beyond the tomb where the form lies we once so fondly cherished. It is not dead, but sleepeth, and we watch, but must weep, too, sometimes, for the night is cold and lonely in the place of tombs.

We have seen Nature drest in her veil of snowy flowers for the bridal. We have seen her brooding over her joys, a young mother in the pride and fullness of beauty. We have seen her bearing her offspring to their richly ornamented sepulchre, and lately as if kneeling with folded hands in the stillness of prayer, while the bare trees and frozen streams bore witness to her patience.

O much, much have we seen, and a little learned. Such is the record of the private mind, and yet as the bright snake-skin is cast many sigh and cry

> "The wiser mind
> Mourns less for what Time takes away
> Than what he leaves behind."

1ST JANUARY, 1846

But for ourselves, we find there is kernel in the nut, though its ripening be deferred till the late frosty weather, and it prove a hard nut to crack, even then. Looking at the individual, we see a degree of growth, or the promise of such. In the child there is a force which will outlast the wreck and reach at last the promised shore. The good man, once roused from his moral lethargy, shall make atonement for his fault, and endure a penance that will deepen and purify his whole nature. The poor lost ones claim a new trial in a new life, and will there, we trust, seize firmer hold on the good for the experience they have had of the bad.

> "We never see the Stars
> Till we can see naught else."

The seeming losses are, in truth, but as pruning of the vine to make the grapes swell more richly.

But how is it with those larger individuals, the Nations, and that Congress of such, the Worlds?—We must take a broad and superficial view of these, as we have of private life, and in neither case can more be done. The secrets of the confessional, or rather of the shrine, do not come on paper, unless in poetic form.

So we will not try to search and mine, but only to look over the world from an ideal point of view.

Here we find the same phenomena repeated; the good nation is yet somehow so sick at heart that you are not sure its goodness will ever produce a harmony of life; over the young nation, (our own,) rich in energy and full of glee, brood terrible omens; others, as Poland and Italy, seem irrecoverably lost.— They may revive, but we feel as if it must be under new forms.

Forms come and go, but principles are developed and displayed more and more. The cauldron simmers, and so great is the fire that we expect it soon to boil over, and new Fates appear for Europe.

Spain is dying by inches; England shows symptoms of having passed her meridian; Austria has taken opium, but she must awake ere long; France is in an uneasy dream—she knows she has been very sick, has had terrible remedies administered, and ought to be getting thoroughly well, which she is not. Louis

Philippe watches by her pillow, doses and bleeds her, so that she cannot fairly try her strength and find whether something or nothing has been done. But Louis Philippe and Metternich must soon, in the course of Nature, leave this scene, and then there will be none to keep out air and light from the chamber, and the patients will be roused and ascertain their true condition.

No power is in the ascending course except the Russian, and that has such a condensation of brute force, animated by despotic will, that it seems sometimes as if it might by and by stride over Europe and face us across the water. Then would be opposed to one another the two extremes of Autocracy and Democracy, and a trial of strength would ensue between the two principles more grand and full than any ever seen on this planet, and of which the result must be to bind mankind by one chain of convictions. Should indeed Despotism and Democracy meet as the two slave-holding powers of the world the result can hardly be predicted. But there is room in the intervening age for many changes, and the Czars profess to wish to free their serfs as our Planters do to free their slaves, and we suppose with an equal sincerity, but the need of sometimes professing such desires is a deference to the progress of Principles which bid fair to have their era yet.

We hope for such an era steadfastly, notwithstanding the deeds of darkness that have made this year forever remarkable in our annals. Our Nation has indeed shown that the lust of gain is at present her ruling passion. She is not only resolute but shameless about it, and has no doubt or scruple as to laying aside the glorious office, assigned her by Fate of Herald of Freedom, Light and Peace to the civilized world.

Yet we must not despair! Even so the Jewish king, crowned with all gifts that Heaven could bestow, was intoxicated by their plenitude, and went astray after the most worthless idols. But he was not permitted to forfeit finally the office designed for him—he was drawn or dragged back to it; and so shall it be with this nation. There are trials in store which shall amend us.

We must believe that the pure blood shown in the time of our Revolution still glows in the heart, but the body of our nation is full of foreign elements. A large proportion of our citizens, or their parents, came here for worldly advantage, and

IST JANUARY, 1846

have never raised their minds to any idea of destiny or duty. More money—more land! is all the watchword they know. They have received the inheritance earned by the Fathers of the Revolution, without their wisdom and virtue to use it. But this cannot last. The vision of those prophetic souls must be realized, else the nation could not exist; every Body must at least "have Soul enough to save the expense of salt," or it cannot be preserved alive.

What a year it has been with us! Texas annexed, and more annexations in store; Slavery perpetuated, as the most striking new feature of these movements. Such are the fruits of American love of liberty! Mormons murdered and driven out, as an expression of American freedom of conscience. Cassius Clay's paper expelled from Kentucky; that is American freedom of the press. And all these deeds defended on the true Russian grounds: "We (the stronger) know what you (the weaker) ought to do and be, and it *shall* be so."

Thus the Principles which it was supposed some ten years back had begun to regenerate the world, are left without a trophy for this past year, except in the spread of Ronge's movement in Germany, and that of Associative and Communist principles, both here and in Europe, which, let the worldling deem as he will about their practicability, he cannot deny to be animated by faith in God and a desire for the good of Man. We must add to these the important symptoms of the spread of Peace Principles.

Meanwhile if the more valuable springs of action seem to lie dormant for a time, there is a constant invention and perfection of the means of action and communication which seems to say "Do but wait patiently; there is something of universal importance to be done by and by, and all is preparing for it to be universally known and used at once." Else what avail magnetic telegraphs, steamers and railcars traversing every rood of land and ocean. Phonography and the mingling of all literatures till North embraces South and Denmark lays her head upon the lap of Italy. Surely there would not be all this pomp of preparation as to the means of communion, unless there were like to be something worthy to be communicated.

Amid the signs of the breaking down of barriers, we may mention the Emperor Nicholas letting his daughter pass from the Greek to the Roman church for the sake of marrying her to the Austrian Prince. Again, similarity between him and us: he, too, is shameless; for while he signs this marriage contract with one hand, he holds the knout in the other to drive the Roman Catholic Poles into the Greek Church. But it is a fatal sign for his empire. 'T is but the first step that costs, and the Russians may look back to the marriage of the Grand Duchess Olga, as the Chinese will to the cannonading of the English, as the first sign of dissolution in the present form of national life.

A similar token is given by the violation of etiquette of which Mr. Polk is accused in his Message. He, at the head of a Government, speaks of Governments and their doings straight forward as he would of persons, and the tower, stronghold of the Idea of a former age, now propped up by etiquettes and civilities only, trembles to its foundation.

Another sign of the times is the general panic which the decay of the Potato causes. We doubt this is not without a providential meaning, and will call attention still more to the wants of the people at large. New and more provident regulations must be brought out, that they may not again be left with only a potato between them and starvation. By another of these whimsical coincidences between the histories of Aristocracy and Democracy, the supply of *truffles* is also failing. The land is losing the "nice things" that the Queen (truly a young Queen) thought might be eaten in place of bread. Does not this indicate a period in which it will be felt that there must be provision for all—the rich shall not have their truffles if the poor are driven to eat nettles, as the French and Irish have in bygone ages?

The poem of which this is a prose translation lately appeared in Germany. It is written by Moritz Hartmann and contains the *gist* of the matter.

Mistress Potato

There was a great stately house full of people who have been running in and out of its lofty gates, ever since the gray times of Olympus. There they wept, laughed, shouted, mourned, and, like day and night, came the usual changes of joys with plagues and sorrows. Haunting that great house up and down, making, baking, and roasting, covering and waiting on the table, has there lived a vast

IST JANUARY, 1846

473

number of years a loyal serving-maid of the olden time—her name was Mrs. Potato.

She was a still little old mother, who wore no baubles or laces, but always had to be satisfied with her plain, every-day clothes, and unheeded, unhonored, oftentimes jeered at and forgotten, she served all day at the kitchen fire and slept at night in the worst room. When she brought the dishes to table she got rarely a thankful glance, only at times some very poor man would in secret shake kindly her hand.

Generation after generation passed by; as the trees blossom, bear fruit and wither, but faithful remained the old housemaid, always the servant of the last heir.

But one morning, hear what happened. All the people came to table and lo! there was nothing to eat, for our good old Mistress Potato had not been able to rise from her bed. She felt sharp pains creeping through her poor old bones. No wonder she was worn out at last! She had not in all her life dared take a day's rest, lest so the poor should starve. Indeed it is wonderful that her good will should have kept her up so long. She must have had a great constitution to begin with.

The guests had to go away without breakfast. They were a little troubled but hoped to make up for it at dinner time.

But dinner time came and the table was empty, and then, indeed, they began to inquire about the welfare of Cookmaid Potato.

And up into her dark chamber where she lay on her poor bed came Great and Little, Young and Old, to ask after the good creature.

"What can be done for her?" "Bring warm clothes, medicine, a better bed." "Lay aside your work to help her." "If she dies we shall never again be able to fill the table," and now, indeed, they sang her praises.

O what a fuss now about the sick bed in that moist and mouldy chamber! and out doors it was just the same,—priests with their masses, processions, and prayers, and all the world ready to walk to penance, if Mistress Potato could but be saved.

And the doctors in their wigs, and counselors in masks of gravity sat there to devise some remedy to avert this terrible ill.

As when a Most Illustrious Dame is recovering from birth of a son, bulletins inform the world of the health of Mistress Potato, and, not content with what they so learn, couriers and lacqueys besiege the door, nay, the king's coach is stopping there.

Yes! yes! the humble poor Maid, 'tis about her they are all so frightened! Who would ever have believed it in days when the table was nicely covered?

The gentlemen of pens and books, priests, kings, lords and ministers, all have senses to scent out famine. Natheless Mistress Potato gets no better. May God help her for the sake, not of such people, but of the poor.

For such, it is a proof they should prize that all must crumble and fall to ruin, if they will work and weary to death the poor maid who cooks in the kitchen.

She lived for you in the dirt and ashes, provided daily for poor and rich; you ought to humble yourselves for her sake. Ah, could we hope that you would take a hint and *next time* pay some heed to the housemaid before she was worn and wearied to death.!!

So sighs rather than hopes Moritz Hartmann.—The wise ministers of England indeed seem much more composed than he supposes them. They are like the old man who, when he saw the avalanche coming down upon his village, said, "It is coming, but I shall have time to fill my pipe once more."—*He* went in to do so and was buried beneath the ruins. But Sir Robert Peel, who is so deliberate, has, doubtless, manna in store for those who have lost their customary food.

Another sign of the times is, that there are left on the earth none of the last dynasty of geniuses, rich in so many imperial heads. The world is full of talent, but it flows downward to water the plain.—There are no towering hights, no Mont Blancs now. We cannot recall one great genius at this day living. The time of prophets is over, and the era they prophesied must be at hand; in its conduct a larger proportion of the human race shall take part than ever before. As Prime Ministers have succeeded Kings in the substantials of monarchy, so now shall a House of Representatives succeed Prime Ministers.

Altogether, it looks as if a great time was coming, and that time one of Democracy. Our country will play a ruling part. Her Eagle will lead the van, but whether to soar upward to the sun or to stoop for helpless prey, who now dares promise? At present she has scarce achieved a Roman nobleness, a Roman liberty, and whether her Eagle is less like the Vulture and more like the Phenix than was the fierce Roman bird, we dare not say. May the New Year give hopes of the latter, even if the bird need first to be purified by fire. *

Review

MOSSES FROM AN OLD MANSE: By NATHANIEL HAWTHORNE—In Two Parts. New-York: Wiley & Putnam. 1846.

WE have been seated here the last ten minutes, pen in hand, thinking what we can possibly say about this book that will not be either superfluous or impertinent.

Superfluous, because the attractions of Hawthorne's writings cannot fail of one and the same effect on all persons who possess the common sympathies of men. To all who are still happy in some groundwork of unperverted Nature, the delicate, simple, human tenderness, unsought, unbought and therefore precious morality, the tranquil elegance and playfulness, the humor which never breaks the impression of sweetness and dignity, do an inevitable message which requires no comment of the critic to make its meaning clear. Impertinent, because the influence of this mind, like that of some loveliest aspects of Nature, is to induce silence from a feeling of repose. We do not think of any thing particularly worth saying about this that has not been so fitly and pleasantly said.

Yet it seems *un*fit that we, in our office of chronicler of intellectual advents and apparitions, should omit to render open and audible honor to one whom we have long delighted to honor. It may be, too that this slight notice of ours may awaken the attention of those distant or busy who might not otherwise search for the volume, which comes betimes in the leafy month of June.

So we will give a slight account of it, even if we cannot say much of value. Though Hawthorne has now a standard reputation, both for the qualities we have mentioned and the beauty of the style in which they are embodied, yet we believe he has not been very widely read. This is only because his works have not been published in the way to insure extensive circulation in this new, hurrying world of ours. The immense extent of country over which the reading (still very small in proportion to the mere working) community is scattered, the rushing and pushing of our life at this electrical stage of development, leave no work a chance to be speedily and largely known that is not trumpeted and placarded. And, odious as are the features of a forced and artificial circulation, it must be considered that it does no harm in the end. Bad books will not be read if they are bought instead of good, while the good have an abiding life in the log-cabin settlements and Red River steamboat landings, to which they would in no other way penetrate. Under the auspices of Wiley and Putnam, Hawthorne will have a chance to collect all his own public about him, and that be felt as a presence which before was only a rumor.

The volume before us shares the charms of Hawthorne's earlier tales; the only difference being that his range of subjects is a little wider. There is the same gentle and sincere companionship with Nature, the same delicate but fearless scrutiny of the secrets of the heart, the same serene independence of petty and artificial restrictions, whether on opinions or conduct, the same familiar, yet pensive sense of the spiritual or demoniacal influences that haunt the palpable life and common walks of men, not by many apprehended except in results. We have here to regret that Hawthorne, at this stage of his mind's life, lay no more decisive hand upon the apparition—brings it no nearer than in former days.—We had hoped that we should see, no more as in a glass darkly, but face to face. Still, still brood over his page the genius of revery and the nonchalance of Nature, rather than the ardent earnestness of the human soul which feels itself born not only to see and disclose, but to understand and interpret such things. Hawthorne intimates and suggests, but he does not lay bare the mysteries of our being.

The introduction to the "Mosses," in which the old Manse, its inhabitants and visitants are portrayed, is written with even more than his usual charm of placid grace and many strokes of his admirable good sense. Those who are not, like ourselves, familiar with the scene and its denizens, will still perceive how true that picture must be; those of us who are thus familiar will best know how to prize the record of objects and influences unique in our country and time.

"The Birth Mark" and "Rappaccini's Daughter" embody truths of profound importance in shapes of aerial elegance. In these, as here and there in all these pieces, shines the loveliest ideal of love and the beauty of feminine purity, (by which we mean no mere acts or abstinences, but perfect single truth felt and done in gentleness) which is its root.

"The Celestial Railroad," for its wit, wisdom, and the graceful adroitness with which the natural and material objects are interwoven with the allegories, has already won its meed of admiration.—"Fire-worship" is a most charming essay for its domestic sweetness and thoughtful life. "Goodman Brown" is one of those disclosures we have spoken of, of the secrets of the breast. Who has not known such a trial that is capable indeed of sincere aspiration toward that only good, that infinite essence, which men call God. Who has not known the hour when even that best-beloved image cherished as the one precious symbol left, in the range of human nature, believed to be still pure gold when all the rest have turned to clay, shows, in severe ordeal, the symptoms of alloy. Oh hour of anguish, when the old familiar faces grow dark and dim in the lurid light—when the gods of the hearth, honored in childhood, adored in youth, crumble, and nothing, nothing is left which the daily earthly feelings can embrace—can cherish with unbroken Faith! Yet some survive that trial more happily than young Goodman Brown. They are those who have not sought it—have never of their own accord walked forth with the Tempter into the dim shades of Doubt. Mrs. Bull-Frog is an excellent humorous picture of what is called to be "content at last with substantial realities"!! The "Artist of the Beautiful" presents in a form that is, indeed, beautiful, the opposite view as to what *are* the substantial realities of life. Let each man choose between them according to his kind. Had Hawthorne written "Roger Malvin's Burial" alone, we should be pervaded with the sense of the poetry and religion of his soul.

As a critic, the style of Hawthorne, faithful to his mind, shows repose, a great reserve of strength, a slow secure movement. Though a very refined, he is also a very clear writer, showing, as we said before, a placid grace, and an indolent command of language.

And now, beside the full, calm yet romantic stream of his mind, we will rest. It has refreshment for the weary, islets of fascination no less than dark recesses and shadows for the imaginative, pure reflections for the pure of heart and eye, and,

478 NEW YORK SHORT PUBLISHED WORKS

like the Concord he so well describes, many exquisite lilies for him who knows how to get at them. *

Review

MEMOIRS. OFFICIAL AND PERSONAL; WITH SKETCHES OF TRAVEL AMONG THE NORTHERN AND SOUTHERN INDIANS; embracing a War Excursion, and Descriptions of Scenes along the Western Borders. By THOMAS L. M'KENNEY, late Chief of the Bureau of Indian Affairs, Author of the History of the Indian Tribes of North America, &c. Two volumes in one. New-York: Paine & Burgess, 60 John-st. 1846.

YESTERDAY, the 4th July, we passed in looking through this interesting work. The feelings and reflections it induced were in harmony with the aspect of the day, a day of gloom, of searching chill and dripping skies. We were very sorry for all the poor laborers and children whom the weather deprived of pleasure on the pleasantest occasion of their year—most of all for those poor children of the Farm Schools on this, perhaps, the first holiday of their dull, narrow little lives. But the mourning aspect of the day seemed to us most appropriate. The boys and boyish young men were letting off their crackers and reveling in smoke and hubbub all day long; a din not more musical, of empty panegyric and gratulation, was going on within the halls of oratory; the military were parading our profaned banners. But the sweet heavens, conscious of the list of wrongs by which this nation, in its now three-score years and ten of independent existence, has abused the boon, veiled themselves in crape and wept.

The nation may wrap itself in callousness and stop its ears to every cry except that of profit or loss; it may build its temples of wood and stone, and hope, by formal service of the lips, to make up for that paid to Mammon in the spirit, but God is not mocked; it is all recorded, all known. The want of honor and even honorable sentiment shown by this people in the day of repudiation; the sin of Slavery and the conduct of the slaveholder, who, at first pretending that he wished, if possible, to put an end to this curse of unlawful bondage, has now unveiled his falsehood by the contrivance and consummation

MEMOIRS OF THOMAS L. M'KENNEY 479

of a plan to perpetuate it, if possible, through all ages; the intolerance and bigotry which disgrace a country whose fundamental idea affords them no excuse, shown in a thousand ways and on every side, but, of late, in a most flagrant form, through the murder of the Mormon leader, the expulsion of his followers, and their persecution even while passing out of these borders, persecution of precisely the same kind, excused on the same grounds, as that with which the Egyptians pursued the Hebrews, add to these the war which at present engages us, at whose very triumphs those who have steady intellect or steady principle must look with an aching heart, and which the Louisiana *Marseillais* is fain to celebrate in such terms as these:

> "Levez vous! fils de l'Amerique,
> La patric invoque vos bras,
> Verrez vous le *faible Mexique*,
> Ravager, piller vos Etats!"

"Rise, sons of America, your country demands your aid, will you see *feeble* Mexico ravage, pillage your States!"

And even in this city they were not ashamed to pen and sing verses calling on the citizen to fight in defence of "liberty," as if it were not the Mexicans alone, the *feeble* Mexicans, that were fighting in defence of their rights, and we for liberty to do our pleasure.

But of all these plague-spots there is none from which we feel such burning pain of shame and indignation, as from the conduct of this nation toward the Indians. Spoliation, aggression, falsehood of the blackest character, a hundred times repeated, each time with increased shamelessness, mark every step of this intercourse. If good men have sometimes interposed, it is but as a single human arm might strive to stay the torrent. The sense of the nation has been throughout, Might makes Right. We will get what we want at any rate. What does it signify what becomes of the Indians? They are red. They are unlike us in character and person.—Let them save themselves if they can, the Indian dogs. We will get all we want at any rate. For the last twenty-five years these proceedings have assumed a still darker shade, when it has been the effort of public and private avarice alike to drive the Indians beyond the Mississippi—when treaties have been made by treachery, signed only by a minority of their tribes, then enforced by our Government so long as they served its purpose, broken then and new ones made and adhered to with the same fidelity. How bitter is the satire of the Indian phrase, "*A White Man's Treaty!*" How just and natural the reply to the missionary who urged upon them the religious benefit of becoming Christians. "Christians!—Why the white men are Christians!"

Most of the facts on these subjects contained in Col. M'Kenney's book we knew before, but they are here detailed in their full force by one intimately connected, often an eye-witness, and whose benevolence, liberal views, and manly sympathy had made him a "beloved brother" to the red man.—He can conclusively show the falsehood of the pretext that they are incapable of civilization, a pretext, indeed, refuted by all who please to look at it by the prospects of the Cherokees, if they had not been so wickedly arrested in their progress. He can show how open they are to the advice of any friend who they think has judgment combined with sympathy for their sad and difficult position. This reliance is expressed toward Col. M'Kenney with the most touching simplicity by these stalwart men, childlike because representing a race reduced to the weakness of childhood.

"Brother: We have opened our ears wide to your talk; we have not lost a word of it. We were happy and our hearts grew big, when we heard you had come to our country. We have always thought of you as our friend; we have confidence in you; we have listened more close, because we think so much of you; we know well you would not deceive us, and we believe you know what is best for us and for our children. Brother, do not you forsake us. Our friends, as you told us, are few—we have none to spare—*we know that.*"

How deeply affecting are the images in the magnificent speech of the Choctaw chief!

Speech of Col. Cobb,

Head Mingo of the Choctaws, East of the Mississippi, in reply to the Agent of the United States.

MEMOIRS OF THOMAS L. M'KENNEY 481

"Brother—We have heard your talk as from the lips of our father, the great white chief at Washington, and my people have called upon me to speak to you. The red man has no books, and when he wishes to make known his views, like his father before him, he speaks from his mouth. He is afraid of writing. When he speaks he knows what he says; the Great Spirit hears him. Writing is the invention of the pale-faces; it gives birth to error and to feuds. The Great Spirit talks— we hear him in the thunder—in the rushing winds and the mighty waters—but he never writes.

"Brother—When you were young we were strong, we fought by your side; but our arms are now broken. You have grown large; my people have become small.

"Brother—My voice is weak; you can scarcely hear me; it is not the shout of a warrior, but the wail of an infant. I have lost it in wailing over the misfortunes of my people. These are their graves, and in those aged pines you hear the ghosts of the departed. Their ashes are here, and we have been left to protect them. Our warriors are nearly all gone to the far country west; but here are our dead. Shall we go, too, and give their bones to the wolves?

"Brother—Two sleeps have passed since we heard you talk. We have thought upon it. You ask us to leave our country, and tell us it is our father's wish. We would not desire to displease our father. We respect him, and you his child. But the Choctaw always thinks. We want time to answer.

"Brother—Our hearts are full. Twelve winters ago our chiefs sold our country. Every warrior that you see here was opposed to the treaty. If the dead could have been counted, it could never have been made; but, alas! tho' they stood around, they could not be seen or heard. Their tears came in the rain drops, and their voices in the wailing wind, but the pale-faces knew it not, and our land was taken away.

"Brother—We do not now complain. The Choctaw suffers, but never weeps. You have the strong arm, and we cannot resist: but the pale-face worships the Great Spirit. So does the red man. The Great Spirit loves truth. When you took our country you promised us land. There is your promise in the book. Twelve times have the trees dropped their leaves, yet we have received no land. Our houses have been taken from us. The white man's plow turns up the bones of our fathers. We dare not kindle our fires; and yet you said we might remain, and you would give us land.

"Brother—Is this *truth*? But we believe now our great father knows our condition, he will listen to us. We are as mourning orphans in our country; but our father will take us by the hand. When he fulfils his promise, we will answer his talk. He means well. We know it. But we cannot think now. Grief has made children of us.—When our business is settled, we shall be men again, and talk to our great father about what he has proposed.

"Brother, you stand in the moccasins of a great chief, you speak the words of a mighty nation, and your talk was long. My people are small, their shadow scarcely reaches to your knee; they are scattered and gone; when I shout, I hear my voice in the depth of the woods, but no answering shout comes back. My words, therefore, are few. I have nothing more to say, but to request you to tell what I have said to the tall chief of the pale-faces, whose brother* stands by your side."

Still more affecting, however, is the address of Lowrey, the now acting chief of the Cherokees, to the Christian community of the U. S., published in our papers a few days since. It is affecting, not from its eloquence like the preceding, but from its broken-hearted subdued tone as overpoweringly pathetic, from this once great, strong, seemingly indomitable race, as when the perishing Cæsar cries, "Give me some drink, Titinius,— like a sick girl." He appeals to the Christian community, which to-day has been dozing in the churches over texts of scripture which they apply only to the by gone day, while there is before them at this moment such a mighty appeal for sympathy, for justice, such wrong to be set right, such service to be done to the commands of Christ, Love one another—Feed my lambs—Go forth to the Gentile.—O Jesus! how dare we say to thee, Lord, Lord?—Can there be hope of avoiding the repulse—"Depart from me, I never knew ye."

Col. M'Kenney, in showing the mistakes that have been made, and the precious opportunities lost of doing right and good to the Indians, shows also that, at this very moment, another such opportunity is presented, probably the last. We bespeak attention to this plan. We do not restate it here, preferring the public should be led to it by gradual steps, through his own book, which we hope to see in general circulation. We shall content ourselves with repeating that the time to attend to the subject, get information and act, is NOW, or never. A very short time and it will be too late to release ourselves, in any measure, from the weight of ill doing, or preserve any vestiges

---

* William Tyler, of Virginia, brother of the late President of the United States, one of the Choctaw Commissioners.

of a race, one large portion of the creation of God, and whose life and capacities ought by all enlightened and honest, not to say religious, minds to be held infinitely precious, if only as a part of the history of the human family.

The details of conduct in General Jackson are very characteristic. That a man so incompetent should have been placed in so responsible a position at such a crisis, merely because he had a ray of genius, some fine instincts, and represented the war spirit in the country, was very sad and fatal. Happy those who opposed it, vanquished though they be! The account of Osceola's and the Agent's conduct relatively at the time when the Indian thrust his knife into the treaty, on being urged, as if he had been a sullen schoolboy, *to make his mark*, is a history in little of the whole relation between the two races. No wonder Osceola, on his death bed, painted his face red, in token of eternal enmity to the whites.

The narrative of the delivery to the whites of RED BIRD, his conduct on that occasion, the just and intelligent appreciation of the motives which actuated him in shedding the blood of Gagnier, nothing being extenuated, nothing set down in malice or in ignorance, make this narrative one of the few truly valuable memorials that remain on this subject. To Col. M'Kenney we are also indebted for the story of Potalesbarro in its original simple traits of pure instinctive magnanimity.

This work is embellished with many appropriate designs, and, as frontispiece to the second volume, boasts a colored lithograph portrait of POCAHONTAS, from an undoubted original, painted in London in 1616. The face is extremely lovely, the eye has the wild, sweet look of the Indian women, with more fullness of soul than they usually possess; the lips too, are full, the upper one too much so for regular beauty, but very expressive of tenderness and generosity. The skin has that golden lustre which makes the Indian complexion as beautiful, compared with the swarthy or dingy red, as the softest blonde is, compared to the coarse or tarnished skins so common among Europeans. The hair is rich and slightly curled; the dress, a rich green, lined and faced with white, leaving bare the neck and the lower part of the arms, is very beautiful and no less becoming. The possession of so fair a copy of a beloved original would, of itself, alone, make the book a desirable possession to many.

484   NEW YORK SHORT PUBLISHED WORKS

All men love Pocahontas for the angelic impulse of tenderness and pity that impelled her to the rescue of Smith. We love her for a sympathy with our race which seemed instinctive and marked her as an instrument of Destiny. Yet we pity her, too, for being thus made a main agent in the destruction of her own people, and feel the fate of Philip, Pontiac, Tecumseh, Nappier, who died in defence of the stock from which they sprang. Of the tender mercies which were to be the reward of every kindness conferred by the red upon the white man, we have a sample in the way in which Smith meets the lovely heroine who had saved his life in *his* native land. She, alone among strangers, rushes to him, calls him *father*, secure of a kind welcome to his heart. He, entrenched in cold conventional restraints, takes her hand and leads her to a chair, addresses her as Miss or Madam, and freezes back at once the warm gushing stream of her affections with the ice of civic life.

A comment upon this is found in the position of the Indian boys brought up by Col. M'Kenney, and especially in the catastrophe of McDonald.

The book, adorned with the portrait of Pocahontas, is enriched by many traits especially calculated to interest women. Among these is the punishment of an Indian for ill treatment of his mother-in-law, received with acclamation by the women of the tribe, as bringing a new era in their destiny. We could have wished, however, that the punishment had been something else than the degradation of the brave to the position of a woman. The Indian custom to that effect being the most powerful expression of the contempt in which they hold the sex, ought not to have been countenanced in an attempt to rectify this way of thinking. The book is appropriately dedicated to two women. The first volume, with a portrait of the author for its frontispiece beneath which might have been inscribed as a proud title which few can boast. The Indian's Friend, is dedicated to Mrs. Madison, and an autograph letter from her in reply, forms an interesting prefix to its pages. The second, with the portrait of Pocahontas, is dedicated to Mrs. Saunders, of Salem, Mass. as having also shown herself with talents, time and money, a friend to the Indians, a happiness which we envy her, and must wish her many competitors more powerful and leisurely than ourselves in its enjoyment.

ORMOND AND WIELAND

Honors are paid to the character of John Ross, which it gives us great pleasure to see, as confirmation of what we have always felt. There is a tone not to be mistaken in the papers which Ross has addressed to the public—a grave, majestic sorrow, a resolute honor, justice, and courage to act as love and duty prompt in a losing cause to the last, an excellent discernment, and a serenely tempered wisdom. We have often wished to extend the hand of friendship to this man, and assure him that there was one pale face who, not having seen, yet knows him, and prizes his efforts as they deserve. We may name, in the late Dr. Channing, another who felt thus toward Ross from the perusal of his writings.

We solicit an extensive perusal of this book; the interest of its contents will repay the money and trouble that may be thus expended. We scarcely dare hope that any thing righteous will be done in consequence, for our hopes as to National honor and goodness are almost wearied out, and we feel obliged to turn to the Individual and to the Future for consolation. Yet, oh Father! might we pray that thou wouldst grant a ray of pure light in this direction, and grant us to help let it in! It were a blessed compensation for many sorrows, many disappointments. At all events, none who have leisure and heart to feel on these subjects may stand excused from bearing open testimony to the truth, whether it avail or no. *

Review

ORMOND; OR, THE SECRET WITNESS.

WIELAND; OR, THE TRANSFORMATION. BY CHARLES BROCKDEN BROWN. Library of Standard Romance. W. Taylor & Co. 2 Astor House.

WE rejoice to see these reprints of Brown's novels, as we have long been ashamed that one who ought to be the pride of the country, and who is, in the higher qualities of the mind, so far in advance of our other novelists, should have become almost inaccessible to the public.

It has been the custom to liken Brown to Godwin. But there was no imitation, no second hand in the matter. They were congenial natures, and whichever had come first might have lent an impulse to the other. Either mind might have been conscious of the possession of that peculiar vein of ore without thinking of working it for the mint of the world, till the other, led by accident, or overflow of feeling, showed him how easy it was to put the reveries of his solitary hours into words and upon paper for the benefit of his fellow men.

"My mind to me a kingdom is."

Such a man as Brown or Godwin has a right to say that. It is no scanty, turbid rill, requiring to be daily fed from a thousand others or from the clouds! Its plenteous source rushes from a high mountain between bulwarks of stone. Its course, even and full, keeps ever green its banks, and affords the means of life and joy to a million gliding shapes, that fill its deep waters, and twinkle above its golden sands.

Life and Joy! Yes, Joy! These two have been called the dark Masters, because they disclose the twilight recesses of the human heart. Yet their gravest page is joy compared with the mixed, shallow, uncertain pleasures of vulgar minds. Joy! because they were all alive and fulfilled the purposes of being. No sham, no imitation, no convention deformed or veiled their native lineaments, checked the use of their natural force. All alive themselves, they understood that there is no joy without truth, no perception of joy without real life. Unlike most men, existence was to them not a tissue of words and seemings, but a substantial possession.

Born Hegelians, without the pretensions of science, they sought God in their own consciousness, and found him. The heart, because it saw itself so fearfully and wonderfully made, did not disown its Maker. With the highest idea of the dignity, power and beauty of which human nature is capable they had courage to see by what an oblique course it proceeds, yet never lose faith that it would reach its destined aim. Thus their darkest disclosures are not hobgoblin shows, but precious revelations.

Brown is great as ever human writer was in showing the self-sustaining force of which a lonely mind is capable. He takes one person, makes him brood like the bee, and extract from the common life before him all its sweetness, its bitterness, and its nourishment.

We say makes *him*, but it increases our own interest in Brown that, a prophet in this respect of a better era, he has usually placed this thinking royal mind in the body of a woman. This personage too is always feminine, both in her character and circumstances, but a conclusive proof that the term *feminine* is not a synonym for *weak*. Constantia, Clara Wieland, have loving hearts, graceful and plastic natures, but they have also noble thinking minds, full of resource, constancy, courage. The Marguerite of Godwin, no less, is all refinement, and the purest tenderness, but she is also the soul of honor, capable of deep discernment, and of acting in conformity with the inferences she draws. The Man of Brown and Godwin has not eaten of the fruit of the tree of knowledge and been driven to sustain himself by the sweat of his brow for nothing, but has learned the structure and laws of things, and become a being, natural, benignant, various, and desirous of supplying the loss of innocence by the attainment of virtue. So his Woman need not be quite so weak as Eve, the slave of feeling or of flattery: she also has learned to guide her helm amid the storm across the troubled waters.

The horrors which mysteriously beset these persons, and against which, so far as outward facts go, they often strive in vain, are but a representation of those powers permitted to work in the same way throughout the affairs of this world. Their demoniacal attributes only represent a morbid state of the intellect, gone to excess from want of balance with the other powers. There is an intellectual as well as a physical drunkenness and which, no less, impels to crime. Carwin, urged on to use his ventriloquism, till the presence of such a strange agent wakened the seeds of fanaticism in the breast of Wieland, is in a state no more foreign to nature than that of the wretch executed last week, who felt himself drawn as by a spell to murder his victim because he had thought of her money and the pleasures it might bring him, till the feeling possessed his brain that hurls the gamester to ruin. The victims of such agency are like the soldier of the Rio Grande, who, both legs shot off and his life-blood rushing out with every pulse, replied serenely to his pitying comrades that "he had now that for which the soldier enlisted." The end of the drama is not in this world, and the fiction which rounds off the whole to harmony and felicity before the curtain falls, sins against truth, and deludes the reader. The Nelsons of the human race are all the more exposed to the assaults of Fate that they are decorated with the badges of well-earned glory. Who but feels as they fall in death, or rise again to a mutilated existence, that the end is not yet? Who, that thinks, but must feel that the recompense is, where Brown places it, in the accumulation of mental treasure, in the severe assay by fire that leaves the gold pure to be used sometime—somewhere.

Brown, man of the brooding eye, the teeming brain, the deep and fervent heart; if thy country prize thee not and has almost lost thee out of sight, it is that her heart is made shallow and cold, her eye dim, by the pomp of circumstance, the love of gross outward gain. She cannot long continue thus for it takes a great deal of soul to keep a huge body from disease and dissolution. As there is more soul thou wilt be more sought, and many will yet sit down with thy Constantia to the meal and water on which she sustained her full and thoughtful existence who could not endure the ennui of aldermanic dinners, or find any relish in the imitation of French cookery. To-day many will read the words, and some have a cup large enough to receive the spirit, before it is lost in the sand on which their feet are planted.

Brown's high standard of the delights of intellectual communion and of friendship correspond with the fondest hopes of early days. But in the relations of real life, at present, there is rarely more than one of the parties ready for such intercourse as he describes. On the one side there will be dryness, want of perception or variety, a stupidity unable to appreciate life's richest boon when offered to its grasp, and the finer nature is doomed to retrace its steps, unhappy as those who having force to raise a spirit cannot retain or make it substantial, and stretch out their arms only to bring them back empty to the breast.

We were glad to see those reprints, but angry to see them so carelessly done. Casting the eye lightly over the page we find *feign* for *fain*, *illegibility* for *eligibility* and the like. Under the cheap system, the carelessness in printing and translating grows

Farewell

FAREWELL to New-York City, where twenty months have presented me with a richer and more varied exercise for thought and life than twenty years could in any other part of these United States.

It is the common remark about New-York that it has, at least, nothing petty or provincial in its methods and habits. The place is large enough; there is room enough and occupation enough for men to have no need or excuse for small cavils or scrutinies. A person who is independent and knows what he wants, may lead his proper life here unimpeded by others.

Vice and Crime, if flagrant and frequent, are less thickly coated by Hypocrisy than elsewhere. The air comes sometimes to the most infected subjects.

New-York is the focus, the point where American and European interests converge. There is no topic of general interest to men that will not betimes be brought before the thinker by the quick turning of the wheel.

Too quick that revolution, some object. Life rushes wide and free, but *too fast*; yet it is in the power of every one to avert from himself the evil that accompanies the good. He must build for his study, as did the German poet, a house beneath the bridge, and, then, all that passes above and by him will be heard and seen, but he will not be carried away with it.

Earlier views have been confirmed and many new ones opened. On two great leadings,—the superlative importance of promoting National Education by hightening and deepening the cultivation of individual minds, and the part which is assigned to Woman in the next stage of human progress in this country, where most important achievements are to be effected, I have received much encouragement, much instruction, and the fairest hopes of more.

On various subjects of minor importance, no less than these, I hope for good results from observation with my own eyes of

Life in the Old World, and to bring home some packages of seed for Life in the New.

These words I address to my friends, for I feel that I have some. The degree of sympathetic response to the thoughts and suggestions I have offered through the columns of this paper has indeed surprised me, conscious as I am of a natural and acquired aloofness from many, if not most, popular tendencies of my time and place. It has greatly encouraged me, for none can sympathize with thoughts like mine who are permanently ensnared in the meshes of sect or party; none who prefer the formation and advancement of mere opinions to the free pursuit of Truth. I see, surely, that the topmost bubble or sparkle of the cup is no voucher for the nature of its contents throughout, and shall, in future, feel that in our age, nobler in that respect than most of the preceding, each sincere and fervent act or word is secure, not only of a final, but a speedy, response.

I go to behold the wonders of art, and the temples of old religion. But I shall see no forms of beauty and majesty beyond what my Country is capable of producing in myriad variety, if she has but the soul to will it; no temple to compare with what she might erect in the Ages, if the catch-word of the time, a sense of DIVINE ORDER, should become, no more a mere word or effigy, but a deeply rooted and pregnant Idea in her life. Beneath the light of a hope that this may be, I ask of my friends once more a kind Farewell. *

American Literature
ITS POSITION IN THE PRESENT TIME, AND PROSPECTS
FOR THE FUTURE

Some thinkers may object to this essay, that we are about to write of that which has, as yet, no existence.

For it does not follow because many books are written by persons born in America that there exists an American literature. Books which imitate or represent the thoughts and life of Europe do not constitute an American literature. Before such can exist, an original idea must animate this nation and fresh currents of life must call into life fresh thoughts along its shores.

We have no sympathy with national vanity. We are not anxious to prove that there is as yet much American literature. Of those who think and write among us in the methods and of the thoughts of Europe, we are not impatient; if their minds are still best adapted to such food and such action. If their books express life of mind and character in graceful forms, they are good and we like them. We consider them as colonists and useful schoolmasters to our people in a transition state; which lasts rather longer than is occupied in passing, bodily, the ocean which separates the new from the old world.

We have been accused of an undue attachment to foreign continental literature, and, it is true, that in childhood, we had well nigh "forgotten our English," while constantly reading in other languages. Still, what we loved in the literature of continental Europe was the range and force of ideal manifestation in forms of national and individual greatness. A model was before us in the great Latins of simple masculine minds seizing upon life with unbroken power. The stamp both of nationality and individuality was very strong upon them; their lives and thoughts stood out in clear and bold relief. The English character has the iron force of the Latins, but not the frankness and expansion. Like their fruits, they need a summer sky to give them more sweetness and a richer flavour. This does not apply to Shakspeare, who has all the fine side of English genius, with the rich colouring, and more fluent life, of the Catholic countries. Other poets, of England also, are expansive more or less, and soar freely to seek the blue sky, but take it as a whole, there is in English literature, as in English character, a reminiscence of walls and ceilings, a tendency to the arbitrary and conventional that repels a mind trained in admiration of the antique spirit. It is only in later days that we are learning to prize the peculiar greatness which a thousand times outweighs this fault, and which has enabled English genius to go forth from its insular position and conquer such vast dominion in the realms both of matter and of mind.

Yet there is, often, between child and parent, a reaction from excessive influence having been exerted, and such an one we have experienced, in behalf of our country, against England. We use her language, and receive, in torrents, the influence of her thought, yet it is, in many respects, uncongenial and injurious to our constitution. What suits Great Britain, with her insular position and consequent need to concentrate and intensify her life, her limited monarchy, and spirit of trade, does not suit a mixed race, continually enriched with new blood from other stocks the most unlike that of our first descent, with ample field and verge enough to range in and leave every impulse free, and abundant opportunity to develope a genius, wide and full as our rivers, flowery, luxuriant and impassioned as our vast prairies, rooted in strength as the rocks on which the Puritan fathers landed.

That such a genius is to rise and work in this hemisphere we are confident; equally so that scarce the first faint streaks of that day's dawn are yet visible. It is sad for those that foresee, to know they may not live to share its glories, yet it is sweet, too, to know that every act and word, uttered in the light of that foresight, may tend to hasten or ennoble its fulfilment.

That day will not rise till the fusion of races among us is more complete. It will not rise till this nation shall attain sufficient moral and intellectual dignity to prize moral and intellectual, no less highly than political, freedom, not till, the physical resources of the country being explored, all its regions studded with towns, broken by the plow, netted together by railways and telegraph lines, talent shall be left at leisure to turn its

AMERICAN LITERATURE 493

energies upon the higher department of man's existence. Nor then shall it be seen till from the leisurely and yearning soul of that riper time national ideas shall take birth, ideas craving to be clothed in a thousand fresh and original forms.

Without such ideas all attempts to construct a national literature must end in abortions like the monster of Frankenstein, things with forms, and the instincts of forms, but soulless, and therefore revolting. We cannot have expression till there is something to be expressed.

The symptoms of such a birth may be seen in a longing felt here and there for the sustenance of such ideas. At present, it shows itself, where felt, in sympathy with the prevalent tone of society, by attempts at external action, such as are classed under the head of social reform. But it needs to go deeper, before we can have poets, needs to penetrate beneath the springs of action, to stir and remake the soil as by the action of fire.

Another symptom is the need felt by individuals of being even sternly sincere. This is the one great means by which alone progress can be essentially furthered. Truth is the nursing mother of genius. No man can be absolutely true to himself, eschewing cant, compromise, servile imitation, and complaisance, without becoming original, for there is in every creature a fountain of life which, if not choked back by stones and other dead rubbish, will create a fresh atmosphere, and bring to life fresh beauty. And it is the same with the nation as with the individual man.

The best work we do for the future is by such truth. By use of that, in whatever way, we harrow the soil and lay it open to the sun and air. The winds from all quarters of the globe bring seed enough, and there is nothing wanting but preparation of the soil, and freedom in the atmosphere, for ripening of a new and golden harvest.

We are sad that we cannot be present at the gathering in of this harvest. And yet we are joyous, too, when we think that though our name may not be writ on the pillar of our country's fame, we can really do far more towards rearing it, than those who come at a later period and to a seemingly fairer task. *Now*, the humblest effort, made in a noble spirit, and with religious hope, cannot fail to be even infinitely useful. Whether we introduce some noble model from another time and clime, to encourage aspiration in our own, or cheer into blossom the simplest wood-flower that ever rose from the earth, moved by the genuine impulse to grow, independent of the lures of money or celebrity; whether we speak boldly when fear or doubt keep others silent, or refuse to swell the popular cry upon an unworthy occasion, the spirit of truth, purely worshipped, shall turn our acts and forbearances alike to profit, informing them with oracles which the latest time shall bless.

Under present circumstances the amount of talent and labour given to writing ought to surprise us. Literature is in this dim and struggling state, and its pecuniary results exceedingly pitiful. From many well known causes it is impossible for ninety-nine out of the hundred, who wish to use the pen, to ransom, by its use, the time they need. This state of things will have to be changed in some way. No man of genius writes for money; but it is essential to the free use of his powers, that he should be able to disembarrass his life from care and perplexity. This is very difficult here; and the state of things gets worse and worse, as less and less is offered in pecuniary meed for works demanding great devotion of time and labour (to say nothing of the ether engaged) and the publisher, obliged to regard the transaction as a matter of business, demands of the author to give him only what will find an immediate market, for he cannot afford to take any thing else. This will not do! When an immortal poet was secure only of a few copyists to circulate his works, there were princes and nobles to patronize litera-ture and the arts. Here is only the public, and the public must learn how to cherish the nobler and rarer plants, and to plant the aloe, able to wait a hundred years for its bloom, or its garden will contain, presently, nothing but potatoes and pot-herbs. We shall have, in the course of the next two or three years, a convention of authors to inquire into the causes of this state of things and propose measures for its remedy. Some have already been thought of that look promising, but we shall not announce them till the time be ripe; that date is not distant, for the difficulties increase from day to day, in consequence of the system of cheap publication, on a great scale.

The ranks that led the way in the first half century of this republic were far better situated than we, in this respect. The country was not so deluged with the dingy page, reprinted from

AMERICAN LITERATURE

Europe, and patriotic vanity was on the alert to answer the question, "Who reads an American book?" And many were the books written, worthy to be read, as any out of the first class in England. They were, most of them, except in their subject matter, English books.

The list is large, and, in making some cursory comments, we do not wish to be understood as designating *all* who are worthy of notice, but only those who present themselves to our minds with some special claims. In history there has been nothing done to which the world at large has not been eager to award the full meed of its deserts. Mr. Prescott, for instance, has been greeted with as much warmth abroad as here. We are not disposed to undervalue his industry and power of clear and elegant arrangement. The richness and freshness of his materials is such that a sense of enchantment must be felt in their contemplation. We must regret, however, that they should have been first presented to the public by one who possesses nothing of the higher powers of the historian, great leading views, or discernment as to the motives of action and the spirit of an era. Considering the splendour of the materials the books are wonderfully tame, and every one must feel that having once passed through them and got the sketch in the mind, there is nothing else to which it will recur. The absence of thought, as to that great picture of Mexican life, with its heroisms, its terrible but deeply significant superstitions, its admirable civic refinement, seems to be quite unbroken.

Mr. Bancroft is a far more vivid writer; he has great resources and great command of them, and leading thoughts by whose aid he groups his facts. But we cannot speak fully of his historical works, which we have only read and referred to here and there.

In the department of ethics and philosophy, we may inscribe two names as likely to live and be blessed and honoured in the later time. These are the names of Channing and of Emerson.

Dr. Channing had several leading thoughts which corresponded with the wants of his time, and have made him in it a father of thought. His leading idea of "the dignity of human nature" is one of vast results, and the peculiar form in which he advocated it had a great work to do in this new world. The spiritual beauty of his writings is very great; they are all distinguished for sweetness, elevation, candour, and a severe devotion to truth. On great questions, he took middle ground, and sought a panoramic view; he wished also to stand high, yet never forgot what was above more than what was around and beneath him. He was not well acquainted with man on the impulsive and passionate side of his nature, so that his view of character was sometimes narrow, but it was always noble. He exercised an expansive and purifying power on the atmosphere, and stands a godfather at the baptism of this country.

The Sage of Concord has a very different mind, in every thing except that he has the same disinterestedness and dignity of purpose, the same purity of spirit. He is a profound thinker. He is a man of ideas, and deals with causes rather than effects. His ideas are illustrated from a wide range of literary culture and refined observation, and embodied in a style whose melody and subtle fragrance enchant those who stand stupified before the thoughts themselves, because their utmost depths do not enable them to sound his shallows. His influence does not yet extend over a wide space; he is too far beyond his place and his time, to be felt at once or in full, but it searches deep, and yearly widens its circles. He is a harbinger of the better day. His beautiful elocution has been a great aid to him in opening the way for the reception of his written word.

In that large department of literature which includes descriptive sketches, whether of character or scenery, we are already rich. Irving, a genial and fair nature, just what he ought to be, and would have been, at any time of the world, has drawn the scenes amid which his youth was spent in their primitive lineaments, with all the charms of his graceful jocund humour. He has his niche and need never be deposed; it is not one that another could occupy.

The first enthusiasm about Cooper having subsided, we remember more his faults than his merits. His ready resentment and way of showing it in cases which it is the wont of gentlemen to pass by in silence, or meet with a good humoured smile, have caused unpleasant associations with his name, and his fellow citizens, in danger of being tormented by suits for libel, if they spoke freely of him, have ceased to speak of him at all. But neither these causes, nor the baldness of his plots, shallowness of thought, and poverty in the presentation of character, should make us forget the grandeur and originality of his sea-sketches,

AMERICAN LITERATURE 497

nor the redemption from oblivion of our forest-scenery, and the noble romance of the hunter-pioneer's life. Already, but for him, this fine page of life's romance would be almost forgotten. He has done much to redeem these irrevocable beauties from the corrosive acid of a semi-civilized invasion.*

Miss Sedgwick and others have portrayed, with skill and feeling, scenes and personages from the revolutionary time. Such have a permanent value in proportion as their subject is fleeting. The same charm attends the spirited delineations of Mrs. Kirkland, and that amusing book, "A New Purchase." The features of Hoosier, Sucker, and Wolverine life are worth fixing; they are peculiar to the soil, and indicate its hidden treasures; they have, also, that charm which simple life, lived for its own sake, always has, even in rude and all but brutal forms.

What shall we say of the poets? The list is scanty; amazingly so, for there is nothing in the causes that paralyze other kinds of literature that could affect lyrical and narrative poetry. Men's

---

* Since writing the above we have read some excellent remarks by Mr. W. G. Simms on the writings of Cooper. We think the reasons are given for the powerful interest excited by Hawk Eye and the Pilot, with great discrimination and force.

"They both think and feel, with a highly individual nature, that has been taught, by constant contemplation, in scenes of solitude. The vast unbroken ranges of forest to its one lonely occupant press upon the mind with the same sort of solemnity which one feels condemned to a life of partial isolation upon the ocean. Both are permitted that degree of commerce with their fellow beings, which suffices to maintain in strength the sweet and sacred sources of their humanity. * * * The very isolation to which, in the most successful of his stories, Mr. Cooper subjects his favourite personages, is, alone, a proof of his strength and genius. While the ordinary writer, the man of mere talent, is compelled to look around him among masses for his material, he contents himself with one man, and flings him upon the wilderness. The picture, then, which follows, must be one of intense individuality. Out of this one man's nature, his moods and fortunes, he spins his story. The agencies and dependencies are few. With the self-reliance which is only found in true genius, he goes forward into the wilderness, whether of land or ocean; and the vicissitudes of either region, acting upon the natural resources of one man's mind, furnish the whole material of his work-shop. This mode of performance is highly dramatic, and thus it is that his scout, his trapper, his hunter, his pilot, all live to our eyes and thoughts, the perfect ideals of moral individuality."

No IX. Wiley and Putnam's Library of American books.—Views and Reviews by W. G. Simms.

hearts beat, hope, and suffer always, and they must crave such means to vent them; yet of the myriad leaves garnished with smooth stereotyped rhymes that issue yearly from our press, you will not find, one time in a million, a little piece written from any such impulse, or with the least sincerity or sweetness of tone. They are written for the press, in the spirit of imitation or vanity, the paltriest offspring of the human brain, for the heart disclaims, as the ear is shut against them. This is the kind of verse which is cherished by the magazines as a correspondent to the tawdry pictures of smiling milliners' dolls in the frontispiece. Like these they are only a fashion, a fashion based on no reality of love or beauty. The inducement to write them consists in a little money, or more frequently the charm of seeing an anonymous name printed at the top in capitals.

We must here, in passing, advert also to the style of story current in the magazines, flimsy beyond any texture that was ever spun or even dreamed of by the mind of man, in any other age and country. They are said to be "written for the seamstresses," but we believe that every way injured class could relish and digest better fare even at the end of long days of exhausting labour. There are exceptions to this censure; stories by Mrs. Child have been published in the magazines, and now and then good ones by Mrs. Stephens and others; but, take them generally, they are calculated to do a positive injury to the public mind, acting as an opiate, and of an adulterated kind, too.

But to return to the poets. At their head Mr. Bryant stands alone. His range is not great, nor his genius fertile. But his poetry is purely the language of his inmost nature, and the simple lovely garb in which his thoughts are arranged, a direct gift from the Muse. He has written nothing that is not excellent, and the atmosphere of his verse refreshes and composes the mind, like leaving the highway to enter some green, lovely, fragrant wood.

Halleck and Willis are poets of society. Though the former has written so little, yet that little is full of fire,—elegant, witty, delicate in sentiment. It is an honour to the country that these occasional sparks, struck off from the flint of commercial life, should have kindled so much flame as they have. It is always a consolation to see one of them sparkle amid the rubbish of daily life. One of his poems has been published within the last year, written, in fact, long ago, but new to most of us, and it

AMERICAN LITERATURE 499

enlivened the literary thoroughfare, as a green wreath might some dusty, musty hall of legislation.

Willis has not the same terseness or condensed electricity. But he has grace, spirit, at times a winning pensiveness, and a lively, though almost wholly sensuous, delight in the beautiful.

Dana has written so little that he would hardly be seen in a more thickly garnished galaxy. But the masculine strength of feeling, the solemn tenderness and refined thought displayed in such pieces as the "Dying Raven," and the "Husband and Wife's Grave," have left a deep impression on the popular mind.

Longfellow is artificial and imitative. He borrows incessantly, and mixes what he borrows, so that it does not appear to the best advantage. He is very faulty in using broken or mixed metaphors. The ethical part of his writing has a hollow, second-hand sound. He has, however, elegance, a love of the beautiful, and a fancy for what is large and manly, if not a full sympathy with it. His verse breathes at times much sweetness; and, if not allowed to supersede what is better may promote a taste for good poetry. Though imitative, he is not mechanical.

We cannot say as much for Lowell, who, we must declare it, though to the grief of some friends, and the disgust of more, is absolutely wanting in the true spirit and tone of poesy. His interest in the moral questions of the day has supplied the want of vitality in himself; his great facility at versification has enabled him to fill the ear with a copious stream of pleasant sound. But his verse is stereotyped; his thought sounds no depth, and posterity will not remember him.

R. W. Emerson, in melody, in subtle beauty of thought and expression, takes the highest rank upon this list. But his poems are mostly philosophical, which is not the truest kind of poetry. They want the simple force of nature and passion, and, while they charm the ear and interest the mind, fail to wake far-off echoes in the heart. The imagery wears a symbolical air, and serves rather as illustration, than to delight us by fresh and glowing forms of life.

We must here mention one whom the country has not yet learned to honour, perhaps never may, for he wants artistic skill to give complete form to his inspiration. This is William Ellery Channing, nephew and namesake of Dr. C., a volume of whose poems, published three or four years ago in Boston, remains unknown, except to a few friends, nor, if known, would they probably, excite sympathy, as those which have been published in the periodicals have failed to do so. Yet some of the purest tones of the lyre are his, the finest inspirations as to the feelings and passions of men, deep spiritual insight, and an entire originality in the use of his means. The frequently unfinished and obscure state of his poems, a passion for forcing words out of their usual meaning into one which they may appropriately bear, but which comes upon the reader with an unpleasing and puzzling surprise, may repel, at first glance, from many of these poems, but do not mar the following sublime description of the beings we want, to rule, to redeem, to re-create this nation, and under whose reign alone can there be an American literature, for then only could we have life worth recording. The simple grandeur of this poem as a whole, must be felt by every one, while each line and thought will be found worthy of earnest contemplation and satisfaction after the most earnest life and thought.

> Hearts of Eternity! hearts of the deep!
> Proclaim from land to sea your mighty fate;
> How that for you no living comes too late;
> How ye cannot in Theban labyrinth creep;
> How ye great harvests from small surface reap;
> Shout, excellent band, in grand primeval strain,
> Like midnight winds that foam along the main,
> And do all things rather than pause to weep.
> A human heart knows naught of littleness,
> Suspects no man, compares with no man's ways,
> Hath in one hour most glorious length of days,
> A recompense, a joy, a loveliness;
> Like eaglet keen, shoots into azure far,
> And always dwelling nigh is the remotest star.

A series of poems, called "Man in the Republic," by Cornelius Mathews, deserves a higher meed of sympathy than it has received. The thoughts and views are strong and noble, the exhibition of them imposing. In plastic power this writer is deficient. His prose works sin in exuberance, and need consolidating and chastening. We find fine things, but not so arranged as to be seen in the right places and by the best light.

AMERICAN LITERATURE 501

In his poems Mr. Mathews is unpardonably rough and rugged; the poetic substance finds no musical medium in which to flow. Yet there *is* poetic substance which makes full chords, if not a harmony. He holds a worthy sense of the vocation of the poet, and worthily expresses it thus:—

> To strike or bear, to conquer or to yield
> Teach thou! O topmost crown of duty, teach,
> What fancy whispers to the listening ear,
> At hours when tongue nor taint of care impeach
> The fruitful calm of greatly silent hearts;
> When all the stars for happy thought are set,
> And, in the secret chambers of the soul,
> All blessed powers of joyful truth are met;
> Though calm and garlandless thou mayst appear,
> The world shall know thee for its crowned seer.

A considerable portion of the hope and energy of this country still turns towards the drama, that greatest achievement when wrought to perfection of human power. For ourselves, we believe the day of the regular drama to be past; and, though we recognize the need of some kind of spectacle and dramatic representation to be absolutely coincident with an animated state of the public mind, we have thought that the opera, ballet, pantomime and briefer, more elastic forms, like the *vaudeville* of the French theatre, or the *proverb* of the social party, would take the place of elaborate tragedy and comedy.

But those who find the theatres of this city well filled all the year round by an audience willing to sit out the heroisms of Rolla, and the sentimentalism and stale morality of such a piece as we were doomed to listen to while the Keans were here, ("Town and Country" was its name,) still think there is room for the regular drama, if genius should engage in its creation. Accordingly there have been in this country, as well as in England, many attempts to produce dramas suitable for action no less than for the closet. The actor, Murdoch, about to devote himself with enthusiasm and hope to prop up a falling profession, is to bring out a series of plays written, not merely *for* him, but because his devotion is likely to furnish fit occasion for their appearance. The first of these, "Witchcraft, a tragedy," brought out successfully upon the boards at Philadelphia, we

502   NEW YORK SHORT PUBLISHED WORKS

have read, and it is a work of strong and majestic lineaments; a fine originality is shown in the conception, by which the love of a son for a mother is made a sufficient *motiv* (as the Germans call the ruling impulse of a work) in the production of tragic interest; no less original is the attempt, and delightful the success, in making an aged woman a satisfactory heroine to the piece through the greatness of her soul, and the magnetic influence it exerts on all around her, till the ignorant and superstitious fancy that the sky darkens and the winds wait upon her as she walks on the lonely hill-side near her hut to commune with the Past, and seek instruction from Heaven. The working of her character on the other agents of the piece is depicted with force and nobleness. The deep love of her son for her, the little tender, simple ways in which he shows it, having preserved the purity and poetic spirit of childhood by never having been weaned from his first love, a mother's love, the anguish of his soul when he too becomes infected with distrust, and cannot discriminate the natural magnetism of a strong nature from the spells and lures of sorcery, the final triumph of his faith, all offered the highest scope to genius and the power of moral perception in the actor. There are highly poetic intimations of those lowering days with their veiled skies, brassy light, and sadly whispering winds, very common in Massachusetts, so ominous and brooding seen from any point, but from the idea of witchcraft, invested with an awful significance. We do not know, however, that this could bring it beyond what it has appeared to our own sane mind, as if the air was thick with spirits, in an equivocal and surely sad condition, whether of purgatory or downfall; and the air was vocal with all manner of dark intimations. We are glad to see this mood of nature so fitly characterized.

The sweetness and *naiveté* with which the young girl is made to describe the effects of love upon her, as supposing them to proceed from a spell, are also original, and there is no other way in which this revelation could have been induced that would not have injured the beauty of the character and position. Her visionary sense of her lover, as an ideal figure, is of a high order of poetry, and these facts have very seldom been brought out from the cloisters of the mind into the light of open day.

AMERICAN LITERATURE 503

The play is very deficient as regards rhythm; indeed, we might say there is no apparent reason why the lines should begin with capital letters. The minor personages are mere caricatures, very coarsely drawn; all the power is concentrated on the main characters and their emotions. So did not Shakspeare, does not ever the genuine dramatist, whose mind teems with "the fulness of forms." As Raphael in his most crowded groups can put in no misplaced or imperfect foot or hand, neither neglect to invest the least important figure of his backgrounds with every characteristic trait, nor could spare the invention of the most beautiful *coiffure* and accessories for the humblest handmaid of his Madonnas, so doth the great artist always clothe the whole picture with full and breathing life, for it appears so before his mental eye. But minds not perfectly artistical, yet of strong conceptions, subordinate the rest to one or two leading figures, and the imperfectly represented life of the others incloses them, as in a frame.

In originality of conception and resting the main interest upon force of character in a woman, this drama naturally leads us to revert to a work in the department of narrative fiction, which, on similar grounds, comes to us as a harbinger of the new era. This book is "Margaret, or the Real and Ideal," a work which has appeared within the past year; and, considering its originality and genuineness, has excited admiration and sympathy amazingly soon. Even some leading reviews, of what Byron used to speak of as the "garrison" class, (a class the most opposite imaginable to that of Garrison abolitionists,) have discussed its pretensions and done homage to its merits. It is a work of great power and richness, a genuine disclosure of the life of mind and the history of character. Its descriptions of scenery and the common people, in the place and time it takes up, impart to it the highest value as a representative of transient existence, which had a great deal of meaning. The beautiful simplicity of action upon and within the mind of Margaret, Heaven lying so clearly about her in the infancy of the hut of drunkards, the woods, the village, and their ignorant, simply human denizens, her unconscious growth to the stature of womanhood, the flow of life impelled by her, the spiritual intimations of her dreams, the prophecies of music in the character of Chilion, the *naive* discussion of the leading

504   NEW YORK SHORT PUBLISHED WORKS

reform movements of the day in their rudimental forms, the archness, the humour, the profound religious faith, make of this book an aviary from which doves shall go forth to discover and report of all the green spots of promise in the land. Of books like this, as good, and still better, our new literature shall be full; and, though one swallow does not make a summer, yet we greet, in this one "Yankee novel," the sufficient earnest of riches that only need the skill of competent miners to be made current for the benefit of man.

Meanwhile, the most important part of our literature, while the work of diffusion is still going on, lies in the journals, which monthly, weekly, daily, send their messages to every corner of this great land, and form, at present, the only efficient instrument for the general education of the people.

Among these, the Magazines take the lowest rank. Their object is principally to cater for the amusement of vacant hours, and, as there is not a great deal of wit and light talent in this country, they do not even this to much advantage. More wit, grace, and elegant trifling, embellish the annals of literature in one day of France than in a year of America.

The Reviews are more able. If they cannot compare, on equal terms, with those of France, England, and Germany, where, if genius be rare, at least a vast amount of talent and culture are brought to bear upon all the departments of knowledge, they are yet very creditable to a new country, where so large a portion of manly ability must be bent on making laws, making speeches, making rail-roads and canals. They are, however, much injured by a partisan spirit, and the fear of censure from their own public. This last is always slow death to a journal; its natural and only safe position is *to lead*; if, instead, it bows to the will of the multitude, it will find the ostracism of democracy far more dangerous than the worst censure of a tyranny could be. It is not half so dangerous to a man to be immured in a dungeon alone with God and his own clear conscience, as to walk the streets fearing the scrutiny of a thousand eyes, ready to veil, with anxious care, whatever may not suit the many-headed monster in its momentary mood. Gentleness is dignified, but caution is debasing; only a noble fearlessness can give wings to the mind, with which to soar beyond the common ken, and learn what may be of use to the crowd below. Writers have nothing to do but to love truth fervently, seek justice according to their ability, and then express what is in the mind; they have nothing to do with consequences, God will take care of those. The want of such noble courage, such faith in the power of truth and good desire, paralyze mind greatly in this country. Publishers are afraid; authors are afraid; and if a worthy resistance is not made by religious souls, there is danger that all the light will soon be put under bushels, lest some wind should waft from it a spark that may kindle dangerous fire.

For want of such faith, and the catholic spirit that flows from it, we have no great leading Review. The North American was once the best. While under the care of Edward Everett, himself a host in extensive knowledge, grace and adroitness in applying it, and the power of enforcing grave meanings by a light and flexible satire that tickled while it wounded, it boasted more force, more life, a finer scope of power. But now, though still exhibiting ability and information upon special points, it is entirely deficient in great leadings, and the *vivida vis*, but ambles and jogs at an old gentlemanly pace along a beaten path that leads to no important goal.

Several other journals have more life, energy and directness than this, but there is none which occupies a truly great and commanding position, a beacon light to all who sail that way. In order to do this, a journal must know how to cast aside all local and temporary considerations when new convictions command, and allow free range in its columns, to all kinds of ability, and all ways of viewing subjects. That would give it a life, rich, bold, various.

The life of intellect is becoming more and more determined to the weekly and daily papers, whose light leaves fly so rapidly and profusely over the land. Speculations are afloat, as to the influence of the electric telegraph upon their destiny, and it seems obvious that it should raise their character by taking from them in some measure, the office of gathering and dispersing the news, and requiring of them rather to arrange and interpret it.

This mode of communication is susceptible of great excellence in the way of condensed essay, narrative, criticism, and is the natural receptacle for the lyrics of the day. That so few good ones deck the poet's corner, is because the indifference or unfitness of editors, as to choosing and refusing, makes this place, at present, undesirable to the poet. It might be otherwise.

The means which this organ affords of diffusing knowledge and sowing the seeds of thought where they may hardly fail of an infinite harvest, cannot be too highly prized by the discerning and benevolent. Minds of the first class are generally indisposed to this kind of writing; what must be done on the spur of the occasion and cast into the world so incomplete, as the hurried offspring of a day or hour's labour must generally be, cannot satisfy their judgment, or do justice to their powers. But he who looks to the benefit of others, and sees with what rapidity and ease instruction and thought are assimilated by men, when they come thus, as it were, on the wings of the wind, may be content, as an unhonoured servant to the grand purposes of Destiny, to work in such a way at the Pantheon which the Ages shall complete, on which his name may not be inscribed, but which will breathe the life of his soul.

The confidence in uprightness of intent, and the safety of truth, is still more needed here than in the more elaborate kinds of writing, as meanings cannot be fully explained nor expressions revised. Newspaper writing is next door to conversation, and should be conducted on the same principles. It has this advantage: we address, not our neighbour, who forces us to remember his limitations and prejudices, but the ideal presence of human nature as we feel it ought to be and trust it will be. We address America rather than Americans.

A worthy account of the vocation and duties of the journalist, is given by Cornelius Mathews. Editors, generally, could not do better than every New Year's day to read and insert the following verses.

> As shakes the canvass of a thousand ships,
> Struck by a heavy land-breeze, far at sea,
> Ruffle the thousand broad sheets of the land,
>   Filled with the people's breath of potency.
>
> A thousand images the hour will take,
>   From him who strikes, who rules, who speaks, who sings,
> Many within the hour their grave to make,
>   Many to live, far in the heart of things.

AMERICAN LITERATURE

A dark-dyed spirit he, who coins the time,
  To virtue's wrong, in base disloyal lies,
Who makes the morning's breath, the evening's tide,
  The utterer of his blighting forgeries.

How beautiful who scatters, wide and free,
  The gold-bright seeds of loved and loving truth!
By whose perpetual hand, each day supplied,
  Leaps to new life the empire's heart of youth.

To know the instant and to speak it true,
  Its passing lights of joy, its dark, sad cloud,
To fix upon the unnumbered gazer's view,
  Is to thy ready hand's broad strength allowed.

There is an inwrought life in every hour,
  Fit to be chronicled at large and told.
'Tis thine to pluck to light its secret power,
  And on the air its many-colored heart unfold.

The angel that in sand-dropped minutes lives,
  Demands a message cautious as the ages,
Who stuns, with dusk-red words of hate his ear,
  That mighty power to boundless wrath enrages.

This feeling of the dignity of his office, honour and power in fulfilling it, are not common in the journalist, but, where they exist, a mark has been left fully correspondent to the weight of the instrument. The few editors of this country who, with mental ability and resource, have combined strength of purpose and fairness of conduct, who have never merged the man and the gentleman in the partisan, who have been willing to have all sides fully heard, while their convictions were clear on one, who have disdained groundless assaults or angry replies, and have valued what was sincere, characteristic and free, too much to bend to popular errors they felt able to correct, have been so highly prized that it is wonderful that more do not learn the use of this great opportunity. It will be learned yet; the resources of this organ of thought and instruction begin to be understood, and shall yet be brought out and used worthily.

We see we have omitted honoured names in this essay. We have not spoken of Brown, as a novelist by far our first in point of genius and instruction as to the soul of things. Yet his works have fallen almost out of print. It is their dark, deep gloom that prevents their being popular, for their very beauties are grave and sad. But we see that Ormond is being republished at this moment. The picture of Roman character, of the life and resources of a single noble creature, of Constantia alone, should make that book an object of reverence. All these novels should be republished; if not favorites, they should at least not be lost sight of, for there will always be some who find in such powers of mental analysis the only response to their desires.

We have not spoken of Hawthorne, the best writer of the day, in a similar range with Irving, only touching many more points and discerning far more deeply. But we have omitted many things in this slight sketch, for the subject, even in this stage, lies as a volume in our mind, and cannot be unrolled in completeness unless time and space were more abundant. Our object was to show that although by a thousand signs, the existence is foreshown of those forces which are to animate an American literature, that faith, those hopes are not yet alive which shall usher it into a homogeneous or fully organized state of being. The future is glorious with certainties for those who do their duty in the present, and, lark-like, seeking the sun, challenge its eagles to an earthward flight, where their nests may be built in our mountains, and their young raise their cry of triumph, unchecked by dullness in the echoes.

EUROPEAN SHORT PUBLISHED
WORKS 1846–1850

LIVERPOOL AND MANCHESTER

Letters from England

Passage in the Cambria—Lord and Lady Falkland—Capt. Judkins—
Liverpool—Manchester—Mechanics' Institute—The Dial—Peace and
War—The Working-Men of England—Their Tribute to Sir Robert Peel—
The Royal Institute—Statues—Chester—Bathing.

AMBLESIDE, Westmoreland, 23d August, 1846.

I TAKE the first interval of rest and stillness to be filled up by
some lines for The Tribune. Only three weeks have passed since
leaving New-York, but I have already had nine days of wonder
in England, and, having learned a good deal, suppose I may
have something to tell.

Long before receiving this, you know that we were fortunate
in the shortest voyage ever made across the Atlantic—only ten
days and sixteen hours from Boston to Liverpool. The weather
and all circumstances were propitious; and, if some of us
were weak of head enough to suffer from the smell and jar of
the machinery, or other ills by which the Sea is wont to avenge
itself on the arrogance of its vanquishers, we found no pity. The
stewardess observed that she thought "any one tempted God
Almighty who complained on a voyage where they did not even
have to put guards to the dishes!"

As many contradictory counsels were given us with regard
to going in one of the steamers in preference to a sailing vessel,
I will mention here, for the benefit of those who have not yet
tried one, that he must be fastidious indeed who could complain
of the Cambria. The advantage of a quick passage and certainty
as to the time of arrival, would, with us, have outweighed
many ills; but, apart from this, we found more space than we
expected and as much as we needed for a very tolerable degree
of convenience in our sleeping-rooms, better ventilation than
Americans in general can be persuaded to accept, general

509

cleanliness and good attendance. In the evening, when the wind was favorable, and the sails set so that the vessel looked like a great winged creature darting across the apparently measureless expanse, the effect was very grand, but ah! for such a spectacle one pays too dear; I far prefer looking out upon "the blue and foaming sea" from a firm green shore.

Our ship's company numbered several pleasant members, and that desire prevailed in each to contribute to the satisfaction of all, which, if carried out through the voyage of life, would make this earth as happy as it is a lovely abode. At Halifax we took in the Governor of Nova-Scotia, returning from his very unpopular administration. His lady was with him, a daughter of William IV, and the celebrated Mrs. Jordan. The English on board, and the Americans, following their lead, as usual, seemed to attach much importance to her left-handed alliance with one of the dullest families that ever sat upon a throne (and that is a bold word, too;) none to her descent from one whom Nature had endowed with her most splendid regalia, genius that fascinated the attention of all kinds and classes of men, grace and winning qualities that no heart could resist. Was the cestus buried with her, that no sense of its preëminent value lingered, as far as I could perceive, in the thoughts of any except myself?

We had a foretaste of the delights of living under an aristocratical Government at the Custom-House, where our baggage was detained, and we waiting for it weary hours, because of the preference given to the mass of household stuff carried back by this same Lord and Lady Falkland.

Capt. Judkins of the Cambria, an able and prompt Commander, was the one who insisted upon Douglass being admitted to equal rights upon his deck with the insolent slaveholders, and assumed a tone toward their assumptions, which, if the Northern States had had the firmness, good sense and honor to use would have had the same effect, and put our country in a very different position from that she occupies at present. He mentioned with pride that he understood the New-York Herald called him "the Nigger Captain," and seemed as willing to accept the distinction as Colonel McKenney is to wear as his last title that of "the Indian's friend."

At the first sight of the famous Liverpool Docks, extending miles on each side of our landing, we felt ourselves in a slower,

LETTERS FROM ENGLAND 511

solider, and not on that account less truly active state of things than at home. That impression is confirmed. There is not as we travel that rushing, tearing and swearing, that snatching of baggage, that prodigality of shoe-leather and lungs that attend the course of the traveler in the United States; but we do not lose our "goods," we do not miss our car. The dinner if ordered in time, is cooked properly and served punctually, and at the end of the day, more that is permanent seems to have come of it than on the full-drive system. But more of that and with a better grace at a later day.

The day after our arrival we went to Manchester. There we went over the magnificent warehouse of —— Phillips, in itself a Bazaar enough to furnish provision for all the wants and fancies of thousands. In the evening we went to the Mechanics' Institute and saw the boys and young men in their classes. I have since visited the Mechanics' Institute at Liverpool, where more than seventeen hundred pupils are received, and with more thorough educational arrangements; but the excellent spirit, the desire for growth in wisdom and enlightened benevolence is the same in both. For a very small fee the mechanic, clerk or apprentice, and the women of their families can receive various good and well-arranged instruction, not only in common branches of an English Education, but in mathematics, composition, the French and German languages, the practice and theory of the Fine Arts, and they are ardent in availing themselves of instruction in the higher branches. I found large classes, not only in architectural drawing, which may be supposed to be followed with a view to professional objects, but landscape also, and as large in German as in French. They can attend many good lectures and concerts without additional charge, for a due place is here assigned to Music as to its influence on the whole mind. The large and well-furnished libraries are in constant requisition, and the books in most constant demand are not those of amusement, but of a solid and permanent interest and value. Only for the last year in Manchester and for two in Liverpool, have these advantages been extended to girls; but now that part of the subject is looked upon as it ought to be, and begins to be treated more and more as it must and will be wherever true civilization is making its way. One of the handsomest houses in Liverpool has been purchased for the girls' school, and room and good arrangement been

EUROPEAN SHORT PUBLISHED WORKS

afforded for their work and their play. Among other things they are taught, as they ought to be in all American schools, to cut out and make dresses.

I had the pleasure of seeing quotations made from our Boston "Dial" in the address in which the Director of the Liverpool Institute, a very benevolent and intelligent man, explained to his disciples and others its objects, and which concludes thus:

> But this subject of self-improvement is inexhaustible. If traced to its results in action, it is, in fact, "The Whole Duty of Man." Here, however, we must stop. Much remains, of which there may be an opportunity to speak hereafter. Meantime, I have sought to impress one great principle, rather than to dwell on minor points, however useful:—a principle which, to us in our relations here, is unspeakably important, identifying, as it does, intellectual improvement with moral obligation and moral progress. What farther of detail it involves and implies, I know that you will, each and all, think out for yourselves. Beautifully has it been said—"Is not the difference between spiritual and material things just this; that in the one case we must watch details, in the other, keep alive the high resolve, and the details will take care of themselves? Keep the sacred central fire burning, and throughout the system, in each of its acts, will be warmth and glow enough."*

To sum up in a few words what I wish now to say. If you seek the power of speech and thought, (and they reciprocally aid each other) let the service of your fellows ever be in view; and in this service be not too curious to inquire whether, how, and when, your own happiness will be the result; be prepared even for unhappiness; in this world both are but means: if prosperity renders benevolence more beneficent, adversity renders it more sympathetic; if joy is the sunshine which makes your purposes of good bear the richest fruit, sorrow is a wind that will increase their strength, and strike their roots deeper into the heart. All outward fortune will thus contribute variously, but not unequally to your moral welfare.

For myself, if I be asked what my purpose is in relation to you, I would briefly reply; it is that I may help, be it ever so feebly, to train up a race of young men, who shall escape vice by rising above it; who shall love truth because it is truth, not because it brings them wealth or honor; who shall regard life as a solemn thing, involving too weighty responsibilities to be wasted in idle or frivolous pursuits; who shall recognize in their daily labors not merely a tribute to the "hard necessity of daily bread," but a field for the development of

---

* The Dial, vol. I, p. 199. October, 1840, Musings of a Recluse.

their better nature by the discharge of duty; who shall judge in all things for themselves, bowing the knee to no sectarian or party watchwords of any kind; and who, while they think for themselves, shall feel for others, and regard their talents, their attainments, their opportunities, their possessions, as blessings held in trust for the good of their fellow-men. It may seem vain to aim at so high things with so humble means; but we must work with such means and such powers as we have; it is for us to seek what is right, it is for another to fix the measure of success which shall attend our search.

I found that The Dial had been read with earnest interest by some of the best minds in these especially practical regions, that it had been welcomed as a representative of some sincere and honorable life in America and thought the fittest to be quoted under this motto

"What are noble deeds but noble thoughts realized?"

Among other signs of the times we bought Bradshaw's Railway Guide, and opening it found extracts from the writings of our countrymen Elihu Burritt and Charles Sumner, on the subject of Peace, occupying a leading place in the "Collect" for the month, of this little hand-book, more likely, in an era like ours, to influence the conduct of the day than would an illuminated breviary. Now that peace is secured for the present between our two countries, the spirit is not forgotten that quelled the storm. Greeted on every side with expressions of feeling about the blessings of peace, the madness and wickedness of War, that would be deemed romantic in our darker land, I have answered to the speakers, "But you are mightily pleased, and illuminate for your victories in China and Ireland, do you not?" and they, unprovoked by the taunt, would mildly reply, "*We* do not, but it is too true that a large part of the nation fail to bring home the true nature and bearing of those events, and apply principle to conduct with as much justice as they do in the case of a nation nearer to them by kindred and position. But we are sure that feeling is growing purer on the subject day by day, and that there will soon be a large majority against war on any occasion or for any object."

I heard a most interesting letter read from a tradesman in one of the country towns, whose daughters are self-elected instructors of the people in the way of cutting out from books and pamphlets fragments on the great subjects of the day, which they send about in packages, or paste on walls and doors. He said that one such passage pasted on a door, he had seen read with eager interest by hundreds to whom such thoughts were, probably, quite new, and with some of whom it could scarcely fail to be as a little seed of a large harvest. Another good omen I found in written tracts by Joseph Barker, a working-man of the town of Wortley, published through his own printing-press. I have one of these before me, "On the blessings of Free Trade," whose opening passage conveys in brief and simple fashion the kind of instruction most needed by America.

Respected Chairman, my Friends.—All I ask is that you will hear me with patience. I acknowledge that on various religious questions my opinions are different from those of most professors of religion; but I cannot consider myself as blamable on that account. My desire is in all things to know what is true and to reduce it to practice in my life. All I care for is to know what is right and do it. It is true I judge for myself what *is* right; but I leave others at liberty to do the same. I differ from others, but I allow others to differ from me; and there is not one of you but what differs as widely from me, as I differ from you: why then should we not bear with one another? Why cannot we each enjoy our liberty with thankfulness, and leave the rest to God. I am accountable to God both for my opinions and practices, and that is enough. If I do wrong, God will punish me, and you have no need to wish to help him; and if I do right He will reward me, and you cannot hinder Him. And *you* also are accountable to God, and should rather be carefully preparing for your own reckoning, than judging whether others are prepared or not. If we can *mend* each other's religious opinions, let us do so at the proper time; but don't let us hate or persecute each other. Let us teach each other in gentleness and love, and then leave each other in the hands of God. To our own master we stand or fall.

I meet you at present as friends of liberty, as persons who rejoice in the freedom and the welfare of mankind. We meet to express our joy and thankfulness for that measure of freedom in trade which has been lately granted to us. I stand forth to declare the joy and thankfulness of my own soul, and to state my reasons for them. I stand forth to express my hopes and wishes, and to show how they may be realized. *   *   *   *

This is not mere talk, noise and bluster, it is the echo of a mighty voice from the very heart of the nation. Like the simple close of Sir R. Peel's speech on resigning the office of Premier, to retire to higher honors, it has that highest eloquence of a plain and adequate sense of great facts. We will not deny ourselves the pleasure of adding the working-man's tribute to the statesman who has acted in the spirit of truth, of honor, of the genuine religion of manhood, for a purpose which shall bear its harvest where no golden corn-field waves.

"I must add a few words about Sir Robert Peel. I know but little of his former life, and I shall therefore say nothing about it. But his conduct of late has been such as to incline me to believe that he has long been a lover of liberty and peace, of knowledge and righteousness, a well-wisher to the people of this empire, and to mankind at large. He has had his fears no doubt, as all reformers have; he has been afraid of offending his party, and of losing his friends; he has been afraid of losing his influence, and lessening his power to do good; yet still, in my judgment, he has leaned to the side of freedom and equity, and longed for the welfare of the people. I do not at all agree with those who give him credit for nothing but a selfish policy and superior tact and talent in what he has done; I believe him to be a truly well-meaning man, and to have been influenced by an earnest desire to promote the welfare of his countrymen and the welfare of the world. His conduct for some time past has been truly noble and admirable.—The way in which he removed the pressure of taxation from the poor to the rich; the manner in which he conducted himself in reference to the Oregon dispute; the eagerness, the anxiety, the resolution, the straight-forwardness, the great patience and perseverance with which he toiled and pleaded for Free Trade; the manly, the *Christian* fortitude with which he braved reproach and persecution; the sacrifices which he made for its sake; the firmness and calmness with which he endured the cruel and disgraceful taunts and insults of his enemies, deserve the highest praise. They have affected me very much. I never felt such a respect for a Statesman before in all my life. It is impossible that he should be a hypocrite. I should as readily think of questioning the sincerity, the integrity of the Apostle Paul as of Sir Robert Peel. If the conduct of Sir Robert Peel for a length of time past does not prove him to be a good, an upright man; a lover of truth and righteousness; a friend to peace and freedom; a real well-wisher to the improvement and the welfare of his country and his kind, then a tree can no longer be known by its fruits;

then a fountain can no longer be known by its streams. For myself I look on Sir Robert Peel as one of the greatest and best-deserving men of our times. There is not a Statesman on earth in whom I have greater confidence. I believe him to be a sterling, Christian man, and I hope that the insults and persecutions with which he has met, and with which he may continue to meet, will only perfect his character, and prepare him for still greater usefulness in days to come.

No doubt Sir Robert has his weakness, his failings; but so have the best of men. He has allowed himself to be influenced at times by his fears; but so have all reformers, from the days of Abraham to the present hour. He has hoped to gain by policy what could only be gained by self-sacrifice; but all good men have indulged such hopes. He has delayed good measures in hopes of winning over his party by time and the force of truth; but the bravest reformers that ever lived have done the same. I do not believe him to be perfect; much less do I believe him to have been always so; but I still regard him as a great, good man, a *friend* as well as a benefactor to his race.

There are many other things in the history of Sir R. Peel very much to his credit, besides those to which I have alluded, but I cannot even refer to them at present.

But what of his conduct toward O'Connell? I answer; it is only fair to suppose, that as he was one of a party who were not all as noble or as enlightened as himself, he might consent to certain measures which he did not quite approve. I cannot myself but construe his motives charitably. I like to illumine the darker portions of his life by the brighter, and not to obscure the brighter portions by the darker or the doubtful. In short, I have a right good, comfortable opinion of Sir R. Peel, and I am glad I have. I offer him my hearty thanks for his efforts in the cause of freedom and human happiness; I congratulate him on his great and glorious triumph; and I pray most heartily that God may spare his life, and favor him richly with the choicest of his blessings, and make him a still greater benefactor to his kind.

As for Cobden and his fellow-laborers, there is no need that I should dwell upon their merits. Almost every one praises them. Sir Robert Peel has made the greatest sacrifices, and has been the greatest sufferer; I therefore sympathize the most with him."   *   *   *   *   *   *   *

How great, how imperious the need of such men, of such deeds, we felt more than ever, while compelled to turn a deaf ear to the squalid and shameless beggars of Liverpool, or talking by night in the streets of Manchester to the girls from the Mills, who were strolling bare-headed, with coarse, rude and reckless air through the streets, seeing through the windows of its gin-palaces the women seated drinking, too dull to carouse. The homes of England! their sweetness is melting into fable; only the new Spirit in its holiest power can restore to those homes their boasted security of "each man's castle," for Woman, the warder, is driven into the street, and has let fall the keys in her sad plight. Yet, darkest hour of night is nearest dawn, and there seems reason to believe that

> "There's a good time coming."

Blest be those who aid—who doubt not that

> "Smallest helps, if rightly given,
> Make the impulse stronger;
> 'Twill be strong enough one day."

Other things we saw in Liverpool—the Royal Institute, with the statue of Roscoe by Chantrey, and in its collection from the works of the early Italian artists and otherwise, bearing traces of that liberality and culture by which the man, happy enough to possess them, and, at the same time engaged with his fellow-citizens in practical life, can do so much more to enlighten and form them than Prince or Noble possibly can with far larger pecuniary means. We saw the statue of Huskisson in the Cemetery. It is fine as a Portrait Statue, but as a work of Art wants firmness and grandeur. I say it is fine as a portrait statue, though we were told it is not like the original; but it is a fine conception of an individuality which might exist, if it does not yet. It is by Gibson, who received his early education in Liverpool. I saw there, too, the body of an infant borne to the grave by women; for it is a beautiful custom here that those who have fulfilled all other tender offices to the little being, should hold to it the same relation to the very last.

From Liverpool we went to Chester, one of the oldest cities in England, a Roman station, Cestrea then, and abode of the "Twentieth Legion," "the Victorious." Tiles bearing this inscription, heads of Jupiter, other marks of their occupation have, not long ago, been detected beneath the sod. The town also bears the marks of Welsh invasion and domestic struggles. The shape of a cross in which it is laid out, its walls and towers, its four arched gateways, its ramparts and ruined towers, mantled with ivy, its old houses with biblical inscriptions, its cathedrals—in one of which tall trees have grown up amid the arches, a fresh garden plot with flowers, bright green and red, has taken place of the altar and a crowd of reveling swallows supplanted the sallow choirs of a former priesthood—present a *tout-ensemble* highly romantic in itself and charming, indeed, to trans-Atlantic eyes. Yet not to all eyes would it have had charms, for one American traveler, our companion on the voyage, gravely assured us that we should find the "castles and that sort of thing all humbug," and that if we wished to enjoy them it would "be best to sit at home and read some *handsome* work on the subject."

At the hotel in Liverpool and that in Manchester I had found no bath, and asking for one at Chester, the chambermaid said with earnest good will, that "they had none, but she thought she could get me a note from her master to the Infirmary!! if I would go there." Luckily I did not generalize quite as rapidly as travelers in America usually do, and put in the note book—"*Mem*: None but the sick ever bathe in England;" for in the next establishment we tried, I found the plentiful provision for a clean and healthy day, which I had read would be met *every where* in this country.

All else I must defer to my next, as the mail is soon to close. *

SCOTLAND, MARY QUEEN OF SCOTS, AND BEN LOMOND

Things and Thoughts in Europe No. V

Perth—Traveling by Coach—Loch Leven—Queen Mary—Loch Katrine—The Trosachs—Rowardennan—A Night on Ben Lomond (Lost)—Scotch Peasantry, &c.

BIRMINGHAM, Sept. 30th, 1846.

I WAS obliged to stop writing at Edinburgh before the better half of my tale was told, and must now begin there again, to speak of an excursion into the Highlands, which occupied about a fortnight.

THINGS AND THOUGHTS IN EUROPE V 519

We left Edinburgh by coach for Perth, and arrived there about three in the afternoon. I have reason to be very glad that I visit this island before the reign of the stage-coach is quite over. I have been every where on the top of the coach, even one day of drenching rain, and enjoy it highly.—Nothing can be more inspiring than this swift, steady progress over such smooth roads, and placed so high as to overlook the country freely, with the lively flourish of the horn preluding every pause. Traveling by railroad is in my opinion the most stupid process on earth; it is sleep without the refreshment of sleep, for the noise of the train makes it impossible either to read, talk or sleep to advantage. Here the advantages are immense; you can fly through this dull trance from one beautiful place to another, and stay at each during the time that would otherwise be spent on the road. Already the Artists, who are obliged to find their home in London, rejoice that all England is thrown open to them for sketching ground, since, whereas, formerly they were obliged to confine themselves to a few "green and bowery" spots in the neighborhood of the metropolis, they can now avail themselves of a day's leisure at a great distance and with choice of position. But while you are in the car, it is to me that worst of purgatories, the purgatory of dullness.

Well, on the coach we went to Perth, and passed through Kinross, and saw Loch Leven, and the island where Queen Mary passed those sorrowful months, before her romantic escape under care of the Douglas. As this unhappy, lovely woman stands for a type in history, death, time, and distance do not destroy her attractive power; like Cleopatra, she has still her adorers; nay, some are born to her in each new generation of men. Lately she has for her chevalier the Russian Prince Labanoff, who has spent fourteen years in studying upon all that related to her, and thinks now that he can make out a story and a picture about the mysteries of her short reign, which shall satisfy the desire of her lovers to find her as pure and just as she was charming. I have only seen of his array of evidence so much as may be found in the pages of Chambers's Journal, but that much does not disturb the original view I have taken of the case, which is that from a Princess educated under that Medici and Guise influence, engaged in the meshes of secret intrigue to favor the

Roman Catholic faith, her tacit acquiescence, at least, in the murder of Darnley, after all his injurious conduct toward her, was just what was to be expected. From a poor, beautiful young woman, longing to enjoy life, exposed both by her position and her natural fascinations to the utmost bewilderment of flattery whether prompted by interest or passion, her other acts of folly are most natural, and let all who feel inclined harshly to condemn her remember the verse,

> Then gently scan your brother man,
> Still gentler sister woman——

Surely in all the stern pages of life's account-book there is none on which a more terrible price was exacted for every precious endowment. Her rank and reign only made her powerless to do good, and exposed her to danger; her talents only served to irritate her foes and disappoint her friends; this most charming of women was the destruction of her lovers: married three times, she had never any happiness as a wife, but in both the connections of her choice found that either she had never possessed or could not retain, even for a few weeks, the love of the men she had chosen, so that Darnley was willing to risk her life and that of his unborn child to wreak his wrath upon Rizzio, and that after a few weeks with Bothwell she was heard "calling aloud for a knife to kill herself with." A mother twice, and of a son and daughter; both the children were brought forth in loneliness and sorrow, and separated from her early, her son educated to hate her, her daughter at once immured in a convent. Add the eighteen years of her imprisonment, and the fact that this foolish, prodigal world, when there was in it one woman fitted by her grace and loveliness to charm all eyes and enliven all fancies, let her be shut up to water with her tears her dull embroidery during all the full rose-blossom of her life, and you will hardly get beyond this story for a tragedy not noble but pallid and forlorn.

Such were the bootless, best thoughts I had while looking at the dull blood-stain and blocked-up secret stair of Holyrood, at the ruins of Loch Leven castle, and afterward at Abbotsford where the picture of Queen Mary's head, as it lay on the pillow when severed from the block, hung opposite to a fine caricature of "Queen Elizabeth dancing high and disposedly." In this last the face is like a mask—so frightful is the expression of cold craft, irritated vanity and the malice of a lonely breast in contrast with the attitude and elaborate frippery of the dress. The ambassador looks on dismayed; the little page can scarcely control the laughter which swells his boyish cheeks. Such can win the world which better hearts (and such Mary's was, even if it had a large black speck in it) are most like to lose.

It was a most lovely day in which we entered Perth, and saw in full sunshine its beautiful meadows, among them the North Inch, the famous battle ground commemorated in "The Fair Maid of Perth," adorned with graceful trees like those of the New-England country towns. In the afternoon we visited the modern Kinfauns, the stately home of Lord Grey. The drive to it is most beautiful, on the one side the Park, with noble hights that skirt it, on the other through a belt of trees was seen the river and the sweep of that fair and cultivated country. The house is a fine one, and furnished with taste, the library large, and some good works in marble.—Among the family pictures one arrested my attention, the face of a girl full of the most pathetic sensibility, and with no restraint of convention upon its ardent, gentle expression. She died young.

Returning, we were saddened, as almost always on leaving any such place, by seeing such swarms of dirty women and dirtier children at the doors of the cottages almost close by the gate of the avenue. To the horrors and sorrows of the streets in such places as Liverpool, Glasgow, and, above all, London, one has to grow insensible or die daily; but here in the sweet, fresh, green country, where there seems to be room for every body, it is impossible to forget the frightful inequalities between the lot of man and man, or believe that God can smile upon a state of things such as we find existent here. Can any man who has seen these things dare to blame the Associationists for their attempt to find prevention against such misery and wickedness in our land? Rather will not every man of tolerable intelligence and good feeling commend, say rather revere, every earnest attempt in that direction; nor dare interfere with any, unless he has a better to offer in its place?

Next morning we passed on to Crieff, in whose neighborhood we visited Drummond Castle, the abode, or rather one of the abodes, of Lord Willoughby D'Eresby. It has a noble park, through which you pass by an avenue of two miles long. The old keep still is ascended to get the fine view of the surrounding country; and during Queen Victoria's visit her Guards were quartered there. But what took my fancy most was the old-fashioned garden, full of old shrubs and new flowers, with its formal parterres in the shape of the family arms, and its clipped yew and box trees. It was fresh from a shower, and now glittering and fragrant in bright sunshine.

This afternoon we pursued our way, passing through the plantations of Ochtertyre, a far more charming place to my taste than Drummond Castle, freer and more various in its features. Five or six of these fine places lie in the neighborhood of Crieff, and the traveler may give two or three days to visiting them with a rich reward of delight. But we were pressing on to be with the lakes and mountains rather, and that night brought us to St. Fillan's, where we saw the moon shining on Loch Earn.

All this region and that of Loch Katrine and the Trosachs which we reached next day, Scott has described exactly in "The Lady of the Lake;" nor is it possible to appreciate that poem without going thither, neither to describe the scene better than he has done after you have seen it. I was somewhat disappointed in the pass of the Trosachs itself; it is very grand, but the grand part lasts so little while. The opening view of Loch Katrine, however, surpassed expectation. It was late in the afternoon when we launched our little boat there for Ellen's isle.

The boatmen recite, though not *con molto espressione*, the parts of the poem which describe these localities. Observing that they spoke of the personages, too, with the same air of confidence, we asked if they were sure that all this really happened. They replied, "Certainly; it had been told from father to son through so many generations." Such is the power of genius to interpolate what it will into the regular log-book of Time's voyage.

Leaving Loch Katrine the following day we entered Rob Roy's country, and saw on the way the house where Helen MacGregor was born and Rob Roy's sword, which is shown in a house by the wayside.

We came in a row-boat up Loch Katrine, though both on that and Loch Lomond you *may* go in a hateful little steamer with a squeaking fiddle to play Rob Roy Mac Gregor O. I walked almost all the way through the pass from Loch Katrine to Loch Lomond; it was a distance of six miles; but you feel as if you could walk sixty in that pure, exhilarating air. At Inversnaid we took boat again to go down Loch Lomond to the little inn of Rowardennan, from which the ascent is made of Ben Lomond, the greatest elevation in these parts. The boatmen are fine, athletic men: one of these we had with us to-night, a handsome young man of two or three-and-twenty, sang to us some Gaelic songs. The first, a very wild and plaintive air, was the expostulation of a girl whose lover has deserted her and married another. It seems he is ashamed and will not even look at her when they meet upon the road. She implores him, if he has not forgotten all that scene of by-gone love, at least to lift up his eyes and give her one friendly glance. The sad *crooning* burden of the stanzas in which she repeats this request was very touching. When the boatman had finished, he hung his head and seemed ashamed of feeling the song too much; then when we asked for another he said he would sing another about a girl that was happy. This one was in three parts. First, a tuneful address from a maiden to her absent lover. Second, his reply, assuring her of his fidelity and tenderness. Third, a strain which expresses their joy when reunited. I thought this boatman had sympathies which would prevent his tormenting any poor women, and perhaps make some one happy, and this was a pleasant thought since probably in the Highlands as elsewhere—

> "Maidens lend an ear too oft
> To the careless wooer;
> Maidens' hearts are *always soft*!
> Would that men's were truer."

I don't know that I quote the words correctly, but that is the sum and substance of a masculine report on these matters.

The first day at Rowardennan not being propitious to ascending the mountain, we went down the lake to sup, and got very tired in various ways, so that we rose very late next morning. Then we found a day of ten thousand for our purpose, but unhappily a large party had come with the sun and engaged all the horses so that, if we went, it must be on foot. This was something of an enterprise for me, as the ascent is four miles and toward the summit quite fatiguing; however, in the pride of newly gained health and strength, I was ready, and set forth with Mr. S. alone. We took no guide—and the people of the house did not advise it as they ought. They told us afterward they thought the day was so clear that there was no probability of danger, and they were afraid of seeming mercenary about it. It was, however, wrong, as they knew what we did not, that even the shepherds can be lost in these hills, if a mist comes on; that a party of gentlemen were so a few weeks before, and only by accident found their way to a house on the other side, and that a child which had been lost was not found for five days, long after its death. We, however, nothing doubting, set forth, ascending slowly, and often stopping to enjoy the points of view, which are many, for Ben Lomond consists of a congeries of hills, above which towers the true Ben or highest peak, as the head of a many-limbed body.

On reaching the peak, the sight was one of beauty and grandeur such as imagination never painted. You see around you no plain ground, but on every side constellations or groups of hills exquisitely dressed in the soft purple of the heather, amid which gleam the lakes like eyes that tell the secrets of the earth and drink in those of the heavens. Peak beyond peak caught from the shifting light all the colors of the prism, and on the farthest angel companies seemed hovering in their glorious white robes.

Words are idle on such subjects; what can I say but that it was a noble vision that satisfied the eye and stirred the imagination in all her secret pulses? Had that been, as afterward seemed likely, the last act of my life, there could not have been a finer decoration painted on the curtain which was to drop upon it.

About four o'clock we began our descent. Near the summit the traces of the path are not distinct, and I said to Mr. S. after a while, that we had lost it. He said he thought that was of no consequence, we could find our way down. I said I thought it was, as the ground was full of springs that were bridged over in the pathway. He accordingly went to look for it, and I stood still because I was so tired I did not like to waste any labor.

THINGS AND THOUGHTS IN EUROPE V 525

Soon he called to me that he had found it, and I followed in the direction where he seemed to be.—But I mistook, overshot it and saw him no more.

In about ten minutes I became alarmed and called him many times. It seems he on his side did the same, but the brow of some hill was between us, and we neither saw nor heard one another.

I then thought I would make the best of my way down and I should find him when I arrived. But in doing so I found the justice of my apprehension about the springs, as so soon as I got to the foot of the hills I would sink up to my knees in bog, and have to go up the hills again, seeking better crossing places. Thus I lost much time; nevertheless in the twilight I saw at last the Lake and the Inn of Rowardennan on its shore.

Between me and it lay direct a high heathery hill, which I afterward found is called "The Tongue," because hemmed in on three sides by a water-course. It looked as if, could I only get to the bottom of that, I should be on comparatively level ground. I then attempted to descend in the water-course, but finding that impracticable, climbed on the hill again and let myself down by the heather, for it was very steep and full of deep holes. With great fatigue I got to the bottom, but when I was about to cross the water-course there it looked very deep, and I felt afraid; it looked so deep in the dim twilight. I got down as far as I could by the root of a tree and threw down a stone; it sounded very hollow, and I was afraid to jump. The shepherds told me afterward, if I had I should probably have killed myself, it was so deep and the bed of the torrent full of sharp stones.

I then tried to ascend the hill again, for there was no other way to get off it, but soon sank down utterly exhausted. When able to get up again and look about me, it was completely dark. I saw far below me a light that looked about as big as a pin's head, that I knew to be from the inn at Rowardennan, but heard no sound except the rush of the waterfall, and the sighing of the night-wind.

For the first few minutes that I perceived I had got to my night's lodging, such as it was, the prospect seemed appalling. I was very lightly clad—my feet and dress were very wet—I had only a little shawl to throw round me, and a cold autumn wind had already come, and the night-mist was to fall on me, all fevered and exhausted as I was. I thought I should not live through the night, or if I did, live always a miserable invalid. I had no chance to keep myself warm by walking, for, now it was dark, it would be too dangerous to stir.

My only chance, however, lay in motion, and my only help in myself, and so convinced was I of this, that I did keep in motion the whole of that long night, imprisoned as I was on such a little perch of that great mountain. *How* long it seemed under such circumstances only those can guess who may have been similarly circumstanced. The mental experience of the time, most precious and profound—for it was indeed a season lonely, dangerous and helpless enough for the birth of thoughts beyond what the common sunlight will ever call to being, may be told in another place and time.

For about two hours I saw the stars, and very cheery and companionable they looked; but then the mist fell and I saw nothing more, except such apparitions as visited Ossian on the hill-side when he went out by night and struck the bosky shield and called to him the spirits of the heroes and the white-armed maids with their blue eyes of grief.—To me, too, came those visionary shapes; floating slowly and gracefully, their white robes would unfurl from the great body of mist in which they had been engaged, and come upon me with a kiss pervasively cold as that of Death. What they might have told me, who knows, if I had but resigned myself more passively to that cold, spirit-like breathing!

At last the moon rose. I could not see her, but her silver light filled the mist. Then I knew it was two o'clock, and that, having weathered out so much of the night, I might then rest; and the hours hardly seemed long to me more.

It may give an idea of the extent of the mountain, that though I called every now and then with all my force, in case by chance some aid might be near, and though no less than twenty men with their dogs were looking for me, I never heard a sound except the rush of the waterfall and the sighing of the night-wind, and once or twice the startling of the grouse in the heather. It was sublime indeed—a never-to-be-forgotten presentation of stern, serene realities.

At last came the signs of day, the gradual clearing and breaking up; some faint sounds from I know not what; the little flies, too, arose from their bed amid the purple heather and bit me; truly they were very welcome to do so. But what was my disappointment to find the mist so thick that I could see neither lake nor inn, nor any thing to guide me. I had to go by guess, and, as it happened, my Yankee method served me well. I ascended the hill, crossed the torrent in the waterfall, first drinking some of the water which was as good at that time as ambrosia. I crossed in that place because the waterfall made steps, as it were, to the next hill; to be sure they were covered with water, but I was already entirely wet with the mist, so that it did not matter. I then kept on scrambling, as it happened, in the right direction, till about seven some of the shepherds found me.—The moment they came all my feverish strength departed though if unaided I dare say it would have kept me up during the day, and they carried me home, where my arrival relieved my friends of distress far greater than I had undergone, for I had had my grand solitude, my Ossianic visions and the pleasure of sustaining myself, while they had had only doubt amounting to anguish and a fruitless search through the night.

Entirely contrary to my expectations I only suffered for this a few days, and was able to take a parting look at my prison as I went down the lake with feelings of complacency. It was a majestic looking hill, that Tongue, with the deep ravines on either side, and the richest robe of heather I have seen any where.

Mr. S. gave all the men who were looking for me a dinner in the barn, and he and Mrs. S. ministered to them, and they talked of Burns, really the national writer, and known by them, apparently, as none other is, and of hair-breadth 'scapes by flood and fell. Afterwards they were all brought up to see me, and it was pleasing indeed to see the good breeding and good feeling with which they deported themselves on the occasion. Indeed, this adventure created quite an intimate feeling between us and the people there. I had been much pleased with them before, in attending one of their dances, at the genuine independence and politeness of their conduct. They were willing and pleased to dance their Highland flings and strathspeys for our amusement, and did it as naturally and as freely as they would have offered the stranger the best chair.

All the rest must wait awhile. I cannot economize time to keep up my record in any proportion with what happens, nor

528 EUROPEAN SHORT PUBLISHED WORKS

can I get out of Scotland on this page, as I had intended, without utterly slighting many gifts and graces. *

LONDON AND PARIS, FRENCH THEATER AND LITERATURE

Things and Thoughts in Europe No. X

More of London—The Model-Prison at Pentonville—Bathing Establishment for the Poor—Also one for washing Clothes—The Crèches of Paris, for Poor People's Children—Old Drury in London—Sadler's Wells—English and French Acting compared—M'lle Rachel—French Tragedy—Rose Cheny—Dumas—Guizot—The Presentation at Court of the young Duchess—Ball at the Tuileries—American and French Women—Leverrier—The Sorbonne—Arago—Celebrated Lecturers—Discussions on Suicide and the Crusades—Rémusat—The Academy—La Mennais—Béranger—Reflections.

PARIS.

WHEN I wrote last I could not finish with London, and there remain yet two or three things I wish to speak of before passing to my impressions of this wonder-full Paris.

I visited the model-prison at Pentonville; but though in some respects an improvement upon others I have seen—though there was the appearance of great neatness and order in the arrangements of life—kindness and good judgment in the discipline of the prisoners—yet there was also an air of bleak forlornness about the place, and it fell far short of what my mind demands of such abodes considered as Redemption schools. But as the subject of prisons is now engaging the attention of many of the wisest and best, and the tendency is in what seems to me the true direction, I need not trouble myself to make crude and hasty suggestions; it is a subject to which persons who would be of use should give the earnest devotion of calm and leisurely thought.

The same day I went to see an establishment which gave me unmixed pleasure; it is a bathing establishment put at a very low rate to enable the poor to avoid one of the worst miseries of their lot, and which yet promises *to pay*. Joined with this is an establishment for washing clothes, where the poor can go and hire, for almost nothing, good tubs, water ready heated,

THINGS AND THOUGHTS IN EUROPE X   529

the use of an apparatus for rinsing, drying and ironing, all so admirably arranged that a poor woman can in three hours get through an amount of washing and ironing that would, under ordinary circumstances, occupy three or four days. Especially the drying closets I contemplated with great satisfaction, and hope to see in our own country the same arrangements throughout the cities and even in the towns and villages.— Hanging out the clothes is a great exposure for women, even when they have a good place for it, but when, as is so common in cities, they must dry them in the house, how much they suffer! In New-York I know those poor women who take in washing endure a great deal of trouble and toil from this cause; I have suffered myself from being obliged to send back what had cost them so much toil, because it had been, perhaps inevitably, soiled in the drying or ironing, or filled with the smell of their miscellaneous cooking. In London it is much worse. An eminent physician told me he knew of two children whom he considered to have died because their mother, having but one room to live in, was obliged to wash and dry clothes close to their bed when they were ill. The poor people in London naturally do without washing all they can, and beneath that perpetual fall of soot the result may be guessed. All but the very poor in England put out their washing, and this custom ought to be universal in civilized countries, as it can be done much better and quicker by a few regular laundresses than by many families, and "the washing day" is so malignant a foe to the peace and joy of households that it ought to be effaced from the calendar. But, as long as we are so miserable as to have any very poor people in this world, *they* cannot put out their washing, because they cannot earn enough money to pay for it, and, preliminary to something better, washing establishments like this of London are desirable.

One arrangement that they have here in Paris will be a good one, even when we cease to have any very poor people, and, please Heaven, also to have any very rich. These are the *Crèches*—houses where poor women leave their children to be nursed during the day while they are at work. I have not yet been to see one of these, and must postpone speaking of them more fully to another letter.

530 EUROPEAN SHORT PUBLISHED WORKS

I must mention that the superintendent of the washing establishment observed, with a legitimate triumph, that it had been built without giving a single dinner or printing a single puff—an extraordinary thing, indeed, for England!

To turn to something a little gayer—the embroidery on this tattered coat of civilized life—I went into only two theatres, Old Drury—once the scene of great glories, now of execrable music and more execrable acting. If anything can be invented more excruciating than an English Opera, such as was the fashion at the time I was in London, I am sure no sin of mine deserves the punishment of bearing it.

At Sadler's Wells I saw a play which I had much admired in reading it, but found still better in actual representation; indeed, it seems to me there can be no better acting play: this is "The Patrician's Daughter," by J. W. Marston. The movement is rapid yet clear and free, the dialogue natural, dignified and flowing—the characters marked with few but distinct strokes. Where the tone of discourse rises with manly sentiment or passion, the audience applauded with bursts of generous feeling that gave me great pleasure, for this play is one that, in its scope and meaning, marks the new era in England; it is full of an experience which is inevitable to a man of talent there, and is harbinger of the day when the noblest commoner shall be the only noble possible in England.

But how different all this acting to what I find in France! Here the theatre is living; you see something really good, and good throughout. Not one touch of that stage strut and vulgar bombast of tone which the English actor fancies indispensable to scenic illusion is tolerated here. For the first time in my life I saw something represented in a style uniformly good, and should have found sufficient proof, if I had needed any, that all men will prefer what is good to what is bad, if only a fair opportunity for choice be allowed. When I came here, my first thought was to go and see Mademoiselle Rachel. I was sure that in her I should find a true genius, absolutely the diamond, and so it proved.—I went to see her seven or eight times, always in parts that required great force of soul and purity of taste even to conceive them, and only once had reason to find fault with her. On one single occasion I saw her violate the harmony of the character to produce effect at a particular moment; but almost invariably I found her a true artist, worthy Greece, and worthy at many moments to have her conceptions immortalized in marble.

Her range even in high tragedy is limited. She can only express the darker passions, and grief in its most desolate aspects. Nature has not gifted her with those softer and more flowery attributes that lend to pathos its utmost tenderness. She does not melt to tears or calm or elevate the heart by the presence of that tragic beauty that needs all the assaults of Fate to make it show its immortal sweetness. Her noblest aspect is when sometimes she expresses truth in some severe shape, and rises, simple and austere, above the mixed elements around her. On the dark side, she is very great in hatred and revenge. I admired her more in PHEDRE than in any other part in which I saw her; the guilty love inspired by the hatred of a goddess was expressed in all its symptoms with a force and terrible naturalness that almost suffocated the beholder. After she had taken the poison, the exhaustion and paralysis of the system—the sad, cold, calm submission to Fate—were still more grand.

I had heard so much about the power of her eye in one fixed look, and the expression she could concentrate in a single word, that the utmost results could only satisfy my expectations. It is, indeed, something magnificent to see the dark cloud give out such sparks, each one fit to deal a separate death, but it was not that I admired most in her.—It was the grandeur, truth and depth of her conception of each part, and the sustained purity with which she represented it.

For the rest, I shall write somewhere a detailed *critique* upon the parts in which I saw her. It is she who has made me acquainted with the true way of viewing French tragedy. I had no idea of its powers and symmetry till now, and have received from the revelation high pleasure and a crowd of thoughts.

The French language from her lips is a divine dialect; it is stripped of its national and personal peculiarities and becomes what any language must—moulded by such a genius—the pure music of the heart and soul. I never could remember her tone in speaking any word; it was too perfect; you had received the thought quite direct. Yet, had I never heard her speak a word, my mind would be filled by her attitudes. Nothing more graceful can be conceived, nor could the genius of sculpture surpass her management of the antique drapery.

She has no beauty except in the intellectual severity of her outline, and bears marks of race that will grow stronger every year, and make her ugly before long. Still it will be a *grandiose*, gipsy, or rather Sibyline ugliness, well adapted to the expression of some tragic parts. Only it seems as if she could not live long; she expends force enough upon a part to furnish out a dozen common lives.

Though the French tragedy is well acted throughout, yet unhappily there is no male actor now with a spark of fire, and these men seem the meanest pigmies by the side of Rachel—so on the scene, beside the tragedy intended by the author, you see also that common tragedy, a woman of genius who throws away her precious heart, lives and dies for one unworthy of her. In parts this effect is productive of too much pain. I saw Rachel one night with her brother and sister. The sister imitated her so closely that you could not help seeing she had a manner, and an imitable manner. Her brother was in the play her lover; a wretched automaton, and presenting the most unhappy family likeness to herself. Since then I have hardly cared to go and see her. We could wish with geniuses as with the Phenix—to see only one of the family at a time.

In the pathetic or sentimental drama Paris boasts another young actress, nearly as distinguished in that walk as Rachel in hers. This is Rose Cheny, whom we saw in her 98th personation of *Clarissa Harlowe*, and afterward in Genevieve and the *Protegé sans le savoir*—a little piece written expressly for her by Scribe. The "Miss Clarisse" of the French drama is a feeble and partial reproduction of the heroine of Richardson; indeed the original in all its force of intellect and character would have been too much for the charming Rose Cheny, but, to the purity and lovely tenderness of Clarissa she does full justice. In the other characters she was the true French girl, full of grace and a mixture of naiveté and cunning, sentiment and frivolity, that is winning and *piquant*, if not satisfying. Only grief seems very strange to those bright eyes; we do not find that they can weep much and bear the light of day, and the inhaling of charcoal seems near at hand to their brightest pleasures.

THINGS AND THOUGHTS IN EUROPE X 533

At the other little theatres you see excellent acting and a sparkle of wit unknown to the world out of France. The little pieces in which all the leading topics of the day are reviewed are full of drolleries that make you laugh at each instant. *Poudre-Coton* is the only one of these I have seen; in this, among other jokes, Dumas, in the character of Monte-Christo and in a costume half Oriental, half juggler, is made to pass the other theatres in review while seeking candidates for his new one.

Dumas appeared in court yesterday and defended his own cause against the editors who sue him for evading some of his engagements. I was very desirous to hear him speak and went there in what I was assured would be very good season, but a French audience, who knew the ground better, had slipped in before me, and I returned, as has been too often the case with me in Paris, having seen nothing but endless staircases, dreary vestibules, and *gens d'armes*. The hospitality of *la grande nation* to the stranger is, in many respects, admirable. Galleries, libraries, cabinets of coins, museums, are opened in the most liberal manner to the stranger, warmed, lighted, ay, and guarded, for him almost all days in the week; treasures of the past are at his service; but when anything is happening in the present, the French run quicker, glide in more adroitly, and get possession of the ground. I find it not the most easy matter to get to places even when there is nothing going on—there is so much tiresome fuss of getting *billets* from one and another to be gone through; but when something is happening it is still worse. I missed hearing M. Guizot in his speech on the Montpensier marriage, which would have given a very good idea of his manner, and which, like this defence of M. Dumas, was a skillful piece of work as regards evasion of the truth. The good feeling toward England which had been fostered with so much care and toil seems to have been entirely dissipated by the mutual recriminations about this marriage, and the old dislike flames up more fiercely for having been hid awhile beneath the ashes. I saw the little Duchess, the innocent or ignorant topic of all this disturbance, when presented at Court. She went round the circle on the arm of the Queen. Though only fourteen she looks twenty, but has something fresh, engaging, and girlish about her. I fancy it will soon be rubbed out under the drill of the royal household.

I attended not only at the presentation but at the ball given at the Tuileries directly after; these are fine shows, as the suite of apartments is very handsome, brilliantly lighted, the French ladies surpassing all others in the art of dress; indeed, it gave me much pleasure to see them; certainly there are many ugly ones, but they are so well dressed and have such an air of graceful vivacity, that the general effect was of a flower-garden. As often happens, several American women were among the most distinguished for positive beauty; one from Philadelphia, who is by many persons considered the prettiest ornament of the dress circle at the Italian Opera, was especially marked by the attention of the King. However, these ladies, even if here a long time, do not attain the air and manner of French-women; the magnetic fluid that envelops them is less brilliant and exhilarating in its attractions.

It was pleasant to my eye, which has always been so wearied in our country by the sombre masses of men that overcloud our public assemblies, to see them now in so great variety of costume, color and decoration.

Among the crowd wandered Leverrier in the costume of Academician, looking as if he had lost, not found, his planet. French *savants* are more generally men of the world and even men of fashion than those of other climates; but, in his case, he seemed not to find it easy to exchange the music of the spheres for the music of fiddles.

Speaking of Leverrier leads to another of my disappointments. I went to the Sorbonne to hear him lecture, nothing dreaming that the old pedantic and theological character of those halls was strictly kept up in these days of light. An old guardian of the inner temple seeing me approach had his speech all ready, and, manning the entrance, said with a disdainful air, before we had time to utter a word, "Monsieur may enter if he pleases, but Madame must remain here," (*i. e.* in the court-yard.) After some exclamations of surprise I found an alternative in the Hotel de Clugny, where I passed an hour very delightfully while waiting for my companion. The rich remains of other centuries are there so arranged that they can be seen to the best advantage; many of the works in ivory, china and carved wood are truly splendid or exquisite. I saw a dagger with jeweled hilt which talked whole poems to my mind. In the various

THINGS AND THOUGHTS IN EUROPE X   535

"Adorations of the Magi" I found constantly one of the wise men black, and with the marked African lineaments. Before I had half finished, my companion came and wished me at least to visit the lecture-rooms of the Sorbonne now that the talk, too good for female ears, was over. But the guardian again interfered to deny me entrance. "You can go, Madame," said he "to the College of France; you can go to this and t'other place, but you cannot enter here." "What, sir," said I, "is it your institution alone that remains in a state of barbarism?" "Que voulez vous, Madame," he replied, and, as he spoke, his little dog began to bark at me. "Que voulez vous, Madame, c'est la regle,"—"What would you have, Madame, IT IS THE RULE,"—a reply which makes me laugh even now, as I think how the satirical wits of former days might have used it against the bulwarks of learned dullness.

I was more fortunate in hearing Arago, and he justified all my expectations. Clear, rapid, full and equal, his discourse is worthy its celebrity, and I felt repaid for the four hours one is obliged to spend in going, in waiting and in hearing, for the lecture begins at half past one and you must be there before twelve to get a seat, so constant and animated is his popularity.

Generally the most celebrated lecturers are silent at this moment. Michelet is ill. Mickiewicz, highly vaunted by discriminating hearers for a various and inspired eloquence, is absent. Sated with lectures in our own country, I have not felt willing to give my hours to the less distinguished, even although for me, as stranger and Columbian ignoramus; I know they would have many a kernel worth disengaging from the husks, if strength and time were more abundant.

I have attended with some interest two discussions at the Athenée—one on Suicide, the other on The Crusades. They are amateur affairs where, as always at such times, one hears much nonsense and vanity, much making of phrases and sentimental mental grimace; but there was one excellent speaker, adroit and rapid as only a Frenchman could be. With admirable readiness, skill and rhetorical polish, he examined the arguments of all the others and built upon their failures a triumph for himself. His management of the language, too, was masterly, and French is the best of languages for such a purpose—clear, flexible, full of sparkling points and quick, picturesque turns, with a subtle blandness that makes the dart tickle while it wounds. Truly he pleased the fancy, filled the ear and carried us pleasantly along over the smooth, swift waters; but then came from the crowd a gentleman, not one of the appointed orators of the evening, but who had really something in his heart to say—a grave, dark man, with Spanish eyes, and the simple dignity of honor and earnestness in all his gesture and manner. He said in few and unadorned words his say, and the sense of a real presence filled the room and those charms of rhetoric faded, as vanish the beauties of soap-bubbles from the eyes of astonished childhood.

I was present on one good occasion at the Academy the day that M. Rémusat was received there in the place of Royer Collard. I looked down from one of the tribunes upon the flower of the celebrities of France, that is to say, of the celebrities which are authentic, *comme il faut*. Among them were many marked faces, many fine heads; but, in reading the works of poets we always fancy them about the age of Apollo himself, and I found with pain some of my favorites quite old, and very unlike the company on Parnassus as represented by Raphael. Some, however, were venerable, even noble, to behold. Indeed the literary dynasty of France is growing old, and here, as in England and Germany, there seems likely to occur a serious gap before the inauguration of another, if indeed another is coming.

However, it was an imposing sight; there are men of real distinction now in the Academy, and Molière would have a fair chance if he were proposed to-day. Among the audience I saw many ladies of fine expression and manner as well as one or two *Precieuses Ridicules*, a race which is never quite extinct.

M. Rémusat, as is the custom on these occasions, painted the portrait of his predecessor; the discourse was brilliant and discriminating in the details, but the orator seemed to me to neglect drawing some obvious inferences which would have given a better point of view for his subject.

A *seance* to me much more impressive and interesting was one which borrowed nothing from dress, decorations, or the presence of titled pomp. I went to call on La Mennais, to whom I had a letter. I found him in a little study; his secretary was writing in a larger room through which I passed. With him was a somewhat citizen-looking, but vivacious, elderly man, whom I was at first sorry to see, having wished for half an hour's undisturbed visit to the apostle of Democracy. But how quickly were those feelings displaced by joy when he named to me the great national lyrist of France, the unequaled Béranger. I had not expected to see him at all, for he is not one to be seen in any show place; he lives in the hearts of the people, and needs no homage from their eyes. I was very happy in that little study in presence of these two men, whose influence has been so great, so real. To me Béranger has been much; his wit, his pathos, his exquisite lyric grace, have made the most delicate strings vibrate, and I can feel, as well as see, what he is in his nation and his place. I have not personally received anything from La Mennais, as, born under other circumstances, mental facts to which he, once the pupil of Rome, has passed through such ordeals, are at the basis of all my thoughts. But I see well what he has been and is to Europe, and of what great force of nature and spirit. He seems suffering and pale, but in his eyes is the light of the future.

These are men who need no flourish of trumpets to announce their coming—no band of martial music upon their steps—no obsequious nobles in their train. They are the true kings, the theocratic kings, the judges in Israel. The hearts of men make music at their approach; the mind of the age is the historian of their passage; and only men of destiny like themselves shall be permitted to write their eulogies, or fill their vacant seat.

Wherever there is a genius like his own, a germ of the finest fruit still hidden beneath the soil, the "*Chante pauvre petit*" of Béranger shall strike, like a sunbeam, and give it force to emerge, and wherever there is the true Crusade—for the spirit, not the tomb of Christ—shall be felt an echo of the "*Que tes armes soient benis jeune soldat*" of La Mennais. *

PARIS, LYONS, NAPLES

Things and Thoughts in Europe No. XIII

Music in Paris—Chopin and the Chevalier Neukomm—Adieu to Paris—A Midnight Drive in a Diligence—Lyons and its Weavers—Their Manner of Life—A Young Wife—The Weavers' Children—The Banks of the Rhone—Dreary Weather for Southern France—The old

Roman Amphitheatre at Arles—The Women of Arles—Marseilles—The Passage to Genoa—Italy—Genoa and Naples—Baia—Vesuvius—The Italian Character at Home—The Passage from Leghorn in a small Steamer—Narrow Escape—A Confusion of Languages—The Degradation of the Neapolitans.

In the last days at Paris I was fortunate in hearing some delightful music. A friend of Chopin's took me to see him, and I had the pleasure, which the delicacy of his health makes a rare one for the public, of hearing him play. All the impressions I had received from hearing his music imperfectly performed were justified, for it has marked traits which can be veiled but not travestied: but to feel it as it merits, one must hear himself; only a person as exquisitely organized as he can adequately express these subtle secrets of the creative spirit.

It was with a very different sort of pleasure that I listened to the Chevalier Neukomm, the celebrated composer of "David," which has been so popular in our country. I heard him improvise on the *Orgue Expressif*, and afterward on a great organ which has just been built here by Cavaillé for the Cathedral of Ajaccio. Full, sustained, ardent, yet exact, the stream of his thought bears with it the attention of hearers of all characters, as his character, full of *bonhommie*, open, friendly, animated and sagacious, would seem to have something to present for the affection and esteem of all kinds of men. One was the minstrel, the other the orator of music; we want them both—the mysterious whispers and the resolute pleadings from the better world which calls us not to slumber here, but press daily onward to claim all our heritage.

Paris! I was sad to leave thee, thou wonderful focus, where ignorance ceases to be a pain, because there we find such means daily to lessen it. It is the only school where I ever found abundance of teachers who could bear being examined by the pupil in their special branches. I must go to this school more before I again cross the Atlantic, where often for years I have carried about some trifling question without finding the person who could answer it. Really deep questions we must all answer for ourselves—the more the pity not to get more quickly through with a crowd of details, where the experience of others might accelerate our progress.

Parting by *diligence*, we pursued our way from twelve o'clock on Thursday till twelve at night on Friday, thus having a large share of magnificent moonlight upon the unknown fields we were traversing. At Chalons we took boat and reached Lyons betimes that afternoon. So soon as refreshed, we sallied out to visit some of the garrets of the weavers. As we were making inquiries about these, a sweet little girl who heard us offered to be our guide. She led us by a weary, winding way, whose pavement was much easier for her feet in their wooden *sabots* than for ours in Paris shoes, to the top of a hill from which we saw for the first time "the blue and arrowy Rhone." Entering the high buildings on this high hill, I found each chamber tenanted by a family of weavers, all weavers, wife, husband, sons, daughters—from nine years old upward—each was helping. On one side were the looms, nearer the door the cooking apparatus, the beds were shelves near the ceiling: they climbed up to them on ladders. My sweet little girl turned out to be a wife of six or seven years' standing, with two rather sickly looking children; she seemed to have the greatest comfort that is possible amid the perplexities of a hard and anxious lot, to judge by the proud and affectionate manner in which she always said "mon maré," and by the courteous gentleness of his manner toward her.— She seemed, indeed, to be one of those persons on whom "the Graces have smiled in their cradle" and to whom a natural loveliness of character makes the world as easy as it can be made while the evil spirit is still so busy choking the wheat with tares. I admired her graceful manner of introducing us into those dark little rooms, and she was affectionately received by all her acquaintance. But alas! that voice, by nature of such bird-like vivacity, repeated again and again, "Ah! we are all very unhappy now." "Do you sing together or go to evening schools?" "We have not the heart.—When we have a piece of work we do not stir till it is finished, and then we run to try and get another; but often we have to wait idle for weeks.—It grows worse and worse, and they say it is not likely to be any better. We can think of nothing but whether we shall be able to pay our rent. Ah! the work-people are very unhappy now." This poor, lovely little girl, at an age when the merchants' daughters of Boston and New-York are just making their first experiences of "society," knew the price of every article of food and clothing that is wanted by such a household to a farthing, her thought by day and her dream by night was, whether she should long be able to procure a scanty supply of these, and Nature had gifted her with precisely those qualities, which, unembarrassed by care, would have made her and all she loved really happy, and she was fortunate now, compared with many of her sex in Lyons—of whom a gentleman who knows the class well said to me, "When their work fails they have no resource except in the sale of their persons. There are but these two ways open to them, of weaving or prostitution to gain their bread." And there are those who dare to say that such a state of things is *well enough*, and what Providence intended for man—who call those who have hearts to suffer at the sight, energy and zeal to seek its remedy, visionaries and fanatics! To themselves be woe, who have eyes and see not, ears and hear not, the convulsions and sobs of injured Humanity!

My little friend told me she had nursed both her children— though almost all of her class are obliged to put their children out to nurse; "but," said she, "they are brought back so little, so miserable, that I resolved, if possible, to keep mine with me."— Next day in the steamboat I read a pamphlet by a physician of Lyons in which he recommends the establishment of *Creches* not merely, like those of Paris, to keep the children by day, but to provide wet nurses for them. Thus by the infants receiving nourishment from more healthy persons, and who, under the supervision of directors, would treat them well, he hopes to counteract the tendency to degenerate in this race of sedentary workers, and to save the mothers from too heavy a burden of care and labor, without breaking the bond between them and their children, whom, under such circumstances, they could visit often and see them taken care of—as they, brought up to know nothing except how to weave, cannot take care of them.— Here, again, how is one reminded of Fourier's observations and plans, still more enforced by the recent developments at Manchester as to the habit of feeding children on opium, which has grown out of the position of things there.

Descending next day to Avignon, I had the mortification of finding the banks of the Rhone still sheeted with white, and there waded through melting snow to Laura's tomb. We did not see Mr. Dickens's Tower and Goblin; it was too late in the day—but we saw a snow-ball fight between two bands of the military in the Castle-yard that was gay enough to make a goblin laugh. And next day, on to Arles, still snow, snow and cutting blasts in the South of France, where everybody had promised us bird-songs and blossoms to console us for the dreary winter of Paris. At Arles, indeed, I saw the little saxifrage blossoming on the steps of the Amphitheatre, and fruit-trees in flower amid the tombs. Here was the first time I saw the great hand-writing of the Romans in its proper medium of stone, and I was content. It looked as grand and solid as I expected, as if life in those days was thought worth the having, the enjoying and the using. The sunlight was warm this day; it lay deliciously still and calm upon the ruins. One old woman sat knitting where twenty-five thousand persons once gazed down in fierce excitement on the fights of men and lions. Coming back, we were refreshed all through the streets by the sight of the women of Arles. They answered to their reputation for beauty; tall, erect and noble, with high and dignified features, and a full, earnest gaze of the eye, they looked as if the Eagle still waved its wings over their city. Even the very old women still have a degree of beauty, because when the colors are all faded and the skin wrinkled, the face retains this dignity of outline. The men do not share in these characteristics; some Priestess, well beloved of the powers of old religion, must have called down an especial blessing on her sex in this town.

Hence to Marseilles—where is little for the traveler to see, except the mixture of Oriental blood in the crowd of the streets. Thence by steamer to Genoa. Of this transit, he who has been on the Mediterranean in a stiff breeze well understands I can have nothing to say, except "I suffered." It was all one dull, tormented dream to me and, I believe, to most of the ship's company—a dream too of thirty hours' duration, instead of the promised sixteen.

The excessive beauty of Genoa is well known, and the impression upon the eye alone was correspondent with what I expected, but, alas! the weather was still so cold I could not realize that I had actually touched those shores to which I had looked forward all my life, where it seemed that the heart would expand, and the whole nature be turned to delight. Seen by a cutting wind, the marble palaces, the gardens, the magnificent water-view of Genoa failed to charm, "I *saw, not felt*, how beautiful they were." Only at Naples have I found *my* Italy, and here not till after a week's waiting—not till I began to believe that all I had heard in praise of the climate of Italy was fable, and that there is really no Spring anywhere except in the imagination of poets. For the first week was an exact copy of the miseries of a New-England Spring; a bright sun came for an hour or two in the morning just to flatter you forth without your cloak, and then—and then—came up a villanous, horrible wind, exactly like the worst East wind of Boston, breaking the heart, racking the brain and turning hope and fancy to an irrevocable green and yellow hue in lieu of their native rose.

However, here at Naples I *have* at last found *my* Italy; I have passed through the Grotto of Pausilippo, visited Cuma, Baia, and Capré—ascended Vesuvius, and found all familiar, except the sense of enchantment, of sweet exhilaration this scene conveys.

"Behold how brightly breaks the morning!"

and yet all new, as if never yet described, for Nature here, most prolific and exuberant in her gifts, has touched them all with a charm unhackneyed, unhackneyable, which the boots of English dandies cannot trample out, nor the raptures of sentimental tourists daub or fade. Baia had still a hid divinity for me, Vesuvius a fresh baptism of fire, and Sorrento—oh Sorrento was beyond picture, beyond poesy, for the greatest Artist had been at work there in a temper beyond the reach of human art.

Beyond this, reader, my old friend and valued acquaintance on other themes, I shall tell you nothing of Naples, for it is a thing apart in the journey of life, and, if represented at all, should be so in a fairer form than offers itself at present. Now the actual life here is over, I am going to Rome, and expect to see that fane of thought the last day of this week.

At Genoa and Leghorn, I saw for the first time Italians in their homes. Very attractive I found them, charming women, refined men, eloquent and courteous. If the cold wind hid Italy, it could not the Italians. A little group of faces, each so full of character, dignity, and what is so rare in an American face, the capacity for pure, exalting passion, will live ever in my memory—the fulfillment of a hope!

THINGS AND THOUGHTS IN EUROPE XIII   543

We came from Leghorn in an English boat, highly recommended, and as little deserving of such praise as many another bepuffed article. In the middle of a fine, clear night, she was run into by the mail steamer, which all on deck perfectly saw coming upon her, for no reason that could be ascertained except that the man at the wheel said *he* had turned the right way, and it never seemed to occur to him that he could change when he found the other steamer had taken the same direction. To be sure the other steamer was equally careless, but as a change on our part would have prevented an accident that narrowly missed sending us all to the bottom, it hardly seemed worth while to persist for the sake of convicting them of error.

Neither the Captain nor any of his people spoke French, and we had been much amused before by the chambermaid acting out the old story of "Will you lend me the loan of a gridiron?" A Polish lady was on board with a French waiting-maid, who understood no word of English. The daughter of John Bull would speak to the lady in English, and, when she found it of no use, would say imperiously to the *suivante*—"Go and ask your mistress what she will have for breakfast." And now when I went on deck there was a parley between the two steamers, which the Captain was obliged to manage by such interpreters as he could find; it was a long and confused business. It ended at last in the Neapolitan steamer taking us in tow for an inglorious return to Leghorn. When she had decided upon this she swept round, her lights glancing like sagacious eyes, to take us. The sea was calm as a lake; the sky full of stars; she made a long detour with her black hull, her smoke and lights, which look so pretty at night, then came round to us like the bend of an arm embracing. It was a pretty picture, worth the stop and the fright—perhaps the loss of twenty-four hours, though I did not think so at the time. At Leghorn we changed the boat, and, retracing our steps, came now at last to Naples,—to this priest-ridden, misgoverned, full of dirty, degraded men and women, yet still most lovely Naples,—of which the most I can say is that the divine aspect of Nature *can* make you forget the situation of Man in this region, which was surely intended for him as a princely child, angelic in virtue, genius and beauty, and not as a begging, vermin-haunted, image-kissing Lazzarone. *

POEM IN THE PEOPLE'S JOURNAL

To a Daughter of Italy

Rome, Oct., 1847.

To guard the glories of the Roman reign,
Statesmen and warriors had toil'd in vain;
If vestal[1] hands had fail'd to tend the fire,
That sacred emblem of pure strong desire.

If higher honors wait the Italian name—
If the fire strive to rise again to flame—
Vestals anew are call'd that glow to fan,
And rouse to fervent force the soul of man.

Amid the prayers I hourly breathe for thee,
Most beautiful, most injured Italy!

---

[1] Vesta was the tutelar deity of Rome; under her protection the Romans believed the city impregnable—the city remained virgin: It was a fortress; a home in which the brave could confide. That Rome might never be invaded by a hostile power, a body of votaries were selected to keep alive the sacred fire. Fire is the natural symbol of Divine energy; those nations who have sought through it to express their ideas of the Divine regulation of affairs have either, like our Indians, extinguished, at stated periods, all the fires which had served the mere daily purposes of life, to re-light them from the fire on the altar, as by a ray from the sun, or, like the Romans, they have contented themselves with never suffering the fire on the altars to be extinguished. The Romans confided this sacred emblem of the highest duty to the care of women; one of these women who failed to her vows, suffered the severest of penalties, because she was supposed to have assumed and failed in the highest responsibility. It was therefore that these white-robed women took place at the public ceremonies beside the rulers, the magistrates and emperors. We flatter ourselves, now-a-days, with putting a larger construction upon these matters; it may be doubted, rather, whether the same deep religious sense animates us that was veiled beneath those forms. However that may be, the woman must be very dull, or very thoughtless, who crosses without emotion the threshold of the vestals at Pompeii, or places herself where they once sat on a level with the monarchs in these great amphitheatres. The vestals of to-day should be of a different sort; it is time that asceticism should cease to be considered the shield of purity. Purity is nature—health—development; but we want vestals, in the sense of human beings faithful to the duty which the full heart and mature mind have once assumed, women that will not let die the sacred fire that has been kindled in a great moment.

TO A DAUGHTER OF ITALY 545

None has a deeper root within the heart,
Than to see woman duly play her part:[2]
To the advancing hours[3] of this great day
A Morning Star[4] be she, to point the way;
The Virgin Mother[5] of a blessed birth,
The Isis[6] of a fair regenerate earth,
And, where its sons achieve their noblest fame,
Still, Beatrice[7] be the woman's name.

[2] One of the few women who write in Italy, Isabella Rossi has felt this and published an appeal to the same effect in the *Alba of Florence*. Lo! here also is seen one of the faint streaks that herald the Dawn (Alba): the song of the lark is not yet heard.

[3] The Hours are represented as women; and who has looked here in Rome upon their vigorous life and majesty, as they follow the *Aurora* of Guido—in their dewy freshness and lyric exhilaration—as they follow the *Aurora* of Guercino, without longing to be *such* an Hour; thus, to scatter roses and drive away the dark, before the path of the sun?

[4] Venus is the Morning Star; she has elevated herself from her birth on the brink of the inconstant wave, to be the pure Urania, the most softly luminous of the planets.

[5] It has been wittily said that the religion of Italy was not so much Christianism as *Marianism*. And certainly this tender worship of the idea of woman is the prevalent one in this country. The Virgin is the inspirer, the consoler; she sustains men amid their earthly griefs—for her bosom has been pierced with many swords—and she knows what is needed by those who are wounded; she is the friend to lead them to heaven—for, as her beautiful motherly form floats upward, still her eyes seek the sons of men below, unable to be happy till they follow. As woman, nursing the hope of a glorious future—as woman, stong in faith amid seeming disappointment—as woman, fitted for the interpreter between God and man, she represents what this age most needs to know, deeply to feel, wisely to interpret, devoutly to act out.

[6] In the later years of the Roman commonwealth, when Rome was enriched by the spoils of a thousand conquests, she sought to appropriate the ideas as well as the material spoils of other nations, and adopted among other means many of their forms of worship. Among these none was more popular than that of Isis,—Isis, the Egyptian expression of the influence of woman, which had a depth of meaning beyond the appreciation of the Greeks and Romans; it remained a mystery to them, but, on that account, only the more captivating and alluring to their thoughts. The finest mythos about Isis is that her husband, Osiris (Apollo,—light, genius) having been murdered and cut to pieces by the power of evil, she wanders, unwearied, to collect the scattered members, as, if all can be reassembled through this patient devotion of love: the Supreme Power has promised Osiris resurrection to a new and higher life. Thus would we wish the action of woman in this sense upon Italy.

[7] The greatest mind of Italy, a mind in its insight as to eternal relations, I dare to say, as yet unequalled in the history of our planet, Dante, saw woman

POSTSCRIPT

Italy herself is represented as woman, and what heart will not tremble at the appeal of one of her noblest sons, to the poet in her behalf.

"Hast thou no songs in thy soul to console us, poet? Sing to us, like Kollac the Bohemian—sing like Mickiewicz: they too, have sung in chains, but their songs are repeated, if in a low voice, yet with love, with devotion, wherever two men suffer and hope in the country which they have sung. Be like them; make for thyself a symbol, an image of angel, or of woman, beautiful, and sad: give her eyes blue as her heavens, a look sometimes radiant as a sun; diffuse around her the perfume of her orange-trees; write on her brow with thy poet's hand, fault and repentance. Let her be as the fallen angel which aspires towards heaven. Then love her, and make us love her. Take her in thy arms, and restore her by the force of love. Sing, weep, and pray with her, but pray with faith, pray with hope; let it be the prayer of men about to rise from their knees, full of strength and devotion; not that of the slave who bends, and basely sinks beneath his chain.

That the sons of Italy may answer to such appeals, let the daughters be worthy to demand it—to be her daughters as the Iphigenia and Macaria of old, who understood the cause of their country, and felt that—

> To be fond of life,
> Becomes me not.

when a higher reason claims the sacrifice.

In copying the words above, from one of the noblest sons of Italy, the words of Joseph Mazzini, I remember with great indignation to have seen extracted in *Galignani's Messenger*, (a paper which, without talent to originate anything good or bad, by a base instinct, delights to copy into its columns whatever is adverse to the cause of progress,) a paragraph from

---

as the Morning Star of his young career, and found that star still his conductor in Paradise; so that the vision of beauty which hallowed his earliest thoughts, appeared to his latest the pure white light of Divine wisdom. To him the name for woman was not only mistress, mother, consoler, but BEATRICE.

TO A DAUGHTER OF ITALY

a leading English journal, which says Italy is weaned from "the sanguinary schemes of Mazzini and his associates." To couple the epithet, sanguinary, with the name of Mazzini, would be simply absurd, as to speak of the darkness of light, were the paragraph written by some Austrian hireling, but in a country where no tyranny veils truth, such an expression seems to bespeak a love of falsehood, or a vindictive spirit in the writer. Italy is *not* weaned from Mazzini; her youth—those who are to be the animating spirit of the future—revere his name. Despite of prohibition and restriction, his thought has penetrated here; and his unwavering faith has warmed and exalted the heart of his country. The moderate party which at present moves in Italy, certainly hopes salvation by means which are not Mazzini's. One so deeply penetrated as he with the truth that shall be as a truism to the coming age, but which as yet finds few souls strong enough to understand and embrace it in all its meaning—the truth that liberty is an inborn right of man—cannot demand it as a boon at the hands of princes. The noble heart of the present pontiff has opened an unexpected door. It remains to be seen whether old bottles will contain the new wine; but those who are now in Italy, whether they hope this or not, must rejoice for the hour in the fine action of love for this good man, this truly pious Pius, on the heart of the nation, and that a degree of liberty of the press, and the rudiments of civil institutions, are introducing some light into the joy that has rested on the lower orders. It does not follow that this people disowns the blood of the martyrs which has been shed seeking Italian liberty by other means. It does not follow that they look coldly on those who have sealed a holy faith by a life of renunciation, of zealous effort. Were it so, Italy would, indeed, be unworthy of happiness; but she is not so base, so ignorant who loves her, as English paragraph-writers fancy.

And, if many members of the moderate party, wedded to another mode of proceeding, might dread the presence of Mazzini, fearing he would seek to outgo their present methods, it is our belief that there is *one* who would at least comprehend his spirit, and that, whatever might be the fears of satellites educated to tremble in the shadow of the Austrian vulture, the heart, the mind, the faith of so pure a lover of mankind would, were sincere and personal intercourse possible, be duly prized by Pius IX.

A dawn of hope smiles on Italy, but the difficulties that lower on her path are also immense. She may yet have need to recall all her true sons to her banner, and it will then be seen if it is too sanguinary to be willing to give life, hope, joy, all for the sake of one's country. For the rest, Mazzini is one of the men of Ideas, born to give impulse to a coming age. It is not easy for such to find in their own times many to understand their great thoughts and plans, but pure and ardent hearts will not fail to seek their influence, though it be necessary to cross desert seas and track the wilderness before it can be reached.

S. Margaret Fuller

THINGS AND THOUGHTS IN EUROPE XVIII 549

AMERICAN TOURISTS AND EUROPEAN
AND AMERICAN POLITICS

Things and Thoughts in Europe No. XVIII

Reflections for the New Year—Americans Abroad—America—Europe: France, England, Poland, Italy, Russia, Austria–their Policy—Still Europe toils and struggles—All these bode a new Outbreak—The Eagle of America stoops to Earth, and shows the character of the Vulture—Abolition—The Youth of the Land–Anticipations of their Usefulness.

THIS letter will reach the United States about the 1st of January; and it may not be impertinent to offer a few New-Year's reflections. Every new year, indeed, confirms the old thoughts, but also presents them under some new aspects.

The American in Europe, if a thinking mind, can only become more American. In some respects it is a great pleasure to be here. Although we have an independent political existence, our position toward Europe, as to Literature and the Arts, is still that of a colony, and one feels the same joy here that is experienced by the colonist in returning to the parent home. What was but picture to us becomes reality; remote allusions and derivations trouble no more: we see the pattern of the stuff, and understand the whole tapestry. There is a gradual clearing up on many points, and many baseless notions and crude fancies are dropped. Even the post-haste passage of the business American through the great cities, escorted by cheating couriers, and ignorant *valets de place*, unable to hold intercourse with the natives of the country, and passing all his leisure hours with his countrymen, who know no more than himself, clears his mind of some mistakes—lifts some mists from his horizon.

There are three species: first, the servile American—a being utterly shallow, thoughtless, worthless. He comes abroad to spend his money and indulge his tastes. His object in Europe is to have fashionable clothes, good foreign cookery, to know some titled persons, and furnish himself with coffee-house gossip, which he wins importance at home by retailing among those less traveled, and as uninformed as himself.

I look with unspeakable contempt on this class—a class which has all the thoughtlessness and partiality of the exclusive classes in Europe, without any of their refinement, or the chivalric feeling which still sparkles among them here and there. However, though these willing serfs in a free age do some little hurt, and cause some annoyance at present, it cannot last: our country is fated to a grand, independent existence, and, as its laws develop, these parasites of a bygone period must wither and drop away.

Then there is the conceited American, instinctively bristling and proud of—he knows not what.—He does not see, not he, that the history of Humanity for many centuries is likely to have produced results it requires some training, some devotion, to appreciate and profit by. With his great clumsy hands, only fitted to work on a steam-engine, he seizes the old Cremona violin, makes it shriek with anguish in his grasp, and then declares he thought it was all humbug before he came, and now he knows it; that there is not really any music in these old things; that the frogs in one of our swamps make much finer, for *they* are young and alive. To him the etiquettes of courts and camps, the ritual of the Church, seem simply silly—and no wonder, profoundly ignorant as he is of their origin and meaning. Just so the legends which are the subjects of pictures, the profound myths which are represented in the antique marbles, amaze and revolt him; as, indeed, such things need to be judged of by another standard from that of the Connecticut Blue-Laws. He criticises severely pictures, feeling quite sure that his natural senses are better means of judgment than the rules of connaisseurs—not feeling that to see such objects mental vision as well as fleshly eyes are needed, and that something is aimed at in Art beyond the imitation of the commonest forms of Nature.

This is Jonathan in the sprawling state, the booby truant, not yet aspiring enough to be a good school-boy. Yet in his folly there is meaning; add thought and culture to his independence, and he will be a man of might: he is not a creature without hope, like the thick-skinned dandy of the class first specified.

The Artistes form a class by themselves. Yet among them, though seeking special aims by special means, may also be found the lineaments of these two classes, as well as of the third, of which I am to speak.

THINGS AND THOUGHTS IN EUROPE XVIII   551

3d. The thinking American—a man who, recognizing the immense advantage of being born to a new world and on a virgin soil, yet does not wish one seed from the Past to be lost. He is anxious to gather and carry back with him all that will bear a new climate and new culture. Some will dwindle; others will attain a bloom and stature unknown before. He wishes to gather them clean, free from noxious insects. He wishes to give them a fair trial in his new world. And that he may know the conditions under which he may best place them in that new world, he does not neglect to study their history in this.

The history of our planet in some moments seems so painfully mean and little, such terrible bafflings and failures to compensate some brilliant successes—such a crashing of the mass of men beneath the feet of a few, and these, too, often the least worthy— such a small drop of honey to each cup of gall, and, in many cases, so mingled, that it is never one moment in life purely tasted,— above all, so little achieved for Humanity as a whole, such tides of war and pestilence intervening to blot out the traces of each triumph, that no wonder if the strongest soul sometimes pauses aghast! No wonder if the many indolently console themselves with gross joys and frivolous prizes. Yes! those men *are* worthy of admiration who can carry this cross faithfully through fifty years; it is a great while for all the agonies that beset a lover of good, a lover of men; it makes a soul worthy of a speedier ascent, a more productive ministry in the next sphere. Blessed are they who ever keep that portion of pure, generous love with which they began life! How blessed those who have deepened the fountains, and have enough to spare for the thirst of others! Some such there are; and, feeling that, with all the excuses for failure, still only the sight of those who triumph gives a meaning to life or makes its pangs endurable, we must arise and follow.

Eighteen hundred years of this Christian culture in these European Kingdoms, a great theme never lost sight of, a mighty idea, an adorable history to which the hearts of men invariably cling, yet are genuine results rare as grains of gold in the river's sandy bed! Where is the genuine Democracy to which the rights of all men are holy? where the child-like wisdom learning all through life more and more of the will of God? where the aversion to falsehood in all its myriad disguises of cant, vanity, covetousness, so clear to be read in all the history of Jesus of

Nazareth? Modern Europe is the sequel to that history, and see this hollow England, with its monstrous wealth and cruel poverty, its conventional life and low, practical aims; see this poor France, so full of talent, so adroit, yet so shallow and glossy still, which could not escape from a false position with all its baptism of blood; see that lost Poland and this Italy bound down by treacherous hands in all the force of genius; see Russia with its brutal Czar and innumerable slaves; see Austria and its royalty that represents nothing, and its people who, as people, are and have nothing! If we consider the amount of truth that has really been spoken out in the world, and the love that has beat in private hearts—how Genius has decked each spring-time with such splendid flowers, conveying each one enough of instruction in its life of harmonious energy, and how continually, unquenchably the spark of faith has striven to burst into flame and light up the Universe—the public failure seems amazing, seems monstrous.

Still Europe toils and struggles with her idea, and, at this moment, all things bode and declare a new outbreak of the fire, to destroy old palaces of crime! May it fertilize also many vineyards!—Here at this moment a successor of St. Peter, after the lapse of near two thousand years, is called "Utopian" by a part of this Europe, because he strives to get some food to the mouths of the *leaner* of his flock. A wonderful state of things, and which leaves as the best argument against despair that men do not, *cannot* despair amid such dark experiences—and thou, my country! will thou not be more true? does no greater success await thee? All things have so conspired to teach, to aid! A new world, a new chance, with oceans to wall in the new thought against interference from the old!—Treasures of all kinds, gold, silver, corn, marble, to provide for every physical need! A noble, constant, starlike soul, an Italian, led the way to its shores, and, in the first days, the strong, the pure, those too brave, too sincere for the life of the Old World hastened to people them. A generous struggle then shook off what was foreign and gave the nation a glorious start for a worthy goal. Men rocked the cradle of its hopes, great, firm, disinterested men who saw, who wrote, as the basis of all that was to be done, a statement of the rights, the inborn rights of men, which, if fully interpreted and acted upon, leaves nothing to be desired.

THINGS AND THOUGHTS IN EUROPE XVIII   553

Yet, oh Eagle, whose early flight showed this clear sight of the Sun, how often dost thou near the ground, how show the vulture in these later days! Thou wert to be the advance-guard of Humanity, the herald of all Progress; how often hast thou betrayed this high commission! Fain would the tongue in clear triumphant accents draw example from thy story, to encourage the hearts of those who almost faint and die beneath the old oppressions. But we must stammer and blush when we speak of many things. I take pride here that I may really say the Liberty of the Press works well, and that checks and balances naturally evolve from it which suffice to its government. I may say the minds of our people are alert, and that Talent has a free chance to rise. It is much. But dare I say that political ambition is not as darkly sullied as in other countries? Dare I say that men of most influence in political life are those who represent most virtue or even intellectual power? Is it easy to find names in that career of which I can speak with enthusiasm? Must I not confess in my country to a boundless lust of gain? Must I not confess to the weakest vanity, which bristles and blusters at each foolish taunt of the foreign press; and must I not admit that the men who make these undignified rejoinders seek and find popularity so? Must I not confess that there is as yet no antidote cordially adopted that will defend even that great, rich country against the evils that have grown out of the commercial system in the old world? Can I say our social laws are generally better, or show a nobler insight to the wants of man and woman? I do, indeed, say what I believe, that voluntary association for improvement in these particulars will be the grand means for my nation to grow and give a nobler harmony to the coming age. But it is only of a small minority that I can say they as yet seriously take to heart these things; that they earnestly meditate on what is wanted for their country,—for mankind,—for our cause is, indeed, the cause of all mankind at present. Could we succeed, really succeed, combine a deep religious love with practical development, the achievements of Genius with the happiness of the multitude, we might believe Man had now reached a commanding point in his ascent, and would stumble and faint no more. Then there is this horrible cancer of Slavery, and this wicked War, that has grown out of it. How dare I speak of these things here? I listen to the same arguments against the emancipation of Italy, that are used against the emancipation of our blacks; the same arguments in favor of the spoliation of Poland as for the conquest of Mexico. I find the cause of tyranny and wrong every where the same—and lo! my Country the darkest offender, because with the least excuse, foresworn to the high calling with which she was called,—no champion of the rights of men, but a robber and a jailer; the scourge hid behind her banner; her eyes fixed, not on the stars, but on the possessions of other men.

How it pleases me here to think of the Abolitionists! I could never endure to be with them at home, they were so tedious, often so narrow, always so rabid and exaggerated in their tone. But, after all, they had a high motive, something eternal in their desire and life; and, if it was not the only thing worth thinking of it was really something worth living and dying for to free a great nation from such a terrible blot, such a threatening plague. God strengthen them and make them wise to achieve their purpose!

I please myself, too, with remembering some ardent souls among the American youth who, I trust, will yet expand and help to give soul to the huge, over fed, too hastily grown-up body. May they be constant. "Were Man but constant he were perfect!" it has been said; and it is true that he who could be constant to those moments in which he has been truly human—not brutal, not mechanical—is on the sure path to his perfection and to effectual service of the Universe.

It is to the youth that Hope addresses itself, to those who yet burn with aspiration, who are not hardened in their sins. But I dare not expect too much of them. I am not very old, yet of those who, in life's morning, I saw touched by the light of a high hope, many have seceded. Some have become voluptuaries; some mere family men, who think it is quite life enough to win bread for half a dozen people and treat them decently; others are lost through indolence and vacillation. Yet some remain constant. "I have witnessed many a shipwreck, yet still beat noble hearts."

I have found many among the youth of England, of France—of Italy also—full of high desire, but will they have courage and purity to fight the battle through in the sacred, the immortal band? Of some of them I believe it and await the proof. If a few succeed amid the trial, we have not lived and loved in vain.

To these, the heart of my country, a Happy New Year! I do not know what I have written, I have merely yielded to my

THINGS AND THOUGHTS IN EUROPE XIX   555

feelings in thinking of America; but something of true love must be in these lines—receive them kindly, my friends; it is, by itself, some merit for printed words to be sincere. *

LIVING IN "THE REAL ROME"

Things and Thoughts in Europe No. XIX

The Climate of Italy—Review of First Impressions—Rome in its various Aspects—The Pope—The Cemetery of Santo Spirito—The Ceremonies at the Chapels—The Women of Italy—The Festival of the Milanese Saint–An Incident in the Chapel—English Residents in the Seven-Hilled City—Mrs. Trollope a resident of Florence—The Pope as he communicates with his People—The Position of Affairs—Lesser Potentates—The Inauguration of the New Council–the Ceremonies thereto appertaining—The American Flag in Rome—A Ball—A Feast, and its Reverse—The Funeral of a Councilor.

ROME, Dec. 17, 1847.

THIS seventeenth day of December I rise to see the floods of sunlight blessing us as they have almost every day since I returned to Rome—two months and more; with scarce three or four days of rainy weather. I see the fresh roses and grapes still each morning on my table, though both these I expect to give up at Christmas.

This autumn is "*something like*," as my country men say at home. Like *what*, they do not say, so I always supposed they meant like the ideal standard. Certainly this weather corresponds with mine, and I begin to believe the climate of Italy is really what it has been represented. Shivering here last Spring in an air no better than the cruel east wind of Puritan Boston, I thought all the praises lavished on

"Italia, O Italia!"

would turn out to be figments of the brain, and that even Byron, usually accurate beyond the conception of plodding pedants, had deceived us when he says you have the happiness in Italy to

"See the sun set sure he'll rise to-morrow,"

and not according to a view which exercises a withering influence on the enthusiasm of youth in my native land be forced to regard each pleasant day as a "*weather-breeder.*"

How delightful, too, is the contrast between this time and the Spring in another respect! Then I was here, like travelers in general, expecting to be driven away in a short time. Like others, I went through the painful process of sight-seeing, so unnatural everywhere, so counter to the healthful methods and true life of the mind. You rise in the morning knowing there are around you a great number of objects worth knowing, which you may never have a chance to see again. You go every day, in all moods, under all circumstances; you feel, probably, in seeing them, the inadequacy of your preparation for understanding or duly receiving them; this consciousness would be most valuable if you had time to think and study, being the natural way in which the mind is lured to cure its defects—but you have no time, you are always wearied, body and mind, confused, dissipated, sad. The objects are of commanding beauty or full of suggestion, but you have no quiet to let that beauty breathe its life into your soul— no time to follow up these suggestions and plant for your proper harvest. Many persons run about Rome for nine days and then go away; they might as well expect to see it so, as to appreciate the Venus by throwing a stone at it. I stayed in Rome nine weeks and came away unhappy as he who, having been taken in the visions of night through some wondrous realm, wakes unable to recall anything but the hues and outlines of the pageant, the real knowledge, the recreative power induced by familiar love, the assimilation of its soul and substance—all the true value of such a revelation—is wanting, and he remains a poor Tantalus, hungrier even when he most needed to be fed.

No; Rome is not a nine-days' wonder, and those who try to make it such lose the ideal Rome (if they ever had it) without gaining any notion of the real. For those who travel, as they do everything else—only because others do—I do not speak to them; they are nothing. Nobody counts in the estimate of the human race who has no character.

For one, I now really live in Rome, and I begin to see and feel the real Rome. She reveals herself now; she tells me some of her life. Now I never go out to see a sight, but I walk every day, and here I cannot miss of some object of consummate interest to end a walk. In the evenings, which are long now, I am at leisure to follow up the inquiries suggested by the day.

As one becomes familiar, ancient and modern Rome—at first so painfully and discordantly jumbled together, are drawn apart to the mental vision. You see where objects and limits anciently were; the superstructures vanish, and you recognize the local habitation of so many thoughts. When this begins to happen it is that one feels first truly at ease in Rome. Then the old Kings, the Consuls, and Tribunes, the Emperors, drunk with blood and gold, the warriors of eagle sight and remorseless beak, return for us, and the toga'd procession finds room to sweep across the scene; the seven hills tower, the innumerable temples glitter, and the Via Sacra swarms with triumphal life once more.

Ah! how joyful to see once more *this* Rome, instead of the pitiful, peddling, Anglicised Rome, first viewed in unutterable dismay from the coupé of the vettura: a Rome all full of taverns, lodging houses, cheating chambermaids, vilest vile *valets de place* and fleas!! A Niobe of Nations, indeed! ah, why! secretly the heart blasphemed, did the Sun omit to kill her, too, when all the glorious race which wore her crown, fell beneath his ray!

Thank heaven, it is possible to wash away all this dirt and come at the marble yet.

Then the later Papal Rome: it requires much acquaintance, much thought, much reference to books, for the child of Protestant, Republican America to see where belong the legends illustrated by rite and picture, the sense of all the rich tapestry where it has a united and poetic meaning, where it is broken by some accident of history. For all these things, a senseless mass of juggleries to the uninformed eye, are really growths of the human spirit struggling to develop its life, and full of instruction for those who learn to understand them.

Then Modern Rome—still ecclesiastical, still darkened and damp in the shadow of the Vatican, but where bright hopes gleam now amid the ashes. Never was a people who have had more to corrupt them—bloody tyranny, and incubus of priestcraft, the invasions, first of Goths, then of trampling emperors and kings, then of sight-seeing foreigners, everything to turn them from a sincere, hopeful, fruitful life, and they are much corrupted, but still a fine race. I cannot look merely with a pictorial eye on the lounge of the Roman Dandy, the bold,

Juno gait of the Roman Contadina. I love them, (Dandies and all?) I believe the natural expression of these fine forms will animate them yet. Certainly there never was a people that showed a better heart than they do in this day of love, of purely moral influence. It makes me very happy to be for once in a place ruled by a father's love, and where the pervasive glow of one good, generous heart is felt in every pulse of every day.

I have seen the Pope several times since my return, and it is a real pleasure to see him in the thoroughfares, where his passage is always greeted as that of *the* living soul.

The first week of November there is much praying for the dead here in the Chapels of the Cemeteries. I went to Santo Spirito. This Cemetery stands high, and all the way up the slope was lined with beggars petitioning for alms, in every attitude and tone, (I mean tone that belongs to the professional beggar's gamut, for that is peculiar,) and under every pretext imaginable, from the quite legless elderly gentleman to the ragged ruffian with the roguish twinkle in his eye, who has merely a slight stiffness in one arm and one leg. I could not help laughing; it was such a show; greatly to the alarm of my attendant, who declared they would kill me, if ever they caught me alone, but I was not afraid. I am sure the endless falsehood in which such creatures live must make them very cowardly. We entered the Cemetery; it was a sweet, tranquil place, lined with cypresses, and soft sunshine lying on the stone coverings where repose the houses of clay in which once dwelt joyous Roman hearts—for the hearts here do take pleasure in life. There were several Chapels; in one boys were chanting, in others people on their knees silently praying for the dead. In another was one of the groups in wax exhibited in such Chapels through the first week of November. It represented St. Carlo Borromeo as a beautiful young man in a long scarlet robe, pure and brilliant, as was the blood of the martyrs, relieving the poor who were grouped around him—old people and children, the halt, the maimed, the blind; he had called them all in to the feast of love; the Chapel was lighted and draped so as to give very good effect to this group; the spectators were mainly children and young girls, listening with ardent eyes, while their parents or the Nuns explained to them the group, or told some story of the Saint. It was a pretty scene, only marred by the presence of a villanous looking man, who ever and anon shook the poor's box. I cannot understand the bad taste of choosing him, when there were *frati* and priests enough of expression less unprepossessing.

I next entered a court-yard, where the stations, or different periods in the Passion of Jesus, are painted on the wall. Kneeling around at these were many persons: here a Franciscan, in his brown robe and cord; there a pregnant woman, uttering, doubtless, some tender aspiration for the welfare of the yet unborn dear one; there some boys, with gay yet reverent air; while all the while these fresh young voices were heard chanting. It was a beautiful moment, and despite the wax saint, the ill-favored friar, the professional mendicants, and my own removal, wide as pole from pole, from the position of mind indicated by these forms, their spirit touched me and I prayed too—prayed for the distant, every way distant—for those who seem to have forgotten me, and with me all we had in common—prayed for the dead in spirit, if not in body—prayed for myself, that I might never walk the earth

"The tomb of my dead self,"

and prayed in general for all unspoiled and loving hearts, no less for all who suffer and find yet no helper.

Going out, I took my road by the Cross, which marks the brow of the hill. Up the ascent still wound the crowd of devotees, and still the beggars beset them. Amid that crowd how many lovely, warm hearted women! The women of Italy are intellectually in a low place, *but*—they are unaffected; you can see what Heaven meant them to be, and I believe they will be yet the mothers of a great and generous race. Before me lay Rome—how exquisitely tranquil in the sunset! Never was an aspect that for serene grandeur could vie with that of Rome at sunset.

Next day was the feast of the Milanese saint, whose life has been made known to some Americans by Manzoni, when speaking in his popular novel of the cousin of St. Carlo, Federigo Borromeo. The Pope came in state to the Church of St. Carlo, in the Corso. The show was magnificent; the church is not very large, and was almost filled with the Papal court and guards, in all their splendid harmonies of color. An Italian child was next me, a little girl of four or five years, whom her mother had brought to see the Pope. As in the intervals of gazing the child smiled and made signs to me, I nodded in return and asked her name: "Virginia," said she; "and how is the Signora named?" "Margherita." "My name," she rejoined, "is Virginia Gentili." I laughed, but did not follow up the cunning, graceful lead— still I chatted and played with her now and then. At last, she said to her mother, "La Signora e molto cara," (the Signora is very dear,) or, to use the English equivalent, *a darling*; "show her my two sisters." So the mother, herself a fine-looking woman, introduced two handsome young ladies, and with the family I was in a moment pleasantly intimate for the hour.

Before me sat three young English ladies the pretty daughters of a noble Earl; their manners were a strange contrast to this Italian graciousness, best expressed by their constant use of the offish pronoun that—"*See that man*," (i. e. some high dignitary of the church,) "Look at that dress," dropped constantly from their lips. Ah! without being a Catholic one may well wish Rome was not dependent on English sight-seers who violate her ceremonies with acts that bespeak their thoughts full of wooden shoes and warming-pans. Can any thing be more sadly expressive of times out of joint than the fact that Mrs. Trollope is a resident in Italy? Yes! she is fixed permanently in Florence, as I am told, pensioned at the rate of two thousand pounds a year to trail her slime over the fruit of Italy. She is here in Rome this winter, and after having violated the virgin beauty of America, will have for many a year her chance to sully the imperial matron of the civilized world. What must the English public be, if it wishes to pay two thousand pounds a year to get Italy Trollopified?

But, to turn to a pleasanter subject. When the Pope entered, borne in his chair of state amid the pomp of his tiara and his white and gold robes, he looked to me thin, or as the Italians murmur anxiously at times *consumato*, or wasted. But during the ceremony he seemed absorbed in his devotions, and at the end I think he had become exhilarated by thinking of St. Carlo, who was such another lover of the human race as himself, and his face wore a bright glow of faith. As he blessed the people he raised his eyes to Heaven, with a gesture quite natural: it was the spontaneous act of a soul which felt that moment more than usual its relation with things above it, and sure of support from a higher Power. I saw him to still greater advantage a little while

THINGS AND THOUGHTS IN EUROPE XIX   561

after when riding on the Campagna with a young gentleman who had been ill; we met the Pope on foot, taking exercise. He often quits his carriage at the gates and walks in this way. He walked rapidly, robed in a simple white drapery, two young priests in spotless purple walked on either side; they gave silver to the poor who knelt beside the way, while the beloved Father gave his benediction. My companion knelt; he is not a Catholic but he felt that "this blessing would do him no harm." The Pope saw at once he was ill and gave him a mark of interest with that expression of melting love, the true, the only charity, which assures all who look on him that were his power equal to his will, no living thing would ever suffer more. This expression the artists try in vain to catch; all busts and engravings of him are caricatures; it is a magnetic sweetness, a lambent light that plays over his features, and of which only great genius or a soul tender as his own would form an adequate image.

The Italians have one term of praise peculiarly characteristic of their highly endowed nature.—They say of such and such, "*Ha una phisonomia simpatica*,"—"He has a sympathetic expression;" and this is praise enough. This may be preëminently said of that of Pius IX. *He* looks, indeed, as if nothing human could be foreign to him. Such alone are the genuine kings of men.

He has shown undoubted wisdom, clear-sightedness, bravery and firmness, but it is above all, his generous human heart that gives him his power over this people. His is a face to shame the selfish, redeem the skeptic, alarm the wicked and cheer to new effort the weary and heavy-laden.—What form the issues of his life may take is yet uncertain: in my belief they are such as he does not think of; but they cannot fail to be for good.—For my part, I shall always rejoice to have been here in this time. The working of his influence confirms all my theories, and it is a positive treasure to me to have seen him. I have never been presented, not wishing to approach so real a presence in the path of mere etiquette; I am quite content to see him standing amid the crowd, while the band plays the music he has inspired.

"Sons of Rome, awake!"

Yes, awake, and let no police officer put you again to sleep in prison, as has happened to those who were called by the Marseillaise.

562   EUROPEAN SHORT PUBLISHED WORKS

Affairs look well here. The King of Sardinia has at last, though with evident distrust and heartlessness, entered the upward path in a way that makes it difficult to return. The Duke of Modena, the most senseless of all these ancient gentlemen, after publishing a declaration which made him more ridiculous than would the bitterest pasquinade penned by another, that he would fight to the death against Reform, finds himself obliged to lend an ear as to the league for the Customs; and if he joins that, other measures follow of course. Austria trembles; and, in fine, cannot sustain the point of Ferrara. The King of Naples, after having shed much blood, for which he has a terrible account to render, (ah! how many sad, fair romances are to tell already about the Calabrian difficulties!) still finds the spirit fomenting in his people; he cannot put it down; the dragon's teeth are sown, and the lazzaroni may be men yet! The Swiss affairs have taken the right direction, and good will ensue, if other powers act with decent honesty, and think of healing the wounds of Switzerland, rather than merely of tying her down, so that she cannot annoy them.

In Rome, here, the new Council is inaugurated, and elections have given tolerable satisfaction. Already struggles, by-passed in other places, begin to be renewed here as to gas lights, introduction of machinery, &c. We shall see at the end of the Winter how they have gone on. At any rate, the wants of the people are in some measure represented; and already the conduct of those who have taken to themselves so large a portion of the loaves and fishes on the very platform supposed to be selected by Jesus for a general feeding of his sheep, begins to be the subject of spoken as well as whispered animadversion. Torlonia is assailed in his bank, Campana amid his urns or his Monte di Pieti—but these assaults have yet to be verified.

On the day when the Council was to be inaugurated, great preparations were made by representatives of other parts of Italy, and also foreign nations friendly to the cause of Progress. It was considered to represent the same thought as the feast of 12th Sept. in Tuscany, the dawn of an epoch when the people should find their wants and aspirations represented and guarded. The Americans showed a warm interest; the gentlemen subscribing to buy a flag (the United States having

THINGS AND THOUGHTS IN EUROPE XIX 563

none before in Rome) and the ladies meeting to make it. The same distinguished individual, indeed, who at Florence, made a speech to prevent "the American Eagle being taken out on so trifling an occasion," with similar perspicuity and superiority of view, on the present occasion was anxious to prevent "rash demonstrations, which might embroil the United States with Austria;" but the rash youth here present rushed on, ignorant how to value his Nestorian prudence—fancying, hot-headed simpletons, that the cause of Freedom was the cause of America and her Eagle at home, wherever the Sun shed a warmer ray, and, there was reason to hope, a happier life for Man. So they hurried to buy their silk—red, white and blue, and inquired of recent arrivals how many States there are this Winter in the Union, in order to making the proper number of stars. A magnificent spread Eagle was procured, not without difficulty, as this, once the eyrie of the king of birds, is now a rookery rather, full of black ominous fowl, ready to eat the harvest sown by industrious hands. This eagle having previously spread its wings over a piece of furniture where its back was sustained by the wall was somewhat deficient in a part of its anatomy. But we flattered ourselves he should be held so high that no Roman eye, if disposed, could carp and criticise. When lo! just as the banner was ready to unfold its young glories in the home of Horace, Virgil and Tacitus, an ordinance appeared, prohibiting the display of any but the Roman ensign.

This ordinance was, it is said, caused by representations made to the Pope that the Obscurantists, ever on the watch to do mischief, meant to make this the occasion of disturbance; as it is their policy to seek to create irritation here; that the Neapolitan and Lombardo–Venitian flags would appear draped with black, and thus the signal be given for tumult. I cannot help thinking these fears were groundless, that the people, on their guard, would have indignantly crushed at once any of these malignant efforts. However that may be, no one can ever be really displeased with any measure of the Pope, knowing his excellent intentions. But the limitation of the festival deprived it of the noble character of the brotherhood of nations and an ideal aim, worn by that of Tuscany. The Romans, chilled and disappointed, greeted their Councilors with but little enthusiasm. The procession, too, was but a poor affair for Rome.

564 EUROPEAN SHORT PUBLISHED WORKS

Twenty-four carriages had been lent by the princes and nobles, at the request of the city, to convey the Councilors. I found something symbolical in this. Thus will they be obliged to furnish from their old grandeur the vehicles of the new ideas. Each deputy was followed by his target and banner. When the deputy for Ferrara passed, many garlands were thrown upon his carriage. There has been deep respect and sympathy felt for the citizens of Ferrara; they have conducted so well under their late trying circumstances. They contained themselves, knowing that the least indiscretion would give a handle for aggression to the enemies of the good cause. But the daily occasions of irritation must have been innumerable, and they have shown much power of wise and dignified self-government.

After the procession passed, I attempted to go on foot from the Café Novo in the Corso to St. Peter's, to see the decorations of the streets, but it was impossible. In that dense but most vivacious, various and good-humored crowd, with all best will on their part to aid the foreigner, it was impossible to advance. So I saw only themselves; but that was a great pleasure. There is so much individuality of character here that it is a great entertainment to be in the crowd.

In the evening there was a ball given at the Argentina. Lord Minto was there; Prince Corsini, now Senator; the Torlonias, in uniform of the Civic Guard; Princess Torlonia, in a sash of their colors, given her by the Civic Guard, which she waved often in answer to their greetings. But the beautiful show of the evening was the Trasteverini dancing the Saltarello in their most brilliant costume. I saw them thus to much greater advantage than ever before; several were nobly handsome, and danced admirably; it was really like Pinelli.

The Saltarello enchants me; in this is really the Italian wine, the Italian sun. The first time I saw it danced one night very unexpectedly near the Colosseum; it carried me quite beyond myself, so that I most unamiably insisted on staying while the friends in my company, not heated by enthusiasm like me, were shivering and catching cold from the damp night-air. I dare say they remember it against me, nevertheless I cherish the memory of the moments wickedly stolen at their expense; for it is only the first time seeing such a thing that you enjoy that peculiar delight. But since, I love to see and study it much.

THINGS AND THOUGHTS IN EUROPE XXV 565

The Pope, in receiving the Councilors, made a speech; such as the King of Prussia entrenched himself in on a similar occasion, only much better and shorter; implying that he meant only to improve, not to *reform*, and should keep things *in statu quo*, safe locked with the keys of St. Peter. This little speech was made, no doubt, more to reassure Czars, Emperors and Kings than from the promptings of the spirit. But the fact of its necessity, as well as the inferior freedom and spirit of the Roman journals to those of Tuscany, seems to say that the Pontifical Government, though from the accident of this one man's accession, it has taken the initiative to better times, yet may not, after a while, from its very nature, be able to keep in the vanguard.

A sad contrast to the feast of this day was presented by the same persons, a fortnight after, following the body of Silvani, one of the Councilors, who died suddenly. The Councilors, the different Societies of Rome, a corps *frati* bearing tapers, the Civic Guard with drums slowly beating, the same state carriages with their liveried attendants all slowly, sadly moving, with torches and banners, drooped along the Corso in the dark night. A single horseman, with his long white plume and torch reversed, governed the procession: it was the Prince Aldobrandini. The whole had that grand effect, so easily given by this artist-people, who seize instantly the natural poetry of an occasion and with unanimous tact hasten to represent it. More and much anon. *

THE REVOLUTIONS OF 1848 IN ITALY

Things and Thoughts in Europe No. XXV

Review of the course of Pius IX—Mamiani—The People's Disappointed Hopes—The Monuments in Milan, Naples, etc.—The King of Naples and his Troops—Calamities of the War—The Italian People—Charles Albert—Deductions—Summer among the Mountains of Italy.

ROME, December 2, 1848.

Messrs. Greeley & McElrath:
EASY is the descent to ill.

566   EUROPEAN SHORT PUBLISHED WORKS

I have not written for six months, and within that time what changes have taken place on this side "the great water." Changes of how great dramatic interest historically—of bearing infinitely important ideally.

I wrote last when Pius IX. had taken the first stride on the downward road. He had proclaimed himself the foe of farther Reform measures, when he implied that Italian independence was not important in his eyes, when he abandoned the crowd of heroic youth who had gone to the field with his benediction, to some of whom his own hand had given crosses. All the Popes, his predecessors, had meddled with, most frequently instigated, war; now came one who must carry out, literally, the doctrines of the Prince of Peace, when the war was not for mercy, or the aggrandizement of individuals, but to redeem national, to redeem human, rights from the grasp of foreign oppression.

I said some cried "traitor," some "imbecile," some "wept," but in the minds of all, I believe, at that time grief was finally predominant. They could no longer depend on him they had thought their best friend. They had lost their father.

Meanwhile his people would not submit to the inaction he urged. They saw it was not only ruinous to themselves, but base and treacherous to the rest of Italy. They said to the Pope, "This cannot be; you must follow up the pledges you have given, or, if you will not act to redeem them, you must have a Ministry that will." The Pope, after he had once declared to the contrary, ought to have persisted. He ought to have said, "I cannot thus belie myself, I cannot put my name to acts I have just declared to be against my conscience."

The Ministers of the people ought to have seen that the position they assumed was utterly untenable; that they could not advance with an enemy in the background cutting off all supplies. But some patriotism, and some vanity exhilarated them, and the Pope, having weakly yielded, they unwisely began their impossible task. Mamiani, their chief, I esteem a man, under all circumstances, unequal to such a position—a man of rhetoric, merely. But no man could have acted, unless the Pope had resigned his temporal power, the Cardinals been put under sufficient check, and the Jesuits and emissaries of Austria driven from their lurking-places.

A sad scene began. The Pope—shut up more and more in his palace, the crowd of selfish and insidious advisers darkening round, enslaved by a confessor—he who might have been the liberator of suffering Europe, permitted the most infamous treacheries to be practiced in his name. Private letters were written to the foreign powers denying the acts he outwardly sanctioned; the hopes of the people were evaded or dallied with; the Chamber of Deputies permitted to talk and pass measures which they never could get funds to put into execution; legions to form and maneuver, but never to have the arms and clothing they needed. Again and again the people went to the Pope for satisfaction. They got only—benediction.

Thus plotted and thus worked the scarlet men of sin, playing the hopes of Italy off and on, while *their* hope was of the miserable defeat consummated by a still worse traitor at Milan on the 6th August. But, indeed, what could be expected from the "SWORD OF PIUS IX." when Pius IX. himself had thus failed to his high vocation. The King of Naples bombarded his city and set on the lazzaroni to rob and murder the subjects he had deluded by his pretended gift of the Constitution. Pius proclaimed that he longed to embrace *all* the Princes of Italy. He talked of peace when all knew for a great part of the Italians there was no longer hope of peace except in the sepulchre, or Freedom.

The taunting manifestoes of Welden are a sufficient comment on the conduct of the Pope. "As the Government of His Holiness is too weak to control his subjects"—"As, singularly enough, a great number of Romans are found fighting against us, contrary to the *expressed* will of their Prince,"—such were the excuses for invasions of the Pontifical dominions and the robbery and insult by which they were accompanied. Such invasions, it was said, made His Holiness very indignant; he remonstrated against these; but we find no word of remonstrance against the tyranny of the King of Naples—no word of sympathy for the victims of Lombardy, the sufferings of Verona, Vicenza, Padua, Mantua, Venice.

In the affairs of Europe there are continued signs of the plan of the retrograde party to effect similar demonstrations in different places at the same hour. The 15th May was one of these marked days. On that day the King of Naples made use of the insurrection he had contrived to excite to massacre his people,

568 EUROPEAN SHORT PUBLISHED WORKS

and find an excuse for recalling his troops from Lombardy. The same day a similar crisis was hoped in Rome from the declarations of the Pope, but that did not work at the moment exactly as the foes of enfranchisement hoped.

However, the wounds were cruel enough. The Roman volunteers received the astounding news that they were not to expect protection or countenance from their Prince; all the army stood aghast that they were no longer to fight in the name of Pio. It had been so dear, so sweet to love and reverence really the Head of their Church, so inspiring to find their religion for once in accordance with the aspirations of the soul. They were to be deprived, too, of the aid of the disciplined Neapolitan troops and their artillery, on which they had counted. How cunningly all this was contrived to cause dissension and dismay may easily be seen.

The Neapolitan General Pepe nobly refused to obey, and called on the troops to remain with him. They wavered; but they are a pampered army, personally much attached to the King, who pays them well and indulges them at the expense of his people, that they may be his support against that people when in a throe of Nature it rises and strives for its rights. For the same reason, the sentiment of patriotism was little diffused among them in comparison with the other troops. And the alternative presented was one in which it required a very clear sense of higher duty to act against habit. Generally, after wavering a while, they obeyed and returned. The Roman States which had received them with so many testimonials of affection and honor, were not slack to show a correspondent aversion and contempt on their retreat. The towns would not suffer their passage; the hamlets were unwilling to serve them even with fire and water. They were filled at once with shame and rage; one officer killed himself, unable to bear it; in the unreflecting minds of the soldiers, hate sprung up for the rest of Italy, and especially Rome, which will make them admirable tools of tyranny in case of civil war.

This was the first great calamity of the war. But apart from the treachery of the King of Naples and the dereliction of the Pope, it was impossible it should end thoroughly well. The people were in earnest, and have shown themselves so; brave, and able to bear privation. No one should dare, after the proofs of the Summer, to reiterate the taunt, so unfriendly frequent on foreign lips at the beginning of the contest, that the Italian can boast, shout, and fling garlands, but not *act*. The Italian always showed himself a noble and a brave, even in foreign service, and is doubly so in the cause of his country. But efficient heads were wanting. The Princes were not in earnest; they were looking at expediency. The Grand Duke, timid and prudent, wanted to do what was safest for Tuscany; his Ministry, *"Moderate"* and prudent, would have liked to win a great prize at small risk. They went no farther than the people pulled them. The King of Sardinia had taken the first bold step, and the idea that treachery on his part was premeditated cannot be sustained; it arises from the extraordinary aspect of his measures, and the knowledge that he is not incapable of treachery, as he proved in early youth. But now it was only his selfishness that worked to the same results. He fought and planned, not for Italy but the house of Savoy, which his Balbis and Giobertis had so long been prophesying was to reign supreme in the new great Era of Italy. These prophecies he more than half believed, because they chimed with his ambitious wishes; but he had not soul enough to realize them; he trusted only in his disciplined troops; he had not nobleness enough to believe he might rely at all on the sentiment of the people. For his troops he dared not have good Generals; conscious of meanness and timidity, he shrank from the approach of able and earnest men; he was only afraid they would, in helping Italy, take her and themselves out of his guardianship. Antonini was insulted, Garibaldi rejected; other experienced leaders, who had rushed to Italy at the first trumpet-sound, could never get employment from him. As to his generalship, it was entirely inadequate, even if he had made use of the first favorable moments. But his first thought was not to strike a blow at the Austrians before they recovered from the discomfiture of Milan, but to use the panic and need of his assistance to induce Lombardy and Venice to annex themselves to his kingdom. He did not even wish seriously to get the better till this was done, and when this was done, it was too late. The Austrian army was recruited, the Generals had recovered their spirits, and were burning to retrieve and avenge their past defeat. The conduct of Charles Albert had been shamefully evasive in the first months. The account given by Franzini, when challenged in the Chamber of Deputies at Turin, might be summed up thus: "Why, gentlemen, what would you have? Every one knows that the army is in excellent condition, and eager for action. They are often reviewed, hear speeches, and sometimes get medals. We take places always, if it is not difficult. I myself was present once when the troops advanced; our men behaved gallantly, and had the advantage in the first skirmish, but afterward the enemy pointed on us artillery from the hights, and naturally, we retired. But as to supposing that his Majesty Charles Albert is indifferent to the success of Italy in the war, that is absurd. He is the Sword of Italy; he is the most magnanimous of Princes! he is seriously occupied about the war; many a day I have been called into his tent to talk it over, before he was up in the morning!"

Sad was it that the heroic Milan, the heroic Venice, the heroic Sicily, should lean on such a reed as this, and by hurried acts, equally unworthy as unwise, sully the glory of their shields. Some names, indeed, stand out quite free from this blame. Mazzini, who kept up a combat against folly and cowardice, of day by day and hour by hour, with almost supernatural strength, warned the people constantly of the evils which their advisers were drawing upon them. He was heard then only by a few, but in this "Italia del Popolo" may be found many prophecies exactly fulfilled, as those of "the golden haired love of Phœbus" during the struggles of Ilium. He himself, in the last sad days of Milan, compared his lot to that of Cassandra. At all events, his hands are pure from all that ill. What could be done to arouse Lombardy he did, but the "Moderate" party unable to wean themselves from old habits, the pupils of the wordy Gioberti thought there could be no safety unless under the mantle of a Prince. They did not foresee that he would run away and throw that mantle on the ground.

Tommaseo and Manin also were clear in their aversion to these measures; and with them, as with all who were resolute in principle at that time, a great influence has followed.

It is said Charles Albert feels bitterly the imputations on his courage, and says they are most ungrateful when he has exposed the lives of himself and his sons in the combat. Indeed, there ought to be made a distinction between personal and mental courage. The former Charles Albert may possess, may have too

THINGS AND THOUGHTS IN EUROPE XXV 571

much, of what this still aristocratic world calls "the feelings of a gentleman" to shun exposing himself to a chance shot now and then. An entire want of mental courage he has shown. His decisive battle was made so by giving up the moment Fortune turned against him. It is shameful to hear so many say this result was inevitable, just because the material advantages were in favor of the Austrians. Pray, was never a battle won against material odds? It is precisely such that a good leader, a noble man, may expect to win. Were the Austrians driven out of Milan because the Milanese had that advantage? The Austrian would again have suffered repulse from them, but for the baseness of this man, on whom they had been cajoled into relying: a baseness that deserves the pillory; and on a pillory will the "magnanimous," as he was meanly called in face of the crimes of his youth and the timid selfishness of his middle age, stand in the sight of posterity. He made use of his power only to betray Milan; he took from the citizens all means of defence, and then gave them up to the spoiler; he promised to defend them "to the last drop of his blood," and sold them the next minute; even the paltry terms he made he has not seen maintained. Had the people slain him in their rage, he well deserved it at their hands; and all his conduct since had confirmed that sudden verdict of passion.

Of all this great drama I have much to write, but elsewhere, in a more full form, and where I can duly sketch the portraits of actors little known in America. The materials are over-rich. I have bought my right in them by much sympathetic suffering; yet, amid the blood and tears of Italy, 't is joy to see some glorious new births.—The Italians are getting cured of mean adulation and hasty boasts; they are learning to prize and seek realities; the effigies of straw are getting knocked down, and living, growing men, take their places. Italy is being educated for the Future: her leaders are learning that the time is past for trust in Princes and precedents—that there is no hope except in Truth and God; her lower people are learning to shout less and think more.

Though my thoughts have been much with the public in this struggle for life, I have been away from it during the Summer months, in the quiet valleys, on the lonely mountains. There, personally undisturbed, I have seen the glorious Italian Summer wax and wane: the Summer of Southern Italy, which I did not see last year. On the mountains it was not too hot for me, and I enjoyed the great luxuriance of vegetation. I had the advantage of having visited the scene of the war minutely last Summer, so that, in mind, I could follow every step of the campaign; while around me were the glorious reliques of old times, the crumbling theater or temple of the Roman day; the bird's-nest village of the Middle Ages—on its purple hight shone the sun and moon of Italy in changeless lustre. It was great pleasure to me to watch the gradual growth and change of the seasons, so different from ours. Last year I had not leisure for this quiet acquaintance. Now I saw the fields first dressed in their carpets of grain, enameled richly with the red poppy and blue corn-flower—in that sunshine how resplendent! Then swelled the fig, the grape, the olive, the almond; and my food was of these products of this rich clime. For near three months I had grapes every day; the last four weeks enough daily for two persons for a cent! Exquisite salad for two persons' dinner and supper, a cent. All other products of the region in the same proportion. One who keeps still in Italy, and lives as the people do, may really have much simple luxury for very little money; though both travel and, to the inexperienced foreigner, life in the cities are expensive. *

REVOLUTIONARY ROME

Things and Thoughts in Europe XXVI

Thoughts of the Italian Race, the Seasons, and Rome—Changes—The Death of the Minister Rossi—The Church of San Luigi dei Francesi—St. Cecilia and the Domenichino Chapel—The Piazza del Popolo, The Troops, Preparatory Movements toward the Quirinal—The Demonstration on the Palace—The Church: Its Position and Aims—The Pope's Flight, &c.—Social Life—Communication with America—The New Year.

Rome, December 2, 1848.

Messrs. Greeley & McElrath:

Not till I saw the snow on the mountains grow rosy in the Autumn sunset did I turn my steps again toward Rome. I was very ready to return. After three or four years of constant

THINGS AND THOUGHTS IN EUROPE XXVI 573

excitement this six months of seclusion had been welcome; but now I felt the need of meeting other eyes beside those, so bright and so shallow, of the Italian peasant. Indeed, I left what was most precious that I could not take with me; still it was a compensation that I was again to see Rome. Rome that almost killed me with her cold breath of last Winter, yet still with that cold breath whispered a tale of import so divine. Rome so beautiful, so great; her presence stupifies, and one has to withdraw to prize the treasures she has given. City of the Soul! yes, it is *that*; the very dust magnetizes you, and thousand spells have been chaining you in every careless, every murmuring moment. Yes! Rome, however seen, thou must be still adored; and every hour of absence or presence must deepen love with one who has known what it is to repose in thy arms.

Repose! for whatever be the revolutions, tumults, panics, hopes of the present day, still the temper of life here is Repose. The great Past enfolds us, and the emotions of the moment cannot here importantly disturb that impression. From the wild shout and throng of the streets the setting sun recalls us as it rests on a hundred domes and temples—rests on the Campagna, whose grass is rooted in departed human greatness. Burial-place so full of spirit that Death itself seems no longer cold; oh let me rest here, too! Rest, here, seems possible; meseems myriad lives still linger here, awaiting some one great summons.

The rivers had burst their bounds, and beneath the moon the fields round Rome lay, one sheet of silver. Entering the gate while the baggage was under examination I walked to the gate of a villa. Far stretched its overarching shrubberies, its deep-green bowers; two statues with foot advanced and uplifted finger, seemed to greet me; it was near the scene of great revels, great splendors in the old time; there lay the gardens of Sallust, where were combined palace, theater, library, bath and villa. Strange things have happened now, the most attractive part of which—the secret heart—lies buried or has fled to animate other forms: for of that part historians have rarely given a hint, more than they do now of the truest life of our day, that refuses to be embodied by the pen; it craves forms more mutable, more eloquent than the pen can give.

I found Rome empty of foreigners: most of the English have fled in affright—the Germans and French are wanted at home—the Czar has recalled many of his younger subjects; he does not like the schooling they get here. That large part of the population which lives by the visits of foreigners was suffering very much—trade, industry, for every reason, stagnant. The people were every moment becoming more exasperated by the impudent measures of the Minister Rossi, and their mortification at seeing Rome represented and betrayed by a foreigner. And what foreigner? A pupil of Guizot and Louis Philippe. The news had just reached them of the bombardment and storm of Vienna. Zucchi, the Minister-of-War, left Rome to put down over-free manifestations in the Provinces, and impede the entrance of the troops of the Patriot Chief, Garibaldi, into Bologna. From the Provinces came soldiery, called by Rossi to keep order at the opening of the Chamber of Deputies. He reviewed them in the face of the Civic Guard; the Press began to be restrained; men were arbitrarily seized and sent out of the kingdom; the public indignation rose to its hight; the cup overflowed.

The 15th was a beautiful day and I had gone out for a long walk. Returning at night, the old Padrona met me with her usual smile a little clouded, "Do you know," said she, "that the Minister Rossi has been killed?" [No Roman said *murdered*.]

"Killed!"

"Yes—with a thrust in the back. A wicked man, surely, but is that the way to punish CHRISTIANS?"

"I cannot," observed a Philosopher, "sympathize under any circumstances with so immoral a deed; but surely the manner of doing it was *grandiose*."

The people at large was not so refined in their comments as either the Padrona or the Philosopher; but soldiers and populace alike ran up and down singing "Blessed the hand that rids the earth of a tyrant."

"Certainly, the manner *was* grandiose."

The Chamber was awaiting the entrance of Rossi. Had he lived to enter, he would have found the Assembly, without a single exception, ranged upon the Opposition benches. His carriage approached, attended by a howling, hissing multitude. He smiled, affected unconcern, but must have felt relieved when his horses entered the courtyard gate of the *Cancelleria*. He did not know he was entering the place of his execution. The horses stopped; he alighted in the midst of a crowd; it jostled

THINGS AND THOUGHTS IN EUROPE XXVI   575

him as if for the purpose of insult; he turned abruptly and received as he did so the fatal blow. It was dealt by a resolute, perhaps experienced, hand; he fell and spoke no word more.

The crowd, as if all previously acquainted with the plan, as no doubt most of them were, issued quietly from the gate and passed through the outside crowd—its members, among whom was he who dealt the blow, dispersing in all directions.—For two or three minutes this outside crowd did not know that anything special had happened.—When they did, the news was at the moment received in silence. The soldiers in whom Rossi had trusted, whom he had hoped to flatter and bribe, stood at their posts and said not a word.—Neither they nor any one asked "Who did this? Where is he gone?" The sense of the people certainly was that it was an act of summary justice on an offender whom the laws could not reach, but they felt it to be indecent to shout or exult on the spot where he was breathing his last. Rome, so long supposed the Capital of Christendom, certainly took a very pagan view of this act, and the piece represented on the occasion at the theaters was "The Death of Nero."

The next morning I went to the church of St. Andrea della Valle, where was to be performed a funeral service, with fine music, in honor of the victims of Vienna; for this they do here for the victims all round—"victims of Milan," "victims of Paris," "victims of Naples," and now "victims of Vienna." But to-day I found the church closed, the service put off—Rome was thinking about her own victims.

I passed into the Ripetta, and entered the church of *San Luigi dei Francesi*. The Republican flag was flying at the door; the young Sacristan said the fine musical service which this church gave formerly on St. Philip's day, in honor of Louis Philippe, would now be transferred to the Republican Anniversary, the 25th of February. I looked at the monument Chateaubriand erected when here, to a poor girl who died last of her family, having seen all the others perish round her. I entered the Domenichino Chapel, and gazed anew on those magnificent representations of the Life and Death of St. Cecilia. She and St. Agnes are my favorite saints. I love to think of those angel visits which her husband knew by the fragrance of roses and lilies left behind in the apartment. I love to think of his visit to the Catacombs, and all that followed. In this picture St. Cecilia,

576   EUROPEAN SHORT PUBLISHED WORKS

as she stretches out her arms toward the suffering multitude, seems as if an immortal fount of purest love sprung from her heart. She gives very strongly the sense of an inexhaustible love—the only love that is much worth thinking about.

Leaving the church I passed along toward the *Piazza del Popolo*, "Yellow Tiber rose," but not high enough to cause "distress," as he does when in a swelling mood rather than "mantle" it. I heard the drums beating, and, entering the Piazza, I found the troops of the line already assembled, and the Civic Guard marching in by platoons; each *battaglione* saluted as it entered by trumpets and a fine strain from the hand of the Carbineers.

I climbed the Pincian to see better. There is no place so fine for anything of this kind as the Piazza del Popolo, it is so full of light, so fair and grand, the obelisk and fountain make so fine a center to all kinds of groups.

The object of the present meeting was for the Civic Guard and troops of the line to give pledges of sympathy preparatory to going to the Quirinal to demand a change of Ministry and of measures. The flag of the Union was placed in front of the obelisk; all present saluted it; some officials made addresses; the trumpets sounded, and all moved toward the Quirinal.

Nothing could be gentler than the disposition of the crowd. They were resolved to be played with no longer, but no threat was heard or thought.—They believed that the Court would be convinced by the fate of Rossi that the retrograde movement it had attempted was impracticable. They knew the retrograde party were panic-struck, and hoped to use the occasion to free the Pope from their meshes. All felt that Pius IX. had fallen irrevocably from his high place of the friend of Progress and father of Italy; but still he was personally beloved, and still his name, so often shouted in hope and joy, had not quite lost its *prestige*.

I returned to the house, which is very near the Quirinal. On one side I could see the Palace and gardens of the Pope, on the other the Piazza Barberini and street of the Four Fountains. Presently I saw the carriage of Prince Barberini drive hurriedly into his court-yard gate, the footman signing to close it, a discharge of firearms was heard, and the drums of the Civic Guard beat to arms.

The Padrona ran up and down crying with every round of shot, "Jesu Maria, they are killing the Pope! O! poor Holy

THINGS AND THOUGHTS IN EUROPE XXVI   577

Father—Tita, Tita, (out of the window to her husband,) what *is* the matter?"

The lord of creation disdained to reply.

"Oh! Signora, pray, pray, ask Tita what is the matter?" I did so. "I don't know, Signora; nobody knows."

"Why don't you go on the mount and see?"

"It would be an imprudence, Signora; nobody will go."

I was just thinking to go myself when I saw a poor man borne by, badly wounded, and heard that the Swiss were firing on the people. Their doing so was the cause of whatever violence there was, and it was not much.

The people had assembled, as usual, at the Quirinal, only with more form and solemnity than usual. They had taken with them several of the Chamber of Deputies, and they sent an embassy, headed by Galetti, who had been in the late Ministry, to state their wishes. They received a peremptory negative. They then insisted on seeing the Pope, and pressed on the palace. The Swiss became alarmed, and fired from the windows, from the roof. They did this, it is said, without orders, but who could, at the time, suppose that? If it had been planned to exasperate the people to blood, what more could have been done? As it was, very little was shed; but the Pope, no doubt, felt great panic. He heard the report of fire-arms—heard that they tried to burn a door of the palace. I would lay my life that he could have shown himself without the slightest danger; nay, that the habitual respect for his presence would have prevailed, and hushed all tumult. He did not think so, and to still it once more degraded himself and injured his people, by making promises he did not mean to keep.

He protests now against those promises as extorted by violence, a strange plea, indeed, for the representative of St. Peter!

Rome is all full of the effigies of those over whom violence had no power. There is an early Pope about to be thrown into the Tiber; violence had no power to make him say what he did not mean. Delicate girls, men in the prime of hope and pride of power—they were all alike about that. They could be done to death in boiling oil, roasted on coals, or cut to pieces; but they could not say what they did not mean. These formed the true Church; it was these who had power to disseminate the religion of Him, the Prince of Peace, who died a bloody death of torture between sinners, because He never could say what He did not mean.

A little church outside the gate of St. Sebastian commemorates this affecting tradition of the Church; Peter, alarmed at the persecution of the Christians, had gone forth to fly, when in this spot he saw a bright figure in his path and recognized his Master traveling toward Rome.

"Lord," he said, "whither goest thou?"

"I go," replied Jesus, "to die, with my people."

Peter comprehended the reproof. He felt that he must not a fourth time deny his Master, yet hope for salvation. He returned to Rome to offer his life in attestation of his faith.

The Roman Catholic Church has risen a monument to the memory of such facts. And has the present Head of that Church quite failed to understand their monition?

Not all the Popes have so failed, though the majority have been intriguing, ambitious men of the world. But even the mob of Rome—and in Rome there *is* a true mob of unheeding cabbage-sellers, who never had a thought before beyond contriving how to satisfy their animal instincts for the day—said, on hearing the protest, "There was another Pius, not long since, who talked in a very different style. When the French threatened him, he said, 'You may do with me as you see fit, but I cannot consent to act against my convictions.'"

In fact, the only dignified course for the Pope to pursue was to resign his temporal power. He could no longer hold it on his own terms; but to that he clung; and the counselors around him were men to wish him to regard *that* as the first of duties. When the question was of waging war for the independence of Italy, they regarded him solely the head of the Church; but when the demand was to satisfy the wants of his people, and ecclesiastical goods were threatened with taxes, then he was the Prince of the State, bound to maintain all the selfish prerogative of by-gone days for the benefit of his successors. Poor Pope! how has his mind been torn to pieces in these later days. It moves compassion. There can be no doubt that all his natural impulses are generous and kind, and in a more private station he would have died beloved and honored; but to this he was unequal; he has suffered bad men to surround; and by their misrepresentations and insidious suggestions, at last entirely to

THINGS AND THOUGHTS IN EUROPE XXVI   579

cloud his mind. I believe he really thinks now the Progress movement tends to anarchy, blood, all that looked worst in the first French Revolution. However that may be I cannot forgive him some of the circumstances of this flight. To fly to Naples to throw himself in the arms of the bombarding monarch, blessing him and thanking his soldiery for preserving that part of Italy from anarchy—to protest that all his promises at Rome were null and void, when he thought himself in safety to choose a commission for governing in his absence, composed of men of princely blood, but as to character so null that everybody laughed and said he chose those who could best be spared if they were killed; (but they all ran away directly;) when Rome was thus left without any Government, to refuse to see any deputation, even the Senator of Rome, whom he had so gladly sanctioned,—these are the acts either of a fool or a foe. They are not his acts, to be sure, but he is responsible, he lets them stand as such in the face of the world, and weeps and prays for their success.

No more of him! His day is over. He has been made, it seems unconsciously, an instrument of good his regrets cannot destroy. Nor can he be made so important an instrument of ill. These acts have not had the effect the foes of freedom hoped. Rome remained quite cool and composed; all felt that they had not demanded more than was their duty to demand, and were willing to accept what might follow. In a few days all began to say, "Well, who would have thought it? The Pope, the Cardinals, the Princes are gone, and Rome is perfectly tranquil, and one does not miss anything, except that there are not so many rich carriages and liveries."

The Pope may regret too late that he ever gave the people a chance to make this reflection. Yet the best fruits of the movement may not ripen for long. It is one which requires radical measures, clear-sighted, resolute men: these last, as yet, do not show themselves in Rome. The new Tuscan Ministry has three men of superior force in various ways: Montanelli, Guerrazzi, D'Aguila; such are not as yet to be found in Rome.

But should she fall this time, (and she must either advance with decision and force, or fall—since to stand still is impossible,) the people have learned much; ignorance and servility of thought are lessened—the way is paving for final triumph.

And my country, what does she? You have chosen a new President from a Slave State, representative of the Mexican War. But he seems to be honest, a man that can be esteemed, and is one really known to the people; which is a step upward, after having sunk last time to choosing a mere tool of party.

Pray send here a good Ambassador—one that has experience of foreign life, that he may act with good judgment; and, if possible, a man that has knowledge and views which extend beyond the cause of party politics in the United States; a man of unity in principles, but capable of understanding variety in forms. And send a man capable to prize the luxury of living in, or knowing Rome: it is one that should not be thrown away on a person who cannot prize or use it. Another century, and I might ask to be made Ambassador myself, ('tis true, like other Ambassadors, I would employ clerks to do the most of the duty,) but woman's day has not come yet. They hold their clubs in Paris, but even George Sand will not act with women as they are. They say she pleads they are too mean, too treacherous. She should not abandon them for that, which is not nature but misfortune. How much I shall have to say on that subject if I live, which I hope I shall not, for I am very tired of the battle with giant wrongs, and would like to have some one younger and stronger arise to say what ought to be said, still more to do what ought to be done. Enough! if I felt these things in privileged America, the cries of mothers and wives beaten at night by sons and husbands for their diversion after drinking, as I have repeatedly heard them these past months, the excuse for falsehood, "I *dare not* tell my husband, he would be ready to kill me," have sharpened my perception as to the ills of Woman's condition and remedies that must be applied. Had I but genius, had I but energy, to tell what I know as it ought to be told! God grant them me, or some other more worthy woman, I pray.

But the hour of sending to the post approaches, and I must leave these great matters for some practical details. I wish to observe to my friends and all others, whom it may concern, that a banking-house here having taken Mr. Hooker, an American, into partnership, some facilities are presented for intercourse with Rome, which they may value. Mr. Hooker undertakes to have pictures copied, and to purchase those little objects of virtu

THINGS AND THOUGHTS IN EUROPE XXVI   581

peculiar to Rome, for those who cannot come themselves, as I suppose few would wish to at this time. He has the advantage of a general acquaintance with the artists to be employed, and an experience, that, no doubt, would enable him to do all this with better advantage than any stranger can for himself. It is also an excellent house to have to do with in money matters, reasonable, exact, and where none of the petty trickery or neglect so common at Torlonia's need be apprehended. They have now made arrangements with Livingston, Wells & Co. for the transmission of letters. Many addressed to me have been lost, I know not how; and I should like my friends to send to me when they can through this channel. Men who feel able can pay their letters through in this way, which has been impossible before. I have received many letters marked *paid through*, and I fear my friends in America have often paid what was quite useless, as no arrangements had been made for forwarding the letters post-paid to Rome. Those who write now can pay their letters to Florence, if they have friends there, through *Livingston, Wells & Co.* to care *Maquay, Pakenham & Co. Florence.* To us of Rome they can be sent through the same, to care of *Pakenham, Hooker & Co. Rome.*

Those of our friends, (I speak of the poor artists as well as myself,) who cannot afford to pay, should at least forbear to write on thick paper and under an envelop, the unnecessary use of which doubles the expense of the letter. I am surprised to find even those who have been abroad so negligent in these respects. I might have bought all the books of reference I needed, and have been obliged to do without money that could have been saved by attention from my friends to these particulars.

Write us two, three, four sheets if you will, on this paper, without crossing. Then if one pays a couple of dollars for a letter, at least one has something for the money: and letters are too important to happiness; we cannot afford to be without knowledge of your thoughts, your lives; but it is hard, in people who can scarcely find bread, to pay for coarse paper and an envelop the price of a beautiful engraving, and know at the same time that they are doomed to leave Rome unable to carry away a single copy of what they have most loved here, for possession or for gift. So write, dear friends, much and often, but dont ruin us for nothing.

582   EUROPEAN SHORT PUBLISHED WORKS

Don Tirlone, the *Punch* of Rome, has just come in. This number represents the Fortress of Gaëta; outside hangs a cage containing a parrot (Pappagallo), the plump body of the bird is surmounted by a noble large head with benign face and Papal head-dress. He sits on the perch now with folded wings, but the cage door, in likeness of a loggia, shows there is convenience to come forth for the purposes of benediction, when wanted. Outside, the King of Naples, dressed as Harlequin, plays the organ for instruction of the bird (unhappy penitent, doomed to penance,) and grinning with sharp teeth observes: "He speaks in my way now." In the background a young Republican holds ready the match for a barrel of gunpowder, but looks at his watch waiting the moment to ignite it.

A happy New-Year to my country! may she be worthy of the privileges she possesses, while others are lavishing their blood to win them—that is all that need be wished for her at present. *

PROCLAMATION OF THE ROMAN REPUBLIC

Things and Thoughts in Europe No. XXVIII

Gioberti, Mamiani and Mazzini—Formation of the Constitutional Assembly—The Right of Suffrage—A Procession—The Proclamation of the Republic—Results—The Decree of the Assembly—The Americans in Rome; Difference of Impressions—The Fight of the Grand Duke of Tuscany—Charles Albert—The Present State of Rome—Reflections and Conclusions—Latest Intelligence.

ROME, Evening of Feb. 20, 1849.

THE League between the Italian States, the DIET which was to establish it, had been the thought of Gioberti, had found its instrument at Rome in Mamiani. Its Deputies were to be named by Princes or Parliaments, their mandate to be limited by the then institutions of the several States, measures of mutual security and some modifications in the way of reform would be the utmost that could be hoped from it. The scope of this party did not go beyond more vigorous prosecution of the War for Independence, and the establishment of good Institutions for the several Principalities on a basis of assimilation.

Mazzini, the great radical thinker of Italy, was on the contrary persuaded that Unity not union was necessary to this country. He had taken for his motto GOD AND THE PEOPLE, and believed in no other powers. He wished an Italian Constitutional Assembly, selected directly by the People, and furnished with an unlimited mandate to decide what form was now required by the needs of the Peninsula. His own wishes, certainly, aimed at the Republic; but the decision remained with the Representatives of the People.

The thought of Gioberti had been at first the popular one, as he, in fact, was the seer of the so-called Moderate party. For myself I always looked upon him as entirely a charlatan, who covered his want of all real force by the thickest embroidered mantle of words. Still, for a time, he corresponded with the wants of the Italian mind. He assailed the Jesuits, and was of real use by embodying the distrust and aversion that brooded in the minds of men against these most insidious and inveterate foes to liberty and progress. This triumph, at least, he may boast: that sect has been obliged to yield; its extinction seems impossible, of such life-giving power was the fiery will of Loyola. In the *Primato* he had embodied the lingering hope of the Catholic Church; Pio IX. had answered to the appeal, had answered only to show its futility. He had run through Italy as courier for Charles Albert, when the so basely styled Magnanimous entered, pretending to save her from the stranger, really hoping to take her for himself. His own cowardice and treachery neutralized the hope, and Charles Albert, abject in his disgrace, took a retrograde Ministry. This the country would not suffer, and obliged him after a while to reässume at least the position of a year since by taking Gioberti for his Premier. But it soon became evident that the Ministry of Charles Albert was in the same position as had been that of Pio IX. The hand was powerless when the head was indisposed. Meantime the thought of Mazzini had echoed through Tuscany from the revered lips of Montanelli; it reached the Roman States, and, though at first propagated by foreign impulse, yet, as soon as understood, was welcomed as congenial. Montanelli had nobly said, addressing Florence, "We could not regret that the realization of this project should take place in a sister city, still more illustrious than ours." The

Romans took him at his word; the Constitutional Assembly for the Roman States was elected with a double mandate, that the Deputies might sit in the Constitutional Assembly for all Italy whenever the other Provinces could send theirs. They were elected by universal suffrage. Those who listened to Jesuits and Moderates predicted that the project would fail of itself. The people were too ignorant to make use of the liberty of suffrage.

But ravens now-a-days are not the true prophetic birds. The Roman Eagle recommences her flight, and it is from its direction only that the High Priest may draw his augury. The people is certainly as ignorant as centuries of the worst government, the neglect of popular education, the enslavement of speech and the Press, could make it; yet it has an instinct to recognize measures that are good for it. A few weeks' schooling at some popular meetings, the clubs, the conversations of the National Guards in their quarters or on patrol, was sufficient to concert measures so well that the people voted in larger proportion than at contested elections in our country, and made a very good choice.

The opening of the Constitutional Assembly gave occasion for a fine procession. All the troops in Rome defiled from the Campidaglio; among them many bear the marks of suffering from the Lombard war. The banners of Sicily, Venice and Bologna waved proudly; that of Naples was veiled with crape. I was in a balcony in the Piazza Di Venizia; the Palazzo Di Venizia, that sternest feudal pile, so long the headquarters of Austrian machinations, seemed to frown as the bands each in passing struck up the *Marseillaise*. The nephew of Napoleon and Garibaldi, the hero of Montevideo, walked together, as Deputies. The Deputies, a grave band, mostly advocates or other professional men, walked without other badge of distinction than the tricolored scarf. I remembered the entrance of the Deputies to the Council only fourteen months ago, in the magnificent carriages lent by the Princes for the occasion; they too were mostly Nobles and their liveried attendants followed, carrying their scutcheons. Princes and Counselors have both fled or sunk into nothingness: in those Counselors was no Counsel.—Will it be found in the present? Let us hope it! What we see to-day has much more the air of reality than all that parade of scutcheons, or the pomp of dress

THINGS AND THOUGHTS IN EUROPE XXVIII 585

and retinue with which the Ecclesiastical Court was wont to amuse the people.

A few days after followed the proclamation of the Republic. An immense crowd of people surrounded the *Palazzo della Cancelleria*, within whose court-yard Rossi fell, while the debate was going on within. At one o'clock in the morning of the 9th February, the Republic was resolved upon and the crowd rushed away to ring all the bells.

Early next morning I rose and went forth to seek the Republic. Over the Quirinal I went, through the Forum to the Capitol. There was nothing to be seen except the magnificent calm emperor, the tamers of horses, the fountain, the trophies, the lions, as usual; among the marbles for living figures, a few dirty, bold women, and Murillo boys in the sun just as usual. I passed into the Corso; there were men in the liberty cap; of course the lowest and vilest had been the first to assume it; all the horrible beggars persecuting as impudently as usual. I met some English; all their comfort was, "It would not last a month."—"They hoped to see all those fellows shot yet."—The English clergyman, more mild and legal, only hopes to see them (as the Ministry, Deputies, &c.) *hung*.

Mr. Carlyle would be delighted with his countrymen. They are entirely ready and anxious to see a Cromwell for Italy. They, too, think it is no matter what happens in "the back parlor," when the people starve. What signifies that, if there is "order" in the front? How dare they make a noise to disturb us yawning at billiards!

I met an American. He "had no confidence in the Republic." Why? Because he "had no confidence in the People." Why? Because "they were not like *our* People." Ah! Jonathan and John—excuse me, but I must say the Italian has a decided advantage over you in the power of quickly feeling generous sympathy, as well as some other things which I have not time now to particularize. *Mais nous nous reverrons.* I have memoranda from you both in my note-book.

At last the procession mounts the Campidaglio. It is all dressed with banners. The tricolor surmounts the Palace of the Senator; the Senator himself has fled. The Deputies mount the steps, and one of them reads, in a clear, friendly voice, the following words:

586 EUROPEAN SHORT PUBLISHED WORKS

FUNDAMENTAL DECREE OF THE CONSTITUTIONAL
ASSEMBLY OF ROME.

ARTICLE I. The Papacy has fallen in fact and in right from the temporal Government of the Roman State.

ART. II. The Roman Pontifex shall have all the necessary guaranties for independence in the exercise of his spiritual power.

ART. III. The form of Government of the Roman State shall be a pure Democracy, and will take the glorious name of Roman Republic.

ART. IV. The Roman Republic will have with the rest of Italy the relations exacted by a common nationality.

Between each of these expressive sentences the speaker paused; the great bell of the Capitol gave forth its solemn melodies; the cannon answered; while the crowd shouted, *Viva la Republica! Viva Italia!*

The imposing grandeur of the spectacle to me gave new force to the thought that already swelled my heart; my nerves thrilled, and I longed to see in some answering glance a spark of Rienzi, a little of that soul which made my country what she is. The American at my side remained impassive. Receiving all his birthright from a triumph of Democracy, he was quite indifferent to this manifestation on this consecrated spot. Passing the Winter in Rome to study Art, he was insensible to the artistic beauty of the scene—insensible to this new life of that spirit from which all the forms he gazes at in galleries emanated. He "did not see the *use* of these popular demonstrations."

Again, I must mention a remark of his as a specimen of the ignorance in which Americans usually remain during their flighty visits to these scenes, where they associate only with one another. And I do it the rather as this seemed a really thoughtful, intelligent man; no vain, vulgar trifler. He said—

"*The people* seem only to be looking on; they take no part."

"What people?" said I.

"Why, these round us; there is no other people."

There are a few beggars, errand-boys and nurse-maids.

"The others are only soldiers."

"Soldiers! The Civic Guard; all the decent men in Rome."

Thus it is that the American, on many points, becomes more ignorant for coming abroad, because he attaches some value to his crude impressions and frequent blunders. It is not thus that

THINGS AND THOUGHTS IN EUROPE XXVIII 587

any seed-corn can be gathered from foreign gardens. Without modest scrutiny, patient study and observation, he spends his money and goes home with a new coat perhaps, but a mind befooled rather than instructed. It is necessary to speak the languages of these countries and know personally some of their inhabitants in order to form any accurate impressions.

The flight of the Grand Duke of Tuscany followed. In imitation of his great exemplar he promised and smiled to the last, deceiving Montanelli, the pure and sincere, at the very moment he was about to enter his carriage, into the belief that he persevered in his assent to the liberal movement. His position was certainly very difficult, but he might have left it like a gentleman, like a man of honor. 'Twas pity to destroy so lightly the good opinion the Tuscans had of him. Now Tuscany meditates union with Rome.

Meanwhile, Charles Albert is filled with alarm. He is indeed betwixt two fires. Gioberti has published one of his prolix, weak addresses, in which he says that in the beginning of every revolution you must fix a limit beyond which you will not go; that, for himself, he has done it—others are surpassing his mark and he will not go any farther. Of the want of thought, of insight to historic and all other truths which distinguishes the "illustrious Gioberti," this assumption is a specimen. But it makes no difference; he and his Prince must go sooner or later, if the movement continues, nor is there any prospect of its being stayed unless by foreign intervention. This the Pope has not yet, it is believed, solicited, but there is little reason to hope he will be spared that crowning disgrace. He has already consented to the incitement of civil war. Should an intervention be solicited, all depends on France. Will she basely forfeit every pledge and every duty, to say nothing of her true interest? It seems that her President stands doubtful, intending to do what is for *his* particular interest; but if his interest proves opposed to the republican principle, will France suffer herself again to be hoodwinked and enslaved? It is impossible to know, she has already shown such devotion to the mere prestige of a name.

On England no dependence can be placed. She is guided by no great idea; her Parliamentary leaders sneer at sentimental policy, and the "jargon" of ideas. She will act, as always, for her own interest; and the interest of her present Government

588 EUROPEAN SHORT PUBLISHED WORKS

is becoming more and more the crushing of the democratic tendency. They are obliged to do it at home both in the back and the front parlor; it would not be decent as yet to have a Spielberg just at home for obstreperous patriots, but England has so many ships, it is just as easy to transport them to a safe distance. Then the Church of England, so long an enemy to the Church of Rome, feels a decided interest with it on the subject of temporal possessions. The rich English traveler, fearing to see the Prince Borghese stripped of one of his palaces for a hospital or some such low use, thinks of his own twenty-mile park and the crowded village of beggars at its gate, and muses: "I hope to see them all shot yet, these rascally republicans."

How I wish my country would show some noble sympathy when an experience so like her own is going on. Politically she cannot interfere; but formerly when Greece and Poland were struggling, they were at least aided by private contributions. Italy, naturally so rich, but long racked and impoverished by her oppressors, greatly needs money to arm and clothe her troops. Some token of sympathy, too, from America would be so welcome to her now. If there were a circle of persons inclined to trust such to me, I might venture to promise the trust should be used to the advantage of Italy. It would make me proud to have my country show a religious faith in the progress of ideas, and make some small sacrifice of its own great resources in aid of a sister cause, now.

But I must close this letter, which it would be easy to swell to a volume from the materials in my mind. One or two traits of the hour I must note. Mazzarelli, chief of the present Ministry, was a prelate, and named spontaneously by the Pope before his flight. He has shown entire and frank intrepidity. He has laid aside the title of Monsignor, and appears before the world as a layman.

Nothing can be more tranquil than has been the state of Rome all Winter. Every wile has been used by the obscurantists to excite the people, but their confidence in their leaders could not be broken. A little mutiny in the troops, stimulated by letters from their old leaders, was quelled in a moment. The day after the proclamation of the Republic, some zealous ignoramuses insulted the carriages that appeared with servants in livery. The Ministry published a grave admonition, that democracy meant liberty, not license, and that he who infringed upon an innocent freedom of action in others must be declared traitor to his country. Every act of the kind ceased instantly. An intimation that it was better not to throw large comfits or oranges during the Carnival, as injuries have thus been sometimes caused, was obeyed with equal docility.

On Sunday last placards affixed in the high places summoned the city to invest Giuseppe Mazzini with the rights of a Roman Citizen. I have not yet heard the result. The Pope made Rossi a Roman Citizen; he was suffered to retain that title only one day. It was given him 14th Nov. he died the 15th. Mazzini enters Rome at any rate for the first time in his life as deputy to the Constitutional Assembly; it would be a noble poetic justice, if he could enter also a Roman Citizen.

24th.—The Austrians have invaded Ferrara, taken $200,000 and six hostages and retired. This step is no doubt intended to determine whether France will resent the insult, or whether she will betray Italy. It shows also the assurance of the Austrian that the Pope will approve of an armed intervention. Probably before I write again these matters will reach some decided crisis. *

"I WRITE YOU FROM BARRICADED ROME"

Undaunted Rome

ROME, 6th May, 1849.

I WRITE you from barricaded Rome. The Mother of Nations is now at bay against them all.

Rome was suffering before. The misfortunes of other regions of Italy, the defeat at Novara, preconcerted in hope to strike the last blow at Italian independence, the surrender and painful condition of Genoa, the money difficulties—insuperable, unless the Government could secure confidence abroad as well as at home—prevented her people from finding that foot-hold for which they were ready. The vacillations of France agitated them, still they could not seriously believe she would ever act the part she has. We must say France, because, though many honorable men have washed their hands of all share in the perfidy, the Assembly voted funds to sustain the expedition to Civita Vecchia, and the Nation, the Army have remained quiescent.

No one was, no one could be, deceived as to the scope of this expedition. It was intended to restore the Pope to the temporal sovereignty, from which the People, by the use of suffrage, had deposed him. No doubt the French, in case of success, proposed to temper the triumph of Austria and Naples, and stipulate for conditions that might soothe the Romans and make their act less odious. Also they were probably deceived by the representations of Gaeta, and believed that a large party, which had been intimidated by the republicans, would declare in favor of the Pope when they found themselves likely to be sustained. But this last pretext may in no way avail them. They landed at Civita Vecchia, and no one declared for the Pope. They marched on Rome. Placards were affixed within the walls by hands unknown, calling upon the Papal party to rise within the town. Not a soul stirred. The French had no excuse left for pretending to believe that the present Government was not entirely acceptable to the people. Notwithstanding, they assail the gates, they fire upon St. Peter's, and their balls pierced the Vatican. They were repulsed as they deserved, retired in quick and shameful defeat, as surely the brave French soldiery could not, if they had not been demoralized by a sense of what an infamous course they were pursuing. France, eager to destroy the last hope of Italian emancipation, France the alguazil of Austria, the soldiers of republican France, firing upon republican Rome! If there be angel as well as demon powers that interfere in the affairs of men, those bullets could scarcely fail to be turned back against their own breasts. Yet Roman blood has flowed also; I saw how it stained the walls of the Vatican Gardens on the 30th April—the first anniversary of the appearance of Pius IX's too famous encyclic letter. Shall he, shall any Pope ever again walk peacefully in these gardens. Impossible! The temporal sovereignty of the Popes was gone, by their shameless, merciless measures taken to restore it. The spiritual dominion falls too into irrevocable ruin.

What may be the issue, at this moment we cannot guess. The French have retired to Civita Vecchia, but whether to reëmbark

UNDAUNTED ROME

591

or to await reïnforcements we know not. The Neapolitan force has halted within a few miles of the walls; it is not large, and they are undoubtedly surprised at the discomfiture of the French. Perhaps they wait for the Austrians, but we do not yet hear that these have entered Romana. Meanwhile Rome is strongly barricaded, and, though she cannot stand always against a world in arms, she means at least to try. Mazzini is at her head; she has now a guide "who understands his faith," and all there is of noble spirit will show itself. We all feel very sad, because the idea of bombs barbarously thrown in, and street-fight in Rome is peculiarly dreadful. Apart from all the blood and anguish inevitable at such times, the glories of Art may perish, and mankind be forever despoiled of the most beautiful inheritance. Yet I would defend Rome to the last moment. She must not be false to the higher hope that has dawned upon her. She must not fall back again into servility and corruption. And no one is willing. The interference of the French has roused the weakest to resistance. "From the Austrians, from the Neapolitans," they cried, "we expected this; but from the French, it is too infamous, it cannot be borne," and they all ran to arms and fought nobly.

The Americans here are not in a pleasant situation. Mr. Cass, the Chargé of the United States, stays here without recognizing the Government. Of course, he holds no position at the present moment that can enable him to act for us. Beside, it gives us pain that our country, whose policy it justly is to avoid physical interference with the affairs of Europe, should not use a moral influence. Rome has, as we did, thrown off a Government no longer tolerable; she has made use of the suffrage to form another; she stands on the same basis as ourselves. Mr. Rush did us great honor by his ready recognition of a principle as represented by the French Provisional Government; had Mr. Cass been empowered to do the same, our country would have acted nobly, and all that is most truly American in America would have spoken to sustain the sickened hopes of European democracy. But of this more when I write next. Who knows what I may have to tell another week? *

592   EUROPEAN SHORT PUBLISHED WORKS

THE FRENCH ARMY BOMBS AND OCCUPIES ROME

Things and Thoughts in Europe No. XXXIII

Siege of Rome—Heat—Night Attacks—The Bombardment—The Night Breach—Defection—Entry of the French—Slaughter of the Romans—The Hospitals—Destruction by Bombs—Cessation of Resistance—Oudinot's Stubbornness—Garibaldi's Troops— Their Muster on the Scene of Rienzi's Triumph—Garibaldi—His Departure—"Respectable" Opinion—The Protectors Unmasked— Cold Reception—A Priest Assassinated—State of Siege Declared— Republican Education—Disappearance of French Soldiers—Clearing the Hospitals—Priestly Baseness—Insult to the American Consul— His Protest and Departure—Disarming the National Guard—Position of Mr. Cass—Petty Oppression—Expulsion of Foreigners—Effect of French Presence—Address to the People—Visit to the Scene of Strife—American Sympathy for Liberty in Europe.

ROME, July 6, 1849.

IF I mistake not, I closed my last letter just as the news arrived here that the attempt of the Democratic party in France to resist the infamous proceedings of the Government had failed, and thus Rome, as far as human calculation went, had not a hope for her liberties left. An inland city cannot long sustain a siege when there is no hope of aid. Then followed the news of the surrender of Ancona, and Rome found herself quite alone— for, though Venice continued to hold out, all communication was cut off.

The Republican troops, almost to a man, left Ancona, but a long march separated them from Rome.

The extreme heat of these days was far more fatal to the Romans than their assailants, for, as fast as the French troops sickened, their place was taken by fresh arrivals. Ours also not only sustained the exhausting service by day, but were harrassed at night by attacks, feigned or real.—These commonly began about 11 or 12 o'clock at night, just when all who meant to rest were fairly asleep. I can imagine the harassing effect upon the troops, from what I feel in my sheltered pavilion, in consequence of not knowing a quiet night's sleep for a month.

The bombardment became constantly more serious. The house where I live was filled as early as the 20th with persons obliged to fly from the *Piazza di Gesù*, where the fiery rain fell thickest. The night of the 21st–22d, we were all alarmed about 2 o'clock A. M. by a tremendous cannonade. It was the moment when the breach was finally made by which the French entered.—They rushed in, and, I grieve to say, that by the only instance of defection known in the course of the siege, those companies of the regiment Union, which had in charge a casino on that point, yielded to panic and abandoned it. The French immediately entered and intrenched themselves. That was the fatal hour for the city. Every day afterward, though obstinately resisted, they gained, till at last, their cannon being well placed, the city was entirely commanded from the Janicular, and all thought of further resistance was idle.

This was true policy to avoid the street fight, in which the Italian, an unpracticed soldier, but full of feeling and sustained from the houses, would have been no match for their disciplined troops. After the 22d, the slaughter of the Romans became every day more fearful. Their defenses were knocked down by the heavy cannon of the French, and, entirely exposed in their valorous onsets, great numbers perished on the spot. Those who were brought into the Hospitals were generally grievously wounded, very commonly subjects for amputation. My heart bled daily more and more at these sights, and I could not feel much for myself, though now the balls and bombs began to fall round me also. The night of the 28th the effect was truly fearful, as they whizzed and burst near me. As many as 30 fell upon or near the *Hotel de Russia*, where Mr. Cass has his temporary abode. The roof of the studio in the pavilion, tenanted by Mr. Stermer, well known to the visitors of Rome, for his highly-finished cabinet pictures, was torn to pieces. I sat alone in my much-exposed apartment thinking "if one strikes me, I only hope it will kill me at once, and that God will transport my soul to some sphere where Virtue and Love are not tyrannized over by egotism and brute force, as in this." However, that night passed; the next, we had reason to expect a still more fiery salute to the Pincian, as here alone remained three or four pieces of cannon which could be used. But the morning of the 30th, in a contest at the foot of the Janicular, the line, old Papal troops, naturally not in earnest like the free corps, refused to fight against odds so terrible, the heroic

594   EUROPEAN SHORT PUBLISHED WORKS

Manara fell, with hundreds of his devoted Lombards. Garibaldi saw his best officers perish, and himself went in the afternoon to say to the Assembly that further resistance was unavailing.

The Assembly sent to Oudinot, but he refused any conditions, refused even to guarantee a safe departure to Garibaldi, his brave foe. Notwithstanding, a great number of men left the other regiments to follow the leader, whose courage had captivated them and whose habit of superiority to difficulties commanded their entire confidence. Toward the evening of Monday, 2d July, it was known that the French were preparing to cross the river and take possession of all the city. I went into the Corso with some friends; it was filled with citizens and military, the carriage was stopped by the crowd near the Doria palace; the lancers of Garibaldi galloped along in full career, I longed for Sir Walter Scott to be on earth again, and see them; all are light, athletic, resolute figures, many of the forms of the finest manly beauty of the South, all sparkling with its genius and ennobled by the resolute spirit, ready to dare, to do, to die. We followed them to the piazza of St. John Lateran. Never have I seen a sight so beautiful, so romantic and so sad. Whoever knows Rome knows the peculiar solemn grandeur of that piazza, scene of the first triumph of Rienzi, the magnificence of the "mother of all churches," the Baptistery with its porphyry columns, the Santa Scala with its glittering mosaics of the early ages, the obelisk standing fairest of any of those most imposing monuments of Rome, the view through the gates of the Campagna, on that side so richly strewn with ruins. The sun was setting, the crescent moon rising, the flower of the Italian youth were marshaling in that solemn place. They had been driven from every other spot where they had offered their hearts as bulwarks of Italian Independence; in this last strong hold they had sacrificed hecatombs of their best and bravest in that cause; they must now go or remain prisoners and slaves. *Where* go, they knew not, for except distant Hungary there is not now a spot which would receive them, or where they can act as honor commands. They had all put on the beautiful dress of the Garibaldi legion, the tunic of bright red cloth, the Greek cap, or else round hat with Puritan plume, their long hair was blown back from resolute faces; all looked full of courage; they had counted the cost before they entered on this perilous struggle; they had weighed life and all its material advantages against Liberty, and made their election; they turned not back, nor flinched at this bitter crisis. I saw the wounded, all that could go, laden upon their baggage cars, some were already pale and fainting, still they wished to go. I saw many youths, born to rich inheritance, carrying in a handkerchief all their worldly goods; the women were ready, their eyes too were resolved, if sad. The wife of Garibaldi followed him horse-back, he himself was distinguished by the white bournouse; his look was entirely that of a hero of the middle ages, his face still young, for the excitements of his life, though so many, have all been youthful, and there is no fatigue upon his brow or cheek. Fall or stand, one sees in him a man engaged in the career for which he is adapted by nature. He went upon the parapet and looked upon the road with a spy-glass, and, no obstruction being in sight, he turned his face for a moment back upon Rome, then led the way through the gate. Hard was the heart, stony and seared the eye that had no tear for that moment. Go! fated, gallant band, and if God care not indeed for men as for the sparrows, most of ye go forth to perish. And Rome, anew the Niobe! Must she lose also these beautiful and brave that promised her regeneration and would have given it, but for the perfidy, the overpowering force of the foreign intervention.

I know that many "respectable" gentlemen would be surprised to hear me speak in this way. Gentlemen who perform their "duties to society" by buying for themselves handsome clothes and furniture with the interest of their money, speak of Garibaldi and his men as "brigands" and "vagabonds." Such are they, doubtless, in the same sense as Jesus, Eneas and Moses were. To me men who can throw so slightly aside the ease of wealth, the joys of affection, for the sake of what they deem honor, in whatsoever form, are the "respectable." No doubt there are in these bands a number of men of lawless minds, and who follow this banner only because there is for them no other path. But the greater part are the noble youths who have fled from the Austrian conscription, or fly now from the renewal of the Papal suffocation, darkened by the French protection.

As for the protectors, they entirely threw aside the mask, as it was always supposed they would, the moment they had possession of Rome.

I do not know whether they were really so bewildered by their priestly councilors as to imagine they would be well received in a city which they had bombarded, and where twelve hundred men were lying wounded by their assault. To say nothing of the justice or injustice of the matter, it could not be supposed that the Roman people, if it had any sense of dignity, would welcome them. However, I was not out, as what countenance I have I would not give on such an occasion; but an English lady, my friend, told me they seemed to look expectingly for the strong party of friends they had always pretended to have within the walls. The French officers looked up to the windows for ladies, and she being the only one they saw, saluted her. She made no reply. They then passed into the Corso. Many were assembled, the softer Romans being unable to control a curiosity the Milanese would have disclaimed, but preserving an icy silence. In an evil hour, a foolish priest dared to break it by the cry of *Viva Pio Nono*. The populace, roused to fury, rushed on him with their knives. He was much wounded; one or two others were killed in the rush. The people howled, then, and hissed at the French, who, advancing their bayonets, and clearing the way before them, fortified themselves in the piazzas. Next day the French troops were marched to and fro through Rome to inspire awe into the people, but it has only created a disgust amounting to loathing, to see that, with such an imposing force, and in great part fresh, the French were not ashamed to use bombs also, and kill women and children in their beds. Oudinot, then, seeing the feeling of the people, and finding they pursued as a spy any man who so much as showed the way to his soldiers—that the Italians went out of the cafés if Frenchmen entered; in short, that the people regarded him and his followers in the same light as the Austrians, has declared the state of siege in Rome—the Press is stifled—everybody is to be in the house at 9½ P. M. and, whoever in any way insults his men, or puts any obstacle in their way, is to be shot.

The fruits of all this will be the same as elsewhere: temporary repression will sow the seeds of perpetual resistance; and never was Rome in so fair a way to be educated for the Republican form of Government as now.

Especially could nothing be more irritating for an Italian population, in the month of July, than to drive them to their homes at half-past nine. After the insupportable heat of the day, their only enjoyment and refreshment is found in evening walks, and chats together as they sit before their cafés, or in groups outside some friendly door. Now they must hurry home when the drum beats at 9 o'clock. They are forbidden to stand or sit in groups, and this by their bombarding *protector*! Comment is unnecessary.

French soldiers are daily missing; of some it is known that they have been killed by the Trastevirini for daring to make court to their women.—Of more than a hundred and fifty, it is only known that they cannot be found; and in two days of French "order" more acts of violence have been committed than in two months under the Triumvirate.

The French have taken up their quarters in the court-yards of the Quirinal and Venetian Palaces, which are full of the wounded, many of whom have been driven well nigh mad, and their burning wounds exasperated by the sound of their drums and trumpets—the constant sense of their insulting presence. The wounded have been warned to leave the Quirinal at the end of eight days, though there are many who cannot be moved from bed to bed without causing them great anguish and peril, nor is it known that any other place has been provided as a hospital for them. At the palace of Venice the French have searched for three emigrants that they wished to imprison, even in the apartments where the wounded were lying; they ran their bayonets into the matresses; they have taken for themselves beds given by the Romans to the hospital—not public property, but private gift. The hospital of Santo Spirito was a Governmental establishment and, in using a part of it for the wounded, its director, Monsignore, had been retained, because he had the reputation of being honest and not illiberal. But as soon as the French entered he, with true priestly baseness, sent away the women nurses, saying he had no longer money to pay them— transported the wounded into a miserable, airless basement, that had before been used as a granary and appropriated the good apartments to the use of the French!

July 8.—The report of this morning is that the French yesterday violated the domicile of our Consul, Mr. Brown, pretending to search for persons hidden there; that Mr. Brown, banner in one hand and sword in the other, repelled the assault, and fairly drove them down stairs; that then he made them an appropriate speech, though in a mixed language of English, French and Italian; that the crowd vehemently applauded Mr. Brown, who already was much liked for the warm sympathy he had shown the Romans in their aspirations and their distresses; that he then donned his uniform and went to Oudinot to make his protest. How this was received I know not, but understand Mr. B. departed with his family yesterday evening.

Will America look as coldly on the insult to herself as she has on the struggle of this injured people?

To-day an edict is out to disarm the National Guard. The generous "protectors" wish to take all the trouble upon themselves. Rome is full of them; at every step are met groups in the uniform of France, with faces bronzed in the African war, and so stultified by a life without enthusiasm and without thought, that I do not believe Napoleon would recognize them as French soldiers.—The effect of their appearance compared with that of the Italian free corps is that of body as compared with spirit. It is easy to see how they could be used to purposes so contrary to the legitimate policy of France, for they do not look more intellectual, more fitted to have opinions of their own, than the Austrian soldiery.

July 10.—The plot thickens. The exact facts with regard to the invasion of Mr. Brown's house, I have not been able to ascertain. I suppose they will be published, as Oudinot has promised to satisfy Mr. Cass. I must add in reference to what I wrote sometime ago of the position of our envoy here, that the kind and sympathetic course of Mr. Cass toward the Republicans in these troubles, his very gentlemanly and courteous bearing, have from the minds of most removed all unpleasant feelings. They see that his position was very peculiar; sent to the Papal Government, finding here the Republican, and just at that moment violently assailed. Unless he had extraordinary powers he naturally felt obliged to communicate further with our Government before acknowledging this. I shall always regret, however, that he did not stand free to occupy the high position that belonged to the representative of the United States at that moment, and peculiarly because it was by a Republic that the Roman Republic was betrayed.—But, as I say, the plot thickens. Yesterday three families were carried to prison because a boy crowed like a cock at the French soldiery from the windows of the house they occupied. Another, because a man pursued took refuge in their court-yard. Yesterday, the city being mostly disarmed, came the edict to take down the arms of the Republic, "emblems of anarchy." But worst of all they have done is an edict commanding all foreigners who had been in the service of the Republican Government to leave Rome within twenty-four hours. This is the most infamous thing done yet, as it drives to desperation those who stayed because they had so many to go with and no place to go to, or because their relatives lie wounded here: no others wished to remain in Rome under present circumstances.

I am sick of breathing the same air with men capable of a part so utterly cruel and false. As soon as I can I shall take refuge in the mountains, if it be possible to find an obscure nook unpervaded by these convulsions. Let not my friends be surprised if they do not hear from me for some time. I may not feel like writing. I have seen too much sorrow, and alas! without power to aid. It makes me sick to see the palaces and streets of Rome full of these injurious foreigners, and to see the already changed aspect of her population. The men of Rome had begun, filled with new hopes, to develop unknown energy—they walked quick, their eyes sparkled, they delighted in duty, in responsibility; in a year of such life their effeminacy would have been vanquished—now, dejectedly, unemployed, they lounge along the streets, feeling that all the implements of labor, all the ensigns of hope, have been snatched from them. Their hands fall slack, their eyes rove aimless, the beggars begin to swarm again, and the black ravens who delight in the night of ignorance, the slumber of sloth, as the only sureties for their rule, emerge daily more and more frequent from their hiding places.

The following Address has been circulated from hand to hand:

TO THE PEOPLE OF ROME

Misfortune, brothers, has fallen upon us anew. But it is trial of brief duration—it is the stone of the sepulcher which we shall throw away after three days, rising victorious and renewed, an immortal

Nation. For with us are God and Justice—God and Justice, who cannot die, but always triumph, while Kings and Popes, once dead, revive no more.

As you have been great in the combat, be so in the days of sorrow—great in your conduct as citizens, of generous disdain, of sublime silence. Silence is the weapon we have now to use against the Cossacks of France and the Priests, their masters.

In the streets do not look at them; do not answer if they address you.

In the cafés, in the eating-houses, if they enter, rise and go out.

Let your windows remain closed as they pass.

Never attend their feasts, their parades.

The harmony of their musical bands be for you tones of slavery, and, when you hear them, fly.

Let the liberticide soldier be condemned to isolation; let him atone in solitude and contempt for having served priests and kings.

And you, Roman women—master-piece of God's work!—deign no look, no smile to those satellites of an abhorred Pope! Cursed be she who, before the odious satellites of Austria, forgets that she is Italian! Her name shall be published for the execration of all her people! And even the courtezans! let them show love for their country, and thus regain the dignity of citizens!

And our word of order, our cry of reunion and emancipation, be now and ever, VIVA LA REPUBLICA!

This incessant cry, which not even French slaves can dispute, shall prepare us to administer the bequest of our martyrs, shall be consoling dew to the immaculate and holy bones that repose, sublime holocaust of faith and of love, near our walls, and make doubly divine the Eternal City. In this cry we shall find ourselves always brothers, and we shall conquer. Viva Rome, the Capital of Italy! Viva the Italy of the People! Viva the Roman Republic!   A ROMAN.

Dated *Rome, July* 4, 1849.

For this day's anniversary, so joyously celebrated in our land, was that of the entrance of the French into Rome.

I know not whether the Romans will follow out this programme with constancy as the sterner Milanese have done. If they can, it will draw upon them endless persecutions, countless exactions, but at once educate and prove them worthy of a nobler life.

Yesterday I went over the scene of conflict. It was fearful even to *see* the casinos *Quattro Venti* and *Vascello*, where the French and Romans had been several days so near one another,

THINGS AND THOUGHTS IN EUROPE XXXIII 601

all shattered to pieces, with fragments of rich stucco and painting still sticking to rafters between the great holes made by the cannonade, and think that men had stayed and fought in them when only a mass of ruins. The French, indeed, were entirely sheltered the last days; to my unpracticed eyes the extent and thoroughness of their works seemed miraculous, and gave me first clear idea of the incompetency of the Italians to resist organized armies. I saw their commanders had not even known enough of the art of war to understand how the French were conducting the siege.—It is true their resources were at any rate inadequate to resistance; only continual sorties would have arrested the progress of the foe, and to make them and man the wall their forces were inadequate. I was struck more than ever by the heroic valor of *ours*, let me say, as I have said all along, for go where I may, a large part of my heart will ever remain in Italy. I hope her children will always acknowledge me as a sister, though I drew not my first breath here. A contadini showed me where thirty seven braves are buried beneath a heap of wall that fell upon them in the shock of one cannonade. A marble nymph, with broken arm, looked sadly that way from her sun-dried fountain, some roses were blooming still, some red oleanders amid the ruin. The sun was casting its last light on the mountains on the tranquil, sad Campagna, that sees one leaf turned more in the book of Woe. This was in the Vascello. I then entered the French ground, all mapped and hollowed like a honey-comb. A pair of skeleton legs protruded from a bank of one barricade; lower a dog had scratched away its light covering of earth from the body of a man, and discovered it lying face upward all dressed; the dog stood gazing on it with an air of stupid amusement. I thought at that moment, recalling some letters received, "O men and women of America, spared these frightful sights, these sudden wrecks of every hope, what angel of Heaven do you suppose has time to listen to your tales of morbid woe? If any find leisure to work for men to-day, think you not they have enough to do to care for the victims here."

I see you have meetings, where you speak of the Italians, the Hungarians. I pray you *do something*; let it not end in a mere cry of sentiment. That is better than to sneer at all that is liberal, like the English; than to talk of the holy victims of patriotism as "anarchists" and "brigands,"—but it is not enough. It ought not

602   EUROPEAN SHORT PUBLISHED WORKS

to content your consciences. Do you owe no tithe to Heaven for the privileges it has showered on you, for whose achievement so many here suffer and perish daily? Deserve to retain them, by helping your fellow-men to acquire them. Our Government must abstain from interference, but private action is practicable, is due. For Italy, it is in this moment too late, but all that helps Hungary helps her also, helps all who wish the freedom of men from an hereditary yoke now become intolerable. Send money, send cheer—acknowledge as the legitimate leaders and rulers those men who represent the people, who understand its wants, who are ready to die or to live for its good. Kossuth I know not, but his people recognize him; Manin I know not, but with what firm nobleness, what persevering virtue, he has acted for Venice!—Mazzini I know, the man and his acts, great, pure and constant,—a man to whom only the next age can do justice, as it reaps the harvest of the seed he has sown in this.—Friends, countrymen, and lovers of virtue, lovers of freedom, lovers of truth!—be on the alert; rest not supine in your easier lives, but remember

> "Mankind is one,
> And beats with one great heart."

"THE NEXT REVOLUTION, HERE AND ELSEWHERE, WILL BE RADICAL"

Italy

FLORENCE, Jan. 6, 1850.

LAST winter began with meteors and the rose-colored Aurora Borealis. All the winter was steady sunshine, and the Spring that followed no less glorious, as if Nature rejoiced in and daily smiled upon the noble efforts and tender, generous impulses of the Italian people. This winter, Italy is shrouded with snow. Here in Florence the oil congeals in the closet beside the fire— the water in the chamber—just as in our country-houses of New-England, as yet uncomforted by furnaces. I was supposing this to be confined to colder Florence, but a letter, this day received, from Rome says the snow lies there two feet deep, and water freezes instantly if thrown upon the pavement. I hardly know how to believe it—I who never saw but one slight powdering of snow all my two Roman winters, scarce enough to cover a Canary bird's wing.

Thus Nature again sympathizes with this injured people, though, I fear me, many a houseless wanderer wishes she did not. For many want both bread, and any kind of shelter this winter, an extremity of physical deprivation that had seemed almost impossible in this richest land. It had seemed that Italians might be subjected to the extreme of mental and moral suffering, but that the common beggar's plea, "*I am hungry*," must remain a mere poetic expression. 'Tis no longer so; for it proves possible for the wickedness of man to mar to an indefinite extent the benevolent designs of God. Yet, indeed, if indefinitely not infinitely. I feel now that we are to bless the very extremity of ill with which Italy is afflicted. The cure is sure, else death would follow.

The barbarities of reaction have reached their hight in the kingdom of Naples and Sicily. Bad government grows daily worse in the Roman dominions. The French have degraded themselves there enough to punish them even for the infamous treachery of which they were guilty. Their foolish national vanity, which prefers the honor of the uniform to the honor of the man, has received its due reward, in the numberless derisions and small insults it has received from a bitterer, blacker vice, the arrogance of the priests. President, envoys, ministers, officers, have all debased themselves; have told the most shameless lies; have bartered the fair fame slowly built up by many years of seeming consistency, for a few days of brief authority, in vain. Their schemes, thus far, have ended in disunion, and should they now win any point upon the right reverend cardinal vices, it is too late. The seeds for a vast harvest of hatreds and contempts are sown over every inch of Roman ground, nor can that malignant growth be extirpated, till the wishes of Heaven shall waft a fire that will burn down all, root and branch, and prepare the earth for an entirely new culture. The next revolution, here and elsewhere, will be radical. Not only Jesuitism must go, but the Roman Catholic religion must go. The Pope cannot retain even his spiritual power. The influence of the clergy is too perverting, too foreign to every hope of advancement and health. Not only the Austrian, and every potentate of foreign blood, must be deposed, but every man who assumes an arbitrary lordship over fellow man, must be driven out. It will be an uncompromising revolution. England cannot reason nor ratify nor criticize it—France cannot betray it—Germany cannot bungle it—Italy cannot bubble it away—Russia cannot stamp it down nor hide it in Siberia. The New Era is no longer an embryo; it is born; it begins to walk—this very year sees its first giant steps, and can no longer mistake its features. Men have long been talking of a transition state—it is over—the power of positive, determinate effort is begun. A faith is offered—men are everywhere embracing it; the film is hourly falling from their eyes and they see, not only near but far, duties worthy to be done. God be praised! It was a dark period of that sceptical endeavor and work, only worthy as helping to educate the next generation, was watered with much blood and tears. God be praised! that time is ended, and the noble band of teachers who have passed this last ordeal of the furnace and den of lions, are ready now to enter their followers for the elementary class.

At this moment all the worst men are in power, and the best betrayed and exiled. All the falsities, the abuses of the old political forms, the old social compact, seem confirmed. Yet it is not so: the struggle that is now to begin will be fearful, but even from the first hours not doubtful. Bodies rotten and trembling cannot long contend with swelling life. Tongue and hand cannot be permanently employed to keep down hearts. Sons cannot be long employed in the conscious enslavement of their sires, fathers of their children. That advent called EMMANUEL begins to be understood, and shall no more so foully be blasphemed. Men shall now be represented as souls, not hands and feet, and governed accordingly. A congress of great, pure, loving minds, and not a congress of selfish ambitions, shall preside. Do you laugh, Editor of the "*Times*?" (Times of the Iron Age.) Do you laugh, Roman Cardinal, as you shut the prison-door on woman weeping for her son martyred in the cause of his country? Do you laugh, Austrian officer, as you drill the Hungarian and Lombard youth to tremble at your baton? Soon you, all of you, shall "*believe* and tremble."

ITALY

I take little interest now in what is going on here in Italy. It is all leavened with the same leaven, and ferments to the same end. Tuscany is stupified. They are not discontented here, if they can fold the hands yet a little while to slumber. The Austrian tutelage is mild. In Lombardy and Venice they would gladly make it so, but the case is too difficult. The sick man tosses and tumbles. The so called Italian moderates are fighting at last, (not battles, they have not energy for that,) but skirmishes in Piedmont. The result cannot be doubtful; we need not waste time and paper in predicting it.

Joy to those born in this day: In America is open to them the easy chance of a noble, peaceful growth, in Europe of a combat grand in its motives, and in its extent beyond what the world ever before so much as dreamed. Joy to them; and joy to those their heralds, who, if their path was desert, their work unfinished, and their heads in the power of a prostituted civilization, to throw as toys at the feet of flushed, triumphant wickedness, yet holy-hearted in unasking love, great and entire in their devotion, fall or fade, happy in the thought that there come after them greater than themselves, who may at last string the harp of the world to full concord, in glory to God in the highest, for peace and love from man to man is become the bond of life. *

UNPUBLISHED WRITINGS

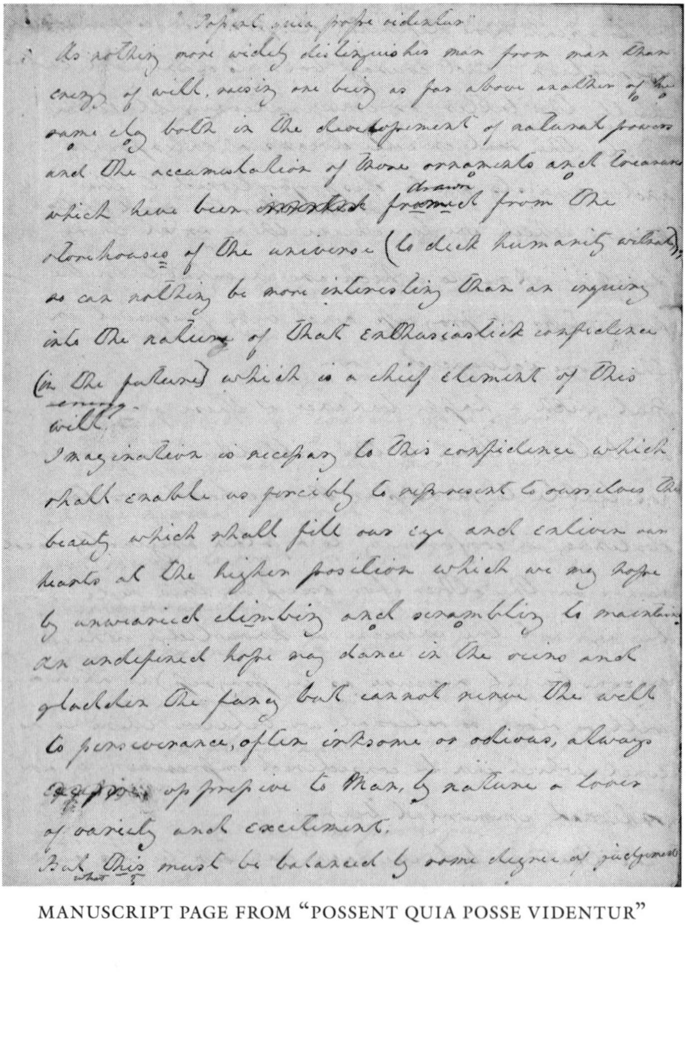

MANUSCRIPT PAGE FROM "POSSENT QUIA POSSE VIDENTUR"

"*Possent quia posse videntur*"

c. pre-fall 1819

As nothing more widely distinguishes man from man than energy of will, raising one being as far above another of the same clay both in the developement of natural powers and the accumulation of those ornaments and treasures which have been framed from the storehouses of the universe to deck humanity withal, so can nothing be more interesting than an inquiry into the nature of that enthusiastick confidence in the future which is a chief element of this will.

Imagination is necessary to this confidence which shall enable us forcibly to represent to ourselves the beauty which shall fill our eye and enliven our hearts at the higher position which we may hope by unwearied climbing and scrambling to maintain. An undefined hope may dance in the veins and gladden the fancy but cannot nerve the will to perseverance, often irksome or odious, always oppressive to Man, by nature a lover of variety and excitement.

But this must be balanced by some degree of judgement or to speak more definitely disposition to practical observation— and courage both to dare and endure, chiefly the latter or imagination will either waste the soul in idle dreams of enterprizes and conquests quite disproportioned to the powers which are to achieve them or embitter the mind under those disappointments which are inevitable in the first steps of progress and very frequent in the more advanced.

But with a happy balance of these qualities we believe that to the will thus invigorated, not liable to rashness on the one hand nor to obstinacy in conforming to a plan originally laid down on the other, (for excess on this side is a bar against the increase of knowledge which we constantly require as we progress,) to such a will, so strong, so rational we believe there is no limit which can be considered imprisoning by an immortal being.

Not that we believe each man can be his own Destiny, that he can fix his eyes upon a certain earthly object and say I will attain it. Much of this is possible and circumstances will bend greatly to favour the bold and wary—His action upon them will be, we do believe, as powerful as theirs on him. But this action must always be mutual. They may overcloud his eye and impair his powers. The object of his strivings may elude his grasp. Leonidas saved his country by a strong exertion of will inspired by the most generous sentiment. Brutus nerved his soul to break those ties most sacred to one like him and failed. Resolved, united hearts freed America—The strongest exertion, the most generous concentration of will for a similar purpose left Poland in blood and chains at the feet of a tyrant.

Yet still the will is powerful, infinitely powerful.— Disappointment, hope deferred may rack the heart, the prize long withheld or entirely denied us may elude our grasp—But if our will be indeed that heaven-born power which deserves at last to conquer destiny, it will do so—Many may lose the race— it is not *always* to the swift but it is sometimes—the *coward* never enters the lists,—the *weakling* failing once never enters them *again*—But the truly strong of will returns invigorated by the contest, calmed, not saddened by failure and wiser from its nature—He may fail a second time but he shall at last obtain it. True! its possession may no longer have power to thrill his heart with the anticipated rapture: his expanded mind longs onward for something farther, perhaps for something quite dissimilar. But if true to himself and to his aim he will have learned in its pursuit what is the genuine happiness and glory— for a thorough and sustained exertion of our powers must advance us in the scale of being and fit us more thoroughly for the station suited to us by at once developing and teaching to ourselves the nature of our talents—We may even go further and say that the desired prize is seldom denied to the grasp of the earnest and persevering individual at some point of his career if not in the form he at first sought it, in some other. If he have grown too wise to value it shall he grieve at his improvement? The most brave and steadily ambitious may never wield the sceptre of a Napoleon, the youth most devoted to oratory may, never meeting great occasions and an excitable audience, fail to become a Demosthenes, the most unwearied student of nature and the Arts may miss the glory of an Angelo but it is not in the power of circumstance to prevent the earnest will from shaping round itself the character of a great, a wise, or a good man.

Theme corrected by father; the only one I have kept; It shows very plainly what our mental relation was.

Autobiographical Romance
1840

PARENTS

My father was a lawyer and a politician. He was a man largely endowed with that sagacious energy, which the state of New England society, for the last half century, has been so well fitted to develop. His father was a clergyman, settled as pastor in Princeton, Massachusetts, within the bounds of whose parish-farm was Wachuset. His means were small, and the great object of his ambition was to send his sons to college. As a boy, my father was taught to think only of preparing himself for Harvard University, and when there of preparing himself for the profession of Law. As a Lawyer, again, the ends constantly presented were to work for distinction in the community, and for the means of supporting a family. To be an honored citizen, and to have a home on earth, were made the great aims of existence. To open the deeper fountains of the soul, to regard life here as the prophetic entrance to immortality, to develop his spirit to perfection,—motives like these had never been suggested to him, either by fellow-beings or by outward circumstances. The result was a character, in its social aspect, of quite the common sort. A good son and brother, a kind neighbor, an active man of business—in all these outward relations he was but one of a class, which surrounding conditions have made the majority among us. In the more delicate and individual relations, he never approached but two mortals, my mother and myself.

His love for my mother was the green spot on which he stood apart from the common-places of a mere bread-winning, bread-bestowing existence. She was one of those fair and flower-like natures, which sometimes spring up even beside the most dusty highways of life—a creature not to be shaped into a merely useful instrument, but bound by one law with the blue sky, the dew, and the frolic birds. Of all persons whom I have known, she had in her most of the angelic,—of that spontaneous love for

AUTOBIOGRAPHICAL ROMANCE

every living thing, for man, and beast, and tree, which restores the golden age.

DEATH IN THE HOUSE

My earliest recollection is of a death,—the death of a sister, two years younger than myself. Probably there is a sense of childish endearments, such as belong to this tie, mingled with that of loss, of wonder, and mystery; but these last are prominent in memory. I remember coming home and meeting our nursery-maid, her face streaming with tears. That strange sight of tears made an indelible impression. I realize how little I was of stature, in that I looked up to this weeping face;— and it has often seemed since, that—full-grown for the life of this earth, I have looked up just so, at times of threatening, of doubt, and distress, and that just so has some being of the next higher order of existences looked down, aware of a law unknown to me, and tenderly commiserating the pain I must endure in emerging from my ignorance.

She took me by the hand and led me into a still and dark chamber,—then drew aside the curtain and showed me my sister. I see yet that beauty of death! The highest achievements of sculpture are only the reminder of its severe sweetness. Then I remember the house all still and dark,—the people in their black clothes and dreary faces,—the scent of the newly-made coffin,—my being set up in a chair and detained by a gentle hand to hear the clergyman,—the carriages slowly going, the procession slowly doling out their steps to the grave. But I have no remembrance of what I have since been told I did,—insisting, with loud cries, that they should not put the body in the ground. I suppose that my emotion was spent at the time, and so there was nothing to fix that moment in my memory.

I did not then, nor do I now, find any beauty in these ceremonies. What had they to do with the sweet playful child? Her life and death were alike beautiful, but all this sad parade was not. Thus my first experience of life was one of death. She who would have been the companion of my life was severed from me, and I was left alone. This has made a vast difference in my lot. Her character, if that fair face promised right, would have been soft, graceful and lively; it would have tempered mine to a gentler and more gradual course.

OVERWORK

My father,—all whose feelings were now concentred on me,— instructed me himself. The effect of this was so far good that, not passing through the hands of many ignorant and weak persons as so many do at preparatory schools, I was put at once under discipline of considerable severity, and, at the same time, had a more than ordinarily high standard presented to me. My father was a man of business, even in literature; he had been a high scholar at college, and was warmly attached to all he had learned there, both from the pleasure he had derived in the exercise of his faculties and the associated memories of success and good repute. He was, beside, well read in French literature, and in English, a Queen Anne's man. He hoped to make me the heir of all he knew, and of as much more as the income of his profession enabled him to give me means of acquiring. At the very beginning, he made one great mistake, more common, it is to be hoped, in the last generation, than the warnings of physiologists will permit it to be with the next. He thought to gain time, by bringing forward the intellect as early as possible. Thus I had tasks given me, as many and various as the hours would allow, and on subjects beyond my age; with the additional disadvantage of reciting to him in the evening, after he returned from his office. As he was subject to many interruptions, I was often kept up till very late; and as he was a severe teacher, both from his habits of mind and his ambition for me, my feelings were kept on the stretch till the recitations were over. Thus frequently, I was sent to bed several hours too late, with nerves unnaturally stimulated. The consequence was a premature development of the brain, that made me a "youthful prodigy" by day, and by night a victim of spectral illusions, nightmare, and somnambulism, which at the time prevented the harmonious development of my bodily powers and checked my growth, while, later, they induced continual headache, weakness and nervous affections, of all kinds. As these again re-acted on the brain, giving undue force to every thought and every feeling, there was finally produced a state of being both too active and too intense, which wasted my constitution, and will bring me,—even although I have learned to understand and regulate my now morbid temperament,—to a premature grave.

No one understood this subject of health then. No one knew why this child, already kept up so late, was still unwilling to retire. My aunts cried out upon the "spoiled child, the most unreasonable child that ever was,—if brother could but open his eyes to see it,—who was never willing to go to bed." They did not know that, so soon as the light was taken away, she seemed to see colossal faces advancing slowly towards her, the eyes dilating, and each feature swelling loathsomely as they came, till at last, when they were about to close upon her, she started up with a shriek which drove them away, but only to return when she lay down again. They did not know that, when at last she went to sleep, it was to dream of horses trampling over her, and to awake once more in fright; or, as she had just read in her Virgil, of being among trees that dripped with blood, where she walked and walked and could not get out, while the blood became a pool and plashed over her feet, and rose higher and higher, till soon she dreamed it would reach her lips. No wonder the child arose and walked in her sleep, moaning all over the house, till once, when they heard her, and came and waked her, and she told what she had dreamed, her father sharply bid her "leave off thinking of such nonsense, or she would be crazy,"— never knowing that he was himself the cause of all these horrors of the night. Often she dreamed of following to the grave the body of her mother, as she had done that of her sister, and woke to find the pillow drenched in tears. These dreams softened her heart too much, and cast a deep shadow over her young days; for then, and later, the life of dreams,—probably because there was in it less to distract the mind from its own earnestness,—has often seemed to her more real, and been remembered with more interest, than that of waking hours.

Poor child! Far remote in time, in thought, from that period, I look back on these glooms and terrors, wherein I was enveloped, and perceive that I had no natural childhood.

BOOKS

Thus passed my first years. My mother was in delicate health, and much absorbed in the care of her younger children. In the house was neither dog nor bird, nor any graceful animated form of existence. I saw no persons who took my fancy, and real life offered no attraction. Thus my already over-excited mind found no relief from without, and was driven for refuge from itself to the world of books. I was taught Latin and English grammar at the same time, and began to read Latin at six years old, after which, for some years, I read it daily. In this branch of study, first by my father, and afterwards by a tutor, I was trained to quite a high degree of precision. I was expected to understand the mechanism of the language thoroughly, and in translating to give the thoughts in as few well-arranged words as possible, and without breaks or hesitation,—for with these my father had absolutely no patience.

Indeed, he demanded accuracy and clearness in everything: you must not speak, unless you can make your meaning perfectly intelligible to the person addressed; must not express a thought, unless you can give a reason for it, if required; must not make a statement, unless sure of all particulars—such were his rules. "But," "if," "unless," "I am mistaken," and "it may be so," were words and phrases excluded from the province where he held sway. Trained to great dexterity in artificial methods, accurate, ready, with entire command of his resources, he had no belief in minds that listen, wait, and receive. He had no conception of the subtle and indirect motions of imagination and feeling. His influence on me was great, and opposed to the natural unfolding of my character, which was fervent, of strong grasp, and disposed to infatuation, and self-forgetfulness. He made the common prose world so present to me, that my natural bias was controlled. I did not go mad, as many would do, at being continually roused from my dreams. I had too much strength to be crushed,—and since I must put on the fetters, could not submit to let them impede my motions. My own world sank deep within, away from the surface of my life; in what I did and said I learned to have reference to other minds. But my true life was only the dearer that it was secluded and veiled over by a thick curtain of available intellect, and that coarse, but wearable stuff woven by the ages,—Common Sense.

In accordance with this discipline in heroic common sense, was the influence of those great Romans, whose thoughts and lives were my daily food during those plastic years. The genius

AUTOBIOGRAPHICAL ROMANCE

of Rome displayed itself in Character, and scarcely needed an occasional wave of the torch of thought to show its lineaments, so marble strong they gleamed in every light. Who, that has lived with those men, but admires the plain force of fact, of thought passed into action? They take up things with their naked hands. There is just the man, and the block he casts before you,—no divinity, no demon, no unfulfilled aim, but just the man and Rome, and what he did for Rome. Everything turns your attention to what a man can become, not by yielding himself freely to impressions, not by letting nature play freely through him, but by a single thought, an earnest purpose, an indomitable will, by hardihood, self-command, and force of expression. Architecture was the art in which Rome excelled, and this corresponds with the feeling these men of Rome excite. They did not grow,—they built themselves up, or were built up by the fate of Rome, as a temple for Jupiter Stator. The ruined Roman sits among the ruins; he flies to no green garden; he does not look to heaven; if his intent is defeated, if he is less than he meant to be, he lives no more. The names which end in "*us*," seem to speak with lyric cadence. That measured cadence,—that tramp and march,—which are not stilted, because they indicate real force, yet which seem so when compared with any other language,—make Latin a study in itself of mighty influence. The language alone, without the literature, would give one the *thought* of Rome. Man present in nature, commanding nature too sternly to be inspired by it, standing like the rock amid the sea, or moving like the fire over the land, either impassive, or irresistible; knowing not the soft mediums or fine flights of life, but by the force which he expresses, piercing to the centre.

We are never better understood than when we speak of a "Roman virtue," a "Roman outline." There is somewhat indefinite, somewhat yet unfulfilled in the thought of Greece, of Spain, of modern Italy; but ROME! it stands by itself, a clear Word. The power of will, the dignity of a fixed purpose is what it utters. Every Roman was an emperor. It is well that the infallible church should have been founded on this rock, that the presumptuous Peter should hold the keys, as the conquering Jove did before his thunderbolts, to be seen of all the world. The Apollo tends flocks with Admetus; Christ teaches by the lonely lake, or plucks wheat as he wanders through the fields some Sabbath morning. They never come to this stronghold; they could not have breathed freely where all became stone as soon as spoken, where divine youth found no horizon for its all-promising glance, but every thought put on, before it dared issue to the day in action, its *toga virilis.*

Suckled by this wolf, man gains a different complexion from that which is fed by the Greek honey. He takes a noble bronze in camps and battle-fields; the wrinkles of council well beseem his brow, and the eye cuts its way like the sword. The Eagle should never have been used as a symbol by any other nation: it belonged to Rome.

The history of Rome abides in mind, of course, more than the literature. It was degeneracy for a Roman to use the pen; his life was in the day. The "vaunting" of Rome, like that of the North American Indians, is her proper literature. A man rises; he tells who he is, and what he has done; he speaks of his country and her brave men; he knows that a conquering god is there, whose agent is his own right hand; and he should end like the Indian, "I have no more to say."

It never shocks us that the Roman is self-conscious. One wants no universal truths from him, no philosophy, no creation, but only his life, his Roman life felt in every pulse, realized in every gesture. The universal heaven takes in the Roman only to make us feel his individuality the more. The Will, the Resolve of Man!—it has been expressed,—fully expressed!

I steadily loved this ideal in my childhood, and this is the cause, probably, why I have always felt that man must know how to stand firm on the ground, before he can fly. In vain for me are men more, if they are less, than Romans. Dante was far greater than any Roman, yet I feel he was right to take the Mantuan as his guide through hell, and to heaven.

Horace was a great deal to me then, and is so still. Though his words do not abide in memory, his presence does: serene, courtly, of darting hazel eye, a self-sufficient grace, and an appreciation of the world of stern realities, sometimes pathetic, never tragic. He is the natural man of the world; he is what he ought to be, and his darts never fail of their aim. There is a perfume and raciness, too, which makes life a banquet, where the wit sparkles no less that the viands were bought with blood.

Ovid gave me not Rome, nor himself, but a view into the enchanted gardens of the Greek mythology. This path I followed, have been following ever since; and now, life half over, it seems to me, as in my childhood, that every thought of which man is susceptible, is intimated there. In those young years, indeed, I did not see what I now see, but loved to creep from amid the Roman pikes to lie beneath this great vine, and see the smiling and serene shapes go by, woven from the finest fibres of all the elements. I knew not why, at that time,—but I loved to get away from the hum of the forum, and the mailed clang of Roman speech, to these shifting shows of nature, these Gods and Nymphs born of the sunbeam, the wave, the shadows on the hill.

As with Rome I antedated the world of deeds, so I lived in those Greek forms the true faith of a refined and intense childhood. So great was the force of reality with which these forms impressed me, that I prayed earnestly for a sign,—that it would lighten in some particular region of the heavens, or that I might find a bunch of grapes in the path, when I went forth in the morning. But no sign was given, and I was left a waif stranded upon the shores of modern life!

Of the Greek language, I knew only enough to feel that the sounds told the same story as the mythology;—that the law of life in that land was beauty, as in Rome it was a stern composure. I wish I had learned as much of Greece as of Rome,—so freely does the mind play in her sunny waters, where there is no chill, and the restraint is from within out; for these Greeks, in an atmosphere of ample grace, could not be impetuous, or stern, but loved moderation as equable life always must, for it is the law of beauty.

With these books I passed my days. The great amount of study exacted of me soon ceased to be a burden, and reading became a habit and a passion. The force of feeling, which, under other circumstances, might have ripened thought, was turned to learn the thoughts of others. This was not a tame state, for the energies brought out by rapid acquisition gave glow enough. I thought with rapture of the all-accomplished man, him of the many talents, wide resources, clear sight, and omnipotent will. A Cæsar seemed great enough. I did not then know that such men impoverish the treasury to build the palace.

I kept their statues as belonging to the hall of my ancestors, and loved to conquer obstacles, and fed my youth and strength for their sake.

Still, though this bias was so great that in earliest years I learned, in these ways, how the world takes hold of a powerful nature, I had yet other experiences. None of these were deeper than what I found in the happiest haunt of my childish years,—our little garden. Our house, though comfortable, was very ugly, and in a neighborhood which I detested,—every dwelling and its appurtenances having a *mesquin* and huddled look. I liked nothing about us except the tall graceful elms before the house, and the dear little garden behind. Our back door opened on a high flight of steps, by which I went down to a green plot, much injured in my ambitious eyes by the presence of the pump and tool-house. This opened into a little garden, full of choice flowers and fruit-trees, which was my mother's delight, and was carefully kept. Here I felt at home. A gate opened thence into the fields,—a wooden gate made of boards, in a high, unpainted board wall, and embowered in the clematis creeper. This gate I used to open to see the sunset heaven; beyond this black frame I did not step, for I liked to look at the deep gold behind it. How exquisitely happy I was in its beauty, and how I loved the silvery wreaths of my protecting vine! I never would pluck one of its flowers at that time, I was so jealous of its beauty, but often since I carry off wreaths of it from the wild-wood, and it stands in nature to my mind as the emblem of domestic love.

Of late I have thankfully felt what I owe to that garden, where the best hours of my lonely childhood were spent. Within the house everything was socially utilitarian; my books told of a proud world, but in another temper were the teachings of the little garden. There my thoughts could lie callow in the nest, and only be fed and kept warm, not called to fly or sing before the time. I loved to gaze on the roses, the violets, the lilies, the pinks; my mother's hand had planted them, and they bloomed for me. I culled the most beautiful. I looked at them on every side. I kissed them, I pressed them to my bosom with passionate emotions, such as I have never dared express to any human being. An ambition swelled my heart to be as beautiful,

AUTOBIOGRAPHICAL ROMANCE   621

as perfect as they. I have not kept my vow. Yet, forgive, ye wild asters, which gleam so sadly amid the fading grass; forgive me, ye golden autumn flowers, which so strive to reflect the glories of the departing distant sun; and ye silvery flowers, whose moonlight eyes I knew so well, forgive! Living and blooming in your unchecked law, ye know nothing of the blights, the distortions, which beset the human being; and which at such hours it would seem that no glories of free agency could ever repay!

There was, in the house, no apartment appropriated to the purpose of a library, but there was in my father's room a large closet filled with books, and to these I had free access when the task-work of the day was done. Its window overlooked wide fields, gentle slopes, a rich and smiling country, whose aspect pleased without much occupying the eye, while a range of blue hills, rising at about twelve miles distance, allured to reverie. "Distant mountains," says Tieck, "excite the fancy, for beyond them we place the scene of our Paradise." Thus, in the poems of fairy adventure, we climb the rocky barrier, pass fearless its dragon caves, and dark pine forests, and find the scene of enchantment in the vale behind. My hopes were never so definite, but my eye was constantly allured to that distant blue range, and I would sit, lost in fancies, till tears fell on my cheek. I loved this sadness; but only in later years, when the realities of life had taught me moderation, did the passionate emotions excited by seeing them again teach how glorious were the hopes that swelled my heart while gazing on them in those early days.

Melancholy attends on the best joys of a merely ideal life, else I should call most happy the hours in the garden, the hours in the book closet. Here were the best French writers of the last century; for my father had been more than half a Jacobin, in the time when the French Republic cast its glare of promise over the world. Here, too, were the Queen Anne authors, his models, and the English novelists; but among them I found none that charmed me. Smollett, Fielding, and the like, deal too broadly with the coarse actualities of life. The best of their men and women—so merely natural, with the nature found every day—do not meet our hopes. Sometimes the simple picture, warm with life and the light of the common sun, cannot fail

622 UNPUBLISHED WRITINGS

to charm,—as in the wedded love of Fielding's Amelia,—but it is at a later day, when the mind is trained to comparison, that we learn to prize excellence like this as it deserves. Early youth is prince-like: it will bend only to "the king, my father." Various kinds of excellence please, and leave their impression, but the most commanding, alone, is duly acknowledged at that all-exacting age.

Three great authors it was my fortune to meet at this important period,—all, though of unequal, yet congenial powers,—all of rich and wide, rather than aspiring genius,—all free to the extent of the horizon their eye took in,—all fresh with impulse, racy with experience; never to be lost sight of, or superseded, but always to be apprehended more and more.

Ever memorable is the day on which I first took a volume of SHAKSPEARE in my hand to read. It was on a Sunday.

—This day was punctiliously set apart in our house. We had family prayers, for which there was no time on other days. Our dinners were different, and our clothes. We went to church. My father put some limitations on my reading, but—bless him for the gentleness which has left me a pleasant feeling for the day!—he did not prescribe what was, but only what was *not*, to be done. And the liberty this left was a large one. "You must not read a novel, or a play;" but all other books, the worst, or the best, were open to me. The distinction was merely technical. The day was pleasing to me, as relieving me from the routine of tasks and recitations; it gave me freer play than usual, and there were fewer things occurred in its course, which reminded me of the divisions of time; still the church-going, where I heard nothing that had any connection with my inward life, and these rules, gave me associations with the day of empty formalities, and arbitrary restrictions; but though the forbidden book or walk always seemed more charming then, I was seldom tempted to disobey.—

This Sunday—I was only eight years old—I took from the book-shelf a volume lettered SHAKSPEARE. It was not the first time I had looked at it, but before I had been deterred from attempting to read, by the broken appearance along the page, and preferred smooth narrative. But this time I held in my hand "Romeo and Juliet" long enough to get my eye fastened to the page. It was a cold winter afternoon. I took the book to the parlor fire, and had there been seated an hour or two, when my father looked up and asked what I was reading so intently. "Shakspeare," replied the child, merely raising her eye from the page. "Shakspeare,—that won't do; that's no book for Sunday; go put it away and take another." I went as I was bid, but took no other. Returning to my seat, the unfinished story, the personages to whom I was but just introduced, thronged and burnt my brain. I could not bear it long; such a lure it was impossible to resist. I went and brought the book again. There were several guests present, and I had got half through the play before I again attracted attention. "What is that child about that she don't hear a word that's said to her?" quoth my aunt. "What are you reading?" said my father. "Shakspeare" was again the reply, in a clear, though somewhat impatient, tone. "How?" said my father angrily,—then restraining himself before his guests,—"Give me the book and go directly to bed."

Into my little room no care of his anger followed me. Alone, in the dark, I thought only of the scene placed by the poet before my eye, where the free flow of life, sudden and graceful dialogue, and forms, whether grotesque or fair, seen in the broad lustre of his imagination, gave just what I wanted, and brought home the life I seemed born to live. My fancies swarmed like bees, as I contrived the rest of the story;—what all would do, what say, where go. My confinement tortured me. I could not go forth from this prison to ask after these friends; I could not make my pillow of the dreams about them which yet I could not forbear to frame. Thus was I absorbed when my father entered. He felt it right, before going to rest, to reason with me about my disobedience, shown in a way, as he considered, so insolent. I listened, but could not feel interested in what he said, nor turn my mind from what engaged it. He went away really grieved at my impenitence, and quite at a loss to understand conduct in me so unusual.

—Often since I have seen the same misunderstanding between parent and child,—the parent thrusting the morale, the discipline, of life upon the child, when just engrossed by some game of real importance and great leadings to it. That is only a wooden horse to the father,—the child was careering to distant scenes of conquest and crusade, through a country of elsewhere unimagined beauty. None but poets remember their youth; but the father who does not retain poetical apprehension of the world, free and splendid as it stretches out before the child, who cannot read his natural history, and follow out its intimations with reverence, must be a tyrant in his home, and the purest intentions will not prevent his doing much to cramp him. Each new child is a new Thought, and has bearings and discernings, which the Thoughts older in date know not yet, but must learn.—

My attention thus fixed on Shakspeare, I returned to him at every hour I could command. Here was a counterpoise to my Romans, still more forcible than the little garden. My author could read the Roman nature too,—read it in the sternness of Coriolanus, and in the varied wealth of Cæsar. But he viewed these men of will as only one kind of men; he kept them in their place, and I found that he, who could understand the Roman, yet expressed in Hamlet a deeper thought.

In CERVANTES, I found far less productive talent,—indeed, a far less powerful genius,—but the same wide wisdom, a discernment piercing the shows and symbols of existence, yet rejoicing in them all, both for their own life, and as signs of the unseen reality. Not that Cervantes philosophized,—his genius was too deeply philosophical for that; he took things as they came before him, and saw their actual relations and bearings. Thus the work he produced was of deep meaning, though he might never have expressed that meaning to himself. It was left implied in the whole. A Coleridge comes and calls Don Quixote the pure Reason, and Sancho the Understanding. Cervantes made no such distinctions in his own mind; but he had seen and suffered enough to bring out all his faculties, and to make him comprehend the higher as well as the lower part of our nature. Sancho is too amusing and sagacious to be contemptible; the Don too noble and clear-sighted towards absolute truth, to be ridiculous. And we are pleased to see manifested in this way, how the lower must follow and serve the higher, despite its jeering mistrust and the stubborn realities which break up the plans of this pure-minded champion.

The effect produced on the mind is nowise that described by Byron:—

"Cervantes smiled Spain's chivalry away," &c.

AUTOBIOGRAPHICAL ROMANCE 625

On the contrary, who is not conscious of a sincere reverence for the Don, prancing forth on his gaunt steed? Who would not rather be he than any of the persons who laugh at him?—Yet the one we would wish to be is thyself, Cervantes, unconquerable spirit! gaining flavor and color like wine from every change, while being carried round the world; in whose eye the serene sagacious laughter could not be dimmed by poverty, slavery, or unsuccessful authorship. Thou art to us still more the Man, though less the Genius, than Shakspeare; thou dost not evade our sight, but, holding the lamp to thine own magic shows, dost enjoy them with us.

My third friend was MOLIÈRE, one very much lower, both in range and depth, than the others, but, as far as he goes, of the same character. Nothing secluded or partial is there about his genius,—a man of the world, and a man by himself, as he is. It was, indeed, only the poor social world of Paris that he saw, but he viewed it from the firm foundations of his manhood, and every lightest laugh rings from a clear perception, and teaches life anew.

These men were all alike in this,—they loved the *natural history* of man. Not what he should be, but what he is, was the favorite subject of their thought. Whenever a noble leading opened to the eye new paths of light, they rejoiced; but it was never fancy, but always fact, that inspired them. They loved a thorough penetration of the murkiest dens, and most tangled paths of nature; they did not spin from the desires of their own special natures, but reconstructed the world from materials which they collected on every side. Thus their influence upon me was not to prompt me to follow out thought in myself so much as to detect it everywhere, for each of these men is not only a nature, but a happy interpreter of many natures. They taught me to distrust all invention which is not based on a wide experience. Perhaps, too, they taught me to overvalue an outward experience at the expense of inward growth; but all this I did not appreciate till later.

It will be seen that my youth was not unfriended, since those great minds came to me in kindness. A moment of action in one's self, however, is worth an age of apprehension through others; not that our deeds are better, but that they produce a renewal of our being. I have had more productive moments and of deeper joy, but never hours of more tranquil pleasure than those in which these demi-gods visited me,—and with a smile so familiar, that I imagined the world to be full of such. They did me good, for by them a standard was early given of sight and thought, from which I could never go back, and beneath which I cannot suffer patiently my own life or that of any friend to fall. They did me harm, too, for the child fed with meat instead of milk becomes too soon mature. Expectations and desires were thus early raised, after which I must long toil before they can be realized. How poor the scene around, how tame one's own existence, how meagre and faint every power, with these beings in my mind! Often I must cast them quite aside in order to grow in my small way, and not sink into despair. Certainly I do not wish that instead of these masters I had read baby books, written down to children, and with such ignorant dulness that they blunt the senses and corrupt the tastes of the still plastic human being. But I do wish that I had read no books at all till later,—that I had lived with toys, and played in the open air. Children should not cull the fruits of reflection and observation early, but expand in the sun, and let thoughts come to them. They should not through books antedate their actual experiences, but should take them gradually, as sympathy and interpretation are needed. With me, much of life was devoured in the bud.

FIRST FRIEND

For a few months, this bookish and solitary life was invaded by interest in a living, breathing figure. At church, I used to look around with a feeling of coldness and disdain, which, though I now well understand its causes, seems to my wiser mind as odious as it was unnatural. The puny child sought everywhere for the Roman or Shakspeare figures, and she was met by the shrewd, honest eye, the homely decency, or the smartness of a New England village on Sunday. There was beauty, but I could not see it then; it was not of the kind I longed for. In the next pew sat a family who were my especial aversion. There were five daughters, the eldest not above four-and-twenty,—yet they had the old fairy, knowing look, hard, dry, dwarfed, strangers to the All-Fair,—were working-day residents in this beautiful planet. They looked as if their thoughts had never strayed beyond the jobs of the day, and they were glad of it. Their mother was one of those shrunken, faded patterns of woman who have never done anything to keep smooth the cheek and dignify the brow. The father had a Scotch look of shrewd narrowness, and entire self-complacency. I could not endure this family, whose existence contradicted all my visions; yet I could not forbear looking at them.

As my eye one day was ranging about with its accustomed coldness, and the proudly foolish sense of being in a shroud of thoughts that were not their thoughts, it was arrested by a face most fair, and well-known as it seemed at first glance,—for surely I had met her before and waited for her long. But soon I saw that she was a new apparition foreign to that scene, if not to me. Her dress,—the arrangement of her hair, which had the graceful pliancy of races highly cultivated for long,—the intelligent and full picture of her eye, whose reserve was in its self-possession, not in timidity,—all combined to make up a whole impression, which, though too young to understand, I was well prepared to feel.

How wearisome now appears that thorough-bred *millefleur* beauty, the distilled result of ages of European culture! Give me rather the wild heath on the lonely hill-side, than such a rose-tree from the daintily clipped garden. But, then, I had but tasted the cup, and knew not how little it could satisfy; more, more, was all my cry; continued through years, till I had been at the very fountain. Indeed, it was a ruby-red, a perfumed draught, and I need not abuse the wine because I prefer water, but merely say I have had enough of it. Then, the first sight, the first knowledge of such a person was intoxication.

She was an English lady, who, by a singular chance, was cast upon this region for a few months. Elegant and captivating, her every look and gesture was tuned to a different pitch from anything I had ever known. She was in various ways "accomplished," as it is called, though to what degree I cannot now judge. She painted in oils;—I had never before seen any one use the brush, and days would not have been too long for me to watch the pictures growing beneath her hand. She played the harp; and its tones are still to me the heralds of the promised land I saw before me then. She rose, she looked, she spoke; and the gentle swaying motion she made all through life has gladdened memory, as the stream does the woods and meadows.

As she was often at the house of one of our neighbors, and afterwards at our own, my thoughts were fixed on her with all the force of my nature. It was my first real interest in my kind, and it engrossed me wholly. I had seen her,—I should see her,—and my mind lay steeped in the visions that flowed from this source. My task-work I went through with, as I have done on similar occasions all my life, aided by pride that could not bear to fail, or be questioned. Could I cease from doing the work of the day, and hear the reason sneeringly given,— "Her head is so completely taken up with —— that she can do nothing"? Impossible.

Should the first love be blighted, they say, the mind loses its sense of eternity. All forms of existence seem fragile, the prison of time real, for a god is dead. Equally true is this of friendship. I thank Heaven that this first feeling was permitted its free flow. The years that lay between the woman and the girl only brought her beauty into perspective, and enabled me to see her as I did the mountains from my window, and made her presence to me a gate of Paradise. That which she was, that which she brought, that which she might have brought, were mine, and over a whole region of new life I ruled proprietor of the soil in my own right.

Her mind was sufficiently unoccupied to delight in my warm devotion. She could not know what it was to me, but the light cast by the flame through so delicate a vase cheered and charmed her. All who saw admired her in their way; but she would lightly turn her head from their hard or oppressive looks, and fix a glance of full-eyed sweetness on the child, who, from a distance, watched all her looks and motions. She did not say much to me—not much to any one; she spoke in her whole being rather than by chosen words. Indeed, her proper speech was dance or song, and what was less expressive did not greatly interest her. But she saw much, having in its perfection the woman's delicate sense for sympathies and attractions. We walked in the fields, alone. Though others were present, her eyes were gliding over all the field and plain for the objects of beauty to which she was of kin. She was not cold to her seeming companions; a sweet courtesy satisfied them, but it hung about her like her mantle that she wore without thinking of it; her thoughts were free, for these civilized beings can really live two lives at the same moment. With them she seemed to be, but her hand was given to the child at her side; others did not observe me, but to her I was the only human presence. Like a guardian spirit she led me through the fields and groves, and every tree, every bird greeted me, and said, what I felt, "She is the first angel of your life."

One time I had been passing the afternoon with her. She had been playing to me on the harp, and I sat listening in happiness almost unbearable. Some guests were announced. She went into another room to receive them, and I took up her book. It was Guy Mannering, then lately published, and the first of Scott's novels I had ever seen. I opened where her mark lay, and read merely with the feeling of continuing our mutual existence by passing my eyes over the same page where hers had been. It was the description of the rocks on the sea-coast where the little Harry Bertram was lost. I had never seen such places, and my mind was vividly stirred to imagine them. The scene rose before me, very unlike reality, doubtless, but majestic and wild. I was the little Harry Bertram, and had lost her,—all I had to lose,—and sought her vainly in long dark caves that had no end, plashing through the water; while the crags beetled above, threatening to fall and crush the poor child. Absorbed in the painful vision, tears rolled down my cheeks. Just then she entered with light step, and full-beaming eye. When she saw me thus, a soft cloud stole over her face, and clothed every feature with a lovelier tenderness than I had seen there before. She did not question, but fixed on me inquiring looks of beautiful love. I laid my head against her shoulder and wept,—dimly feeling that I must lose her and all,—all who spoke to me of the same things,—that the cold wave must rush over me. She waited till my tears were spent, then rising, took from a little box a bunch of golden amaranths or everlasting flowers, and gave them to me. They were very fragrant. "They came," she said, "from Madeira." These flowers stayed with me seventeen years. "Madeira" seemed to me the fortunate isle, apart in the blue ocean from all of ill or dread. Whenever I saw a sail passing in the distance,—if it bore itself with fulness of beautiful certainty,—I felt that it was going to Madeira. Those

thoughts are all gone now. No Madeira exists for me now,—
no fortunate purple isle,—and all these hopes and fancies are
lifted from the sea into the sky. Yet I thank the charms that
fixed them here so long,—fixed them till perfumes like those
of the golden flowers were drawn from the earth, teaching me
to know my birth-place.

I can tell little else of this time,—indeed, I remember little,
except the state of feeling in which I lived. For I *lived*, and when
this is the case, there is little to tell in the form of thought. We
meet—at least those who are true to their instincts meet—a
succession of persons through our lives, all of whom have some
peculiar errand to us. There is an outer circle, whose existence
we perceive, but with whom we stand in no real relation. They
tell us the news, they act on us in the offices of society, they
show us kindness and aversion; but their influence does not
penetrate; we are nothing to them, nor they to us, except as a
part of the world's furniture. Another circle, within this, are
dear and near to us. We know them and of what kind they are.
They are to us not mere facts, but intelligible thoughts of the
divine mind. We like to see how they are unfolded; we like to
meet them and part from them; we like their action upon us
and the pause that succeeds and enables us to appreciate its
quality. Often we leave them on our path, and return no more,
but we bear them in our memory, tales which have been told,
and whose meaning has been felt.

But yet a nearer group there are, beings born under the same
star, and bound with us in a common destiny. These are not
mere acquaintances, mere friends, but, when we meet, are
sharers of our very existence. There is no separation; the same
thought is given at the same moment to both,—indeed, it is
born of the meeting, and would not otherwise have been called
into existence at all. These not only know themselves more,
but *are* more for having met, and regions of their being, which
would else have laid sealed in cold obstruction, burst into leaf
and bloom and song.

The times of these meetings are fated, nor will either party
be able ever to meet any other person in the same way. Both
seem to rise at a glance into that part of the heavens where the
word can be spoken, by which they are revealed to one another
and to themselves. The step in being thus gained, can never be

lost, nor can it be re-trod; for neither party will be again what the other wants. They are no longer fit to interchange mutual influence, for they do not really need it, and if they think they do, it is because they weakly pine after a past pleasure.

To this inmost circle of relations but few are admitted, because some prejudice or lack of courage has prevented the many from listening to their instincts the first time they manifested themselves. If the voice is once disregarded it becomes fainter each time, till, at last, it is wholly silenced, and the man lives in this world, a stranger to its real life, deluded like the maniac who fancies he has attained his throne, while in reality he is on a bed of musty straw. Yet, if the voice finds a listener and servant the first time of speaking, it is encouraged to more and more clearness. Thus it was with me,—from no merit of mine, but because I had the good fortune to be free enough to yield to my impressions. Common ties had not bound me; there were no traditionary notions in my mind; I believed in nothing merely because others believed in it; I had taken no feelings on trust. Thus my mind was open to their sway.

This woman came to me, a star from the east, a morning star, and I worshipped her. She too was elevated by that worship, and her fairest self called out. To the mind she brought assurance that there was a region congenial with its tendencies and tastes, a region of elegant culture and intercourse, whose object, fulfilled or not, was to gratify the sense of beauty, not the mere utilities of life. In our relation she was lifted to the top of her being. She had known many celebrities, had roused to passionate desire many hearts, and became afterwards a wife; but I do not believe she ever more truly realized her best self than towards the lonely child whose heaven she was, whose eye she met, and whose possibilities she predicted. "He raised me," said a woman inspired by love, "upon the pedestal of his own high thoughts, and wings came at once, but I did not fly away. I stood there with downcast eyes worthy of his love, for he had made me so."

Thus we do always for those who inspire us to expect from them the best. That which they are able to be, they become, because we demand it of them. "We expect the impossible— and find it."

My English friend went across the sea. She passed into her former life, and into ties that engrossed her days. But she has never ceased to think of me. Her thoughts turn forcibly back to the child who was to her all she saw of the really New World. On the promised coasts she had found only cities, careful men and women, the aims and habits of ordinary life in her own land, without that elegant culture which she, probably, over-estimated, because it was her home. But in the mind of the child she found the fresh prairie, the untrodden forests for which she had longed. I saw in her the storied castles, the fair stately parks and the wind laden with tones from the past, which I desired to know. We wrote to one another for many years;—her shallow and delicate epistles did not disenchant me, nor did she fail to see something of the old poetry in my rude characters and stammering speech. But we must never meet again.

When this friend was withdrawn I fell into a profound depression. I knew not how to exert myself, but lay bound hand and foot. Melancholy enfolded me in an atmosphere, as joy had done. This suffering, too, was out of the gradual and natural course. Those who are really children could not know such love, or feel such sorrow. "I am to blame," said my father, "in keeping her at home so long merely to please myself. She needs to be with other girls, needs play and variety. She does not seem to me really sick, but dull rather. She eats nothing, you say. I see she grows thin. She ought to change the scene."

I was indeed *dull*. The books, the garden, had lost all charm. I had the excuse of headache, constantly, for not attending to my lessons. The light of life was set, and every leaf was withered. At such an early age there are no back or side scenes where the mind, weary and sorrowful, may retreat. Older, we realize the width of the world more, and it is not easy to despair on any point. The effort at thought to which we are compelled relieves and affords a dreary retreat, like hiding in a brick-kiln till the shower be over. But then all joy seemed to have departed with my friend, and the emptiness of our house stood revealed. This I had not felt while I every day expected to see or had seen her, or annoyance and dulness were unnoticed or swallowed up in the one thought that clothed my days with beauty. But now she was gone, and I was roused from habits of reading or reverie to feel the fiery temper of the soul, and to learn that it must have vent, that it would not be pacified by shadows, neither meet

AUTOBIOGRAPHICAL ROMANCE

without consuming what lay around it. I avoided the table as much as possible, took long walks and lay in bed, or on the floor of my room. I complained of my head, and it was not wrong to do so, for a sense of dulness and suffocation, if not pain, was there constantly.

But when it was proposed that I should go to school, that was a remedy I could not listen to with patience for a moment. The peculiarity of my education had separated me entirely from the girls around, except that when they were playing at active games, I would sometimes go out and join them. I liked violent bodily exercise, which always relieved my nerves. But I had no success in associating with them beyond the mere play. Not only I was not their school-mate, but my book-life and lonely habits had given a cold aloofness to my whole expression, and veiled my manner with a hauteur which turned all hearts away. Yet, as this reserve was superficial, and rather ignorance than arrogance, it produced no deep dislike. Besides, the girls supposed me really superior to themselves, and did not hate me for feeling it, but neither did they like me, nor wish to have me with them. Indeed, I had gradually given up all such wishes myself; for they seemed to me rude, tiresome, and childish, as I did to them dull and strange. This experience had been earlier, before I was admitted to any real friendship; but now that I had been lifted into the life of mature years, and into just that atmosphere of European life to which I had before been tending, the thought of sending me to school filled me with disgust.

Yet what could I tell my father of such feelings? I resisted all I could, but in vain. He had no faith in medical aid generally, and justly saw that this was no occasion for its use. He thought I needed change of scene, and to be roused to activity by other children. "I have kept you at home," he said, "because I took such pleasure in teaching you myself, and besides I knew that you would learn faster with one who is so desirous to aid you. But you will learn fast enough wherever you are, and you ought to be more with others of your own age. I shall soon hear that you are better, I trust."

Fictional Autobiographical Fragment

c. 1841–42

MY mother never recovered from the death of this child. She had watched her too anxiously through her illness, and her life was a slender stem that would not bear more than one blow from the axe. Beside, her whole life was in her children, for her marriage was the not uncommon one of a lovely young girl, ignorant of herself, and of her capacities for feeling, to a man of suitable age and position because he chose her. He was honorable, kind-hearted, well-educated (as it is called) and of good sense, but a mere man of business who had never dreamed of what such a woman as she needs in domestic life. He kept her in a good house, with a good wardrobe, was even in his temper, and indulgent to her wishes, but he did not know what it was to be companionable, the friend, much less the lover, and if he had, he would not have had time, for his was the swift crowded course of an American business life. So she pined and grew dull, she knew not why, something was wanting she could not tell what, but there was a dreariness, a blank, she tormented herself that she was so ungrateful to a kind Providence, which had given her so much for want of which the many suffer: she tried to employ herself for the poor, she gave her heart to her children. Still she languished and the first blow found so little life to resist it, that she fell a speedy victim.

Perhaps it was well so, and yet I know not. Beside my own feeling of infinite loss there has been a bitter sense that had she lived there was enough in me corresponding with her unconscious wants to have aroused her intellect and occupied her affections. Perhaps her son might have made up to her for want of that full development of feeling which youth demands from love. I have read her girlish letters and verses, which fell from her young life as easily as drops of dew from a morning sky, and I have understood all that her exquisite nature promised. Such a woman I have not elsewhere met, reserved and pure as a pearl, but winning and musical as the gentle ripple of some

FICTIONAL AUTOBIOGRAPHICAL FRAGMENT 635

lake, hidden amid friendly trees. 'Twere too bitter to feel that all her lovely young life was wasted in the sand, but that all around I see such mutilation of lives, that I must transfer my hope for the most to future spheres.

I did not see her dead, but she, too, no doubt was beautiful. Her picture hangs before me now, an object of no less worship than in my lonely childhood. Its beauty is very girlish, with soft tendrils of brown hair curling from a small feminine head, sweet but timid blue eyes, a mouth of little force, but around which hovers the promise of boundless love. The expression of the head asks, and expects, without demanding tenderness. The brow is as ideal as those that Raphael loved to draw, it gives to the whole aspect an expression of unbroken purity, as of a being incapable of knowing or resenting evil. Mother, before thy virgin nature sin would hide its head, passion would have been checked from its wild extremes at the thought of celestial goodness, and the intellect laid aside its harness of proof to repose amid a green and flowering nature.

They kept me from her in her illness, nor, remembering how much I had been excited at the funeral of my sister, was it thought best I should see her given back to earth. So I know her only in this picture, and in the sweet, vague feeling that those tender eyes have often bent over my face, especially just as I was about to enter the enchanted realms of sleep. But this is, perhaps, my most precious possession. A man of genius who has written too little makes a poor heart-broken boy, thus recals his mother, "Once I was lost in the vineyard and could not find my way back. At last I heard her calling me, and following the voice, soon saw her beautiful motherly face above the green vine-leaves.—Oh, it was all so fair and *so long ago.*" This do I feel also.—The works of art which represent these family relations seem like these thoughts of my mother as beautiful and as long ago. But I am fortunate to have these images of mother and sister. They have been kept fresh in my mind amid the uncongenial surroundings of after days. The feelings that have sprung from them have fostered the conviction that the family is a divine order, and not a mere school of preparation. Here we do not often meet the persons who are to compose our true family, but the glimpses we obtain of what is possible to such relations here, are to me the earnest that, in that

636 UNPUBLISHED WRITINGS

state of perfect development which we call heaven, these shall be perfected, and the family ties attain the beauty and mutual adaptation of a stellar group in the pure blue.

A friend of mine thinks himself happy that he lost his mother at his birth. "For thus," says he, "I became the child of an angel." No doubt it is more easy to preserve the ideal meaning of a love whose "death has set its seal," than of one constantly subject to the mutations of experience. Yet those cannot hide truth from the earnest mind, though they may obscure it for a season. I would not think my love could not have stood the test of experience. But I accept these early losses, as fit introduction to a life whose whole teaching has been how to renounce, and yet believe, and whose whole meaning yet revealed may be comprized in the one word Patience,—But what a Patience? one inert, cold, and unproductive? or one rich in daily thought and holy hope? Thou, my friend, wilt say at the end thy thought of the state of my mind. We do not know ourselves in any state till on the eve of quitting it, and I will not too confidently interpret on my text but this I know that converse with many climates, many men, many books, also many aspirations, many griefs, and reactions of a nature not easily subdued have led me to revere and wish to adopt this one watch-word of Patience.

CHAPTER II

My father was a sincere mourner. Although he did not understand his wife, and would never have discerned the feelings that early drank the oil from her lamp, he felt her loveliness and purity. It was, indeed, a genuine choice, for he was a man who clearly knew his own mind and of a genuine though superficial character. He went on a long journey and took me with him. I was not five years old, and had little remembrance of this time, till not long since, passing through the same region, sweet pictures of former days rose to view and I found myself looking about as for familiar objects.

We returned, but to a desolate house. My father had taken two elder sisters to live with him, and manage his household, [   ]

A Credo
1842

———————————

THERE is a spirit uncontainable and uncontained,—Within it all manifestation is contained, whether of good (accomplishment), or evil (obstruction). To itself its depths are unknown. By living it seeks to know itself, thus evolving plants, animals, men, suns, stars, angels, and, it is to be presumed an infinity of forms not yet visible in the horizon of this being who now writes.

Its modes of operation are twofold.

First as genius inspires genius,—love love,—angel mother brings forth angel-child. This is the uninterrupted generation or publication of spirit taking upon itself congenial forms.

—Second

Conquering obstruction, finding the like in the unlike. This is a secondary generation, a new dynasty, as virtue for simplicity, faith for oneness, charity for pure love.

Then begins the genesis of Man, as through his consciousness he attests the laws which regulated the divine genesis. The Father is justified in the Son.

The mind of man asks "why was this second development?— Why seeks the divine to exchange best for better, bliss for hope, domesticity for knowledge?" We reject the plan in the universe which the Spirit permitted as the condition of conscious life.

We reject it in the childhood of the soul's life.—The cry of infancy is why should we seek God when he is always there, why seek what is ours as soul's through indefinite pilgrimages, and burdensome cultures.

The intellect has no answer to this question, yet as we through faith and purity of deed enter into the nature of the Divine it is answered from our own experience. We understand though we cannot explain the mystery of something gained where all already is.

God we say is Love, if we believe this we must trust him. Whatever has been permitted by the law of being must be *for* good, and only *in time not good*. We do trust him and are led forward by experience. Sight gives experience of outward life, faith of inward. We then discern however faintly the necessary harmony of the two lives. The moment we have broken through an obstruction, not accidentally but by the aid of Faith we begin to realize why any was permitted. We begin to interpret the Universe and deeper depths are opened with each soul that is convinced. For it would seem that the Divine expressed his meaning to himself more distinctly in man than in the other forms of our sphere, and through him uttered distinctly the Hallellujah which the other forms of nature only intimate.

Wherever man remains imbedded in nature, whether from sensuality or because he is not yet awakened to consciousness, the purpose of the whole remains unfulfilled, hence our displeasure when man is not, in a sense, *above* nature. Yet when he is not so closely bound with all other manifestations, as duly to express their spirit, we are also displeased. He must be at once the highest form of nature and conscious of the meaning she has been striving successively to unfold through those below him.

Centuries pass,—whole races of men are expended in the effort to produce one that shall realize this idea and publish spirit in the human form. But here and there there is a degree of success. Life enough is lived through a man to justify the great difficulties and obstruction attendant on the existence of Mankind.

Then through all the realms of thought vibrates the affirmation "This is my beloved son in whom I am well pleased" and many souls encouraged and instructed offer themselves to the baptism, whether of water, whether of fire.

I do not mean to lay an undue stress upon the position and office of man, merely because I am of his race, and understand best the scope of his destiny. The history of the earth, the motions of the heavenly bodies suggest already modes of being higher than his, and which fulfil more deeply this office of interpretation. But I do suppose his life to be the rivet on one series of links in the great chain, and that all these higher existences are analogous to his. Music suggests them, and when carried on these strong wings through realms which on the ground we discern but dimly, we presee how the next step in the soul's upward course shall interpret man to the universe as he now interprets these forms beneath himself. For there is ever evolving a consciousness of consciousness, and a soul of the soul. To know is to bring to light somewhat yet to be known. And as we elucidate the previous workings of spirit, we ourselves become a new material for its development.

Man is himself one tree in the garden of the spirit. From his trunk grow many branches, social contracts, art, literature, religion &c. The trunk gives the history of the human race, it has grown up higher into the heavens, but its several acorns, though each expressed the all, did not ripen beyond certain contours and a certain size.

In the history of matter, however, laws have been more and more clearly discerned, and so in the history of spirit, many features of the God Man have put forth, several limbs disengaged themselves. One is what men call revelation; different from other kinds only in being made through the acts and words of men.

Its law is identical whether displaying itself as genius or piety, but its modes of expression are distinct dialects though of similar structure.

The way it is done is this. As the oak desires to plant its acorns, so do souls to become the fathers of souls. Some do this through the body, others through the intellect. The first class are citizens;—the second artists, philosophers, law givers, poets, saints.—All these are Anointed, all Emmanuel, all Messiah, so far as they are true to the law of their incorruptible existence, brutes and devils so far as they are subjected to that of their corruptible existence.

But yet farther, as wherever there is a tendency, a form is gradually evolved as its type, as the rose represents the flower-world and is its queen, as the lion and eagle compress within themselves the noblest that is expressed in the animal kingdom, as the telescope and microscope express the high and searching desires of man; and the organ and orrery his completeness, so has each tribe of thoughts and lives its law upon it to produce a king, a form which shall stand before it a visible representation of the aim of its strivings. It gave laws with Confucius and Moses, it tried them with Brahma, it lived its life of eloquence in the Apollo, it wandered with Osiris. It lived one life as Plato,

640 UNPUBLISHED WRITINGS

another as Michel Angelo or Luther. It has made gods, it has developed men. Seeking, making it produced ideals of the developments of which humanity is capable, and one of the highest, nay in some respects the very highest it has yet known was the life of Jesus of Nazareth.

I suppose few are so much believers in his history as myself. I believe, (*in my own way*) in the long preparation of ages and the truth of prophecy, I see a necessity in the character of Jesus why Abraham should be the founder of his nation, Moses its lawgiver, and David its king and poet. I believe in the genesis, as given in the Old Testament. I believe in the prophets, and that they foreknew not only what their nation required, but what the development of universal man required, a Redeemer, an atoner, one to make voluntarily at the due crisis the sacrifice Abraham would have made of the child of his old age, a lamb of God taking away the sins of the world. I believe that Jesus came when the time was ripe, that he was peculiarly a messenger and son of God. I have nothing to say in denial the story of his birth, whatever the true circumstances were *in time* he was born of a virgin, and the tale expresses a truth of the soul. I have no objection to the miracles, except where they do not happen to please me, why should not a soul so consecrate and intent develope new laws, and make matter plastic. I can imagine him walking the waves and raising the dead without any violation of my usual habits of thought. He could not remain in the tomb, they say, surely not, death is impossible to such a being. He remained upon earth and all who have met him since *on the way* have felt their souls born within them. He ascended to Heaven, surely, it could not be otherwise.

But when I say to you, also, that though I think all this really happened, it is of no consequence to me whether it did or not, that the ideal truth such illustrations present to me, is enough, and that if the mind of St John, for instance, had conceived the whole and offered it to us as a poem, to me, as far as I know, it would be just as real, you see how wide the gulf that separates me from the Christian church.

Yet you also see that I believe in the history of the Jewish nation and its denouement in Christ, as presenting one great type of spiritual existence. It is very dear to me and occupies

A CREDO

a large portion of my thoughts. I have no trouble. So far from the sacrifice required of Abraham, for instance, striking me as it does Mr Parker I accept it as prefiguring a thought to be fully expressed by the death of Christ, (yet forget not that they who passed their children through the fire to Moloch were pious also, and not more superstitious than an *exclusive* devotion to Christ has made many of his followers.) "Do you not place Christ then in a higher place than Socrates, for instance or Michel Angelo?"

Yes! because if his life was not truer, it was deeper, and he is a representative of the ages. But then I consider the Greek Apollo as one also!

Have men erred in following Christ as a leader.

Perhaps rarely. So great a soul must make its mark for many centuries. Yet only when men are freed from him, and interpret him by the freedom of their own souls, open to visits of the Great Spirit from every side can he be known as he is.

"With your view do you not think he placed undue emphasis on his own position"? In expression he did so, but this is not in my way either. I should like to treat of this separately in another letter.

Where he was human, not humanly-divine, and where men so received him, there was failure, and is mist and sect,—but never where he brought them to the Father.

But they knew not what they did with him then, and do not now.

For myself I believe in Christ because I can do without him; because the truth he announces I see elsewhere intimated; because it is foreshadowed in the very nature of my own being. But I do not wish to do without him. He is constantly aiding and answering me. Only I will not lay any undue and exclusive emphasis on him. When he comes to me I will receive him; when I feel inclined to go by myself, I will. I do not reject the church either:—let men who can with sincerity live in it. I could not—for I believe far more widely than any body of men I know.

And as nowhere I worship less than in the places set apart for that purpose,—I will not seem to do so. The blue sky seen above the opposite roof preaches better than my brother, because, at present, a freer, simpler medium of religion. When great souls

642　　UNPUBLISHED WRITINGS

arise again that dare to be entirely free, yet are humble gentle and patient, I will listen, if they wish to speak. But that time is not nigh;—those I see around me, here & in Europe, are mostly weak and young.

Would I could myself say with some depth what I feel as to religion in my very soul. It would be a clear note of calm security. But for the present I think you will see how it is with me as to Christ. I am grateful here, as every where, where spirit bears fruit in fulness. It attests the justice of my desires; it kindles my faith; it rebukes my sloth; it enlightens my resolve. But so does the Apollo, and a beautiful infant, and the summer's earliest rose. It is only one modification of the same harmony. Jesus breaks through the soil of the world's life, like some great river through the else inaccessible plains and valleys. I bless its course. I follow it, but it is a part of the All. There is nothing peculiar about it, but its form.

I will not loathe sects, persuasions, systems, though I cannot abide in them one moment. I see most men are still in need of them. To them their banners, their tents; let them be Platonists, Fire worshippers, Christians; let them live in the shadow of past revelations. But I Oh Father of our Souls.—The One— seek thee. I seek thee in these forms; and in proportion as they reveal thee more, they lead me beyond themselves. I would learn from them all, looking to thee. I set no limits from the past to my own soul or any soul. Countless Ages may not produce another worthy to loose the shoes of Jesus of Nazareth; yet there will surely come another manifestation of that Word, that was in the beginning, for it is not dead, but sleepeth; and if it lives, must declare itself.

All future manifestations will come, like this,—not to destroy the law and the prophets but to fulfil. But as An Abraham called for a Moses, & a Moses for a David, so does Christ for another ideal. This ideal I believe you had in your mind let him not go. We want a life more complete and various than that of Christ, we have had the Messiah to teach and reconcile; let us have a Man to live out all the symbolical forms of human life with the calm beauty and physical fulness of a Greek God, with the deep consciousness of a Moses, with the holy love and purity of Jesus.

　　Amen.

A CREDO

Addenda.

I have not shown with any distinctness how the very greatness of the manifestation in Jesus calls for a greater. But this as the extreme emphasis given by himself to his office, should be treated of separately in a letter or essay On the processes of Genius in declaring itself.

I have not shown my deep feeling of his life as a genuine growth, so that his words are all living & they come exactly to memory with all the tone and gesture of the moment, true runes of a divine oracle. It is the same with Shakspeare, and in a less degree with Dante.

I have not spoken of men clinging to him, from the same weakness that makes them so dependent on a priesthood, or make idols of the objects of affection. In him hearts seek *the* Friend, Minds *the* Guide. But this is weakness in religion, as elsewhere. No prop will do

"The Soul must do its own immortal work."

and books, lovers, friends, mediators fly from us only to return, when we can do without them. But when we can use and learn from them, yet feel able to do without them they will depart no more. If I were to preach on this subject I would take for a text the words of Jesus.

"*Nevertheless* I tell you the truth—It is expedient for you that I go away; for if I go not, the Comforter will not come unto you; but if I depart, I will send him unto you."

To Beethoven

Saturday eveg 25th Novr 1843

MY only friend

How shall I thank thee for again tonight breaking the chains of my sorrowful slumber. I did not expect it. For months now I have been in a low state of existence. Nothing profited me, nothing budded or blossomed in my garden. I was not sad; the arrow did not rankle in my heart as sometimes it does, but it lay there a cold dull substance where foreign pressure seemed to prevent pulsation from its harmony, life from its abundance.

My eyes are always clear, dear friend, I always see that the universe is rich, if I am poor. I see the insignificance of my sorrows. In my will I am not a captive, in my intellect not a slave. I know the richness of my inheritance though I cannot take possession of it. It is not my fault that the palsy of my affections benumbs my whole life. I would disregard it if I could.

And here indeed, my lot is accursed, yes, my friend let me curse it. The curse like the ill is but for the time. I know what the Eternal justice promises.—But in this one sphere it is sad. Thou didst say thou hadst no friend but thy art,—but that one is enough.—I have no art in which to vent the swell of a soul as deep as thine, Beethoven, and of kindred frame. *Thou* wilt not think me presumptuous in this saying as another might. I have always known that thou wouldst welcome, wouldst know me, as no other who ever lived upon the earth since its first creation would.

Thou wouldst forgive me, Master, that I have not been true to my eventual destiny, and therefore suffered on every side the "pangs of despised love."—Thou didst the same. But thou didst borrow from those errors the inspiration of thy genius; why is it not thus with me? Is it because as a woman I am bound by a physical law which prevents the soul from manifesting itself. Sometimes the moon seems mockingly to say so,—to say that I too shall not shine unless I can find a sun. O cold and barren moon, tell a different tale, and give me a son of mine own.

TO BEETHOVEN

But thou, Oh blessed Master, dont answer all my questions and make it my privilege to be. Like a humble wife to the sage or poet, it is my triumph that I can understand, can receive thee wholly, like a mistress I arm thee for the fight, like a young daughter I tenderly bind thy wounds.

Thou art to me beyond compare, for thou art all I want. No heavenly sweetness of Jesus, no many leaved Raphael no golden Plato is any thing to me compared with thee. The infinite Shakspeare, the stern Angelo, Dante bitter sweet like thee, are no longer dear in thy presence. And beside these names, there are none others that could vibrate in thy crystal sphere.—Thou hast all of them and that ample surge of life beside that great winged being which they only dreamed of.

There is none greater than Shakspeare, for he is a God, but his creations are successive, thy Fiat comprehends them all.

Beethoven, my heart beats, I live again, for I feel that I am worthy audience for thee, and that my being would be reason enough for thine.

I met thy mood and mine last summer in nature on those wide impassioned plains flower and crag bestrown. There the tide of emotion had rolled over and left the vision of its smiles and sobs as I saw tonight from thee.

Oh, if thou wouldst take me wholly to thyself, I am lost in this world where I sometimes meet angels but of a different star from mine. Forgive me that I love them who cannot love me. Even so does thy spirit call upon, plead with all spirits. But thou dost triumph and bring them all in, my triumphs are but for the moment, thine eternal.

Master! I have this summer envied the oriole which had even a swinging nest in the high bough. I have envied the least flower that came to seed, though that seed were strown to the wind. But I envy none when I am with thee. Tonight I had no wish for thee: it was long since we had met. I did not expect to feel again, I was so very cold; tears had fallen; but they were Hamlet tears of speculation. Thy touch made me again all human. O save and give me to myself and thee.

Chamois

c. 1844

I HAVE passed the coldest heights, through the gloomiest ravines, along the paths that tremble with a strong sigh of the wind. As I bounded upwards, the evening star seemed ready to descend upon my forehead. The atmosphere nearest heaven was not too bracing for my eager breast. Still upwards, onwards, the breast swells more and more with rapture. Where the ark rested on the snow-peak of Ararat, there would I climb.

But I see not the ark,—and the eternal snows have lost the pure and roseate hues that distance gave. Fixed and dull they stretch before me, they stretch into the distance, but do not lead the eye thither. Clefts in the blue ice call the eye downwards, as to an obscure, a mysterious death.

But onward still,—on that even impossible crag. I shall find the moment for which I come, I shall find myself. See how wildly it rises, wildly desiring, loneliest spot,—virgin in loneliness, untrodden, unreached, since the birth of Time. But my boldest foot shall find a hold upon the crag. I will make the impossible mine own.

'Tis done,—and with resolve strong as death I have sprung to this life. I find a home on the height which turned hope dizzy.— For I needed not the anchor of Hope,—I know nor hope nor fear,—but make the *must* of my bosom, that of all destiny.

It is mine.—What is mine? An untrodden solitude. Yes,—I have found myself,—I am alone with myself,—and the genius of my life has fled. "Thou needest me not,"—he cried,— and shook his purple wings to flee. "On this spot thou canst overlook all the region,—from this spot look straight into the eyes of Heaven, nearer than can any created thing.

"None can compare with thee,—none can think of thee,— for none can conceive the spot where thou art. Yes, thou canst now be alone, in loneliness entirely unprofaned, was it not for this thou didst so bound forward? and defy all rivals, to be 'alone with the Alone'"?

But an unutterable sadness seizes me,—and the crag wails and wails. One barren thought encompasses me,—where is love, the presence of a God?

"What needs love? Love is compromise, is prophecy.—Thou art alone in Truth. Leave Love behind for those who still aspire."

No, I will return and bring it hither.

But how is this? I cannot return.—The chasm is impassable. Genius of life, pause yet a moment on the wing, can I not return?

GENIUS.

"Never,—save the baseness of repentance dash thee to pieces in the chasm.

The spirit of resolve, the onward, upward soul may pass such gulfs—but their powers desert them if they look back. Knowest thou not the curse recorded from all time, on those that look back?"

THE CHAMOIS NATURE:—"but I cannot pause. I meant only to ask for a moment of loneliness,—a moment has shown me all,—the below, the above, myself, the all—what then remains? If I stay here I am not myself—already I die,—for already I question. Shall Death be prolonged? It cannot,—for Death is but a moment's pause."

GENIUS—

"Wait in death till thou art called."

CHAMOIS NATURE.

Then chain me to the rock,—for still the bounding, seeking spirit forces me to flee, back,—since I cannot forward.

GENIUS.

"Chain thyself by Truth,—because thou *canst not* recede. Farewell.—"

CHAMOIS NATURE.

"I cannot recede,—no, I cannot. I cannot choose *that*; there is no atom of my life that could choose that. But oh! this fire of delay"!—

CHORUS OF STARS.—

Lo! the Sun departs,—the hues steal from the fields of earth, he pauses yet a moment on the threshold to look upon her. Thus have we seen the lover pause, taking a last look of her he loved, who lived in him alone—who lives a living death out of his presence; why must he depart and leave her thus lost, thus colorless?—Proud in his beautiful anguish, he will not question,

648 UNPUBLISHED WRITINGS

he will not speak; so strong, yet Fate is stronger; so beauteous, yet cannot abide to keep his love beautiful.

He pauses on the threshold,—kingly, though a vanquished King.—

He folds around him his golden robes; they borrow lustre,—they gleam and swell with the impassioned heave of his breast.

But she, his love, sits weeping; her head leans on her hand; her dark locks fall lower and lower,—yet she feels his look, and strives to smile. In that last smile of pathetic love, the earth becomes the angel of herself. How many youthful souls have hailed that last smile of day upon the earth, as the sole moment worth knowing, among the gaudy shows of existence. Then love completes wedlock in "blessedness not happiness"; and Cyprian calls Justina his bride at last, amid the martyr flames, for God, and not desire, have given her to him.—

But it is all over now. He is gone, the lonely bridegroom, the vanquished king,—and gentle, pitying Night has wiped away the tears of earth, and turned them all to pearls. The two will meet again; *could* they but realize how soon, it would seem almost undeservedly soon.—All Nature sleeps in a dream of dew and perfume, the wind still sustains her dream by its long symphonies.

But hark! there is a jar,—a mis-tuned chord, and that one of the noblest. List what it may be.—

Chamois nature.—

Oh why is it? *why?* Why thus far and no farther? My whole nature was ready for Godhood,—and I sink momently into death.—Why here on this sacred height?

I had feared nothing, doubted nothing, forborne nothing, if I might but on.—Genius of my life, return and answer me; the anguish of my doubt, the weight of my chain, increase ages in each moment. Genius, return! I must hear the voice,—know again the beat of mine own accustomed heart.—

Stars.—

Silence, vain mourner! Hear the All! It speaks through us,—for we, now central, once like thee seeking a sphere, know all, say all to the ready soul.

Abandon the genius of thy life. Abandon thine own nature. They served thee true while thou wert but expression,—the growth into outwardness, of a thought.

But it *is* expressed,—that Chamois thought. Let it lie in the past.—

Crushed in the embrace of God, let thy individual nature slowly perish,—the martyr's death. Each pure tear shall be, like us, after its appointed ages, a Star and Sun. Weep thou, freely,—but let them be the tears of nature unfulfilled, not of contentious will.

Offer thy breast freely for an altar of sacrifice; from that high lonely crag, the fires shall be seen afar, a beacon to all who watch, and weep, and pray by night. Could those who are forever bound in the celestial harmony envy,—we too might envy thee, as thou enviest the past. For our days of merit are over, we cannot deserve, we know too well the meaning of all. We cannot ascend, for we circle in true spheres.—

We will shine coldly on thee, burning so fiercely there; yet the two fires, of agony, of purity, will be the same when thou canst make them so. When the unvanquished atom which men call soul, lies, sweet, though unsubdued, amid the smouldering ruins of the human nature, and says to us *unappealingly* my brothers,—then, then!—

Chamois thought, thought of saddest music

Farewell!—

JOURNALS

Rome 1st Jany 1849

This year cannot fail to be rich in events most important for Italy, Europe, the world

Rome has at last become the focus of the Italian revolution & I am here. I shall in this book make brief notes of the events of the day, to be filled out as journal at my leisure.

The Pope is still absent at Gaeta and in his absence the temporal power of the Papacy has recd the last blow. The Constituente Romana was proclaimed on Friday 29th Nov 1848. It will be followed by the Constituente Italiana, which ought in the natural order of things to constitute Italy one and one republic. There may be many breakers yet before that shore

MANUSCRIPT PAGE FROM ROME DIARY

Poems and Selections from Journal Fragments
1833–1844

---

c. 1833

2[d] May. More than a fortnight since I wrote last—yet have I read several books. One on Egypt filled my head completely I attempted to write something about it, enjoyed it the first time the second grew cold—invention flagging—style tame—oh! I am very wretched—I cannot finish it—there it must lie in my desk with my other plans, tragedies forsooth? What fiend has put into my head and heart this purpose of writing—I cannot write—yet something I was born for—O Lord, Lord show me what it was—It cannot be to educate these children—or *that* would make me happy when I do my best—Once I thought I knew what I wanted—I had two wishes both of them were thwarted, my heart bled—O God thou knowest that I have striven to be reconciled to thy will but I fear—I fear that when the fount of hope dried up energy invention all the bright intellectual gifts vanished too—Must it be so O God must I descend into the grave without fame as without happiness.

—

c. 1833

Shall I never have an hour of self-complacency. Shall all these bitter tears, this heart-burning and silent pain end in nothing—Chance people admire me and call me good and bright—This is mockery—cutting irony to my consciousness— receive letters telling me that I am laying up treasures in heaven or that I must "revel in intellectual pride" &c—No matter what they say—In my own eyes I am imbecile, abased—yet I have still—A heart to comprehend true greatness. Study of noble souls to know their goodness—Why cannot I add one to the glorious company. Enough—Enough—I can pour out my lamentations fast enough—That poor consumptive girl—that

wretched worn-out woman are happier than I—They have no
ambition, no strong sensibilities forever wounded—no keen
tastes rarely gratified—no panting after the Divinity without
reliance on his goodness—

—

Octr 1839.

In a fair garden of a distant land
Where autumn skies the softest blue outspread
   A lovely crimson Dahlia reared her head
To drink the lustre of the season's prime,
   And drink she did until her cup oerflowed
With ruby redder than the sunset cloud.

—

   Near to her root she saw the fairest Rose
That ever oped her soul to sun and wind,
   And still the more her sweets she did disclose
The more her queenly heart of sweets did find,
   Not only for her worshipper the Wind,
But for Bee, Nightingale, and Butterfly,
   Who would with ceaseless wing about her ply
Nor ever cease to seek what found we still must find.

—

   Upon the other side, nearer the ground,
A paler flowret on a slender stem,
   That cast so exquisite a fragrance round
As seemed the minute blossom to contemn,
   Seeking an ampler urn to hold its sweetness
And in a statelier shape to find completeness.

—

   Who could refuse to hear that keenest voice.
   Although it did not bid the heart rejoice;
The Dahlia bowed her head, forgot the Sun,
   And, though the Nightingale had just begun
His hymn—the Evening Breeze began to woo
When at the charming of the evening dew
The flowret could its secret soul disclose,
   By that revealing touched, the queenly Rose
Forgot them both a deeper joy to hope,
And list the love-note of the Heliotrope.

—

c. 1840

Content thee—for without content
The sharpest edge of joy is gone,
It is a couch of roses, sent
From Heaven for man to rest upon,

Oh lie then but an hour with me—
And let sky-ranging Fantasy
Rest silent: Eager Hope, be dumb,
And with it warm desire, the womb,
    Whence cometh future sorrow—
All these shall visit thee tomorrow,
Drink present quiet whilst thou may—
The choice is not with thee alway.

—

c. 1840

There is something very propitious to good writing in the form of dialogue.

The regular build of an Essay (maugre the unpretending name) is dangerous.

It tempts to round the piece into a whole by filling up the gaps between the thoughts with—Words—words—words.—

Often, too often do I wish to die? My spirit sinks and my whole heart grieves!

My day is poor of thought and deed, my body is a burden not an instrument. I have few thoughts, too much feeling, o that I should live to write this.

—

c. 1840s

Fate is law, and the man that discovereth the law that rules him and follows it shall be firm when other things shake. It is like the presiding star astrologers feigned. It shall lead you to dangers and through them,—

—

c. May 1844

I feel within myself an immense power, but I cannot bring it out. I stand a barren vine stock from which no grape will swell though the richest wine is slumbering in its root.

I never doubt my eventual perfection, but I doubt whether this life be my climate or will ripen my fruit.

—

c. May 1844

I said I felt an immense power. It may seem a joke, but I *do* feel something corresponding to that tale of the Destinies falling in love with Hermes.

—

c. May 1844

I was always wishing to cast myself into the arms of some other nature. The burden of my thoughts oppressed me, and I was forced to throw it off by intercourse with natures which had not the art to measure of mine,—This was womanish I own. And, on looking back, I see there was not one who could directly aid me. It was their misfortune, not their fault. I am not yet a man. I yet long for the gush of mingling souls to fill the broad channel of one bright stream—the fiery action of mind on mind giving to all that comes between them the eager aspiration of flame.

from S. M. Fuller's bouquet.—Journal
c. 1836–1837

These two little engravings were given me by a friend one eve g at Mrs Farrar's Jany 1836 before I had quite resigned the hope of going with Mrs F. to Europe.

—

Heidelberg

The stately castle in the calm moonlight,
A chronicle of the romantic day,
    Wakes up my thoughts to warm and stirring life
Striving to paint the fair or warlike forms
    Which animated this now voiceless pile.

Reality might bring another mood
    And, as the picture stimulates the fancy,
The place itself, perhaps would soothe the heart;
    A fragrant summer's eve upon that flood!

Beneath the loving eye of such a moon!
    And one whose thoughts, though unexpressed, I know
To muse with me! Had it such hours in store
    I of the coming year would ask no more.

Would not each instant rouse some heavenly wish
Which, treasured in the soul, would hallow it
    And keep it safe through scenes of other temper?
—For from the past those who know Memory's power
Can oft refresh the sultry present hour:
    Thus, mid the throng of petty purposes,
Mean feelings, low pursuits, and sensual pleasures
    Which haunt the common day and seek to stifle
The ethereal spark in Man, we would recal
    The sweetness and the meaning of this scene
Earnest to make *our* purposes and pleasures
    As noble and enduring as the pile,
Calm as the moonlight, pure as were the breezes,

Direct and earth-enriching as the stream
Harmonious as the whole with central Beauty.
Without such impulses if *I* must strive
Yet love of them will "save my soul alive."

Jan^y—1836—

—

Drachenfels

Loneliness so profound
'Tis almost desolation here I see
Awe struck I gaze around
While common life seems far apart to be.

Not only common life
All human interest from this spot is far
The hum of business—the passions' strife
Love's music, and the stirring notes of war.

On other heights I've stood
And traced with curious eye the haunts of Man,
Seen to a thread shrunk the wide-rolling flood,
Cities to specks,—existence to a span,

And felt the moment proud,
The mind dilating with the wider view
Faintly presaged through earth-bred mist and cloud
Our joys when eagle winged we shall our youth renew.

But no aspiring hope,
No eager joy, nor rich remembrance here
Could bless me—Here no heavenly gate can ope
No visions of ethereal birth appear.

A high mysterious mood
Breathes from the scene like that which might be known
To some keen spirit from the shackles flown
Of human flesh and blood,

New to its present lot
A moment poised in space
Where, known terrestrial laws prevailing not,
It finds not yet its place.

The abstract and the lone
This spot can teach, yet *how* I cannot tell
    The hieroglyphic spell
Will not the bonds of common language own.

    Those who the might have known
  Of such a scene, and felt the fancy moved
    By a force feared yet loved
From these vague words can know my thought alone.

    Home of the Dragon brood
None shall thy secret penetrate save he
Who from their laughing demon mystery
The phantoms of his being daring woo'ed,

    And, seeking Truth alone
While he the Angel in his being feels
    Shrinks not from what reveals
    Another power which Time cannot disown.

    Like thee, O crag, that power,
When all material powers shall pass away
    Melting in heavenly day
    At the dread trumpet hour,

    'Neath the All-seeing Eye
Mysterious no more, like vapour driven
    Before the eye of this our visible Heaven,
Shall yield with all Time's fabrics to Eternity.

from Reflections Journal
c. 1839

Poesy—the expression of the sublime and beautiful, whether in measured words or in the fine arts. The human mind apprehending the harmony of the universe and making new combination by its laws.

Poetry—the sublime and beautiful expressed in measured language. It is closely allied with the fine arts. It should sing to the ear, point to the eye and exhibit the symmetry of architecture. If perfect, it will satisfy the intellectual and moral faculties, no less than the heart and the senses. It works chiefly by simile and melody. It is to prose as the garden to the house. Pleasure is the object of the one, convenience of the other. The flowers and fruits may be copied on the furniture of the house, but if their beauty be not subordinated to utility, they lose the charm of beauty and degenerate into finery. The reverse is the case in the garden.

—

Woman is the flower, man the bee. She sighs out melodious fragrance and invites the winged laborer. He drains her cup, carries off the honey. She dies on the stalk. He returns to the hive well fed and praised as an active member of the community.

—

I held in my hand the cup. It was full of hot liquid, the air was cold. I delayed to drink, and its vital heat, its soul curled upwards in delicatest wreaths. I looked delighted on their beauty, but while I waited, the essence of the draught was wasted on the cold air; it would not wait for me; it longed too much to utter itself, and, when my lip was ready, only a flat, worthless sediment remained of what had been.

Faen so &c

The son of the Gods has sold his birthright. He has received therefor one, not merely the fairest, but the sweetest and holiest of earth's daughters. Yet is it not a fit exchange. His pinions droop powerless, he must no longer soar amid the golden stars. No matter, he thinks—I will take her to some green and flowery isle. I will pay the penalty of Adam for the sake of the daughter of Eve. For her I will make the earth fruitful by the sweat of my brow. No longer my hands shall bear the coal to the lips of the inspired singer, no longer my voice modulate its tones to the accompaniment of spheral harmonies. My hands lift the clod of the valley which now dares cling to them with brotherly familiarity. And for my soiling dreary taskwork all the day I receive—food.

But the smile with which she greets me at set of sun, is it not worth all that sun has seen me endure. Can angelic delights surpass those which I possess when pacing the shore with her, watched by the quiet Moon, listen to the tide of the world surging up impatiently against the Eden it cannot conquer. Truly, the joys of heaven were gregarious and low in comparison. This, this alone is exquisite, because exclusive and peculiar.

Ah Seraph—but the winter's frost must rip thy vine. A viper lurks beneath the flowers to sting the foot of thy child, and pale decay must steal over the cheek thou dost adore. In the realm of Ideas all was imperishable. Be blest, while thou canst;—O love thee, fallen Seraph, but thou shouldst not have sold thy birthright.

All for love and the world well lost. That sounds so true. But Genius when it sells itself gives up not only the world but the Universe.

Yet does not Love comprehend the Universe? The Universe is Love: Why should I weary my eye with scanning the parts, when I can clasp the whole this moment to my beating heart?

But if the intellect be repressed, the idea will never be brought out from the feeling. The amaranth wreath will in thy grasp be changed to one of roses, more fragrant, indeed, but withering with a single sun.

I have thought much whether Goethe did well in giving up Lili. That was the crisis in his existence. From that era dates his existence as a Weltweise; the heroic element vanished irrecoverably from his character; he became an Epicurean and a Realist, plucking flowers and hammering stones instead of looking up to the stars.

How could he look through the blinds and see her sitting alone in her beauty, yet give her up for so slight reasons. He was right as a genius, but wrong as a character.

—

C. —— has written wonders about the mystery of personality. Why do we so love it?—In the first place, each wishes to embrace a whole and this seems the readiest way. The intellect soars, the heart clasps, from putting "a girdle around the earth in twenty minutes" thou would'st return to thy own green little isle of emotion, and be the loving and playful fay rather than the delicate Ariel.

Then these persons are plants, organic. We can predict their growth according to their own law. From the cotyledon young girl we can predict the lustre, the fragrance of the future flower. It waves gracefully to the breeze, the dew rests upon its petals, the bee busies himself in them and flies away after a brief rapture, richly laden. When it fades, its leaves fall softly on the bosom of mother earth to all whose feelings it has so closely conformed. It has lived as a part of nature, its life was music, and we open our hearts to the melody.

Says Goethe "Why dost thou mourn, beloved, that thy beauty is transitory. It is the law which nature has stamped upon all beauty."

But characters like thine and mine are mineral. We are the bone and sinew, those the smiles and glances of earth. We lie nearer the Mighty heart, and boast an existence more enduring than they. The sod lies heavy on us, or, if we show ourselves, the melancholy moss clings to us. If we are to be made into palaces and temples, we must be hewn and chiselled by instruments of unsparing sharpness. The process is mechanical and unpleasing, the noises which accompany it discordant and obtrusive, the artist is surrounded by rubbish. Yet we may be polished to marble smoothness. In our veins may lie the diamond, the ruby, perhaps the emblematic carbuncle.

The flower is pressed to the bosom with intense emotion, but in the home of love it withers and is cast by.

The gem is worn with less love, more pride, if we enjoy its sparkle the joy is partly from calculation of its value, but, if it is lost, we regret it long.

For myself, my name is Pearl. I lay at the beginning amid slime and foul prodigies from which only my unsightly shell protected me. I was cradled and brought to my present state amid disease and decay. Only the experienced diver could have known that I was there and brought me to the strand where I now am valued as pure, *round*, and, if less brilliant than the diamond, yet an ornament for a kingly head. If I were again immersed in the element where I dwelt first, now that I am stripped of my protecting shell, I should blacken into deformity.

For you, I presume by your want of steady light, and by the brilliancy of sparks which are occasionally struck from you, that you are either a flint, or a rough diamond. If the former, I hope you are at home in some friendly tinder box, instead of lying in the highway to answer the hasty hoof of the trampling steed. If a diamond, I hope to meet you in some imperishable crown, where we may long remain together, you lighting up my pallid orb, I tempering your blaze.

Pearl.

I do not remember ever before to have created any thing in a dream which I could not analyze and find it made up from what I had seen, but last night I invented a flower. How sorry I am to be out of the practice of painting flowers, else I might give an idea of this

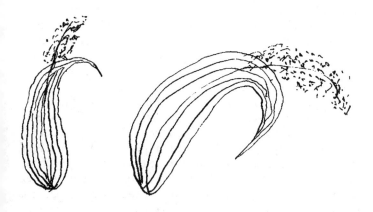

Such was its shape, the flower was cream color dotted with amber, the broad-ribbed leaf of a glistening, a very delicate green. It was of great size and looked very beautiful in my dream. No doubt I have seen perhaps enlarged it from some little friend of the woods and meadows. I mention it that I may know it when we meet again. All the rest was very prosaic. Sometimes for weeks I dream of the beautiful objects of Nature, and then again for a long time of prating social life and its petty vexations.

—

Went to bed ill with pain in the *right* side of my head. Could not get to sleep for a long time, when I did, dreamt that the Egyptian, who has so often tormented me into the nervous headach, sat by my side and kept alluring a gigantic butterfly who was hovering near to rest upon her finger. He approached, but, declining her skinny finger, flapped his crimson wings for a moment, then settled on the *left* side of my forehead; I tried in vain to drive him away; he plunged his feet, bristling with feelers, deeper and deeper into my forehead till my pain rose to agony. I awoke with my hand on the left side of my forehead to which the pain had changed. After the usual applications had been made I again fell asleep. Now I was in a room of a large hotel, very ill. On the bed was a pink counterpane, such as was in the little room where I endured so many weeks of nervous headach without complaining to any body. I wandered out, I know not why, and could not find my way back. I went through the usual distresses of going into strange rooms &c, at last, in despair and quite exhausted, lay down in an entry. Many persons passed by, some looked scornfully at me, others tried to lift me but I was too heavy and at last was left lying on the floor. I was in great pain in the back. I was wrapt in a long robe, but my feet were bare they seemed growing cold as marble. I thought I must die in this forlorn condition, and tried to resign myself to bear it well. At last a sweet female form approached she sat down by me on the cold, damp, brick floor. I cried, O Amy, and laid my head on her bosom. I wept long and bitterly. She had dark eyes and regular features the face I never saw before, but the feeling I had was the same as when Anna in the fever drew me up out of the pit of blood. It is the true feeling of feminine influence, the same which Goethe wished to illustrate by his tale of the child charming the lion, the influence of benignity, purity and faith. As I have masculine traits, I am naturally often relieved by women in my imaginary distresses. When I awoke the warmth was gone from the stone* which had been placed at my feet, they were marble cold, the pain had gone into the spine and my pillow was drenched with tears.

This dream seems, as mine, from the nature of my illness must be, very illustrative of the influence of the body on the mind when will and understanding are not on the alert to check it. Let those who undervalue the moral power of will analyze their dreams and see what they become without it.

Another time I dreamt that my body was a dungeon and a beautiful angel escaped at the head. That was a time when the pain in the spine was very bad.

People appear in their true characters in my dreams. How divine were the two youthful ones of R. They were the most I ever knew of him—the revelation of Poetry in the one, the divine enthusiasm of the dark downcast eyes in the other.

* Not a tombstone

from Bound Journal
c. 1839–1840

How many of my fine plans lie apparently frost bitten in the bud. There always seems excuse for doing nothing. But I think I ought to keep some record, perhaps some of them may come to flower, if ever I get honorably through this Life I have proposed and can shake aside my load of cares.

My four tragedies are slumbering peacefully in my trunk. They cannot again be touched at present.

—

A book called Fragments or some such name composed of sketches of character short stories and essays on art and the passions still attracts my hopes, for this my materials are already rich and simply require arrangement. "The poem is written, all but the verses."

—

Elschen's story which she has given me leave to use. But that must not be yet, not till there are none to sneer, and none to grieve. I will have it told some still moonlight evening on the bosom of some far away lake to an intelligent ear.

Motto
She grew not wise
Nor grows &c
But in Elschen's case, she was not to blame but the iron weight of *reason* which was let fall prematurely on her youth.

F. H's story amid the Hory mountains. I know this so well and have learnt him so by heart. I think I can unfold him from his infatuated youth to the cold piece of intellectual furniture he is now. His friendship with that stern youth would be the best part, better than his ideal love, or contempt for his jacobin guardian.—

—

Mrs —s two love affairs told me by herself when her hair was silver. One at 16 the other at 46, both of infinite beauty and full of significance. She had been married between to a man she did not love, and had many children, but, for a wonder, was not degraded by this grand mistake in life.

The Pilgrimages of Leila

As a Gnome / Power
As a Sylph / Beauty
As a Daemon / Goodness and Wisdom
Her return to human nature.
Motto from Hesiod——

This would be a true poem and give the kernel both of art and Nature, if I could sing it as it has been sung to me on the seaside and in the wild wood.

Essays—on the Advantages of Sickness—
On the dangers of ill-health.——

1st Deepening powers of sympathy, at the same time turning mind inward and favoring concentration. Active energy blunted, but delicacy of perception increased.

2d, Selfishness—care of detail, want of noble courage, gradual recaling in of obtuseness of feeling till at last the master is for the house & not the house for the master.

Sept 25.
It is now proposed that I should conduct a magazine which would afford me space and occasion for every thing I may wish to do. If I only dare tax my health and spirits with the undertaking.
　While I hold it in my eye new plans rise before me.
　The introduction which it is proposed that I shall write will afford me fine oppory to point out what is the true office of the Critic and what I think our position is here as thinkers to leaven this vast mass of actors.

—

　If there be in the hive more than one queen, one must perish.
　The whole swarm go up with that one in a pyramidal form of which that one is the apex.

So it is while in the sight of mortals, but afterwards we know not, for they cannot impregnate her except in upper air.

Fourier thinks the universe a bee hive & the bee should be a symbol of perfected life (as the beetle among the ancients was of the early stages in nature).

But the female glow worm is clothed with light that she may attract the male.

Even Milton makes Eve think Adam, at first, less beautiful than herself.

—

I accept all these persons say of my writing with certain limitations. The advice or opinions of friends are only useful to one who has steadfastness enough to use them in his own way. She may modify but must never alter the line of action to which Nature impels you.

17th   I did envy those who had kept within the protecting bound of a private life, but I will not. I will want severest trials.

—

17th April 1840.

Every body finds fault with me just now, some in one way, some in another—With regard to this new journal not only shall I be exposed to make enemies on every side, but be stripped for a time of the reputation I have enjoyed for talents and knowledge—We are in a sad position Raoul & I & other poor authors whose works have been talked of too much while yet in the port-folio; the public when it has a fair oppory to judge them is disappointed just in proportion to the vivacity of its prestige. It had nursed its fancy with promises of what those works should be and is very angry that they do not realize its hopes—

Then a woman of tact and brilliancy like me has an undue advantage in conversation with men, They are astonished at our instincts. They do not see where we got our knowledge and while they tramp on in their clumsy way we wheel and fly and dart hither and thither and seize with ready eye all the weak points (like Saladin in the desert). It is quite another thing when we come to write, and without suggestion from another mind to declare the positive amount of thought that is in us. Because we seemed to know all they think we can tell all—and finding we can tell so little lose faith in their first opinion of us *which natheless was true.*

Then these gentlemen are surprized that I write no better because I talk so well. But I have served a long apprenticeship to the one, none to the other. I will write well yet, but never I think so well as I talk for then I feel inspired and the means are pleasant; my voice excites me, my pen never.

I shall by no means be discouraged, nor take what they say for gospel, but try to sift from it all the truth & use it. I feel within myself the strength to dispense with all illusions and I will manifest it. I will stand steady and rejoice in the severest probations!

from 1842 Journal

—————————

August 18–September 25, 1842
Thursday. Ellery brought down Ellen's picture & put it in my room. It is a hard painting, but simple and true, the upper part of the face is very like, and he has got the purity of the brow and the shape of the eyelids which are so peculiar. The mouth is too rigid. E. H. says it fails in "that look of the *appealing child* that Ellen has."

Waldo brought me at once the inkhorn and pen. I told him if he kept me so strictly to my promise, I might lose my ardor, however I began at once to write for him, but not with much success, the subject has lost its charm. Lidian came in to see me before dinner: she wept for the lost child, and I was tempted to do the same, which relieved much from the oppression I have felt since I came. Though I can never meet Lidian on such subjects, I felt for her today and she liked to have me. Waldo showed me all he and others had written, about the child, there is very little from W's own observation, though he was with him so much. He has not much eye for the little signs in children that have such great leadings. The little there is is good. I found he had written out last autumn's passage

"Mamma. May I have this bell which I have been making to stand by the side of my bed?

Yes, it may stand there.

But, mamma, I am afraid it will alarm you. It may sound in the middle of the night, and it will be heard over the whole town, it will sound like some great glass thing which falls down and breaks all to pieces; it will be louder than a thousand hawks; it will be heard across the water, and in all the countries; it will be heard all over the world."

I liked this because it was exactly so he talked spinning away without end, and with large beautiful earnest eyes. But most of the stories are of short sayings. This is good in M. Russell's

1842 JOURNAL 671

journal of him. She had been telling him a story that excited him & then he told her this

"How his horse went once into a long long wood, and how he looked through a squirrel's eye and saw a great giant, and the giant was himself." He thought of this many times afterwards.

I hate to hear them compare little Edith with him, though she is a sweet child. Ellen is of another blood: she is her aunt Brown's child. But I shall never care for another in this house.

Waldo & I went to walk to Walden pond, as usual, & staid till near sunset on the water's brink beneath the pines. It was a very lovely afternoon, great happy clouds floating, a light breeze rippling the water to our feet: it was altogether sweet, and not out of memory, as is too often the case between us, but from the present moment & to be remembered. We go but very little way on our topics, just touch & taste and leave the cup not visibly shallower. Waldo said once his were short flights from bough to bough, & so it is not up into the blue. I feel more at home with him constantly, but we do not act powerfully on one another. He is a much better companion than formerly, for once he would talk obstinately through the walk, but now we can be silent and see things together. We talked on the subject of his late letter, the threatenings of the time which come to so little, and of some individual cases where Sorrow is still the word, of those who began with such high resolve. Too high I said, & W. agreed. We spoke of the prayer of a friend Lord use me only for high purposes, no mean ones.—We must not dictate to the spirit.

This evening Ellery called me out to the east clover slip, from which there is a wide view over the meadows. The moon was nearly at full. He told me a great deal about himself. He got excited, as in painting a picture. He said the changes of his life made figures to him of himself on his canvass just as of other people, that it was endless change, urged on by a fate, that he disappointed every one, and most me, and there was no hope of its ever being otherwise.

Friday. I kept at my writing almost all day, but with small success. I cannot get hold of my subject in a way to suit me. I shall not be able to do at all what I intended. The richness of material is a disadvantage. I am obliged to reject too much and this chills me.

Elizabeth came to see me this afternoon. I grieve to see her fine frame subject to such rude alarms. But she truly said "I am not a failed experiment, for in the bad hours I do not forget what I thought in the better."

In the evening I took a walk with W. Looking at the moon in the river he said the same thing as in his letter, how each twinkling light breaking there summons to demand the whole secret, and how "promising, promising nature never fulfils what she thus gives us a right to expect." I said I never could meet him here, the beauty does not stimulate me to ask *why?*, and press to the centre, I was satisfied for the moment, full as if my existence was filled out, for nature had said the very word that was lying in my heart. Then we had an excellent talk: We agreed that my god was love, his truth. W. said that these statements alternate, of course, in every mind, the only difference was in which you were most at home, that he liked the pure mathematics of the thing.

—

Saturday Dear Richard has been here a day or two, and his common sense, and homely affection are grateful after these fine people with whom I live at swords points (though for the present turned downwards.) It is well to thee and thou it after talking with angels and geniuses. Richard and I spent the afternoon at Walden, & got a great bunch of flowers, a fine thunder shower gloomed gradual up, & turned the lake inky black, but no rain came till sunset. Reading Mr Alcott's letters makes me ache, it is miserable to see his boyish infatuation and his swelling vanity, already worse than ever. George Bradford was pleased by his idealizing his tie of marriage so in the distance, but, remembering what I do, it was as disagreeable to me as the rest. This afternoon I spent with W. in the study. I have not seen him before for two or three days, as he has been away, & then other people have been here. Apropos to the letters he read me his portrait of Mr A, which is masterly, and suppresses nothing, though I should throw things into very different relations. Apropos to William's letters, we had an excellent talk about God and the world. W. hates Fate as much as I do though in a different way.—It was pouring hard & quite cold: he had on his blue cloak falling in large straight folds; in that he looks as if he had come to his immortality, as a statue.

1842 JOURNAL 673

I inclose here a letter received from Hawthorne in answer to a question put at Ellery's earnest request, and with it one from Sophia received several days since. It is a striking contrast of tone between the man and woman so sincerely bound together by one sentiment.

Sunday. A heavy rain. I must stay at home. I feel sad.—Mrs Ripley was here today, but I only saw her a while in the afternoon and spent the day in my room. Sunday I do not give to my duty writing, as indeed I finished yesterday, after a sort, the article on ballads. Though a patchwork thing, it has craved time to do it.

Tomorrow to fresh fields and pastures new.

I have thoughts but no room or time to write them.

All these eve gs it has rained and we could not go out. Ellery has come into my room, but it has not been pleasant. The indoor darkness seemed to cloud his mind: he was entirely different from what he is beneath the open sky. The first night he began by railing at me as artificial. "It dont strike me when you are alone with me, he says, but it does when others are present. You dont follow out the fancy of the moment, you converse, you have treasured thoughts to tell, you are disciplined, artificial." I pleaded guilty, and observed that I supposed it must be so, with one of my continuity of thought or earnestness of character.—As to that, says he, I shall not like you the better for your excellence. I dont know what is the matter, I feel strongly attracted towards you, but there is a drawback in my mind, I dont know exactly what. You will always be wanting to grow forward, now I like to grow backward too. You are too ideal. Ideal people anticipate their lives, and they make themselves and every body around them restless, by always being beforehand with themselves, & so on in the very tone of William's damning letter.

I listened attentively, for what he said was excellent, following up the humor of the moment he arrests admirable thoughts on the wing. But I cannot but see, that what they say of my or other obscure lives is true of every prophetic, of every tragic character,—And then I like to have them make me look on that side, and reverence the lovely forms of nature, & the shifting moods, and the clinging instincts. But I must not let them disturb me. There is one only guide, the voice in the heart that asks—Was thy wish sincere? If so thou canst not stray from nature, nor be so perverted but she will make thee true again. I must take my own path, and learn from them all, without being paralyzed for to day. We need great energy, and self-reliance to endure to day. My age may not be the best, my position may be bad, my character ill formed, but thou, Oh Spirit, hast no regard to aught but the seeking heart, and if I try to walk upright will thou guide me? What despair must he feel who after a whole life passed in trying to build up himself, resolves that it would have been far better, if he had kept still as the clod of the valley, or yielded easily as the leaf to every breeze. A path has been appointed me. I have walked in it as steadily as I could. "I am what I am." That which I am not, teach me in the others. I will bear the pain of imperfection, but not of doubt. Waldo must not shake me in my worldliness, nor William in the fine motion that has given me what I have of life, nor this child of genius, make me lay aside the armour without which I had lain bleeding on the field long since, but if they can keep closer to Nature, and learn to interpret her as souls, also,—let me learn from them what I have not.

The spirit ascends through every form of nature into man, and no doubt here should make the complete animal instinctive man before unfolding his higher nature. But it was no accident that the serpent entered Eden, that the regular order of things was destroyed, that a painful throe accompanies every precious truth. When the soul has mastered it all, when it has learnt the secret in all its series, then there shall be no more breaks, no sluggishness, no premature fruit, but every thought be unfolded in its due order. Till then let us stand where our feet are placed and learn bit by bit, secure that it must be the destiny of each man to fill the whole circle.

Ellery said when we found a snake in the path that it was the *criticism* in the universe. It was not ugly, not loathsome; no, handsome and adroit in its motions, but it made you cold.

Monday. All the rain is over: it is a day of broad sunshine, spirited but warm breezes, great floating clouds. I made a holyday of it out in the woods. Much did I long "divinely to intend" the mind on subjects all-important to it, but I could not. I could get no steady light, only sighs for it were in a purer spirit than formerly. I am not in that state of clear vision I was two years ago, nor in that state of sweet feeling I was last summer, but Heaven be praised the clouds are rising that have lain low upon my soul all this fair summer.

I read some of William's letters. How fair and grand the vision that flits before him. I think it is true that he draws nearer. He has many thoughts that if he could hold them fast, and follow them patiently would bring balm in the

—

Sept

This golden afternoon I walked with Waldo to the hemlocks. There we sat down and staid till near sunset. He read me verses.—Dichtung und Wahrheit is certainly the name for his life, for he does not care for facts, except so far as the immortal essence can be distilled from them. He has little sympathy with mere life: does not seem to see the plants grow, merely that he may rejoice in their energy.

We got to talking, as we almost always do, on Man and Woman, and Marriage.—W. took his usual ground. Love is only phenomenal, a contrivance of nature, in her circular motion. Man, in proportion as he is completely unfolded is man and woman by turns. The soul knows nothing of marriage, in the sense of a permanent union between two personal existences. The soul is married to each new thought as it enters into it. If this thought puts on the form of man or woman, if it last you seventy years, what then? There is but one love, that for the Soul of all Souls, let it put on what cunning disguises it will, still at last you find yourself lonely,—*the Soul.*

There seems to be no end to these conversations: they always leave us both where they found us, but we enjoy them, for we often get a good expression.

Waldo said "Ask any woman whether her aim in this union is to further the genius of her husband; and she will say yes, but her conduct will always be to claim a devotion day by day that will be injurious to him, if he yields." "Those who hold their heads highest," quoth he, with a satirical side glance, "would do no better, if they were tried." I made no reply, for it is not worthwhile to, in such cases, by *words.*

676   JOURNALS

2^d It is a most brilliant day, & I stole the morning from my writing to take Lidian and then Mamma to ride. L. has had a slow fever which has confined her to her chamber almost ever since I came, & I have not been attentive to her as I should have been, if I had thought she cared about it. I did not go into her room at all for a day or two, simply because I was engaged all the time and kept expecting to see her down stairs. When I *did* go in, she burst into tears, at sight of me, but laid the blame on her nerves, having taken opium &c. I felt embarrassed, & did not know whether I ought to stay or go. Presently she said something which made me suppose she thought W. passed the evenings in talking with me, & a painful feeling flashed across me, such as I have not had, all has seemed so perfectly understood between us. I said that I was with Ellery or H. T. both of the eve gs & that W. was writing in the study.

I thought it all over a little, whether I was considerate enough. As to W. I never keep him from any such duties, any more than a book would.—He lives in his own way, & he dont soothe the illness, or morbid feelings of a friend, because he would not wish any one to do it *for him*. It is useless to expect it; what does it signify whether he is with me or at his writing. L. knows perfectly well, that he has no regard for me or any one that would make him wish to be with me, a minute longer than I could fill up the time with thoughts.

As to my being more his companion that cannot be helped, his life is in the intellect not the affections. He has affection for me, but it is because I quicken his intellect.—I dismissed it all, as a mere sick moment of L's.

Yesterday she said to me, at dinner, I have not yet been out, will you be my guide for a little walk this afternoon. I said "I am engaged to walk with Mr E. but"—(I was going to say, I will walk with you first,) when L. burst into tears. The family were all present, they looked at their plates. Waldo looked on the ground, but soft & serene as ever. I said "My dear Lidian, certainly I will go with you." "No! she said I do not want you to make any sacrifice, but I do feel perfectly desolate, and forlorn, and I thought if I once got out, the fresh air would do me good, and that with you, I should have courage, but go with Mr E. I will not go."

I hardly knew what to say, but I insisted on going with her, & then she insisted on going so that I might return in time for my other walk. Waldo said not a word: he retained his sweetness of look, but never offered to do the least thing. I can never admire him enough at such times; he is so true to himself. In our walk and during our ride this morn g L. talked so fully that I felt reassured except that I think she will always have these pains, because she has always a lurking hope that Waldo's character will alter, and that he will be capable of an intimate union; now I feel convinced that it will never be more perfect between them two. I do not believe it will be less: for he is sorely troubled by imperfections in the tie, because he dont believe in any thing better.—And where he loved her first, he loves her always. Then the influence of any one with him would be just in proportion to independence of him, combined with pure love of him for his own sake. Yet in reply to all L. said, I would not but own that though I thought it was the only way, to take him for what he is, as he wishes to be taken, and though my experience of him has been, for that very reason, so precious to me, I dont know that I could have fortitude for it in a more intimate relation. Yet nothing could be nobler, nor more consoling than to be his wife, if one's mind were only thoroughly made up to the truth.—As for myself, if I have not done as much as I ought for L. it is that her magnanimity has led her to deceive me. I have really thought that she was happy to have me in the house solely for Waldo's sake, and my own, and she is, I know, in the long account, but there are pains of every day which I am apt to neglect for others as for myself.— But Truth, spotless Truth, and Prayer and Love shall yield a talisman to teach me how to steer.

I suppose the whole amount of the feeling is that women cant bear to be left out of the question. And they dont see the whole truth about one like me, if they did they would understand why the brow of Muse or Priestess must wear a shade of sadness. On my side I dont remember them enough. They have so much that I have not, I cant conceive of their wishing for what I have. (*enjoying* is not the word: these I know are too generous for that) But when Waldo's wife, & the mother of that child that is gone thinks me the most privileged of women, & that E. H. was happy because her love was snatched away for a life long separation, & thus she can know none but ideal love: it does seem a little too insulting at first blush.—And yet they are not altogether wrong.

Friday

Ellery has seemed in a real pet with me for two or three days. I dont know what I did, some trifling thing. On Monday E & I went to walk, it was a calm bright afternoon. I felt full of music, & at first I did not enjoy being with E. for he was full of whimsies, & I felt as if I should rather have followed out my own course of feeling. At Walden we sat down among the bushes, & there E. was amusing me with his fancies of possible life upon the lake, & had just built his cottage, where he wrote verses from eight in the morning till four in the afternoon, summoning his attendant who hovered during the day on the edge of the wood by notes graduated on a key bugle to express his wants,—when Waldo dashed through the trees, and came down close to us. He made the same lovely apparition, as when he came down the bank where I was sitting with Hawthorne the other day, cleaving the shade like a sunbeam, the same lovely light in his eye and happy smile on his lips—I see written in his journal, "And now before the flush quite fades from my cheek, let me write &c" and this sweet girlishness is expressive of these brief visitations of loveliest youth to his face, where generally is seen only the purist, the critic, or the cold idealist. The other day he asked me to ride to Cambridge with him. I did not wish to go, but when I saw him setting off without me, I could not be willing, & said, Oh I ought to have gone: it will be so desolate here all day without you. He blushed like a silly little child & said "That it go up stairs & it will find a battledore & shuttlecock to console it." I laughed & thought we should certainly never cease to be young. We may wear out a body: it may get worn and hard, but the look of the infant will pierce through the old disguise, & so on ad infinitum. Today he said "What, are you here. I knocked at your door for you to go with me, & as you did not answer I thought you were asleep". I made some answer on the impulse of the moment that I was sorry I was not with him, perhaps this displeased E. or something that I said next day, but he seemed unwilling even to look at me for two or three days & at last I wrote him a note which he answered in these verses.

1842 JOURNAL 679

They made me weep, for they show such a sense of how it really is with me, a tender feeling which few have had the perception to yield me. In the afternoon, E. H. came to see me, and made me late with my walk. When I did go I found Ellery in the wood, walking lightly, & with a sweet smile on his lips, as one upborne by pleasant fancies, & striking his cane against every little thing, which shows electricity at the fingers' ends.—He joined me and told me that he had got a "capital" letter from Caroline, told me many things in it, & that she wanted him so much to come to Naushon. He wanted my advice whether to go, & if he did *how* to go, for it must be at once as Ellen might be here the middle of next week.—He said he had never done any thing for C., never come when she wished him to, and he thought he had a duty to her, & now was his last chance, for he did not expect to be able to see her & Ellen together, & "when I am once united to E. again, I shall never be separated from her." "She is the flower of my life. I must keep her at my side", said he with a smile of even angelic tenderness. He showed a clearness as to his relations with the two that satisfied and surprised me, nor do I now think he will ever *regret* his choice.—I felt that the meeting would be the greatest satisfaction both to him & C. & was entirely in favor of his going, & he did go next morn g. But I expected him back on Tuesday, for he said nothing should induce him to stay later as E. might arrive on Wednesday.

—

Friday. A day of black rain again and I am made exceedingly anxious by letters which make me almost sure that Ellen will come to night & Ellery not returned. Every day since Tuesday I have been more anxious lest some ill has happened to him, & besides, if he is well & safe. I think if Ellen arrives & finds him absent on such an errand, when she has come all this way to him alone, & he ought to be ready to receive her, it will deal a death blow to their peace. I wrote to N. B. & Boston to get news of him, then tried to turn my mind to other things. I could not go on with my own work, so wrote little piece on Tennyson for the Dial, & then sketch of Mr Alcott at Waldo's request. His own is excellent, though it requires, I think, mine and Carlyle's & a dozen others to balance it.

After. Waldo came into my room to read me what he has written in his journal about marriage, & we had a long talk. He listens with a soft wistful look to what I say, but is nowise convinced. It was late in a dark afternoon, the fine light in that red room always so rich, cast a beautiful light upon him, as he read and talked. *Since* I have found in his journal two sentences that represent the two sides of his thought.

In time

"Marriage should be a covenant to secure to either party the sweetness and the handsomeness of being a calm continuing inevitable benefactor to the other."

In eternity

"Is it not enough that souls should meet in a law, in a thought, obey the same love, demonstrate the same idea. These alone are the nuptials of minds.

I marry you for better, not for worse, I marry impersonally."

I shall write to him about it.

At night Mamma & Lidian came down too & sat in my room. I was no longer engrossed in writing & talk, & my anxiety increased as the hour for the stage was approaching lest Ellen should arrive unaccompanied by Ellery. W. declared it was impossible to happen, but I saw well enough he was as anxious as I.

At last the stage stopped in a violent rain. W. went to the door & sure enough it was my poor little prodigal. "Is Mr Channing here" "No, but Margaret is" & in he brought her.

I thought I should faint, but recovered myself directly. I did not wish to frighten her & I did not let her know where Ellery was gone. She behaved sweetly, though so disappointed at not finding him. I saw at once that she was less selfish than formerly.

Waldo was now distressed *for me*: he called me out, & offered to go down to Boston this very evening, & bring me back news if I would. But I would not let him & then he said he should go in the morning early. I shall never forget the tender sympathy he showed me at this time. We talked sometime & when I came back I found I had left Ellen too long alone. She felt as if E. must be ill, & she had better go to him in B. next morning. "He may not be there" said I. "Why, he must," says she "where else could he be?" I made no reply—how people can ever bear the task of dissembling or concealing I cant think, one minute of it is so painful.

I passed a wretched night, yet was much entertained, for she talked all through the night & I wanted to hear about what she had to say. In the middle of the night she got up unpacked her trunk to get it & set E's picture (an ugly thing that I should not think she would value) on the mantelpiece that she might see it. Then an hour or two after she said "M. are you asleep," "No"—"I hope you will like Ellery so that he may enjoy being with you: he needs the stimulus of such minds. He values Cary's very much: he reads her letters a great deal: Do you know whether he has seen her?"—I believe, he has, said I, & I *thought* "poor deluded innocent"—Then I thought over all these relations once more, but I still came to the same result that I always do. If I were Waldo's wife, or Ellery's wife, I should acquiesce in all these relations, since they needed them. I should expect the same feeling from my husband, & I should think it little in him not to have it. I felt I should never repent of advising Ellery to go whatever happened. Well, he came back next day, and All's Well that Ends Well. It was I that suppose always thought that he & others will surely do as they intend, & that's a great mistake.

Mamma & Lidian sympathized with me almost with tears, Waldo looked radiant, & H. T. as if his tribe had won a victory. Well it was a pretty play, since it turned out no tragedy at last. Ellery told Ellen at once how it was, and she took it just as she ought.

This day H. Hedge passed with us, and in the afternoon I went with him to Cambridge. I did not enjoy seeing him while we were at Concord. Seeing him & S. Ward with Waldo, I understand why he should always suspect them of being mere men of the world and men of talent: they are so with him; he sits with his lovely courteous *un*confiding smile and *sees* them merely, & they are seen not known. But the moment I am alone with either it is another thing. H's manner so glassy and elaborate before, full of soul, the tones of his voice entirely different. We had an excellent talk on all the great themes before men at this present. H. emphasizes the Church & the Race as William does. I see that side, but care more for the other. What is done here at home in my heart is my religion. I said to H. I see not one step before me, and my only act is to live to day, and not hasten to conclusions. Let others choose their way, I feel that mine is to keep my equipoise as steadfastly as I may, to see, to think, a faithful sceptic, to reject nothing but accept nothing till it is affirmed in the due order of mine own nature. I belong nowhere. I have pledged myself to nothing. God and the soul and nature are all my creed, subdivisions are unimportant.—As to your Church, I do not deny the church, who can that holds communion on themes of permanent interest as I do with several minds. I have my church where I am by turns priest & lay man. I take these simpler modes, if the world prefers more complex, let it. I act for myself, but prescribe for none other.

Cambridge & its people seemed very strange this eve g after the ideal, the true community life at Concord.—With William, with Sarah Clarke, I am in church, with Waldo and Ellery in community.

Next morn g wrote a letter to Mother & saw the boys then H. came for me. An eagle had perched on the vane of Mr Newell's church, & we found the whole town *standing* under this unaccustomed minister. The bird of the Sun kept majestically still, he had been stationed there to be stared at for more than an hour, only now and then opening a wing. Will the prim little parson dare to hold forth beneath such auspices?

At Brookline I listened with curiosity to H's sermons. In fact it is not more wonderful for a disciple of Hegel to preach, than for a Buddhist to feel gratitude. They were written with high finish: their mechanism excellent. The doctrine was good; the one, to encourage the good in oneself, rather than make a fuss about the evil, the other I must tread the winepress alone, true, but touched so slightly on what I know and feel.

Dined at Judge Jackson's. If it were possible to decide what insanity is, I should say my dear Marianne is slightly so. Perhaps it will never increase. Susan's face is all sunk in the eyes. The woman is merged in the mother, beautiful, yet it pleases me not. Be the more a woman for being a mother. It is a queenly child she has got. I could not look at it enough! the majesty of its gesture and gaze are imposing. Little Edith is unborn as yet compared with this child. An admirable physique: each of her motions was an encouragement. I was deeply interested in seeing

1842 JOURNAL 683

the idiot boy. I see Bulwer, Miss Martineau & Shakespeare are truer to nature than I would have supposed. The moon is his God: every tale of this kind recals the Thessalian fable. It was a sweet picture, the saintly sister singing hymns while his hands were clasped on his breast in ecstacy.

At Waltham were good talk. The inspiration of the individual need not be sacrificed in favor of that of the race. We can just as well have both.

Oh I am tired of this journal: it is a silly piece of work. I will never keep another such. Write thoughts, the sum of all this life, or turn it into poetic form: this meagre outline of fact has no value in any way:

I gave the aftn & eve g to Lidian: she read to me of little Waldo and talked well.

She said the Angels look on what you do, perhaps with as much disdain as you and Waldo would on Mrs. Hemans. Whatever has spoken to us of one human heart has a right to exist.

I confess, I replied, but ever, ever we are striving to the more excellent. Forgive if we are narrow and cold on the way. Yet should we mend.

When we found snakes the other day, Ellery said they were the criticism of the universe, handsome, easy in motion, cold and odious.

He said Mr E. is quite wrong about books: He wants them all good, now I want many bad. Literature is not merely a collection of gems, but a great system of interpretation.

This hangs well together with L's idea. When she read me W's answer to my questions, & said when he would not answer so as to meet her wants, she thought Christ would if he were there. I told her yet just so did Christ answer *his* disciples again and again Feed my lambs & nothing more, no explanations, no going out of himself to meet their wants. Both she and Mamma were struck by this, but L. will not remember it.

I gave her a poem the other night, in answer to a good deal of this talk, of which here is a copy.

Nothing makes me so anti-Christian, & so anti-marriage as these talks with L. She lays such undue stress on the office of Jesus, & the demands of the heart.

Waldo had got through with his tedious prose, & to day he got into the mood to finish his poem. Just at night he came into the red room to read the passage he had inserted. This is to me the loveliest way to live that we have. I wish it would be so always that I could live in the red room, & Waldo be stimulated by the fine days to write poems & come the rainy days to read them to me. My time to go to him is late in the evening. Then I go knock at the library door, & we have our long word walk through the growths of things with glimmers of light from the causes of things. Afterward, W. goes out & walks beneath the stars to compose himself for his pillow, & I open the window, & sit in the great red chair to watch them. The only thing I hate is our dining together. It is never pleasant and some days I dislike it so that I go out just before dinner & stay till night in the woods, just to break the routine. I do not think a person of more complete character would feel or make the *dinner* bell such a vulgarity as W. does, but with him these feelings are inevitable.

He has put more of himself into Saadi and the other poem Masque than in any thing he has written before.

On "yet it doth not seem to me
      That the high gods love tragedy"
His voice was beautiful.

He seems indeed to have entirely dismissed the other province. Whenever in his journal he speaks of his peculiar character & limitations he has written in the margin "*Accept*", and Saadi is one acceptance throughout.

Late in the eve g, he came in again, to read me some lines he had been adding. When he had done he asked me how I got such a cold. I could not but laugh then to see that grief was the *last* thing Saadi ever thought of, and I told him Lidian had been making me cry. "What" said he "my boy"? I told him afterward how I was affected for I did not wish him to think it was all for the child's sake, but I dont know that I did well for Saadi the joygiver walked in deep shadow for one or two days after.

—

Sunday. All this morning I spent in reading W's journals for the last year, or rather in finishing them, for I have had them by me for weeks. This afternoon I meant to have gone into the woods and finished Ellery's book, but I went into the library after dinner & staid till night: it was our last talk and my best. We talked over many things in the journal, especially a good lead was given by "Sickness is generally the coat in which genius is drest," an unusual remark for W.—We talked too of Bulwer & the people of talent,—W grows more merciful day by day. I ought to go away now these last days I have been fairly intoxicated with his mind. I am not in full possession of my own. I feel faint in the presence of too strong a fragrance. I think, too, he will be glad to get rid of me. Elizth asked if he would not be sad when I was gone. I told her, no, relieved rather,—for all the things he says in his Essays on these subjects are true of himself. I took tea with Ellen & Ellery & then went in to see E. H. Waldo came for me, but Ellery came down to my room afterward, & E.H. rose betimes next morning and came down to breakfast with us. Mamma and Lidian went to Boston with me. Farewell, dearest friend, there has been dissonance between us, & may be again, for we do not fully meet, and to me you are too much & too little by turns, yet thanks be to the Parent of Souls, that gave us to be born into the same age and the same country and to meet with so much of nobleness and sweetness as we do, & I think constantly with more and more.

Going down I had a thorough talk with Lidian. I shall never trouble myself any more: it is not just to her. But I will do more in attending to her, for I see I could be of real use. She says she feels I am always just to her, but I might be more.

from October 1842 Journal

Monday the anniversary of Sam's marriage. I know not yet what to think of this event which dawned so poetically on me. From it the music has not flowed that I expected, nor is my own mind now in harmony with those that seemed so fatally bound to it, yet that heart of love which beat then could not err, only we must grow wiser every day, else the true will become false.

—

entirely to Mr. Green's care to look over his prints &c the whole eveg in peace. I like to look at things with him; he cares for a great deal which I do not value, and looks at details much more than I do, (perhaps, because he understands them so much better,) but all his thoughts and feelings are genuine, he never speaks he knows not what, and understands when to be silent.—

A series of heads of distinguished French people in and after the Revolution interested me much & I wished I could have them to look at while rereading Carlyle's book—

Many things interested me at the time which are not worth writing about, but nothing fixed my attention so much, as a large engraving of Me Recamier in her boudoir. I have so often thought over the intimacy between her and Me de Stael. It is so true that a woman may be in love with a woman, and a man with a man. It is so pleasant to be sure of it because undoubtedly it is the same love that we shall feel when we are angels when we ascend to the only fit place for the Mignon's where

Sie fragen nicht nach Mann und Weib—

It is regulated by the same law as that of love between persons of different sexes, only it is purely intellectual and spiritual, unprofaned by any mixture of lower instincts, undisturbed by any need of consulting temporal interests, its law is the desire of the spirit to realize a whole which makes it seek in another being for what it finds not in itself. Thus the beautiful seeks

OCTOBER 1842 JOURNAL 687

the strong, and the strong the beautiful, the mute seek the eloquent &c the butterfly settles always on the dark flower. Why did Socrates love Alcibiades?—why did Korner love Schneider? how natural is the love of Wallenstein for Max, that of Me de Stael for de Recamier, mine for Anna Barker. I loved Anna for a time I think with as much passion as I was then strong enough to feel—Her face was always gleaming before me, her voice was echoing in my ear, all poetic thoughts clustered round the dear image. This love was a key which unlocked for me many a treasure which I still possess, it was the carbuncle (emblematic gem) which cast light into many of the darkest caverns of human nature.—She loved me, too, though not so much, because her nature was "less high, less grave, less large, less deep" but she loved more tenderly, less passionately. She loved me, for I well remember her suffering when she first would feel my faults and knew one part of the exquisite veil rent away, how she wished to stay apart and weep the whole day. Then again that night when she leaned on me and her eyes were such a deep violet blue, so like night, as they never were before, and we both felt such a strange mystic thrill and knew what we had never known before. Now well too can I now account for that desire which I often had to get away from her and be alone with nature, which displeased her so, for she wished to be with me all the time. I do not love her now with passion, for I have exhausted her idea, and she does not stimulate my fancy, she does not represent the Beautiful to me now, she is only one beautiful object. Then she has never had a chance to get a hold on my heart by the thousand links of intimacy, we have been so little together; all was from the elective affinities. But still I love her with a sort of pallid, tender romance and feel towards her as I can to no other woman. I thought of all this as I looked at Me Recamier and had one thought beside which has often come into my mind, but I will not write it down; it is so singular that I have often thought I would never express it in any way; I am sure no human being but myself would understand it—

Me Recamier is half-reclining on a sofa. She is draped in white drapery which clings very gracefully to her round but elegantly slender form, her beautiful neck and arms are bare, her hair knotted up so as to show the contour of her truly feminine head to great advantage. A book lies carelessly on her lap, one hand yet holds it at the place where she left off, her lovely face is turned towards us; she appears to muse on what she has been reading. It seems when you see a woman in a picture with a book, that she is doing exactly that for which she was born. The book gives such an expression of purity to the female figure. A large window partially veiled by a white curtain gives a view, of a city, at some little distance, on one side stand the harp and piano;—there are just books enough for a lady's boudoir— There is no picture except one of De Recamier herself as De Stael Corinne; this is absurd, but the absurdity is interesting as recalling the connexion. You imagine her to have been reading one of De Stael's books and to be now pondering what those brilliant words of her gifted friend, which so electrify her, can mean. Every thing in the room is in keeping; nothing appears to have been put there because other people have it; but there is nothing which shows a taste more noble and refined than you would expect from the fair Frenchwoman; all is elegant, modern, in harmony with the delicate habits and superficial culture which you would look for in its occupant.—

Note two delightful moonlight walks round the cove the evegs of 9th and fifth of April. The hour was the same in both (eleven p.m.), but the two pictures presented by the basin entirely different owing to the change in the position of the moon.

—

Sam was away, and I slept with Anna the first time for two years. It was exquisitely painful to feel that I loved her less than when we before were thus together in confiding sleep, and she too is now so graceful and lovely, but the secret of my life is sealed to her forever. I never speak of the inmost experience, but listen to her graceful talk. I took pleasure in sleeping on Sam's pillow and before closing my eyes solicited that visions like his might come to me but I had a frightful dream of being imprisoned in a ship at sea, the waves all dashing round, and knowing that the crew had resolved to throw me in. While in horrible suspense, many persons that I knew came on board. At first they seemed delighted to see me & wished to talk but when I let them know my danger, & intimated a hope that they might save me, with

OCTOBER 1842 JOURNAL 689

cold courtliness glided away. Oh it was horrible these averted faces and well dressed figures turning from me, from captive, with the cold wave rushing up into which I was to be thrown.

We breakfasted in the little room S. has fitted up for a study. I am glad he has done this at last & he has good ones too.

Little Anna is quite sweet just now; she has been ill, is very pale & her eyes look large and melancholy.

We went to hear James; after the sermon a vote was put up for Latimer the Slave, now in prison, and James's few words of remark and little prayer were so just, simple, and in so wise and true a tone, as drew tears from many eyes, mine for instance. I felt at the time so rich, so free, and blest to know how to pray for the unfortunate.

James & Sarah came to see us this afternoon. Anna walked over the bridge with me; it was a mellow pensive sunset, I like this bridge as much as ever, sights from it have been to me the parents of infinite suggestion and still the distant line seems worthy to engirdle a little world of love and thought and goodness.

A letter from Concord tonight. 30th Octr, little Waldo's birthday he says.

from *Journal Fragments*

c. 1840, 1844

———————————

Feb 26th

I. B. at last meeting
Some one quoted this saying,

Woman has a cell less in the brain and a chord more in the heart (than man).

I did not like this because of the attempt at finery and epigrammatic, therefore false as crack sayings are wont to be, and yet again I do like it as expressing that the distinction of sex lies not in opposition but in distribution and proportion of attributes. Whether this dualism will always continue I know not but at present we cannot conceive of active happiness without it. To find oneself in another nature, likeness and unlikeness, Sun acting on the earth are conjugal,—sun and moon fraternal.

In savage life we see that what we suppose to be the true relation is not preserved, Woman does not adorn and sanctify life, she drudges and serves.

But the true relation would seem to be that expressed in Schiller's Bell. In childhood they learn together and not unequally while merely putting forth antennae and gathering food. The time for action arrives—the youth rushes out into a wider sphere to discipline the powers which are by and by to make his circlet a representation of the universe. The maiden stays at home and tends the rose tree (ie cultivates beauty) and in the domestic sphere prepares herself for the succession of petty efforts which are the destiny of woman.

I have no objection to a succession of petty efforts instead of a few great deeds, if all harmonized by law, if each be really a line or stanza of a poem.

Woman as woman is deficient in concentration, but I see no reason why she should not improve in this respect. Her instinctive nature, her life of love, her sensitive organization— all seem to make it impossible she should concentrate too much.

JOURNAL FRAGMENTS

Let her then cultivate it as far as she may,—There can be no firm self-trust without it, and as the poet is by nature equally deficient in it why should it hurt woman as woman, more than poet as poet.

Let woman think of herself as soul still more than as woman and with a general conformity to her lot in indifferent particulars, never dare stifle what God has given.

Yet I love each mode of existence in its own place and with all my allowance for the infinite gradations on this scale am conscious of a movement of aversion, when a voice too soft, a gesture too pliant, in look too fluid is seen in man or a gesture too large, a glance too determined, a voice too sonorous in woman. Yet are there moments in the life of each when it seems legitimate to assume the character of the other.

Are they not, as notes of music are,
Made for each other though dissimilar
&c

He momently grows mild
While she assumes a bolder gait
To wander at his side.

Such is the mutual influence,

Man more	Woman more
Genius	Taste
Active Will	passive Will
Determined purpose	delicacy of rejection
Versatile Energy	power of adaptation
He collects	She arranges
He strikes out new materials	She harmonizes them for him
He has the strife	She is the aim
He more for Truth & power	She for Beauty & Love.

Yet is it more & less all through, I see no attribute exclusively feminine.

I confess myself quite unable to account for no woman having been able to produce a great work of art. In woman

692   JOURNALS

Speak of Goethe's remarks here.

generally I see habits of life, a sensitiveness to the impression of every hour, a want of tenacity of fibre which account for it, beside that the natural history of the sex is that at the period when men begin to be artists, they begin to be mothers, an engrossing and still more disturbing profession. But I see and have read of so many in female form who are not women in character, and whose efforts were no wise checked that it does seem unaccountable that the annals of the sex do not produce a single instance of the purely objective existence of the artist.

Women could be queens captains, learned, for all these are comparatively social, but they

—

c. May 1844

therefore the thought of God is torpid within me.

I can see no way, nor no hope that this story can ever be made beautiful to me, that I can ever be wholly reconciled with the Past. I have got to go on, as resolutely as I can, and perhaps I shall be helped.

I have not been able to pray, dost thou, my friend, pray for me. Oh, if I were sure thou didst really love me, that it would be permanent, I could find solace with thee but now——

In the chamber of death I prayed, in very early years. Give me truth. Cheat me on by no illusion. Oh the granting of this prayer is sometimes terrible to me. I walk over the burning ploughshares, and they *do* sear my feet.

Yet nothing but truth will do, no love that is not eternal, and as large as the universe, no philanthropy in executing whose behests. I myself became unhealthy, no creative genius which bursts asunder my life to leave it a poor black chrysalid behind.

And yet this last is too true of my life.

O it is wonderful to look back and see how, with *such* an aspiration as I have always had, my outward form has been blighted, and distorted, my mental powers impeded, my soul steeped in anguish. Fate thou art *all but* omnipotent. Thou art not that. I must, shall conquer, though now I feel so weary, and so sad, I have not a right to say I will.

JOURNAL FRAGMENTS 693

With the intellect I always have always shall overcome, but that is not the half of the work. The life, the life Oh, my God! shall the life *never* be sweet!

Apropos to the little sketch W found at the Mill *1ˢᵗ April* of the youth and maiden reading together, and which he has put into his journal I added these lines,

> When leaves were falling thickly in the pale November day,
> A bird dropt here this feather upon her pensive way;
> Another bird has found it in the chill snowy April day.
> It brings to him the music of all her summer's lay:
> Thus sweet birds, though unmated, do never sing in vain,
> The lovely notes they utter to free them from their pain,
> Caught up by the echoes, ring through the blue dome,
> And, by good spirits guided, pierce to some gentle home.
> The pencil moved prophetic together now they read
> In the fair book of Nature and find the hope they need.
> The wreath woven by the river is by the seaside worn
> And one of fate's best arrows to its due mark is borne.

M. F.

29ᵗʰ May, 1844.

—

I have seen several fair and noble beings.

I have fully prized the treasures of each, but none was for me. I sat in

the anguish of Tantalus,
Now I will wait!
Yet how natural the desire
Let me gather from the Earth, one full-grown, fragrant flower
Let it bloom within my bosom, through its one blooming hour
Let it die within my bosom, and to its parting breath
Mine shall answer, *having lived*, I shrink not now from Death.
It is this niggard halfness that turns my heart to stone
Tis the cup seen not tasted that makes the infant moan.
Let me for once press firm my lips upon the Moment's brow
Let me for once distinctly feel *I am all happy now.*
And bliss shall seal a blessing upon that moment's brow.

But the heart must have the soul's full free, unfaltering assent to this draught, else the asp lurks at the bottom of the cup.

694 JOURNALS

—

Today Sunday 3ᵈ Jun. I write the following.

To the Apollo on my pin

I thank the hand which gave this gift to me,
The Delphian image of my destiny.

Tis not the Sun-God, radiantly calm,
Whose tameless wheels over this worldlet run
Calling to life the poison as the balm,
White birds to worship, wily snakes to shun.

'Tis not the Pythian with shaft just sped,
Avenging sunbeam from that spotless fire,
Form of stern loveliness, a beauteous dread,
The sounding bow more than the sounding lyre.

It is the Shepherd Singer heavenly sweet,
At sight of whom mild flocks and rustic men
Left their green pastures when his snowy feet
Turned rather downward through the rocky glen
To where the beach with ocean wild & wide
A larger consciousness of life supplied.

It is the Shepherd Singer heavenly sad,
Who vainly loved so many lovely forms
They answered not, or answering fell mad,
And whitest halcyons boded darkest storms
Imprisoning bark doth fondest bosom wrong,
And naught is left the Singer but his song.

It is enough, melodiously sad!
More than enough, harmoniously glad!

Earth strings the lyre, but not from earth alone
Find'st thou vibration for its faintest tone.
Love filled the eye, but when beheld too near,
We lose the diamond lustre of the tear.
When into Genius, Love flows back again
One lyric flame from breasts of many men
We see the Son back to his home aspire

The Delphian baptized in his own life's fire,
Thus the Anointed pleases well his Sire
Soul poem for the Universal Lyre.

———

Monday June 10th.
This day last year we reached Chicago, between eight and nine
in the evening, and all the scenes of that day have been floating
before my mind amid the trifles of this.

Henry Hedge has been here tonight—Repeating to me his
poem of the Crucifix. It has beauty of form, but no depth in
the spirit.

Virgin Mother, Mary mild!
It was thine to see the child
    Gift of the Messiah dove,
Pure blossom of idea love,
    Break, upon the "guilty cross",
The seeming promise of his life:
    Of faith, of hope, of love a loss
Deepened all thy bosom's strife
    Brow down-bent and heart-strings torn.
Fainting, by frail arms upborne.

———

But tis mine, oh Mary mild,
To tremble lest the heavenly child
    Crucified within my heart
    Ere of earth he take his part
Leave my life that horror wild
    The Mother who has slain her child.
Let me to the tomb repair,
    Find the angel watching there,
Ask his aid to walk again
    Undefiled with brother men.

Once my heart within me burned
At the least whisper of thy voice:
    Though my love was unreturned,
    Happy in a holy choice;
    Once my lamp was constant trimmed
    And my fond resolve undimmed.

> Fan again the Parsee fire,
> Let it light my funeral pyre,
> Purify the veins of earth
> Temper for a phoenix birth.

God, thou knowest what I mean. Lead me through the labyrinth till I face the monster whose presence I feel in the secret depths. May I neither slay nor be slain, but return to the light an instructed being, able to meet this solemn Future.

—

17th. Ellery here & that strange woman she of the Sperit of whom I know not decisively what to think.

Obliged to spend morng in arrangements. Mother went to Beverly at one. I do hope she will get pleasure & health.

A most entertaining letter from Arthur. He had been in the thick of Mormonism at Nauvoo. Been much with Lady Emma & Smith's mother & children, & at the meeting where they cried Coronach for his death.

Some headach still, but this aftn & evening got afloat in my writing.

Saw the moon for first time in an exquisite sunset sky, but over my left shoulder, & was superstitious eno to be disturbed thereby.

> O waxing moon
> Shed influence mild
> Loved August moon
> Grieve not thy child.
>
> I must perforce follow thee
> Demon of my nativity,
> But oh, succor me,
> Angel of my futurity
>
> My Genius, hover near
> Drive away these thoughts of fear.
> If I indeed be all alone
> Cherish the more thy daughter lone
> Make the woman all thy own.

Is some fate leading to donzella lagune I am laying a plan as if I had never had that thought.

JOURNAL FRAGMENTS

Let the man defend
Till this strife and dark doubt end.

Make me purer
Stronger surer—

O let not deadly fear
Creep so very near.
Centipede and scorpion
So near thy daughter's pillow lone
Send thy dove to brood
Over her shadowy solitude

There must be Love
Below around above
Let the great mind
Untiring rush to find
Steadfast stand to bind,
Till the soft heart the needed peace may find.

from Manuscript Tracing Journal
1844

Tuesday 2^d July. Sarah returned from town with the news that in consequence of their bad preperation of her plate for the etchings all her labor for these last ten days is lost.

She sat down directly to draw again.

This morning in giving S. Raphael's Descent from the Cross I gave her a little poem descriptive of it. The Invocation to the Virgin with which it begins is the same with that of one in my last vol. of journal but there it turns to penitential psalm for me, here to interpretation.

> Virgin Mother Mary mild:
> It was thine to see the child
>   Gift of the Messiah dove,
> Pure blossom of ideal love,
>   Break, upon the guilty cross
> The seeming promise of his life!
>   Of faith, of hope, of love a loss
> Deepened all thy bosom's strife
>   Brow down beat and heart strings torn.
> Fainting, by frail arms upborne,
>
>   All those startled figures show
> That they did not apprehend
>   The thought of him who there lies low.
>   On whom those sorrowing eyes they bent:
> They do not feel this holiest hour,
>   Their hearts soar not to read the power
> Which this deepest of distress
>   Alone could give to save and bless.
>
>   Soul of that fair, now ruined form
> Thou who hadst force to bide the storm,
>   Must again descend to tell
> Of thy life the hidden spell.
>   Though their hearts within them burned,
> The flame rose not till he returned

> Just so all our dead ones lie,
> Just so call our thoughts on high,
> Thus we linger on the earth,
> and dully miss death's heavenly birth.

I went in aft^n to Mt Auburn with the second vol of the Countess of Rudolstadt. It is not good, except in a few passages. Sand shines only in the analysis of the passions and a noble freedom of character, she is but green in the mysteries of high philosophy & shows the grisette when she tries to write of Jacob Behmen.

I had not much of a time in the garden of groves, & was interrupted by two gallant gentlemen in the best hour; however, one feels better out in the breeze & seeing the "sege Gipfel" of the trees and better for having been out.

—

July 4th.

I wrote a letter to Cary & carried it with some others to the office but it was shut. I was disappointed, I hoped I might find one there that would do me good.

O I need some help. No I need a full a godlike embrace from some sufficient love. I know not why, but the wound of my heart has reopened yesterday & today. My head aches.

Last year this day was the Ganymede day. The full music of soul amid that resplendent beauty of nature. I remember every one of the golden sands of that day. All its pictures of supernatural loveliness pass before my eyes.

Here all looks so mean! The air is cold, hostile, the color sharp & painful as always in these cold summer days.

I read Tennyson a little while this morning. I love him, I will write to him this evening.

I have been writing about the horse but not well. This is not one of my muse times of energy. Needs more joy, or sorrow, for that dull, haunting pain don't suit my constitution.

Sometime I shall write again about this & give it another turn.

Meanwhile

> On the boundless plain careering
> By an unseen compass steering

Wildly flying, re-appearing.
With untamed fire their broad eyes glowing
    In every step a grand pride showing,
Of no servile moment knowing,
    Happy as the trees & flowers
In their instinct-cradled hours,
    Happier in fuller powers,
    See the wild horse nobly ranging
Nature varying not changing
    Lawful in their lawless ranging.
    But hark, what boding crouches near?
On the horizon now appear
    Centaur forms of force & fear.
    On their enslaved brethren borne
With bit & whip of tyrant scorn,
    To make new captives as forlorn.
    Wildly snort the astonished throng
Stamp & wheel & fly along
    Those Centaur powers they know are strong.
    But the lasso, skilful cast,
Holds one only captive fast
    Youngest weakest left the last,
    How thou trembled then, Konic!
Thy full breath came short & thick,
    Thy heart to bursting beat so quick;
    Thy strange brethren peering round,
By those tyrants held & bound,
    Tyrants fell whom falls confound;
    With rage & pity fill thy heart
Death shall be thy chosen part
    Ere such slavery tame thy heart.
    But—strange unexpected joy!
They seem to mean him no annoy
    Gallop off, both man & boy.
    Let the wild horse freely go,—
Almost he shames it should be so,
    So lightly prized himself to know.
    All delusion 'tis, O steed!
Never again, upon the mead
    Shalt thou a free wild horse feed.
    The mark of man doth blot thy side
The fear of man hath dulled thy pride
    Thy master soon shall on thee ride.

Thy brethren of the free plain,
Joyful speeding back again
  With proud career & flowing mane,
Find thee branded, left alone,
  And their hearts are turned to stone,
  They keep thee in their midst alone.
Cruel the intervening years,
  Seeming freedom stained by fears,
  Till the captor re-appears;
Finds thee with thy broken pride;
  Amid thy peers still left aside,
  Unbeloved & unallied;
Finds thee ready for thy fate;
  For joy & hope 'tis all too late,
  Thou'rt wedded to the sad estate.

Wouldst have the princely spirit bowed
  Whisper only, speak not loud,
  Mark & leave him in the crowd:
Thou need'st not spies nor jailors have,
  The free will serve thee like the slave,
  Coward shrinking from the brave;
And thy cohorts, when they come
  To take the weary captive home
  Need only beat the retreating drum.

To herself.
Sometime, on a fairer plain
May these captives live again.
Where no tyrant stigmas stain,

Marriage will then have broke the rod,
Where wicked foot has never trod
  The verdure sacred to a God.

To the captive, not utterly forsaken,
only, Konnick, that noble heart,
To the dark predestined part
  Its own temper must impart.

Move as nobly, centaur-driven
As when, ungiving and ungiven,
Thou didst greet thy native heaven.

JOURNALS

> To the trumpet cry ha-ha!
> Scent the battle field afar
> Thy day dawns from that bloody war.
>
> Day of hope, as day of doom,
> opening realms where will be soon
> For all to live and need no tomb.

5 o'clock. How the day fleets, I have let Abby go to town to be Independent till ten, & there is not a disturbing sound. Sweet is the unbroken loneliness. I seem nearer home than usual.

At my window looking out on the river the world seems beautiful, yet oh! so full of dust & bustle. The river smiles sweetly mildly.

Now I have been able to write out the piece to Sarah, though it is not good as the subject demands, but I can never tell whether my thought will weave her robe of linsey woolsey or satin. We must take what the hour gives, so here—

To Sarah

> Our friend has likened thee to the sweet fern,
> Which with no flower salutes the ardent day,
> Yet, as the wanderer pursues his way
> While the dews fall, & hues of sunset burn,
> Sheds forth a fragrance from the deep green brake
> Sweeter than the rich scents that gardens make.
>
> ---
>
> Like thee, the fern loves well the hallowed shade
> Of trees that quietly aspire on high,
>   Amid such groves was consecration made
> Of vestals tranquil as the vestal sky:
>   Like thee, the fern doth better love to hide
> Beneath the leaf the treasure of its seed
>   Than to display it, with an idle pride,
> To any but the careful gatherer's heed;
>   A treasure known to philosophic ken,
>   Garnered in nature, asking nought of men:
> Nay! can invisible the wearer make
> Who would, unnoted, in life's game partake.

But I will liken thee to the sweet bay,
  Which I first learned in the Cohasset woods
To name upon a sweet, though pensive day
  Passed in their ministering solitudes.
I had grown weary of the anthem high
  Of the full wave cheering the patient rocks,
I had grown weary of the sob & sigh
  Of the dull ebb after emotion's shocks;
My eye was weary of the glittering blue
  And the unbroken horizontal line,
My mind was weary, tempted to pursue
  The circling waters in their wide design;
Like snowy sea-gulls, stooping to the wave,
  Or, rising buoyant to the utmost air,
To dart, to circle, airily to lave,
  Or wave-like, float in foam-born lightness fair;
I had swept onward like the wave so full,
Like sea-weed, now, left on the shore so dull.

  I turned my steps to the retreating hills,
Rejected sand from that great haughty sea,
  Watered by nature with consoling rills
And gradual drest with grass, & shrub, & tree;
  They seemed to welcome me with timid smile
That said, "We'd like to soothe you for awhile.
You seem to have been treated by the sea
In the same way that long ago were we."

They had not much to boast, those gentle slopes;
  For the wild gambols of the sea-sent breeze
Had mocked at many of their quiet hopes
  And bent & dwarfed their fondly cherished trees;
Yet even in these marks of bypast wind
There was a tender stilling for my mind.
  Hiding within a small but thickset wood,
  I soon forgot the haughty chiding flood;
  The sheep bell's tinkle on the drowsy ear
  With the bird's chirp, so short, & light, & clear,
  Composed a melody that filled my heart
  With flower-like growths of childish artless art
And of the tender tranquil life I lived a part.

It was an hour of pure tranquillity
Like to the autumn sweetness of thine eye
　Which pries not, seeks not, & yet clearly sees,
Which woos not, beams not, yet is sure to please.

Hours passed, & sunset called me to return
Where its sad glories on the cold wave burn.
　Rising from my kind bed of thick-strown leaves
A fragrance the astonished sense receives
　Ambrosial, searching, yet untiring mild
Of that soft scene the soul was it, or child?
　'Twas the sweet bay I had unwitting spread
A pillow for my senseless throbbing head
　And which, like all the sweetest things, demands
To make it speak the grasp of alien hands.

　All that this scene did at that moment tell
I since have read, O wise mild friend, in thee;
　Pardon the rude grasp its sincerity,
And feel that I, at least, have known thee well;
　Grudge not the green leaves ravished from thy stem
　Their music should I live, muse-like, to tell,
Thou wilt, in fresher green forgetting them,
　Send others to console me for farewell.
Thou wilt see why the dim word of regret
Was made the one to rhyme with Margaret.

But to the Oriental parent tongue
　Sunrise of Nature, does my chosen name
My name of Leila, as a spell belong
　Teaching the meaning of each temporal blame.
I chose it by the sound, not knowing why,
　But, since I know that Leila stands for night,
I own that sable mantle of the sky
　Through which pierce, gem-like, points of distant light.
"As sorrow truths, so night brings out her stars."
(O add not, Bard, that "those stars shine too late")
While Earth grows green amid the ocean jars
And trumpets set shall wake the slain of her long century wars.

Leila in the Arabian zone
Dusky, languishing and lone
Yet full of light are her deep eyes
And her gales are lovers sighs

So in Egyptian clime
Grows an Isis calm sublime
   Blue black is her robe of night
   But blazoned o'er with points of light
   The horns that Io's brow deform
   With Isis take a crescent form
   And as a holy moon inform
The magic Sistrum arms her hand
   And at her deep eye's command
   Brutes are raised to thinking men
Soul growing, to her soul filled ken.

Dian of the lonely life
Hecate fed on gloom and strife.
   Phebe on her throne of air
   Only Leila's children are.

   Patient serpent, circle round
   Till in death thy life is found;
      Double form of godly prime
      Holding the whole thought of time,
      When the perfect two embrace,
      Male and female, black and white
      Soul is justified in space,
      Dark made fruitful by the light,
      And centred in the diamond Sun
      Time, eternity, are one.

Through brute nature, upward rising
Seed upstriving to the light,
   Revelations still surprizing
     Inwardness is grown insight.
     Still I slight not the first stages
Dark, but God-directed ages
   In my nature leonine
     Toiled and learned a soul divine,
    Put forth an aspect chaste, serene
    Nature's virgin mother queen
Assumes at last the destined wings
Earth and heaven together brings
   While her own form the riddle tells
That baffled all the wizard spells
Drawn from intellectual wells
Cold water where Truth never dwells
It was fable told you so
Seeks her in common daylight's glow.

          My seal ring:—
Mercury has cast aside
   The signs of intellectual pride,
Freely offers thee the soul,
   Art thou noble to receive?
Canst thou give or take the whole
   Nobly promise and believe?
Then those wholly human art
A spotless radiant ruby heart,
And the golden chain of love
Has bound thee to the realm above.
   If there be one small mean doubt
One serpent thought that fled not out
Take instead the serpent rod
Thou art neither man nor god;
Guard thee from the powers of evil
Who cannot trust vows to the Devil:
Walk thy slow and spell-bound way,
Keep on thy mask, or shun the day,
Let go my hand upon the way.

MANUSCRIPT TRACING JOURNAL 707

July Fourth 1844

Good night, Fourth July
I have kept you duly
Setting myself free
Even from thee, Amerikey.

  Just so, I trow, that wight,
  Julius Cesar hight,
  Who gave this month his name,
  Gold letters in a rich frame,
  Would have soared high above thee
  Levelling Amerikey,
  And built above a dome
  Such as crowned old Rome
  Full of conquered riches
  And adorned with hero niches
Too high to be reached by Irishmen in ditches.

Yet think not, Amerikey,
  I dont love humanity,
Nor value independence,
If it be fact and not pretence
  That you have such a thing:
I know you have no king,
  But have you noblemen?
  Or have you gentlemen?
  Far more, have you *Men*?—
No! why then, Amerikey,
  I pray you tell to me
  Why you make such a noise
  With rockets, guns, and boys!—
  All the use of earth,
  Is to god-men to give birth
  And if you cannot say
That you've done this, for shame, be still, I pray.

—

This has been a solemn sweet day. The first black rain we have
had, all the others have been bright light summer rains. I have
been ill, too, and in a way that always binds me deep in nature.
I am much earthy, yet sometimes my soul forgets the body a
great deal. At these times it is again born & swathed in body &

I feel a mysterious but not painful shudder, as I hold the golden
girdle for the next birth. The moon is waxing.—

> Lead, lunar ray:
> To the crossing of the way
> Where to secret rite
> Rises the armed Knight
> My champion for the fight.
>
> Fall heavier, still, sweet rain!
> Free from their pain
> Plants which still in earth
> Are prisoned back from birth
> Teach the sun their worth.
>
> Soul, long lie thus still,
> Cradled in the will.
> Which to this motley ball,
> Sphere so great, so small,
> Did thee call.
>
> ———
>
> Suns have shone on thee
> brooding thy mystery;
> Now this sweet rain
> Frees from the pain
> Of birth the golden grain.
>
> ———
>
> Yet within the nest
> Patience still were best
> Birds of my thought!
> Food shall be brought
> To you by mother thought.
>
> ———
>
> Let your wings grow strong
> For the way is long
> To the distant zone
> Where glows the throne
> Of your phenix king so lone.
>
> ———
>
> Nestle still, keep still,
> Cradled by the will
> Which must daily ye fill,
> If while callow, ye keep still.

from Italy 1849 Journal

Rome 1st Jany 1849

This year cannot fail to be rich in events most important for Italy, Europe, the world.

Rome has at last become the focus of the Italian revolution & I am here. I shall in this book make brief notes of the events of the day, to be filled out as journal at my leisure.

The Pope is still absent at Gaeta and in his absence the temporal power of the Papacy has recd the last blow. The *Constituente Romano* was proclaimed on Friday 29th Nov 1848. It will be followed by the *Costituente Italiana*, which ought in the natural order of things to constitute Italy one and one republic. There may be many breakers yet before that shore is reached, but it must finally be attained since no other can yield safety for the ship's crew. May the difficulties yet to be overcome lead to union and teach them the soberness of wisdom necessary to reconstruct.

I believe now that I have seen so much of Italy that the power of the priests must be entirely overthrown before any thing solid can be done for this people. But every thing tends to destroy their authority only as it has long been founded only on habit and not on illusion, an appeal to reason will not suffice.

A hundred discharges of artillery from the Castle St Angelo announced the *Constituente*. The next evening the Piazza del Popolo was illuminated, with lights all round (except on the Pincian) & a great fire in the piazza which sent up its beautiful tribute of sparks to the deepest black blue sky, the most thoughtful fair sky I ever saw in Italy from which hung the crescent moon. The orchestra was the platform of the obelisk; the lights of the musicians were reflected in the fountain. A fair scene. The people were very quiet & showed little feeling about the great step that had been taken. Also in the Corso were few lights except those of the Casinos, while they were so eager to illuminate last winter for every trifle. *Then* they understood better.

—

Eveg   tomorrow celebration of the Kings Magi coming to adore the infant of Bethlehem.

What mockery! Now if kings & priests knew that such a child was to be born, they would not go but send, not presents of gold & myrrh but assassins to stifle the child.

At midnight to the fair of St Eustachio, a pretty scene, well worth describing.

6th   Instead of the Pope comes from him an excommunication against those engaged in the movements of the 15th 16th Nov r and in the changes to which they have led and are leading *in somma* against the major part of Romans whether in this city or the provinces. I have not yet seen the document, but it is said to be worded in all the most foolish phrases of ancient superstition. The people received it with jeers, tore it at once from the walls and yesterday (Sunday) evening carried it in procession through the Corso wrapped round a candle's end, the only light of the procession, they ran along giggling and mumbling in imitation of priestly chants detachments occasionally digressing to throw copies into some privy. Such is the finale of St Peterdom!

Same eve g took a fair view of Piazza Navona, where is the church of the young Agnes, so powerful in her purity. Palazzo Doria, Palazzo Braschi! How strange it seems that the people has so long submitted to see a few men living in these superb edifices while they lived in putrid cellars or smoky cabins. O it is frightful that they have been able to bear it so many thousand years.

Entered to see the Marrionnettes. The farce was as anti-ecclesiastical as the Tartuffe of Molière and the audience laughingly echoed the ejaculations of the hypocrite "Pazienza" "O che mondo, che mondo" "O che secolo." The marrionnettes, unable to correspond exactly in their gestures to the words supposed to issue from their mouths were so ludicrous a picture of that large portion of beings in the human form, slaves of fashion and opinion.

An assembly has been held, a kind of electoral caucus, to contrive means.

8th   visited to day the Arch of Gallienas, the Trophies of Marius and the Temple of Minerva Medica. All near Ponta Mazzine as is also a fine fragment of aqueduct within the walls.

Have now finally seen the mandate of the Pope, it is not a formal excommunication, but an advise that all who take part in that "detestable" act of the Constitutional Assembly will be excommunicated.

It is the silliest document possible, an astonishment in this age.

Extract of a letter from Lago Maggiore.

"Also in this region is opened a collection in favor of Venice. All has been done by Sig^a Laura Mantegazzi di Canero. This generous woman, after having with such courage, with so much love and bounty snatched from death, cared and sustained the Legionaries of Garribaldi who call her the Angel of Luini and Marazzone, has taken upon herself the burden of making a giro around Lago Maggiore and through all the province of Novara for the benefit of the sublime beggar. She has made and continues it. Neither vigor of the season nor weakness of sex impede her, she knocks at the door of the poor, mounts the stair of the rich, despises the growlings of the retrograde, smiles at the rudeness of the ignorant, content always if she can only draw from each Italian the charity of 30 soldi per month. Nor has the pious desire been disappointed. Almost all gave the obol, many were beyond duty generous. She can already dispose of five thousand *lire italiane* per month. The Duke of Savoy gives 60 per month."

——

20th 21st The suffrages for C. A. have been given & all passed off peaceably. The first day Sunday they came in slowly each waiting to see what the other would do or unable like lazy Romans as they are to give up their usual lounge a festa day. Monday the votes came in plentifully disappointing the retrogrades who with their usual perspicacity seeing only what *is* at the moment, and never what is to be next moment had said there would not be an adequate number of votes to elect two reps.

Both eve gs they went to the Capitol which was illuminated, carrying the urns with civica banners music, torches, evvivas and all that sort of thing. Marcus Aurelius looks rather astonished & refuses to sustain the tri-color in his hand, it always drops & droops most pitifully.

News from France all reactionary Royalists hoping now to make Bonaparte unpopular & bring back the Duke of Bordeaux. Well may Considerant say the body politic, civilization has wounds so deep it seems impossible to cure them: they are always breaking out afresh.

—

31st It appears that Zucchi stands in arms at Ponte Cervo, what troops can be mustered are sent against him.

I went out towards Ponte Molle to meet the first detachment of the Legion that comes from Venice to protect Rome. A great crowd of people went out and a large detachment of Civica with bands and banners. It was painful to contrast their fair fresh condition with the battered meagre pallid appearance of those who have been in the field. It is those, alas! whose trumpets I heard as they went forth through this very gate del Popolo nine months ago. They might well curse Pio IX. Their banners now worn and faded like themselves bore the cross with *In hoc signo vinces.* It was from this very point that Constantine first saw the fiery sign.

—

Republic declared 9th Feb y 1849 on a Friday.

10th Feb y News arrives of the flight of the grand duke from Tuscany, he says not from *fear* but from scruples of conscience at finding himself amenable to the excommunication!! Like Pio he left an autograph letter leaving *his familiars* in care of the ministry.

The news was received with gladness and a provisional government immed y created in the persons of Montanelli Guerazzi and Mazzini.

He fled with all his family from Sienna by Porta St Stefano where a ship was ready for him. It is not known where he is gone.

—

10 March Mazzini's speech in the Assembly. Bonaparte——

15th March Mazzini in the Assembly Project for the war, for reps to the General assembly.

17th It appears certain that the Roman ambassadors have not been rec d in Paris, that the French government will not be friendly to the Italian republics.

18th Charles Albert has declared war.

Ten days after he was defeated at Novara abdicated in favor of his son Victor Emanuel II & fled into Spain.

ITALY 1849 JOURNAL

Victor Emanuel sues for peace and takes up with the most shameful terms of armistice.

Genoa refuses to join, is besieged & bombarded by the Sardinian troops very valorous against *her*. She did not resist desperately; the richer inhabitants could not endure the idea of having the city destroyed! Quarters houses that did not resist were plundered by the Piedmontese soldiery. Many acted in the same infamous way *towards* Italians in the vicinity of Novara. Shows how much confidence may be put in the good judgment or truth of Ital n newspaper writers there has been no end to their panegyrics as to the right sentiment of the Piedmontese army.

Now without shame they talk of the priests having demoralized them at confession & make all the excuses they can without any regard to what they said before.

Now Genoa Piedmont are all submiss, the press is to be muzzled the clubs shut up, the parliament is prorogued, the reactionary ministry formed.

A reaction has succeeded in Florence—Many think Guerazzi has in the last betrayed the republican party. I do not know; they are so ready to say those things here. At any rate the republican party has been proved to be a small minority in Tuscany.

Now follows the infamy of France sending here her troops to restore the pope. The consummation of her downward course; do what she will, she can sink no lower.

It is the 29th April, the anniversary of the Pope's Encyclic letter. The tragedy so begun is tending to a close. Rome is barricaded, the foe daily hourly expected. Will the Romans fight. Outwardly they express great ardor, the chamber of deputies has warmly & unanimously voted to resist, at the review of the Civic guard yesterday they gave great promise, yet somehow I doubt them all.

From my window I see now where they are bringing boards I suppose to make a support for cannon, & it seems to be such play for men & boys alike.

LETTERS

TASSO'S OAK, ROME

FIRST LETTER

To Timothy Fuller

dear Father
    it is a heavy storm i hope you will not have to come home in
it little eugene is aslep whil i am writing.
    Ps caroline has been here in the rain

April 24, 1817?

"I DO NOT LIKE SARAH, CALL ME MARGARET ALONE"

To Timothy Fuller

Cambridge. 16 January 1820

My dear father
    I received your letter of the 29th about a week ago. I should
have written to you much sooner but have been very busy. I
begin to be anxious about my letter of the 28th which you do
not mention having received in any of your letters. If it has not
miscarried it reached you a fortnight ago. Your letter to me was
dated the day after mine was written but you do not mention
it in any of your letters to Mamma.—
    I attend a school which is kept by Aunt Abigail for *Eugene*
and *myself* and my *cousins* which with writing and singing
schools and my lessons to Uncle Elisha takes up *most* of my
time—
    I *have* not written to Miss *Kilshaw yet as* there is no
opportunity of sending our letters. *Deep rooted* indeed is my
affection for her May it flourish an *ever* blooming flower till our
kindred spirits absolved from earthly day mount together to
those blissful regions where never again we shall be seperated.
I am not romantic, I am not making professions when I say
I love Ellen better than my life. I love her better and reverence
her more for her misfortunes. Why should I not she is as lovely
as sweet tempered as before. These were what I loved before
and as she possesses all these now why should my love diminish.

717

Ought it not rather to increase as she has more need of it. It is for herself alone I grieve for the loss of fortune She will be exposed to many a trial a temptation she would otherwise have escaped Not but I know she will go through them all No But I shall feel *all* her sorrows—

You will let me read Zeluco? will you not and no conditions. Have you been to the theatre this winter? Have they any oratorios at Washington?—I am writing a new tale called The young satirist. You must expect the remainder of this page to be filled with a series of unconnected intelligence My beautiful pen now makes a large mark I will write no farther. 17th January 1820

Yesterday I threw by my pen for the reason mentioned above. Have you read Hesitation yet. I knew you would (though you are no novel reader) to see if they were rightly delineated for I am possessed of the greatest blessing of life a good and kind father. Oh I can never repay you for all the love you have shown me But I will do all I can

We have had a dreadful snowstorm today. I never look around the room and behold all the comforts with which Heaven has blessed me without thinking of those *wretched* creatures who are wandering in all the snow without food or shelter. I am too young No I am not. In nine years a great part of my life I can remember but two good actions done those more out of sefishness than charity. There is a poor woman of the name of Wentworth in Boston she would willingly procure a subsistence but has not the means. My dear father a dollar would be a great sum to this poor woman. You remember the handsome dollar that I know your generosity would have bestowed on when I had finished my Deserted Village I shall finish it well and desire nothing but the pleasure of giving it to her. My dear father send it to me immediately I am going into town this week I have a thousand things to say but neither time or paper to say them in.

Farewel my dear Father I am Your affectionate daughter

MARGARET FULLER

P S I do not like Sarah, call me Margaret alone, pray do!

TO SUSAN PRESCOTT 719

"THE AVENUES OF GLORY ARE SELDOM ACCESSIBLE"

To the Marquis de Lafayette

Sir,

I expect the pleasure of seeing you tonight. If I should not be disappointed, the timidity appropriate to youth and the presence of many strangers will probably prevent me from expressing the ardent sentiment of affection and enthusiastic admiration which pervades my soul whenever I think of you; I cannot resist the desire of placing my idea before your mind if it be but for a moment; I cannot resist the desire of saying, "La Fayette I love I admire you;" I am sure that this expression of feeling, though from one of the most insignificant of that vast population whose hearts echo your name, will not be utterly inconsequent to you; I am sure that not one of that people in whose cause you consumed, amid the toils and hardships of a camp, the loveliest years of human existence and from whom you are now receiving a tribute of gratitude unparalleled in the annals of history as your extraordinary life, is inconsequent to you. Sir the contemplation of a character such as yours fills the soul with a noble ambition. Should we both live, and it is possible to a female, to whom the avenues of glory are seldom accessible, I will recal my name to your recollection

Accept the sincere homage of a youthful heart and dear friend of my country, farewell.

SARAH MARGARETT FULLER.

June 16, 1825?

"I AM DETERMINED ON DISTINCTION"

To Susan Prescott

Cambridge, 11 July 1825

Having excused myself from accompanying my honored father to church, which I always do in the afternoon, when possible, I devote to you the hours which Ariosto and Helvetius ask of my eyes,—as, lying on my writing-desk, they put me in mind that they must return this week to their owner.

You keep me to my promise of giving you some sketch of my pursuits. I rise a little before five, walk an hour, and then practise on the piano, till seven, when we breakfast. Next I read French,—Sismondi's Literature of the South of Europe,—till eight, then two or three lectures in Brown's Philosophy. About half-past nine I go to Mr. Perkins's school and study Greek till twelve, when, the school being dismissed, I recite, go home, and practise again till dinner, at two. Sometimes, if the conversation is very agreeable, I lounge for half an hour over the dessert, though rarely so lavish of time. Then, when I can, I read two hours in Italian, but I am often interrupted. At six, I walk, or take a drive. Before going to bed, I play or sing, for half an hour or so, to make all sleepy, and, about eleven, retire to write a little while in my journal, exercises on what I have read, or a series of characteristics which I am filling up according to advice. Thus, you see, I am learning Greek, and making acquaintance with metaphysics, and French and Italian literature.

"How," you will say, "can I believe that my indolent, fanciful, pleasure-loving pupil, perseveres in such a course?" I feel the power of industry growing every day, and, besides the all-powerful motive of ambition, and a new stimulus lately given through a friend. I have learned to believe that nothing, no! not perfection, is unattainable. I am determined on distinction, which formerly I thought to win at an easy rate; but now I see that long years of labor must be given to secure even the "*succes de societe*,"—which, however, shall never content me. I see multitudes of examples of persons of genius, utterly deficient in grace and the power of pleasurable excitement. I wish to combine both. I know the obstacles in my way. I am wanting in that intuitive tact and polish, which nature has bestowed upon some, but which I must acquire. And, on the other hand, my powers of intellect, though sufficient, I suppose, are not well disciplined. Yet all such hindrances may be overcome by an ardent spirit. If I fail, my consolation shall be found in active employment.

"I WISH TO TALK WITH YOU NOW ABOUT THE GERMANS"

To James Freeman Clarke

7th August 1832.

Dear James,

Where are you, and what doing? and *why* dont you come here? I feel quite lost; it is so long since I have talked myself—To see so many acquaintances, to talk so many words and never tell my mind completely on any subject. To say so many things which do not seem *called out* makes me feel strangely *vague* and *moveable.*—

'Tis true the time is probably near when I must live alone to all intents and purposes—separate entirely my acting from my thinking world, take care of my ideas without aid (c'est a dire except from the "illustrious dead") answer my own questions, correct my own feelings and do all that "hard work" for myself—How tiresome 'tis to find out all one's self-delusion—I thought myself so very independent because I could conceal *some* feelings at will and did not need the *same* excitement as other young characters did—And I am not independant nor never shall be while I can get any-body to minister to me. But I shall go where there is never a spirit to come if I call ever so loudly—But I dont wish to anticipate the time when stones and running brooks shall be my only companions—and I wish to talk with you now about the *Germans*

I have not got any-body to speak to that does not talk common-place—And I wish to talk about such an uncommon person—About Novalis!—a wondrous youth—and who has only written *one volume.* That is pleasant! I feel as if I could pursue my natural mode with him, get acquainted, then make my mind easy in the belief that I know all that is to be known. And he died at twenty-nine, and as with Korner your feelings may be single, you will never be called upon to share his experience and compare his future feelings with his present. And his life was so full and so still.

—Then it is a relief after feeling the immense superiority of Goethe. It seems to me as if the mind of Goethe had embraced the universe—I have felt that so much lately in reading his lyrick poems—I am enchanted while I read; he comprehends every feeling I ever had so perfectly, expresses it so beautifully, but when I shut the book, it seems as if I had lost my personal identity—All my feelings linked with such an immense variety that belong to beings I had thought so different. What can I bring? There is no answer in my mind except "It is so" or "It will be so" or "No doubt such and such feel so"—Yet while my judgement becomes daily more tolerant towards others the same attracting and repelling work is going on in my feelings. But I persevere in reading the great sage some part of every day, hoping the time will come when I shall not feel so overwhelmed and leave off this habit of wishing to grasp the whole and be content to learn a little every-day as becomes so mere a pupil. But now the one-sidedness, imperfection and glow of a mind like Novalis's seem refreshingly human to me. I have wished fifty times to write some letters giving an account first of his very pretty life and then of his one volume as I re-read it chapter by chapter—If you will pretend to be very much interested perhaps I will get a better pen and write them to you. But you know I must have people interested that I may speak. And I wish to ask you, now I think of it whether you feel as I expect people to feel about the *tasteless want of reserve* exhibited in my hand-writing. I see I shall never improve—Now though I sat down with the best resolves I have written this letter just as usual. And so in my journal and even extract-books If I were a princess I would have a secretary and never write another line—I always fancy whoever reads this hand-writing must see all my faults. And I dont like to have them seen without my consent.—

I called on *Miss Smith* when in town but forgot to ask about your letter in proper times. Mark this—Amelia was charmed with your visit which you thought such a failure— "Such is the nature of social intercourse" Did you ever receive my invite for that Sunday eveg to meet Helen It is well you did not come. She was very angry with me again and probably you might have come in for a share—So much thunder and lightning is rather fatiguing—I dont think I shall venture near her soon

Mr Henry has returned to Cambridge and many other little things have happened which I cant take the trouble to write— Miss Woodward told me she had lately seen and liked you very much "Indeed she had always been interested in you on account of your family &c" Did you like *her?*—Have you seen Elizh—She is well and divides her time between hard piano practice and the study of *Johnson* and Mrs *Chapone!*—

This is a sad blotting half-sheet I have taken, but I shall send this whole scrawl. I feel so much more natural since I began to write that I dare say I have nothing more to tell you and you need not come here. But write if you have encountered anything new or pretty. I must not expect die Grosse und Schöne.— With love to Sarah if she be with you yours

M.

WRITING A BIOGRAPHY OF GOETHE

To James Freeman Clarke

Groton 19th April 1836—

Dear Friend,

Your letter imparted to me a pure satisfaction; the heart seemed to speak in it without reserve—Sometimes it seems as if you had a feeling of pride which stood between you and me, or some other feeling!—'Tis but a film—yet sufficient to prevent you from radiating much heat upon my earth-bound state.

Who is the imaginative love. Give name and date!—I am shocked to perceive you think I am *writing* the life of Goethe—No! indeed! I shall need a great deal of preparation before I can have it clear in my head.—I have taken a great many notes but I shall not begin to write it till it all lies mapped out before me. I have no materials for ten years of his life— from the time he went to Weimar up to the Italn journey— Besides! I wish to see the books that have been written about him in Germany by friend or foe—I wish to look at the matter from all sides—New lights are constantly dawning upon me and I think it possible I shall come out far enough from the Carlyle view perhaps from yours and will distaste you which will trouble me.

In a brief, but seemingly, calm and authentic notice of Goethe's life which I met with in an English publication the other day I find it stated that his son was illegitimate, that he lived out of wedlock with the mother for twenty years and only married her on acct of the son as late as 1806—I confess this has greatly pained and troubled me—I had no idea that the mighty "Indifferentist" went so far with his experimentalizing in *real life*. I had not supposed he "*was*" all he "*writ*," and have always maintained that stories which have been told me as coming from Dr Follen which represented him as a man of licentious life could not be true because he was living at a court whose outward morality, at least, must be pure under the auspices of a princess like the Grand duchess Amelia.—In the same publication many, not agreeable, hints are thrown out respecting those very ten years which I know so little about.

How am I to get the information I want unless I go to Europe—To whom should I write to choose my materials—I have thought of Mr Carlyle but still more of Goethe's friend Von Muller—I dare say he would be pleased at the idea of a life of G. written in this hemisphere and be very willing to help me. If you have any-thing to tell me you will and not mince matters—Of course my impressions of Goethe's works cannot be influenced by information I get about his *life* but as to this latter I suspect I must have been hasty in my inferences—I apply to you without scruple—These are subjects on which *gentlemen* and *ladies* usually talk a great deal but apart from one another— you, however, are well aware that I am very destitute of what is commonly called modesty. With regard to this, how fine is the remark of our present subject. "Courage and modesty are virtues which every sort of society reveres because they are virtues which cannot be counterfeited, also they are known by the *same hue*"—When that blush does not come naturally into my face I do not drop a veil to make people think it is there All this may be very "*unlovely*" but it is *I*. As to sending the 40 vols, do not, till you know certainly that I shall not go to Europe—That will be decided the first of June and I will write and tell you—When I wrote for the Goethe I thought it *was* decided but it is not. My mind is much harassed by anxiety and suspense—add to this that my health has been most miserable for two or three months back. So I do not accomplish much—If I thought my constitution was really broken and that I must never again know my natural energy of body and mind I should be almost overcome, but the physician says it is only the extreme cold winter acting on a frame debilitated by a severe illness and all the painful emotion which came after and that the summer will probably restore me.

What subjects do you wish me to write upon for your mag. and how can I send if I *do* write. It seems to me I have but little to give the West. I have left myself no room for critiques on your writing but by and by I will do what you desire—Would you not like me to wait till I have read your N. American piece. Be assured you have heart and mind sympathy from me.—I should like to come to the West very much perhaps if I do not go abroad, I might for a time if I could do something to pay my way. Perhaps you do not know that I am to have scarce any money.—I suppose if I have health I can earn it as others do—I have a protege that I wish you could get a place for. She is a farmer's daughter, far from elegant or pretty but with a sterling heart and mind and really good education. She knows Latin, French and Italian and could teach the common English branches and something of Mathematics I have taken some pains with her and feel a desire that her earnest wish to go and teach at the South or West should be gratified.—She is persuaded it would do her good and I know enough of the misery of being baffled and hemmed in on every side by seemingly insignificant barriers to feel an interest in giving her a chance to try her experiment too. She would make a good governess or assistant—if any thing of the sort falls in your way think of *her* an thou lovest *me*.

I know you must hate these crossed letters—

M. F.

I have been reading, with delight, Herschell's discourse on Nat. Philosophy—Do you know it?

DEFENDING TRANSCENDENTALISM

To Caroline Sturgis

Providence Rhode Island
16th Novr 1837—

My dear Caroline,

When I saw your Father in September I felt a natural delicacy about interfering in your affairs, (although conscious of very pure and kind motives) and apologized, to which he replied by begging me not, and saying that he must always consider any manifestation of interest from me in your behalf as a *kindness and a favor—*

When I spoke of your coming here and asked if it would be agreeable to him, he replied *it would extremely so*, that *he could have no objection except from the fear that I might be taking too much care upon myself.*—When I asked if he would *object to your boarding at the City Hotel* with me, and gave some reasons for fearing he might, he said that he had *perfect confidence in your discretion*, and that any *arrangement I might think proper for myself he should also esteem proper for you*, and left me, requesting *to hear from me on the subject as soon as I should decidedly know what arrangements I could make.*

Remembering all this distinctly (for I was much pleased by your father's manner and spoke of it to several of our mutual friends and by repetition even his words were impressed on my memory,) I cannot but feel strong indignation at the statements contained in your letter, at the levity and discourtesy with which I *seem* to be treated, and at the unnecessary trouble which has been given me.

I have nothing to say as to what you shall do. My feelings towards you are unchanged. They are those of warm affection and interest for your welfare. I know not of another young person of whom, under my present circumstances, I would have taken similar charge. I have avoided taking one into the house who would have given me very little trouble, and whose friends were earnestly desirous of having her under my influence—I may venture to say that my motives with regard to you were those of disinterested, and uncommon kindness, and ought to have been met in a very different manner.

The question as to whether you shall come rests with yourself and your family. Here or any-where I shall be glad to receive you. I might cease *to visit you* but should always be happy to have you visit me. I live at Mrs Susan Aborn's, Aborn St.— Any hackman when you leave the cars would know where it is. I should not wish to receive you before Tuesday unless you can mail a letter so that I can get it on Saty to tell me that you can come on Monday. We have no Sunday mail, I believe. And

TO RALPH WALDO EMERSON

this much ceremony, at least, is due me and quite necessary as I must inform my hostess about your coming.—

As to transcendentalism and the nonsense which is talked by so many about it—I do not know what is meant. For myself I should say that if it is meant that I have an active mind frequently busy with large topics I hope it is so—If it is meant that I am honored by the friendship of such men as Mr Emerson, Mr Ripley, or Mr Alcott, I hope it is so—*But* if it is meant that I cherish any opinions which interfere with domestic duties, cheerful courage and judgement in the practical affairs of life, I challenge any or all in the little world which knows me to prove such deficiency from any acts of mine since I came to woman's estate.—

You are at liberty to show this letter if you please to your parents. I permit but do not *require* it, because I think as your letter was written in haste some expressions may have given me exaggerated notions—You are on the spot, and can judge; do as you think proper.

Let me once more, before I close, repeat to you the assurances of my affection. If you have dallied with me, I know it is not your fault—You would never wilfully interfere with my comfort or feelings in any way and are incapable of treating me in an indelicate manner. But at the same time, if you do not come, I shall not write again. I do not wish to be needlessly agitated by exchanging another letter on this topic—I will let you know when I am in Boston and see you there at least once—Sincerely your friend

S. M. FULLER.

"I WANT TO SEE YOU AND STILL MORE TO HEAR YOU"

To Ralph Waldo Emerson

Providence 1st March 1838—

My dear friend,

Many a Zelterian epistle have I mentally addressed to you full of sprightly scraps about the books I have read, the spectacles I have seen, and the attempts at men and women with whom

728 LETTERS

I have come in contact. But I have not been able to put them on paper, for even when I have attempted it, you have seemed so busy and noble, and I so poor and dissipated that I have not felt worthy to address you.

At present I am not at all Zelterian in my mood but very sombre and sullen. I have shut the door for a few days and tried to do something—You have *really* been doing something! And that is why I write—I want to see you and still more to hear you. I must kindle my torch again. Why have I not heard you this winter? I feel very humble just now yet I dare to say that being lives not who would have received from your lectures as much as I should. There are noble books but one wants the breath of life sometimes. And I see no divine person. I myself am more divine than any I see—I think that is enough to say about them—I know Dr Wayland now, but I shall not care for him. He would never understand me, and, if I met him, it must be by those means of suppression and accommodation which I at present hate to my hearts core. I hate every-thing that is reasonable just now, "wise limitations" and all. I have behaved much too well for some time past; it has spoiled my peace. What grieves me too is to find or fear my theory a cheat—I cannot serve two masters, and I fear all the hope of being a worldling and a literary existence also must be resigned—Isolation is necessary to me as to others. Yet I keep on "fulfilling all my duties" as the technical phrase is except to myself.—But why do I write thus to you who like nothing but what is good i e cheerfulness and fortitude? It is partly because yours is an image of my oratory. I suppose you will not know what this means. and if I do not jest when I write to you I must *pray*. And partly as a preliminary to asking you, unsympathizing, unhelpful, wise good man that you are to do several things for me. I hear you are to deliver one of your lectures again in Boston. I would have you do it while I am there. I shall come on Wednesday next and stay till the following Monday Perhaps you will come to see me, for though I am not as good as I was, yet as I said before, I am better than most persons *I* see and, I dare say, better than most persons *you* see. But perhaps you do not need to see anybody, for you are acting and nobly—If so you need not come yourself, but send me your two lectures on Holiness and Heroism to read while in Boston. Let me have

TO LIDIAN JACKSON EMERSON 729

these two lectures to read *at any rate*, whether you come or no. Do not disappoint me. I will treat them well and return them safe. I shall be at Mr Sturgis's all the time. I shall come out on Thursday to hear you at Cambridge, but they wrote me that lecture would be on the Heart and not so fine as some of yours.

I have not read any books except what every body reads, Gardiner on Music (thank *you* for that; it was a great deal to me.) Carlyle as noble as I hoped, absorbing me quite for a fortnight, Lamb's letters, Whately's Rhetoric.

Lately I have been amusing myself with looking at you through two pair of spectacles of very dissimilar construction in Brownson's review and the Democratic. I have a disciple of yours in my German class—a very lovely young man. He has never seen you but gets regular bulletins of you from some friend in Boston—I suppose I could get them animated into inviting you to speak to the Larvae here if you would come. Several gentlemen promised me their aid, if there was a chance of getting you. Adieu Sanctissime. Tell Lidian that the thought of her holiness is very fragrant to me. Tell your son that if he has grown less like Raphael's cherubs I will never forgive him. Tell my dear Elizabeth that I love her just as I did last August, but shall probably never write to her—

Devoutly if not worthily yours

S. M. FULLER.

"FRET NOT THAT KINDEST HEART"

To Lidian Jackson Emerson

Sunday morng—

Dear Lidian,

Fret not that kindest heart because of my evil doing. Your remark was rather the occasion than the cause for any pain I felt. I was in a state of weak sensitiveness while at your house, which I probably shall not get free from till I have enjoyed for some time the benefits of seclusion and repose.

I trust and believe that you will always show your esteem for me by the same freedom you have formerly used. I, on my side,

730 LETTERS

should cease to come, if I could not speak and act as naturally as I always have. But there is no fear of that, I think.

I shall write to Mr F. and will make the desired inquiries about Sophia—I shall, however, probably leave Providence at the end of next term.—I wish I could feel more joy at the prospect of escape from uncongenial pursuits and the oppressive intercourse with vulgar minds. But I cease from a noble effort to consult my own health and feelings. I have done and suffered much without attaining my object, or removing one evil which formerly afflicted me, and I cannot be joyful.

I hope the little charmer is better It was sad to see a cloud on him. With affectionate remembrance to your goodly company I am yours as ever

S. M. FULLER.

August 19, 1838

"MY PLAN FOR THE PROPOSED CONVERSATIONS"

To Sophia Ripley?

Jamaica Plain,
27th August, 1839—

My dear friend,

I find it more difficult to give on paper a complete outline of my plan for the proposed conversations than I expected. There is so much to say that I cannot make any statement satisfactory to myself within such limits as would be convenient for your purpose. As no one will wish to take the trouble of reading a long manuscript, I shall rather suggest than tell what I wish to do, and defer a full explanation to the first meeting. I wish you to use this communication according to your own judgment; if it seems to you too meagre to give any notion of the plan, lay it aside and interpret for me to whomsoever it may concern.

The advantages of such a weekly meeting might be great enough to repay the trouble of attendance if they consisted only in supplying a point of union to well-educated and thinking women in a city which, with great pretensions to mental refinement, boasts at present nothing of the kind and where

TO SOPHIA RIPLEY? 731

I have heard many of mature age wish for some such means of stimulus and cheer, and these people for a place where they could state their doubts and difficulties with hope of gaining aid from the experience or aspirations of others. And if my office were only to suggest topics which would lead to conversation of a better order than is usual at social meetings and to turn back the current when digressing into personalities or commonplaces so that—what is invaluable in the experience of each might be brought to bear upon all. I should think the object not unworthy of an effort. But my own ambition goes much farther. Thus to pass in review the departments of thought and knowledge and endeavor to place them in due relation to one another in our minds. To systematize thought and give a precision in which our sex are so deficient, chiefly, I think because they have so few inducements to test and classify what they receive. To ascertain what pursuits are best suited to us in our time and state of society, and how we may make best use of our means for building up the life of thought upon the life of action.

Could a circle be assembled in earnest desirous to answer the great questions. What were we born to do? How shall we do it? which so few ever propose to themselves 'till their best years are gone by. I should think the undertaking a noble one, and if my resources should prove sufficient to make me its moving spring, I should be willing to give it a large portion of those coming years which will as I hope be my best. I look upon it with no blind enthusiasm, nor unlimited faith, but with a confidence that I have attained a distinct perception of means which if there are persons competent to direct them, can supply a great want and promote really high objects. So far as I have tried them yet they have met with success so much beyond my hopes, that my faith will not be easily shaken, or my earnestness chilled.

Should I however be disappointed in Boston I could hardly hope that such a plan could be brought to bear upon general society in any other city of the U.S. But I do not fear if a good beginning can be had, I am confident that twenty persons cannot be brought together for better motives than those of vanity or pedantry to talk upon such subjects as we propose without finding in themselves great deficiencies which they will be very desirous to supply. Should the enterprize fail, it will be either from incompetence in me or that sort of vanity in others which wears the garb of modesty. On the first of these points I need not speak. I can scarcely have felt the wants of others so much without feeling my own still more deeply. And from the depth of my feeling and the earnestness it gave such power as I have thus far exerted has come. Of course those who propose to meet me feel a confidence in me. And should they be disappointed I shall regret it not solely or most on my own account, I have not given my gage without weighing my capacity to sustain defeat. For the other I know it is very hard to lay aside the shelter of vague generalities, the cant of coterei criticism and the delicate disdains of *good society* and fearless meet the light although it flow from the sun of truth. Yet, as without such generous courage nothing can be done, or learned I cannot but hope to see many capable of it. Willing that others should think their sayings crude, shallow or tasteless if by such unpleasant means they may secure real health and vigor which may enable them to see their friends undefended by rouge or candlelight.

Since I saw you I have been told that several persons are desirous to join, if only they need not talk. I am so sure that the success of the whole depends on conversation being general that I do not wish any one to join who does not intend, *if pos-sible*, to take an active part. No one will be forced, but those who do not talk will not derive the same advantages with those who openly state their impressions and consent to learn by blundering as is the destiny of Man here below. And general silence or side talks would paralyze me. I should feel coarse and misplaced if I were to be haranguing too much. In former instances I have been able to make it easy and even pleasant to twenty five out of thirty to bear their part, to question, to define, to state and examine their opinions. If I could not do as much now I should consider myself unsuccessful and should withdraw. But I should expect communication to be effected by degrees and to do a great deal myself at the first meetings.

My method has been to open a subject as for instance *Poetry* as expressed in
External Nature,
The Life of man
Literature

The Fine Arts
or History of a nation to be studied in
Its religious and civil institutions
Its literature and arts,
The characters of its great men
and after as good a general statement as I know how to make select a branch of the subject and lead others to give their thoughts upon it.

When they have not been successful in verbal utterance of their thoughts I have asked for them in writing. At the next meeting I read these aloud and canvassed their adequacy without mentioning the names of the writers. I found this less and less necessary as I proceeded and my companions acquired greater command both of thoughts and language, but for a time it was useful. I hope it may not be necessary now, but if it should great advantages may be derived from even this limited use of the pen.

I do not wish at present to pledge myself to any course of subjects. Except generally that they will be such as literature and the arts present in endless profusion. Should a class be brought together, I should wish first to ascertain our common ground and in a few meetings should see whether it be practicable to follow up the design in my mind which would look as yet too grand on paper. Let us see whether there will be any organ and if so note down the music to which it may give breath.

I believe I have said as much as any one will wish to read. I am ready to answer any questions which may be put and will add nothing more here except

always yours truly,

S. M. FULLER.

"MY CLASS IS SINGULARLY PROSPEROUS"

To Unknown Correspondent

25 Nov 1839

My class is singularly prosperous I think. I was so fortunate as to rouse at once the tone of simple earnestness which can scarcely, when once awakened, cease to vibrate. All seem in a glow and quite as receptive as I wish They question and examine, yet follow leadings; and thoughts (not opinions) have been trumps every time. There are about 25 members, and every one, I believe, full of interest. The first time, ten took part in the conversation; the last still more. Mrs Bancroft came out in a way that surprized me. She seems to have shaken off a wonderful number of films. She showed pure vision, sweet sincerity, and much talent. Mrs Josiah Quincy keeps us in good order and takes care yt "Xy" and "morality" are not forgotten. The first time was the genealogy of heaven and earth, then the will (Jupiter); the Understanding, (Mercury)

Second, the celestial inspiration of genius, perception and transmission of divine law (Apollo) the terrene inspiration the impassioned abandonment of Genius (Bacchus) of the thunderbolt, the Caduceus, the ray, and the grape having disposed of as well as might be, we came to the wave, and the seashell it moulds; to Beauty, and Love, her parent her child

I assure you there is more Greek than Bostonian spoken at the meetings, and we may have pure honey of Hymettus to give you yet. I have been happy *a mourir*. Four hundred and seventy designs of Raffalle in my possession for a week.

"WHEN I WRITE, IT IS INTO ANOTHER WORLD"

To William Henry Channing

Jamaica Plain,
22d March, 1840—

My dear friend,

This eveg is not a very good time to answer your letter, but I must take it, *faute de mieux*, because I want to say to you. Though your plan be a brave one, and I would wish to become acquainted with Ernest as speedily as possible, yet if you be not ready at once to commence your pilgrimage with him, send some short pieces. I do not ask as James was wont for "bundles" of fine original compositions but make use of the modester words *some* or *several* and I pray you heed my request, for with this first number we want room for choice. I have myself a great deal written but as I read it over scarce a word seems pertinent to the place or time. When I meet people I can adapt myself to them, but when I write, it is into another world, not a better one perhaps, but one with very dissimilar habits of thought to this where I am domesticated. How much those of us who have been much formed by the European mind have to unlearn and lay aside, if we would act here. I would fain do something worthily that belonged to the country where I was born, but most times I fear it may not be.

What others can do, whether all that has been said is the mere restlessness of discontent, or there are thoughts really struggling for utterance will I think be tested now. A perfectly free organ is to be offered for the expression of individual thought and character. There are no party measures to be carried, no particular standard to be set up. A fair calm tone, a recognition of universal principles will, I hope pervade the essays in every form I hope there will neither be a spirit of dogmatism nor of compromise. That this periodical will not aim at leading public opinion, but at stimulating each man to think for himself, to think more deeply and more nobly by letting them see how some minds are kept alive by a wise self-trust. I am not sanguine as to the amount of talent which will be brought to bear on this publication. I find all concerned rather indifferent, and see no great promise for the present. I am sure we cannot show high culture, and I doubt about vigorous thought. But I hope we shall show free action as far as it goes and a high aim. It were much if a periodical could be kept open to accomplish no outward object, but merely to afford an avenue for what of free and calm thought might be originated among us by the wants of individual minds.

James promises nothing but if I can get him here I shall expect some sound rough fruit of American growth. From Mr Emerson we may hope good literary criticisms, but his best thoughts must, I suppose take the form of lectures for the present.

But you will see I wish you were here that I might talk with you once. I cannot write well to any one to whom I do not write constantly. But we shall write constantly to our friends in print now. When I have finished "Ernest" I will seal and send a letter I writ you last summer provided it seems fit for an appendix to the record of your search.

736   LETTERS

My dear friend, you speak of your sense of "unemployed force."—I feel the same. I never, never in life have had the happy feeling of really doing any thing. I can only console myself for these semblances of actions by seeing that others seem to be in some degree aided by them. But Oh! really to feel the glow of action, without its weariness, what heaven it must be! I cannot think, can you, that all men in all ages have suffered thus from an unattained Ideal. The race must have been worn out ere now by such corrosion. May you be freed from it! for me, my constant ill-health makes me daily more inadequate to my desires and my life now seems but a fragment. At such hours we take refuge in the All, we know that somewhere in Nature this vitality stifled here is manifesting itself. But individuality is so dear we would fain sit beneath our own vines and fig trees.

Farewell, pray write to me again if it suits you so to do. I should answer all the letters, a compliment I do not always pay. My respects to Miss Channing. Mother and sister are not near me now, but they think of you ever with respect and love.

Yours

S. MARGARET FULLER.

"DID YOU NOT ASK FOR A 'FOE' IN YOUR FRIEND?"

To Ralph Waldo Emerson

29 Sept 1840

I have felt the impossibility of meeting far more than you; so much, that, if you ever know me well, you will feel that the fact of my abiding by you thus far, affords a strong proof that we are to be much to one another. How often have I left you despairing and forlorn. How often have I said, this light will never understand my fire; this clear eye will never discern the law by which I am filling my circle; this simple force will never interpret my need of manifold being.

Dear friend on one point misunderstand me less. I do not love power other than every vigorous nature delights to feel itself living. To violate the sanctity of relations, I am as far from it as you can be. I make no claim. I have no wish which is not dictated by a feeling of truth. Could I lead the highest Angel

TO RALPH WALDO EMERSON 737

captive by a look, that look I would not give, unless prompted by true love. I am no usurper. I ask only mine own inheritance. If it be found that I have mistaken its boundaries, I will give up the choicest vineyard, the fairest flower-garden, to its lawful owner. [   ]

In me I did not think you saw the purity, the singleness, into which, I have faith that all this darting motion, and restless flame shall yet be attempered and subdued. I felt that you did not for me the highest office of friendship, by offering me the clue of the labyrinth of my own being. Yet I thought you appreciated the fearlessness which shrinks from no truth in myself and others, and trusted me, believing that I knew the path for myself. O it must be that you have felt the worth of that truth which has never hesitated to infringe our relation, or aught else, rather than not vindicate itself. If you have not seen this stair on which God has been so untiringly leading me to himself, you have indeed been wholly ignorant of me. Then indeed, when my soul, in its childish agony of prayer, stretched out its arms to you as a father, did you not see what was meant by this crying for the moon; this sullen rejection of playthings which had become unmeaning? Did you then say "I know not what this means; perhaps this will trouble me; the time will come when I shall hide my eyes from this mood;"—then you are not the friend I seek.

But did not you ask for a "foe" in your friend? Did not you ask for a "large formidable nature"? But a beautiful foe, I am not yet, to you. Shall I ever be? I know not. My life is now prayer. Through me sweetest harmonies are momently breathing. Shall they not make me beautiful,—Nay, beauty! Shall not all vehemence, all eccentricity, be purged by these streams of divine light? I have, in these hours, but one pain; the sense of the infinite exhausts and exalts: it cannot therefore possess me wholly; else, were I also one wave of gentlest force. Again I shall cease to melt and flow; again I shall seek and pierce and rend asunder.

But oh, I am now full of such sweet certainty, never never more can it be utterly shaken. All things have I given up to the central power, myself, you also; yet, I cannot forbear adding, dear friend. I am now so at home, I know not how again to wander and grope, seeking my place in another Soul. I need to

738 LETTERS

be recognized. After this, I shall be claimed, rather than claim, yet if I speak of facts, it must be as I see them.

To L. my love. In her, I have always recognized the saintly element. *That*, better than a bible in my hand, shows that it cannot be to me wholly alien. Yet am I no saint, no anything, but a great soul born to know all, before it can return to the creative fount.

Yesterday, I saw Mr R. He had, on reflection, taken my frankness in the true way; we are much nearer, and, I think, shall go on better and better. Say no word of this or of aught personal to————. His vanity makes him perfidious, without his intending it.

REJECTING A DIAL SUBMISSION

To Henry David Thoreau

1st Decr.

I am to blame for so long detaining your manuscript. But my thoughts have been so engaged that I have not found a suitable hour to reread it as I wished till last night. This second reading only confirms my impression from the first. The essay is rich in thoughts, and I should be *pained* not to meet it again. But then the thoughts seem to me so out of their natural order, that I cannot read it through without *pain*. I never once feel myself in a stream of thought, but seem to hear the grating of tools on the mosaic. It is true as Mr E. says, that essays not to be compared with this have found their way into the Dial. But then those are more unassuming in their tone, and have an air of quiet good-breeding which induces us to permit their presence. Yours is so rugged that it ought to be commanding. Yet I hope you will give it me again, and if you see no force in my objections disregard them.

S. M. FULLER.

1840

BEETHOVEN'S FIFTH SYMPHONY

To William Henry Channing

[   ] it is to be that I shall have something positive to do for you, before I depart. If so, it will compensate for past obstructions.

I hope you will go to the Ripleys for a time and that you will be in perfect peace there to work and to think.

Mr Parker preached a grand sermon yesterday at Purchase St. It was on Idolatries. He wound up with the Idolatry of Jesus.—As they thought of giving him a call he wished to let them know all his thoughts as explicitly as they lay before himself. When he came down, he was in a fine glow; *you* would have said he looked *manly*. I quite loved him.

Saturday evening I heard one of Beethoven's great symphonies. Oh William, what majesty what depth, what tearful sweetness of the human heart, what triumphs of the Angel mind! Into his hands he drew all the forces of sound, then poured them forth in tides such as ocean knows not, then the pause which said It is very good and the tender touch which woke again the springs of life. When I read his life I said I will never repine. When I heard this symphony I said I will triumph more and more above the deepening abysses. The life is large which can receive a Beethoven. I lived that hour.—There are many true men. I have you to be my friend.—I begin to revive, though I have had too much fatigue lately and my head still aches and aches. You are right to suppose I have been ill, in the month of January I lost too much blood in one of my nervous attacks and have been somewhat too ethereal and too pensive ever since. [   ]

April 5, 1841

740   LETTERS

HANDING OVER EDITORSHIP OF THE DIAL

To Ralph Waldo Emerson

Boston,
9th April, 1842.

Dear Waldo,

I understand you have given notice to the Public, that, the Dial is to be under your care in future, and I am very glad of this for several reasons, though I did not like to express my feeling as you seemed reluctant to bind yourself in any way. But a year is short time enough for a fair trial.

Since it is now understood that you are Pilot, it is not needful for me to make the observations I had in view. The work cannot but change its character a good deal, but it will now be understood there is a change of director, too. The only way in which this is of importance to me is that I think you will sometimes reject pieces that I should not. For you have always had in view to make a good periodical and represent your own tastes, while I have had in view to let all kinds of people have freedom to say their say, for better, for worse.

Should time and my mood be propitious, I should like to write some pages on the amusements here this past winter, and a notice at some length of Hawthorne's Twice told tales. I was much interested by the Gipsey book, but dont incline to write about it—Longfellow sent us his poems, and if you have toleration for them, it would be well to have a short notice written by some one (*not* me)—I will have them sent to you and the little prayer book also. If you do not receive the latter, it will be because I could not get it, not because I have forgotten your wish. Please mention in your next, whether you did not find "Napoleon." I do not see it among my papers, and think I must have given it you.

As to pecuniary matters, Miss Peabody I have found more exact and judicious than I expected, but she is variable in her attention, because she has so many private affairs. She will do very well under your supervision, but a connection with her offers no advantages for the spread of your work whatever it may be. But you have always thought the Dial required nothing of this kind. Much, much do I wish for myself I could find a publisher who is honest, and has also business talents. Such a connexion ought to be permanent. But I can hear of no person in Boston or elsewhere that it is desirable to be connected with, so I suppose I must still jog on as before, this dubious pace. But if ever you get any light in this quarter, pray impart.

I should think the Dial affairs were now in such a state that you could see clear into the coming year, and might economize about it considerably.

Well! I believe this is all I have to say, not much truly.

I leave town Monday eveg and go to Cambridge for a few days. On Friday or Saturday I go to Canton to board with an Aunt of mine for four or five weeks. I think I shall be there perfectly retired and quiet; it suits my convenience in many respects to go. I wish I could feel as if the Muse would favor me there and then, but I feel at present so sad and languid, as if I should not know an hour of bright life again. It will be pity if this hangs about me just at the time when I might obey inspirations, if we had them, but these things are beyond control, and the demon no more forgets us than the angel. I will make myself no more promises *in time*. If you have any thing to say to me I should receive a letter here as late as Friday morng, if directed to Miss Peabody's care. Afterward direct to me at Canton. Care Charles Crane.

I thank you and Lidian for your invitation and know well your untiring hospitality. Should it seem well so to do, I will come. I cannot now tell how I shall feel. After Canton I shall go to Providence, for a few days, then to N. Bedford to pass a week with Aunt Mary Rotch. Farewell, dear Waldo, yours as ever,

Margaret.

I still have thoughts of going to the West, but shall not know about it for some weeks.

PEABODY'S WEDDING TO NATHANIEL HAWTHORNE

To Sophia Peabody

Saturday June 4th.

My dear Sophia,

After reading your letter I wanted to write a few lines, as we met in such a hasty, interrupted fashion. Yet not much have

I to say, for great occasions of bliss, of bane,—tell their own story, and we would not, by unnecessary words, come limping after the true sense. If ever mortal was secure of a pure and rational happiness which shall grow and extend into immortal life, I think it is you, for the love that binds you to him you love is wise and pure and religious, it is a love given not chosen, and the growth not of wants and wishes, but of the demands of character. Its whole scope and promise is very fair in my eyes. And for daily life, as well as in the long account, I think there will be great happiness, for if ever I saw a man who combined delicate tenderness to understand the heart of a woman, with quiet depth and manliness enough to satisfy her, it is Mr Hawthorne. How simple and rational, too, seems your plan of life. You will be separated only by your several pursuits and just enough daily to freshen the founts of thought and feeling; to one who cannot think of love merely in the heart, or even in the common destiny of two souls, but as necessarily comprehending intellectual friendship, too, it seems the happiest lot imaginable that lies before you. But, if it should not be so, if unexpected griefs or perils should arise, I know that mutual love and heavenly trust will gleam brightly through the dark. I do not *demand* the earnest of a future happiness to all believing souls. I wish to temper the mind to believe, without prematurely craving *sight*, but it is sweet when here and there some little spots of garden ground reveal the flowers that deck our natural Eden,—sweet when some characters can bear fruit without the aid of the knife, and the first scene of that age-long drama in which each child of God must act to find himself is plainly to be deciphered, and its cadences harmonious to the ear.

I wish you could have begun your new life so as to have had these glorious June days in Concord. The whole earth is decked for a bridal. I see not a spot on her full and gold bespangled drapery. All her perfumes breathe, and her eye glows with joy. I saw a *rose* this morning, and I fear the beautiful white and Provence roses will bloom and wither before you are ready to gather them.

My affectionate remembrance to your friend. You rightly felt how glad I should be to be thought of in the happy hour and plan for the future. As far as bearing an intelligent heart I think

I deserve to be esteemed a friend. And thus in affection and prayer dear Sophia yours

MARGARET F.

1842

"I HAVE NOT LIVED MY OWN LIFE"

To George T. Davis

Cambridge
17th Decr 1842.

Dear George,

I have thought of you many times since we parted on that dreary night in that dreary street. I did not like to bid you good bye so, and next day, when I found I had unexpectedly an hour at noon, regretted that I could not send for you to come and see me if you would.—Yesterday was one of my very sick days, and I had time to think and thought of you so much, that I must write and ask you to write to me

I am not fond of dwelling on the past, and prefer pressing onward to the things that are before. But objects round me now irresistably recal the days when we were so much together. The house where I live stands in the orchard of the old Dana house, and is shaded by trees on which I looked from my window. The view is the same, the river so slow and mild, the gentle hills, the sunset over Mt. Auburn, I love to look on it. My father would often try to check my pride, or as he deemed it my *arrogance* of youthful hope and pride by a picture of the ills that might come on me,—and all have come of which he spoke, sickness, poverty, the failure of ties and all my cherished plans, but none of these changes have had the effect he prophesied. I feel the same heart within my breast, I prize the same objects, though more deeply, and I may say more wisely. For the same persons I am still interested, nor have I been deceived in any of them, there is not one I have ever loved who did not possess the groundwork of character, and has not in some degree justified my election, for all of them as for myself, I am emboldened to an immortal hope. The best of what I could say to you on this subject I have expressed in some papers which I have prepared as I agreed with you I would and shall give you when you come to town. You must then bring your children as you promised and show me. I love to know these new lives in which my friends bloom again.—I feel that the darkest hue on my own lot is that I have neither children, nor yet am the parent of beautiful works by which the thought of my life might be represented to another generation. Yet even this is not dark to me, though it sometimes makes me pensive.—I have not lived my own life, neither loved my own love, my strength, my sympathies have been given to others, their lives are my aims. If here I could call nothing my own, it has led me to penetrate deeper into the thought which pervades all. I have not been led to limit my thoughts to a span, nor fix my affections with undue order on some one set of objects. So all things are equalized at last.—I cannot help regretting sometimes that I can do so little for any one, so little for my nearest and dearest to soothe their pains, or remove obstacles from their path. Yet is *that little* not often to be met with. I can say from the depth of my heart, never cease to hope and trust if you deserve you will at last be satisfied. I can understand each mind in its own way, for I see men in their several natures; and not by any rule taken from my own character and experience. This those who love me know, and you do, I am sure, though you said, as we parted, that the sympathy of friendship was superficial, if it did not answer with warmth to some things you said, especially of *ambition*, you will see the reason when you come. Write to me at once if you can, and let me know how the green fields look beneath December snows. Always affectionately your

COUSIN M.

I was surprised to hear from James you had not read Tennyson.—Do read him at once. He has solved his own problems.

VISITING THE TERRITORY OF WISCONSIN

To Richard F. Fuller

Milwaukee, 29th July, 1843.

My dear Richard,

I should have written to you long since, but that I expected to receive a letter from you. No formal engagement was made, 'tis true but I thought you would feel the wish to communicate to me somewhat of yourself during the summer. It has been a painful surprize to me that Mother should never once write. I have felt very anxious about her health, and about yours, but a letter received from Ellen, a day or two since, implies, though it does not say that you are none of you ill. She tells me, too, you are gone to Groton where I hope you will live as you did last summer, and regain the natural temper of body and mind of which Cambridge, with its artificial and mechanical disciplines, threatens to deprive you.

I see by the list of those to whom the Bowdoin prizes were awarded that the essay to which you devoted so much time and study did not gain one. This failure I know could not fail to be dispiriting at the moment, but I trust you recovered from it in the manly spirit you thought you should. You will not suspect me who am your true and manly friend, of any insincere soothing when I say that the award of Cambridge is no test of what the world's will be. Seeing Carey's name at the head of the list, and knowing what he is from those well capable to judge, I cannot regret that you should fail before a tribunal so sensible to his merits. I feel that your abilities are excellent, your ambition deeper and purer than is usual at your age or any other, and I have no doubt of your eventual success with yourself, and with the world, if you do not unsettle your health on the way.

Daily I thought of you during my visit to the Rock River territory. It is only five years since the poor Indians have been dispossessed of this region of sumptuous loveliness, such as can hardly be paralleled in this world. No wonder they poured out their blood freely before they would go. On one island, belonging to Mr Hinshaw, a gentleman with whom we staid, are still to be found their "caches" for secreting provisions, the wooden troughs in which they pounded their corn, the marks of their tomahawks upon felled trees. When he first came he found the body of an Indian woman, in a canoe, elevated on high poles, with all her ornaments on. This island is a spot where nature seems to have exhausted her invention in crowding it with all kinds of growths, from the most rich trees down to the most delicate plants. It divides the river which there sweeps along in clear and glittering current betwixt noble parks, richest green lawns, pictured rocks, crowned with old hemlocks, or smooth bluffs three hundred feet high, the most beautiful of all. Two of these, the Eagle's nest, and the Deer's walk, still the habitual resort of the grand and beautiful creatures from which they are named, were the scene of some of the happiest hours of my life. I had no idea from verbal description of the beauty of these bluffs, nor can I hope to give any to others. They lie so magnificently bathed in sunlight; they touch the heavens with so sharp and fair a line!—This is one of the finest parts of the river but it seems beautiful enough to fill any heart and eye all along its course, and nowhere broken or injured by the hand of man.—And there, I thought, if we two could live and you have a farm which would not be a twentieth part the labor of a N England farm, and would pay twenty times as much for the labor, and have our books and our pens, and a little boat on the river, how happy we might be for four or five years, at least *as* happy as fate permits mortals to be. For we, I think, Richard, are really congenial, and if I could hope permanent peace on the earth, I might hope it with you.

You will be glad to hear that I feel overpaid for coming here. Much is my life enriched by the images of the great Niagara, of the vast lakes, the heavenly sweetness of the prairie scenes, and above all by the lovely region where I would so gladly have lived. My health too is materially benefitted. I hope to come back better fitted for toil and care, as well as with the beauteous memories to sustain me in them—Let me find you well and bright, too, do not let me be met by sorrow—I have recd a letter from Mother since I began this Where it has been lingering I cant conceive; it bears date 29th June. Affectionately always your sister

MARGARET.

"THE CARBUNCLE"

To Caroline Sturgis

Friday evening, May 3d

I hasten to inform thee, Caroline, how well thou art guarded with talismans. The Greek meaning of Amethyst is Antidote against intoxication. It was used by the ancients as a talisman for this, also to give good thoughts and understanding.

The Agate preserves against the sting of the Scorpion, and, worn on the left arm, or hand, makes the owner wise and attractive. If laid under the head of the sleeper, it brings him manifold dream-pictures.

How sweet it is after the thunder-shower! but you are not among the blossoming trees.

Just now, looking in Pericles and Aspasia for something else (which I could not find) I came upon the poem, "You build your nest Aspasia" &c I had forgotten how beautiful it is; look and see if it be not the right kind of nest.

You gave me this book, and Festus, if ever you find a book as good, or (possible?) better, be sure and give me that too.

MARGARET.

The *diamond* is an antidote against poison, wild beasts, and evil spirits. The Dantes in their thick forests need the diamond.

The Carbuncle is called so from carbo, because like a live coal.

> Slow wandering on a tangled way
> To their lost child pure spirits say
>   The diamond marshal thee by day;
> By night the carbuncle defend
>   Hearts-blood of a bosom friend;
> On thy brow the Amethyst,
>   Violet of secret earth,
> When by fullest sunlight kist
>   Best reveals its regal worth,
> And when that haloed moment flies
> Shall keep thee steadfast, chaste and wise.

1844

"YOU ARE INTELLECT, I AM LIFE"

To Ralph Waldo Emerson

The Parsonage, 13th July.
It seems rather odd, dear Waldo, to send you a rude thing like this, just as you have been showing me your great results, sculptured out into such clear beauty.

But your excellence never shames me, nor chills my next effort, because it is of a kind wholly unattainable to me, in a walk where I shall never take a step. You are intellect, I am life. My flowers and stones however shabby interest *me*, because they stand for a great deal *to me*, and would, I feel, have a hieroglyphical interest for those of like nature with me. Were I a Greek and an artist I would polish my marbles as you do, as it is, I shall be content whenever I am in a state of unimpeded energy and can sing at the top of my voice, I dont care what. Whatever is truly felt has some precious meaning. I derive a benefit from hearing your pieces as I should from walking in the portico of a temple, amid whose fair columns the air plays freely. From it I look out upon an azure sea. I accept the benignant influence. It will be eight years next week since I first came to stay in your house. How much of that influence have I there received! Disappointments have come but from a youthful ignorance in me which asked of you what was not in your nature to give. There will be little of this, if any, in future. Surely! these essays should be a sufficient protest against such *illusions.*

The piece I send you pleases me as the "Herberts" and that "Dialogue" did as being each the thought of a day. Here are three days of life in the past year during which my mind pursued its natural course uninterrupted from sun to sun. They please me by recalling these three bright days. Anyone who, in reading them, considered it as spending the day with me might find an interest in them, if in my mind at all.

The horse, konic belongs to Frank Shaw. S. Ward it was who likened Sarah to the sweet fern. The Sistrum I have shown you, and I believe the Serpent, triangles, and rays which I had drawn for me. The other two emblems were ascribed to me by others, and the Winged Sphynx I shall have engraved and use, if ever

TO ELIZABETH HOAR

749

I get to look as steadily as she does. Farewell, O Grecian Sage, though not my Oedipus.

I wish I could have Edith up here a little while, some day. I want to see her with Una,—but I suppose she could not walk so far, could she?

The Egyptians embodied the Sphynx as in body a lion, in countenance of calm human virgin beauty. It was reserved for the Greek to endow her with wings.

I have just had a very pleasant visit from Henry. No Atlantides though!

1844

VISITING SING SING PRISON

To Elizabeth Hoar

Oct [28?] 1844

We have just been passing Sunday at Sing Sing. We went with William Channing: he staid at the chaplain's we at the prison. It was a noble occasion for his eloquence and I never felt more content than when at the words "Men and Bretheren," all those faces were upturned like a sea swayed by a single wind and the Shell of brutality burst apart at the touch of love divinely human. He visited several of them in their cells and the incidents that came were moving.

On Sunday they are all confined in their cells after 12 at noon that their keepers may have rest from their weekly fatigues, but I was allowed to have some of the women out to talk with and the interview was very pleasant. They were among the so called worst, but nothing could be more decorous than their conduct, and frank too. All passed much as in one of my Boston Classes. I told them I was writing about Woman and as my path had been a favoured one I wanted to ask some information of those who had been tempted to pollution and sorrow. They seemed to reply in the same spirit in which I asked. Several however expressed a wish to see me alone, as they could then say *all*, and they could not bear to before one another: and I intend to go there again, and take time for this. It is very gratifying

LETTERS

to see the influence these few months of gentle and intelligent treatment have had on these women: indeed it is wonderful, and even should the State change its policy, affords the needed text for treatment of the subject.

WOMAN IN THE NINETEENTH CENTURY

To William Henry Channing

Sunday eveg
17th Novr 1844.

At last, my dear William, I have finished the pamphlet. The last day it kept spinning out beneath my hand. After taking a long walk early on one of the most noble exhilarating sort of mornings I sat down to write and did not put the last stroke till near nine in the evening Then I felt a delightful glow as if I had put a good deal of my true life in it, as if, suppose I went away now, the measure of my foot-print would be left on the earth. That was several days ago, and I do not know how it will look on revision, for I must leave several days more between me and it before I undertake that, but think it will be much better than if it had been finished at Cambridge, for here has been no headach, and leisure to choose my hours.

It will make a pamphlet rather larger than a number of the Dial, and would take a fortnight or more to print. Therefore I am anxious to get the matter *en train* before I come to N. Y. that I may begin the 1st Decr for I want to have it out by Christmas. Will you then see Mr Greeley about it the latter part of this week or the beginning of next. He is absent now, but will be back by that time and I will write to him about it. Perhaps he will like to undertake it himself.

The estimate you sent me last summer was made expecting an edition of fifteen hundred, but I think a thousand will be enough. The writing, though I have tried to make my meaning full and clear, requires, shall I say? too much culture in the reader to be quickly or extensively diffused. I shall be satisfied if it moves a mind here and there and through that others; shall be well satisfied if an edition of a thousand is disposed of in the course of two or three years

TO EUGENE FULLER

If the expense of publication should not exceed a hundred or even a hundred and fifty dollars, I should not be unwilling to undertake it, if thought best by you and Mr G. But I suppose you would not think that the favorable way as to securing a sale.

If given to a publisher I wish to dispose of it only for one edition. I should hope to be able to make it constantly better while I live and should wish to retain full command of it, in case of subsequent editions. [   ] to be made up before coming here. If Mr. G. really did expect him to write whig editorials, that, I agree with you, he could not do, but I do not think he has ascertained Mr. G's design, and he will go home without doing so.

[   ] seeing him, for the [   ] But I ha[   ] lives none with whom I stand at present in mental relations who does not know the whole of my thought about him E said he could alter nothing, still it [   ]

Last night I kept dreaming of you delivering your discourse I heard whole sentences and many tones of voice so I had the benefit of this day's utterance before those who heard it perchance

Adieu dear friend.

HORACE GREELEY AND THE NEW-YORK TRIBUNE

To Eugene Fuller

N. Y. 9th March, 1845.

Dearest Eugene,

Your Arkansas letter was received with great joy. It was long since I had heard from yourself and, as usual, I cannot obtain much information from the family. It is true I deserve not from them, as the necessity of doing so much other writing makes me a bad correspondent to them and to every one.

I am glad too to hear of your health, and that, with the ennui of so long a journey at such a time, you were able to make some profit. Profit always sounds like your coming back to us, which, amid the whirl of a busy life, I cannot cease to wish, and which Mother has only too much leisure to dream about.

I do not know much of the family, except that Mother is still troubled with dyspepsea, but, in other regards, not sick. Ellen well, and the child, they say most lovely, Richard doing well. For me, I have never been so well situated. As to a home the place where we live is old and dilapidated but in a situation of great natural loveliness. When there, I am perfectly secluded, yet every one I wish to see comes to see me, and I can get to the centre of the city in half an hour. The house is kept in a Castle Rackrent style, but there is all affection for me and desire to make me at home, and I do feel so, wh could scarcely have been expected from such an arrangement. My room is delightful; how I wish you could sit at its window with me and see the sails glide by!

As to the public part; that is entirely satisfactory. I do just as I please, and as much or little as I please, and the Editors express themselves perfectly satisfied, and others say that my pieces *tell* to a degree, I could not expect. I think, too, I shall do better and better. I am truly interested in this great field which opens before me and it is pleasant to be sure of a chance at half a hundred thousand readers.

Mr Greeley I like, nay more, love. He is, in his habits, a slattern and plebeian, and in his heart, a nobleman. His abilities, in his own way, are great. He believes in mine to a surprizing extent. We are true friends.

It was pleasant you should see that little notice in that wild place. The book is out, and the theme of all the newspapers and many of the journals. Abuse public and private is lavished upon its views, but respect expressed for me personally. But the most speaking fact and the one wh satisfies me, is that the whole edition was sold off in a week to the booksellers and $85 handed to me as my share. Not that my object was in any wise money, but I consider this the signet of success. If one can be heard that is enough! I shall send you 2 copies one for yourself and one to give away, if you like. If you noticed it in a N. O. paper, you might create a demand for it there; the next edition will be out in May. In your next letter tell me your address, that I may know what to do when I wish to send parcels to you.

I wish you would write a series of letters about what you have seen in Arkansas and the S. West, that I might use in the Tribune, if I thought best. I think you would do this well.

Write one, at least, about this late tour as a sample and tell about Wild Cat &c *out full.*

I hear a great deal of music, having free entrance every where from my connection with the paper. Most of the Italian Opera corps is now at N. O. and I hope you will hear them perform Semiramide, with which I was enchanted I am glad you love music as well as ever. Farewell, and Heaven bless my dear brother is always the prayer of

MARGARET.

I am almost perfectly well at present.

If you see the Weekly Tribune you will find all my pieces marked with a Star. I began 1st Decr.

"I FEEL CHOSEN AMONG WOMEN"

To James Nathan

Sunday afternoon.

The true lovely time is come at last. The leaves and grasses are out, so that the wind can make soft music as it sweeps along instead of the rattling and sobbing of winter. A dear little shower is refreshing the trees and they grow greener and fairer every moment in gratitude. (I write so badly because the wind shakes my paper too as well as the other leaves, but I cant bear to shut the window.)

You must use your moderation about our interviews, and as you know best. I like best to rely entirely upon you, yet keep time as much as possible with the enchanting calls of outward nature. It is nothing to be together in the parlor or in the street, and we are not enough so among the green things Today the lilacs are all in blossom, and the air is full of a perfume which causes extasy.

I hear you with awe assert the power over me and feel it to be true. It causes awe, but not dread, such as I felt sometime since at the approach of this mysterious power, for I feel deep confidence in my friend and know that he will lead me on in a spirit of holy love, and that all I may learn of nature and the soul will be legitimate. The destiny of each human being is no doubt great and peculiar, however obscure its rudiments to our present sight, but there are also in every age *a few* in whose lot the meaning of that age is concentrated. I feel that I am one of those persons in my age and sex. I feel *chosen among women*. I have deep mystic feelings in myself and intimations from elsewhere. I could not, if I would, put into words these spirit-facts, indeed they are but swelling germs as yet, and all I do for them is to try to do nothing that might blight them. Yet as you say you need to forget *your* call, so have I need of escaping from this overpowering sense. But when forced back upon myself as now, though the first turnings of the key were painful, yet the inner door makes rapturous music too upon its golden hinge. What it hides you perhaps know, as you read me so deeply; indeed, some things you say seem as if you did. Yet *do not*, unless you *must*. You look at things so without their veils, yet that seems noble and antique to me. I do it when you hold me by the hand, yet when I feel how you are thinking, I sometimes inly say Psyche was but a mortal woman, yet as the bride of Love, she became a daughter of the Gods too. But had she learned in any other way this secret of herself, all had been lost, the plant and flower and fruit.

But it is impossible to say these things at least for me. They are myself, but not clearly defined to myself. With you, all seems to assume such palpable reality, though you do not forget its inner sense either. I love to hear you read off the secret, and yet you sometimes make me tremble too.

I confide in you, as this bird now warbling without confides in me. You will understand my song, but you will not translate it into language too human. I wish, I long to be human, but divinely human. Let the soul invest every act of its abode with somewhat of its own lightness and subtlety. Are you my guardian to domesticate me in the body, and attach it more firmly to the earth. Long it seemed that it was only my destiny to say a few words to my youth's companions and then depart. I hang lightly as an air plant. Am I to be rooted on earth, oh choose for me a good soil and a sunny place, that I may be a green shelter to the weary and bear fruit enough to pay for staying.

A revoir à dieu

May 4?, 1845

TO JAMES NATHAN

"AN APPROACHING SEPARATION, PRESSES ON MY MIND"

To James Nathan

Friday evening, May 23d
dear friend, I do not, just now, find any thing to write; the fact of an approaching separation, presses on my mind, and makes me unable to make the best use of the hours that remain.

I will therefore borrow from the past. Many little things have made me feel as if there had been a gradual and divinely moved preparation for our meeting. Today I took out of the portfolio some leaves written last autumn among the mountains and found there these lines which will impress you from their consonance, in some respects, with what you have since uttered to me. Many such things I write down; they seem dictated to me, and are not understood fully at the time. They are of the things which are received mystically long before they are appreciated intellectually.

Perhaps you had better destroy them, not now, for you will hardly be at leisure for them yet, but sometime when you feel ready, as they are so intimately personal.

I wish you would ask me to explain the difference the Greeks made between the moon as Hecate and as Diana, and the allusions to the girdle of Apollo, and at the conclusion to Tantalus; there are beautiful things in the Greek mythology which you will appreciate.

I feel it is true what you say that in the new and greater religion we shall rise above the need of this mythology, for all which they intimated in poetry we must realize in life, but as yet I cling to these beautiful forms as I do to the green and flowery earth, and again will say, linger with me here awhile.

Our friend, here, asks anxiously *whether you are gone yet?* She expresses a great desire to hear you play on your guitar once more, and I am glad you left it; we will pass an hour together so. She is really quite content about us now.

I am not well. You cannot bend your mind on me now. I know it is not because you love me less but because there are necessarily so many things, at present, to distract, but I feel it; the strength that was only given is gone. Or rather it was

not given only lent, but you would have given it if you could,
I know.

Later

I have copied out the poem and hope there are no words
miswrit, but cannot read it over, do not smile at all, liebste, I am
a little afraid of your smiles, and it is only in the deepest recess of
our mutual life I could have shown it you, for to me it is prophecy

Among the mountains, October 1844.

Afternoon in the dell where was a broken fall and many-voiced
With evergreens and red and golden trees,
At varying elevations grouped around,
   Its basin hid and cool and circular,
On which the leaves rested as dreamily
   As if the stream could never wake again;
The mountains towered around, purple and rose,
The Sun, still climbing, vainly sought to peer
   Into that still recess.
     My soul sank there
A prayer that Intellect with its broad light
   Will ne'er reveal, nor even clearly know
But Nature holds it to her secret heart.

Evening, moonlight.
     To the Face seen in the Moon.
Oft, from the shadow of my earthly sphere,
I looked to thee, Orb of pale pearly light,
   To loose the weariness of doubt and fear
In thy soft Mother's smile so pensive bright.
   Thou seemedst far and safe and chastely living,
Grace-full and thought-full, loving, beauty giving;
   But, if I steadfast gaze upon thy face,
   A human secret, like our own, I trace.
For, through the woman's smile looks the male eye
   So mildly, steadfastly, but mournfully,
He holds the *bush* to point as to his cave
   Teaching anew the truth so bright, so grave.
   "Escape not from the riddle of the Earth,
Through mortal pangs to win immortal birth,
   Both man and woman from the natural womb

TO JAMES NATHAN

Must slowly win the secrets of the tomb
    And then, together rising, fragrant, clear,
The worthy Angel of a better sphere.
    Diana's beauty shows what Hecate wrought,
Apollo's lustre rays the zodiac thought
    In Leo regal, as in Virgo pure,
As Scorpio secret, as the Archer sure.
    In unpolluted beauty mutual shine
Earth, Moon, and Sun, the Human Thought Divine.
For Earth is purged by tameless central fire,
    And Moon in Man has told her hid desire,
    And Time has found himself eternal Sire,
    And the Sun sings All on his ray-strung lyre."

    Steady bear me on
    Counting life's pulses all alone
Till all is felt and known and done.
    Thus far have I conquered Fate
    I have learned to wait.
Nor in these early days snatch at the fruits of late.
    The man from the Moon
Looks not for an instant noon,
But from its secret heart
    Slow evolves the Art
Of that full consummation needed part.

    For thee, my Apollo.
        The girdle I weave,
    From whose splendid hollow
Thy young breast shall its impulse receive.
    I am the mother of thy spirit-life,
    And so in law thy wife
    And thou art my sire.
For all this treasured fire
    Learns from thee
    Its destiny.
And our full mutual birth
Must free this earth.
From our union shall spring
    The promised King
Who, with white sail unfurled
Shall steer through heavens of soul an unpolluted world.
    In that world
Earth's Tale shall be

A valued page
Of poesy.
As Grecian bards
Knew how to praise
The kingly woes
Of darker days,
And Tantalus, soaring where the mist is over blown
Meets on his hard-won throne a Juno of his own.

1845

"I SHALL NOT ALTER A LINE OR A WORD"

To Evert A. Duyckinck

June 28th

private
To Mr Duyckinck

I received a note yesterday from Mr Wiley, requesting that I would omit the article on Festus from the forthcoming volumes and "all other matter of a controversial character or likely to offend the religious public."

Now you well know that I write nothing which might not offend the so-called religious public. I am too incapable of understanding their godless fears and unhappy scepticism to have much idea of what would offend them. But there are probably sentences in every piece, perhaps on every page, which, when the books are once published, will lead to censure.

I consented to take counsel as to the selection of pieces with *you*, because you can understand. As there is a superabundance of matter, and whatever is not published now will be hereafter I was willing to take counsel as to the selection from the pieces. But I hope it is clearly understood that in those I *do* publish, I shall not alter a line or a word, on such accounts They will stand precisely as they were originally written and if you think Mr Wiley will not be content to take the consequences you had better stop the transaction now.

Also in the department of Foreign literature I must be guided by my own judgment. The articles on Goethe and others, probably contain things far more likely to offend than those in the

TO EVERT A. DUYCKINCK 759

piece on Festus, but I will not omit them, if I publish at all, for they are some of my best pieces, and I do not wish the volumes to be made up of indifferent matter.

I could not, if I would, act in this temporizing manner; it is too foreign to my nature. But I do not believe in it as a matter of policy. The attractive force of my mind consists in its energy, clearness and I dare to say it, its catholic liberality and fearless honor. Where I make an impression it must be by being most myself. I ought always to ignore vulgar prejudices, and I feel within myself a power which will sustain me in so doing and draw to me sufficient and always growing sympathy.

I do not believe it is *wise* to omit the piece on Festus or that on Shelley. Those who care for what I write at all, will care most for such pieces. It seems unhandsome towards Mr Bailey, who is now the first of the younger living English poets, to omit him and name others. There is only one consideration that makes me willing in that case, which is that, on looking the piece over, I find the extracts make it too long and could not well be omitted. I consent then in the case of those two pieces.—I would also like to have you if you think it desirable hold counsel with Mr Wiley, as to the articles on Swedenborgianism and the Wesleys. There is nothing in them controversial as, of course, there could not be in any thing I write, viewing all sects, as I do merely as expressions of human opinion and character. But they are on matters theological, though not viewed from a theological point. I wish to publish them because they have some merit, but I do not care particularly about it. Only make Mr Wiley understand that where I *do* care I shall insist, and that I give him no vouchers that there shall be nothing to offend his religious public in the book. I shall publish the articles just as they stand, without any attention to such considerations or not at all. If he is not content with that, we had better stop now. If we do, however, I shall publish an account of this transaction for I wish in every way to expose the restrictions upon mental freedom which threaten to check the progress of genius or of a religious sentiment worthy of God and man in this country.

I have read the play with great pleasure. The view of character and statements of magnetic influence from soul to soul is truly noble. The accounts by the girl of her love are fine poetry, so are those of the sympathizing aspects of nature with those dark

760   LETTERS

mental seasons. There is *no metre*, rhythm though the poem assumes to be written in it. Tell the author's name; is it yours? I shall prize it.

I have recd only two proofs, as yet. I shall expect a note from you tomorrow night.

If we go on, (and I suppose we shall, only I want it to be on a firm and honorable basis) I can supply all the rest of the Engh literature part on Tuesday. Farewell, my good friend, for I feel as if you were such to me, though we have not seen much of one another yet. But I know your soul is truly liberal and fair.

S. M. F.

1846

ENGLAND AND PARIS

To Caroline Sturgis

[   ] I find how true for me was the lure that always drew me towards Europe. It was no false instinct that said I might here find an atmosphere needed to develope me in ways *I* need. Had I only come ten years earlier; now my life must ever be a failure, so much strength has been wasted on obstructions which only came because I was not in the soil most fitted to my nature, however, though a failure, it is less so than with most others and the matter not worth thinking about. Heaven has room enough and good chances enough in store, no doubt, and I can live a great deal in the years that remain.

As soon as I got to England, I found how right we were in supposing there was elsewhere a greater range of interesting character among the men, than with us. I do not find, indeed, any so valuable as three or four among the most marked we have known, no Waldo, none so beautiful as William when he is *the angel*, more like Charles on the Egyptian side, none so beauty-ful as S. was when he *was Raphael*, but so many that are strongly individual and have a fund of hidden life.

In Westmoreland I knew and have since been seeing in London, a man such as would interest you a good deal; his name is Atkinson, some call him the "Prince of the English

Mesmerizers" and he has the fine instinctive nature you may suppose from that.

He is a man about thirty, in the fulness of his powers, body and mind. He is tall and firmly formed, his head of the Christ-like sort as seen by Leonardo, mild and composed, but power-ful and sagacious. He does not think, but perceives and acts. He is intimate with the artists, having studied architecture himself as a profession, but has some fortune on which he lives, sometimes stationary and acting in the affairs of other men, sometimes wandering about the world and learning. He seems bound by no tie, yet looks as if he had children in every place.

I saw also a man, an artist, severe and antique in his spirit; he seemed burdened by the sorrows of aspiration, yet very calm, as secure in the justice of Fate. What he does is bad, but full of a great desire. His name is Scott. I saw also another, a pupil of Dela Roche, very handsome, and full of a voluptuous enjoyment of Nature; him I liked a little in a different way.

By far the most beauteous person I have seen is Joseph Mazzini. If you ever see "Sanders People's Journal," you can read articles by him that will give you some notion of his mind, especially one on his friends the two Bandieras and Rufini, headed "Italian Martyrs."—He is one in whom holiness has purified, but nowhere dwarfed the man. I shall make a little sketch of him in a public way for the Tribune. I do not like to say more of him here now. I can do it better when I have seen him more, which I shall do in the course of time.

I saw some girls in London that interested me. Anna Howitt, daughter of W. and Mary Howitt about 22 has chosen the profession of an artist; she has an honorable ambition, talent, and is what is called a sweet pretty girl. Margaret Gillies is older; she has given up many things highly valued by English women to devote herself to Art, and attained quite a high place in the profession; her pictures are full of grace, rather sentimental, but that she is trying to shake off. For the rest she is an excellent, honest girl. But the one whom I like *very* much is Eliza Fox, only daughter of the celebrated W. J. She is about five and twenty; she also is an artist and has begun a noble independent life. she seems very strong and simple, yet delicate in the whole tissue of her. I could not find time to talk with her as I wanted but whenever I did she grew upon me. Whenever I did I thought of you and Jane and lamented that you did not embark on the wide stream of the world as artists, then all that has been so beautiful in your lives would have been embodied for others, too, who needed it so much. Eliza has a friend, also an English woman, now living at Rome of whom she spoke with such cordial esteem that I shall look for her when there. they both have had a great deal to contend with. They say men *will not* teach girls drawing with any care, and beside they find it so difficult to get chances to draw from living models.

I saw another fine girl; she was not an artist, but has a great deal of life, and she is so tall, strong and beautiful, like the nymphs. But there is not room to tell you about *her* or much about any thing.

The three months in England were months of the most crowded life, especially the six weeks in London. I came here, resolved to rest, for I am almost sick. A strange place to rest, some would think, but till my letters are presented no one knows me, and I shall not send them for some days. We are *getting dressed* (I do not wonder as I look around me here at the devotion of a French woman to her *mise* it is truly *deliceuse* as they call it with that absurd twinkle of their pretty eyes.) Rachel is acting. I have a letter to her and one to George Sand, but I do not want to see them, till I get to speaking French a little. Today we have come to our private lodging a very cheerful elegant apartment in the Hotel Rougement, where I shall speak French all the time, beside taking a master, and I hope to improve a good deal in a few days. Goodnight, as this must wait till next Steamer I shall add to it just before sending.

November 16?, 1845

MEETING THOMAS CARLYLE

To Ralph Waldo Emerson

Paris 16 Novr, 1846

I meant to write on my arrival in London, six weeks ago—But as it was not what is technically called "the season", I thought I had best send all my letters of introduction at once, that I might glean what few good people I could. But more than I expected were there; these introduced others, and in three days I got engaged in such a crowd of acquaintance that I had hardly time to dress and none to sleep during all the weeks I was in London.

I enjoyed this time extremely. I find myself much in my element in European Society. It does not indeed come up to my ideal; but so many of the encumbrances are cleared away that used to weary me in America, that I can enjoy a freer play of faculty, and feel, if not like a bird in the air, at least as easy as a fish in water.

On my very first arrival I encountered in Liverpool and Manchester, a set of devout readers of the Dial, still more of Emerson. Of the latter I found many wherever I went. In Westmoreland I found an English gentleman, one of the rich landowners, who live so charmingly that they scarce learn the need of thought, who yet had drawn from the Essays the impulse to a higher being, and knew them by heart, if not by head, so that he could have made a book of Excerpts in the style of Fanny

In Edinburgh I met Dr Brown. He is still quite a young man, but with a high ambition, and I should think commensurate powers; but all is yet in the bud with him. He has a friend, David Scott, a painter full of imagination and very earnest in his views of Art. I had some pleasant hours with them; and the last night which they and I passed with De Quincey a real Grand Conversatione, quite in the Landor style, which lasted in full harmony some hours.

Of the Scotch People whom I saw you will find notices in the Tribune, as also of my Highland Tour and my hair-breadth escape with life on one of the peaks of Ben-Lomond—Of the people I saw in London you will wish me to speak first of the Carlyles. Mr C came to see me at once, and appointed an evening to be passed at their house. That first time I was delighted with him. He was in a very sweet humor, full of wit and pathos, without being overbearing or oppressive. I was quite carried away with the rich flow of his discourse; and the hearty noble earnestness of his personal being brought back the charm which once was upon his writing, before I wearied of it. I admired his Scotch, his way of singing his great full sentences, so that each one was like the stanza of a narrative ballad. He let me talk a little now and then, enough to free my lungs, and change my position, so that I did not get tired.

That evening he talked of the present state of things in England, giving light witty sketches of the men of the day, fanatics and others—and some sweet homely stories he told of things he had known of the Scotch Peasantry. Of you he spoke worthily, as he seldom writes to you, and most unlike the tone of his prefaces, so that for the moment, I was quite reconciled to him.

Especially he told with beautiful feeling a story of some poor farmer or artisan in the country, who on Sunday lays aside the cark and care of that dirty English world, and sits reading the Essays, and looking upon the Sea.

I left him that night, intending to go out very often to their house.—I assure you there never was any thing so witty as Carlyle's description of [   ] it was enough to kill one with laughing. I on my side contributed the story of [   ] to his fund of anecdote on this subject, and it was fully appreciated. Carlyle is worth a thousand of you for that, he is not ashamed to laugh when he is amused, but goes on in a cordial human fashion.

The second time Mr C had a dinner-party, at which was a witty french flippant sort of man Lewes, author of a History of Philosophy, and now writing a life of Goethe, a task for which he must be as unfit as irreligion and sparkling shallowness can make him. But he told stories admirably, and was allowed sometimes to interrupt Carlyle, a little, of which one was glad, for that night he was in his more acrid mood, and, though much more brilliant than the former evening, became wearisome, at least to my mind which disclaimed and rejected almost every-thing he said

For a couple of hours he was talking about poetry, and the whole harangue was one eloquent proclamation of the defects in his own mind. Tennyson wrote in verse because the schoolmasters had taught him that it was great to do so, and had thus unfortunately been turned from the true path for a man. Burns had in like manner been turned from his vocation, Shakespeare had not had the good sense to see that it would have been better to write straight on in prose, and

TO RALPH WALDO EMERSON 765

such nonsense which though amusing eno' at first, he ran to death after a while. The most amusing part is always when he comes back to some refrain as in the French Revolution of the *Sea-Green*; in this instance it was Petrarch in *Laura*, the last word pronounced with his ineffable sarcasm of drawl. Although he said this over fifty times I could not ever help laughing when *Laura* would come, Carlyle running his chin out when he spoke it, and his eyes glancing till they looked like the eyes and beak of a bird of prey. Poor Laura! Lucky for her that her poet had already got her safely canonized beyond the reach of this Teufelsdrockh vulture.

The worst of hearing Carlyle is that you cannot interrupt him. I understand the habit and power of haranguing have increased very much upon him, so that you are a perfect prisoner when he has once got hold of you. To interrupt him is a physical impossibility; if you get a chance to remonstrate for a moment, he raises his voice and bears you down. True, he does you no injustice, and with his admirable penetration sees the disclaimer in your mind, so that you are not morally delinquent; but it is not pleasant to be unable to utter it. The latter part of the evening, however, he paid us for this by a series of sketches in his finest style of railing and raillery of modern French Literature, not one of them, perhaps, perfectly just, but all drawn with the finest, boldest strokes, and, from his point of view, masterly. All were depreciating, except that of Béranger. Of him he spoke with perfect justice, because with hearty sympathy.

I had, afterward, some talk with Mrs. C., whom hitherto I had only *seen*, for who can speak while her husband is there? I like her very much;—she is full of grace, sweetness, and talent. Her eyes are sad and charming. [   ]

After this, they went to stay at Lord Ashburton's, and I only saw them once more, when they came to pass an evening with us. Unluckily, Mazzini was with us, whose society, when he was there alone, I enjoyed more than any. He is a beauteous and pure music; also, he is a dear friend of Mrs. C.; but his being there gave the conversation a turn to "progress" and ideal subjects, and C. was fluent in invectives on all our "rose-water imbecilities." We all felt distant from him, and Mazzini, after some vain efforts to remonstrate, became very sad. Mrs. C. said

766 LETTERS

to me, "These are but opinions to Carlyle; but to Mazzini, who has given his all, and helped bring his friends to the scaffold, in pursuit of such subjects, it is a matter of life and death."

All Carlyle's talk, that evening, was a defence of mere force,— success the test of right;—if people would not behave well, put collars round their necks;—find a hero, and let them be his slaves, &c. It was very Titanic, and anti-celestial. I wish the last evening had been more melodious. However, I bid Carlyle farewell with feelings of the warmest friendship and admiration. We cannot feel otherwise to a great and noble nature, whether it harmonize with our own or not. I never appreciated the work he has done for his age till I saw England. I could not. You must stand in the shadow of that mountain of shams, to know how hard it is to cast light across it.

Honor to Carlyle! *Hoch!* Although in the wine with which we drink this health, I, for one, must mingle the despised "rose-water."

And now, having to your eye shown the defects of my own mind, in the sketch of another, I will pass on more lowly,— more willing to be imperfect,—since Fate permits such noble creatures, after all, to be only this or that. It is much if one is not only a crow or magpie;—Carlyle is only a lion. Some time we may, all in full, be intelligent and humanly fair.

"YOU WISHED TO HEAR OF GEORGE SAND"

To Elizabeth Hoar

Paris, 18 January 1847

You wished to hear of George Sand, or, as they say in Paris, "Madame Sand." I find that all we had heard of her was true in the outline; I had supposed it might be exaggerated. She had every reason to leave her husband,—a stupid, brutal man, who insulted and neglected her. He afterwards gave up their child to her for a sum of money. But the love for which she left him lasted not well, and she has had a series of lovers, and I am told has one now, with whom she lives on the footing of combined means, independent friendship. But she takes rank in society like a man, for the weight of her thoughts, and has just given her daughter in marriage. Her son is a grown-up young man, an artist. Many women visit her, and esteem it an honor. Even an American here, and with the feelings of our country on such subjects, Mrs.——, thinks of her with high esteem. She has broken with La Mennais, of whom she was once a disciple.

I observed to Dr. François, who is an intimate of hers, and loves and admires her, that it did not seem a good sign that she breaks with her friends. He said it was not so with her early friends; that she has chosen to buy a chateau in the region where she passed her childhood, and that the people there love and have always loved her dearly. She is now at the chateau, and, I begin to fear, will not come to town before I go. Since I came, I have read two charming stories recently written by her. Another longer one she has just sold to *La Presse* for fifteen thousand francs. She does not receive nearly as much for her writings as Balzac, Dumas, or Sue. She has a much greater influence than they, but a less circulation.

She stays at the chateau, because the poor people there were suffering so much, and she could help them. She has subscribed *twenty thousand francs* for their relief, in the scarcity of the winter. It is a great deal to earn by one's pen: a novel of several volumes sold for only fifteen thousand francs, as I mentioned before.

"I WISH TO BE FREE AND ABSOLUTELY TRUE
TO MY NATURE"

To Marcus and Rebecca Spring

Rome April 10th 1847

I was by my nature destined to walk by the inner light alone. It has led, will lead me sometimes on a narrow plank across deep chasms, if I do not see clear, if I do not balance myself exactly I must then fall and bleed and die. For this intellectually I am always prepared. I wish to be free and absolutely true to my nature, and if I cannot live so I do not wish to live. I may shrink from pain, but I must not be really afraid of it.

From infancy I have foreseen that my path must be difficult, it has been less so than I expected. Still I feel in myself immense trials possible to me and can only hope to be inwardly ripened for them. If they do not come in this world they will in another, it is not for me to fix the time of their coming but only to avoid wasting my strength in frivolous excitements in factitious duties and try to keep the strings of action fresh and strong within me.

I have never sought love as a passion; it has always come to me as an angel bearing some good tidings I have wished to welcome the messenger noble, but never to detain it, or cling with a weak personality to a tie which had ceased to bind the soul, I believe I should always do the same, however I might suffer from loss or void in the intervals of love, if I did not I can only say I should act very unworthily and I hope I should be punished till I returned to my better self.

I do not know whether I have loved at all in the sense of oneness, but I have loved enough to feel the joys of presence the pangs of absence, the sweetness of hope, and the chill of disappointment. More than once my heart has bled, and my health has suffered from these things but mentally I have always found myself the gainer, always younger and more noble. I have no wish about my future course but that it should be like the past, only always more full and deeper.

You ask me if I love M. I answer he affected me like music or the richest landscape, my heart beat with joy that he at once felt beauty in me also. When I was with him I was happy; and thus far the attraction is so strong that all the way from Paris I felt as if I had left my life behind, and if I followed my inclination I should return at this moment and leave Italy unseen

Still I do not know but I might love still better tomorrow; I have never yet loved any human being so well as the music of Beethoven yet at present I am indifferent to it. There has been a time when I thought of nothing but Michael Angelo, yet the other day I felt hardly inclined to look at the forms his living hand had traced on the ceiling of the Sistine. But when I loved either of these great Souls I abandoned myself wholly to it, I did not calculate, I shall do so in life if I love enough.

"I FIND MYSELF SO HAPPY HERE ALONE AND FREE"

To Richard F. Fuller

Rome,
29th Octr 1847.

My dear Richard

A private oppoy offering to send letters to America, I have prepared some notes for my friends, but as the gentleman goes first to Naples and Paris, he will not sail till 4th Decr and it is not worth-while to write to you as the news of me will then be old. A single letter I can send by post. I am trying all I can to economize in these little things, anxious to keep the Roman expenses for six months within the limits of four hundred dollars. Rome is not as cheap a place as Florence, but then I would not give a pin to live in Florence. We have just had glorious times with the October feasts when all the Roman people were out. I am now truly happy here, really *in* Rome, so quiet and familiar no longer, like the mob, a staring, sight-seeing stranger riding about finely dressed in a coach to see the Muses and the Sibyls. I see these things now in the natural manner and am happy. Yes I *am* happy here. Goodbye, dear Richard, heaven bless you and show you how to act. Keep free of false ties they are the curse of life. I find myself so happy here alone and free.

MARGARET.

REVOLUTION

To William Henry Channing

Rome, 29 March 1848

I have been engrossed, stunned almost, by the public events that have succeeded one another with such rapidity and grandeur. It is a time such as I always dreamed of, and for long secretly hoped to see. I rejoice to be in Europe at this time, and shall return possessed of a great history. Perhaps I shall be called to act. At present, I know not where to go, what to do. War is everywhere. I cannot leave Rome, and the men of Rome are

770   LETTERS

marching out every day into Lombardy. The citadel of Milan
is in the hands of my friends, Guerriere, &c., but there may be
need to spill much blood yet in Italy. France and Germany are
not in such a state that I can go there now. A glorious flame
burns higher and higher in the heart of the nations.

"I HAVE DONE . . . THINGS THAT MAY INVOKE CENSURE"

To Jane Tuckerman King

Rome April 1848

The Gods themselves walk on earth, here in the Italian
Spring. Day after day of sunny weather lights up the flowery
glades and Arcadian woods. The fountains, hateful during the
endless rains, charm again. At Castle Fusano I found heaths
in full flower I felt cheered. Such beauty is irresistible. But ah
dearest, the drama of my fate is very deep, and the ship plunges
deeper as it rises higher. You would be amazed, I believe, could
you know how different is my present phase of life, from that
in which you knew me; but you would love me no less; for it is
still the same planet that shews such different climes.

You know me, because you never in your life wounded me,
in the slightest way; you are always dear, and our intercourse
always noble.

I touched your mental life at a point of light. I am not in
so high a state of soul at present, as when you knew me: I am
enlarging the circle of my experiences. I deepen the sources,
but do not soar. But I always understand, and am always true.

I am very happy here; tranquil, and alone in Rome. I love
Rome more every hour; but I do not like to write details, or
really to let any one know any thing about it. I pretend to,
perhaps, but in reality, I do not betray the secrets of my love.

Whatever may be the future developments of my life, *you*
will always love me, and prize my friendship. Much has changed
since we met; my character is not in what may be called the
heroic phase, now. I have done, and may still do, things that
may invoke censure; but in the foundation of character, in my
aims, I am always the same:—and I believe you will always have

confidence that I act as I ought and must,—and will always value my sympathy.

"EVERYTHING CONFIRMS ME IN MY RADICALISM"

To Costanza Arconati Visconti

Rome 27 May 1848

This is my last day at Rome. I have been passing several days at Subiaco and Tivoli, and return again to the country to-morrow. These scenes of natural beauty have filled my heart, and increased, if possible, my desire that the people who have this rich inheritance may no longer be deprived of its benefits by bad institutions.

The people of Subiaco are poor, though very industrious, and cultivating every inch of ground, with even English care and neatness;—so ignorant and uncultivated, while so finely and strongly made by Nature. May God grant now, to this people, what they need!

An illumination took place last night, in honor of the "Illustrious Gioberti." He is received here with great triumph, his carriage followed with shouts of "*Viva Gioberti, morte ai Jesuiti!*" which must be pain to the many Jesuits, who, it is said, still linger here in disguise. His triumphs are shared by Mamiani and Orioli, self-trumpeted celebrities, self-constituted rulers of the Roman state,—men of straw, to my mind, whom the fire already kindled will burn into a handful of ashes.

I sit in my obscure corner, and watch the progress of events. It is the position that pleases me best, and, I believe, the most favorable one. Everything confirms me in my radicalism; and, without any desire to hasten matters, indeed with surprise to see them rush so like a torrent, I seem to see them all tending to realize my own hopes.

My health and spirits now much restored, I am beginning to set down some of my impressions. I am going into the mountains, hoping there to find pure, strengthening air, and tranquillity for so many days as to allow me to do something.

"POOR ONE, ALONE, ALL ALONE!"

To Charles King Newcomb

22d June 48

My dear Charles,

It was a very pleasing surprize this morng to see your hand writing. You speak of you and your Mother having written, but I have never recd any letter from either, nor any answer to the questions I have asked our mutual friends about you. I remember just about the time you wrote 15th May, I sent a message to your Mother in a letter written to America and thought at the same time I wish I could know about Charles now.

You ask if I never feel home-sickness. I have at times fits of deep longing to see persons and objects in America. At times my ear and eye grow weary of the sound of a foreign tongue, and the features of a foreign race. But then my affections and thoughts have become greatly interested in some things here, and I know if I once go to the U. S. I can never come back.

Then you know, dear Charles, *I* have no "home," no peaceful roof to which I can return and repose in the love of my kindred from the friction of care and the world. My Mother has love enough and would gladly prepare me such an one, but I know she has not money. Returning to the U. S. seems return to a life of fatigue, to which I feel quite unequal, while I leave behind many objects in whose greatness and beauty I am able for a time to forget these things. Thus I prize the present moment and get what I can from it. I may be obliged to return ere long, for nothing in outward life favors my plans, nor do any letters bring any but bad news.

At present my outward environment is very beautiful. I am in the midst of a theatre of mountains, some of them crowned with snow, all of very noble shapes. Along three sides run bridle paths, fringed with olive and almond groves and vineyards; here and there gleams a church or shrine. Through the valley glides a little stream, along its banks here and there little farm houses; vegetation is most luxuriant in this valley. This town is on a slope of one of the hills, it is a little place, much ruined, having been once a baronial residence, the houses of these

TO CHARLES KING NEWCOMB

barons are gone to decay; there are churches now unused, with faded frescoes over the arched portals, and the open belfry and stone wheel-window that are so beautiful. Out of town sweet little paths lead away through the fields to Convents, one of Passionists, another of Capuchins, both seem better than the monks found near great cities; it looks very peaceful to see their draped forms pacing up the hills, and they have a healthy red in the cheek, unlike the vicious sallowness of monks of Rome. They get some life from their gardens and birds, I suppose. In the churches still open are pictures, not by great masters, but sweetly domestic, which please me much. There is one of the Virgin offering the nipple to the child Jesus; his little hand is on her breast, but he only plays and turns away; others of Santa Anna teaching the Virgin, a sweet girl of ten years old, with long curling auburn hair to read, the Virgin leans on her mother's lap; her hair curls on the book. There is another of the Marriage of the Virgin, a beautiful young man, one of three suitors, and like her as if her cousin, looks sadly on while she gives her hand to Joseph. There is often sweet music in these churches, they are dresst with fresh flowers, and the mountain breeze sweeps through them so freely, they do not smell too strong of incense.

Here I live with a lively Italian woman who makes me broth of turnips and gets my clothes washed in the stream. I shall stay here sometime, if the beautiful solitude continue to please. The country people say "Povera, sola, soletta," poor one, alone, all alone! the saints keep her," as I pass. They think me some stricken deer to stay so apart from the herd. But the cities are only 3 days off, if I wish to go, full of wars and the rumors of wars and all sorts of excitements, which have proved beyond my strength to share for the present. Good bye, dear Charles. I have written little, you know it is but little one can write in a letter. Address always Greene and Co. they will forward the letter. My love to your Mother and sisters. I was pleased you mentioned Cary. I wish she would write

Ever yours

MARGARET.

774 LETTERS

WAITING TO DELIVER HER CHILD

To Giovanni Angelo Ossoli

Rieti,
22 agosto 48

Sto un poco meglio, caro, ma si posso passare cosi il giorno meno soffrente, al contrario m'annoja che questo pare dire bisogna aspettare ancora.

Aspettare!! che noja sempre. Ma—si stava sicura fare bene, vorrei molto passare questa prova avanti tuo arrivo, ma quando penso che è possibile per me morire sola senza che poteva toccare una cara mano, voglio piu aspettare. Cosi spero tua presenza la domenica mattina

Io vedo pel giornale che il Papa fa sospendere la partenza della truppa, lui agisce come io pensavo, e mi piace molto adesso per ti non entrare ancora. Fra poco questi affari staran più certi; tu puoi prender ere qualche risoluzione più a vantaggio che adesso.

Cerca si puoi sentire alcuni dettagli di Milano Non sarebbe possibile nel caffè degli Belle Arti? m'incresce molto pel destino dei cari amici, come deven soffrire adesso.

Penso anche tanto di te, spero che sei meno tormentato, si noi stavam insiemi sarebbe un consolo ma Adesso tutto va male, ma non e possibile che va cosi sempre, sempre. Addio, amore. Mi dispiace che bisogna passare tanti giorni avanti tua venuta, tanti tanti. Mi piace che ho adesso il piccolo ritratto, lo riguardo sovente. Dio ti conserva.

Rieti,
August 22 '48

I'm a little better, dear, but if I can get through the day with less suffering, on the contrary it annoys me that this seems to mean that we still must wait.

Wait!! What a bore. But—if I were sure of faring well, I would like to get through this ordeal before you arrive, but when I think it is possible for me to die alone without touching a dear hand, I prefer to wait longer. So I hope you will be here Sunday morning.

TO GIOVANNI ANGELO OSSOLI

I see from the newspaper that the Pope is suspending the troop's departure, just as I thought, and now I'm very glad that you haven't joined yet. These matters will soon become more certain; you will be able to make decisions more to your advantage than now.

See if you can find out any details about Milan. Wouldn't that be possible at the Caffe delle Belle Arti? I'm very sorry for the fate of my dear friends, how they must be suffering now.

I think often of you as well, I hope you are less anguished, it would be a consolation if we could be together, but—now everything is going badly, but it's not possible that it will always, always be this way. Goodbye, my love. I am sorry to have to wait so many days before you come, so so many. I am glad I now have your small portrait, I look at it often. May God keep you.

"THIS DEAR BABY IN MY ARMS"

To Giovanni Angelo Ossoli

Rieti 7 Settembre 1848

Cmo Consorte

Io sto bene molto meglio che io sperava. Il Bambino anche va bene ma piange molto ancora, e spero che sarè più tranquillo quando tu vieni. Per altro voglio che per me sii tranquillo, e ti darò spesso mie nuove scrivendoti di nuovo ben presto. La mia lettera che hai per Parigi potrai affrancarla alla Posta.

Tutti di questa famiglia dove io mi trovo ti salutano. Dandoti un abbraccio, ed un bagio in questo caro Pupo che ho nelle braccia sono Tua Affma

MARGHERITA

Rieti September 7, 1848

Dearest Consort,

I am well, far better than I had hoped. The Child is also doing well, but he still cries a lot, and I hope he will be calmer when you arrive. I do not want you to worry about me, moreover, and I will write again very soon, sending you often my news. My letter for Paris that you have can be stamped at the post office.

The entire family where I am staying sends their regards. Embracing and kissing you through this dear Baby in my arms, I am Your Affectionate

Margherita

"THE BEST FRIENDS, . . . MUST BE WOMEN"

To Giuseppe Mazzini

Rome
3 March, 1849.

Dear Mazzini,

Though knowing you occupied by the most important affairs, I again feel impelled to write a few lines. What emboldens me is the persuasion that the best friends,—in point of perfect sympathy and intelligence the only friends,—of a man of ideas and of marked character, must be women. You have your mother; no doubt you have others, perhaps many; of that I know nothing; only I like to offer also my tribute of affection.

When I think that only two years ago, you thought of coming into Italy with us in disguise, it seems very glorious, that you are about to enter Republican Rome as a Roman Citizen. It seemed almost the most sublime and poetical fact of history. Yet, even in the first thrill of joy, I felt, "He will think his work but beginning now"

When I read from your hand these words "il lungo esilio testè ricominciato, la vita non confortata fuorchè d'affetti lontani e contesi, e la speranza lungamente protratta e il desiderio che commincia a farmisi supremo di dormire finalmente in pace, dachè non ho potuto vivere in terra mia"

When I read these words they made me weep bitterly and I thought of them always with a great pang at the heart. But it is not so, dear Mazzini. You do not return to sleep under the sod of Italy, but to see your thought springing up all over her soil. The gardeners seem to me, in point of instinctive wisdom or deep thought, mostly incompetent to the care of the garden, but an idea like this will be able to make use of any implements, it is to be hoped will educate, the men by making them work. It is not this, I believe, which still keeps your heart so melancholy, for I seem to read the same melancholy in your answer to the Roman assembly. You speak of "few and late years," but some full ones still remain; a century is not needed, nor ought the same man, in the same form of thought, to work too long on an age. He would mould and bend it too much to himself, better for him to die and return incarnated to give the same truth aid on yet another side. Jesus of Nazareth died young; but had he not spoken and acted as much truth as the world could bear in his time? A frailty, a perpetual short-coming, motion in a curve line, seems the destiny of this earth. The excuse awaits us elsewhere; there must be one, for it is true, as said Goethe, that "Care is taken that the trees grow not up into heaven." Then, like you, appointed ministers, must not be the less earnest in their work, yet to the greatest, the day, the moment is all their kingdom. God takes care of the increase.

Farewell! For your sake I would wish at this moment to be an Italian and a man of action. But *though an American*, I am not even *a woman of action*; so the best I can do is to pray with the whole heart. Heaven bless dear Mazzini, cheer his heart and give him worthy helpers to carry out its holy purposes!

"I AM NOT WHAT I SHOULD BE ON THIS EARTH"

To William Henry Channing

Rome, March 10th 1849

> Father of light, conduct my feet
>   Through life's dark, dangerous road;
> Let each advancing step still bring
>   Me nearer to my God.

These clumsy lines from some hymn, I learned in childhood are always recurring. Ah! how very sad it is, that all these precious first feelings that were meant to kindle steady fire on the altar of my life were wasted.

I am not what I should be on this earth. I could not be.

My nature has need of profound and steadfast sentiment, without this it could have no steadfast greatness, no creative power.

778 LETTERS

I have been since we parted the object of great love from the noble and the humble. I have felt it towards both; Yet a kind of chastened libertine I rove, pensively, always, in deep sadness, often O God help me; is all my cry. Yet I have very little faith in the paternal love, I need; the government of the earth does seem so ruthless or so negligent.

I am tired of seeing men err and bleed. I am tired of thinking, tired of hoping. I take an interest in some plans, *our* socialism, for instance, for it has become mine, too, but the interest is shallow as the plans. They are needed, they are even good, but man will still blunder and weep, as he has done for so many thousand years.

Coward and footsore, gladly would I creep into some green recess, apart from so much meddling and so much knowing, where I might see a few not unfriendly faces, where not more wretches would come than I could relieve.

Yes! I am weary, and faith soars and sings no more. Nothing is left good of me, except at the bottom of the heart, a melting tenderness. She loves much.

Thus I now die daily, and well understand the dejections of other troubled spirits with whom in times past I have communed.

"NO SECRET CAN BE KEPT"

To Caroline Sturgis Tappan

16th March, 1849.

My loved Caroline

Your letter received yesterday, so full of sweetness and acquainting me so well with the facts of your life brought true consolation: forgive, if in the inclosed, I utter something like a reproach, that I knew through others first this great fact in your life. I ought not to have felt so, But all the while I was hoping myself, I thought of you too, and expected this news from your next letter. When it told me nothing, I thought it was not so, then when others came and told me, I felt sad. Since I have had this troubled feeling, I will not suppress it, but send the inclosed letter, otherwise not of worth, that you may know me no better than I am.

Now then your little one is there. Will not William write me the day and hour and what kind of weather there was when it came. I hope to hear soon.

I am very glad to hear how your life is likely to be and that you will be with your baby among mountains. Mine too saw mountains when he first looked forward into the world. Rieti, not only an old classic town of Italy, but one founded by what are now called the aborigines, is a hive of very ancient dwellings with soft-colored red brown roofs, a citadel and several towers. It is in a plain twelve miles in diameter one way, not much less the other, entirely encircled with mountains of the noblest form, casinos and hermitages gleam here and there on their lower slopes. This plain is almost the richest in Italy and full of vineyards. Rieti is near the foot of the hills on one side, the rapid Velino makes almost the circuit of its walls on its way to Terni. *I too had my apartment, shut out from the family on the bank of this river. I too saw the mountains,* as I lay on my restless couch. I had a *piazza, or as they call them here loggia which hung over the river,* where I walked most of the night, for I was not like you, I could not sleep at all those months. I do not know how I lived.

In Rieti the ancient Umbrians were married thus. In presence of friends the man and maid received together the gifts of *fire and water.* The bridegroom then conducted to his house the bride. At the door he gave her the keys and entering threw behind him nuts as a sign that he renounced all the frivolities of boyhood.

But I intend to write all that relates to the birth of Angelino in a little book, which I shall, I hope, show you sometime. I have begun it and then stopped; it seemed to me he would die. If he lives, I shall finish it, before the details are at all faded in my mind.

Rieti is a place where I should have liked to have him born, and where I should like to have him now, but 1st the people are so wicked, the most ferocious and mercenary population of Italy. I did not know this when I went there. I expected to be solitary and quiet among poor people. But they looked on *the marchioness* as an ignorant *Inglese,* and they fancy all *Inglesi* have wealth untold. Me they were bent on plundering in every way; they are so still. They made me suffer terribly in the first days and disturb me greatly still in visits to my darling. To add to my trouble, the legion Garribaldi is now stationed there, in which so many desperadoes are enlisted. The Neapolitan troops 6 miles off are far worse, and in case of conflict I should fear for the nurse of Angelino, the loveliest young woman there. I cannot take her from her family. I cannot change him to another place without immense difficulty in every way. That I could not nurse him was owing to the wickedness of these people, who threw me into a fever the first days. I shall tell you about it sometime. There is something very singular and fateful in the way all has wrought to give me more and more sorrow and difficulty. Now I only live from day to day watching the signs of the times; when I asked you for the money I meant to use it to stay with him in Rieti, but now I do not know whether I can stay there or not. If it proves impossible, I shall at all risks, remove him. I may say every day is to me one of mental doubt and conflict; how it will end, I do not know. I try to hold myself ready every way body and mind for any necessity.

You say no secret can be kept in the civilized world and I suppose not long, but it is very important to me to keep this, for the present, if possible, and by and by to have the mode of disclosure at my option. For this, I have made the cruellest sacrifices; it will, indeed, be just like the rest, if they are made of none effect.

After I wrote to you I went to Rieti. The weather was mild when I set out, but by the fatality that has attended me throughout, in the night changed to a cold, unknown in Italy and remained so all the time I staid. There was, as is common in Italy, no fireplace except in the kitchen. I suffered much in my room with its brick floor, and windows through which came the cold wind freely. My darling did not suffer, because he was a little swaddled child like this and robed in wool beside, but I did very much. When I first took him in my arms he made no sound but leaned his head against my bosom, and staid so, he seemed to say how could you abandon me, what I felt you will know only when you have your own. A little girl who lived in the house told me all the day of my departure he could not be comforted, always refusing the breast and looking at the door; he has been a strangely precocious infant; I think it was through sympathy with me, and that in that regard it

TO CAROLINE STURGIS TAPPAN 781

may be a happiness for him to be with these more plebian, instinctive, joyous natures. I saw he was more serene, that he was not sensitive as when with me, and slept a great deal more. You speak of my being happy; all the solid happiness I have known has been at times when he went to sleep in my arms. You say when Ellen's beautiful life had been so wasted, it hardly seemed worthwhile to begin another. I had all those feelings too. I do not look forward to his career and his manly life; it is *now* I want to be with him, before passion, care and bafflings begin. If I had a little money I should go with him into strict retirement for a year or two and live for him alone. This I cannot do; all life that has been or could be natural to me is invariably denied. God knows why, I suppose.

I receive with profound gratitude your thought of taking him, if any thing should happen to us. Should I live, I dont know whether I should wish him to be an Italian or American citizen; it depends on the course events take here politically but should we die, the person to whom he would naturally fall is a sister of his father a person of great elegance and sweetness but entirely limited in mind. I should not like that. I will think about it. Before he was born I did a great deal having the idea I might die and all my spirit remain incarnated in him, but now I think I shall live and carry him round myself as I ride on my ass into Egypt. We shant go so mildly as this yet.

You talk about your mangers, Carrie, but that was only for a little, presently came Kings with gold cups and all sorts of things. Joseph pawned them; with part of the money he bought this nice donkey for the journey; and they lived on the rest till Joseph could work at his trade, we have no donkey and it costs a great deal to travel in diligences and steamers, and being a nobleman is a poor trade in a ruined despotism just turning into a Republic. I often think of Dicken's marchioness playing whist in the kitchen. So I play whist every where.

Speaking of the republic, you say do I not wish Italy had a great man. Mazzini is a great man; in mind a great poetic statesman, in heart a lover, in action decisive and full of resource as Cesar. Dearly I love Mazzini, who also loves me. He came in just as I had finished this first letter to you. His soft radiant look makes melancholy music in my soul; it consecrates my present life that like the Magdalen I may at the important hour

782 LETTERS

shed all the consecrated ointment on his head. There is one, Mazzini, who understands thee well, who knew thee no less when an object of popular fear than now of idolatry, and who, if the pen be not held too feebly, will make that posterity shall know thee, too.

Ah well! what is the use of writing, dear Caroline. A thousand volumes would not suffice for what I have to say. Pray for You? oh much I have, for my love for you is deep, I trust immortal. May you hold a dear one safe in your arms! and all go sweetly as it has gone

> I could not wish thy better state
> Was one of my degree
> But we may mourn that evil fate
> Made such a churl of me.

Could I envy it would be this peace with the own one, but God grant it to Carrie, since thou wert such a niggard as to steal it from me. At least make some good use of it; don't give it to fools only.

Adieu, love, my love to William your husband with the fair noble face. You can always show him my letters if he cares to read them, then burn—and when you are once more able [   ] to

MARGARET

Although I think y[r]emember that I shall be [   ] for it is, indeed, a great physical crisis.

No American here knows that I ever was in Rieti. They suppose I passed the summer at Subiaco.

"IN THE EVENT WE BOTH DIE"

To Giovanni Angelo Ossoli

Quanto m'incresce, amore, mancar ti ieri e possibile anch, oggi, si tu puoi venire. Vado a Casa Diez, si possibile cerchi la, ultimo piano, si sto la ancora o son andato al spedale. Dio ti conserva Quanto ho sofferta a vedere i feriti, e non posso

TO GIOVANNI ANGELO OSSOLI 783

conoscere si qualche cosa ti accade, ma bisogna sperare. Ho ricevuta la lettera di Rieti, nostro Nino sta perfettamente bene, grazia per questo.

Mi fa di bene che almeno i Romani han fatto qualche cosa, si solamente tu puoi stare. In evento del morte di tutti dui ho lasciata una carta col certificato di Angelino e alcune righe pregando i Sto curare per lui. Si per qualche accidente io moriro tu puoi riprendere questa carta si vuoi da me, come da tua moglie. Ho voluta per Nino andare in America, ma tu farari come ti pare. Era nostro dovere combinare questo meglio. Ma speriamo che non sara bisogno. Sempre benedicendo la tua

MARGHERITA

Si tu vivi e io moro, stai sempre devotissimo per Nino. Si tu ami mai un altra, ancora pensi primo per lui, io prego, prego, amore.

How sorry I am, my love, to have missed you yesterday, and perhaps today as well, if you are able to come. I am going to Casa Diez. If possible, look for me there, on the top floor if I am still there, or at the hospital if I have gone there. May God preserve you. How I suffered seeing the wounded, and I have no way of knowing if something happens to you, but one must hope. I received the letter from Rieti, our Nino is fine, thankfully.

It does me good to know that at least the Romans have done something, as long as you survive. In the event we both die, I have left a note with Angelino's birth certificate and a few words begging the Storys to take care of him. Should I by any chance die, you can take back the note from me if you like, as from your wife. I wanted Nino to go to America, but you should do as you please. It was our duty to arrange this better. But let us hope it won't be necessary. Blessing you as always,

Margherita

If you live and I die, always be devoted to Nino. If you ever love another woman, still think of him first, I beg you, I beg you, my love.

June 1849

"ROME IS BEING DESTROYED"

To Ralph Waldo Emerson

Rome, 10 June 1849

I received your letter amid the round of cannonade and musketry. It was a terrible battle fought here from the first till the last light of day. I could see all its progress from my balcony. The Italians fought like lions. It is a truly heroic spirit that animates them. They make a stand here for honor and their rights, with little ground for hope that they can resist, now they are betrayed by France.

Since the 30th April, I go almost daily to the hospitals, and, though I have suffered,—for I had no idea before, how terrible gunshot-wounds and wound-fever are,—yet I have taken pleasure, and great pleasure, in being with the men; there is scarcely one who is not moved by a noble spirit. Many, especially among the Lombards, are the flower of the Italian youth. When they begin to get better, I carry them books, and flowers; they read, and we talk.

The palace of the Pope, on the Quirinal, is now used for convalescents. In those beautiful gardens, I walk with them,— one with his sling, another with his crutch. The gardener plays off all his waterworks for the defenders of the country, and gathers flowers for me, their friend.

A day or two since, we sat in the Pope's little pavilion, where he used to give private audience. The sun was going gloriously down over Monte Mario, where gleamed the white tents of the French light-horse among the trees. The cannonade was heard at intervals. Two bright-eyed boys sat at our feet, and gathered up eagerly every word said by the heroes of the day. It was a beautiful hour, stolen from the midst of ruin and sorrow; and tales were told as full of grace and pathos as in the gardens of Boccaccio, only in a very different spirit,—with noble hope for men, with reverence for woman.

The young ladies of the family, very young girls, were filled with enthusiasm for the suffering, wounded patriots, and they wished to go to the hospital to give their services. Excepting the three superintendents, none but married ladies were permitted to serve there, but their services were accepted. Their governess

TO RALPH WALDO EMERSON

then wished to go too, and, as she could speak several languages, she was admitted to the rooms of the wounded soldiers, to interpret for them, as the nurses knew nothing but Italian, and many of these poor men were suffering, because they could not make their wishes known. Some are French, some German, and many Poles. Indeed, I am afraid it is too true that there were comparatively but few Romans among them. This young lady passed several nights there.

Should I never return,—and sometimes I despair of doing so, it seems so far off, so difficult, I am caught in such a net of ties here,—if ever you know of my life here, I think you will only wonder at the constancy with which I have sustained myself; the degree of profit to which, amid great difficulties, I have put the time, at least in the way of observation. Meanwhile, love me all you can; let me feel, that, amid the fearful agitations of the world, there are pure hands, with healthful, even pulse, stretched out toward me, if I claim their grasp.

I feel profoundly for Mazzini; at moments I am tempted to say, "Cursed with every granted prayer,"—so cunning is the daemon. He is become the inspiring soul of his people. He saw Rome, to which all his hopes through life tended, for the first time as a Roman citizen, and to become in a few days its ruler. He has animated, he sustains her to a glorious effort, which, if it fails, this time, will not in the age. His country will be free. Yet to me it would be so dreadful to cause all this bloodshed, to dig the graves of such martyrs.

Then Rome is being destroyed; her glorious oaks; her villas, haunts of sacred beauty, that seemed the possession of the world forever,—the villa of Raphael, the villa of Albani, home of Winkelmann, and the best expression of the ideal of modern Rome, and so many other sanctuaries of beauty,—all must perish, lest a foe should level his musket from their shelter. *I* could not, could not!

I know not, dear friend, whether I ever shall get home across that great ocean, but here in Rome I shall no longer wish to live. O, Rome, *my* country! could I imagine that the triumph of what I held dear was to heap such desolation on thy head!

"I HAVE UNITED MY DESTINY WITH THAT OF
AN OBSCURE YOUNG MAN"

To Costanza Arconati Visconti

Reading a book called "The Last Days of the Republic in Rome," I see that my letter, giving my impressions of that period, may well have seemed to you strangely partial. If we can meet as once we did, and compare notes in the same spirit of candor, while making mutual allowance for our different points of view, your testimony and opinions would be invaluable to me. But will you have patience with my democracy,—my revolutionary spirit? Believe that in thought I am more radical than ever. The heart of Margaret you know,—it is always the same. Mazzini is immortally dear to me,—a thousand times dearer for all the trial I saw made of him in Rome;—dearer for all he suffered. Many of his brave friends perished there. We who, less worthy, survive, would fain make up for the loss, by our increased devotion to him, the purest, the most disinterested of patriots, the most affectionate of brothers. You will not love me less that I am true to him.

Then, again, how will it affect you to know that I have united my destiny with that of an obscure young man,—younger than myself; a person of no intellectual culture, and in whom, in short, you will see no reason for my choosing; yet more, that this union is of long standing; that we have with us our child, of a year old, and that it is only lately I acquainted my family with the fact.

If you decide to meet with me as before, and wish to say something about the matter to your friends, it will be true to say that there have been pecuniary reasons for this concealment. But *to you* in confidence I add, this is only half the truth; and I cannot explain or satisfy my dear friend farther—I should wish to meet her independent of all relations; but as we live in the midst of "society," she would have to enquire for me now as *Margaret Ossoli* that being done, I should like to say nothing farther on the subject.

However you may feel about all this, dear Madame Arconati, you will always be the same in my eyes. I earnestly wish you may not feel estranged, but only, if you do, I would rather for you to act upon it. Let us meet as friends, or not at all—In all events I remain ever yours,

MARGARET

August 1849

"ON THE BRINK OF LOSING MY LITTLE BOY"

To Caroline Sturgis Tappan

Rieti 28 Aug 49.

I have been on the brink of losing my little boy. During all the siege of Rome I could not see him, and though the Physician wrote reassuring letters I often seemed to hear him calling me amid the roar of the cannon, and he seemed to be crying. When I came I found mine own fast waning to the tomb. All that I have undergone seemed little to what I felt seeing him unable to smile or lift his little wasted hand Now by incessant care day and night I have brought him back (who knows if indeed that be a deed of love?) into this difficult world. I hope that the cruel law of my life will at least not oblige me to be separated from him—

"IT WAS ONLY GREAT LOVE FOR YOU THAT KEPT ME SILENT"

To Margarett Crane Fuller

Dearest Mother,

I received your letter a few hours before leaving Rome. Like all of yours, it refreshed me, and gave me as much satisfaction as anything could, at that sad time. Its spirit is of eternity, and befits an epoch when wickedness and perfidy so impudently triumph, and the best blood of the generous and honorable is poured out like water, seemingly in vain.

I cannot tell you what I suffered to abandon the wounded to the care of their mean foes; to see the young men, that were faithful to their vows, hunted from their homes,—hunted like wild beasts; denied a refuge in every civilized land. Many of those I loved are sunk to the bottom of the sea, by Austrian cannon, or will be shot. Others are in penury, grief, and exile. May God give due recompense for all that has been endured!

My mind still agitated, and my spirits worn out, I have not felt like writing to any one. Yet the magnificent summer does not smile quite in vain for me. Much exercise in the open air, living much on milk and fruit, have recruited my health, and I am regaining the habit of sleep, which a month of nightly cannonade in Rome had destroyed.

Receiving, a few days since, a packet of letters from America, I opened them with more feeling of hope and good cheer, than for a long time past. The first words that met my eye were these, in the hand of Mr. Greeley:—"Ah, Margaret, the world grows dark with us! You grieve, for Rome is fallen;—I mourn, for Pickie is dead."

I have shed rivers of tears over the inexpressibly affecting letter thus begun. One would think I might have become familiar enough with images of death and destruction; yet somehow the image of Pickie's little dancing figure, lying, stiff and stark, between his parents, has made me weep more than all else. There was little hope he could do justice to himself, or lead a happy life in so perplexed a world; but never was a character of richer capacity,—never a more charming child. To me he was most dear, and would always have been so. Had he become stained with earthly faults, I could never have forgotten what he was when fresh from the soul's home, and what he was to me when my soul pined for sympathy, pure and unalloyed. The three children I have seen who were fairest in my eyes, and gave me most promise of the future, were Waldo, Pickie, Hermann Clarke;—all nipped in the bud. Endless thoughts has this given me, and a resolve to seek the realization of all hopes and plans elsewhere, which resolve will weigh with me as much as it can weigh before the silver cord is finally loosed. Till then, Earth, our mother, always finds strange, unexpected ways to draw us back to her bosom,—to make us seek anew a nutriment which has never failed to cause us frequent sickness.

This brings me to the main object of my present letter,—a piece of intelligence about myself, which I had hoped I might be able to communicate in such a way as to give you *pleasure*. That

TO MARGARETT CRANE FULLER 789

I cannot,—after suffering much in silence with that hope,—is like the rest of my earthly destiny.

The first moment, it may cause you a pang to know that your eldest child might long ago have been addressed by another name than yours, and has a little son a year old.

But, beloved mother, do not feel this long. I do assure you, that it was only great love for you that kept me silent. I have abstained a hundred times, when your sympathy, your counsel, would have been most precious, from a wish not to harass you with anxiety. Even now I would abstain, but it has become necessary, on account of the child, for us to live publicly and permanently together; and we have no hope, in the present state of Italian affairs, that we can do it at any better advantage, for several years, than now.

My husband is a Roman, of a noble but now impoverished house. His mother died when he was an infant, his father is dead since we met, leaving some property, but encumbered with debts, and in the present state of Rome hardly available, except by living there. He has three older brothers, all provided for in the Papal service,—one as Secretary of the Privy Chamber, the other two as members of the Guard Noble. A similar career would have been opened to him, but he embraced liberal principles, and, with the fall of the Republic, has lost all, as well as the favor of his family, who all sided with the Pope. Meanwhile, having been an officer in the Republican service, it was best for him to leave Rome. He has taken what little money he had, and we plan to live in Florence for the winter. If he or I can get the means, we shall come together to the United States, in the summer;—earlier we could not, on account of the child.

He is not in any respect such a person as people in general would expect to find with me. He had no instructor except an old priest, who entirely neglected his education; and of all that is contained in books he is absolutely ignorant, and he has no enthusiasm of character. On the other hand, he has excellent practical sense; has been a judicious observer of all that passed before his eyes; has a nice sense of duty, which, in its unfailing, minute activity, may put most enthusiasts to shame; a very sweet temper, and great native refinement. His love for me has been unswerving and most tender. I have never suffered a pain that he could relieve. His devotion, when I am ill, is to be compared only with yours. His delicacy in trifles, his sweet domestic graces, remind me of E——. In him I have found a home, and one that interferes with no tie. Amid many ills and cares, we have had much joy together, in the sympathy with natural beauty,—with our child,—with all that is innocent and sweet.

I do not know whether he will always love me so well, for I am the elder, and the difference will become, in a few years, more perceptible than now. But life is so uncertain, and it is so necessary to take good things with their limitations, that I have not thought it worth while to calculate too curiously.

However my other friends may feel, I am sure that *you* will love him very much, and that he will love you no less. Could we all live together, on a moderate income, you would find peace with us. Heaven grant, that, on returning, I may gain means to effect this object. He, of course, can do nothing, while we are in the United States, but perhaps I can; and now that my health is better, I shall be able to exert myself, if sure that my child is watched by those who love him, and who are good and pure.

What shall I say of my child? All might seem hyperbole, even to my dearest mother. In him I find satisfaction, for the first time, to the deep wants of my heart. Yet, thinking of those other sweet ones fled, I must look upon him as a treasure only lent. He is a fair child, with blue eyes and light hair; very affectionate, graceful, and sportive. He was baptized, in the Roman Catholic Church, by the name of Angelo Eugene Philip, for his father, grandfather, and my brother. He inherits the title of marquis.

Write the name of my child in your Bible, Angelo Ossoli, *born September* 5, 1848. God grant he may live to see you, and may prove worthy of your love!

More I do not feel strength to say. You can hardly guess how all attempt to express something about the great struggles and experiences of my European life enfeebles me. When I get home,—if ever I do,—it will be told without this fatigue and excitement. I trust there will be a little repose, before entering anew on this wearisome conflict.

I had addressed you twice,—once under the impression that I should not survive the birth of my child; again during the siege of Rome, the father and I being both in danger. I took Mrs. Story, and, when she left Rome, Mr. Cass, into my confidence. Both were kind as sister and brother. Amid much

pain and struggle, sweet is the memory of the generous love
I received from William and Emelyn Story, and their uncle. They
helped me gently through a most difficult period. Mr. Cass, also
who did not know me at all, has done everything possible for me.

August 31, 1849

"HE IS TO ME A SOURCE OF INEFFABLE JOYS"

To Costanza Arconati Visconti

Florence 16 Oct 49
My loved friend, I read your letter with greatest content. I did
not know but there might seem something offensively strange
in the circumstances I mentioned to you. Goethe says, there
is nothing men pardon so little as singular conduct for which
no reason is given; and remembering this, I have been a little
surprized at the even increased warmth of interest with which
the little American society of Florence has received me, with
the unexpected accessories of husband and child, asking no
questions, and seemingly content to find me so. With you I
indeed thought it would be so, because you are above the world;
only, as you have always walked in the beaten path, though with
noble port and feet undefiled, yet I thought you might not like
your friends to be running about in these blind alleys. It glads
my heart indeed that you do not care and we may meet in love.

You speak of our children. Ah, dear friend, I do, indeed, feel
we shall have deep sympathy there. I do not believe mine will be
a brilliant child, like Gian Martino. Indeed, I see nothing particular about him, yet he is to me a source of ineffable joys, far
purer, deeper than any thing I ever felt before, like what Nature
had sometimes given, but more intimate, more sweet. He loves
me very much, his little heart clings to mine. I trust, if he lives
to sow there no seeds which are not good, to be always growing
better for his sake. His father, too, will be a good father. He
has very little of what is called intellectual development, but
unspoiled instincts, affections pure and constant, a quiet sense
of duty, which to me, who have seen much of the great faults
in characters of enthusiasm and genius, seems of highest value.

792   LETTERS

When you write by post, please direct *Marchesa Ossoli*, as all the letters come to that address. I might lose yours without it. I did not explain myself on that point. The fact is, it seems to me silly for a radical like me, to be carrying a title; and yet, while Ossoli is in his native land, it seems disjoining myself from him not to bear it. You spoke of my always addressing you in form: now for you, it seems appropriate, and, though the least of your honors, it would pain me to have it omitted. You were born so. You are really the lady of large lands; you and your husband both feel the duties that come with position of command, and, I am sure, if you look back with pride to ancestors, it is not, as many do, to lean upon their merits, but to emulate them. For me, it is a sort of thing that does not naturally belong to me, and unsustained by fortune, is but a *souvenir* even for Ossoli. Yet it has seemed to me for him to drop it, an inherited title, would be in some sort to acquiesce in his brothers' disclaiming him, and dropping a right he may possibly wish to maintain for his child. How does it seem to you? I am not very clear about it. If O. dropt the title, it would be a suitable moment in becoming an inhabitant of republican America.

"OSSOLI IS FORMING SOME TASTE FOR BOOKS"

To Emelyn Story

[   ] talk with Mrs. S. Today we have been out to the casa di Ogli and found its little chapel full of contadine (their lovers were waiting outside the door); they looked charming in their black veils, their straw hat was worn to the door and then hung on the arm with shy glancing eyes and cheeks pinched rosy by the cold. For it is cold here as N England. On foot we have explored a great part of the environs, before I had no idea of their beauty. When here with the Springs I took only the regular drives, as prescribed for all ladies and gentlemen that travel. This evening we came home by a path that led to the banks of the Arno; the dome, the snowy mountains, were glorious in the rosy tint and haze just before sunset. What a difference it makes to come home to a child; how it fills up all the gaps of life, just in the way that is most consoling, most refreshing. I used to feel sad at that time; the day

TO ELIZABETH BARRETT BROWNING 793

had not been nobly spent, I had not done my duty to myself and others; then I felt so lonely, now I never feel lonely, for even if my little boy dies, our souls will remain eternally united. then I feel *infinite* hope for him, hope that he will serve God and man more loyally than I have and seeing how full he is of life, how much he can afford to throw away, I feel the inexhaustableness of nature and console myself for my own incapac[   ]

I see Mr and Mrs Browning often, but Mrs B. will not be able to go out any more, being again *enceinte*, their baby is surpassingly pretty. Our intercourse as yet has not amounted to much, being taken too much in snatches. She seems to me just as you described her. Mr B. is entertaining, very cordial in his manner, but my intercourse with him I find singularly external. I know not that I ever had such with any person of substance. They speak of you both with very great partiality (let not that word read as equivoque) and desire to be commended unto you.

Madame Arconati is near me; we have had some hours of great content together, but in the last weeks her only child has been dangerously ill. I have no other acquaintance except in the American Circle, and should not care to make any unless singularly desirable, for I want all my time for the care of my child, for my walks and visits to objects of art, in which again I can find pleasure, and in the evening for study and writing. Ossoli is forming some taste for books, which I never expected, also he is studying English. He learns it of Horace Sumner to whom he teaches Italian in turn.

c. November 1849

REMEMBERING EDGAR ALLAN POE

To Elizabeth Barrett Browning

Casa Libri
Thursday 6th Decr

Dear Mrs Browning,
    Thanks for sending me the names. I find I had already the same cap pattern, but it looked so pretty on your baby's head I did not recognize it.

I am very sorry the nurse did not come upstairs with him; if you send her again will you tell her to do so, that he may exchange a few looks with mine. I think babies seem amazed at one another, they are not in haste to make acquaintance, probably they still feel what a world lies hidden in each person, they are not yet made callous by those habits of hasty unfeeling intercourse soon formed by what is called society.

It seemed to me when I was last at your house, as if a curtain fell down between us. A great sadness fell upon me, just after Mr Browning came in; it did not seem to come from him; he seemed cheerful and glowing after his walk, but some cause changed suddenly the temper of my soul, so that I could hardly realize what was passing and the cloud did not leave me for several hours. Did you share any such influence. I think probably it was confined to me, but have noted the day and hour in my diary, in case any interpretation should later be tendered.

Those fragments expressed the almost universal feeling towards Poe; several women loved him, but it seemed more with passionate illusion which he amused himself by inducing than with sympathy; I think he really had no friend. I did not know him, though I saw and talked with him often, but he always seemed to me shrouded in an assumed character. Still as I did not know him, and do not accept the opinions of others till my own impressions have confirmed them, as I did know he had much to try his spirit I always treated him cordially. He seemed to feel that *I* was not prejudiced against him; he once said that he had faith in me, that he thought me not only incapable of baseness, but incapable of understanding it; that this was from him a strong expression of esteem, shows what his life had been. He said in a sketch he published of me that he thought me capable of great affection. Now, seeing these bitter waters poured out even upon his tomb, I have remembered these things and regretted that I never tried whether more friendliness from me might have been useful to him; but it is only the millionth time I have let occasions pass where suffering fellow men might have been soothed or helped Pardon that the leaf is soiled. I had not observed it. Ever truly yours

M. Ossoli

1849

"THIS FALSE STATE OF SOCIETY"

To William Henry Channing

Florence 17th December 1849.

It is now a month since I had your little letter, and always I have been waiting to answer in vague expectation of some kind of a crisis. I know not what but it has long seemed that in the year 1850, I should stand on some important plateau in the ascent of life, should be allowed to pause for awhile, and take more clear and commanding views than ever before. I feel however no marked and important change as yet, and it is not worth while to wait too long.

My love for Ossoli is most pure and tender, nor has any one, except little children or mother, ever loved me as genuinely as he does. To you, dear William I was obliged to make myself known; others have loved me with a mixture of fancy and enthusiasm excited by my talent at embellishing subjects. He loves me from simple affinity; he loves to be with me, and serve and soothe me. Our relation covers only a part of my life, but I do not perceive that it interferes with anything I ought to have or be; I do not feel any way constrained or limited or that I have made any sacrifice. Younger I might, because I should have been exposed to love some other in a way that might give him pain, but I do not now feel apprehensive of that. There is more danger for him, as he is younger than I; if he should, I shall do all that this false state of society permits to give him what freedom he may need. I have thought a great deal about this; there are things I do not wish to put on paper. I daresay I shall tell them to you when we meet. You speak as if I might return to America without him. I thought of it at one time, knowing it would be very trying for him to go with me, that when I first am with my former friends, he may have many lonely hours. Beside he had then an employment in Rome and we needed the money. I thought I would go and either write for him to come to me, or return to Italy. But now that cannot be. He could not at present reenter Rome without danger; he is separated from his employment and his natural friends, nor is any career open for him in Italy at present. Then I could not think of taking away the child for several months; his heart is fixed on the child as fervently as mine. Then it would not only be very strange and sad to me to be without his love and care for weeks and months, but I should feel very anxious about him under present circumstances. I trust we shall find means to make the voyage together and remain together. In our country he will have for resources, his walks and quiet communings with nature, which is always so great a part of his life; he will have the child, and I think my family, expecially my mother, will love him very dearly and he will be learning the language with them. I suppose I must myself be engaged in the old unhealthy way, life will probably be a severe struggle. I hope I shall be able to live through it, and not neglect my child, nor Ossoli. He has suffered enough; it has ploughed furrows in his life since first we met. He has done all he could and cannot blame himself. Our destiny is sad; we must brave it as we can. I hope we shall always feel mutual tenderness, and Ossoli has a simple child-like piety that will make it easier for him.

You speak of my whole future, that future here on earth now seems to me short. It may be terribly trying but it will not be so very long now. Indeed, now I have the child, I am often sad fearing I may not stay long enough

As to my writing do not expect any thing very good of it I suppose there are impressions worth the general hearing about as far as they are correct and I am anxious to do historical justice to some facts and persons, but I am not aware that there will be *that* of advantage to a thinker. I do not know for I cannot read it over, but believe I have scarce expressed what lies deepest in my mind. I take no pains about this or other things but let the Genius lead. I did struggle to lead a simple, natural life *at home*, and learning of my child, writing only when imperatively obliged by the mind that insisted on utterance, but was defeated and now I strive no more. Eternity is ours, beloved William—we will be true and full living beings yet—

Ever yours—

"I LIKE ALSO MUCH LIVING WITH MY HUSBAND"

To Arthur Hugh Clough

Florence
16th Feby 1850

Dear Mr Clough,

I am going to write, principally with the view of getting a letter back, so you must not disappoint me.

You wrote that you might see me here, might come every now and then to Italy. But you must come to America rather. I think I shall go there this summer. Dearly as I love Italy and incomplete as is my acquaintance with her yet, I do not like to be here at this time of incubus. Often I forget it, but on reawaking to a sense of the realities round me it is crushing to think, to feel all that is smothered down in mens minds. I care least for these cowed and coward Florentines; they are getting only what they deserve, but do not like to be among them.

The judicious conduct of the Austrians here is quite admirable. One would not think that men installed where they are not wanted and ought not to be could seem so gentlemanly The troops are kept in great order, still from the very nature of the case the Tuscans gather with each day fresh cause for gloomy brooding. The Austrians at this moment seem in great dread of an outbreak, but I suppose it could only be some trifling street fuss as yet

Yes I shall like to go back and see our "eighteen millions of bores," with their rail-roads, electric telegraphs, mass movements and ridiculous dilettant phobias, but with ever successful rush and bang. I feel as if I should be the greatest bore of all when I get home, so few will care for the thoughts of my head or the feelings of my heart, but there will be some pairs of eyes to see, and a sense of fresh life unknown here.

I have recd an offer from an Amern publisher for my book, but it is not satisfactory and I think to wait till I go myself, perhaps to burn meanwhile. I am not at all sorry it was not to be published in England, (indeed now I see the question whether foreigners can hold copy right is quite decided against us) and I shall not care if prevented from publishing at all. I dare say the experiences if left for seed corn will grow to something better.

As to money I have not got any yet, but probably should not by the book; if it succeeded tolerably, I should get cheated somehow out of the penny fee.

Casting aside the past and the future, and despite the extreme cold which has tormented me much in an Italn apartment, fit only for May and June, I have enjoyed many bright and peaceful hours this winter. My little baby flourishes in my care; his laughing eyes, his stammered words and capricious caresses afford me the first unalloyed quiet joy I have ever known. Tis true! he must grow up to sorrow and to strive and have less and less the sweet music that seems to flow around him now, if like his mother he will be full of faults and much unreasonable, but I hope there will be in him a conquering, purifying energy too. What we call God seems so very near in the presence of a child; we bless the love that gave this soul to put an end to loneliness, we believe in the justice that is bound to provide it at last with all it needs. I like also much living with my husband. You said in your letter you thought I should at any rate be happier now because the position of an unmarried woman in our time is not desirable; to me on the contrary it had seemed that in a state of society where marriage brings so much of trifling business arrangements and various soporifics the liberty of single life was most precious. I liked to see those I loved only in the best way. With Ossoli I liked when no one knew of our relation, and we passed our days together in the mountains, or walked beautiful nights amid the ruins of Rome. But for the child I should have wished to remain as we were, and feared we should lose much by entering on the jog-trot of domestic life. However, I do not find it so; we are of mutual solace and aid about the dish and spoon part, yet enjoy our free rambles as much as ever. Now I have written a good deal of me, will you write some sincere words of you, at least as much so as you have put in your print. Which makes me always so sorry I threw away the chance of knowing you in Rome. Had I known you before we could have talked then, but I was so pressed with excitements, I had not the soul to make a new acquaintance

Is Mazzini in London; have you seen him? if so, do write me how he is and whatever you may know of him. I think of him with unspeakable affection, but do not wish to write.

Adieu, dear Mr Clough, your friend

MARGARET

"I AM ABSURDLY FEARFUL ABOUT THIS VOYAGE"

To Costanza Arconati Visconti

Florence, 6 April
1850.

[   ] Yesterday I had been bled after more than ten days constant headach, and dangerous pressure on the brain. I was lying feeling relieved yet much exhausted too, when your letter came. You cannot know how much good it did me. Its effect was quite talismanic, as the sight of you has often been, seeming to heal, console and strengthen.

With Guisti was extinguished a spark of the true fire of genius. Now Italy seems to me wholly bereft—Mazzini, Berchet, silent, Giusti dead—The great depart, "And none rise up to fill their vacant seat"—. [   ] I would not for the world have your last thoughts of me mingled with the least unpleasantness, when mine of you must always be all sweet. I say, *last thoughts.* I am absurdly fearful about this voyage. Various little omens have combined to give me a dark feeling. Among others just now, we hear of the wreck of the ship Westmoreland, bearing Powers's Eve. Perhaps we shall live to laugh at these, but in case of mishap, I should perish with my husband and child perhaps to be transferred to some happier state; and my dear mother, whom I so long to see, would soon follow, and embrace me more peaceably elsewhere. You, loved friend, God keep and cherish here and hereafter! is the prayer of your loving and grateful

MARGARET

"I LEAVE ITALY WITH PROFOUND REGRET"

To Lewis Cass Jr.

Florence
2d May, 1850.

Dear Mr Cass,

I shall, most probably, leave Florence and Italy the 8th or 10th of this month and am not willing to depart without saying adieu to yourself. I wanted to write the 30th April, but a succession of petty interruptions prevented. That was the day I saw you first and the day the French first assailed Rome. What a crowded day that was! I had been in the morning to visit Ossoli in the garden of the Vatican, just after my return you entered. I then went to the hospital and there passed the night amid the groans of many suffering, some dying men. What a strange first of May it was as I walked the streets of Rome by the first sunlight of next day! Those were to me grand and impassioned hours. Deep sorrow followed, many embarrassments many pains! Let me once more at parting thank you for the sympathy you showed me amid many of these. A thousand years might pass and you would find it unforgotten by me. I shall be glad however if you have destroyed, or will destroy, letters I wrote you during that period. I was heartsick, weary; the future seemed too difficult, and I too weak to face it. What I felt, what I wrote then is below the usual temper of my mind, and I would be glad to cancel all trace of those weaker moods—

I leave Italy with profound regret and with only a vague hope of returning. I could have lived here always, full of bright visions, and expanding in my faculties, had destiny permitted. May you be happy who remain here! it would be well worth while to be happy in Italy.

I had hoped to enjoy some of the last days, but the weather has been steadily bad since you were in Florence. Since the 4th April, we have not had a fine day and all our little plans for visits to favorite spots, and beautiful objects from which we must long be separated, have been marred!

Adieu! I do not feel like writing much. You will, probably, not have time to answer now, but if you feel inclined sometimes to address me in our country, a permanent address would be to care of S. G. Ward, Boston

I sail in the bark Elizabeth for New York. She is laden with marble and rags, a very appropriate companionship for wares of Italy. She carries Powers's statue of Calhoon. Adieu, remember that we look to you to keep up the dignity of our country; many important occasions are now likely to offer, for the American, (I wish I could write the *Columbian*) man to advocate, more, to *represent* the cause of Truth and Freedom, in face of their foes, and remember me as their lover and your friend

M. O.

CHRONOLOGY

NOTE ON THE TEXTS

NOTES

GENERAL INDEX

INDEX OF FULLER'S POETRY TITLES
AND FIRST LINES

Chronology

1810   Born Sarah Margaret Fuller on May 23, 1810, in Cambridgeport, Massachusetts, the first child of Margarett Crane Fuller and Timothy Fuller. Father, born July 11, 1778, the eldest of five brothers in family of ten children headed by a minister-turned-farmer, graduated from Harvard in 1801 and worked as a country schoolteacher before establishing a law practice in Boston. Mother, born February 15, 1789, is one of three daughters of a village gunsmith; worked as schoolteacher in her late teens. Parents married May 28, 1809.

1812–18   Sister Julia Adelaide born August 18, 1812; dies October 5 the following year. Fuller's first memories are of her sister's corpse laid out for viewing, mother's withdrawal into mourning, and father's subsequent intense focus on Fuller. He begins teaching her to read. Father elected to Massachusetts House of Representatives as a Republican; begins serving in 1813. By age four, Fuller reads fluently; father accelerates home education, introducing Latin at age six, requiring recitations at night after work, and insisting on rapid answers in complete sentences, fostering precocious skill in speech and debate. Brother Eugene born May 14, 1815; brother William Henry born in late 1817. Father elected to U.S. House of Representatives and spends first six months of 1818 in Washington, D.C.; supervises Fuller's education by mail.

1819–25   Father continues annual six-month stints in Washington, D.C., for three terms in Congress. He takes strong antislavery stance against Missouri Compromise; otherwise fails to distinguish himself. Mother joins him for one session, leaving children in care of relatives; father requires Fuller to tutor brothers after school while Fuller continues to study at home. Fuller writes father on January 16, 1820, requesting he call her "Margaret" in future, not "Sarah" or "Sarah Margaret." Sister Ellen Kilshaw born August 7, 1820, named for family friend Fuller adores: a young single woman with musical talent who had returned home to England in 1817, leaving Fuller bereft. Fuller takes piano lessons and begins studying Greek. In 1820, attends nearby

805

806 CHRONOLOGY

co-educational Port School to recite Latin, following college preparatory curriculum designed for boys. Excels in composition, attracting "emulous interest" from classmate Oliver Wendell Holmes as well as derision for her "long, flexile neck," the result of congenital spinal curvature. The next year, enters Dr. Park's rigorous girls' school on Beacon Hill, becoming the star pupil. Brother Arthur Buckminster born August 10, 1822. Fuller is "opinionative," dallies with older Harvard students at dances, and is unpopular with peers; parents withdraw Fuller from Dr. Park's school while searching for another to instill "feminine discipline." Brother Richard Frederick born May 15, 1824. In May, at fourteen, boards for one year at Miss Prescott's school in Groton; continues to be unpopular but admires Prescott. Returns from school in spring 1825; attends Boston reception for Lafayette, June 16; writes unanswered letter expressing hope they will meet. Writes to Prescott in July 1825: "I am determined on distinction." Fuller's formal schooling is finished; she embarks on ambitious course of self-education.

1826–28 Father declines to stand for reelection to U.S. House of Representatives; returns to Massachusetts House of Representatives, becoming Speaker; continues law practice and purchases and moves family to Dana Mansion near Harvard College. Father's expected diplomatic appointment doesn't materialize, disappointing Fuller's hopes for European travel to further her education. Brother James Lloyd born May 11, 1826. Fuller attracts admiring group of female friends and falls under influence of two older women: novelist Lydia Maria Francis, later Child, with whom she undertakes comparative study of John Locke and Germaine de Staël; and Eliza Farrar, author and wife of Harvard professor John Farrar, whose soirées for students and professors Fuller attends. Farrar advises Fuller on dress and comportment to conceal her congenital spinal curvature and introduces Fuller to her cousin Anna Barker from New Orleans. Brother Edward Breck born May 23, 1828, on Fuller's eighteenth birthday; assigned by mother to Fuller's care but is sickly and dies in her arms the following year on September 15.

1829–34 Meets Harvard students George Davis and James Freeman Clarke at Farrar's salon; falls in love with Davis, who

CHRONOLOGY 807

appears to reciprocate but later rejects Fuller. Friendship with Clarke deepens; they learn German together and read Schiller, Novalis, Richter, and Goethe. Translates Goethe's *Torquato Tasso*. In 1831, father sells Dana Mansion, gives up law and politics, and moves family first to Brattle House, Cambridge home of wealthy uncle Abraham Fuller, then, in the spring of 1833, to a farm in Groton, Massachusetts, with plans to retire and write a history of the United States. Fuller distressed by loss of Cambridge intellectual life and suffers first migraine headaches. Required by father to educate six younger siblings at home; father promises trip to Europe as reward when brothers fitted for college. Making Fuller marriageable is no longer in father's plans; devotes himself to farming, assisted by sons and supported by household labor of wife and daughters. Clarke graduates from Harvard Divinity School in 1833 and accepts pastorate in Louisville, Kentucky, as an "evangelist" for Unitarianism in the West. Troubled by lack of vocation, narrowing opportunities, and grueling toil at home, Fuller drafts sermons intended for Clarke, but which turn into "reveries"; initially rejects Clarke's advice that she become a writer, wishing instead to put her skill at elocution to use, but knows that path is closed to women. Stays at Farrars' Cambridge home with Barker, July 1834; spends August at Barker summer estate in Newport, Rhode Island. Encouraged by father to respond to historian George Bancroft's critique of the Roman orator Brutus in October *North American Review*; essay "Brutus," her first publication, appears in the *Boston Daily Advertiser* on November 27.

1835   Publishes three long book reviews in newly founded *Western Messenger*, solicited and edited by Clarke. Childhood friend Frederic Henry Hedge, now a Unitarian minister, sends Fuller's translation of *Torquato Tasso* to Ralph Waldo Emerson, who expresses a desire to meet. Tours Trenton Falls in upstate New York at midsummer with Farrars and Samuel Gray Ward, a Harvard senior and son of a prominent Boston banker, with whom Fuller feels an immediate connection; on return trip visits Barker in Newport and meets English social theorist Harriet Martineau in Cambridge. Tells Martineau she plans to write a biography of Goethe. Farrars propose eighteen-month European tour to begin the following summer with Fuller, Ward, and Barker; in London they will be escorted by Martineau, who returns to England in August. Publishes short story "Lost and Won" with fictionalized George Davis as protagonist in *New England Galaxy* on August 8; Clarke tips off Davis, leaving Fuller mortified. Back home in September, falls gravely ill for nine days, perhaps with typhus; fearing she will die, father assures her of his affection. Three days later father contracts Asiatic cholera, likely from field labor; dies next evening, October 1, at fifty-seven, intestate, not having begun his book. Unexpectedly diminished Fuller estate now in control of tight-fisted uncle, Abraham Fuller. Fuller pledges to care for brothers and sister and negotiates with uncle on mother's behalf for family funds. Writes poems of love and longing to Barker, picturing them together on "some isle far apart from the haunts of men." Due to straitened circumstances, faces loss of trip with Farrars, Barker, and Ward to Europe, where she'd planned to renew friendship with Martineau and research her Goethe biography.

1836   In January falls ill; attributes to shock of father's death. On recovery, plans to make living by pen. Publishes three major articles in *American Monthly*; the second, "Present State of German Literature," is featured as lead article in July. On July 21, travels to Concord for three-week stay with Emerson, their first meeting; the visit is arranged by Elizabeth Peabody, a prominent Boston writer and educator who has taken an interest in Fuller's career. Emerson praises Fuller's poem, "Lines—On the Death of C.C.E.," lamenting the recent death of his brother Charles, published in *Boston Daily Centinel and Gazette*, and reads his first book, *Nature*, aloud to her in manuscript. Two-part essay, "Modern British Poets," published in *American Monthly* in September and October. In fall, stays with uncle Henry Fuller in Boston; gives lessons in German, Italian, and French literature to young women who include Caroline Sturgis, daughter of wealthy Boston merchant; translates aloud from German texts for Rev. William Ellery Channing. Realizes she must teach to support herself and family; accepts position as assistant to Amos Bronson Alcott, teaching academic subjects and recording Alcott's formal conversations with students in his experimental Temple School, a position formerly held by Peabody.

1837–38   Begins teaching in January 1837; quickly sees that Temple School is in trouble and she will not be paid. Resigns to accept

CHRONOLOGY 809

well-paid teaching position at progressive coeducational Greene Street School, soon to open in Providence, Rhode Island. In April, Unitarian minister George Ripley accepts her proposal to translate Eckermann's *Conversations with Goethe* in his series, *Specimens of Foreign Standard Literature*; Ripley expresses interest in publishing her Goethe biography. Emerson gives address at opening of Greene Street School in May. Fuller is in charge of all sixty female students; forms advanced class of older girls to study Greek goddesses as role models, engaging them in dialogue: "I am bringing my opinions to the test." Invited again to Emerson house in Concord in September to attend first meeting of the Transcendental Club at which women are present, a sumptuous meal provided by Lidian Emerson the day after Emerson's Phi Beta Kappa address, "The American Scholar"; Peabody's invitation was rescinded in favor of Fuller. Invites Caroline Sturgis to share rooms in Providence as her private pupil; Sturgis's father forbids it due to Fuller's association with the Transcendentalists. Introduces Sturgis to Emerson, who feels instant affinity. Joins Coliseum Club in Providence; reads paper on "The Progress of Society" with particular attention to the status of women. Holds classes for adults on German literature; translates Eckermann. Falls sick from overwork and resigns from Greene Street School in December 1838.

1839   Completes translation of Eckermann's *Conversations with Goethe* in February for publication in July; Goethe biography advertised as later volume in Ripley's series. Translations of two poems by Goethe published in *Select Minor Poems of Goethe and Schiller*, also in Ripley's series; Fuller is the only female translator, alongside Frederic Henry Hedge, James Freeman Clarke, George Bancroft, William Henry Channing, and others. Family home in Groton is sold; rents Willow Brook property in Jamaica Plain to reside with mother and younger brothers Richard and Lloyd. Writes to George Ripley's prodigiously learned wife, Sophia, on August 27 proposing series of Conversations for women to ask questions: "What were we born to do? How shall we do it?" Peabody helps gather students and collect tuition; Fuller earns $200 for three months of weekly sessions beginning November 6, an impressive sum; topics range from Greek mythology to aesthetics to woman's role in society. Clarke returns to Boston married. Fuller attempts

810   CHRONOLOGY

to deepen ties with Samuel Gray Ward, with whom she had been corresponding since his return from Europe the previous year, when he had been taken up as a protégé by Emerson on Fuller's urging. Though devoted to Fuller as a friend and mentor, Ward clarifies he is not interested romantically. He has fallen in love with Barker while traveling in Europe, but Barker's father forbids the match, disapproving of Ward's intention to pursue a profession in the arts. Introduces Barker, visiting at Willow Brook, to Emerson, who is enchanted: "The wind is not purer than she is." Emerson invites Fuller to edit *The Dial*, proposed new quarterly journal of Transcendentalist writers; she accepts on October 20 while visiting Emerson in Concord.

1840   First series of Conversations extended through spring. Second series begins in fall at Peabody's foreign language bookshop and subscription library, recently opened at 13 West Street, Boston; twenty-five to thirty women attend. Solicits writings from Transcendentalist circle for first issue of *The Dial*, published in July. Fuller's "A Short Essay on Critics" is the lead article; her review of Washington Allston's exhibition, written in new first-person style, largely adulatory but critical of Allston's "grand historical paintings" as inadequate to his "genius," concludes with paired poems by Fuller and Ward. Other poets represented include Emerson; his late first wife, Ellen, and late brother Edward; Henry David Thoreau; and Clarke's sister Sarah and Sturgis's sister Ellen Sturgis Hooper, both members of Fuller's Conversations class. The first chapter of Cincinnati-based Unitarian minister William Henry Channing's "Ernest the Seeker," an intended serial novel about a young man traveling the world in search of faith, is the sole work of fiction. Essays by Theodore Parker, John Sullivan Dwight, and Thoreau are included along with Bronson Alcott's obscurely mystical "Orphic Sayings," which draw critical fire, possibly dooming the journal; it nevertheless continues for another four years. In summer, after an August weekend in which Fuller, Sturgis, and Barker spend "three golden days" alone with Emerson in his Concord home, Fuller believes she has cemented an enduring and exclusive familial bond among a circle of five, including Ward, "as complete as friendship could make it." Emerson, too, believes "ideal relations" have been established, and is as shocked as Fuller when, in early September, Barker and Ward announce plans

CHRONOLOGY   811

to marry in October; Ward will give up his artistic ambitions to become a banker. A disappointed Emerson officiates at the wedding; Fuller is not invited. Postpones second installment of Alcott's "Sayings," originally intended for October *Dial*; rejects Thoreau's essay "The Service" as too rough and invites revision. Second *Dial* issue contributors include Emerson, J. F. Clarke, Sturgis, Hedge, G. Ripley, Hooper, Christopher Pearse Cranch, Ellery Channing, W. H. Channing, and Fuller, who labors over layout and proofs unassisted and so far unpaid. On October 18, George and Sophia Ripley meet with Fuller, Alcott, and Emerson in Concord to propose they join the Ripleys in founding a utopian community at Brook Farm; all three decline. Later that fall, the loss of both Barker and Ward to marriage stirs memories of her father's sudden death, bringing on an emotional and spiritual "winter"; begins writing "Autobiographical Romance," tracing the sources of her present crisis and entering an "era of illumination in my mental life."

1841   Publishes first writings on female capability and woman's fettered position in society, the allegorical tales "The Magnolia of Lake Pontchartrain" and "Leila," in January and April issues of *The Dial*. In February begins translating *Die Günderode*, an epistolary narrative of female friendship by Goethe's acolyte Bettine Brentano von Arnim. At the urging of Emerson and others, offers ten-week series of Conversations on Greek mythology to mixed group of men and women in the Boston home of George and Sophia Ripley beginning March 1. Personalities clash and men dominate discussion; the experiment will not be repeated. The Ripleys depart for Brook Farm in West Roxbury to establish the utopian community Fuller has refused to join, but when the lease on Willow Brook runs out in April, moves brother Lloyd to Brook Farm and sells the family cow to the utopians. Attends first performance of Beethoven's Fifth Symphony in Boston, April 3, an experience that "woke again the springs of life." Visits Brook Farm in May, then departs on the first of several weeks-long working holidays through the summer and early fall: at Newport, Rhode Island, and Newbury, Massachusetts, with Caroline Sturgis; in Concord with the Emersons; and in Cambridge with the Farrars. Enjoys a moonlit boat ride on the Concord River with Thoreau at the oars. Fuller's contributions to *The Dial* increase to nearly 30 percent of the journal's contents: essays, poetry, reviews and notices of books, concerts, exhibitions. "Goethe," a forty-one-page essay published in July, marks her decision to put aside the projected biography; now dreads the thought of "living so long in the shadow of one mind." Completes unpublished memoir, "Autobiographical Romance," while staying with the Emersons in October, concluding that, in the highest form of friendship, "There is no separation; the same thought is given at the same moment to both." In November settles for the winter as a boarder in Uncle Henry Fuller's Boston home. Continues editorial work on *The Dial*, begins new series of Conversations for women, and gives as many as ten weekly lessons in foreign literature to younger women, including Caroline Sturgis.

1842   In January *Dial* publishes her third proto-feminist allegory, "Yuca Filimentosa," along with "Bettine Brentano and Her Friend Günderode," a review-essay of the von Arnim work she has been translating. Explains her method as translator in preface to the volume published by Elizabeth Peabody in March as *Günderode*: to "throw myself . . . into the mood of the writer." On March 17, writes to Emerson that she can't afford to continue as editor of *The Dial*. Emerson accepts the role with Peabody as new publisher, while still mourning the death of his first child, Ralph Waldo Emerson Jr., from scarlatina on January 27. He had written to Fuller the next morning, "Shall I ever dare to love any thing again?" In June, after completing third series of Conversations for women, attends sermon by William Henry Channing, who has returned to Boston from Cincinnati, and writes seventeen-page letter in response to issues he raised, which she titles "A Credo," setting out her own beliefs: "What is done here at home in my heart is my religion." Free from editorial duties, spends portions of the summer with friends, including two weeks in the White Mountains in July with James Freeman Clarke and his wife Anna, renewing the connection with Clarke. Determined to end itinerancy, rents house at 8 Ellery Street in Cambridge beginning September 1 for herself, mother, and youngest brother Richard, who is enrolled at nearby Harvard College. Spends six weeks in Concord with the Emersons beginning August 17, writing "Romaic and Rhine Ballads," the lead essay for October *Dial*. Records in her journal a complex interplay of personalities as the newlyweds Sophia and Nathaniel Hawthorne settle at the

CHRONOLOGY 813

Old Manse, and Fuller's sister Ellen returns to Massachusetts from Ohio, where she had fallen in love and married the poet-journalist Ellery Channing. Ellery's tardy arrival for the couple's planned reunion at the Emerson house throws the household into panic, scarcely lessened when Ellery explains he'd spent several days visiting Caroline Sturgis. Unable to find affordable lodging in Concord, the Channings join the Fullers in Cambridge for the winter. Spends first week of October at Brook Farm to lead Conversations on "Education," impressing one participant: "She knew so much more than all the women and most of the men that she could not disguise her own superiority." A night alone in late October with Anna Barker Ward at the Beacon Hill townhouse Anna shares with husband Samuel Gray Ward, away on business, revives feelings of passion and loss experienced two years before. In November, begins fourth series of Conversations for women with weekly topics including "Mistakes," "Faith," "Creeds," "Woman," "Daemonology," and "Persons who never awake to life in this world."

1843 Accepts invitation for late May travel with James Freeman Clarke, his mother Rebecca, and his sister Sarah, an accomplished artist, to visit Clarke's younger brother William Hull Clarke in Chicago, the first leg of a four-month journey to the West that Fuller expects will provide material for a book. Clarke will leave the women in William's care for further travel in Illinois, Wisconsin, and Michigan. In the weeks leading up to departure, devotes herself to writing "The Great Lawsuit: Man *versus* Men, Woman *versus* Women," the culmination of years of reading, thought, and discussion on issues of gender. "There is no wholly masculine man, no purely feminine woman," she concludes, after explicating societal forces that hinder both men and women in their progress toward achieving "fullness of being." The forty-seven-page treatise appears as lead essay in July *Dial*, winning praise from *New-York Tribune* editor Horace Greeley, who encourages its expansion into a book, and from Thoreau: "a noble piece, rich extempore writing, talking with pen in hand." As her most significant essay is published, Fuller travels by wagon with her companions through the Rock River Valley in northern Illinois. In her journal and letters written from the West to friends and family through the summer, Fuller mourns the plunder of natural resources and decries the forced removals of

814   CHRONOLOGY

indigenous peoples, while expressing awe at sublime nature and sympathizing with newly arrived emigrants eking out a living in harsh conditions. Enjoys the company of William Clarke, developing a romantic attachment similar to that with the young Samuel Gray Ward. Returning through New York City in mid-September, attends a Sunday morning service at William Henry Channing's newly established Christian Union Church and finds Thoreau and Alcott in attendance. Back in Cambridge, is granted a desk in Harvard's library where, "under the covert gaze of the undergraduates who had never before looked upon a woman reading in those sacred precincts," she conducts daily research for her book about the West. Begins final series of Conversations for women on "Education," with reference to texts of Goethe and Spinoza; weekly discussion topics include "Culture," "Ignorance," "Vanity," "Prudence," "Patience," and "Health."

1844   Pressure to complete book on Western travels brings on spate of migraine headaches in early months of the year. William Hull Clarke visits Boston in March; Fuller is disappointed in hopes for his return of her affection and disturbed by his flirtation with Caroline Sturgis, yet increases her resolve to seek "Truth, truth . . . the great preservative." Spends three weeks in New York City in early April; attends Fourierist convention led by George Ripley with William Henry Channing and interviews prospective publishers for her book. Follows Horace Greeley's advice for a dual imprint of Boston and New York publishers in order to attract review attention from New York critics; accepts offer of 10 percent royalties from Little and Brown in Boston, with New York distribution by Charles S. Francis and Company. Concludes fifth and final Conversation series in late April: "a most animated meeting" after which she is "loaded with beautiful gifts" and bouquets of symbolic flowers. On her birthday, May 23, writes final lines of *Summer on the Lakes, in 1843*, a hybrid text mixing reportage, poetry, and fiction, which expands on the sentiments expressed in journals and letters written on the journey, for June 4 book publication: "I think this must be an important era in my life." Second printing published soon after with illustrations by Sarah Clarke. The book earns praise from New York critics including Edgar Allan Poe, for the work's "graphicality," and Evert A. Duyckinck: "the only genuine American book I can think published this season." Caroline Sturgis visits

CHRONOLOGY 815

Fuller in Cambridge for two weeks in June. Spends three weeks in Concord in July, divided between the Hawthornes at the Old Manse and the Channings, Ellen and Ellery, who have found a home there for themselves and their first child, named Margaret Fuller Channing. In her journal, expresses impatience with Emerson's "transcendental fatalism." In August, Greeley, who deemed Fuller "one of the most original as well as intellectual of American Women" in his *Tribune* review of *Summer on the Lakes*, invites Fuller to move to New York City as "head of literary department" of the *New-York Tribune*; continues to urge expansion of "Great Lawsuit" into a book. Arriving in Cambridge on September 15 to press the job offer in person, Greeley receives Fuller's acceptance. Spends October and November at Fishkill Landing on the Hudson River with Caroline Sturgis, revising and expanding "Great Lawsuit" and reading diaries of inmates at Mount Pleasant Female Prison at Sing Sing, then under the direction of reformer Eliza Farnham. Decides to write about the women in her lengthening manuscript; considers them unfairly punished for prostitution, when men have led them into crime, and little different from women who marry for money: "What blasphemes in them must fret and murmur in the perfumed boudoir, for a society beats with one great heart." Visits Sing Sing in late October with Caroline Sturgis and William Henry Channing, a founder of the reformist New York Prison Association. Moves to Greeley family home in Turtle Bay to begin *Tribune* job on December 1, having completed manuscript of *Woman in the Nineteenth Century* for publication by Greeley and his partner Thomas McElrath in New York City. On Christmas Day returns to Sing Sing with W. H. Channing and prison reformers Marcus and Rebecca Spring. Rebecca Spring later recalls that while Channing preached a sermon to the men, Fuller "stood like an inspired person" before the assembled women "and spoke to them not as to criminals, but friends."

1845 Establishes distinctive critical and reportorial voice in front-page *New-York Tribune* columns, expanding scope of subjects from literature and the arts to social issues: prison reform, treatment of the mentally ill, immigration, Black voting rights. Total output reaches 250 columns in twenty months; signs columns with a star. Many columns reprinted in weekly edition circulated nationally to readership beyond the daily paper's 30,000 New York City subscribers: "I am well content at present to aid in the great work of mutual education." *Woman in the Nineteenth Century* published in February, a much expanded version of the original essay. A call to arms challenging men to "remove arbitrary barriers" to women's progress and women to make themselves independent "units" before entering marital unions, it also applauds female antislavery activists. Fuller is pleased that "the opposition and sympathy it excites are both great." First printing of 1,500 sells out rapidly. Fuller writes that she has left "the measure of my foot-print . . . on the earth." Begins treatment for spinal curvature with French mesmeric healer Theodore Leger and finds relief. Mingles with New York literati—Poe, Duyckinck, Lydia Maria Child, Elizabeth Oakes Smith, and others—in the home of Anne Lynch, one of America's foremost salonnières, who Fuller knows as a former member of Providence's Coliseum Club. There, near Washington Square, at a New Year's Eve party soon after her arrival in the city the previous year, she had met James Nathan, a handsome German-Jewish banker with literary aspirations. In February they begin attending concerts and plays in the city; she falls in love, feels "I am with you as never with any other one," and enjoys Nathan's embrace when they sit alone on the riverbank at Turtle Bay. In April, Nathan tells Fuller he must leave for Europe the following month; he is sheltering an unmarried English woman he hopes to reform and must find the "poor maiden" a better living arrangement. Fuller chooses to believe him. Days later, Nathan makes a sexual advance and is rebuffed by a shocked and dismayed Fuller, who had considered their love free of "earth-stain." She wavers, but "cannot" enter into a physical relationship. When Nathan departs for Europe at the end of May, he leaves his dog and guitar in Fuller's care, along with an ambiguous gift: a white veil. Through the summer Fuller awaits news of Nathan's promised return, but he remains abroad. Begins visiting the city's Female Refuge, established by the New York Prison Association to help former inmates find work, and offers counsel to residents: "I like them better than most women I meet." British edition of *Woman in the Nineteenth Century* published in September. The same month, Marcus and Rebecca Spring offer to bring Fuller with them on a European tour, covering her transportation and lodging costs in exchange for serving as companion to their eight-year-old son Edward—pending approval from

CHRONOLOGY 817

Marcus's employers for a fifteen-month leave of absence. Fuller accepts, crying tears of joy at the potential realization of her lifelong dream. In December, moves from the Greeley home to a boardinghouse in lower Manhattan, enabling easier attendance at concerts and the theater and a more active social life centered on Anne Lynch's Saturday night soirees. Writes in her journal that the year 1845 "has rent from me all I cherished, . . . but I have lived at last not only in rapture but in fact."

1846   Predicts in *Tribune* column on January 1 that "our country will play a ruling part" in the "great time coming," an era of democracy—but whether as eagle, vulture, or phoenix, "we dare not say." Continues brisk pace of publication with reviews of works by Hawthorne, George Sand, Leigh Hunt, Robert Browning, Eliza Farnham, Charles Brockden Brown, and former superintendent of Indian Affairs Thomas L. McKenney. Other columns feature accounts of the consecration of Grace Church's new uptown sanctuary at Tenth Street and a lecture by antislavery crusader Cassius Clay; two "ideal sketches" portraying "The Rich Man" in contrast to "The Poor Man"; and a critique of feminine propriety, "Mistress of Herself, Though China Fall." In February, Marcus Spring receives permission to travel and Fuller begins planning for August 6 departure for Europe; persuades Greeley to advance $120 for fifteen monthly dispatches she plans to post from locations on the Springs' itinerary of travel through England, Scotland, France, Italy, Switzerland, and Germany. Proposes publication of a book of selected essays and reviews to Evert Duyckinck, editor of Wiley and Putnam's Library of American Books series, and begins assembling a two-volume collection for simultaneous publication in England and the U.S., expecting the work to be in print for her arrival in August. Tussles with Duyckinck over essays he'd like to omit as controversial on religious grounds: "I shall not alter a line or a word on such accounts." *Papers on Literature and Art*, including one new essay, "American Literature: Its Position in the Present Time, and Prospects for the Future," is finally published in September. By then Fuller has posted her first *Tribune* dispatch, dated August 23, which appears in print on September 24 as "Letters from England." Writes to James Nathan, inviting him to join her party on an excursion in the Trossachs; after sending Fuller his own travel letters in hopes she will help place them for publication and receiving her critical judgment, Nathan informs Fuller he will not see her at all in Europe as he is engaged to marry a German woman. In February, missing Nathan and mourning the lack of any "real, permanent connection with any soul," Fuller had felt like "a wandering intelligence, driven from spot to spot." Now, touring England with a like-minded family and meeting or reacquainting with William Wordsworth, Harriet Martineau, and a young Matthew Arnold, she writes of Nathan's rejection in her journal, "I care not," resolving to "take such disappointments more lightly than I have." In Scotland in late September gets lost overnight while climbing Ben Lomond, resulting in a vivid experience of the sublime: "my grand solitude." In Newcastle, descends into a coal mine to observe colliers' working conditions. Settles with the Springs in London for six weeks starting October 1. Meets numerous literary lights, including Jane and Thomas Carlyle and the exiled Italian political theorist Giuseppe Mazzini, who instantly gains Fuller's sympathy for the cause of a united Italy. Finds English "habits of conversation so superior to those of Americans, I am able to come out a great deal more than I can at home." Reaching Paris in mid-November, struggles with speaking the language she reads fluently; has new dresses made and defers important social calls while practicing her French.

1847   In Paris, as in London, Fuller is already known to progressive-minded writers and editors for *Woman in the Nineteenth Century* and *Papers on Literature and Art*. Her essay "American Literature" is translated for publication in the socialist journal *La Revue Indépendante,* one of whose founders, George Sand, interrupts her own work on a February afternoon for a meeting with Fuller, saying "it is better to throw things aside, and seize the moment." For her part, Fuller "never liked a woman better." On February 14, after despairing of hearing the frequently ill Frédéric Chopin, Sand's paramour, perform in public, Fuller sits in on a lesson and enjoys the composer's conversation as much as his playing. The next day, receives a visit from the Polish poet Adam Mickiewicz and quickly develops a "deep-founded mental connection" with the exiled revolutionary, a staunch advocate of women's rights. The Springs, who had objected to Fuller's meeting with the sexually adventurous Sand, are troubled when Fuller spends most of her last evenings in Paris with Mickiewicz, who tells Fuller she is "the only one to whom it has been given to touch that which is decisive in today's world and to comprehend in advance the world to come." Leaving Paris for Italy in March, Fuller feels "as if I had left my life behind." In Rome on April 1, meets the twenty-six-year-old Marchese Giovanni Angelo Ossoli, youngest son of a noble family with ties to the Pope, who escorts her back to the Springs' apartment on the Corso after she'd become separated from her hosts during a vespers service at Saint Peter's. They spend evenings together walking among Roman ruins. In her fourteenth *Tribune* dispatch, dated May and published under the title "Things and Thoughts in Europe," Fuller describes a torch-bearing parade on April 19, "a river of fire" along the Corso, when Romans celebrated the newly installed Pope Pius IX's establishment of a lay advisory council: a "limited" form of democracy, but "a great measure for Rome." A second "new thing" for Rome, a "popular dinner" held outdoors in the Baths of Titus, marks the return of exiled politicians and men of letters under Pius IX's liberalizing influence. At the end of May, as she is about to depart Rome for Venice with the Springs, Ossoli proposes marriage; although Fuller feels their meeting to have been "singular, fated," she does not consider the offer seriously. In Venice, parts with the Springs to remain in Italy as they move on to Switzerland: "I wish to be free and absolutely true to my nature." Travels to Florence, Milan, the Italian lakes, and Geneva; hikes alone across the Great Saint Bernard Pass. In August, stays on Lake Como with Marchesa Costanza Arconati Visconti, recently returned from political exile; meets poet and novelist Alessandro Manzoni, another political radical. Negotiates payment from Greeley for future *Tribune* dispatches to support herself in Rome, where she returns in October and moves into rented rooms on the Corso with the assistance of Ossoli. Poem "To A Daughter of Italy," Fuller's effort to promote the cause of Italian unification with a British audience, is published in the *People's Journal*. Her October 18 *Tribune* dispatch reiterates the "intoxication of joy" felt in Rome for the initial liberalizing measures of Pius IX and predicts: "our age is one where all things tend to a great crisis, not merely to revolution but to radical reform." Secretly, Fuller and Ossoli become lovers. A *Tribune* dispatch dated December 17 reports: "I now really

820   CHRONOLOGY

live in Rome, and I begin to see and feel the real Rome." By
the end of the month, she is pregnant.

1848   In her twentieth *Tribune* dispatch, published in the U.S.
on February 7, Fuller reports rainy days in Rome as the
New Year approached, and "I find myself without strength,
without appetite, almost without spirits." Dispatch twenty-
two, dated January 27, informs readers that "revolution
has broken out in Naples"; in the following weeks, popular
uprisings spread to Venice and Milan. In Paris, Louis
Philippe is overthrown and a French Republic declared,
Metternich flees Vienna, and King Frederick William IV
of Prussia is forced out of Berlin. In March, receives visits
from Mickiewicz, who is passing through Rome with a
"squadron" of fellow exiles on their way to instigate democratic revolution in Poland; Fuller confides her pregnancy
to him. Writes to W. H. Channing on March 29: "I rejoice
to be in Europe at this time, and shall return possessed of
a great history. Perhaps I shall be called to act." Giuseppe
Mazzini returns to Milan from London in April but
remains wary of Pius IX's seeming liberalism and will not
travel to Rome. In June, Fuller leaves Rome for L'Aquila
and then Rieti, fifty miles north of Rome, to conceal her
pregnancy, telling friends she is going into the countryside
for three months to write a book on the revolutions in
Europe. Corresponds with Ossoli, who has joined the Civic
Guard established by the Pope and must remain in Rome;
expresses love, pleasure in his care and affection, and fears
for her health and survival in childbirth. On September 5,
son Angelo Eugene Philip Ossoli born in Rieti: a child
"too good and beautiful . . . I could die for him." On
November 5, son is baptized in cathedral at Rieti with both
parents in attendance; baptismal register states parents are
married. Fuller and Ossoli continue living separately, hiding
their child and their relationship in order to avoid scandal
and protect Fuller's ability to make a living as a journalist for
an American audience. On November 6, returns to Rome
with Ossoli, leaving son "Nino" with a wet nurse, Chiara
Fiordiponte, and her family in Rieti. Fuller rents top-floor
room at 60 Piazza Barberini. Through the summer, violent
counter-revolutionary forces turn back radical movements
through much of Europe, but in Italy, the tide of revolution
rises, with demands for reform surpassing Pius IX's
moderate measures, leading to the assassination of Pius IX's

CHRONOLOGY 821

deputy, Pellegrino Rossi, on November 15. The Pope flees to Gaeta, outside Naples, under the protection of Ferdinand II, King of the Two Sicilies; Rome prepares for elections and the convening of a Constitutional Assembly. Venice and Tuscany remain in popular control, raising hopes for Italian unification. In early December writes "a sad cry from my lacerated affections" to Caroline Sturgis, now married to William Aspinwall Tappan, telling about Ossoli and son Nino and asking for financial assistance and secrecy. At Christmas, after a separation of nearly two months during which she filed two *Tribune* dispatches reporting on the Roman revolution, Fuller travels to Rieti to spend the holiday with Nino, who "seems to recognize me."

1849   On New Year's Day writes in her journal: "Rome has at last become the focus of the Italian revolution and I am here." On February 9, the Constitutional Assembly votes to proclaim a Roman Republic, a "pure Democracy." On March 5, Mazzini arrives in Rome to take a seat in the Assembly and soon after to serve as one of the triumvirs charged with leading the defense of Rome against likely attack from Austria. The Civic Guard has become the Republic's army, and Ossoli is on active duty. On March 8, Mazzini pays a surprise visit to Fuller; says he hopes to return often, but "the crisis is tremendous, and all will come on him." Mazzini visits again on March 16 when Fuller receives an answering letter from Caroline Sturgis Tappan bringing "true consolation." Tappan offers to serve as Nino's guardian if Fuller should predecease him. Writes to Tappan that "every day is to me one of mental doubt and conflict; how it will end, I do not know." On March 26, having filed three *Tribune* dispatches urging U.S. support of the Roman Republic, leaves Rome for Rieti to see Nino, who is "fat" but "small," and remains until April 16. Giuseppe Garibaldi is training a force of 1,500 men quartered near Rieti to aid in defense of the Republic. On April 24, to the surprise of Mazzini and the triumvirs, an army of 10,000 French soldiers commissioned by the French Assembly under the newly installed President Louis Napoleon arrives in Civitavecchia, a port city thirty-five miles northwest of Rome, aiming to preempt an Austrian invasion, crush the Roman Republican government, and return the Pope to Rome. Fuller moves to the hotel Casa Diez to join a handful of English and Americans remaining in Rome. Confides in American friend Emelyn Story her

822 CHRONOLOGY

marriage to Ossoli and Nino's birth, showing certificates for each, Story later states; asks Story to bring Nino to America if Fuller and Ossoli do not survive. On April 30, French troops begin firing on the Vatican, where Ossoli's regiment is posted, and are successfully turned back; Fuller begins work as "Regolatrice" (director) of Fate Bene Fratelli hospital on Tiber Island, supervising medical staff and offering consolation to the wounded. May 6 *Tribune* dispatch opens: "I write you from barricaded Rome." *Tribune* dispatch dated May 27 reports a truce brokered by Mazzini; June 10 dispatch describes "these sad but glorious days" after France breaks the truce on June 2 and lays siege to the city. "Rome is being destroyed," she writes to Emerson on June 10. Visits Ossoli in Vatican gardens, finds him "haggard" but determined; on June 16, Ossoli is commissioned captain and assigned to lead defense of the Pincian Hill as heavy bombardment continues. Finally, on June 30, the Assembly votes to surrender; on July 2, Fuller witnesses Garibaldi's departure with his regiment, like "a hero of the middle ages." Writes to brother Richard on July 8: "Private hopes of mine are fallen with the hopes of Italy. I have played for a new stake and lost it." Fuller and Ossoli leave Rome for Rieti, where they find Nino near death: no longer able to sustain nursing both Nino and her own baby, Fiordiponte has weaned him onto bread and wine. After many anxious weeks, Nino recovers; Fuller faces necessity of return to the U.S. and an end to secrecy about her personal life. From Rieti writes to W. H. Channing in late July, "I shall never regret the step which has given me the experience of a mother and satisfied domestic wants in a most sincere and sweet companion." To her mother on August 31: "it may cause you a pang to know your eldest child might long ago have been addressed by another name than yours, and has a little son a year old." Describes Ossoli as "a Roman, of a noble but now impoverished family": "In him I have found a home, and one that interferes with no tie." Begins signing letters M.F.O. and assumes the title Marchesa Ossoli. Moves to Florence in late September to join a community of English-speaking expatriates centered on Robert and Elizabeth Barrett Browning; enjoys family life: "What a difference it makes to come home to a child."

1850   In final *Tribune* dispatch, dated January 6, Fuller laments: "all the worst men are in power, and the best betrayed and exiled." Yet she believes "the struggle" in Europe will

CHRONOLOGY   823

continue: "a combat grand in its motives, and in its extent beyond what the world ever before so much as dreamed." She looks to America for the "chance of a noble, peaceful growth," and begins planning her family's return, seeking inexpensive passage on a cargo ship. Continues work on her book, now focused on the Roman Republic's rise and fall, which she plans to publish in the U.S. Enjoys visits at Casa Guidi with the Brownings, whose son is close in age to Nino. In letters home Fuller does not mention a wedding and makes no secret that, as she'd written to W. H. Channing, she entered into the "corrupt social contract" of marriage only for her son's sake. Gossip swirls among her old friends; Sarah Clarke thinks Margaret "more afraid of being thought to have submitted to the ceremony of marriage than to have omitted it." Some feel she should not return to face scandal. Emerson writes a letter advising Fuller to remain abroad, which likely she does not receive before her May departure; nor does she receive a letter from Paulina Wright Davis inviting her to preside over the first National Woman's Rights Convention in October. To Tappan she writes on April 16, "I pity those who are inclined to think ill, when they might as well have inclined the other way, however let them go." On May 17, the three Ossolis and Nino's nurse Celeste Paolini board the barque *Elizabeth* at Livorno, expecting a six-week voyage to New York City; a goat will provide Nino's milk. Before leaving the Mediterranean, Captain Seth Hasty falls sick with smallpox and dies; the ship is quarantined for a week at Gibraltar. The *Elizabeth* sails on with first mate Henry Bangs serving as captain; Nino contracts smallpox at sea and survives. In July, Fuller's final publication, "Recollections of the Vatican," appears in the *United States Magazine and Democratic Review*, recalling the days in 1849 when the Vatican gardens were "full of armed men" as well as an earlier torchlight tour of the Vatican galleries on which she'd viewed "divine images" that would "remain to exhilarate and bless all my after life." On July 19, nearing port before dawn, the *Elizabeth* is blown off course by a fierce storm and runs aground off Fire Island; passengers and crew wait on deck for rescue, but the active figures they see on shore after sunrise are profiteers scavenging goods from the wrecked ship: fabrics, hats, olive oil, almonds. In heavy surf and rising tide, some crew members swim to shore; the Ossolis, unable to swim, continue to wait for rescue until the ship breaks up entirely and they are swept under the waves. On shore, one of Fuller's five trunks is recovered, containing letters from Mazzini and Mickiewicz, correspondence with Ossoli, and her Roman journal, but no document confirming her marriage to Ossoli and no pages of her book manuscript. According to an inventory compiled by Thoreau, who is dispatched by Emerson to the scene of the wreck, a second trunk washes ashore empty; the remaining three trunks, a case of books, and a tin box marked with the initials M.F.O. are lost, as are the bodies of Fuller and Ossoli. Nino's body is buried temporarily in the sand to be removed days later to a cemetery in Cambridge, where his remains are interred alongside those of Edward Breck and Timothy Fuller. On October 23, the over one thousand delegates to the National Woman's Rights Convention who are gathered in Worcester, Massachusetts, to hear speeches by Sojourner Truth, Lucretia Mott, Frederick Douglass, Lucy Stone, and William Lloyd Garrison, honor Fuller with a moment of silence. Davis recalls: "We were left to mourn her guiding hand—her royal presence."

Note on the Texts

This volume gathers two books by Margaret Fuller, *Summer on the Lakes, in 1843* (1844) and *Woman in the Nineteenth Century* (1845), along with thirty-seven of her essays and columns written for *The Dial*, the *New-York Tribune*, and other publications, as well as a large selection of unpublished writings, journals, poetry, and letters, many available previously only in expurgated editions.

SUMMER ON THE LAKES, IN 1843 *and*
WOMAN IN THE NINETEENTH CENTURY

When Fuller was invited by her friend James Freeman Clarke to tour the Great Lakes with him, his mother Rebecca, and his sister Sarah on a four-month excursion to begin in late May 1843, she began to document her experiences in letters and a travel journal, hoping to use these materials to write a book. Upon her return to Cambridge in the fall, she was granted a desk in Harvard's library, where she conducted additional research for her book about the West, writing the final lines on May 23, 1844, her birthday.

Advised by *New-York Tribune* editor Horace Greeley to publish with a dual imprint of Boston and New York publishers in order to attract review attention from New York critics, Fuller accepted an offer of 10 percent royalties from Little and Brown in Boston, with New York distribution by Charles S. Francis and Company.

Summer on the Lakes, in 1843 was published by Little and Brown in Boston and Charles S. Francis and Company in New York on June 4, 1844. A second issue was published almost immediately with seven plates of etchings by Sarah Clarke. Fuller wrote to Sarah Shaw that the plates did not arrive at the printer until some copies of the first issue had already been bound. There was no British edition. The present volume uses the second issue as its text and reproduces the topical running heads, which are likely authorial (see also the discussion of the running heads in *Woman in the Nineteenth Century*, below); however, the page design of the Library of America series does not accommodate all of Fuller's running heads, and those left off are given below, along with the pages in this volume to which they refer:

Geneva: page 30.
Retrospection: pages 51–52.

825

826 NOTE ON THE TEXTS

Haste Makes Waste: page 62.
Philip Van Artevelde: page 78.
Titian's Venus and Adonis: pages 84–85.
Milwaukie (second instance): page 92.
Free Hope: pages 96–97.
Self-Poise: pages 98–99.
Obstacles: page 144.
Mrs. Schoolcraft: page 148.
The Young Warrior: page 152.
Death of Red Shoes: page 156.
Mackenzie: page 170.
The General Scott: page 174.
Dinners: pages 179–80.

As she was preparing to travel to the West, Fuller wrote a forty-seven-page essay that was published as the lead essay in *The Dial* in July 1843, "The Great Lawsuit: Man *versus* Men, Woman *versus* Women." The essay was well received by *Dial* readers, and Horace Greeley wrote to Fuller, encouraging its expansion into a book; the following year, Greeley offered Fuller a job as "head of the literary department" of the *New-York Tribune* and convinced her to move to New York City. Fuller spent October and November 1844 in Fishkill Landing, New York, revising and expanding her essay, and had finished the manuscript by December 1, when she moved into Greeley's family home to begin her *Tribune* job. *Woman in the Nineteenth Century* was published in New York by Greeley and his partner Thomas McElrath in February 1845. A British edition was published by H. G. Clarke and Co. later in 1845; its text is the same as the American edition except for changes to bring about conformity with British conventions of spelling and punctuation.

After Fuller's death in 1850, her brother Arthur Fuller edited a new edition of the book, adding to it a selection of Fuller's articles for the *New-York Tribune*. *Woman in the Nineteenth Century and Kindred Papers Relating to the Sphere, Condition, and Duties of Woman* was published in 1855 with a preface by Arthur Fuller and an introduction by Horace Greeley that both emphasized Fuller's "high, moral and noble characteristics" and her domesticity. Besides altering the author's name to Margaret Fuller Ossoli, the name Fuller assumed when she made her connection to her son's father, Giovanni Angelo Ossoli, public in 1849, this edition made "very slight verbal alterations," according to Greeley's introduction; removed an early footnote on George Sand's androgyny; deleted Fuller's appendices to the book; and also changed twenty-one of the eighty-one topical

NOTE ON THE TEXTS

running heads, giving them a greater emphasis on traditional Christianity and on more common forms of progressive activism for New England women (such as temperance and abolition) and thereby diminishing Fuller's more radical and controversial arguments about free love, socialism, and gender fluidity. Arthur Fuller's 1855 edition, published in Boston by John P. Jewett & Company; in Cleveland, Ohio, by Jewett, Proctor & Worthington; and in New York by Sheldon, Lamport & Co., was reprinted at least nine times from 1857 to 1972.

The present volume uses the 1845 Greeley and McElrath edition as its text and incorporates Fuller's authorial running heads. Running heads not accommodated by the design of the present volume are given below:

Preface: pages 191–92.
Let All the Plants Grow!: page 216.
In Spain: page 222.
Give the Liberty of Law: page 226.
Woman Capable of Friendship: page 232.
William and Mary Howitt: page 238.
The Wife Inevitably Influences the Husband: shortened,
    on page 247, to The Wife Influences the Husband.
Why Grow Old?: pages 251–52.
Cassandra: page 256.
Dr. Channing: pages 260–61.
Can We Trust an Earthly Father?: page 266.
The Daughters of Goethe: page 270.
The Lady in Comus: page 276.
Follow Una, Not Duessa: pages 280–81.
Eugene Sue: page 286.
Exaltados! Exaltadas!: page 290.
Bond-Maids! Brunhildas!: page 294.
Annexation of Texas: pages 297–98.
Be True To-day: pages 305–6.

SHORT PUBLISHED WORKS

In 1839, Ralph Waldo Emerson invited Fuller to edit *The Dial*, a proposed new quarterly journal of Transcendentalist writers. Fuller accepted, and the first issue was published in July of the following year. By 1841, she was contributing nearly 30 percent of the contents of each issue. The journal never gained enough subscriptions for her annual salary to be paid. Fuller served as editor until March 1842, when she wrote to Emerson explaining that she could not afford to

828   NOTE ON THE TEXTS

stay on. *The Dial* continued another two years under the editorship of Emerson before publication ceased.

Beginning in December of that year, when Fuller moved to New York City to take up the position that Horace Greeley had offered her as a columnist for the *New-York Tribune*, and continuing for the next two years, she published more than 250 columns. In August 1846, Fuller departed on a European tour with Marcus and Rebecca Spring. Fuller was to serve as a companion for the Springs' twelve-year-old son, but she arranged with Greeley to write fifteen monthly dispatches from Europe. In the end, however, Fuller remained in Europe for the next four years, and wrote thirty-seven dispatches from Europe for the *Tribune*.

Besides her work for *The Dial* and the *New-York Tribune*, Fuller published several books during these years, including a translation of *Gespräche mit Goethe* (*Conversations with Goethe*) by Johann Peter Eckermann (the present volume contains Fuller's preface to her translation), and *Papers on Literature and Art*, a two-volume collection of Fuller's essays from *The Dial* and the *Tribune* that was published in Wiley and Putnam's Library of American Books series, edited by Evert Duyckinck.

Two essays from *Papers on Literature and Art* are collected in the present volume: "American Literature: Its Position in the Present Time, and Prospects for the Future" and "A Short Essay on Critics." The former was published for the first time in *Papers on Literature and Art*, which is the source of the text used here. The latter was first published in *The Dial* during the time when Fuller was that magazine's editor. In preparing *Papers on Literature and Art* for the printer, Fuller expressed unhappiness with cuts proposed by Wiley, addressing both the contents of the book and materials he deemed unorthodox or offensive. "Where I make an impression it must be by being most myself," Fuller wrote in a letter to Duyckinck, protesting Wiley's interventions (see pages 758–60 in this volume). In the end, Fuller's essays were printed, according to Fuller, "just as they stand," but all essays on German, French, and Italian literature were removed from the contents. The differences between the two texts of "A Short Essay on Critics" are relatively minor, concerning accidentals and a few substantives. Though it is not clear whether Wiley or Fuller was responsible for the changes, the present volume uses as its source *The Dial* text, over which Fuller is known to have exercised full control.

The following is a list of the short works, primarily from *The Dial* and the *New-York Tribune*, that are included in this volume, in the order of their appearance, giving the source of each text.

NOTE ON THE TEXTS

NEW ENGLAND, 1839–1844

"Translator's Preface." S. M. Fuller, *Conversations with Goethe in the Last Years of His Life, Translated from the German of Eckermann* (Boston: Hilliard, Gray, and Co., 1839), vii–xxvi.

"A Short Essay on Critics." *The Dial* 1.1 (1840 [July]): 5–11.

"A Record of Impressions: Produced by the Exhibition of Mr. Allston's Pictures in the Summer of 1839." *The Dial* 1.1 (1840 [July]): 73–83.

"The Magnolia of Lake Pontchartrain." *The Dial* 1.3 (1841 [January]): 299–305.

"Leila." *The Dial* 1.4 (1841 [April]): 462–67.

"Yuca Filamentosa." *The Dial* 2.3 (1842 [January]): 286–88.

From "Bettine Brentano and Her Friend Günderode." *The Dial* 2.3 (1842 [January]): 313–22.

NEW YORK, 1844–1846

"Emerson's Essays." *New-York Daily Tribune*, December 7, 1844: 1.

"French Novelists of the Day: Balzac, George Sand, Eugene Sue." *New-York Daily Tribune*, February 1, 1845: 1.

Review of J. Stanley Grimes, *Etherology; or The Philosophy of Mesmerism and Phrenology. New-York Daily Tribune*, February 17, 1845: 1.

"Our City Charities. Visit To Bellevue Alms House, to the Farm School, the Asylum for the Insane, and Penitentiary on Blackwell's Island." *New-York Daily Tribune*, March 19, 1845: 1.

"Prevalent Idea That Politeness Is Too Great A Luxury to Be Given to the Poor." *New-York Daily Tribune*, May 31, 1845: 2.

Review of Frederick Douglass, *Narrative of the Life of Frederick Douglass, An American Slave. New-York Daily Tribune*, June 10, 1845: 1.

"The Irish Character." *New-York Daily Tribune*, June 28, 1845: 2.

Review of Edgar Allan Poe, *Tales, New-York Daily Tribune*, July 11, 1845: 1.

"The Wrongs of American Women. The Duty of American Women." *New-York Daily Tribune*, September 30, 1845: 1.

Review of Henry Wadsworth Longfellow, *Poems. New-York Daily Tribune*, December 10, 1845: 1.

Review of *The Poetical Works of Percy Bysshe Shelley. New-York Daily Tribune*, December 27, 1845: 1.

"1st January, 1846," *New-York Daily Tribune*, January 1, 1846: 1.

Review of Nathaniel Hawthorne, *Mosses from an Old Manse. New-York Daily Tribune*, June 22, 1846: 1.

Review of Thomas L. M'Kenney, *Memoirs, Official and Personal. New-York Daily Tribune*, July 8, 1846: 1.

830 NOTE ON THE TEXTS

Review of Charles Brockden Brown, *Ormond; Or, the Secret Witness* and *Wieland; Or, the Transformation*. *New-York Daily Tribune,* July 21, 1846: 1.

"Farewell." *New-York Daily Tribune,* August 1, 1846: 2.

"American Literature: Its Position in the Present Time, and Prospects for the Future." S. Margaret Fuller, *Papers on Literature and Art, Part II* (New York: Wiley and Putnam, 1846): 122–42.

EUROPE, 1846–1850

"Letters from England." *New-York Daily Tribune,* September 24, 1846: 2.

"Things and Thoughts in Europe No. V." *New-York Daily Tribune,* November 13, 1846: 1.

"Things and Thoughts in Europe No. X." *New-York Daily Tribune,* March 3, 1847: 1.

"Things and Thoughts in Europe No. XIII." *New-York Daily Tribune,* May 29, 1847: 1.

"To a Daughter of Italy." *The People's Journal* 4 (1847): 327.

"Things and Thoughts in Europe No. XVIII." *New-York Daily Tribune,* January 1, 1848: 1.

"Things and Thoughts in Europe No. XIX." *New-York Daily Tribune,* January 29, 1848: 1.

"Things and Thoughts in Europe No. XXV." *New-York Daily Tribune,* January 19, 1849: 1.

"Things and Thoughts in Europe No. XXVI." *New-York Daily Tribune,* January 26, 1849: 1.

"Things and Thoughts in Europe No. XXVIII." *New-York Daily Tribune,* April 4, 1849: 1.

"Undaunted Rome." *New-York Daily Tribune,* June 5, 1849: 2.

"Things and Thoughts in Europe No. XXXIII." *New-York Daily Tribune,* August 11, 1849: 2.

"Italy." *New-York Daily Tribune* Supplement, February 13, 1850: 1.

UNPUBLISHED WRITINGS AND JOURNALS

Fuller left behind at her death a large number of unpublished manuscripts, which include sketches, dialogues, poetry, essays, and diaries as well as notes she committed to paper that were intended to be expanded upon in her journals or elsewhere; she also kept multigeneric journals or commonplace books that include poetry, sketches, reflections, sentimental friendship albums, and copies of others' writing. After her death, many of Fuller's manuscripts were

NOTE ON THE TEXTS 831

cut up, defaced, rewritten, and bowdlerized for the posthumous two-volume *Memoirs of Margaret Fuller Ossoli*, edited by Ralph Waldo Emerson, William Henry Channing, and James Freeman Clarke (Boston: Phillips, Sampson and Company, 1852). The editors censored material they judged to be culturally lacking in virtue for a woman, effaced material in colored pencils and pens, edited Fuller's prose, and pasted scraps of journal material onto transcriptions of her writings in other hands to send to the printer. Much manuscript material was destroyed in the process. Other manuscripts were treated similarly for posthumous publications overseen by Fuller's brother, Arthur Fuller. Some texts now exist only in transcriptions in other hands or in the *Memoirs*. With a few exceptions, even Fuller's bound journals have been excised or effaced. Much of the loose journal material consists of fragments, often undated. Most of Fuller's journal fragments and other manuscripts are housed in the Houghton Library at Harvard, where the Fuller family deposited their own manuscripts; others are archived at the Boston Public Library, the Massachusetts Historical Society, and the Fruitlands Museum.

Most of the texts in the present volume are available from only one source: some of these are manuscripts or fragments of manuscripts in Fuller's hand, while others are manuscript copies in another hand or else a posthumously published source for which the original manuscript of the text is no longer known to be extant. For those texts transcribed from a manuscript source, the current edition retains Fuller's spelling, capitalization, and punctuation, including her use of dashes or a period with a dash to separate sentences or sentence fragments. Fuller often indicated a new paragraph by leaving space on the end of a line; this edition indents the first line of new paragraphs so indicated. Likewise, Fuller often omitted periods at the end of sentences and paragraphs and indicated the start of a new sentence only by capitalizing the beginning of the next word; this edition supplies periods in those cases. In light of Fuller's practice of normally capitalizing the first word of a sentence, any indistinct punctuation mark that could either be a comma or a period is taken to be a comma if the next word is not capitalized; but if the context indicates a period in such a case, a capital letter is supplied. Contractions and superscript letters, such as "aftn," have been retained, as have ampersands. Fuller's marked cancellations and additions to the manuscript are adopted.

Further discussion of the source of each text is given below.

UNPUBLISHED WRITINGS

"Possent quia posse videntur." Houghton, MS Am 1086 (78). School theme corrected by father. Undated, but written prior to

832 NOTE ON THE TEXTS

the fall of 1819, after which Fuller was no longer educated at home. Autograph manuscript with manuscript revisions by Timothy Fuller, which are not incorporated into the text; these take the form of small circles beneath or underlining of individual letters, suggestions for alternate wordings, corrections to punctuation, and marginal comments such as requests for specificity. However, a notation at the end in Fuller's mature hand is included. An image of one of the manuscript pages may be found on page 608 in this volume. This school theme has not been published except in short excerpts until the present volume.

"Autobiographical Romance." *Memoirs of Margaret Fuller Ossoli*, vol. 1 (Boston: Phillips, Sampson and Company, 1852): 11–57. The editors of this posthumous volume dated this piece to 1840. No manuscript is known to be extant. The text was presented as quoted material within *Memoirs of Margaret Fuller Ossoli*, quotation marks appearing at the beginning of each line and at the end of the text; the present volume omits the quotation marks.

"Fictional Autobiographical Fragment." Houghton, MS Am 1086 (42) as "Autobiographical Remarks and Narrative fragment." Autograph manuscript of loose sheets, dated in this edition to c. 1841–42, as Fuller was in those years engaged in various forms of life writing. The present volume reorders the text from the Houghton Library's arrangement, based on the material evidence of the paper, such as its color, and on narrative sequence; the beginning and end of the text are missing.

"A Credo." Boston Public Library, MS Am 1450, Box 2, Folder 97. Autograph manuscript annotated on the last page in another hand as "Summer of 1842." One sentence in the text was effaced in the manuscript with both light and dark gray inks; in addition, the lighter ink in multiple places clarifies letter formation and makes corrections. These changes were possibly made by William Ellery Channing, the original recipient of Fuller's "Credo," part of a longer correspondence between the two writers about their religious beliefs. This edition restores the canceled sentence (at 642.33, as "This ideal I believe you had in your mind let him not go.") and does not incorporate the changes made by other pens.

"To Beethoven." Houghton, MS Am 1086 (40) as "Journal about and letter to Beethoven." Autograph manuscript, dated November 25, 1843.

"Chamois." Houghton, MS Am 1086 (43) as "[Journal:] Chamois: autograph manuscript?" Undated manuscript in the hand of either Emelyn Story or a copyist hired by Fuller's family after her death. Story was a reliable copyist and reproduced Fuller's characteristic

NOTE ON THE TEXTS 833

spellings. No manuscript of this piece in Fuller's hand is known to be extant. Two other hands have marked corrections to the manuscript in pen and in pencil, possibly for posthumous publication; these corrections have not been incorporated into the text. This edition dates the text to 1844 based on resonances with Fuller's letter of July 1844 to Ralph Waldo Emerson, for which see pages 748–49 in this volume. One of the other hands has also noted on the first page of the manuscript, seemingly for a planned posthumous publication, that the text should be placed at the end of a chapter with a poem, "Sub Rosa Crux," which was written in 1844. "Chamois" has not been published except in short excerpts until the present volume.

JOURNALS

Poems and Selections from Journal Fragments. Houghton, MS Am 1086 (45) as "[Journal: Fragments of Journal] 1833, 1839, 1840: autograph manuscript, ca. 1833–1840." Fragments of autograph manuscript pages, seemingly from multiple journals originally. Notes, revisions, highlighting, strike-throughs, and erasures in red and purple ink and in pencil in other hands are not reproduced in this edition. Some entries were dated by Fuller, mostly in 1839 and 1840; entries dated in this edition to 1833 seem to relate to a separate 1833 journal containing writing on Egypt. The 1844 entries were so dated by Emerson in his Margaret Fuller Ossoli journal (for which see the discussion of Fuller's letters, below).

from S. M. Fuller's bouquet.—Journal. Houghton, MS Am 1086 (98) as "'S M Fuller's bouquet': autograph manuscript journal, undated." Autograph manuscript dated in this edition to c. 1836–1837 based on the publication dates of passages Fuller copied into this journal from other works as well as a reference to her canceled plans to travel to Europe in 1836.

from Reflections Journal. Houghton, MS Am 1086 (49) as "[Journal: Reflections]: autograph manuscript, undated." Autograph manuscript dated c. 1839. One entry is dated April 1839, and Fuller quotes from an 1839 publication as well as from a lecture Emerson delivered in February and May 1839.

from Bound Journal. Houghton MS Am 1086 (85) as "1840 S. M. Fuller: autograph manuscript journal, 1840." Autograph manuscript dated c. 1839–1840 in this edition; entries not included in this edition extend to 1844. Fuller dated one entry April 1840; other entries concern her acceptance of the editorship of *The Dial* in 1839 and drafts for the table of contents for the first two issues of *The Dial* in 1840.

834 NOTE ON THE TEXTS

from 1842 Journal. Joel Myerson, "Margaret Fuller's 1842 Journal: At Concord with the Emersons," *Harvard Library Bulletin* 21.3 (July 1973): 322–24, 327–33, 334–39, 340. The present volume prints the extracts from "1842 Journal" from the text edited by Joel Myerson, but with a few alterations in editorial procedure. In three cases, where an obvious slip of the pen in manuscript was marked by Myerson with "[sic]," the present volume omits the "[sic]" and corrects the slip of the pen: 671.15, it it; 679.17, tenderness." [extra closing quotation]; 685.7, in in. As Fuller habitually indicated new paragraphs only by beginning a new line, the present volume indents the first line of new paragraphs printed flush left by Myerson. Bracketed editorial insertions used by Myerson to identify persons or places, expand contractions and abbreviations, or clarify meaning, have been deleted in the present volume. In instances where canceled, but still legible, words were printed by Myerson with lines through the deleted material, this volume omits the canceled words. And where Myerson indicated insertions Fuller made above the line or in a margin within arrows or other symbols, the present volume accepts Fuller's insertions and prints them without editorial symbols. Bracketed editorial corrections and insertions by Myerson, where they seem to be the only possible reading, are accepted and printed without brackets. One editorial correction has been made: at 683.1, Myerson's correction of "recals" (an acceptable nineteenth-century spelling) to "recalls" has not been reproduced. A full-text version of the complete work is freely available: https://nrs.harvard.edu/URN -3:HUL.INSTREPOS:37364024.

from October 1842 Journal. Robert D. Habich, "Margaret Fuller's Journal for October 1842," *Harvard Library Bulletin* 33.3 (Summer 1985): 283, 286–88, 290–91. The present volume prints the extracts from "October 1842 Journal" from the text edited by Robert D. Habich, but with the same alterations in editorial procedure as outlined for the "1842 Journal" above. One instance where an obvious slip of the pen in manuscript was marked by Habich with "[sic]" has been corrected in this volume and printed without "[sic]": at 688.37, a [for an ampersand]. A full-text version of the complete work is freely available: https://nrs.harvard.edu/URN-3:HUL .INSTREPOS:37363948.

from Journal Fragments. Fruitlands Archives and Research Center, Fm_MS_7, folder 4, items 20–26. Autograph manuscripts, some dated (and reordered from their presentation in the Fruitlands Archive) in this edition based on internal evidence. All of the Fruitlands 1844 fragments are written on different types of paper and could have been composed at different times. The first fragment presented

NOTE ON THE TEXTS 835

(pages 690–92 in this volume) is either a copy of an 1840 document describing or planning for one of Fuller's conversations or an original 1840 document mixed in with the 1844 fragments. See "Margaret Fuller's Boston Conversations: The 1839–1840 Series," ed. Nancy Craig Simmons, *SAR* (1994) for Elizabeth Peabody's transcription of the Conversation that appears to correspond with this document. All fragments show marks in ink and in orange and regular lead pencil that highlight passages, insert pagination, comment on sections, add words, and reform Fuller's letters to provide more clarity to a reader. The content and types of marks suggest they were made by the editors of Fuller's posthumous *Memoirs*; they are ignored in this edition.

from Manuscript Tracing Journal. The bulk of Fuller's 1844 journal, possibly as much as two-thirds of it, is no longer extant. It seems to have survived intact until at least 1910, when, preparing remarks for the centennial celebration of Fuller's birth, Fuller's niece Edith Fuller wrote, "I have before me her journal of 1844." Edith Fuller referred to entries from December 1844 that are no longer extant; the copies that exist contain entries from June through October 1844. When the Fuller family papers were deposited at Harvard in 1926, the original of Fuller's 1844 journal was not among them. The only fragments of the journal that are known to be extant are at the Fruitlands Archives and Research Center, Fm_MS_7, folder 4, items 20–26, mixed in with pages from Fuller's earlier May 1844 journal. The remaining pages of the journal, from which the present edition selects extracts, exist only in a tracing of the original journal made by William Hull Clarke (now in the Massachusetts Historical Society, Perry-Clarke Papers P-321). Clarke had obtained Fuller's original journal from Arthur Fuller's widow in 1876; Clarke wrote to his sister Sarah, who had been Fuller's friend, "Mrs. Arthur Fuller lent me, last winter, one of Margaret's journals, kept in 1844. It is very interesting. . . . I am making a tracing of it on thin paper to paste into a blank book, as I must return the original." Clarke carefully traced over Fuller's own handwriting; however, he also elided material, sometimes but not always indicating where he did so. Because Clarke reproduced the pagination of the original in his tracing, entire pages are known to be missing, and Clarke frequently left out poems, instead referring in marginal notes in his own handwriting to an edition of Fuller's work published posthumously in 1860, *Life Without and Life Within*. It is possible that some of the pages from a section that in Clarke's tracing copy is annotated as "ten pages gone" exist in the Fruitlands fragments, including entries from late August and early September. Clarke also erased references to Caroline Sturgis Tappan and other

836 NOTE ON THE TEXTS

contemporaries in the journal as well as in other Fuller manuscripts he was given; he wrote to Tappan in 1875, "I felt justified to erase your name (or initials) where they appeared." The present edition uses Clarke's tracing as its text; the poems "On the boundless plain careering" and "To Sarah," which Clarke left out of his tracing, have been taken from a copy of the poems made by Emelyn Story at the request of the Fuller family (Houghton MS Am 1086 [60]). The Fuller family attempted to have transcribed all of Fuller's manuscripts in their possession, and Story was a reliable copyist, reproducing Fuller's characteristic spellings.

from Italy 1849 Journal. Houghton, MS Am 1086 (94) as "[Rome diary]: autograph manuscript journal; Rome, 1847–1849." Fuller's Italian journal has not previously been published except in a text that silently omits words or whole passages, until the present volume.

LETTERS

After her death, Fuller's letters received, in many cases, the same treatment as her other manuscripts, with little care given to their preservation. The Fuller family did hire a copyist to duplicate the letters in their possession, but many other letters were destroyed or lost. In the letters that were gathered and published in the *Memoirs of Margaret Fuller Ossoli*, the editors omitted most of the names of the correspondents and persons mentioned within letters, altered punctuation and wording, joined separate letters together, and even rewrote passages. In the process, many of the original letters were cannibalized, destroyed, or lost (Charles Newcomb's letters, for example, disappeared in the post when Emerson mailed them back).

Other letters later came to light in further posthumous publications: Thomas Wentworth Higginson's 1884 biography *Margaret Fuller Ossoli*, which used letters collected by William Henry Channing as well as the Fuller family, some of which are no longer extant; and the 1903 *Love-Letters of Margaret Fuller*, which published for the first time her letters to James Nathan (the originals were later purchased by the Boston Public Library). The letters and other manuscripts collected by the Fuller family were deposited in the Houghton Library, and Higginson's collection went to the Boston Public Library. Other letters exist in the papers of their recipients at the Houghton Library and the New York Public Library.

The source of the text for the letters in the present edition is the six-volume *The Letters of Margaret Fuller*, ed. Robert N. Hudspeth (Ithaca, NY: Cornell University Press, 1983–95). Copyright ©

NOTE ON THE TEXTS

1983–95 by Cornell University Press. Used by permission of the publisher, Cornell University Press. Hudspeth brought together all known extant letters by Fuller, whether in autograph manuscripts; manuscript copies; Emerson's "Margaret Fuller Ossoli" journal, in which he copied extracts from Fuller's letters while he drafted his portion of the posthumous *Memoirs*; or in one of the posthumous printed sources. In some cases, the text for a letter had to be stitched together from several sources; for example, the first half of Fuller's August 1849 letter to Costanza Arconati Visconti only survives in the posthumous *Memoirs*, but Hudspeth was able to join to this a surviving fragment of the end of the letter in a copy in an unknown hand that is housed in the Houghton Library.

The present volume prints the selected letters from the texts edited by Robert N. Hudspeth, but with a few alterations in editorial procedure. Bracketed editorial corrections and insertions of the earlier editors, in which only one obvious possible reading is offered, are accepted and printed without brackets. Where Hudspeth has supplied dates and locations not given by Fuller or otherwise missing from the text at the heads of the letters, the present edition prints these at the end of the letters to distinguish them from Fuller's own letter openings. The three letters in Italian to Giovanni Ossoli, for which Hudspeth includes nineteenth-century translations, presumably done at the request of the Fuller family and published either in full or in part in the posthumous *Memoirs* and in Higginson's biography, are here printed both in the Italian and in new English translations commissioned for the present volume from Virginia Jewiss. In the August 27, 1839, letter to Sophia Ripley, in which Hudspeth stitched together several letter fragments, this edition deletes the final two words in the penultimate fragment so that at 733.28–30, "I am ready to answer any questions which may be proposed Meanwhile put and will add nothing more here" reads "I am ready to answer any questions which may be put and will add nothing more here." Finally, in the May 23, [1845], letter to James Nathan, the line spacing and, in one instance, capitalization of one letter of the poem have been adjusted with reference to the manuscript of the letter at the Boston Public Library (MS Am. 1451, folder 49).

The following is a list of the letters that are included in this volume, in the order of their appearance, giving the volume and page number of the text of each letter in Hudspeth's edition:

To Timothy Fuller, April [24, 1817?], I: 79.
To Timothy Fuller, January 16, 1820, I: 93–95.
To the Marquis de Lafayette, [June? 16? 1825?], I: 150.

838   NOTE ON THE TEXTS

To Susan Prescott, July 11, 1825, I: 151–52.
To James Freeman Clarke, August 7, 1832, VI: 186–88.
To James Freeman Clarke, April 19, 1836, VI: 286–88.
To Caroline Sturgis, November 16, 1837, I: 313–15.
To Ralph Waldo Emerson, March 1, 1838, I: 327–28.
To Lidian Jackson Emerson, [August 19, 1838], I: 340–41.
To Sophia Ripley[?], August 27, 1839, II: 86–89.
To Unknown Correspondent, November 25, 1839, II: 101–2.
To William Henry Channing, March 22, 1840, II: 125–27.
To Ralph Waldo Emerson, September 29, 1840, II: 159–60.
To Henry David Thoreau, December 1, [1840], II: 185.
To William Henry Channing, [April 5, 1841], II: 205–6.
To Ralph Waldo Emerson, April 9, 1842, III: 57–59.
To Sophia Peabody, June 4, [1842], III: 65–66.
To George T. Davis, December 17, 1842, III: 104–6.
To Richard F. Fuller, July 29, 1843, III: 132–33.
To Caroline Sturgis, May 3, [1844], III: 193–94.
To Ralph Waldo Emerson, July 13, [1844], III: 209–10.
To Elizabeth Hoar, October [28?], 1844, III: 237.
To William Henry Channing, November 17, 1844, III: 241–42.
To Eugene Fuller, March 9, 1845, IV: 56–57.
To James Nathan, [May 4?, 1845], IV: 94–96.
To James Nathan, May 23, [1845], IV: 104–7.
To Evert A. Duyckinck, June 28, [1846], IV: 212–14.
To Caroline Sturgis [November 16?, 1846], IV: 239–41.
To Ralph Waldo Emerson, November 16, 1846, IV: 245–49.
To Elizabeth Hoar, January 18, 1847, IV: 256.
To Marcus and Rebecca Spring, April 10, [1847], IV: 262–63.
To Richard F. Fuller, October 29, 1847, IV: 310.
To William Henry Channing, March 29, 1848, V: 58–59.
To Jane Tuckerman King, April 1848, V: 59–60.
To Costanza Arconati Visconti, May 27, [1848], V: 69.
To Charles King Newcomb, June 22, 1848, V: 76–78.
To Giovanni Angelo Ossoli, August 22, 1848, V: 108–9; new English
     translation by Virginia Jewiss.
To Giovanni Angelo Ossoli, September 7, 1848, V: 111; new English
     translation by Virginia Jewiss.
To Giuseppe Mazzini, March 3, 1849, V: 196–98.
To William Henry Channing, March 10, 1849, V: 205–6.
To Caroline Sturgis Tappan, March 16, 1849, V: 207–11.
To Giovanni Angelo Ossoli, [June 1849], V: 235; new English translation
     by Virginia Jewiss.
To Ralph Waldo Emerson, June 10, 1849, V: 239–40.
To Costanza Arconati Visconti [August 1849], V: 249–50.
To Caroline Sturgis Tappan, August 28, 1849, V: 258–59.

NOTE ON THE TEXTS   839

To Margarett Crane Fuller, August 31, 1849, V: 259–62.
To Costanza Arconati Visconti, October 16, 1849, V: 269–70.
To Emelyn Story, [c. November 1849], V: 279–80.
To Elizabeth Barrett Browning, December 6, [1849], V: 288–89.
To William Henry Channing, December 17, 1849, V: 300–301.
To Arthur Hugh Clough, February 16, [1850], VI: 63–65.
To Costanza Arconati Visconti, April 6, 1850, VI: 74.
To Lewis Cass Jr., May 2, 1850, VI: 83–84.

This volume presents the texts of the original printings, manuscripts, or later editions chosen as sources here but does not attempt to reproduce features of their typographic design. The texts are printed without alteration except for the changes previously discussed and the correction of typographical errors. Spelling, punctuation, and capitalization are often expressive features, and they are not altered, even when inconsistent or irregular. The following is a list of typographical errors corrected, cited by page and line number: 10.22, termerity; 29.29, beasteses; 61.18, dream?; 62.29–30, panting it; 68.29, ef; 87.30, not to permitted; 95.12, Scherin; 97.24, faith; 106.19, three.”; 107.10, Weinsburg; 109.34, touch.; 130.18, hedoes; 130.38, lives.; 142.17, and bad; 146.4, get.; 148.39, inconsistences; 151.17, wife.”; 154.26, The Shawano; 164.16, women; 165.24, assemblage.; 185.3, unnecessay; 189.13, *evea*; 201.24, “We are tempted; 210.37, affection,’” said; 216.37, exhibtion; 238.3, other wise; 239.32, others;; 242.37, After he first; 249.28, reformation.’; 257 [running head], Cassanrra; 262.36, vow.; 277.5, that ‘all; 279 [running head], Tmple of Juno; 286.21, basis; 290.30, English, novelist; 294.35, Neckar’s; 303.6, occuption; 312.7, Ch accolga; 312.7, l mio; 314.9, argest; 328.10–11, came the the suit; 357.19, treat us as as; 375.39, A moment; 388.35, me;”; 403.35, makes us; 407.25, nature—; 412.4, show some; 413.6, yet yet; 416.34, blood is now; 419.28, sonmambulist; 429.29, anecdatos; 429.32, others eyes; 430.27, Kinment; 432.21, Planation.; 436.3, Emmett’s; 438.28, Americam; 441.3, a Nasture; 442.8, profession; 442.17, nature,; 444.14, valne; 445.12, sueh; 445.22, Woman; 446.32, pinchback; 447.8, future, And; 447.25, poetic, taste; 447.36, ungenerous, It; 449.4, literatue; 452.18, Evange list; 460.34, thee,; 466.28, eat; 468.5, bless never; 470.24, hope such; 473.20, time time.; 473.26, to help her.; 475.18, has been; 476.36, “Rapaccini’s; 478.1, Cincord; 482.37, vestgies; 484.18, McKenney; 484.23, mother in-law; 487.16, heen; 488.30, intercouse; 491.14, Literatnre; 501.23, pantomine; 505.25, to this; 505.29, bold various; 512.29, will their; 517.3, fable only; 517.14, Chartney; 521.21, covention; 522.27, *not*; 523.34, Rowardennen; 524.2, or me,; 524.19, night; 525.13, Rowardinnan; 526.29, might the; 527.19, and and; 528.10,

840   NOTE ON THE TEXTS

Tuilleries; 528.13, La Mennais—Bèranger; 533.1, act ting; 533.16, *le*;
534.35, delighfully; 535.11, me. "Que; 537.3, Bèranger; 537.8, Bèranger;
537.27, Bèranger; 538.19, Cavaille; 542.14, Cama; 552.13, spring time;
555.7, Santo Spirits; 555.10, Trolloppe; 555.14, Hall; 557.17, pleas!!; 561.23,
clear sightedness; 561.31–32, it a; 562.21, satisfaction, Already; 562.27,
very very; 563.2, distinguised; 563.9, simpleton,; 563.24, or ordinance;
563.27, Oscurantists; 564.32, run; 566.33, exhilarated; 569.25, he was
inly; 570.33, Tommaseo; 574.12, Garribaldi; 576.26, retrogade; 576.27,
panic-struck; 579.36, Guerazzi; 585.21, &c; 587.6, to any; 594.1, Marara;
594.16, light athletic; 595.23, inervention; 599.3, court yard; 601.24,
eaf; 602.8, Send, money; 602.30, peopie; 625.12, Moliére; 634.25,
there, has; 635.26, recal; 635.30, *ago.* This; 636.7, whose death; 638.33,
bodeis; 639.8, art literature; 639.14–15, spirit, Many; 642.36, hunan;
645.30, Least; 646.5, star Seemed; 646.35, "alone with the Alone"?;
653.28, still—"A; 653.30, company Enough; 655.4, Heliotrope,; 655.25,
fiilling; 656.6, root,; 662.8, minutes thou; 662.23, beauty.; 664.22,
ill, On; 665.1–2, lion., the; 665.6, gone. into; 668.5, nature.; 689.21,
he says,; 691.10, aversion, (when; 698.9, That; 699.20, The wound;
702.14, I, can; 703.26, we.; 706.15, niether; 707.29, thier; 709.27, skey;
709.28, skey; 710.27, Moliére.; 728.34, Monda; 728.35, fo; 756.8, 1845;
761.22, Martyrs.—; 794.6, not not yet; 796.15, much.

Notes

In the notes below, the reference numbers denote page and line of this volume (the line count includes headings but not rule lines). No note is made for material included in *Merriam-Webster's Collegiate Dictionary*, except when needed for clarification. Biblical quotations and allusions are keyed to the King James Version, and references to Shakespeare to *The Riverside Shakespeare*, ed. G. Blakemore Evans (Boston: Houghton Mifflin, 1974). Footnotes in the text are by Fuller. For additional textual and explanatory information, see *Margaret Fuller, Critic: Writings from the* New-York Tribune, *1844–1846*, ed. Judith Mattson Bean and Joel Myerson (New York: Columbia University Press, 2000); *"These Sad but Glorious Days": Dispatches from Europe, 1846–1850*, ed. Larry J. Reynolds and Susan Belasco Smith (New Haven, CT: Yale University Press, 1991); and *The Letters of Margaret Fuller*, six volumes, ed. Robert N. Hudspeth (Ithaca, NY: Cornell University Press, 1983–95). Recent studies that helped to inform this edition include Eagan Dean, "*Woman in the Nineteenth Century* and the Politics of Reprinting, 1845–1980," *ESQ: A Journal of Nineteenth-Century American Literature and Culture* 69.1 (2022): 39–72; and Phyllis Cole, "'A Credo': Margaret Fuller and the Transcendentalists," *New England Quarterly* 97.2 (2024). For additional biographical information, see Charles Capper, *Margaret Fuller: An American Romantic Life*, vol. 1, *The Private Years*, and vol. 2, *The Public Years* (Oxford: Oxford University Press, 1992 and 2007); and Megan Marshall, *Margaret Fuller: A New American Life* (Boston: Houghton Mifflin Harcourt, 2013).

SUMMER ON THE LAKES, IN 1843

8.9   Cloten] Foolish character in Shakespeare's *Cymbeline*.

8.11   Jonathan] Eighteenth- and nineteenth-century term for a typical American, especially a rural New Englander.

9.10   Muskau] German travel writer Hermann Ludwig Heinrich Pückler-Muskau (1785–1871).

9.13   Dickens] Charles Dickens wrote a critical travel account of the U.S.: *American Notes for General Circulation* (1842).

10.19   General Porter and Jack Downing] American general Andrew Porter (1743–1813). Jack Downing, character in *The Life and Writings of Major Jack*

841

842   NOTES

Downing, of Downingville, Away Down East in the State of Maine (1833), by Maine humorist and newspaper editor Seba Smith (1792–1868); the book has a section on Sam Patch, who gained fame by jumping into the Niagara River near the bottom of Niagara Falls.

11.16   Recluse of Niagara] Englishman Francis Abbott lived in a cabin at the Falls from 1829 to 1831, avoiding most human contact, until he drowned.

13.8   "barren, barren all"] Cf. *Henry IV, Part 2*, V.iii.7.

15.5   *J., S. and M.*] James Freeman Clarke (1810–1888), his sister Sarah Ann Clarke (1808–1896), and Margaret Fuller.

15.19   Hoffman's] German author E.T.A. Hoffmann (1776–1822).

25.21–22   uva ursi . . . kinnick-kinnick] Evergreen shrubs.

26.14   Catlin's book] *Manners, Customs, and Condition of the North American Indians* (1841) by painter George Catlin.

26.24   Murray's travels] *Travels in North America* (1839) by writer and diplomat Charles Augustus Murray (1806–1895).

26.39   Schoolcraft's Algic Researches] *Algic Researches, comprising inquiries respecting the mental characteristics of the North American Indians* (1839) by American geographer and Michigan Indian agent Henry Rowe Schoolcraft (1793–1864), who married Ojibwe writer Jane Johnston, or Bamewawagezhikaquay (1800–1842).

27.15   stories Mrs. Jameson wrote] *Winter Studies and Summer Rambles in Canada* (1838) by Irish writer Anna Murphy Brownell Jameson (1794–1860).

27.21   Cooper in such inventions as his Uncas] Uncas is a character in *The Last of the Mohicans* (1826) by James Fenimore Cooper.

27.25   Irving's books] *A Tour on the Prairies* (1835) and *Astoria* (1836) by Washington Irving.

27.36   McKenney's Tour to the Lakes] *Sketches of a tour to the lakes: of the character and customs of the Chippeway Indians, and of incidents connected with the treaty of Fond du Lac* (1827) by Thomas Loraine McKenney (1785–1859), first head of the U.S. Bureau of Indian Affairs.

28.8   "The golden and the flame-like flowers."] "The Prairies" (1832), l. 16, by William Cullen Bryant. The quotations below (at 29.3–4 and 30.6–9) are also from Bryant's poem.

29.22   Chamouny or the Trosachs] Chamonix is a valley near Mont Blanc; the Trossachs are a forested region near Ben Lomond (Scottish Highlands). Both were described by writers.

NOTES 843

31.4 "sees what he foresaw."] "Character of the Happy Warrior" (1807), l. 54, by William Wordsworth.

31.32 Madoc] In Welsh legend the medieval prince Madoc sailed to America. Robert Southey wrote the epic poem *Madoc* (1805).

33.5 Trollopian records] English writer Frances (Fanny) Trollope (1779–1863) traveled and lived in the U.S. and wrote an often critical book: *Domestic Manners of the Americans* (1832).

38.34 Rhesus] In Homer's *Iliad*, Rhesus, King of Thrace, was famous for his horses.

39.12–13 "Of itself . . . still be seeking?"] Wordsworth, "Expostulation and Reply" (1798), ll. 27–28.

41.4 in the shadow of the Seven Sisters] Reference unclear. Possibly the constellation Pleiades, or the Seven Sisters Rocks overlooking the River Wye, a scenic area in England.

41.8 West] When the American painter Benjamin West arrived in Rome in 1760 and was shown the Apollo Belvedere, he said, "My God, how like it is to a young Mohawk warrior."

41.25–26 Ganymede to His Eagle . . . THORWALDSEN'S] In Ovid, *Metamorphoses*, book 10, Jove falls in love with the boy Ganymede and, in the shape of an eagle, takes him to Mount Olympus to be cupbearer to the gods. Bertel Thorwaldsen created a statue of Ganymede.

44.8–9 the fatal Nine . . . Delphian] The nine muses in Greek mythology; Delphian refers to the Greek oracle at Delphi, sacred to Apollo, the god of poetry, music, and dance.

50.10 Mrs. Gore's novels] Catherine Grace Frances Gore (1798–1861) wrote "silver fork" novels depicting Regency high society.

50.16 Kinmont] Scottish philosopher and abolitionist Alexander Kinmont (1799–1838).

51.18 Will's coffeehouse] Will's Coffee House was a late-seventeenth-century London gathering spot for such cultural figures as John Dryden.

51.23 Big Thunder] American Indian (perhaps Winnebago) chief, whose embalmed body sat in a stockade on a mound—in accord with tribal tradition—in Belvidere, Illinois (c. 1830).

52.18 Allston's death] The painter Washington Allston; Fuller reviewed his works in "A Record of Impressions produced by the Exhibition of Mr. Allston's Pictures in the Summer of 1839," for which see pp. 359–70 in this volume.

54.15–18 a friend in Massachusetts . . . Triformis] "Triformis" was written by James Freeman Clarke.

844 NOTES

56.4–62.17 "And you, too, love . . . make zigzag fences."] Excerpts from letters and poetry by Fuller's friends, Transcendentalist, poet, and banker Samuel Gray Ward (1817–1907) and poet William Ellery Channing (1818–1901).

63.3 Mariana] Fuller's fictional character Mariana may have autobiographical elements, although this is debated. Mariana is also a character in *Wilhelm Meisters Lehrjahre* (*Wilhelm Meister's Apprenticeship*) (1795–96) by Johann Wolfgang von Goethe.

66.12 Hastings] The British governor-general of India, Warren Hastings (1732–1818), was tried and acquitted for "high crimes and misdemeanours" by the House of Lords.

66.13–15 Methodist preacher . . . rotten egg] Founder of Methodism John Wesley and his fellow preachers were sometimes assaulted as they traveled in Britain in the 1740s and 1750s.

66.26–28 Roman matron . . . "It is not painful, Poetus."] When her husband, Aulus Caecina Paetus, hesitated to kill himself as ordered by the emperor Claudius for his role in a rebellion, Arria stabbed herself and then uttered this line. This wording comes from a footnote to the poem "Poetic Lines, Addressed to a Friend," in *Original Poems*, by Mary Hopkins Pilkington (1811).

67.39 "The Bandit's Bride,"] *The Bandit's Bride: or, The Maid of Saxony, a Romance* (1807) by English novelist Louisa Sidney Stanhope (fl. 1806–27).

73.3–10 "felt . . . this black return,"] Richard Monckton Milnes, "The Lay of the Humble" (1838), ll. 41–48.

74.22 "Whom men love not, but yet regret,"] From "Stanzas Written in Dejection, near Naples" (1824) by Percy Bysshe Shelley.

74.27 Fortunio] *Fortunio* (1838), a novel by Théophile Gautier.

75.23 *Helen of Kirconnel Lee*] Scottish ballad "Helen of Kirkconnel," which Fuller quotes in lines 75.31 and 76.1. The rest are Fuller's words.

78.5 Van Artevelde's Elena] A character in *Philip van Artevelde* (1834) by English writer Henry Taylor (1800–1886).

79.39 Morris Birkbeck] Reformer and abolitionist Morris Birkbeck (1764–1825), who was interested in utopian communities, emigrated to Illinois and wrote books popularizing immigration to the prairies: *Notes on a Journey in America from the Coast of Virginia to the Territory of Illinois* (1817) and *Letters from Illinois* (1818).

83.10–11 You may see a great deal here of Life, in the London sense] Perhaps a reference to Johnson's statement, "when a man is tired of London, he is tired of life; for there is in London all that life can afford," quoted in *The Life of Samuel Johnson, LL.D.* (1791), by James Boswell.

NOTES

845

84.20–21 Titian's Venus and Adonis] One of several versions of a painting by Titian.

87.24 "A thing for human feelings the most trying,"] George Gordon, Lord Byron, *Don Juan* (1819–24), canto III, l. 402.

88.38 Mr. Lowell has put into verse] "A Chippewa Legend" in *Miscellaneous Poems* (1843) by James Russell Lowell.

94.31 jereed] Turkish team sport played on horses.

95.12–14 Die Seherin von Prevorst . . . Kerner] Doctor and spiritualist Andreas Justinus Kerner (1786–1862) described the clairvoyant Friederike Hauffe (1801–1827) in *Die Seherin von Prevorst* (1829). In the following pages (through 123.2), Fuller creates a debate about this phenomenon among four points of view and then summarizes Kerner's account.

96.34 what the French sage calls the "aromal state."] Philosopher and utopian socialist Charles Fourier believed that the freeing of one's magnetic fluid or energy resulted in an open, "aromal state." See also next note.

96.38–97.2 animal magnetism . . . electricity] Theories of mesmerism, derived from Franz Anton Mesmer, held that "animal magnetism" or "animal electricity" was a form of energy pervading the world, that it was a force one person could exert on another (as in hypnotism), and that some people were more open to the electrical impulses abroad in the world.

98.12–13 "Care is taken, . . . not up into heaven,"] Goethe, *Aus meinem Leben: Dichtung und Wahrheit* (*From My Life: Poetry and Truth*, 1811–33).

98.19 Roman emperor address his soul] Hadrian (76–138) wrote this poem to his soul on his deathbed.

98.25 *Self-Poise.*] This character echoes the ideas of Ralph Waldo Emerson, Fuller's friend and her co-editor of the journal *The Dial.*

100.15 Whatever is, is right] Alexander Pope, *An Essay on Man*, epistle I, l. 294.

102.8 Radcliffe] Ann Radcliffe, author of such widely read Gothic novels as *The Mysteries of Udolpho* (1794).

104.2 Amoretti] Italian writer, scientist, and ecclesiastic Carlo Amoretti (1741–1816).

105.13 Canidias] Canidia was a witch in Horace's *Epodes* (30 BCE).

109.23 pabulum vitæ] Latin: food of life.

110.24–26 Blake . . . designs of the Resurrection] William Blake illustrated an edition of *The Complaint: or, Night Thoughts* (1794), by English poet Edward Young (1683–1765). The illustrations included images of Christ's resurrection.

846 NOTES

113.25 Eschenmeyer . . . "Mysteries."] *Mysterien des innern Lebens* (*Mysteries of the Inner Life*, 1830), a commentary on Kerner's *Die Seherin von Prevorst* by German philosopher and doctor Adam Karl August Eschenmayer (1768–1852).

115.25–26 Goethe . . . Wanderjahre . . . Macaria] Goethe published *Wilhelm Meisters Wanderjahre* in 1821–29. A daughter of Hercules, Macaria sacrificed herself to save Athens.

117.5 Townshend] English poet and clergyman Chauncy Hare Townshend (1798–1868), author of *Facts in Mesmerism; with Reasons for a dispassionate Inquiry into it* (1840).

118.6 Cornelius Aggrippa] German doctor and philosopher of the occult Heinrich Cornelius Agrippa (1486–1535).

119.23 Jung Stilling] German writer and physician Johann Heinrich Jung (1740–1817), known as Heinrich Stilling.

120.31 St. Theresa] Saint Theresa of Ávila (1515–1582), a Spanish Carmelite nun and mystic.

128.19 Henry] American-Canadian fur trader Alexander Henry (1739–1824) lived briefly with the Ojibwe and wrote *Travels and Adventures in Canada and the Indian Territories, between the years 1760 and 1776* (1809).

130.2–9 Mr. Schoolcraft . . . Mrs. Schoolcraft] See note 26.39.

130.39 Mrs. Grant] Scottish writer Anne MacVicar Grant (1755–1838) spent ten early years in colonial America, which she described in *Memoirs of an American lady: with sketches of manners and scenery in America, as they existed previous to the Revolution* (1808).

132.11 Carver, in his travels among the Winnebagoes] American explorer of the Great Lakes region Jonathan Carver (1710–1780), author of *Travels through America in the Years 1766, 1767, and 1768* (1778).

133.4 Mackenzie] Scottish fur trader and explorer of Canada Alexander Mackenzie (1764–1820), author of *Voyages from Montreal Through the Continent of North America to the Frozen and Pacific Oceans in 1789 and 1793* (1801).

134.7 Preux] French: Gallant knight.

134.7–8 Lord Edward Fitzgerald] Irish nationalist (1763–1798) who traveled to Detroit, where, according to his biography (Thomas Moore's *The Life and Death of Lord Edward Fitzgerald*, 1831), he was adopted by the Bear clan of the Kanien'kehá:ka (Mohawk).

134.9 Brant] Mohawk leader Thayendanegea, or Joseph Brant (1743–1807), who allied with the British during the Revolution.

NOTES   847

134.17   McKenney] McKenney (see note 27.36) cowrote *History of the Indian Tribes of North America* (1838–44) with James Hall (1793–1868). The following description is in vol.I.

134.27   Zinzendorf] Nikolaus Ludwig Zinzendorf helped to found Moravian communities in Pennsylvania.

137.9   deputation of the Sacs and Foxes] In 1837 Massachusetts governor Edward Everett (1794–1865) received Keokuk, Black Hawk, and other leaders of the Fox and Sac (or Sauk) tribes. Fuller's source may be *The Life and Adventures of Black Hawk: with sketches of Keokuk, the Sac and Fox Indians, and the late Black Hawk War* (1840), by Benjamin Drake (1795–1841).

137.26   Uncas and Magawisca] Characters, respectively, in Cooper's *The Last of the Mohicans* and *Hope Leslie; or, Early Times in the Massachusetts* (1827) by American writer Catharine Maria Sedgwick (1789–1867).

139.8   Combe nor Spurzheim] George Combe (1788–1858), Andrew Combe (1797–1847), and Johann Christoph Spurzheim (1776–1832) popularized phrenology, whose practitioners estimated their clients' faculties and characters by feeling bumps on their heads.

139.28   Where Massasoit sleeps—where Philip fell!] Wampanoag leader Philip (Metacom or Metacomet, c. 1639–1676), Massasoit's son, led several tribes in King Philip's War (1675–76), the last organized military resistance to English settlement in New England.

140.5   Phidian] The work of the influential sculptor Phidias (c. 480–430 BCE) is associated with the classical Greek era.

141.18   EVERETT'S SPEECH] Reprinted in Drake's *The Life and Adventures of Black Hawk* (see note 137.9).

145.1–2   "Needs be that offences . . . whom they come."] Luke 17:1.

145.8   Clevengers's] American sculptor Shobal Vail Clevenger (1812–1843).

145.12   Books as Catlin's] See note 26.14.

147.25   Mrs. Jameson] See note 27.15.

147.39–148.1   Sir William Johnson . . . Mrs. Grant] Irishman William Johnson (c. 1715–1774), a British army officer and British agent to the Iroquois, held land in upstate New York that became a center of trade with the Mohawk. For Grant see note 130.39.

149.17   Adair] Irish fur trader James Adair (c. 1709–1783), author of *The History of the American Indians* (1775).

151.19   Vivian Greyism] *Vivan Grey* (1826) is a novel by Benjamin Disraeli.

152.1   Nanabojou] Nanabozho is an Ojibwe trickster figure and shape-shifter.

848 NOTES

152.11 Life on the Lakes] New York doctor Chandler Robbins Gilman (1802–1865) wrote *Life on the Lakes: Being tales and sketches collected during a trip to the pictured rocks of Lake Superior* (1836).

156.12 Murray and Henry] For Murray, see note 26.24; for Henry, see note 128.19.

159.10 Carver's Travels] See note 132.11.

161.3–5 "Nec nisi materna . . . domabile flamma."] Latin: "Only his maternal part [his body] shall feel the power of Vulcan. That which he drew from me is exempt and free from death, conquerable by no flames." Ovid, *Metamorphoses*, 9.251–53.

162.9 Henry] See note 128.19.

163.20 Rigolette] Character in *Les Mystères de Paris* (*The Mysteries of Paris*, 1842–43) by French writer Eugène Sue (1804–1857).

166.16 Fitzgerald] See note 134.7–8.

166.22 McKenney and Hall's book] Their *History of the Indian Tribes* (see notes 27.36 and 134.17) included lithograph portraits of American Indian leaders based on paintings by American artist Charles Bird King.

166.25 Drake's book] Probably *The Book of the Indians of North America; comprising details in the lives of about five hundred chiefs and others* (1833) by Samuel Gardner Drake (1798–1875).

166.30 Guess] George Guess, also known as Sequoyah (c. 1770–1843), invented the Cherokee syllabary, enabling the Cherokee to have written language.

169.27 John Ross] Cherokee statesman (1790–1866), elected principal chief of the Cherokee Nation in 1828, who opposed the Cherokees' removal to Oklahoma in the 1830s.

170.13 Mackenzie's Travels] See note 133.4.

170.28 massacre at Chicago] The Battle of Fort Dearborn (Chicago) was an episode of the War of 1812, where the Potawatomi attacked and defeated evacuating U.S. troops.

171.33 Georgia] Georgia pushed for Cherokee expatriation through the Removal Act of 1830.

173.25 Allegro and Penseroso] Milton's representations of joy and melancholy in the poems "L'Allegro" and "Il Penseroso," in his *Poems of Mr. John Milton, both English and Latin* (1645).

NOTES

849

175.26–27 Every Cæsar should be able to write his own commentary.] Gaius Julius Caesar's *Commentarii de Bello Gallico* (*The Gallic Wars*, 52–51 BCE) describes his conquest of Gaul.

177.8 To Edith,] Edith Emerson Forbes (1841–1929), daughter of Ralph Waldo and Lidian Emerson.

180.39–181.1 the New Purchase] *The New Purchase: Or, Seven and a Half Years in the Far West* (1843), a fictionalized account of life in Indiana, by American clergyman and educator Baynard Rush Hall (1793–1863).

181.13 Scrope] English writer and amateur painter William Scrope (1772–1852), author of *The Art of Deerstalking* (1838).

183.4 S.] Sarah Clarke (see note 15.5).

184.16–18 "Look before and after." . . . "Pine for what is not."] Shelley, "To a Skylark" (1820), ll. 86–87.

184.35–185.8 its surrender . . . General Hull] General William Hull (1753–1825) fought in the American Revolution and was governor of Michigan Territory before he surrendered Fort Detroit to the British in the War of 1812, for which he was court-martialed.

186.1 Butler's Analogy] *The Analogy of Religion, Natural and Revealed, to the Constitution and Course of Nature* (1736) by English bishop and philosopher Joseph Butler (1692–1752).

186.9–11 Fourier . . . experiment of voluntary association] Fourier (see note 96.34) argued for alleviating social injustice and economic misery by creating cooperative communities through "voluntary association."

WOMAN IN THE NINETEENTH CENTURY

189.3–5 *"Frei durch Vernunft . . . Busen dir verschweig."*] From "Die Künstler" (1789) by Friedrich von Schiller (1759–1805): "Free through reason, strong through laws, / Through gentleness great, and rich through treasures, / Which for a long time your bosom kept silent from you."

189.6–15 *"I meant the day-star . . . free hours."*] From "On Lucy, Countess of Bedford" (1616) by Ben Jonson, ll. 7–16. Fuller changes Jonson's seventh line, "Only a learned and manly soul."

193.2 "Frailty, thy name is WOMAN."] *Hamlet*, I.ii.146.

194.5–8 Siquis tamen, . . . Assensere Dei.] Ovid, *Metamorphoses*, 9.256–59: "'But if there is anyone, if there is anyone, I say, who is going to be sorry that Hercules is made a god, why then, he will begrudge the prize, but he will at least know that it was given deservedly, and will be forced to approve the deed.' The gods assented."

850 NOTES

194.33–35 The candlestick set . . . upon the hill.] Matthew 5:14–15 (from the Sermon on the Mount). Fuller continues to quote from Matthew in the next paragraphs, at 195.36–196.1 (Matthew 7:12, 7) and 196.8 (Matthew 5:48).

195.10–11 "Der stets den . . . favorable to shepherds."] From Schiller's play *Die Jungfrau von Orleans* (*The Maid of Orleans*), Prologue, scene 4.

196.34 Jewish prophet described the Lamb] Either Isaiah 53:7 ("he is brought as a lamb to the slaughter") or John 1:29 ("Behold the Lamb of God")—probably John, as Fuller notes that the time of the prophecy "drew nigh."

197.18–32 "The ministry of man . . . eternity is."] From *Le Ministère de l'Homme-Esprit* (1802) by Louis Claude de Saint-Martin (1743–1803), French philosopher interested in mysticism and spiritualism.

197.35 Crawford's Orpheus] *Orpheus and Cerberus* (1843), statue by American sculptor Thomas Crawford (1814–1857), exhibited at the Boston Athenæum in 1844.

198.1 "Orphic sayings"] Bronson Alcott published "Orphic Sayings" in *The Dial*.

198.34 Bacon] Cf. *The Wisdom of the Ancients* (1609), ch. XXXI, by Francis Bacon.

199.25 citoyen, citoyenne] French: masculine and feminine forms of "citizen."

199.30–31 the poem . . . by Beranger] "La Liberté" (1822) by Pierre-Jean de Béranger.

199.33 "such crimes were committed in her name."] Paraphrase of "O Liberty, what crimes are committed in thy name!," spoken by Marie-Jeanne Roland (1754–1793), democratic republican (Girondin), before being guillotined during the French Revolution.

200.11–12 "Father, forgive them, for they know not what they do."] Luke 23:34.

201.1–16 "Tutti fatti a sembianza . . . immortal spirit."] From *Il Conte di Carmagnola* (1820), by Alessandro Manzoni.

201.29 Landor] Walter Savage Landor (1775–1864), who was supportive of liberal causes.

201.36 Sterling] Scottish writer John Sterling (1806–1844).

202.13 Carabbas] The Master of Carabas is the fictitious title of a poor man whose conniving cat helps him achieve status and wealth in "Puss in Boots," as retold by Charles Perrault in *Les Contes de ma Mère l'Oye* (*Tales of Mother Goose*, 1697).

NOTES 851

207.19 Washingtonian societies] The Washingtonian Temperance Society, with branches in several states, was active in the 1840s and 1850s.

208.38–209.1 talents were given . . . with usury] Cf. Matthew 25:14–30. "Usury" here means simply "interest," not exorbitant interest.

209.5 Miranda] Prospero's daughter in Shakespeare's *The Tempest*. Here Miranda is a partial self-portrait of Fuller, who was educated by her father.

209.30 electric nature] See note 96.38–97.2.

211.25–34 "I meant the day-star . . . free hours."] See note 189.6–15.

212.25 Dejanira] In Greek myth, Dejanira inadvertently killed Hercules with a poisoned robe.

212.38 Richter] Jean Paul Friedrich Richter, known as Jean Paul.

213.25 Plater] Countess Emilia Broel-Plater (1806–1831), Polish Lithuanian revolutionary who fought against the Russian Empire.

215.4 Semiramis] Queen of Assyria, ninth century BCE.

215.11 Eloisa] Héloïse, twelfth-century French writer, philosopher, and abbess who married the theologian Peter Abelard.

215.30 Tasso's prison bars] Torquato Tasso, who was imprisoned for insanity; subject of Goethe's play *Torquato Tasso* (1790), which Fuller translated.

216.1–2 professor's daughter] Novella d'Andrea, fourteenth-century legal scholar who taught at the University of Bologna, where her father was a professor of law, from behind a curtain.

216.2–3 Mrs. Carter and Madame Dacier] Elizabeth Carter (1717–1806), English poet and translator of Greek, French, and Italian texts. Anne Dacier (1647–1720), French classical scholar, translator of the *Iliad* and the *Odyssey*.

216.38–39 "O that those lips . . . heard thee last."] "On Receipt Of My Mother's Picture" (1798), ll. 1–2, by William Cowper.

217.12 "True to the kindred points of Heaven and home."] Wordsworth, "To the Skylark" (1825), l. 12.

217.16 Rosicrucian lamp] Rosicrucianism, a spiritual and esoteric movement beginning in seventeenth-century Germany, ascribed its origins to a medieval founder whose reopened tomb revealed still-burning lamps.

217.24–25 Sita in the Ramayana, . . . Egyptian Isis] Sita, Hindu goddess known for purity in the Hindu epic *Ramayana*. Isis, powerful Egyptian goddess known for magical abilities and wisdom.

218.20–26 "By that great vow . . . his wife."] *Julius Caesar*, II.i.272–75, 285–87. Fuller continues to quote from *Julius Caesar* in the next paragraphs,

852 NOTES

at 218.29–31 (II.i.288–90), 218.34–36 (V.iv.33–35), 219.4–9 (II.i.292–97), and 219.13–18 (IV.ii.119–24).

219.24–34   Nic nisi *maternâ* . . . righteous act approve."] Ovid, *Metamorphoses*, 9.251–56.

220.13–14   "Honor gone . . . never have been born."] Adapted from Goethe, *Sprüche in Reimen, Zahme Xenien und Invektiven* (*Sayings in Rhyme, Tame Scenes, and Invectives*, 1815–42, collected in 1908).

220.28   Macaria] See note 115.25–26.

221.18   *Dame du Comptoir*] French: a saleswoman or sales clerk (standing behind a "comptoir," or counter).

222.2   Petrarch's Hymn] "Praise and Prayer to Maria" (1316–1320) by Francesco Petrarca; see Appendix B, pp. 308–12 in this volume.

222.12–14   "Lady Teresa's Bridal." . . . the Infanta] "The Wedding of Lady Theresa" from *Ancient Spanish Ballads* (1823) by Scottish writer John Lockhart (1794–1854); see Appendix C, pp. 312–14 in this volume. The Infanta is Lady Theresa.

222.28   altvater day] German: old father day, meaning ancient or bygone times.

223.7   Drachenfels] Hill ("Dragon's Rock") on the Rhine River, associated with legends and topped by a ruined castle. See also Fuller's poem "Drachenfels," pp. 658–59 in this volume.

224.25   Panthea] Persian ruler Cyrus II treated his captive Panthea so honorably, according to Xenophon, that she came to respect him and persuaded her husband, his enemy, to fight for him.

224.33–34   "Better a thousand women . . . see the light."] Euripides, *Iphigenia in Aulis*, l. 1,394.

225.32   Ximena] Ximena, wife of eleventh-century Spanish hero El Cid.

226.21–24   "Vor dem Sklaven, . . . chains to break.] From Schiller, "Die Worte des Glaubens" ("Words of Faith," 1798).

226.28–30   Swedenborg's angelic state, . . . enfranchised soul] The ideas here are from *Conjugial Love* (1768) by Emanuel Swedenborg.

226.28–29   heaven where there is no . . . giving in marriage] Cf. Matthew 22:30.

226.31–34   Jene himmlische Gestalten . . . verklarten Leib] From Mignon's song in Goethe's *Wilhelm Meisters Lehrjahre* (1795–96), book 8, ch. 2: "Those heavenly beings, / They do not ask who is man or woman, / And no garments, no folds / Surround the transfigured body."

NOTES

228.14 "Malinche"] Cf. William Hickling Prescott, *The Conquest of Mexico* (1843). "Malinche" is Marina, an Aztec woman enslaved by Cortés who acted as his interpreter.

228.26–28 Britomart and Belphœbe . . . Florimel . . . Una] Characters in *The Fairie Queene* (1596) by Edmund Spenser.

228.34 Macaria] See note 115.25–26.

228.34 Ford] English playwright John Ford (1586–c. 1639).

228.37–40 an Imogen, a Desdemona, a Rosalind . . . Cordelia] Characters in Shakespeare's plays *Cymbeline, Othello, As You Like It, Julius Caesar, Measure for Measure,* and *King Lear.*

229.6–7 "I could not love thee, . . . honor more."] "To Lucasta, Going to the Warres," ll. 11–12 (1649), by Richard Lovelace (1617–1657).

229.11–12 "To heaven, my love, to heaven, and leave you in the storm?"] John Cooke (1608–1660), the solicitor general of the Commonwealth, presided over Charles I's trial and is thought to have said this shortly before his execution following the Restoration of Charles II.

229.14 Colonel Hutchinson's] English Puritan John Hutchinson (1615–1664), a signer of Charles I's death warrant; his wife Lucy (1620–c. 1680) wrote his biography.

229.16 "abler soul"] "The Ecstasy," l. 43 (c. 1590s), by John Donne (1572–1631).

229.18–19 "Were not our souls . . . make them such."] "An Ode upon a Question Moved, Whether Love Should Continue Forever," ll. 123–24 (1665), by Edward Herbert (1583–1648).

229.20 "Broken Heart"] *The Broken Heart* (1633), play by Ford (for whom see note 228.34).

229.28 "If thou art false, O then Heaven mocks itself."] *Othello*, III.iii.278.

229.34 "Frailty, thy name is woman."] *Hamlet*, I.ii.146.

230.8–9 Calderon's Justina] Character in *El Mágico Prodigioso* (1637) by Pedro Calderón de la Barca.

233.19 Roland and his wife] French revolutionary Jean-Marie Roland de La Platière (1734–1793) killed himself when he heard of his wife's execution. For his wife, see note 199.33.

234.9–10 Godwin . . . Mary Wolstonecraft] Radical philosophers William Godwin and Mary Wollstonecraft, author of *A Vindication of the Rights of Woman* (1792).

854 NOTES

234.37 Marguerite, of whom the weak St. Leon] Characters in Godwin's novel *St. Leon* (1799).

235.4 "Mon frère;"] French: My brother.

235.9 Simon and Indiana] Novels (1835, 1832) by George Sand.

236.3–4 "La Roche Mauprat"] *Mauprat*, 1837 novel by Sand.

237.7 Eloisa] See note 215.11.

237.26 Goodwyn Barmby] Unitarian minister and Christian socialist John Goodwyn Barmby (1820–1881).

238.14 Howitts] English writers and reformers William (1792–1879) and Mary Botham (1799–1888) Howitt.

238.25–26 "L'Amie Inconnue" . . . "adored Araminta,"] Araminta is a character in "Angelina; Or, L'Amie Inconnue," in *Moral Tales for Young People, Vol. II* (1802) by Maria Edgeworth (1768–1849).

239.6 Goetz Von Berlichingen] A historical knight as well as character in Goethe's play *Götz Von Berlichingen* (1773).

239.11–17 Manzoni thus dedicates . . . many virtues."] From Manzoni's tragedy *Adelchi* (1822).

240.3 Zinzendorf] See note 134.27. The following quotation is from Zinzendorf's *Natural Reflexions on Several Subjects, in the manner he is used to think within himself* (1747–48).

240.35 "Daughter of God and Man, accomplished Eve!"] Milton, *Paradise Lost*, IV.660.

240.37 Spangenberg] German Moravian August Gottlieb Spangenberg (1704–1792) worked with Zinzendorf.

241.12 The Flying Pigeon] The story of Rantchewaime (Flying Pigeon) is from McKenney and Hall's *History of the Indian Tribes of North America*, vol. I (see notes 166.22 and 134.17).

242.32–34 Cyrus visits . . . her name is Panthea] See note 224.25. The following account is from Xenophon's *Cyropaedia* (c. 370 BCE).

247.20–23 Socrates . . . steadiness of judgment."] From Xenophon's *Symposium* (c. 360s BCE).

247.24 Economics] Xenophon, *Oeconomicus* (c. 360s BCE).

248.28–31 Montague could learn . . . Somerville] English traveler and writer Mary Wortley Montagu (1689–1762); Scottish mathematician Mary Fairfax Somerville (1780–1872).

NOTES

851.9   Martha] In Luke 10:40, Martha is burdened by household drudgery.

252.4   Tasso's Leonora] Eleonora d'Este (1537–1581), Tasso's patron (see note 215.30).

252.30   Iphigenia in Aulis] Fuller means Euripides's *Iphigenia in Tauris* (c. 414 BCE), in which Iphigenia, having been rescued by the goddess Artemis from being sacrificed by her father Agamemnon at Aulis so that his army can sail to the Trojan War, has become a priestess in a temple to Artemis in the country of the Taurians.

253.1   Persica] Persicha or the Persian Sibyl, one of five sibyls painted by Michelangelo on the ceiling of the Sistine Chapel (1508–12).

253.10   Victoria Colonna] Italian poet (1492–1547) who wrote elegies to her husband after his death.

253.20   Mrs. Jameson] See note 27.15; the story is from Jameson's *Winter Studies and Summer Rambles in Canada* (1838).

253.36–37   Joanna Southcott and Mother Anne Lee] English religious leader and prophet Joanna Southcott (1750–1814) and founder of the Shaker movement Mother Anne Lee (1736–1784).

253.38   Ecstatica, Dolorosa] Female figures of religious ecstasy and grief.

254.4   De Maistre] Either French diplomat Joseph de Maistre (1753–1821), who wrote *Soirées de Saint-Petersbourg* (1821), or his brother Xavier (1763–1852), who wrote *La jeune Sibérienne* (1825).

254.7   mothers"] Cf. Goethe's *Faust, Part II* (1832), Act I, where Faust descends into the "realm of the Mothers."

254.9–10   from Behmen down to St. Simon] German mystic Jacob Behmen or Böhme (1575–1624) and French socialist Claude-Henri de Rouvroy, Comte Saint-Simon (1760–1825).

254.17–19   Plato . . . two-fold expression of one thought.] Cf. Plato's *Symposium*, where Socrates tells the myth of an original hermaphrodite being, bifurcated to create the two sexes.

254.23   Timæus] One of Plato's dialogues (c. 360 BCE).

254.33   electrical, the magnetic] See note 96.38–97.2.

255.16   *herissé*] French: bristling, ruffled.

255.28   Rachel] Stage name of French tragic actress Élisa Félix (1821–1858).

255.31   Guercino] Italian painter Giovanni Francesco Barbieri (1591–1666), known as Guercino.

856 NOTES

256.15–18 "she who advances . . . hymn to the Gods,"] Unidentified quotation. Emerson copied these lines into his journal in 1868 with the question "Is it Goethe's?"

256.26 Trojan Dames] Euripides, *The Trojan Women* (415 BCE). The following quotations are from the play.

257.3 *raptus*] Latin: rape, abduction, linked here with English "rapture."

257.19 Seeress of Prevorst] See note 95.12–14.

257.21 Delphos] Location of the oracle of Delphi.

257.37 Guyon] French mystic Jeanne Marie de la Motte Guyon (1648–1717).

258.3–4 only little children . . . kingdom of heaven] Cf. Matthew 18:3.

258.10 Isabella's jewels] Queen Isabella apparently sold her jewels to pay for Columbus's voyages to the Americas.

259.25 What shall I do to enter upon the eternal life?] Luke 10:25.

259.31–32 Lady's Book] American women's magazine *Godey's Lady's Book* (1830–78).

259.37 Grand Duchess Amelia] Anna Amalia of Brunswick-Wolfenbüttel (1739–1807), Duchess of Saxe-Weimar-Eisenach, and Goethe and Schiller's patron, made Weimar a cultural center.

260.2 Angelina Grimke and Abby Kelley] Abolitionists and feminists Angelina Grimké (1805–1879) and Abby Kelley (1811–1867).

260.34 Dr. Channing] The Rev. William Ellery Channing (1780–1842).

261.15 Mrs. Jameson] See note 27.15.

261.34 Kinmont] See note 50.16.

262.17–18 learners of the word . . . hearers only.] Cf. James 1:22.

262.35–36 "With a placid brow, . . . keep thy vow."] Wordsworth, "Liberty," ll. 133–34 (1829).

266.20 Southey's Kehama] *The Curse of Kehama* (1810) by Robert Southey (1774–1843).

266.37 Alcibiades with his phials] Alcibiades stole the drinking cups of a friend. Fuller's point here is unclear.

267.23–25 Swedenborg came . . . New Jerusalem] Cf. Swedenborg's *Apocalypse Revealed* (1766).

269.35–271.26 Frau Aja . . . the Fair Saint] Fuller discusses the women in Goethe's life and then the female characters in his *Faust, Tarquato Tasso,*

NOTES 857

Iphigenia auf Tauris, Wilhelm Meisters Lehrjahre, and *Wilhelm Meisters Wanderjahre*. The quoted lines at 272.21–26 are from *Wilhelm Meisters Wanderjahre*, book 8, ch. 2.

270.30 Lord Herbert] See note 229.18–19.

270.33 the son, child of his degrading connection] Wieland was Goethe's son with his common-law wife Christiane Vulpius (they later married, in 1806).

270.37 M. Henri Blaze] French critic François-Henri-Joseph Blaze (1784–1857).

274.4 Mrs. Jameson] See note 27.15.

276.19 Comus] Milton's masque *Comus* (1634) depicts the spiritual power of chastity.

278.22 Nestorian Sage] Nestor was the wise counsellor of the Greeks in Homer's epics.

279.11 Lady Russell] Writer and critic of corruption Lady Rachel Russell (1636–1723).

280.25–26 "Steep the soul . . . last thee long."] "Shadows," ll. 5–6, by Richard Monckton Milnes (1809–1885).

280.29 Desatir] An apparently ancient Zoroastrian text, probably a forgery, whose English translation was published in 1818.

281.1–2 Duessa . . . Una] See note 228.26–28.

281.11–12 Mr. Adams . . . Miss Foster] Sixth U.S. president John Quincy Adams (1767–1848), who refers to his father, second U.S. president John Adams (1735–1826), and mother, Abigail Adams (1744–1818), in the following passages. Sarah Foster (1802–1886) was the principal teacher at the Washington Female Seminary (Pennsylvania), which Adams visited in 1843.

283.17 "Whom God loves, to him gives he such a wife."] Goethe, *Götz von Berlichingen*, scene 16 (1773).

283.21–23 "Daughter of God . . . IMMORTAL EVE."] Milton, *Paradise Lost*, 4.660 and 9.291.

285.34 Mrs. Child in the case of Amelia Norman.] American reformer and writer Lydia Maria Child (1802–1880) supported Norman when she was charged with (and acquitted of) stabbing her seducer in a public space.

286.8 Eugene Sue] See note 163.20.

286.21–22 "Who bases good . . . that he knows."] Cf. Wordsworth, "Character of the Happy Warrior," ll. 33–34.

NOTES

286.25–29 Fleur de Marie . . . "hump-backed Sempstress"] Characters in Sue's novels.

286.29 "Wandering Jew"] *Le juif errant* (*The Wandering Jew*), 1844–45 novel by Sue.

286.35–36 Sir Charles Grandison] Protagonist of *Sir Charles Grandison* (1753) by English writer Samuel Richardson (1689–1761).

288.37 Madame Necker de Saussure] Swiss writer Albertine Necker de Saussure (1766–1841), educational theorist, advocate for education for women, and friend of Germaine de Staël.

288.38 "A synod of good women should decide,"] Goethe, *Torquato Tasso*, II.i.260. Fuller quotes from her own translation of this scene in *The Dial*, vol. 2 (January 1842).

290.13 "Los Exaltados."] Radical wing of the liberal party in Spain.

291.32 one swallow does not make a summer] Proverb, meaning one positive event does not guarantee a trend.

292.4 "The Whole Duty of Women,"] *The Whole Duty of a Woman; or, A Guide to the Female Sex, from the Age of Sixteen to Sixty, &c.* (1753), written anonymously by English writer William Kenrick (1725–1779), himself known as a dissolute, hack writer.

292.16–17 "Cette vie . . . morale de notre cœur."] French: "This life has no value unless it serves the moral education of our heart." This line, attributed to de Staël, is the epigraph on the title page of Necker's *The Study of the Life of Woman*, translated and published in Philadelphia in 1843. Fuller paraphrases and quotes from this book in the following paragraphs.

293.15–18 Paraguay woman, . . . woman must be;"] Fuller is paraphrasing from the account of a Native woman in Southey's notes to his poem *A Tale of Paraguay* (1825).

293.19 Sir A. Mackenzie] See note 133.4. Southey refers to Mackenzie's book in his notes.

293.21–294.7 "After the first . . . doll to decorate."] Fuller has rearranged the order of the lines by moving the passage on the son before that on the daughter.

294.13–15 Brunhilda . . . Walkyrie] Figure in Norse and Germanic legends; shield maiden.

295.28–296.2 Miss Sedgwick . . . the means and the ends] For Sedgwick, see note 137.26. Fuller seems to refer to Sedgwick's book *Means and Ends; or, Self-Training* (1839).

NOTES

297.18–20 O'Connell from unjust imprisonment, . . . Tara's Hill.] Daniel O'Connell was arrested after demanding Irish independence from Great Britain.

297.25 annexation of Texas!] The admission of Texas into the U.S. as a slave state in 1845 strengthened pro-slavery factions in Congress and led to the war with Mexico (1846–48).

297.38–298.1 Queen Emma . . . Mrs. Hutchinson] Emma, Queen of England, Denmark, and Norway (c. 984–1052), married first to King Æthelred and then Cnut, underwent an ordeal of hot iron to prove her chastity. Anne Hutchinson (1591–1643) was excommunicated by the Massachusetts Bay Colony for preaching as a woman.

298.35 Five Points] A poor area in New York City, often referred to as the epitome of a slum.

301.22 Dodona's oak] In ancient Greece, Dodona was the site of an important oracle of Zeus, where the god spoke through the rustlings of an oak tree.

302.6 Fitzgerald] See note 134.7–8.

303.3–4 maid of Saragossa . . . Emily Plater.] Maria Augustin fought unsuccessfully to defend the Spanish city Saragossa from the French (1800–1809); the Greek towns of Missolonghi and Suli resisted the Turks in the Greek war of independence (1821–29). For Plater, see note 213.25.

304.22 Landor] See note 201.29.

304.26–28 "The gods approve . . . ungovernable love."] Wordsworth, "Laodamia," ll. 74–76 (1815).

306.5 "Though many have . . . noble hearts."] In a November 23, 1848, letter to Marcus Spring, Fuller attributed this quotation to German poet Theodor Körner (1791–1813).

308.14 Thomas Taylor] English translator and Neoplatonist Thomas Taylor (1758–1835) published *The Metamorphosis, or Golden Ass, and Philosophical Works of Apuleius* in 1822.

308.22 Lodi e Preghiere a Maria] Petrarch, "Praise and Prayer to Maria" (1316–20).

312.18 Baldur] Balder, the son of the Norse gods Frigga and Odin.

312.21 LOCKHART'S SPANISH BALLADS] See note 222.12–14.

314.19–20 W. E. Channing, a poem called "Reverence,"] "Reverence" (1843) by Ellery Channing (see note 260.34).

314.25 the author of "Festus,"] *Festus* (1839–45) by English poet Philip James Bailey (1816–1902).

860 NOTES

314.32 TRACTATUS POLITICI] *Tractatus Theologico-Politicus* (1670) by Baruch Spinoza (1632–1677).

322.18 Memoirs] See note 130.39.

323.1 Miranda] See note 209.5.

324.6 "Ah me! that breast, those cheeks, those golden tresses!"] From Euripides, *Iphigenia in Aulis* (408–6 BCE), as are most other quotations in this appendix.

325.5 Guido's Archangel] *The Archangel Michael Defeating Satan* (1635), painting by Italian artist Guido Reni (1575–1642).

327.3 "Supplicants"] *The Suppliants*, or *The Suppliant Women* (423 BCE), by Euripides.

329.9–12 Cooper makes the weak Hetty . . . any woman."] From Cooper's *The Deerslayer* (1841).

329.34–35 "Her prentice han' . . . losses o',"] From "Green Grow The Rashes" (1783), by Robert Burns (1759–1796).

331.24 Apollo Belvidere] A classical marble statue (Roman copy of a Greek original) in the Vatican Museum, the Apollo Belvedere epitomized the art of sculpture in Fuller's period.

331.36 Macaria] See note 115.25–26; the quoted lines are from Euripides's *The Heracleidae* (c. 430 BCE).

332.10 Jeptha's daughter] Cf. Judges 11:30–39. Jeptha sacrifices his daughter to win a battle.

333.11–24 "I heard Him, . . . Toward the morning star."] From "A Dream of Fair Women" (1833–42), by Alfred, Lord Tennyson.

333.25 "Trojan dames"] *The Trojan Women* (415 BCE), by Euripides. The following lines are from this play.

335.19 Beatrice Cenci] Beatrice Cenci (1577–1599) was apparently raped by her abusive father; she and other family members killed him and were executed. Her story and her image, based on a painting ascribed to Reni (see note 325.5), were retold and reproduced in Fuller's era.

SHORT PUBLISHED WORKS

341.10 Eckermann] Johann Peter Eckermann (1792–1854), Goethe's secretary in his last years, recounted Goethe's remarks in *Gespräche mit Goethe* (*Conversations with Goethe*, 1836).

341.15 Mrs. Jameson's . . . Canada."] See note 27.15.

NOTES 861

342.17 Boswell] Eckermann's *Conversations with Goethe* was often compared to James Boswell's 1791 biography of Samuel Johnson.

342.28 Zelter, Schiller, Meyer] German musician and composer Carl Friedrich Zelter (1758–1832) and Swiss painter Johann Heinrich Meyer (1760–1832). For Schiller, see note 189.3–5.

343.6 "Wilhelm Meister" and "Faust"] For *Wilhelm Meister* see note 115.25–26. *Faust* is Goethe's major play, published in two parts in 1808 (revised 1828–29) and in 1832.

344.2 "Blackwood's Magazine,"] Influential Scottish conservative literary journal and review (1817–1980).

344.37 *Die Wahlverwandtschaften*] Goethe's novel *Elective Affinities* (1809).

344.39–40 Natalia and Makaria, . . . Iphigenia] Natalia is a character in Goethe's *Wilhelm Meister's Lehrjahre*. For Makaria (or Macaria), see note 115.25–26. For Iphigenia, see note 252.30.

346.36 the rest.] Fuller adds a footnote here, which this edition omits: "For Goethe's own view of his past conduct, and in his last days, when his life had well nigh become a part of history, see p. 413." At the end of Eckermann's book, Goethe defends his decision not to become politically engaged but to remain focused on his work as a poet—which he claims is also patriotic.

348.33–34 the merchants he met while travelling] Fuller adds a footnote here, which this edition omits: "See p. 192." The passage Fuller refers to follows:

> Freedom consists not in refusing to recognize any thing above us, but in knowing how to respect what is above us; for, by respecting it, we raise ourselves to it, and make manifest that we bear within ourselves the idea of what is higher, and are worthy to be on a level with it.
>
> I have on my journeys met merchants from the north of Germany, who fancied they showed themselves my equals by rudely seating themselves next me at table. That was not the way; but they might have become so, if they had known how to value and treat me properly.

349.18–19 "He was a man, . . . like again."] *Hamlet*, I.ii.187–88.

350.11 *Farbenlehre*] Goethe's book *Zur Farbenlehre* (*Theory of Colors*, 1810).

350.35 Mr. Jeffrey] Scottish Whig Francis Jeffrey (1773–1850), editor of the influential, liberal *Edinburgh Review* (1802–1929).

355.20–21 "sieves and drainers for . . . luxurious readers"] Thomas Carlyle, "Novalis" (1829).

359.2 EXHIBITION OF MR. ALLSTON'S PICTURES] Harding's Gallery in Boston exhibited Washington Allston's works in 1839.

862   NOTES

360.15 Beatrice] In this essay, Fuller reviews these paintings: *Beatrice* (1816–19), *The Valentine* (1809–11), *The Dead Man Restored to Life by Touching the Bones of the Prophet Elisha* (1811–14), *Jeremiah Dictating His Prophecy of the Destruction of Jerusalem to Baruch the Scribe* (1820), *Miriam the Prophetess* (1821), *Saul and the Witch of Endor* (1820), *Evening Hymn* (1835), *Rosalie* (1835), *Italian Shepherd Boy* (1819), *Lorenzo and Jessica* (1832), *Scene from Shakespeare's "The Taming of the Shrew"* (*Katharina and Petruchio*, 1809), *The Sisters* (1816–17), *Donna Mencia in the Robber's Cavern* (1815), *Mother Watching Her Sleeping Child* (1814).

360.21–22 Vicar of Wakefield to Cooper's novels] *The Vicar of Wakefield* (1766) is a novel by Oliver Goldsmith. For Cooper, see note 27.21.

360.30 *mot d'enigme*] French: the answer to the riddle.

361.27 Wilkie or Newton] Scottish painter David Wilkie (1785–1841) and British painter Francis Milner Newton (1720–1794).

362.20 Massacre of the Innocents] Unidentified painting.

363.28 Miriam] In Exodus, Miriam is the sister of Moses and leads the Israelites in a song of celebration after they leave Egypt and cross the Red Sea.

365.2 Norna] In Nordic mythology, the three Nornas, or Norns, are the goddesses of fate or destiny.

365.22–23 Edwin, Lorenzo and Jessica] Lorenzo and Jessica are characters in Shakespeare's *The Merchant of Venice*. "Edwin" is unidentified.

365.27 *epanchement*] French: abandon.

366.15 "blood listening in his frame,"] Cf. the poem "To Constantia Singing" (1824), l. 6, by Shelley.

367.28 Gremio] Gremio is a comic figure in Shakespeare's *The Taming of the Shrew*.

367.38 Scene from Gil Blas] Allston's painting represents an episode in French writer Alain-René Lesage's picaresque novel *L'Histoire de Gil Blas* (1715–35).

368.6 Jews] The exhibition's catalog *Exhibition of Pictures, Painted by Washington Allston, at Harding's Gallery, School Street* (1839), lists three items, two named "Sketch of a Polish Jew," and one *Isaac of York*; all were painted in 1817. Allston retitled *Isaac of York* after the Jewish character in Scott's novel *Ivanhoe* after that novel was published in 1819.

368.8 The Landscapes] The catalog lists twelve landscapes.

369.1 two sonnets] The first sonnet appended to the essay is by Fuller's friend Samuel Gray Ward (see note 56.4–62.17), as is the final paragraph of the essay, beginning with "Today." The second sonnet is by Fuller.

NOTES

863

369.4   The Bride] Allston's painting of Queen Esther, from the biblical Book of Esther.

371.13   "He was fulfilled of all nobleness."] Expression found in Scott's *Kenilworth* (1821).

373.19–22 and 30–31   'Sconosciuto pur cammina . . . in negro.'] From Tasso (see note 215.30), *Gerusalemme Liberata* (*Jerusalem Delivered*, 1581), canto 10, lines 21–24, 37–38. This epic poem was frequently translated in the eighteenth and nineteenth centuries. Fuller changes the words slightly from the original Italian. A 1901 English translation by Henry Morley:

> Unknown, unseen, disguised, travelled he,
> By desert paths and ways but used by few,
> And rode revolving in his troubled thought
> What course to take, and yet resolved on naught. . . .
>
> But when the night cast up her shade aloft
> And all earth's colors strange in sables dyed, . . .

374.4–8   'O that I were . . . that dresseth me.'] The fifth stanza of the poem "Employment" (1633) by George Herbert. Fuller has changed Herbert's "dressed" to the archaic "dresseth."

376.14   'Mothers'] See note 254.7.

378.2   "In a deep vision's intellectual scene."] The first line of Abraham Cowley's poem "The Complaint" (1663). The line is quoted by Wordsworth in "Liberty" (1829), l. 113.

378.14   *fetiche*] French: fetish.

382.3   Dagon] Biblical god of the Philistines, a false idol defeated by the Hebrew god in 1 Samuel 5.1–4.

382.13–14   a Genius . . . a Demon] In Roman and Greek myth, a genius or a demon (or daimon) is a divine spirit accompanying or guiding a place, person, or community.

384.1   Yuca Filamentosa] The Yucca Filamentosa is a white flowering plant native to the southeastern U.S.

384.2–14   "The Spirit builds . . . deep thoughts?"] "Inscription for a Garden" (1843) by Ellery Channing (see note 260.34). Fuller tweaks a few words (e.g., "things" becomes "thoughts").

385.39   Alcmeon] Of the several historical figures in Greek antiquity called Alcmaeon, Fuller seems to be thinking of Alcmaeon of Croton, a fifth-century BCE philosopher and scientist whose research on the body led to medical discoveries.

864   NOTES

387.1–2   Bettine Brentano and Her Friend Günderode] Writer Bettine (or Bettina) Brentano von Arnim (1785–1859) reworked her correspondence with Goethe (see next note) and poet Karoline von Günderode (or Günderrode, 1780–1806) into successful books that some critics have called epistolary novels, although Fuller emphasizes here their autobiographical nature. Fuller published her translation of Arnim's *Die Günderode* (1840) as *Günderode* in 1842.

387.3   letters to Goethe] Arnim's *Goethes Briefwechsel mit einem Kinde* (*Goethe's Correspondence with a Child*, 1835).

390.38–39   "it is the punishment . . . from the gods,"] Salutius (fl. 355–367), *On the Gods and the World.*

391.17   Euphorion] A character in *Faust, Part II* (1832), modelled on a Greek mythological figure, also named Euphorion, who tries to fly but perishes.

391.19–21   Tasso . . . L'Espinasse] For Tasso, see note 215.30. Werther is the protagonist in Goethe's novel *Die Leiden des jungen Werthers* (*The Sorrows of Young Werther*, 1774). Douglas (or Douglass) is a character in Scott's novel *The Abbot* (1820). For Eloisa, see note 215.11. Writer Julie-Jeanne-Éléonore de Lespinasse (1732–1776) presided over a Paris salon and is a participant in the dialogues that make up Denis Diderot's *Le Rêve de d'Alembert* (*The Dream of d'Alembert*, published 1782 and 1830).

391.23   "It will not, nor it cannot come to good."] *Hamlet*, I.ii.163.

392.1   But the letters to Goethe] Fuller reprints the following section of this article in her "Translator's Preface" to *Günderode.*

392.23–24   grandmother Me. La Roche] Sophie von La Roche (1730–1807), author of novels and travel writings, maintained a cultural and literary salon.

393.30   Hermia and Helena] Characters in Shakespeare's *A Midsummer Night's Dream.*

393.31   vale of Enna] Site in Sicily associated with the worship of Ceres and the abduction of Persephone by Hades.

394.26   "Loves where (art) has set its seal,"] Cf. Byron, "And Thou Art Dead, as Young and Fair" (1812), l. 23.

395.35   "descend to meet."] In "The Over-Soul" (*Essays: First Series*, 1841), Emerson writes, "Men descend to meet." This sentence is the last sentence in Fuller's "Translator's Preface" to *Günderode*; the *Dial* article adds two more paragraphs and translated excerpts from the book.

397.6   first series] Emerson's *Essays: First Series* (1841).

403.9   "liberating God"] Emerson calls poets "liberating gods" in his essay "The Poet" in *Essays: Second Series.*

NOTES

865

403.14–21 "Poetry was all written . . . the nations."] From "The Poet."

403.22–30 "As the eyes . . . flowing of nature."] From "The Poet."

403.22 Lyncæus] In Greek mythology, a son of Heracles.

404.2 George Sand . . . Eugene Sue] For Sand, see note 235.9; for Sue, see note 163.20.

404.3 "Wandering Jew,"] See note 286.29.

405.39 Democratic Review] *United States Magazine and Democratic Review* (1837–51), published by John O'Sullivan (1813–1895).

407.22–23 "Eugenie Grandet," . . . "Father Goriot"] Balzac's novels *Eugénie Grandet* (1833), *La Recherche de l'absolu* (1834), and *Le Père Goriot* (1835). "Sweet Pea" is possibly *Le Lys dans la Vallée* (1835).

407.38 "Seraphitus"] Balzac's novel *Séraphîta* (1834), about an androgynous character.

408.38 SCHILLER puts into the mouth of Mary Stuart] Schiller's 1800 play *Maria Stuart* (*Mary Stuart*).

411.28–29 "La Roche . . . Mosaistes,"] Sand's novels *Mauprat* (1837), *André* (1834), *Jacques* (1833), *Les Sept Cordes de la Lyre* (*The Seven Strings of the Lyre*, 1839), *Les Maîtres mosaïstes* (*The Master Mosaic Workers*, 1837).

411.33–36 "Leone Leoni," . . . Fiamma] Sand's novels *Leone Leoni* (1833), *Simon* (1835), and *Spiridion* (1839). Fiamma is a character in *Simon*.

411.37 "E l'onore;"] Italian: And honor.

412.1–2 "Consuelo," with its sequel "Baroness de Rudolstadt"] Sand's novel *Consuelo* (1842–43) and its sequel *La Comtesse de Rudolstadt* (*Countess of Rudolstadt*, 1843).

412.4–5 the Interpreter's house] The house of the Interpreter is one of Christian's first stops in *The Pilgrim's Progress* (1678) by John Bunyan.

412.30 "Mysteries of Paris," "Matilda,"] Sue's novels *Les Mystères de Paris* (*The Mysteries of Paris*, 1842–43) and *Mathilde* (1841).

413.15 Association] Fourier's ideas of associationism, utopian communities based on principles of shared labor, were influential in the U.S. in the 1840s. See also note 186.9–11.

413.30–31 *his* "Wandering Jew" with that of Beranger] The "Wandering Jew" is a figure in one of Béranger's songs (see also note 286.29).

415.2–3 MESMERISM AND PHRENOLOGY] For these terms and animal magnetism (at 415.28–29), see notes 96.38–97.2 and 139.8.

866 NOTES

417.3 Mr. Grimes's] American lawyer and phrenologist J. Stanley Grimes (1807–1903).

420.18–20 Bellevue Alms House . . . Blackwell's Island] Bellevue Alms House, associated with Bellevue Hospital in Manhattan, the oldest public hospital in the country. Blackwell's Island, now Roosevelt Island, held several of New York City's public institutions, including an orphanage, the New York City Lunatic Asylum, and the Penitentiary and Penitentiary Hospital.

424.9 Bloomingdale] Bloomingdale Insane Asylum. In 1841 Bloomingdale became a private hospital, and patients who could not pay were moved to the New York City Lunatic Asylum on Blackwell's Island, which Fuller discusses here as the Asylum for the Insane.

425.11 Sing Sing] Prison in Ossining, NY.

425.38 Tombs] The Halls of Justice and House of Detention held the city's courts, police, and temporary detention cells. Its Egyptian Revival style prompted the nickname "The Tombs."

426.4 Dr. Griscom] John Hoskins Griscom (1809–1874), a physician and sanitary reformer, wrote *The Sanitary Condition of the Laboring Population of New York* (1845).

430.19 Soulié] French novelist and playwright Frédéric Soulié (1800–1847).

430.27–29 Kinmont . . . Dr. Channing] For Kinmont, see note 50.16. For Channing, see note 260.34.

431.5 Garrison . . . Phillips] Abolitionists William Lloyd Garrison (1805–1879), who edited the antislavery newspaper *The Liberator* (1830–65), and Wendell Phillips (1811–1884).

431.27 "Bring no more vain oblations"] Isaiah 1:13.

431.34–35 Kingdom of Heaven . . . larger than a mustard-seed] Cf. Matthew 17:20.

432.13 "Where is thy brother?"] Genesis 4:9. The closing quotation, following this line, is from the second half of ch. 2 in Douglass's *Narrative*.

434.30–32 "Domestic love, almost . . . him to life"] Quoted from "Spirit of the Irish Press," *New-York Daily Tribune*, June 25, 1845, reprinted from *The Nation*, an Irish nationalist newspaper in Dublin.

435.6–7 "Men have died . . . not for love."] *As You Like It*, IV.i.106–8.

435.35 Roumelia] Rumelia was a region of the Ottoman Empire in the Balkans.

NOTES

867

435.40 "The harp of Tara's halls,"] "The Harp That Once Through Tara's Hall" (1821), lyrics by Thomas Moore.

436.3 Emmet's appeal] Robert Emmet (1778–1803) was hanged for leading a Dublin uprising against the British; his "Speech from the Dock" at his 1803 conviction was widely circulated.

436.7 Lord Edward Fitzgerald] See note 134.7–8.

436.40 Currans] Irish patriot, lawyer, orator, and politician John Philpot Curran (1750–1817).

438.30 Burdett's little book] American writer Charles Burdett published the novel *The Elliott Family: Or The Trials Of New York Seamstresses* in 1845.

438.37–439.2 "The Duty of American . . . Catherine Beecher] *The Duty of American Women to Their Country* was published anonymously by Catharine E. Beecher in 1845. Lucy Stone was a women's rights and antislavery activist (1818–1893).

442.15 Mrs. George Lee] Hannah Farmham Sawyer Lee (1780–1865), popular author known for short 1837 novel *Three Experiments of Living*.

444.15–16 Rev. Calvin Stowe] Clergyman and professor (1802–1866), married to Harriet Beecher Stowe, sister of Catharine Beecher. The following quotation is from "Address of Professor Stowe," included in Beecher's *The Duty of American Women*.

446.36 Parnassus] Greek mountain associated with Apollo, music, and poetry.

449.8–11 From the cool cisterns . . . cisterns flow] "Hymn to the Night," ll. 13–16.

449.32–37 Therefore at Pentecost . . . woodlands wide.] "Prelude" from *Voices of the Night*, ll. 43–48.

451.27 Pegnitz] German river.

452.5 Queen Cunigunde's] Perhaps Cunigunde of Luxembourg (c. 975–1033), who married Holy Roman Emperor Henry II (973–1024).

452.7 the poet Melchior, singing Kaiser Maximilian's] German musician Melchior Neusidler (1531–1590); Holy Roman Emperor Maximilian I (1459–1519).

452.13 sainted Sebald] Missionary and patron saint of Nuremberg Sebaldus (ninth or tenth century CE).

452.15 sainted Lawrence] Spanish deacon Lawrence (225–258), who was martyred in Rome.

NOTES

453.6–10 Hans Sachs . . . Adam Paschman's] Sixteenth-century German Meistersingers Hans Sachs and Adam Puschman.

453.30–454.2 Wrapt in thy scarlet . . . but the foot-prints?] "To the Driving Cloud" (1845), ll.3–6.

454.4–7 A feeling of sadness . . . resembles rain.] "The Day is Done" (1844), ll.9–12.

454.9–11 "I will forget her! . . . to the winds.] From the play *The Spanish Student* (1842), III.ii.36–38.

454.18 Preciosas] Preciosa is a character in *The Spanish Student*.

454.29 Excelsior!!] Latin: higher. Also title of Longfellow's poem "Excelsior" (1841).

455.17 Queen Mab] Shelley's poem *Queen Mab; A Philosophical Poem; With Notes* (1813).

456.25 "Have I not kept my vow?"] "Hymn to Intellectual Beauty," l. 62.

456.36 July to the French nation.] The French Revolution of 1830 took place in July.

457.4 *Suspiria de Profundis*] *Suspiria de profundis* (Latin: *Sighs from the Depths*, 1845) by Thomas De Quincey.

457.17–18 "they know not what they do."] Luke 23:34–38.

457.26 Foster] Journalist George G. Foster (1814–1856) edited this edition (perhaps the first American edition) of Shelley's poems. The following lines are from Foster's "Preface," pp. 7–8.

462.30 Tmolus] In Greek myth, a mountain god and son of Ares, who judges a musical contest between Apollo and Pan.

462.32–463.1 Peneus . . . Tempe . . . Pelion's shadow] The Vale of Tempe, through which the Peneus (or Pineios) River runs, was associated with Apollo. Mount Pelion is in the same area.

463.16 Menalus] Mountain sacred to Pan in Arcadia, in Greece's Peloponnese.

463.38–464.5 The crane o'er seas . . . place of peace,—] "To Edward Williams" (1836), ll. 41–47.

464.14–30 "He had fitted up . . . his words.)] From Shelley's "Advertisement" that precedes his long poem *Epipsychidion: Verses addressed to the noble and unfortunate Lady Emilia V—, now imprisoned in the convent of—* (1821). The Greek title means "about a little soul."

464.37–465.6 High, spirit-wingéd . . . profit thee.] *Epipsychidion*, ll. 13–20.

NOTES

869

465.26–31 Pythagorean questions . . . left undone?] From the *Golden Verses*, attributed to Pythagoras. There were several English translations.

466.29–30 four-and-twenty blackbirds . . . before the King."] From "Sing a Song of Sixpence," a traditional English nursery rhyme.

468.16–17 Double, double, / Toil and trouble,] *Macbeth*, IV.i.101–11.

468.35–37 "The wiser mind . . . leaves behind."] Wordsworth, "The Fountain: A Conversation," ll. 34–36. Fuller changes "Age" to "Time."

469.12–13 "We never see . . . naught else."] Cf. Philip James Bailey, "Festus" (1839, 1845), ll. 212–13.

471.13–14 Cassius Clay's paper expelled from Kentucky] U.S. politician Cassius Marcellus Clay (1810–1903) from Kentucky became an abolitionist and published the antislavery newspaper *True American*, whose press was attacked by a mob in 1845.

471.20 Ronge's movement] Catholic priest Johannes Ronge (1813–1887) was suspended from the priesthood for his democratic beliefs; he was involved in the liberalizing movements of the 1840s.

472.7–8 Grand Duchess Olga] Olga Nikolaevna (1822–1892) married Charles I of Württemberg (1823–1891), not Austria, in 1846.

472.16–17 decay of the Potato] The Irish Potato Famine began in 1845.

472.30 Moritz Hartmann] Writer and journalist Moritz Hartmann (1821–1872), born in Bohemia, was a politically active liberal in Germany.

476.5 Red River] The southern Red River, in Texas and Louisiana.

478.1 Concord] The Concord River in Massachusetts.

478.16 Farm Schools] On Blackwell's Island, now Roosevelt Island. See note 420.17–19.

479.5 murder of the Mormon leader] Joseph Smith (1805–1844) was murdered by a mob in Illinois.

479.9 war which at present engages us] The Mexican-American War (1846–48).

480.1–2 treaties have been made . . . minority of their tribes] The Treaty of New Echota (1835), signed by Cherokee leaders representing a minority of the Cherokee, ceded the Cherokee Nation's land in the U.S. Southeast, and led to the forced removal known as the Trail of Tears.

480.9–10 Col. M'Kenney] See note 27.36.

480.34 Col. Cobb] Choctaw leader Samuel Cobb (c. 1786–1864).

870   NOTES

482.11 Lowrey] George Lowrey, or Rising Fawn, Agin'-agi'li (c. 1770–1852), assistant principal chief of the Cherokee Nation.

482.17–18 "Give me some drink . . . sick girl."] *Julius Caesar*, I.ii.127–28.

482.23 Feed my lambs] John 21:15.

482.24–26 Lord, Lord? . . . I never knew ye."] Matthew 7:22–23.

483.17–23 RED BIRD . . . Gagnier . . . Potalesbarro] Red Bird (c. 1788–1828), a Winnebago leader who resisted mining on tribal land and shot the settler Registre Gagnier. Potalesbarro is unidentified.

484.2 rescue of Smith] John Smith's (1580–1631) famous account (in *The Generall Historie of Virginia, New-England, and the Summer Isles*, 1624) of the intervention of Powhatan's daughter Pocahontas to save his life in Virginia has been variously taken as truth, characterized as fiction, and interpreted as Powhatan's ritual inducting of Smith into his confederacy.

484.19 McDonald] Choctaw James Lawrence McDonald (1801–1831) was sponsored in his education by McKenney and by Secretary of War John C. Calhoun and became a lawyer. Rather than support the U.S. government's push to remove the Choctaw, he returned to Choctaw territory, resisted removal, and—finally believing that Choctaw survival hinged on compliance—signed the Treaty of Dancing Rabbit Creek (1830), which authorized removal to Indian Territory (Oklahoma). He took his own life in 1831.

484.33–36 Mrs. Madison . . . Mrs. Saunders] Dolley Todd Madison (1768–1849), wife of U.S. president James Madison. American writer Elizabeth Elkins Sanders (1762–1851) published *Conversations, Principally on the Aborigines of North America* (1828), critical of U.S. removal policies.

485.11 John Ross] Cherokee John Ross, or Guwisguwi, Mysterious Little White Bird (1790–1866), was principal chief of the Cherokee Nation (1828–66) and resisted removal.

485.1 Channing] See note 260.34.

485.26–27 ORMOND . . . WIELAND] The novels *Wieland: or, The Transformation: An American Tale* (1798) and *Ormond; Or, The Secret Witness* (1799) by Charles Brockden Brown were reissued in 1846.

486.10 "My mind to me a kingdom is."] "My Mind to me a Kingdom is" (1588) by English poet and diplomat Edward Dyer (1543–1607).

487.9–12 Constantia, Clara . . . Marguerite of Godwin] Heroines, respectively, of Brown's *Ormond* and *Wieland* and of Godwin's novel *St. Leon* (1799).

487.31 Carwin] Character in Brown's *Wieland*.

NOTES 871

495.11 Mr. Prescott] See note 228.14.

495.34 Dr. Channing] See note 260.34.

497.6 Miss Sedgwick] See note 137.26.

497.10 Mrs. Kirkland] American writer Caroline Kirkland (1801–1864), author of A *New Home—Who'll Follow?* (1839).

498.22–23 Mrs. Child . . . Mrs. Stephens] For Child, see note 285.34. American writer Anne Stephens (1813–1886).

498.33 Willis] American writer and editor Nathaniel P. Willis (1806–1867).

499.6 Dana] American writer Richard Henry Dana Sr. (1787–1879).

499.38–39 William Ellery Channing] Ellery Channing the poet (see note 260.34).

500.19–32 Hearts of Eternity! . . . remotest star.] Channing's "Sonnet IV" in *Poems* (1843).

500.33 "Man in the Republic," by Cornelius Mathews] "Poems on Man in the Republic," by American writer Cornelius Mathews (1817–1889), published in *The Various Writings of Cornelius Mathews* (1843). The following quotation is the fourth stanza of poem XIX in this set, "The Poet."

501.28–29 Rolla . . . Keans] *Rolla* (1833), verse drama by Alfred de Musset. Edmund Kean and his son Charles Kean (1811–1868) toured the U.S. performing plays by Shakespeare and others.

501.34–38 Murdoch . . . "Witchcraft, a tragedy,"] American actor James Edward Murdoch (or Murdock, 1811–1893). *Witchcraft, or the Martyrs of Salem* (1846) by Cornelius Mathews.

503.22 "Margaret, or the Real and Ideal,"] *Margaret: A Tale Of the Real and Ideal, Blight and Bloom* (1845), novel by Unitarian minister and writer Sylvester Judd (1813–1853).

505.19 *vivida vis*] Latin: vivid force, or keen vigor, a phrase frequently quoted from *De Rerum Natura* (*On the Nature of Things*), book I, l. 72, by Lucretius.

506.32–507.20 As shakes the canvass . . . wrath enrages.] The first seven stanzas of Mathews's poem XIII, "The Journalist."

507.37–508.4 Brown . . . Ormond] See note 485.26–27.

509.29 Cambria] British steamer on the Cunard Line.

510.11–12 Governor of Nova-Scotia . . . unpopular administration] Lucius Bentinck Cary, Viscount of Falkland (1803–1884), governor of Nova Scotia from 1840 to 1846; he resisted the introduction of the system of responsible government, which emphasized parliamentary accountability.

872 NOTES

510.13 Mrs. Jordan] Dorothea Jordan (1761–1816), gifted actress and mistress of Prince William, Duke of Clarence (1765–1837, later King William IV), with whom she had ten children, who were given the surname FitzClarence; Cary's wife was Amelia FitzClarence (d. 1858).

510.28 Judkins] Charles H. E. Judkins (1811–1876), captain of the Cambria during Frederick Douglass's 1845 voyage to Britain.

510.37 McKenney] See note 27.36.

511.16 Mechanics' Institute] Mechanics' Institutes offered night classes, especially on technical and scientific topics, and libraries for working men.

512.5 Director of the Liverpool Institute] Reformer William Ballantyne Hodgson (1815–1880).

513.16–17 Bradshaw's Railway Guide] George Bradshaw (1801–1853) published *Bradshaw's Monthly Railway Guide*, timetables for the burgeoning British railway system, starting in 1841.

513.18 Elihu Burritt] Peace activist and editor (1810–1879).

514.8 Joseph Barker] Working-class preacher, printer, and reformer (1806–1875).

515.27 Oregon dispute] Border dispute between the U.S. and the United Kingdom over the Oregon Territory, settled by the 1846 Oregon Treaty.

516.21 O'Connell] See note 297.18–20.

517.8–12 "There's a good time . . . enough one day."] "There's a Good Time Coming," popular poem by Scottish writer Charles Mackay (1814–1889), set to music by English composer Henry Russell (1812/13–1900).

517.13–14 Royal Institute, with the statue of Roscoe by Chantrey] Lawyer, abolitionist, banker, and writer William Roscoe (1753–1831) was a founder of the Liverpool Royal Institute; English sculptor Sir Francis Leggatt Chantrey (1781–1841).

517.20–25 statue of Huskisson . . . by Gibson] British politician and free trade advocate William Huskisson (1770–1830); Welsh sculptor John Gibson (1790–1866).

519.24–26 Loch Leven . . . Douglas] Mary, Queen of Scots (1542–1587) was imprisoned in Lochleven Castle from 1567 to 1568 and escaped with the help of William Douglas (1533–1591), whose family owned the castle.

519.30 Prince Labanoff] Writer and collector Prince Alexandre Labanov-Rostovsky (1788–1877) wrote *Lettres, instructions et mémoires de Marie Stuart* (7 vols., 1844), translated by William Turnbull as *Letters of Mary Stuart* (1845).

NOTES 873

519.36 Chambers's Journal] The influential *Chambers' Edinburgh Journal* was co-edited by William (1800–1883) and Robert (1802–1871) Chambers.

519.38 Guise] French noblewoman Mary of Guise (1515–1560) was queen of Scotland (1538–42) and mother of Mary, Queen of Scots.

520.9–10 Then gently scan . . . sister woman—] "Address to the Unco Guid, or the Rigidly Righteous," ll. 49–50, by Burns.

520.22 Bothwell] James Hepburn, Earl of Bothwell (c. 1534–1578), Mary's third husband.

520.35–36 Holyrood . . . Abbotsford] Holyrood Palace in Edinburgh, Mary's residence during her reign; Abbotsford, Sir Walter Scott's home.

521.11–12 "The Fair Maid of Perth,"] Novel (1828) by Scott.

521.33 Associationists] See note 413.15.

522.27 *con molto espressione*] Italian: with much feeling (used in music directions).

522.35–37 Rob Roy's country . . . Helen MacGregor] Scott's novel *Rob Roy* (1817), in which Helen MacGregor is Roy's wife.

523.28–31 "Maidens lend an ear . . . men's were truer."] Paraphrased from Bryant's poem "Song," ll. 5–8, in *Poems* (1831).

524.5 Mr. S.] Fuller was traveling with Marcus (1810–1874) and Rebecca (1811–1911) Spring, progressive and wealthy friends whose son Fuller tutored during their travels.

526.17 Ossian] Scottish poet and collector of Gaelic poetry James Macpherson (1736–1796) claimed to have discovered the utterances of an ancient Gaelic bard (Ossian), which he published in a popular volume as *Fingal, an Ancient Epic Poem in Six Books* (1762).

528.18 Pentonville] Pentonville Prison (opened 1842) became a model for prisons in Britain and elsewhere; in order to reform prisoners, the design isolated them from each other.

530.7 Old Drury] The Theatre Royal, Drury Lane.

530.15 "The Patrician's Daughter" by J.W. Marston] Play (1842) by lawyer, playwright, and drama critic John Westland Marston (1819–1890).

530.34 Rachel] Stage name of Elisabeth Félix (1821–1858), an acclaimed tragic actress performing in such plays as Racine's *Phèdre* (1677).

532.27–28 Rose Cheny . . . *Clarissa Harlowe*] The identity of Rose Cheny is unclear; an eighteenth-century English actress, Mrs. Gardner (fl. 1763–82),

874 NOTES

also performed under the name Miss Cheney, but this is not that actress. *Clarissa Harlowe* is a stage adaptation of the novel *Clarissa* (1748) by Samuel Richardson.

532.28–29 Genevieve . . . Scribe] Popular playwright and librettist Augustin Eugène Scribe (1791–1861) wrote *Geneviève* (1846) and *La Protégée sans le savoir* (1846).

533.4–5 *Poudre-Coton*] French: Guncotton. Apparently the title of a short topical skit.

533.6 Dumas] Alexandre Dumas *père* (1802–1870).

533.25 *billets*] French: tickets.

534.2 Tuileries] The Tuileries Palace was a royal residence; it was burned by the Paris Commune in 1871.

534.20–21 Leverrier . . . found, his planet.] Astronomer and mathematician Urbain Jean Joseph Le Verrier (1811–1877), who predicted the existence of Neptune.

534.27 Sorbonne] The University of Paris, or perhaps more specifically the College of Sorbonne, the theological college of the university.

534.35 Hotel de Clugny] The Hôtel de Cluny opened as a museum in 1843.

535.7 College of France] The Collège de France, a prestigious, non-degree-granting research institution whose lectures and courses were (and are) free and open to the public.

535.16 Arago] French mathematician and politician François Arago (1786–1853).

536.12 M. Rémusat . . . Royer Collard] Writer and politician Charles François Marie, Comte de Rémusat (1797–1875); politician and philosopher Pierre Paul Royer-Collard (1763–1845).

536.28 *Precieuses Ridicules*] *Les Précieuses ridicules* (*The Affected Young Ladies*, 1659), a one-act satire by Molière.

536.34 *sceance*] I.e., séance, in the sense of a meeting.

536.36 La Mennais] Liberal Catholic priest and political thinker Félicité Robert de La Mennais (or Lamennais, 1782–1854).

537.3 Béranger] See note 413.30–31.

537.26–30 "*Chante pauvre petit*" . . . *jeune soldat*"] "Chante, Chante pauvre petit!" ("Sing, poor little one, sing!") is God's instruction to the poet at the end of each stanza in Béranger's poem "Ma Vocation" ("My Vocation,"

NOTES 875

translated 1850); "Que tes armes soient benis jeune soldat" ("May your weapons be blessed young soldier") is from *Paroles d'un croyant* (*Words of a Believer*, 1834) by La Mennais.

538.16 Chevalier Neukomm] Austrian composer Sigismund von Neukomm (1778–1858) wrote the oratorio *David* (1834).

538.19 Cavaillé] French organ builder Aristide Cavaillé-Coll (1811–1899).

540.39 Laura's tomb] Laura de Noves (c. 1310–1348), who may have been the "Laura" of Petrarch's poems.

540.40 Mr. Dickens's Tower and Goblin] Dickens described his guide to Avignon's Palace of the Popes, a site of the Inquisition, as a "Goblin" (*Pictures from Italy*, ch. 3, 1846).

542.17 "Behold how brightly breaks the morning!"] Song (1820) by French composer Daniel François Esprit Auber (1782–1871).

543.19 *suivante*] French: lady's maid.

544.1 *People's Journal*] *The People's Journal* (1846–48), a London periodical promoting social reform, published by John Saunders (1810–1895).

546.23–26 Iphigenia and Macaria . . . Becomes me not.] See notes 115.25–26 and 252.30; the lines are spoken by Iphigenia.

546.29 Joseph Mazzini] Political thinker and activist Giuseppe Mazzini worked for a unified Italy, founded the Young Italy political movement, and espoused a democratic republic. Fuller met him in London, where he was in exile.

546.30 *Galignani's Messenger*] English-language newspaper published in Paris from 1814 to 1884 by the Galignani family.

550.32 Jonathan] See note 8.11.

553.32–33 our cause is, indeed, the cause of all mankind] Paraphrase of a line in the "Introduction" of Thomas Paine's *Common Sense* (1776): "The cause of America is, in a great measure, the cause of all mankind."

553.38 this wicked War] The Mexican-American War (1846–48), which extended the territory of slavery.

555.29–33 "Italia, O Italia!" . . . rise to-morrow,"] Byron, "Childe Harold's Pilgrimage" (1812–18), canto 4, stanza 42, l. 1, and "Beppo. A Venetian Story" (1818), stanza 43, l. 2.

557.13 Via Sacra] Main street in ancient Rome, leading through the Forum.

559.3 *frati*] Italian: monks.

NOTES

559.19   "The tomb of my dead self,"] Cf. Shelley, "The Sunset," l. 41.

559.32–33   Manzoni . . . novel of the cousin of St. Carlo] *I promessi sposi* (*The Betrothed*, 1827, rev. 1842) by Alessandro Manzoni, for whom see note 201.1–16; the church of St. Carlo is dedicated to St. Carlo Borromeo (1538–1584), an archbishop of Milan who fed and ministered to the Milanese during a famine and plague.

560.21   Mrs. Trollope] See note 33.5.

561.21   Pius IX] Pope Pius IX (Giovanni Maria Mastai Ferretti, 1792–1878).

561.36   "Sons of Rome, awake!"] From "The Awakening of Italy" (1848), a song of the Italian revolutionary movement with text by Italian American newspaper publisher Gian Secchi de Casali (1819–1885) and music by German American composer Herrman S. Saroni (1824–1900); it was translated into English by William Cullen Bryant.

561.39   Marseillaise] Revolutionary song of France.

562.1–4   King of Sardinia . . . Duke of Modena] Charles Albert (1798–1849), King of Piedmont-Sardinia until he abdicated in 1849; Francis V (1819–1875), Duke of Modena until 1859.

562.10   King of Naples] Ferdinand II (1810–1859), king of the Kingdom of the Two Sicilies (Naples and Sicily), began his reign with liberal tendencies but later violently suppressed revolts in both Sicily and southern Italy.

562.15–16   The Swiss affairs] The Sonderbund War (1847), a brief civil war in which the majority Protestant cantons defeated the Catholic cantons, resulted in the Swiss Federal Constitution of 1848.

562.30   Torlonia . . . Campana] Alessandro Torlonia (1800–1886), member of a wealthy family of bankers, was criticized for his management of the bank; Giampietro Campana (1808–1880), art collector and director of the Monte di Pietà, a papal charity that operated as a pawnbroker, was accused of mismanaging its finances.

563.16–27   rookery . . . Obscurantists] Fuller refers in both lines to the Jesuits, who opposed liberal reform.

564.22   the Argentina] The Teatro Argentina offered opera and drama.

564.22–23   Lord Minto . . . Prince Corsini] English politician and diplomat Gilbert Elliot-Murray-Kynynmound, 2nd Earl of Minto (1782–1859); diplomat and political moderate Tommaso Corsini (1767–1856).

564.30   Pinelli] Bartolomeo Pinelli (1781–1835), illustrator and engraver of Roman scenes.

NOTES 877

566.35 Mamiani] Writer and politician Terenzio Mamiani (1799–1885) worked for Italian unification and served in the Roman ministry in 1848.

567.15–18 traitor at Milan . . . King of Naples] After promising to defend Milan in its revolt against the Austrian Empire, Charles Albert (see note 562.1) withdrew, allowing the Austrian army to avenge itself on the Milanese. For the King of Naples, see note 562.10.

567.24 Welden] Franz Ludwig Baron von Welden (1780–1853), lieutenant field marshal during the Austrian suppression of the revolt of northern Italian states.

567.38 15th May] Riots and demonstrations took place both in Vienna and in Paris.

568.16 General Pepe] General Guglielmo Pepe (1783–1855) supported the 1848 revolutions and resigned his commission in the Neapolitan army, fighting in northern Italy as a volunteer.

569.7 Grand Duke] Leopold II (1797–1870), Grand Duke of Tuscany, at first supported liberal reforms, but when Florence declared itself a republic in 1849 he wavered and subsequently invited Austrian troops to occupy the city.

569.17 Balbis and Giobertis] Political moderates and writers Cesare Balbo (1789–1853) and Vincenzo Gioberti (1801–1852) worked at times in Charles Albert's government and advocated for an Italian confederation of separate states, independent of foreign powers.

569.27 Antonini] General Giacomo Antonini (1792–1854), a leader of volunteers against Austrian forces.

570.1 Franzini] Antonio Franzini (1788–1860), Charles Albert's minister of war in 1848.

570.19 Mazzini] See note 546.29.

570.33 Tommaseo and Manin] Writer and liberal politician Niccolò Tommaseo (1802–1874); Daniele Manin (1804–1857) was a leader of the anti-Austrian revolt in Venice.

574.6–10 Rossi . . . Zucchi] Moderate liberal politician Pellegrino Luigi Odoardo Rossi (1787–1848) was papal minister of the interior; General Carlo Zucchi (1777–1863) fought repeatedly against Austrian occupation in the 1820s to 1830s and in 1848 served as papal minister of arms in Rome.

574.38 the *Cancelleria*] The Palazzo della Cancelleria (Palace of the Chancellery), where the parliament of the Roman Republic met.

576.6–7 "Yellow Tiber rose," . . . "mantle"] Cf. Byron, *Childe Harold's Pilgrimage*, canto 4, stanza 79, l. 9.

878 NOTES

577.9   the Swiss] Soldiers serving as the pope's bodyguard.

577.15   Galetti] Lawyer and political activist Giuseppe Galletti (1798–1873).

579.4   this flight.] The pope fled Rome in disguise in November 1848.

579.35–36   Montanelli, Guerrazzi, D'Aguila] Giuseppe Montanelli (1813–1862) and Francesco Domenico Guerrazzi (1804–1873) were leaders of the republican movement in Florence; D'Aguila is probably Sicilian activist Mariano d'Ayala (1808–1877), who accepted a position in Guerrazzi's government in 1848.

580.1–5   new President . . . mere tool of party] President Zachary Taylor (1784–1850), victorious general in the Mexican-American War; the "tool of the party" is President James K. Polk (1795–1849), whose administration pursued the annexation of Texas.

582.1   *Don Tirlone,* the *Punch* of Rome] *Il Don Pirlone* was a satirical newspaper (1848–49) published during the Roman revolution; *Punch* was an influential British satirical magazine.

583.21   *Primato*] *Del primato morale e civile degli italiani* (*On the Civil and Moral Primacy of the Italians,* 1843) argued for the significance of Italian contributions to civilization and urged the creation of a federated Italian government under the pope.

584.28–29   nephew of Napoleon] French ornithologist, republican, and member of the Roman Assembly Charles Lucien Jules Laurent Bonaparte (1803–1857).

585.34   *Mais nous nous reverrons*] French: But we will see each other again.

586.18   Rienzi] Nicola Gabrini (1313–1354), known as Cola di Rienzo or Rienzi, reformist leader of a revolt in Rome and advocate for unification of Italy, seen by nineteenth-century revolutionaries as their predecessor.

587.32   her President] Louis-Napoleon Bonaparte (1808–1873) was elected in 1848 as president of the French Second Republic.

588.4   Spielberg] Spielberg was the Austrian Empire's most notorious prison, used for Italian revolutionaries after 1822.

588.28   Mazzarelli] Liberal Catholic priest Carlo Emanuele dei conti Muzzarelli (1797–1856), whom the pope appointed as *Presidente del Consiglio dei Ministri* (President of the Council of Ministers), stayed in Rome after the pope's flight in 1848 and was asked by the Roman Republic to keep this position.

590.27   alguazil] Spanish (alguacil): police officer.

591.5   Romana] Romagna, province of northern Italy.

NOTES

879

591.30   Mr. Rush] U.S. diplomat Richard Rush (1780–1859), ambassador to France, recognized the French Second Republic after the revolutionary upheaval in February 1848.

592.6   Oudinot's] Lieutenant-General Charles Nicolas Victor Oudinot (1791–1863), commander of the French forces that defeated Rome in 1849.

592.7   Rienzi] See note 586.18.

592.13   Mr. Cass] Chargé d'affaires of the United States to the Papal States, beginning in 1849.

593.12   Janicular] The Janiculan or Janiculum Hill in Rome.

593.36   Pincian] The Pincian Hill in Rome.

594.1   Manara] Luciano Manara (1825–1849), Milanese officer under Garibaldi.

594.11   the Corso] The Via del Corso is a major avenue in Rome.

594.24   the Santa Scala] The Holy Stairs, adjacent to St. John Lateran, were the stairs Christians believed Christ climbed during his trial under Pontius Pilate, later transported to Rome.

595.20–21   Rome, anew the Niobe!] In "Childe Harold's Pilgrimage" (1812–18), canto 4, stanza 79, Byron calls Rome "The Niobe of nations! there she stands, / Childless and crownless, in her voiceless woe."

597.9   Trasteverini] Inhabitants of a working-class Roman neighborhood, Trastevere.

597.13   the Triumvirate] The triumvirate leading the Roman Republic's Constituent Assembly: politician Carlo Armellini (1777–1863); Mazzini (see note 546.29), who came to Rome and joined its revolutionary government; and politician and supporter of Mazzini Aurelio Saffi (1819–1890).

597.19   the Quirinal] The Quirinal Palace, a residence of the pope until 1871.

597.38   our Consul, Mr. Brown] Nicholas Brown III (1792–1859), U.S. consul to the papal court, 1845–53.

598.14–15   the African war] The French completed the conquest of Algeria in 1830–48.

599.29   black ravens] I.e., the Jesuits.

599.37–38   the stone of the sepulcher . . . after three days] Cf. Luke 24:2.

880   NOTES

601.17   contadini] A contadino is an Italian peasant (Fuller uses the plural form here).

604.34   the "*Times*?"] Fuller denounced in several dispatches the London *Times'* reactionary coverage of the 1848 revolutions.

UNPUBLISHED WRITINGS

609.1   *Possent quia posse videntur*] Virgil, *Aeneid* 5:231: "They can because they think they can." "Possent" should have been conjugated as "Possunt."

610.6   Leonidas] King of Sparta (c. 540–480 BCE) and hero of the Battle of Thermopylae.

610.39   Angelo] Italian Renaissance artist Michelangelo di Lodovico Buonarroti Simoni (1475–1564).

615.16   Virgil . . . dripped with blood] Virgil, *Aeneid*, 3:27–48.

617.16–17   Jupiter Stator] Temple of Jupiter Stator in Rome (second or third century BCE), "stator" meaning one who stays, stands, upholds.

618.6   *toga virilis*] Toga ritually put on at the advent of manhood.

618.31–32   the Mantuan] Virgil, from Mantua, is Dante's guide through Hell and Purgatory in Dante's *Divine Comedy* (1321).

620.10   *mesquin*] Spanish, *mezquino*: mean, stingy.

622.1   the wedded love of Fielding's Amelia] Fielding's novel *Amelia* (1751) concerns the early married life of a young couple.

624.26–27   Coleridge . . . Sancho the Understanding] Coleridge discusses Don Quixote and Sancho Panza, characters in Cervantes's novel *Don Quixote* (1606–16), as representing the Kantian terms of Reason and Understanding (terms American Transcendentalists adopted) in *Course of Lectures* (1818–19).

624.39   "Cervantes smiled Spain's chivalry away,"] Byron, *Don Juan* (1824), canto 12, stanza 11, l. 1.

627.30   English lady] Ellen Kilshaw (dates unknown).

629.13   Guy Mannering] Scott's novel *Guy Mannering; or, The Astrologer* (1815).

635.25–30   A man of genius . . . *long ago.*"] Adapted from Friedrich David Gräter, *Honig's Owl-Tower: A German Tale* (1829).

636.7   "death has set its seal,"] A common phrase in the nineteenth-century popular imagination, in sermons or other religious contexts.

NOTES

881

638.27   This is my . . . pleased] Matthew 3:17.

640.30   I say to you] Fuller addresses Channing directly, as she does elsewhere in this piece.

641.3   Mr Parker] Unitarian clergyman Theodore Parker (1810–1860), whose controversial sermon "A Discourse of the Transient and Permanent in Christianity" (1841) precipitated religious debate in Boston.

643.17   "The Soul must do its immortal work."] From the poem "Two Hymns," *The Dial*, II.1 (1841), by Eliza Thayer Clapp (1811–1888).

643.23–25   "*Nevertheless* I tell you . . . unto you."] John 16:7–13.

644.1   To Beethoven] An imaginary letter to the deceased German composer Ludwig van Beethoven (1770–1827).

644.29   "pangs of despised love"] *Hamlet*, I.iii.71.

646.35   "alone with the Alone"] Proclus, *Commentary* on Plato's *Timaeus*, book II.

647.14–15   Knowest thou . . . back?"] Cf. Genesis 19:17–26.

648.14   Cyprian calls Justina] Saints Cyprian and Justina, martyred in Antioch in 304 CE; Justina converted Cyprian, a magician who had tried to seduce her, to Christianity.

JOURNALS

656.11–12   Destinies . . . Hermes] In Christopher Marlowe and George Chapman's poem *Hero and Leander* (1598), based on a Greek myth, Cupid causes the Destinies, or Fates, to fall in love with Mercury, or Hermes, who rejects them.

657.4   Mrs Farrar's] Writer Eliza Ware Farrar (1791–1870); she and her husband, Harvard mathematics professor John Farrar, had offered to take Fuller with them on a European tour.

658.6   Drachenfels] Hill on the Rhine River, meaning "dragon's rock."

660.31   The son of the Gods has sold his birthright.] Fuller is probably referring to Samuel Ward's marriage to Anna Hazard Barker (1813–1900).

661.32–33   amaranth wreath . . . one of roses] Amaranths symbolize immortality; red roses symbolize love.

661.36   Lili] Anna Elisabeth "Lili" Schönemann (1758–1817), beloved by Goethe in his youth.

661.37   Weltweise] German: Philosopher.

882   NOTES

662.7–8   "a girdle around the earth in twenty minutes)] Cf. *A Midsummer Night's Dream*, II.i.175–76.

665.17   R.] Probably Samuel Ward (see note 56.4–62.17), a recurring figure in this journal, whom Fuller referred to as "Raffaello."

666.8   four tragedies] Fuller planned to write a series of tragedies based on historical figures.

666.15   Elschen's] Fuller's friend Elizabeth Wells Randall (1811–1867).

666.24   F. H's story amid the Hory mountains.] Probably Unitarian minister, Transcendentalist, and German literature scholar Frederic Henry Hedge (1805–1890), who studied in Germany in his teens. The Hory mountains are either the Ore Mountains (Czech: *Krušné hory*) on the German-Czech border or the Staré Hory Mountains in central Slovakia.

667.22   a magazine] *The Dial* (1840–44), which Fuller edited in 1840–42.

668.22   Raoul] Probably refers to Emerson.

670.3   Ellery brought down Ellen's picture] Poet William Ellery Channing II (1817–1901) married Fuller's sister Ellen Kilshaw Fuller (1820–1856).

670.7   E. H.] Elizabeth Sherman Hoar (1814–1878), fiancée of Emerson's deceased brother and an intimate of his family.

670.9   Waldo] From his teen years on, Emerson called himself by his middle name.

670.12   the subject] Fuller was writing an essay for *The Dial*, now under Emerson's editorship.

670.12–13   Lidian . . . the lost child] Emerson's wife, Lidian Jackson Emerson (1802–1892), was mourning the loss of their son Waldo earlier that year.

670.34   M. Russell's] Mary Howland Russell (1803–1862), friend of Lidian Emerson.

671.6–8   Edith . . . Ellen . . . aunt Brown's] Edith Emerson Forbes (1841–1929), Ellen Tucker Emerson (1839–1909), and Lidian's sister Lucy Jackson Brown (1798–1868).

672.2   rude alarms] Probably a reference to Hoar's frail health.

672.18   Richard] Fuller's brother Richard Frederick Fuller (1824–1869).

672.25   Mr Alcott's letters] For Alcott, see note 198.1; at this time, Alcott was in England.

NOTES

883

672.27 George Bradford] Transcendentalist and teacher George Partridge Bradford (1807–1890).

672.35 William's] Unitarian clergyman, writer, and reformer William Henry Channing (1810–1884).

673.1–2 Hawthorne . . . Ellery's earnest request] Nathaniel (1804–1864) and Sophia Peabody Hawthorne (1809–1871) refused Ellery Channing's suggestion that he and Ellen board with them in Concord.

673.6–7 Mrs Ripley] Teacher and Transcendentalist Sarah Alden Bradford Ripley (1793–1867).

675.12 Dichtung und Wahrheit] From the title of Goethe's autobiography of his early life, *Aus meinem Leben: Dichtung und Wahrheit* (*From my Life: Poetry and Truth*; 1811–33).

676.2 Mamma] Emerson's mother, Ruth Haskins Emerson (1768–1853).

676.15 H. T.] Henry David Thoreau.

678.40 these verses] No verses appear in the journal here.

679.9–10 Caroline . . . come to Naushon] Transcendentalist Caroline Sturgis Tappan (1818–1888), Fuller's and Emerson's friend, had been in love with Ellery Channing before his marriage; Naushon was a Sturgis family property.

679.34 N. B.] New Bedford, Massachusetts.

680.38 B.] Boston.

681.28 H. Hedge] See note 666.24.

681.30 S. Ward] Samuel Gray Ward (see note 56.4–62.17).

682.15 Sarah Clarke] See note 15.5.

682.19 Mr Newell's church] First Parish Church in Cambridge; Unitarian William Newell (1804–1881), minister.

682.32–34 Judge Jackson's . . . Marianne . . . Susan's] Massachusetts judge Charles Jackson (1775–1855), his wife Susan, and daughter Marianne.

683.6 At Waltham were good talk.] Perhaps with Sarah Ripley (see note 673.4–5).

683.35 here is a copy] No poem is copied into the journal here.

684.19–22 Saadi . . . gods love tragedy"] Emerson's poems "Saadi" (*The Dial*, 3.2) and "Masque" (or "The Poet," unpublished); the following lines are in "Saadi."

884 NOTES

686.2 Sam's marriage] The marriage of Samuel Ward (see note 56.4–62.17) and Anna Barker (see note 660.31) in 1840.

686.8 Mr. Green's] Probably retired military officer William Batchelder Greene (1819–1878), who contributed to *The Dial*.

686.25–26 Mignon's . . . Mann und Weib] See note 226.31–34.

689.6 Little Anna] Samuel and Anna Barker Ward's daughter Anna Barker Ward (1841–1875).

689.8–9 James . . . Latimer the Slave] George Washington Latimer (1819–1897), enslaved in Virginia, escaped with his wife to Boston and was captured and threatened with return to his enslaver; his case prompted abolitionist resistance and resulted in his purchase and freedom. James Freeman Clarke was one of the clergymen who preached at public meetings advocating for Latimer's release.

689.14 James & Sarah] See note 15.5.

689.20–21 little Waldo's birthday] See note 670.12–13.

690.21 Schiller's Bell] Schiller's poem "Das Lied von der Glocke" ("Song of the Bell," 1798).

691.18–20 He momently . . . side.] Fuller loosely quotes from "The Indian's Bride," by Edward Coote Pinkney (1802–1828), published in his *Poems* (1825) and republished in *The Miscellaneous Poems of Edward C. Pinkney* (1844).

691.22 Man more   Woman more] Fuller demarcates the division between these columns with a line.

692.5 they begin to be mothers] In making the point that women's energies are diverted to the demands of motherhood and, therefore, not as available for art, Fuller likely meant to quote from Goethe. Although it is unclear which text she had in mind, Fuller discusses her plans to give readings from Goethe's writings on the fine arts in 1840 letters and journal fragments (not included in this volume).

692.13 social, but they] No manuscript pages remain to complete this journal fragment.

692.15 therefore the thought] The preceding pages of this manuscript fragment are no longer extant.

692.19 dost thou, my friend] Fuller addresses the brother of Sarah and James Freeman Clarke, William Hull Clarke (1812–1878), who acted as her guide and with whom she fell in love during her 1843 trip that served as the basis of *Summer on the Lakes, in 1843*. Fuller felt betrayed when William and Caroline Sturgis later struck up a flirtation in Boston.

NOTES

885

693.4   W] William Hull Clarke.

695.8   Henry Hedge] See note 666.24.

695.11–696.4   Virgin Mother . . . phoenix birth]. Fuller's other version of this poem is in the Manuscript Tracing Journal, pp. 698–99 in this volume.

696.13–14   Arthur . . . Nauvoo . . . Lady Emma] Fuller's brother, Unitarian minister Arthur Buckminster Fuller (1822–1862), spent a few years in Illinois, where Joseph Smith Jr. (1805–1844), the founder of the Church of Latter Day Saints (the Mormons), his wife Emma, and his followers settled in a town they renamed Nauvoo.

696.16   Coronach] Scottish or Irish Gaelic: a funeral song.

696.28–29   donzella lagune] Italian: lady-in-waiting by the lake. As she noted elsewhere in her 1844 journal, Fuller used this term as a code to refer to emotions too painful to express directly. She may be invoking Sir Walter Scott's narrative poem *The Lady of the Lake* (1810).

698.3–5   Sarah . . . the etchings] Sarah Clarke contributed the illustrations to Fuller's book *Summer on the Lakes, in 1843*.

698.7   giving S. Raphael's Descent from the Cross] Fuller seems to have given Sarah Clarke a print of a drawing by Raphael, *The Descent from the Cross*.

698.12–699.4   Virgin Mother . . . heavenly birth.] See also pp. 695–96 in this volume for Fuller's other version of this poem. Fuller published this version as "Lines Suggested by Raphael's Descent from the Cross," in *The Rose of Sharon: A Religious Souvenir for MDCCCXLVI*, ed. Miss S. C. Edgarton (1846).

699.5–11   Mt Auburn . . . the garden of groves] Mount Auburn Cemetery in Cambridge was the first example of the rural cemetery movement in the U.S.

699.5–6   the Countess of Rudolstadt] See note 412.1–2.

699.9–10   Jacob Behmen] German philosopher Jakob Böhme (1575–1624).

699.13   "sege Gipfel"] German (perhaps Segen Gipfel): blessing [of the] mountain peak.

699.16   Cary] Caroline Sturgis; see note 679.9–10.

699.22   the Ganymede day] A day during Fuller's tour of the Midwest; see note 41.25–26.

700.23   Konic] Perhaps German (König): king. See also note 748.34.

702.7   Abby] A domestic servant.

702.18   Our friend has likened thee to the sweet fern] See note 748.35–38.

886 NOTES

703.2 Cohasset] Coastal town south of Boston.

704.33 "As sorrow . . . her stars."] From *Festus: A Poem*, by English poet Philip James Bailey (1816–1902).

706.19 My seal ring:—] Emerson describes Fuller's seal ring, with a figure of Mercury, in *Memoirs of Margaret Fuller Ossoli* (1852).

709.10 *Constituente Romana*] The *Constituente Romana*, republican Rome's governing assembly.

709.23 Castle St Angelo] Castel Sant'Angelo, originally the emperor Hadrian's tomb, later a papal fortress. The following paragraphs name several locations in Rome, including the Corso, a major thoroughfare.

710.6 St Eustachio] Saint Eustace, martyred in 118 under Emperor Hadrian.

710.29 "O che mondo . . . O che secolo."] Italian: What a world! What a century!

711.5 a letter from Lago Maggiore.] The letter writer is unknown. Lago Maggiore is "Lake Maggiore."

711.7 Laura Mantegazzi di Canero] Italian patriot Laura Solera Mantegazza (1813–1873).

711.11 giro] Italian: tour.

711.21 C. A.] Constitutional Assembly.

711.30–32 the Capitol . . . Marcus Aurelius] The civic center of Rome, the Piazza del Campidoglio (designed by Michelangelo), sits on the Capitoline Hill and holds the ancient equestrian statue of Emperor Marcus Aurelius.

711.31 evvivas] Italian: hurrahs.

711.36 Bonaparte . . . Duke of Bordeaux] French president Charles-Louis Napoléon Bonaparte (1808–1873), later Emperor Napoleon III; Louis Philippe I (1773–1850) had been forced to abdicate as king of France in 1848; Louis Philippe's nephew Henri, Count of Chambord and Duke of Bordeaux (1820–1883), was the Legitimist pretender.

711.37 Considerant] Victor Prosper Considerant (1808–1893), French socialist philosopher who collaborated with Fourier and whose pro-labor ideas helped to shape revolutionary thought in France in 1848.

712.3 Zucchi] See note 574.6–10.

712.7 Civica] Civic Guard of Rome, initially permitted by Pope Pius IX.

712.13–14 *In hoc signe vinces* . . . Constantine] In one account, Emperor Constantine (c. 272–337) was converted to Christianity by a vision of a

NOTES 887

cross in the sky with these words (in Greek) over it: "in this sign, you will conquer."

712.23–24 Montanelli Guerrazzi and Mazzini] See notes 562.1 and 562.1–4.

712.34–36 Charles Albert . . . Victor Emanuel II] For Charles Albert, see note 562.1; Victor Emmanuel II (1820–1878), King of Sardinia from 1849 until 1861, when he became king of a united Italy.

LETTERS

717.2 *Timothy Fuller*] Fuller's father (1778–1835), a lawyer, served in the Massachusetts House and Senate and in the U.S. Congress.

717.5–6 eugene . . . caroline] Fuller's brother Eugene Fuller (1815–1859) and, probably, Fuller's cousin Caroline Kuhn (1806–1885).

717.19–21 Aunt Abigail . . . Uncle Elisha] Abigail Crane (1792–1876) and Elisha Fuller (1794–1855), to whom Fuller recited Greek and Latin lessons.

717.23 Miss *Kilshaw*] See note 670.3.

718.6 Zeluco] A 1789 novel by Scottish physician and writer John Moore (1729–1802).

718.14 Hesitation] The novel *Hesitation: or, To marry, or not to marry?* (1819) by Mrs. Ross.

718.30 Deserted Village] A 1770 poem by Oliver Goldsmith.

719.28 *Susan Prescott*] Fuller boarded at Prescott's (1796–1869) girls' school in Groton, Massachusetts.

720.7 Brown's Philosophy] Scottish philosopher Thomas Brown (1778–1820) wrote *Lectures on the Philosophy of the Human Mind* (1820).

720.8 Mr. Perkins's school] George William Perkins (1804–1856) taught school in Cambridgeport, where the Fullers lived.

720.25 a friend] Perhaps Lydia Maria Francis (Child), for whom see note 285.34.

721.2 James Freeman Clarke] See note 15.5.

721.27 Novalis!] Pen name of poet Georg Philipp Friedrich Freiherr von Hardenberg (1772–1801).

721.31 Korner] Playwright Karl Theodor Körner (1791–1813).

722.33 Helen] Helen Davis (1798–1887).

888   NOTES

722.37–723.3   Mr Henry . . . Elizh . . . Mrs *Chapone*!] Perhaps clergyman and writer Caleb Sprague Henry (1804–1884); for Elizabeth Randall, see note 666.15; English writer Hester Mulso Chapone (1727–1801).

723.8   die Grosse und Schöne.—] German: the big and beautiful.

723.9   Sarah] See note 15.5.

724.6   Dr Follen] Charles (Karl) Theodor Christian Friedrich Follen (1796–1840), German immigrant to the U.S. and first professor of German literature at Harvard University.

724.9   Grand duchess Amelia] See note 259.37.

724.15   Von Muller] Weimar statesman Friedrich von Müller (1779–1849).

724.31–32   I shall not go to Europe] The Farrars (see note 657.4) had offered to take Fuller to Europe, but this plan fell through.

725.3   your mag.] Clarke was editing the *Western Messenger* (1835–41) in Cincinnati.

725.28   Herschell's] Astronomer Frederick William Herschel (1738–1822).

725.31   Caroline Sturgis] See note 679.9–10.

727.33   Zelterian] For Zelter, who corresponded with Goethe, see note 342.28.

728.15   Dr Wayland] Francis Wayland (1796–1865), president of Brown University.

729.8   Gardiner on Music] English composer William Gardiner (1770–1853) wrote *The Music of Nature* (1832).

729.13   Brownson's review and the Democratic] Editor and clergyman Orestes Brownson (1803–1876) published a review of Emerson in his journal, the *Boston Quarterly Review*. The other review Fuller mentions (not by Brownson) appeared in the *Democratic Review* (see note 405.39).

729.19–22   Lidian . . . Elizabeth] See notes 670.12–13 and 666.15.

730.3–4   Mr F. . . . Sophia—] Fuller tried unsuccessfully to have Lidian Emerson's niece Sophia Brown (1821–1842) hired at Hiram Fuller's (1814–1880) school, where Fuller was teaching.

730.17   Sophia Ripley] Transcendentalist Sophia Willard Dana Ripley (1803–1861), who participated in the Conversations Fuller plans in this letter.

734.6–9   Mrs Bancroft . . . Mrs Josiah Quincy] Elizabeth Davis Bliss Bancroft (1803–1886); probably Mary Jane Miller Quincy (1806–1874).

NOTES 889

734.21   *a mourir*] French: unto death.

734.22   designs of Raffalle] The painter Raphael.

734.24   *William Henry Channing*] See note 672.35.

734.31   Ernest] W. H. Channing published two parts of "Ernest the Seeker" in *The Dial* (July and October 1840). In this letter Fuller discusses her hopes for *The Dial*.

734.33   James] Clarke, as editor of the *Western Messenger*.

736.17   Miss Channing] W. H. Channing's sister Lucy Ellery Channing (1809–1877).

738.8   Mr R] Perhaps George Ripley, the husband of Sophia Ripley, for whom see note 730.17.

738.16   your manuscript] Fuller, as editor, rejected Thoreau's essay "The Service," which remained unpublished until 1902.

739.6   the Ripleys] George and Sophia Ripley, for whom see note 730.17.

739.8   Mr Parker] See note 641.3.

739.14   one of Beethoven's great symphonies] Beethoven's Fifth Symphony, performed at the Boston Academy of Music (the second performance in the U.S., and the first in Boston).

740.23   Gipsey book] *The Zincali: An Account of the Gypsies of Spain* (1841), by George Borrow.

740.29   "Napoleon"] Unpublished poem by Benjamin Franklin Presbury (1810–1868).

740.31   Miss Peabody] Bookstore owner, writer, and educator Elizabeth Palmer Peabody (1804–1894) was publisher of *The Dial* from January 1842 to July 1843.

741.22–27   Charles Crane . . . Mary Rotch] Charles P. Crane was Fuller's cousin. Eliza Farrar's (see note 657.4) aunt, Mary Rotch (1777–1848), was interested in Transcendentalist ideas; Fuller and others called her "Aunt Mary."

743.6   *George T. Davis*] Fuller had been in love with Davis (1810–1877) some years before.

743.20–21   old Dana house] Fuller had lived there as a teenager.

745.2   *Richard F. Fuller*] Fuller's brother (1824–1869).

745.17   Bowdoin prizes] Harvard College prizes.

745.24   Carey's] Richard's fellow student George Blankern Cary (1824–1846).

890   NOTES

745.33–34   Indians have been dispossessed] The Sac and Fox tribes lost this land to the U.S. in the 1830s.

747.2   Caroline Sturgis] See note 679.9–10

747.14–16   Pericles and . . . your nest Aspasia"] Walter Savage Landor's "imaginary conversation," *Pericles and Aspasia* (1836), CCXXVI, l. 1.

748.3   The Parsonage] The Old Manse in Concord, where Fuller was staying with the Hawthorne family.

748.27–28   "Herberts" and that "Dialogue"] Fuller published her poem "The Two Herberts" in the *Present* 1 (March 1844), and her "Dialogue" in *The Dial* 4 (April 1844).

748.34   the horse konic belongs to Frank Shaw] See Fuller's poem on "Konic" in her journals, pp. 699–702 in this volume; Boston abolitionist Francis George Shaw (1809–1882).

748.35–38   Sarah to the sweet fern. . . . Winged Sphynx] A set of poems Fuller sent Emerson: one on the horse Konic (see previous note); "To Sarah"; "Sistrum"; one accompanying an image of a double triangle, serpent, and rays (see page 705 in this volume); and one about a winged sphynx. The image of the serpent, triangles, and rays became the frontispiece of *Woman in the Nineteenth Century*; see illustration, p. 189 in this volume.

749.3–4   Edith . . . Una] Emerson's and Hawthorne's daughters.

749.9   Henry] Perhaps Henry David Thoreau.

749.13   *Elizabeth Hoar*] See note 670.7.

749.15–16   Sing Sing . . . William Channing] For Sing Sing, see note 425.11; for William Henry Channing, see note 56.4–62.17.

750.9   the pamphlet] Fuller's book *Woman in the Nineteenth Century* (1845).

751.16   E] The passages with missing text refer to Ellery Channing's difficulties in trying to work at Greeley's *New-York Tribune*.

751.24   *Eugene Fuller*] See note 717.5–6.

752.8–9   Castle Rackrent style] *Castle Rackrent* was an 1800 novel by Maria Edgeworth chronicling the mismanagement of their estate by four generations of the Rackrent family.

752.34   N. O.] New Orleans, where Eugene was living at the time.

753.14   *James Nathan*] German banker (1811–1888) temporarily living in New York, with whom Fuller fell in love.

755.30   Our friend] Mary Greeley (1811–1872).

NOTES 891

756.5 liebste] German: dearest. In a later letter to James Nathan (May 26, 1845) Fuller catches her mistake; she has used the feminine form here, and she corrects to "liebster," saying she must have been "seeking the woman in you."

756.31 A human secret, like our own] In Fuller's original version of the poem, written in 1844, this line reads: "A human secret, like my own."

758.11 *Evert A. Duyckinck*] Publisher Evert Augustus Duyckinck (1816–1878), editor at Wiley and Putnam, which published Fuller's collection of essays *Papers on Literature and Art* (1846).

758.16 Festus] Fuller's review of Philip Bailey's *Festus* (see note 314.25).

760.29–31 Waldo . . . William . . . Charles . . . S] Emerson, William Henry Channing, Charles King Newcomb (1820–1894), and Samuel Ward, for whom see note 681.28.

760.35 Atkinson] Phrenologist Henry George Atkinson (1812–1884).

761.15–16 Scott . . . pupil of Dela Roche] Scottish painter David Scott (1806–1849); the pupil of Paul Delaroche was perhaps Edward Armitage (1817–1896).

761.18–22 Joseph Mazzini . . . "Italian Martyrs.] Mazzini published "Italian Martyrs," on fellow revolutionaries Attilo and Emilio Bandiera and Jacopo Ruffini, in *The People's Journal* in two parts in 1833.

761.19 "Sanders People's Journal"] See note 554.1.

761.27–30 Anna Howitt . . . Margaret Gilles] Writer and artist Anna Mary Howitt (1824–1884); artist Margaret Gillies (1803–1887).

761.35–36 Eliza Fox . . . W. J.] English painter Eliza Bridell Fox (1824–1903), daughter of editor and reformer William Johnson Fox (1786–1864).

762.22 Rachel] See note 530.34.

763.21–24 Dr Brown . . . David Scott] Physician John Brown (1810–1882); for Scott, see note 761.15–16.

765.11 Teufelsdrockh] Cf. Carlyle's 1831 novel *Sartor Resartus: The Life and Opinions of Herr Teufelsdröckh in Three Books.*

765.28 Mrs. C.] Writer (though unpublished) Jane Baillie Welsh Carlyle (1801–1866).

765.32 Lord Ashburton's] Banker and politician Alexander Baring, Lord Ashburton (1774–1848).

766.25 Elizabeth Hoar] See note 670.7.

767.5 La Mennais] See note 536.36.

892 NOTES

767.6   Dr. François] Physician and writer Ferdinand François (1806–1868).

767.14   *La Presse*] First mass newspaper in France, founded in 1836.

767.26   Marcus and Rebecca Spring] See note 524.5.

768.22   M.] Adam Mickiewicz, whom Fuller had met in Paris.

769.26   *William Henry Channing*] See note 672.33.

770.2   Guerriere] Journalist and politician Anselmo Guerrieri Gonzaga (1819–1879).

770.7   Jane Tuckerman King] Fuller's former pupil (1821–unknown).

770.12   Castle Fusano] A villa near Ostia.

771.4   Costanza Arconati Visconti] Liberal Milanese aristocrat Costanza Trotti Arconati Visconti (1800–1871).

771.18–22   Gioberti." . . . Mamiani and Orioli] For Gioberti and Mamiani, see notes 569.17 and 566.35; scientist and politician Francesco Orioli (1783–1856).

772.2   *Charles King Newcomb*] See note 760.29–30.

773.35   Cary] Caroline Sturgis Tappan (see note 679.7–8).

774.2   *Giovanni Angelo Ossoli*] Roman liberal (1821–1850) and father of Fuller's child.

776.6   Giuseppe Mazzini] See note 546.29.

776.19   Roman Citizen] In February 1849, the Roman assembly declared Rome a republic, invited Mazzini to Rome, and declared him a Roman citizen.

776.23–27   "il lungo esilio . . . in terra mia"] Italian: "at the beginning of another long exile, life has few comforts but for distant and disputed affections, and long-delayed hope and the desire that is beginning to become supreme in me to finally rest in peace, since I have not been able to live in my own land."

777.12   "Care is taken . . . into heaven."] See note 98.12–13.

779.1   William] Caroline Sturgis married William Aspinwall Tappan (1819–1905).

779.28   Angelino] Fuller's son Angelo Eugene Philip Ossoli (1848–1850).

781.6   Ellen's beautiful life . . . wasted] Caroline Sturgis Tappan's sister Ellen Sturgis Hooper (1812–1848), Transcendentalist poet, died of tuberculosis, leaving three children, including Marian (Clover) Hooper, who later married Henry Adams.

NOTES 893

781.32–33   Dicken's marchioness playing whist] In Dickens's novel *The Old Curiosity Shop* (1841), a character renames his servant a "marchioness" and teaches her a (different) card game.

785.19   "Cursed with every granted prayer,"] Alexander Pope, *Moral Essays,* Epistle ii, l. 147.

787.21   Margarett C. Fuller] Margarett Crane Fuller (1789–1859).

788.16   Pickie] Horace and Mary Greeley's child.

788.30–31   Hermann Clarke] The child of James Freeman and Anna Huidekoper Clarke.

790.39–791.2   Mr. Cass . . . William and Emelyn Story] U.S. diplomat Lewis Cass Jr. (1814–1878), chargé d'affaires to the Papal States in 1849; sculptor and writer William Wetmore Story (1819–1895) and his wife Emelyn Eldredge Story (1820–1894) were American expatriates in Rome.

791.25   Gian Martino] Giovanni Arconati Visconti (1839–1889).

792.24   contadine] Italian: peasants.

793.25   Horace Sumner] Brother (1824–1850) of Charles Sumner; sailed with Fuller to the U.S. on the *Elizabeth* and, along with Fuller, was drowned in the shipwreck off Fire Island, New York.

797.32   my book] Fuller was writing a history of the Italian revolution.

799.16   Giusti] Satirical poet Giuseppe Giusti (1808–1850), member of the revolutionary Tuscan parliament.

799.17   Berchet] Milanese poet Giovanni Berchet (1783–1851).

799.24   Westmoreland, bearing Powers's Eve] The ship *Westmoreland* sank that March; *Eve* was a statue by Hiram Powers.

801.5   Powers's statue of Calhoon.] Fuller's ship the *Elizabeth* carried Powers's statue of John Calhoun.

General Index

Abbotsford, 520
Abbott, Francis, 11
Abby (domestic servant), 702
Abélard, Pierre, 215, 237
Abolitionism, 208, 298, 430–31, 471, 503, 554, 689
Aborn, Susan, 726–27
Abradatus, 242–46, 248
Abraham, 640–42
Achilles, 224, 325, 328–30, 335
Adair, James: *The History of the American Indians*, 149, 153–59, 170
Adam, 221, 254, 283, 661, 668
Adams, Abigail, 281–82
Adams, John, 281–82
Adams, John Quincy, 204, 281–82
Admetus, 617
Adonis, 84–85
Aeneas, 595
Aesculapius, 97, 116
Africa, 535
African Americans, 40, 202–3, 208, 298, 429–34, 510, 553, 689
Agamemnon, 256–57, 323–24, 326–31, 333–34
Agrippa, Heinrich Cornelius, 118
Agustín, María, 303
Ajaccio, Corsica, 538
Albani, Alessandro, 785
Albany, NY, 159
Alcibiades, 266, 687
Alcmaeon of Croton, 385
Alcott, Bronson, 672, 679, 727; "Orphic Sayings," 198
Aldobrandini, Prince (Camillo Borghese), 565, 588
Alexander the Great, 349
Algeria, 598

Allegheny River, 142
Allston, Washington, 52–53, 359–70
Amazons, 212, 315
Ambleside, England, 509
American tourists abroad, 549–51
American Tract Society, 123
Amoretti, Carlo, 104
Amphictyonic League, 352
Amsterdam, Netherlands, 174
Anantooiah tribe, 154–55
Ancona, Italy, 592
Andrea, Novella d', 216
Andromache, 335
Anglicans, 588
Anna-Amalia of Brunswick-Wolfenbüttel, 259, 269, 724
Anne, Queen, 228, 614, 621
Antigone, 220, 323, 333
Antiope, 212
Antonini, Giacomo, 569
Apollo, 51, 84, 112, 128, 218, 255–56, 263, 265, 333, 358, 388, 461–62, 536, 545, 570, 617, 639, 641–42, 694, 734, 755, 757
Apollo Belvedere, 331
Apuleius, 307
Arabia, 308, 369, 705
Arago, François, 535
Ariosto, Ludovico, 346, 719
Arkansas, 751–52
Arles, France, 541
Armellini, Carlo, 597
Armenians, 247
Armitage, Edward, 761
Arnim, Bettina Brentano von, 387–95
Ashburton, Baron (Alexander Baring), 765
Aspasia, 215, 304, 747

894

GENERAL INDEX

Athens, ancient, 169, 207
Atkinson, Henry George, 760–61
Auber, Daniel-François-Esprit, 542
Augustus, 346
Austria, 131, 228, 469, 472, 547, 552,
   562–63, 566–67, 569–71, 574–75,
   584, 589–91, 595–96, 598, 600,
   604–5, 797
Avignon, France, 540
"Awakening of Italy, The" (song),
   561
Aztecs, 169, 228

Bacchus (Dionysus), 734
Bacon, Francis: *The Wisdom of the
   Ancients*, 198
Baia, Italy, 542
Bailey, Philip James: *Festus*, 314,
   318–20, 469, 705, 747, 758–59
Balbo, Cesare, 569
Baldor, 312
Balzac, Honoré de, 404, 406–8,
   412, 414, 767; *Eugènie Grandet*,
   407; *Père Goriot*, 407, 414;
   La Recherche de l'Absolu, 407;
   Seraphitus, 407–8
Bancroft, Elizabeth Davis Bliss, 734
Bancroft, George, 495
Bandiera, Attilo and Emilio, 761
Barker, Anna. *See* Ward, Anna Barker
Barker, Joseph, 514–16
Bark River, 86
Barmby, John Goodwyn and
   Catharine, 237
Barrett, Elizabeth. *See* Browning,
   Elizabeth Barrett
Barry, Comtesse du (Jeanne Bécu),
   225
Beatrice, 545–46
Beecher, Catharine E., 444; *The
   Duty of American Women to
   Their Country*, 438–39, 445
Beethoven, Ludwig van, 277,
   644–45, 768; Symphony No. 5,
   739

Bellevue Alms House, 420–22
Bellevue Hospital, 420
Belvidere, IL, 51
Ben Lomond, 523–27, 763
Béranger, Pierre-Jean de, 413,
   765; "La Liberté," 199; "Ma
   Vocation," 537
Berchet, Giovanni, 799
Bethlehem, 710
Bible, 11, 110, 361, 382, 431, 640, 738,
   790. *See also individual books*
Big Thunder, 51
Birkbeck, Bradford, 82
Birkbeck, Morris, 79, 81–82, 94
Birmingham, England, 518
Black Hawk, 34, 38, 141
Blackwell's (now Roosevelt) Island,
   420
Blackwood's Magazine, 344
Blake, William, 110
Blaze, François-Henri-Joseph, 270
Bloomingdale Insane Asylum, 424
Blue laws, 550
Boadicea (Boudica), 297
Boccaccio, Giovanni, 231, 456,
   784
Böhme, Jakob, 254, 699
Bologna, Italy, 574, 584
Bonaparte, Charles-Lucien, 584
Bonaparte, Louis-Napoléon (later
   Napoléon III), 587, 711–12
Borromeo, Carlo, 558–60
Borromeo, Federigo, 559
Borrow, George: *The Zincali*, 740
Boston, MA, 45, 49, 62, 137, 141,
   159, 191, 281, 368, 400, 499, 509,
   512, 539, 542, 555, 679–80, 685,
   718, 727–29, 731, 734, 740–41,
   749, 801
Boston Daily Mail, 203
Boston Quarterly Review, 729
Boswell, James, 342
Bothwell, Earl of (James Hepburn),
   520
Bowdoin Prizes, 745

896 GENERAL INDEX

Bradford, George Partridge, 672
Brahma, 639
Brant, Joseph, 134
Brittany, 295, 435
Broel-Plater, Emilia, 213–15, 303
Brookline, MA, 682
Brown, Charles Brockden: *Ormond*,
485–89, 508; *Wieland*, 485–89
Brown, John, 763
Brown, Lucy Jackson, 671
Brown, Nicholas, III, 597–98
Brown, Sophia, 730
Brown, Thomas: *Lectures on the
Philosophy of the Human Mind*,
720
Browning, Elizabeth Barrett, 296,
793; letter to, 793–94; "To
George Sand: A DESIRE," 235,
409–10; "To George Sand: A
RECOGNITION," 235–36, 410
Browning, Robert, 793–94
Brownson, Orestes, 729
Brunhilda, 294
Brutus, Marcus Junius, 347, 610
Bryant, William Cullen, 498; "The
Prairies," 28, 30; "Song," 523
Buddhists, 29, 682
Buffalo, NY, 13, 15, 25, 134, 173, 186
Bulwer-Lytton, Edward, 683
Burdett, Charles: *The Elliott Family*,
438, 444–45
Burke, Edmund, 436
Burns, Robert, 527, 764; "Address
to the Unco Guid, or the Rigidly
Righteous," 520; "Green Grow
the Rashes," 329
Burritt, Elihu, 513
Butler, Joseph: *The Analogy of
Religion*, 186
Byron, Lord (George Gordon), 11,
201, 266, 387, 457, 503; "And
Thou Art Dead, as Young and
Fair," 394; "Childe Harold's
Pilgrimage," 555, 576, 595; *Don
Juan*, 87, 624

Caesar, Julius, 707, 781; *Gallic
Wars*, 175
Cagliostro, Alessandro, 183
Cain, 171
Calabria, 562
Calderón, Pedro, 349; *El Magico
Prodigioso*, 230
Calhoun, John C., 801
Cambria, R.M.S., 509–10
Cambridge, MA, 678, 681–82,
717–20, 722, 729, 741, 743, 745,
750
Campagna, 561, 573, 594, 601
Campana, Giampietro, 562
Canada, 8, 162, 164, 173–74, 510
Canidia, 105
Canova, Antonio, 252, 277
Canton, MA, 741
Carlyle, Jane Welsh, 763, 765–66
Carlyle, Thomas, 96, 348, 585, 679,
723–24, 729, 762–66; *The French
Revolution*, 686, 765; "Novalis,"
355; *Sartor Resartus*, 765
Carter, Elizabeth, 216
Carthage, ancient, 171
Carver, Jonathan: *Travels through
America*, 132, 159, 165, 176
Cary, George Blankern, 745
Cass, Lewis, Jr., 591, 593, 598,
790–91; letter to, 800–801
Cassandra, 220, 256, 263, 333–34,
570
Catherine II, Empress of Russia, 215
Catholics, 95, 136, 221, 280, 344,
361, 404, 424, 429, 472, 492,
520, 536–37, 552, 560–61, 568,
578, 583–84, 588, 603, 709–13,
771, 773, 790
Catlin, George: *Manners, Customs,
and Condition of the North
American Indians*, 26, 134, 145,
161, 163, 169–70
Cato, 201, 219
Cavaillé-Coll, Aristide, 538
Celibacy, 279, 294

GENERAL INDEX

Cenci, Beatrice, 335
Ceres (Demeter), 217, 265, 267, 302, 393
Cervantes, Miguel de: *Don Quixote*, 624–25
Chambers' Edinburgh Journal, 519
Chamonix, France, 29
Channing, Ellen Fuller (sister), 670, 679–81, 685, 745, 752, 781
Channing, Ellery (William Ellery Channing II), 499–500, 670–71, 673–74, 676, 678–81, 683, 685, 696, 751; "Inscription for a Garden," 384; "Reverence," 314–18; "Sonnet IV," 500
Channing, Lucy Ellery, 736
Channing, William Ellery, 260–61, 430, 485, 495–96
Channing, William Henry, 672, 674–75, 749, 760; "Ernest the Seeker," 734–35; letters to, 734–36, 739, 750–51, 769–70, 777–78, 795–96
Chantrey, Francis Leggatt, 517
Chapone, Hester Mulso, 723
Charles Albert, King of Sardinia and Duke of Savoy, 562, 567, 569–71, 583, 587, 711–12
Chastity, 275, 277, 285
Chateaubriand, François-René, 575
Cheny, Rose, 532
Cherokee, 157, 166, 169, 480, 482, 485
Chester, England, 517–18
Chicago, IL, 25, 28–29, 51–52, 54, 62, 78, 85, 170, 173, 175, 179, 695
Child, Lydia Maria, 285–86, 498
China, 472, 513
Chinese Americans, 161
Chippewa (Ojibwe), 88, 125, 144, 147, 152, 165, 178
Choctaw, 157, 480–82, 484
Chopin, Frédéric, 538
Christianity, 136–37, 142, 155, 171, 215, 222–23, 229, 241, 275, 325,
344, 444, 455, 480, 482, 515–16, 545, 551, 574, 578, 617, 640–42, 683
Cincinnati, OH, 443–44
Cinderella, 212
Civitavecchia, Italy, 590
Clapp, Eliza Thayer: "Two Hymns," 643
Clarke, Hermann, 788
Clarke, James Freeman ("J."), 15–17, 689, 734, 744; letters to, 721–25; "Triformis," 54–55
Clarke, Sarah Ann ("S."), 15–17, 25, 29, 183, 682, 689, 698, 702, 723, 748
Clarke, William Hull, 692–93
Clay, Cassius, 471
Cleopatra, 519
Cleveland, OH, 17
Clevenger, Shobal Vail, 145
Clough, Arthur Hugh: letter to, 797–99
Clytemnestra, 324, 326–28, 330
Cobb, Samuel, 480–82
Cobden, Richard, 516
Cohasset, MA, 703
Coleridge, Samuel Taylor, 349, 624; "The Rime of the Ancient Mariner," 15
Collège de France, 535
Colonna, Victoria, 253
Columbus, Christopher, 228
Combe, George and Andrew, 139
Conant, Reverend, 30
Concord, MA, 496, 670–85, 689, 742, 748
Concord River, 478
Confucius, 639
Congress, U.S., 432
Connecticut, 550
Considerant, Victor-Prosper, 711
Constantine, 712
Conversations (Fuller), 730–34
Cooke, John, 229

898 GENERAL INDEX

Cooper, James Fenimore, 360, 496–97; *The Deerslayer*, 329; *The Last of the Mohicans*, 27, 137, 497; *The Pilot*, 497
Corn Plant, 168
Corsini, Tommaso, 564
Cortés, Hernán, 228
Costituente Romana, 709–11, 776–77
Cowley, Abraham: "The Complaint," 378
Cowper, William: "On Receipt of My Mother's Picture," 216
Crane, Abigail, 717
Crane, Charles P., 741
Crawford, Thomas: *Orpheus and Cerberus*, 197
Creek (Muscogee), 153–54
Creoles, 63
Crieff, Scotland, 521
Cromwell, Oliver, 585
Currans, John Philpot, 436
Cyprian (saint), 648
Cyrus II, 224, 242, 244–48

Dacier, Anne, 216
D'Aguila, Mariano, 579
Dana, Richard Henry, 499
Dante Alighieri, 122, 231, 344, 349, 367, 643, 645, 747; *The Divine Comedy*, 366, 545–46, 618; *La Vita Nuova*, 464
Darnley, Lord (Henry Stuart), 520
David, 640, 642
Davis, George T.: letter to, 743–44
Davis, Helen, 722
Declaration of Independence, 281
Defoe, Daniel: *Robinson Crusoe*, 37
Dejanira, 212
Delaroche, Paul, 761
Delphi, oracle at, 44, 116, 128, 257, 694–95
Democratic Party, 426
Democratic Review, 204, 405, 729
Denmark, 24, 297, 471

De Quincey, Thomas, 763; *Suspiria de Profundis*, 457
D'Eresby, Willoughby, 522
Desatir, 280
Detroit, MI, 18, 134, 184–86
Deutsche Schnellpost, 203
Dial, The, 191, 397, 512–13, 667, 679, 734–35, 738, 740–41, 750, 763
"Dialogue" (Fuller), 748
Diana (Artemis), 54–55, 217–18, 265, 384, 705, 755, 757
Dickens, Charles, 466; *American Notes for General Circulation*, 9; *The Old Curiosity Shop*, 781; *Pictures from Italy*, 540
Disraeli, Benjamin: *Vivian Grey*, 151; *The Young Duke*, 290
Dixon's Ferry, IL, 34
Dodona, oracle at, 301
Domestic service, 441
Don Pirolone, Il (newspaper), 582
Douglas, William, 519
Douglass, Frederick, 510; *Narrative of the Life of Frederick Douglass, An American Slave*, 429–34
Drachenfels, 223, 658
Drake, Samuel Gardner: *The Book of the Indians of North America*, 166
Driving Cloud, 453–54
Druids, 123
Drummond Castle, 521–22
Dublin Magazine, 95, 120
Dudevant, Casimir, 766
Dudevant, Solange, 766–67
Dumas, Alexandre (*père*), 430, 533, 767
Dutch immigrants, 62, 174, 422
Duyckinck, Evert A.: letter to, 758–60
Dyer, Edward: "My mind to me a Kingdom is," 486

Eastern Orthodox Church, 472
Eckermann, Johann Peter: *Conversations with Goethe*, 341–51

GENERAL INDEX

899

Edgeworth, Maria, 273; "Angelina," 238; *Castle Rackrent*, 752
Edinburgh, Scotland, 518–19, 763
Education for women, 248–49, 258, 300, 439, 442
Egypt, 653, 664, 705, 781; ancient, 217, 244–45, 479, 545, 749, 760
Elektra, 252
Eleonora d'Este, 252
Elizabeth, Queen, 215, 227–28, 521
Elizabeth, R.M.S., 801
Emerson, Edith, 671, 682, 749
Emerson, Ellen Tucker, 671
Emerson, Lidian Jackson, 670, 676–77, 680–81, 683–85, 729, 738, 741; letter to, 729–30
Emerson, Ralph Waldo, 495–96, 499, 668, 670–72, 674–85, 727, 735, 738, 760; *Essays: First Series*, 397, 399, 401, 403, 763–64; *Essays: Second Series*, 397–403, 763–64; *Human Culture* lectures, 728–29; letters to, 727–29, 736–38, 740–41, 748–49, 761–66, 784–85; *Nature*, 397; "The Over-Soul," 395; "The Poet," 403; "Saadi," 684
Emerson, Ruth Haskins, 676, 680–81, 683, 685
Emerson, Waldo, 670–71, 677, 683–84, 689, 729–30, 788
Emma, Queen, 297
Emmet, Robert, 436
England, 19, 26, 30–31, 33–34, 49, 81, 132, 134, 147, 151, 162, 215, 225, 227–29, 258, 279, 286, 297, 343–44, 394, 397, 435–36, 447, 469, 472, 474, 491–92, 495, 504, 509–11, 516–19, 521, 528–30, 533, 536, 542–43, 547, 552, 554, 560, 573, 587–88, 604, 614, 621, 723, 759–66, 797
English immigrants, 81, 88
Epicureanism, 661
Equality, 200, 221, 232, 238, 268, 275, 297, 302

Eschenmayer, Adam Karl August: *Mysterien des innern Lebens*, 113
Essays on Literature and Art (Fuller), 758–60
Esther, 369–70
Etruria, ancient, 218
Euripides, 322; *The Heracleidae*, 331–33; *Iphigenia in Aulis*, 224, 324–31, 546; *Iphigenia in Tauris*, 252; *The Suppliants*, 327; *The Trojan Women*, 256–57, 333–35
Eurydice, 199
Eustache (saint), 710
Eve, 214, 221, 230, 240, 283, 291, 487, 661, 668
Everett, Edward, 137, 141–42, 505
Exodus (biblical book), 200, 236, 300, 363–64, 479

Factory work, 441, 516
Falkland, Viscount (Lucius Bentinck Cary), 510
Farm Schools, 420, 422–24, 478
Farrar, Eliza Ware, 657
Feminine principle, 262–63, 301, 303
Fénelon, François, 257
Ferdinand II, King of Naples, 562, 567–68, 582
Ferrara, Italy, 562, 564
Fichte, Johann Gottlieb, 394
Fielding, Henry, 622; *Amelia*, 622
Fitzgerald, Edward, 134, 166, 302, 436–37
Florence, Italy, 41, 560, 563, 581, 583, 602, 713, 769, 789, 791–801
Flying Pigeon (Ratchewaine), 134, 166–67, 241–42
Follen, Charles (Karl) Theodor, 724
Forbes, Edith Emerson. *See* Emerson, Edith
Ford, John, 228; *The Broken Heart*, 229
Foster, George G., 457–58
Foster, Sarah, 281

GENERAL INDEX

Fourier, Charles, 96, 149, 186, 268–69, 273, 303, 413, 521, 540, 668
Fox, 137, 141, 745–46
Fox, Eliza Bridell, 761–62
Fox, William Johnson, 761
Fox River, 30
France, 91–92, 136, 147, 156, 162, 174, 213–14, 220, 225, 255, 286, 295, 343, 404–14, 428, 430, 456, 469–70, 501, 504, 528–41, 554, 567, 573–75, 587, 589–601, 603–4, 614, 621, 686, 711–13, 762–70, 784–85, 800
Francis V, Duke of Modena, 562
Francis of Assisi, 11
François, Ferdinand, 767
Franzini, Antonio, 570
Frederick William IV, King of Prussia, 565
French immigrants, 62, 128
French Revolution, 199, 409, 579, 686
Friendship, 232–33, 238, 441
Frigga, 312
Fuller, Arthur Buckminster (brother), 696
Fuller, Ellen (sister). *See* Channing, Ellen Fuller
Fuller, Elisha (uncle), 717
Fuller, Eugene (brother), 717; letters to, 751–53
Fuller, Hiram (no relation), 730
Fuller, Margarett Crane (mother), 18–20, 612, 615, 620, 634–36, 682, 696, 717, 736, 745–46, 751–52, 772, 795–96, 799; letter to, 787–91
Fuller, Richard Frederick (brother), 672, 752; letters to, 745–46, 769
Fuller, Timothy (father), 18–21, 209–10, 612, 614, 616, 621–23, 632–34, 636; letters to, 717–18

Gaeta, Italy, 590, 709
Gagnier, Registre, 483

Galen, 112
Galetti, Giuseppe, 577
Galignani's Messenger, 546
Ganymede, 41–44, 699
Gardiner, William: *The Music of Nature*, 729
Garibaldi, Anita, 595
Garibaldi, Giuseppe, 569, 574, 584, 594–95, 711, 780
Garrison, William Lloyd, 431, 503
Gautier, Théophile: *Fortunio*, 74
General Scott (steamboat), 173
Genesis (biblical book), 300, 432
Geneva, IL, 30
Geneva, Switzerland, 292
Genoa, Italy, 541–42, 589, 713
Georgia, 171
German immigrants, 62, 123
Germany, 95, 101–3, 119, 122–23, 152, 203, 222–24, 238, 286, 341–43, 346–47, 350, 352, 394–95, 451–53, 470, 472, 489, 502, 504, 536, 573, 604, 657–59, 721, 723, 770, 785
Gibson, John, 517
Gillies, Margaret, 761
Gilman, Chandler Robinson: *Life on the Lakes*, 152
Gioberti, Vincenzo, 569–70, 582–83, 587, 771
Giusti, Giuseppe, 799
Glasgow, Scotland, 521
Godey's Lady's Book, 259
Godiva, Lady, 297
Godwin, William, 237, 486; *St. Leon*, 234, 487
Goethe, Christine Vulpius, 270, 723–24
Goethe, Johann Wolfgang von, 149, 259, 450, 661–62, 721–24, 758, 764, 791; *Aus meinem Leben*, 98, 777; *Aus meinem Leben: Dichtung und Wahrheit*, 675; and Eckermann's *Conversations with Goethe*, 341–51; *Zur Farbenlehre*, 350; *Faust*, Part I,

GENERAL INDEX 901

270, 343–44; *Faust*, Part 2, 254, 343–44, 391; *Götz von Berlichingen*, 239, 283; *Iphigenia auf Tauris*, 270, 331, 344; *Die Leiden des jungen Werthers*, 391; letters of Bettina Brentano to, 387–92, 394; *Sprüche in Reinem*, 220; *Torquato Tasso*, 288; *Die Wahlverwandtschaften*, 344; *Wilhelm Meisters Lehrjahre*, 226, 270–71, 343–44, 686; *Wilhelm Meisters Wanderjahre*, 115, 269–71, 343–44

Goethe, Wieland, 270, 724

Going Cloud (Key-way-no-wut), 145–46

Goldsmith, Oliver: "The Deserted Village," 718; *The Vicar of Wakefield*, 360

Gonzaga, Anselmo Guerrieri, 770

Gore, Catherine, 50

Gothic, 36

Goths, 557

Graces, 302, 393, 539

Grant, Anne MacVicar: *Memoirs of an American Lady*, 130–32, 148, 322

Gräter, Friedrich David: *Honig's Owl-Tower*, 635

"Great Lawsuit, The" (Fuller), 191

Great Western (steamboat), 62, 184

Greece, 207, 295, 303, 588; ancient, 27, 41, 50, 85, 116, 138, 149, 152, 156, 169; 198, 217–18, 220–21, 224, 228, 233–34, 252, 255–57, 272, 302, 322–35, 344, 346, 366, 382, 384, 393, 400, 446, 461–63, 531, 546, 570, 610, 617–19, 639, 641–42, 683, 734, 748–49, 755, 758

Greek language, 619, 720, 747

Greeley, Horace, 565, 572, 750–52, 788

Greeley, Mary, 755

Greeley, Pickie, 788

Greene, William Batchelder, 686

Greenwood, John, Sr., 11

Grey, Charles, 521

Grey, Jane, 249

Griggsville, IL, 58

Grimes, J. Stanley: *Etherology*, 415–20

Grimké, Angelina, 260–61

Griscom, John Hoskins, 426

Groton, MA, 723, 745

Guercino (Giovanni Barbieri), 255; *Aurora*, 545

Guerrazzi, Francesco Domenico, 579, 712

Guess, George (Sequoyah), 166–67

Guizot, François, 533, 574

Günderode, Karoline von, 392–95

Guyon, Jeanne-Marie de la Motte, 257

Hagar, 300

"Hail, Columbia!", 45

Halifax, Nova Scotia, 510

Hall, Baynard Rush: *The New Purchase*, 180–81, 497

Hall, James: *History of the Indian Tribes of North America*, 134, 166, 171, 183

Halleck, Fitz-Greene, 498

Hartmann, Moritz, 472–74

Harvard University, 176, 612, 745

Hastings, Warren, 66

Hauffe, Frederike, 95–123, 166, 257, 263

Hawthorne, Nathaniel, 508, 673, 678, 742; "The Artist of the Beautiful," 477; "The Birth-mark," 476; "The Celestial Rail-road," 477; "Fire-Worship," 477; *Mosses from an Old Manse*, 475–78; "Mrs. Bullfrog," 477; "Rappaccini's Daughter," 476; "Roger Malvin's Burial," 477; *Twice-Told Tales*, 740; "Young Goodman Brown," 477

GENERAL INDEX

Hawthorne, Sophia Peabody, 673; letter to, 741–43
Hawthorne, Una, 749
Haydn, Joseph: *The Creation*, 336
Hazelwood estate, 35–38
Hecate, 149, 705, 755
Hector, 325
Hecuba, 256–57, 333–34
Hedge, Frederic Henry, 666, 681–82, 695
Hegel, G. W. F., 486, 682
Heidelberg, Germany, 657–58
Heine, Heinrich, 221
"Helen of Kirkconnel" (ballad), 75–77
Helen of Troy, 324, 326, 329
Héloïse, 215, 237, 391
Helvetius, Claude-Adrien, 719
Hemans, Felicia Dorothea, 683
Hennepin, Louis, 13–14
Henry, Alexander, 128, 156, 159, 162–66, 170, 175–76
Henry, Caleb Sprague, 722
Henry IV, King of England, 466
Herbert, George, 270; "Employment," 374; "An Ode upon a Question Moved, Whether Love Should Continue Forever," 229–31
Hercules (Herakles), 161, 194, 212, 219, 263, 272, 332
Herschel, William, 725
Hindus, 217, 242
Hinshaw, Mr., 745–46
Hoar, Elizabeth Sherman, 670, 672, 677–79, 685, 729; letters to, 749–50, 766–67
Hodgson, William Ballantyne, 512
Hoffmann, E. T. A., 15
Holy Land, 297, 710
Holyrood Palace, 520
Homer, 17; *Iliad*, 162, 325, 335, 348; *Odyssey*, 198
Hooker, Mr. (banker), 580

Horace, 563, 618
Howitt, Anna Mary, 761
Howitt, William and Mary Botham, 238, 761
Hugo, Victor, 422
Hull, William, 185
Hungary, 203, 601–2, 604
Huskisson, William, 517
Hutchinson, Anne, 298
Hutchinson, John, 229

Iduna, 291
Illinois, 78–79, 81, 180–81
Illinois (steamboat), 62
Illinois prairies, 28–51, 56–59, 61–62, 80
Illinois River, 58
Immigrants, 17, 25, 31, 62, 79, 81, 85, 88, 94–95, 123, 128, 470–71
India, 217, 221, 242
Indiana, 180–81
Inversnaid, Scotland, 523
Iolaus, 332, 335
Iphigenia, 220, 224, 323–33, 335, 344, 546
Ireland, 24, 35, 39, 295, 297, 434–37, 513, 516, 707
Irish immigrants, 62, 436
Irish Potato Famine, 472–74
Irving, Washington, 496, 508; *Astoria*, 27; *A Tour on the Prairies*, 27
Isabella of Castile, Queen, 227–28, 258
Isaiah (biblical book), 196, 431
Ishmael, 250, 300
Isis, 217, 220, 307–8, 545, 705
Israelites, ancient, 172, 196, 200, 214, 236, 300, 332, 362–64, 369–70, 382, 479, 537, 640–42
Italy, 14, 41, 61, 104, 114, 176, 230–31, 242, 343, 350, 469, 471, 517, 534, 541–48, 552, 554–605, 617, 709–13, 723, 753, 761, 766–801

GENERAL INDEX   903

Jackson, Andrew, 483
Jackson, Charles and Susan, 682
Jackson, Marianne, 682
Jamaica Plain, MA, 351, 730, 734
James (biblical book), 262
Jameson, Anna Brownell, 261; *Loves of the Poets*, 274; *Shakespeare's Heroines*, 274; *Winter Studies and Summer Rambles in Canada*, 27, 147–48, 178, 253, 341, 349, 392
Jeffrey, Francis, 350
Jeptha, 332–33
Jeremiah, 362–63
Jesuits, 404, 563, 566, 583–84, 599, 771
Jesus, 106, 137, 142, 200–201, 222, 297, 362, 467, 470, 482, 537, 551–52, 559, 562, 578, 595, 617, 640–43, 645, 683, 698, 710, 739, 761, 773, 777, 781
Jews, 153, 155, 172, 196, 200, 203, 211, 272, 290, 297, 640
Joan of Arc, 213–14
John (biblical book), 196, 482, 640, 643
Johnson, Samuel, 201, 342, 723
Johnson, William, 147–48
Jonson, Ben: "On Lucy, Countess of Bedford," 189, 211
Jordan, Dorothea, 510
Joseph (husband of Mary), 773, 781
Joseph (son of Jacob), 364
Judd, Sylvester: *Margaret*, 503–4
Judges (biblical book), 332
Judkins, Charles H. E., 510
Julian the Apostate, 147
Juno (Hera), 265, 278, 558, 758
Jupiter (Zeus), 41–44, 219, 264–65, 388, 517, 617, 734
Justina (saint), 648

Kant, Immanuel, 394
Karl I, Prince of Württemberg, 472
Kean, Charles and Edmund, 501

Kelley, Abby, 260
Kenrick, William: *The Whole Duty of a Woman*, 292
Kentucky, 471
Keokuk, 137, 141
Kerner, Andreas Justinus: *Die Seherin von Prevorst*, 95–123, 166, 257, 263
Key-way-no-wut (Going Cloud), 145–46
Kilshaw, Ellen, 627–29, 631–32, 717–18
King, Jane Tuckerman: letter to, 770–71
King Philip's War, 139
Kinmont, Alexander, 50, 261, 430
Kirkland, Caroline, 497
Kishwaukee, IL, 50–51
Kollac the Bohemian, 546
Konic, 700, 748
Körner, Karl Theodor, 306, 687, 721
Kossuth, Lajos, 602
Kuhn, Caroline, 717
Kürnbach, Germany, 103

Labanov-Rostovsky, Alexandre, 519
Lafayette, Marie-Joseph du Motier de, 140; letter to, 719
Lake Erie, 17, 746
Lake Huron, 23, 159, 746
Lake Michigan, 28–29, 54, 62, 83, 123–24, 159, 746
Lake Pontchartrain, 371–77
Lake Superior, 28, 135, 152, 176, 180, 746
Lamb, Charles, 428, 729
La Mennais, Felicité-Robert de, 536–37, 767; *Paroles d'un Croyant*, 537
Landor, William Savage, 201, 304, 763
La Roche, Sophie von, 392
La Rochefoucauld, François de, 255
Latimer, George Washington, 689

904 GENERAL INDEX

Latin language, 616–17
Latins, 491–92
Laura de Noves, 540, 765
Lee, Anne, 253
Lee, Hannah Farnham Sawyer, 442
Leonardo da Vinci, 761
Leonidas, 610
Leopold II, Grand Duke of
Tuscany, 569, 587
Lesage, Alain-René: *L'Histoire de
Gil Blas*, 367
Lespinasse, Julie-Jeanne-Éléonore
de, 391
Le Verrier, Urbain, 534
Lewes, George Henry: *The
Biographical History of
Philosophy*, 764
Linnaeus, Carl, 264
Liverpool, England, 509–11, 516–18,
521, 763
Livorno (Leghorn), Italy, 542–43
Loch Lomond, 522–26
Locke, John, 399
Lockhart, John: *Ancient Spanish
Ballads*, 312
Loki, 291
Lombardy, 563, 567, 569–70, 584,
594, 604–5, 770, 784
London, England, 21, 83, 274,
426, 441, 483, 519, 521, 528–30,
760–63, 799
London *Times*, 604
Longfellow, Henry Wadsworth,
499; *Ballads and Other Poems*,
740; "The Day Is Done," 454;
"Excelsior," 454; "A Gleam of
Sunshine," 451; "Hymn to the
Night," 449; "Lines to the
Planet Mars," 451; "Nuremberg,"
451–53; *Poems*, 445–54; "The
Reaper and the Flowers," 451;
The Spanish Student, 454; "To
the Driving Cloud," 453–54;
"The Village Blacksmith," 451;
"Voices of the Night," 449

Long Grove, IL, 57
Lorelei, 152
Louis XIV, King of France, 206
Louisiana, 371, 479
Louis Philippe, King of France,
469–70, 534, 574–75, 711
Love, 276, 280, 283, 285, 293, 301,
304–5, 441
Lovelace, Richard: "To Lucasta,
Going to the Warres," 229
Lowell, James Russell, 499; "A
Chippewa Legend," 88–89, 91
Löwenstein, Germany, 101–2, 107
Lowrey, George, 482
Loyola, Ignatius of, 583
Luke (biblical book), 145, 200, 251,
457, 599
Luther, Martin, 640
Lyncaeus, 403
Lyons, France, 539–40

Macaria, 115, 220, 228, 271–73,
331–33, 335, 344, 546
Mackay, Charles: "There's a Good
Time Coming," 517
Mackenzie, Alexander, 293; *Voyages
from Montreal through the
Continent of North America*,
133, 170
Mackinac Island, 4, 18, 124–34,
147, 152, 159, 161–65, 173, 175,
178–79, 181–82, 184
Macpherson, James (Ossian),
526–27
Madeira, 629–30
Madison, Dolley Todd, 484
Madoc, 31
Maistre, Joseph de: *Soirées de Saint-
Petersbourg*, 254
Mamiani, Terenzio, 566, 582, 771
Manara, Luciano, 594
Manchester, England, 511, 516, 518,
540, 763
Mandan, 170
Manin, Daniele, 570, 602

GENERAL INDEX

Manitou Island, 23–25
Mantegazza, Laura Solera, 711
Mantua, Italy, 567
Manzoni, Alessandro, 305, 559;
  Adelchi, 239; "Il Conte di
  Carmagnola," 201
Manzoni, Enrichetta, 239
Marcus Aurelius, 711
Maria Theresa, Empress of Austria,
  228
Marina (enslaved Aztec woman),
  228
Marina (fictional character), 63–75,
  77–78
Marital rights, 204–5
Marriage, 202–5, 231–39, 241, 248,
  250, 253, 255, 257, 265, 268, 275,
  279, 283, 287–89, 293–94, 304,
  439–41, 675, 677–78, 680–81,
  683
Mariage de convenance, 279–80
Mars (Ares), 265
"Marseillaise" (song), 561, 584
Marseilles, France, 541
Marston, John Westland: *The
  Patrician's Daughter*, 530
Martha, 251
Martineau, Harriet, 261, 296, 683
Mary, Queen of Scots, 227, 408,
  519–21
Mary, Virgin, 214, 221–23, 230,
  242, 252, 254, 290, 297, 305,
  308–12, 321, 503, 545, 695, 698,
  773, 781
Mary Magdalen, 344
Mary of Guise, 519
Masculinity, 263, 303
Massachusetts, 442, 502, 612
Massachusett tribe, 141
Massasoit, 139
Massinger, Philip, 228, 331
Mathews, Cornelius: "Man in the
  Republic," 500–501, 506–7;
  *Witchcraft, or the Martyrs of
  Salem*, 501–3

Matthew (biblical book), 194–95,
  226, 431, 482, 638
Max (fictional character), 687
Mazzarelli, Carlo Emanuele, 588
Mazzini, Giuseppe, 546–48, 570,
  583, 589, 591, 597, 602, 712, 761,
  765–66, 781–82, 785–86, 799;
  letter to, 776–77
McDonald, James Lawrence, 484
McElrath, Thomas, 565, 572
McKenney, Thomas L., 510; *History
  of the Indian Tribes of North
  America*, 135, 166, 171, 183;
  Memoirs: Official and Personal,
  478–85; *Sketches of a Tour to the
  Lakes*, 27, 145
Mechanics' Institutes, 511–12
Medea, 25
Medes, 200
Medici family, 519
Mediterranean Sea, 541
Mendelssohn, Felix, 37
Menelaus, 324, 326
Mercury (Hermes), 8, 265, 656, 706,
  734
Metacom (Philip), 139, 147, 170,
  484
Methodists, 66
Metternich, Klemens von, 470
Mexican-American War, 479,
  487–88, 553–54, 580
Mexico, 228, 495
Meyer, Heinrich, 342
Michelangelo Buonarroti, 277, 365,
  610, 640–41, 645; *Persian Sibyl*,
  252–53; Sistine Chapel frescoes,
  768
Michelet, Jules, 535
Michigan, 144, 184–86
Mickiewicz, Adam, 535, 546, 768
Middle Ages, 572
Milan, Italy, 559, 567, 569–71, 575,
  596, 600, 770, 775
Milnes, Richard Monckton:
  "Shadows," 280

906   GENERAL INDEX

Milton, John, 279, 346; "L'Allegro" and "Il Penseroso," 173; *Comus*, 276; *Paradise Lost*, 240, 276, 283, 668
Milwaukee, WI, 83–85, 92, 95, 122–24, 745
Mina-va-va-na, 165
Minerva (Athena), 217, 262–65, 333
Minto, Earl of (Gilbert Elliot-Murray-Kynynmound), 564
Miranda (fictional character), 209–10, 213
Miriam, 363–64
Missionaries, 137, 142–44, 161, 171
Mississippi River, 34, 142, 479
Missolonghi, Greece, 303
Missouri River, 142
Modena, Italy, 562
Mohawk, 130–32, 134
Mohawk River, 147, 159
Molière (Jean-Baptiste Poquelin), 625; *Les Précieuses Ridicules*, 536; *Tartuffe*, 710
Montagu, Mary Wortley, 248
Montague, Mary, 131
Montanelli, Giuseppe, 579, 583, 587, 712
Montezuma, 169
Montpensier, Duc de (Antoine-Louis d'Orléans), 533
Moore, John: *Zeluco*, 718
Moore, Thomas: "The Harp That Once Through Tara's Hall," 435–36
Mormons, 471, 479, 696
Moses, 200, 214, 236, 300, 364, 595, 639–40, 642
Motherhood, 216–17, 219, 232, 249–50, 263, 285, 303
Mount Vesuvius, 542
Muckwa (fictional character), 149–51
Müller, Friedrich von, 724
Murdoch, James Edward, 501
Murray, Charles Augustus: *Travels in North America*, 26, 156, 166, 170

Muscogee (Creek), 153–54
Muses, 44, 137, 262–63, 265, 267, 393–95, 769
Muslims, 223
Musset, Alfred de: *Rolla*, 501

Nanabozho, 152
Naples, Italy, 174, 542–43, 562–63, 567–68, 575, 579, 582, 584, 590–91, 603, 769, 780
Napoléon Bonaparte, 23, 405, 584, 598, 610
Nappier, 484
Nathan, James: letters to, 753–58
Native Americans, 6, 8, 17, 25–28, 34, 36, 38, 40–41, 49, 51, 86–94, 123–26, 128–72, 174–76, 178–84, 206, 219, 228, 231, 241–42, 253, 266, 293, 302, 322, 437, 453–54, 478–85, 510, 618, 745–46
Nauvoo, IL, 696
Necker de Saussure, Albertine, 286–87, 294; *The Study of the Life of Woman*, 292
Nelson, Horatio, 488
Neptune (Poseidon), 265
Nero, 575
Nestor, 278, 563
Netherlands, 28, 174
Neukomm, Sigismund von: *David*, 538
New Bedford, MA, 679, 741
Newcomb, Charles King, 760; letter to, 772–73
Newell, William, 682
New Orleans, LA, 430, 752–53
New Spain, 228
Newton, Francis Milner, 361
Newton, Isaac, 263, 416
New York, 426, 750
New York City, 48–49, 203, 274, 298, 420–27, 441, 444, 489, 509, 529, 539, 751–52, 801
New York City House of Detention (The Tombs), 425–26

GENERAL INDEX

New York City Lunatic Asylum, 420, 424, 426
New York Herald, 510
New York Pathfinder, 262
New York Tribune, 340, 434, 509, 751–53, 761, 763
Niagara Falls, 7–14, 159, 746
Nicholas I, Czar, 471–72, 549, 574
Noah, 106, 646
Nohant, France, 767
Nomabbin Lake, 86, 92, 159
Norman, Amelia, 285–86
Norns, 365
Norse mythology, 291, 294, 312, 365
North American Review, 359, 505, 725
Norway, 297
Norwegian immigrants, 31, 123
Novalis (Georg Philipp Friedrich von Hardenberg), 721–22
Novara, Italy, 589, 711–13
Nova Scotia, 510
Nuremberg, Germany, 451–53

Obscurantists, 563
O'Connell, Daniel, 297, 437, 516
Odin, 312
Oedipus, 749
Off, Dr., 107
Ojibwe (Chippewa), 88, 125, 144, 147, 152, 165, 178
"Old maids," 250–52
Old Scrany, 153–54
Olga Nikolaevna, 471–72
Omaha, 453
Oregon, IL, 38–41, 46, 51
Oregon Territory, 515
Orestes, 324, 327–28
Orioli, Francesco, 771
Orpheus, 197–99, 326
Osceola, 169, 483
Osiris, 545, 639
Ossian (James Macpherson), 526–27
Ossoli, Angelo Eugene Philip, 775–76, 779–81, 783, 787, 789–92, 795–96, 798–99

Ossoli, Giovanni Angelo, 786, 789–93, 795–96, 798–800; letters to, 774–76, 782–83
Ottawa, 125
Oudinot, Charles-Nicolas, 594, 596, 598
Ovid: *Metamorphoses*, 161, 194, 219, 619

Padua, Italy, 567
Paetus, Arria and Aulus Caecina, 66
Paine, Thomas: *Common Sense*, 553
Palestine, 297
Palmer, Samuel, 88
Pan, 358, 461–63
Panthea, 224, 242–46
Papponi, 104
Paraguay, 133, 293
Paris, 326, 528–41
Paris, France, 274, 405, 414, 426, 441, 567, 575, 588, 625, 762, 766–68, 775
Parker, Theodore, 641, 739
Parthenon, 169
"Patient serpent, circle round" (Fuller), 705, 748
Paul (apostle), 515
Pawnee, 26
Peabody, Elizabeth Palmer, 740
Peel, Robert, 474, 515–16
Penelope, 213
Penitentiary and Penitentiary Hospital, 424–26
Pennet, 104
Pentonville Prison, 528
People's Journal, 544
Peoria, IL, 61
Pepe, Guglielmo, 568
Pericles, 156, 215, 304, 747
Perkins, William, 720
Persia, ancient, 224, 242–48, 280
Perth, Scotland, 519
Petalesharro, 168–69
Peter (apostle), 388, 552, 565, 577–78, 617

908 GENERAL INDEX

Petrarch, Francesco, 540, 765; "Praise and Prayer to Maria," 222, 308–12
Phidian, 140
Philadelphia, PA, 501, 534
Philip (Metacom), 139, 147, 170, 484
Phillips, Wendell, 431
Phocion, 26, 156, 204
Piedmont, 562, 605, 713
Pindar, 399, 448
Pine Lake, 86, 92
Pinelli, Bartolomeo, 564
Piranesi, Giovanni Battista: *Visions of Antiquity*, 348
Pius IX, Pope, 547, 552, 558–61, 563, 565–68, 576–79, 583, 587–90, 595, 600, 603, 709–13, 775, 784, 789
Plato, 639, 642, 645; *Republic*, 254; *Symposium*, 254; *Timaeus*, 254
Plotinus, 11
Plutarch, 346
Pluto (Hades), 393
Pocahontas, 483–84
Poe, Edgar Allan, 794; "The Murders in the Rue Morgue," 438; *Tales*, 437–38
Poland, 213, 469, 552, 554, 588, 610, 785
Polk, James K., 472
Polygamy, 231, 279
Pompadour, Marquise de (Jeanne-Antoinette Poisson), 225
Pompeii, 544
Pontiac, 147, 170, 484
Pope, Alexander: *Moral Essays*, 785
Porter, Andrew, 10
Potalesbarro, 483
Potawatomi, 91
Poussin, Nicolas, 52
Powers, Hiram: *Eve*, 799; *John C. Calhoun*, 801
Prairie du Chien, WI, 163
Presbury, Benjamin Franklin: "Napoleon," 740
Presbyterians, 136

Prescott, Susan: letter to, 719–20
Prescott, William Hickling, 228, 495
Presse, La, 767
Princeton, MA, 612
Proclus, 264
Prometheus, 196, 407
Property rights, 203–4, 302
Proserpina (Persephone), 198, 217, 393
Prostitutes, 285, 540
Protestants, 557–58
Proverbs (biblical book), 16
Providence, RI, 725–27, 741
Prussia, 470, 565
Pückler-Muskau, Hermann Ludwig Heinrich, 9
Puritans, 361, 492, 555
Pythagoras, 99, 465

Quakers, 207, 238, 268
Québec, Canada, 162
Quincy, Mary Jane Miller, 734

Rachel (Elisabeth Félix), 255, 530–32, 762
Racine, Jean: *Phèdre*, 531
Radcliffe, Ann, 102
Ramayana, 217
Randall, Elizabeth Wells, 666, 723
Raphael (Raffaello Sanzio), 84, 503, 536, 635, 645, 729, 734, 760, 785; *The Descent from the Cross*, 698
Ratchewaine (Flying Pigeon), 134, 166–67, 241–42
Récamier, Juliette, 686–88
Red Bird, 483
Red Jacket, 167, 170
Red River, 476
Red Shoes, 156, 170
Rémusat, Charles-François, 536
Reni, Guido: *Archangel Michael Defeating Satan*, 325; *Beatrice Cenci*, 335
Revolutionary War, 470–71, 610

GENERAL INDEX

909

Revolution of 1830 (France), 456
Revolution of 1848 (Italy), 555–605, 709–13, 769–70, 775–77, 780–81, 784–85, 787–90, 797, 800
Rhea, 264
Rhesus, 38
Rhine River, 152, 223–24
Rhode Island, 203
Rhône River, 539
Richardson, Samuel, 456; *Clarissa*, 532; *Sir Charles Grandison*, 286–87
Richter, Jean Paul Friedrich, 212
Rienzo, Cola di (Nicola Gabrini), 586, 594
Rieti, Italy, 774–76, 778–83, 787
Rio Grande, 487
Ripley, George, 727, 738–39
Ripley, Sarah Alden Bradford, 673
Ripley, Sophia Dana: letter to, 730–33
Risorgimento. See Revolution of 1848 (Italy)
Rizzio, David, 520
Rock River, 34, 38, 40–41, 46, 86, 745
Rocky Mountains, 142
Roland, Marie-Jeanne, 199, 233
Roland de La Platière, Jean-Marie, 233
Romagna, 591
Rome, ancient, 36, 66, 91–92, 98, 159, 168, 171, 175, 200, 215, 218–19, 347, 382, 474, 517, 541, 544–45, 557–58, 563, 575, 610, 616–19, 624, 626, 707, 710–12
Rome, Italy, 41, 61, 197, 537, 542, 544, 555–605, 652, 709–13, 716, 762, 767–71, 773, 776–91, 798, 800
Ronge, Johannes, 471
Roscoe, William, 517
Rosicrucianism, 217
Ross, John (Guwisguwi), 169, 485
Ross, Mrs.: *Hesitation*, 718

Ross Grove, IL, 32
Rossi, Isabella, 545
Rossi, Pellegrino, 574, 576, 585, 589
Rossini, Gioachino: *Semiramide*, 753
Rotch, Mary, 741
Rousseau, Jean-Jacques, 411
Rowardennan, Scotland, 523–27
Royal Institute (Liverpool), 517
Royer-Collard, Pierre-Paul, 536
Ruffini, Jacopo, 761
Rumelia, 435
Rush, Richard, 591
Russell, Mary Howland, 670
Russell, Rachel, 279, 282–83, 298
Russia, 215, 254, 470–72, 552, 574, 604

Sac, 137, 141, 159, 745–46
Saffi, Aurelio, 597
St. Clair River, 17
Saint-Martin, Louis-Claude de: *Le Ministère de l'Homme-Esprit*, 197
St. Petersburg, Russia, 254
Saint-Simon, Comte (Claude-Henri de Rouvroy), 254
Saladin, 668
Sallust, 573
Samson, 138
Samuel (biblical book), 382
Sand, George (Amantine-Lucile-Aurore Dupin), 234–36, 286, 404, 406, 408–12, 414, 580, 762, 766–67; *André*, 411; *La Comtesse de Rudolstadt*, 412, 699; *Consuelo*, 412; *Indiana*, 235; *Jacques*, 411; *Leone Leoni*, 411; *Les Maîtres Mosaïstes*, 411; *Mauprat*, 236, 411; *Les Septs Cordes de la Lyre*, 411; *Simon*, 235, 411; *Spiridion*, 411
Sand, Maurice, 767
Sappho, 215, 391
Saragossa, Spain, 303
Sardinia, 562, 569, 713
Saul, 364

GENERAL INDEX

Sault Ste. Marie, Canada, 162–63, 173–75, 179
Saunders, Elizabeth Elkin, 484
Savannah, GA, 137
Schelling, Friedrich, 394
Schiller, Friedrich von, 342, 344, 346; "Dignity of Woman," 203, 212; *Die Jungfrau von Orleans*, 195; "Die Künstler," 189; "Das Lied von der Glocke," 690; *Maria Stuart*, 408–9; "Die Worte des Glaubens," 226
Schlegel, August von, 349
Schlegel, Friedrich von, 349
Schmidgall, Johann, 101
Schneider, 687
Schönemann, Anna Elisabeth, 661–62
Schoolcraft, Henry Rowe, 130; *Algic Researches*, 26–27
Schoolcraft, Jane Johnston, 130, 132, 134, 148
Scotland, 44, 131, 227, 258, 518–28, 763–64
Scott, David, 761, 763
Scott, Walter, 129, 422, 594; *The Abbot*, 391; *The Fair Maid of Perth*, 521; *Guy Mannering*, 629; *Ivanhoe*, 368; *Kenilworth*, 371; "The Lady of the Lake," 522; *Rob Roy*, 522–23
Scribe, Augustin-Eugène: *Geneviève*, 532; *La Protégée sans le Savoir*, 532
Scrope, William: *The Art of Deerstalking*, 181
Scythians, 138
Sedgwick, Catharine Maria, 295–96, 497; *Hope Leslie*, 137
Semiramis, 215
Sequoyah (George Guess), 166–67
Seraglios, 231, 279–80
Shakespeare, William, 11, 346, 348–49, 387, 416, 492, 503,

622–26, 643, 645, 683, 764; *As You Like It*, 228, 435; *Coriolanus*, 624; *Cymbeline*, 8, 218, 228; *Hamlet*, 193, 229–30, 349, 391, 624; *Henry IV*, Part 2, 13; *Julius Caesar*, 218–19, 482, 624; *King Lear*, 228–29, 407; *Macbeth*, 24, 468; *Measure for Measure*, 228; *enice*, 228, 365; *A Midsummer Night's Dream*, 393; *Othello*, 218, 228–30; *Romeo and Juliet*, 622; *The Taming of the Shrew*, 367; "Venus and Adonis," 84
Shaw, Francis George, 748
Shawano, 153–55
Shelley, Mary: *Frankenstein*, 493
Shelley, Percy Bysshe, 262, 759; "Alastor," 457; *Epipsychidion*, 464–65; "Hymn of Apollo," 461–62; "Hymn of Pan," 461–63; "Hymn to Intellectual Beauty," 456, 458–60; "Julian and Maddalo," 457; "Lines to a Critic," 460; "Lines Written among the Euganean Hills," 363; "The Past," 461; *Poetical Works*, 454–65; "Prometheus," 457; *Queen Mab*, 455, 457; "Stanzas," 463; "Stanzas Written in Dejection, near Naples," 74; "The Sunset," 559; "To Constantia Singing," 366; "To Edward Williams," 463–64
Siberia, 604
Sicily, 562, 584, 603
Sidney, Philip, 279
Silvani, Antonio, 565
Silver Lake, 86, 91–92
Simms, William Gilmore, 497
Sing Sing Prison, 425, 749
Sirens, 198
Sismondi, Jean-Charles-Léonard de, 711
"Sistrum" (Fuller), 748
Sita, 217

GENERAL INDEX

Slavery, 200, 202–5, 208, 226, 262, 266, 297–98, 429–34, 471, 478–79, 510, 553–54, 588, 689
Smith, Emma, 696
Smith, John, 484
Smith, Joseph, 479, 696
Smith, Miss, 722
Smith, Seba: *The Life and Writings of Major Jack Downing*, 10
Smollett, Tobias, 621
Socrates, 97, 247, 641, 687
Somerville, Mary Fairfax, 248
Sonderbund War, 562
Sophocles, 11, 322
Sorbonne (Université de Paris), 534–35
Sorrento, Italy, 542
Soulié, Frédéric, 430
Southcott, Joanna, 253
Southey, Robert: *The Curse of Kehama*, 266; "A Tale of Paraguay," 293
Spain, 63, 123, 169, 174, 222, 225, 227–28, 230, 258, 290, 303, 312–14, 343, 469, 617, 624, 712
Spangenberg, August Gottlieb, 240
Sparta, ancient, 27, 220, 233–34, 610
Spenser, Edmund, 100; *The Faerie Queene*, 117–18, 228, 233–34, 281
Spinoza, Baruch, 232; *Tractatus Theologico-Politicus*, 314–15
Spring, Marcus and Rebecca, 524, 527, 792; letter to, 767–68
Springfield, IL, 58, 82
Spurzheim, Johann Christoph, 139
Staël, Germaine de, 248, 292, 686–88
Stanhope, Louisa Sidney: "The Bandit's Bride," 67–68, 75
Stephens, Anne, 498
Sterling, John, 201
Stilling, Heinrich (Johann Heinrich Jung), 119
Stone, Lucy, 439
Story, Emelyn Eldredge, 783, 790–91; letter to, 792–93

Story, William Wetmore, 783, 791
Stowe, Calvin, 444
Stowe, Harriet Beecher, 444
Sturgis, Caroline. *See* Tappan, Caroline Sturgis
Sturgis, William, 725–27, 729
Stylites, 168
Subiaco, Italy, 771
Sue, Eugène, 314, 320–21, 406, 412–14, 767; *Le Juif Errant*, 286, 404, 412; *Mathilde*, 412; *Les Mystères de Paris*, 163, 412
Suffrage, 225, 297
Suli, Greece, 303
Summer on the Lakes, in 1843 (Fuller), 698
Sumner, Charles, 513
Sumner, Horace, 793
Sweden, 14
Swedenborg, Emanuel, 122, 226, 254, 759; *Apocalypse Revealed*, 267–69
Swedish immigrants, 123
Swiss immigrants, 123
Switzerland, 562
Sylvain (fictional character), 71–75

Tacitus, 563
Tantalus, 556, 755, 758
Tappan, Caroline Sturgis, 679, 681, 699, 773; letters to, 725–27, 747, 760–62, 778–82, 787
Tappan, William Aspinwall, 779, 782
Tartars, 161
Tasso, Torquato, 215, 252, 346, 391, 716; *Gerusalemme Liberata*, 373
Taylor, Henry: *Philip van Artevelde*, 78
Taylor, Thomas, 308
Taylor, Zachary, 580
Tecumseh, 170, 484
Tennyson, Alfred, 679, 699, 744, 764; "A Dream of Fair Women," 333
Teutons, 222

GENERAL INDEX

Texas, 297, 471
Theresa of Ávila, 120, 252
Theseus, 212
Thoreau, Henry David, 676, 681, 749; letter to, 738; "The Service," 738
Thorwaldsen, Bertel, 41
Tieck, Ludwig, 621
Titian (Tiziano Vecelli): *Venus and Adonis*, 84–85
Tivoli, Italy, 771
Tmolus, 462
Tommaseo, Niccolò, 570
Torlonia, Alessandro, 562, 564, 581
"To Sarah" (Fuller), 702, 748
Townshend, Chauncy Hare, 117
Transcendentalism, 727
Treaty of New Echota, 480
Trojan War, 570
Trollope, Frances, 560; *Domestic Manners of the Americans*, 33
Trossachs, 29, 522
True American (newspaper), 471
Tuileries Palace, 534
Turin, Italy, 570
Turks, 279, 303
Tuscany, 562–63, 565, 569, 579, 583, 587, 605, 712–13, 797
"Two Herberts, The" (Fuller), 748
Tyler, John, 482
Tyler, William, 482

Ulysses (Odysseus), 198, 213
Umbria, 779
Unitarians, 25, 30
Urania, 251, 382, 545

Valkyries, 294
Vatican, 8, 552, 557, 559, 565–66, 577–79, 586, 590, 593, 709–13, 800
Venice, Italy, 563, 567, 569–70, 584, 602, 605, 711–12
Venus (Aphrodite), 16, 84–85, 265, 382, 545, 556
Verona, Italy, 567

Vesta, 217–18, 220, 265, 544
Vicenza, Italy, 567
Victoria, Queen, 26, 132, 258, 437, 472, 522
Vienna, Austria, 228, 274, 567, 574–75
Vigny, Alfred de, 405, 414
Vikings, 454
Virgil, 563, 618; *Aeneid*, 609, 615
Visconti, Costanza Arconati, 793; letters to, 771, 786–87, 791–92, 799
Visconti, Giovanni Arconati, 791
Vittorio Emanuele II, King of Sardinia, 712–13
Vulcan (Hephaestus), 265

Wachusett, MA, 612
Walden Pond, 671–72, 678
Wales, 31, 517
Wallenstein, Albrecht Wenzel Eusebius von, 687
Waltham, MA, 683
Ward, Anna Barker, 687, 689
Ward, Anna Hazard Barker, 687–89
Ward, Samuel, 681, 686, 688, 748, 760, 801; "To W. Allston, on Seeing His Bride," 369
War of 1812, 10, 185
Washington, DC, 134, 169–70, 183, 481, 718
Washington, George, 142, 259
Washingtonian Temperance Society, 207
Wa-wa-tam, 156, 162–63, 170
Wayland, Francis, 728
"Wedding of Lady Theresa, The" (ballad), 222, 225, 312–14
Weimar, Germany, 723
Weinsberg, Germany, 107, 113
Welden, Franz Ludwig von, 567
Wesley, John and Charles, 66, 759
West, Benjamin, 41

GENERAL INDEX

913

West, The, 17–18, 24, 85, 123–24,
141–42, 439, 725, 741, 752
Western Messenger, 725
Westmoreland, R.M.S., 799
Whately, Richard: *Elements of
Rhetoric*, 729
Whig Party, 426, 751
White Mountains, 10–11
Wiley, John, 758–59
Wiley & Putnam (publisher), 476,
497
Wilkie, David, 361
William IV, King of England, 510
Willis, Nathaniel P., 498–99
Winckelmann, Johann Joachim, 785
"Winged Sphynx" (Fuller), 748
Winnebago, 126, 132, 152, 176, 483
Wisconsin (steamboat), 185
Wisconsin River, 159
Wisconsin Territory, 83–95, 122–24,
144, 181, 745–46
Witchcraft, 501–3
Wollstonecraft, Mary: *A
Vindication of the Rights of
Woman*, 234, 237
Woman in the Nineteenth Century
(Fuller), 445, 749–52
"Woman's lot," 288
Women: cleanliness of, 296;
degraded, 283–85, 296; education
for, 248–49, 258, 300, 439,
442; Fourier on, 268–69, 273,
303; genius of, 254–55, 262–63;
Goethe on, 269–73; on Illinois
prairie, 47–51; influence of,
206; Italian, 559; marital rights

of, 204–5; Native American,
128–35, 155, 160, 183, 206, 253,
293, 302, 484; "old maids,"
250–52; professions for, 441–44;
property rights of, 203–4, 302;
prostitutes, 285, 540; in public
life, 206–7, 213–16, 227–28,
260; purity of, 275–77, 279,
544; spiritual tendencies of, 254,
256, 259–61; suffrage for, 225,
297; Swedenborg on, 267–69;
as teachers, 442–44; work of,
439–45, 516–17, 529
Women's rights, 305
Woodward, Miss, 722
Wordsworth, William, 96, 266;
"Character of the Happy
Warrior," 31, 286; "Expostulation
and Reply," 39; "The Fountain:
A Conversation," 468;
"Laodamia," 304; "Liberty,"
262; "To the Skylark," 217

Xenophon: *Cyropaedia*, 224,
242–46; *Oeconomicus*, 224,
247–48; *Symposium*, 247
Ximena, 225

Young, Edward: *The Complaint: or,
Night Thoughts*, 110
Yowanne, 155

Zelter, Carl Friedrich, 342, 727–28
Zinzendorf, Nikolaus Ludwig, 134,
240–41
Zucchi, Carlo, 574, 713

Index of Fuller's Poetry Titles and First Lines

Afternoon in the dell where was a broken fall and many-voiced, 756
Among the mountains, October 1844, 756
And has another's life as large a scope?, 336

Book to the Reader, The, 186

Carbuncle, The (see "Slow wandering on a tangled way")
Content thee—for without content, 655

Double Triangle, Serpent and Rays (see "Patient serpent, circle round")
Drachenfels, 658

Each Orpheus must to the depths descend, 198

Familiar to the childish mind were tales, 37
Farewell, ye soft and sumptuous solitudes!, 52
For one, like me, it would be vain, 100
For the Power to whom we bow, 306

Ganymede to His Eagle, 41
Good night, Fourth July, 707
Governor Everett Receiving the Indian Chiefs, 137

Heidelberg, 657

If the same star our fates together bind, 177

In a fair garden of a distant land, 654
I thank the hand which gave this gift to me, 694

July Fourth 1844, 707

Lead, lunar ray, 708
Leila in the Arabian zone, 705
Loneliness so profound, 658

My seal ring:—, 706
My son, with weariness thou seemest spent, 59

Not long enough we gaze upon that face, 369

On the boundless plain careering, 699
Our friend has likened thee to the sweet fern, 702
O waxing moon, 696

Patient serpent, circle round, 705

Sacred Marriage, The, 336
Slow wandering on a tangled way, 747
Solitary and *Traveller,* 59
Some dried grass-tufts from the wide flowery plain, 6
Summer days of busy leisure, 5

the anguish of Tantalus, 693
The stately castle in the calm moonlight, 657
The temple round, 277
Through brute nature, upward rising, 706

914

INDEX OF POETRY TITLES AND FIRST LINES   915

To a Daughter of Italy, 544
To a Friend, 6
To Allston's Picture, "The Bride," 369
To Edith, on Her Birthday, 177
To guard the glories of the Roman
    reign, 544
To Sarah, 702
To see your cousin in her country
    home, 186
To the Apollo on my pin, 694
To the Face seen in the Moon,
    (*see Among the Mountains,
    October 1844*)

Upon the rocky mountain stood
    the boy, 41

Virgin Mother, Mary mild!, 695
Virgin Mother Mary mild, 698

When leaves were falling thickly
    in the pale November day,
    693
When no gentle eyebeam charms,
    178
Who says that Poesy is on the
    wane, 137

*This book is set in 10 point ITC Galliard, a face designed
for digital composition by Matthew Carter and based
on the sixteenth-century face Granjon. The paper is acid-free
lightweight opaque that will not turn yellow or brittle with age.
The binding is sewn, which allows the book to open easily and lie flat.
The binding board is covered in Brillianta, a woven rayon cloth
made by Van Heek–Scholco Textielfabrieken, Holland.
Composition by Westchester Publishing Services.
Printing by Sheridan, Grand Rapids, MI.
Binding by Dekker Bookbinding, Wyoming, MI.
Designed by Bruce Campbell.*

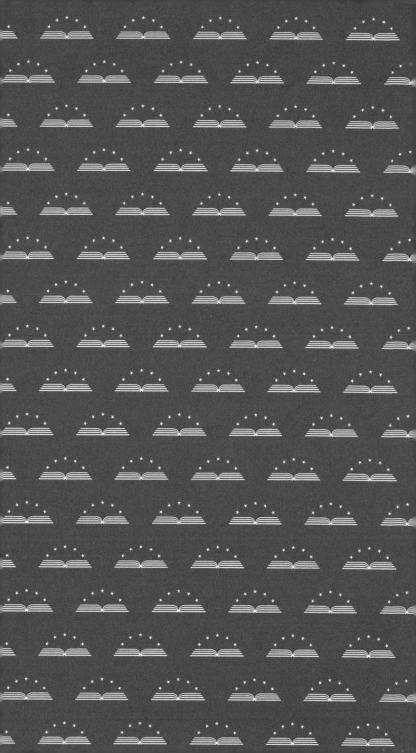